# Retraumatization

# Retraumatization

## Assessment, Treatment, and Prevention

**Edited by Melanie P. Duckworth and Victoria M. Follette**

Routledge
Taylor & Francis Group
New York   London

Routledge
Taylor & Francis Group
270 Madison Avenue
New York, NY 10016

Routledge
Taylor & Francis Group
27 Church Road
Hove, East Sussex BN3 2FA

© 2012 by Taylor and Francis Group, LLC
Routledge is an imprint of Taylor & Francis Group, an Informa business

Printed in the United States of America on acid-free paper
10 9 8 7 6 5 4 3 2 1

International Standard Book Number: 978-0-415-87275-1 (Hardback) 978-0-415-87276-8 (Paperback)

---

**Library of Congress Cataloging-in-Publication Data**

---

Retraumatization : assessment, treatment, and prevention / edited by Melanie P. Duckworth, Victoria M. Follette.
    p. ; cm.
  Includes bibliographical references and index.
  ISBN 978-0-415-87275-1 (hardback : alk. paper) -- ISBN 978-0-415-87276-8 (pbk. : alk. paper)
    1. Post-traumatic stress disorder. 2. Diseases--Relapse. I. Duckworth, Melanie P. II. Follette, Victoria M.
    [DNLM: 1. Stress Disorders, Post-Traumatic--therapy. 2. Recurrence. 3. Stress Disorders, Post-Traumatic--prevention & control. 4. Stress Disorders, Post-Traumatic--psychology. WM 172]

  RC552.P67R48 2011
  616.85'21--dc22                                    2011001064

---

**Visit the Taylor & Francis Web site at**
**http://www.taylorandfrancis.com**

**and the Routledge Web site at**
**http://www.routledgementalhealth.com**

# Contents

# Editors

**Melanie Duckworth, PhD,** received her doctorate in clinical psychology from the University of Georgia and is currently an associate professor in the Department of Psychology at the University of Nevada, Reno. Dr. Duckworth directs the Motor Vehicle Collision and Chronic Pain Research Program at the University of Nevada, Reno. She conducts laboratory-based and clinical research that examines the pre-, peri-, and postcollision variables that predict postcollision physical and psychological recovery and overall quality of life. In 2008, she coedited a book in which medical and psychological health-care providers and legal experts outlined best practices for assessing and managing the sometimes complicated aftermath associated with serious, injury-causing motor vehicle collisions (Duckworth, Iezzi, & O'Donohue, 2008). Dr. Duckworth teaches graduate and undergraduate seminars that address those health behaviors that contribute to chronic physical conditions and directs research related to health-risk behaviors including risky driving and risky sexual engagement. She has published peer-reviewed articles and invited book chapters that address both assessment and treatment of physical and psychological injuries incurred by persons exposed to potentially traumatizing events. Professional publications also include chapters that address the influence of culture on the prevention and treatment of chronic medical conditions and the assessment and cognitive-behavioral treatment of psychological disorders.

**Victoria Follette, PhD,** is recognized as a clinical scientist with a strong foundation in empirical-based therapy and has published edited volumes related to mindfulness in psychotherapy and cognitive-behavioral approaches to trauma therapy. In 2008, she was named as a Foundation Professor at the University of Nevada, Reno, and was also given the Nevada State Psychological Association's award for Outstanding Psychologist. Currently, she is the Chair of the Department of Psychology and is a licensed psychologist in the State of Nevada.

Dr. Follette's clinical and research work has emphasized an examination of the long-term consequences associated with a history of child sexual abuse (Polusny & Follette, 1996). In particular, she has investigated the impact of experiential avoidance in the diverse outcomes associated with various forms of maltreatment in the family of origin (Polusny, Rosenthal, Aban, & Follette, 2004). In addition to investigating intrapersonal impacts of trauma, she has examined interpersonal problems in intimate partner relationships. She coauthored a self-help book on Acceptance and Commitment Therapy (ACT) for individuals with a history of abuse, which can be adapted for group or individual therapy. Dr. Follette supervises a research laboratory at the University of Nevada, Reno, which continues to examine trauma-related outcomes, with a special interest in revictimization.

## REFERENCES

Duckworth, M. P., Iezzi, T., & O'Donohue. W. T. (Eds.). (2008). *Motor vehicle collisions: Medical, psychosocial, and legal consequences.* Oxford, UK: Elsevier.

Polusny, M. A., & Follette, V. M. (1995). Long-term correlates of child sexual abuse: Theory and review of the empirical literature. *Applied and Preventive Psychology, 4,* 143–166.

Polusny, M. A., Rosenthal, M. Z., Aban, I., & Follette, V. M. (2004). Experimental avoidance as a mediator of the effects of adolescent sexual victimization on negative adult outcomes. *Violence and Victims, 19,* 109–120.

# Contributors

**Pamela C. Alexander**
Sherborn, Massachusetts

**Sonja V. Batten**
Veterans Affairs Central Office and
    Uniformed Services University of
    the Health Sciences
Washington, DC

**Jordan T. Bonow**
Department of Psychology
University of Nevada, Reno
Reno, Nevada

**Christine A. Courtois**
Private Practice
Washington, DC

**Lisa S. Doane**
Cleveland State University
Cleveland, Ohio

**William C. Follette**
Department of Psychology
University of Nevada, Reno
Reno, Nevada

**Alan E. Fruzzetti**
Department of Psychology
University of Nevada, Reno
Reno, Nevada

**Devika Ghimire**
Department of Psychology
University of Nevada, Reno
Reno, Nevada

**Stevan E. Hobfoll**
Rush University Medical Center
Chicago, Illinois

**Julia E. Hoffman**
National Center for Posttraumatic
    Stress Disorder (PTSD) and the
    Veterans Affairs (VA) Palo Alto
    Health Care System
Menlo Park, California

**Tony Iezzi**
Behavioral Medicine Service
London Health Sciences Centre
London, Ontario
Canada

**Katherine M. Iverson**
Men's Health Sciences Division
National Center for PTSD
VA Boston Healthcare System and
    Department of Psychiatry
Boston University
Boston, Massachusetts

**Anthony P. King**
Trauma, Stress, and Anxiety
  Research Group
Department of Psychiatry
University of Michigan
Ann Arbor, Michigan

**Harold Kudler**
VA Mental Illness Research,
  Education, and Clinical Center
and
Duke University Medical Center
Durham, North Carolina

**Eric Kuhn**
National Center for PTSD and the
  VA Palo Alto Health Care System
Menlo Park, California

**Heidi La Bash**
Department of Psychology
University of Nevada, Reno
Reno, Nevada

**Jung eun Lee**
Department of Psychology
University of Nevada, Reno
Reno, Nevada

**Israel Liberzon**
Department of Psychiatry
University of Michigan
Ann Arbor, Michigan

**Candice M. Monson**
Department of Psychology
Ryerson University
Toronto, Ontario
Canada

**James A. Naifeh**
Uniformed Services University of
  the Health Sciences
Washington, DC

**Anthony Papa**
Department of Psychology
University of Nevada, Reno
Reno, Nevada

**Josef I. Ruzek**
National Center for PTSD and the
  VA Palo Alto Health Care System
Menlo Park, California

**Jeremiah A. Schumm**
Cincinnati VA Medical Center and
  University of Cincinnati School of
  Medicine
Cincinnati, Ohio

**Erika M. Shearer**
Department of Psychology
University of Nevada, Reno
Reno, Nevada

**Amy E. Street**
Women's Health Sciences Division
National Center for PTSD
VA Boston Healthcare System and
  Department of Psychiatry
Boston University
Boston, Massachusetts

**Claudia Zayfert**
Department of Psychiatry
Dartmouth Medical School
Lebanon, New Hampshire

Chapter 1

# Introduction

*Victoria M. Follette and Melanie P. Duckworth*

Our clinical experience and knowledge of the research literature led us to the decision that there was a clear need for a book that addresses the complexities in treating individuals with multiple trauma experiences. While there is an excellent body of research on the etiology and treatment of trauma symptoms, most notably posttraumatic stress disorder (PTSD), a number of questions remain unanswered. In Brewin's outstanding book, *Posttraumatic Stress Disorder: Malady or Myth?* (2003), he outlines the many controversies that have emerged over time regarding the fundamentals of the etiology of trauma symptoms and suggestions for treatment of immediate and delayed presentation of symptoms. He notes that these controversies are not new but rather can be traced back to Freud's early conceptualizations about the causes of pathology.

At various points in time, "skeptics" have asserted that there really is no foundation for the diagnosis of traumatic stress and that the diagnosis is a "sociopolitical" construction. In more recent controversies, there have been questions about whether the mental health field should focus on victims or perpetrators and whether the goals of treatment, particularly in cases of interpersonal trauma, are related to the identification of legal responsibility for damages or helping victims without regard to how the treatment is associated with the legal system. In part, the involvement of mental health providers in the legal system led to the famous "memory wars" that led to both positive and negative outcomes in trauma research. (See Brewin 2003, for a more complete discussion of the debate.) On the positive side, there were a number of cautions regarding practice that resulted from a careful examination of our scientific knowledge of memory. While this information was critical to the

1

field, many other areas of research in trauma were put on hold while the battle over memory played out. It has even been suggested that some academics changed the focus of their research in order to avoid the heated controversy. It is worth noting that for the majority of trauma survivors, memory for the event is not in question, and the memory issues were germane only in the debates around survivors of child sexual abuse. Discussion of this debate may seem tangential to this book; however, when we discuss retraumatization, there are many instances in which child abuse is the first trauma experience and thus becomes part of the research and clinical analysis.

Debates about memory and the rates of child abuse have not been the only focus of controversy. Some have suggested that we have become a society of victims, and that there has been an excessive focus on the impact of events that should be placed in a normal, albeit painful, set of life experiences. Moreover, many have claimed that mental health practitioners are "diagnosis happy" and that the field has in fact caused damage by diagnosis with the associated implication that all survivors are wounded. This controversy continues, and the issues became relevant in the creation of this book. In some ways, the most significant controversy surrounded whether there should even be a book on this topic. Scholars in the field questioned the need for a book that examines multiple trauma exposures, suggesting that such study may not add to our basic understanding of the underlying processes and of the focus on developing empirically based treatments. Even if one accepts the need for an analysis of retraumatization, a number of definitional issues come into play.

In our advice to our authors, we suggested that they consider a traumatic event is an experience that causes intense physical and psychological stress reactions. Examples of traumatic events included in the book include childhood abuse, loss, violence, physical and psychological assault, serious physical injuries, exposure to war, exposure to natural disasters, and torture. In this book, we define *retraumatization* as traumatic stress reactions, responses, and symptoms that occur consequent to multiple exposures to traumatic events that are physical, psychological, or both in nature. These responses can occur in the context of repeated multiple exposures within one category of events (e.g., child sexual assault and adult sexual assault) or multiple exposures across different categories of events (e.g., childhood physical abuse and involvement in a serious motor vehicle collision during adulthood). These multiple exposures increase the duration, frequency, and intensity of distress reactions. We would like to recognize that the term *retraumatization* has been used in a much more circumscribed way to capture distress that occurs with the retelling of a trauma narrative. Our use of the term *retraumatization* is more literal, emphasizing traumatic stress symptoms that occur in response to traumatic events rather than distress symptoms that occur in the context of treatment. Our definition of retraumatization is intended as a unifying guide across chapters, but we encouraged authors to address other definitions and conceptualizations of *retraumatization* that are germane to their work.

As we consider the definition of *retraumatization*, it is also important to note that the definition of PTSD is in transition with the development of the *Diagnostic and Statistical Manual of Mental Disorders,* 5th edition (*DSM-V*) entering its final phases. Even though PTSD is not the primary focus of this text, a brief review of the diagnosis is relevant to our basic conceptualizations about trauma outcomes. It is worth noting that at a more meta level, there are questions about the fundamental nature of the *DSM,* including suggestions about structural changes and about the utility of a categorical or dimensional system. Additional suggestions include ideas such as the reorganization of the diagnostic groupings with a focus on a variety of shared risk and clinical factors and movement away from a model that is so closely aligned with medical diagnosis. Even though these controversies provide some general context for the debates regarding trauma, we will confine ourselves to some of the specific concerns about the current PTSD diagnosis. McNally (2003) has been a key figure in these discussions and notes a particular concern about the issue of "bracket creep" that is defined in part as an increase in what constitutes exposure to a traumatic stressor. One concern is that individuals whose only exposure to trauma involved witnessing an event should not be included as candidates for the diagnosis of PTSD. In general, the specific nature of what should be included as a Criterion A event and how we can reliably use that criteria have been two key controversies in the continuing evolution of the diagnosis (Weathers & Keane, 2007). Brewin (2003) suggests that one alternative would be to remove the Criterion A event in that the many attempts to define triggering events have only led to an increased *lack* of clarity. However, questions about the adequacy of the current criterion go beyond issues of what constitutes a traumatic event. Instead of a focus on the traumatic event, it has been suggested that the presence or absence of core symptoms, particularly re-experiencing in the present moment, should be the primary criterion for diagnosis.

Brewin, Lanius, Novac, Schnyder, and Galea (2009) provide a useful discussion of several issues that have been raised in regard to the reformulation of the PTSD diagnosis. There are a number of points raised in their paper, and the authors point out three significant concerns directly relevant to the book at hand. First, there has been concern that the experience of normal events has been pathologized, ignoring the fact that exposure to painful events is a part of the normal human experience and that generally people experience a normal path of recovery. Second, they note the concern that the overlap of the PTSD criteria with other diagnoses has lessened its utility. Finally, Brewin et al. also note a biological profile associated with PTSD.

We considered many of these arguments in developing a plan for this text. In our view, although it is clear that exposure to traumatic events puts individuals at risk for developing a variety of psychological disorders including PTSD, it is important to develop an expanded conceptualization of how we consider both number of exposures to potentially traumatic events (PTEs) and the varied outcomes that may occur. Recently, it has become clear that a large percentage of trauma survivors may be exposed to more than one traumatic experience. There is a growing empirical literature examining the impact of repeated exposures to traumatic events on psychological well-being. Multiple exposures to trauma and increases in the duration, frequency, and intensity of exposure to potentially traumatizing experiences are associated with increases in PTSD and related trauma symptomatology, especially in comparison to a single exposure to a traumatic event. The literature provides some evidence on empirically supported treatments for survivors of traumatic experiences, but there are a number of lacunae in that literature. For example, much less is known about repeated exposure to combat stress. The increasing number of individuals who experience multiple deployments has made treatment of these Veterans a significant concern. Moreover, there is documentation of some Veterans reporting both combat stress and sexual trauma related to military service. Also, much less is known about the treatment of individuals who experience multiple sexual traumas. As a result of these questions, it became clear to us that it was time to bring together leaders in this area to document the current state of the field in an edited text.

The purpose of this book is to provide the most current information on the epidemiology, theory, and treatment issues related to multiple trauma experiences. The first section of the proposed book will include chapters that address epidemiological and theoretical issues related to multiple trauma experiences. Other chapters will be designed to specifically address retraumatization occurring across military and interpersonal violence contexts. However, the primary focus of the text is related to the most recent work addressing prevention and treatment approaches for specific populations. Although there is not extensive empirical literature on these groups, the work presented here generally is based on empirically supported concepts.

As clinical scientists, we consider a basic theoretical foundation as the key to building both research questions and clinical interventions. The field has seen a number of advances in the clarity of a number of theories that have been used to conceptualize the long-term impacts of traumatic exposure. We do not intend to present every current theoretical perspective in these chapters, but we have tried to provide chapters that represent some of the fundamental work in the field at this time. However, we certainly acknowledge that there are a number of promising new lines of research emerging that may provide additional depth and breadth to our current conceptualizations of the retraumatization literature.

Cognitive behavioral theory, with its foundation in basic learning principles, has been at the forefront of trauma work for many years. In Zayfert's discussion (Chapter 2), she describes the development of the model for PTSD using Mowrer's two-factor theory, in which both the acquisition of and maintenance of fear are explained. The use of behavioral and cognitive avoidance is considered the primary mechanism for the maintenance of fear related to traumatic stimuli. Kudler (Chapter 3) presents a psychoanalytic perspective of the study of trauma that includes a comprehensive review of the history surrounding some of the seminal work in this area. In a discussion that transcends all perspectives on the conceptualization of traumatic reactions, he points out the distinction between the external and internal representations of the experience. In his discussion of more current analytic perspectives, he makes clear the importance of considering multiple systems that can impact the flexibility of functioning, and that adaptation can lead to balance and growth. The literature surrounding the neurobiological issues related to exposure to trauma has grown dramatically in recent years as developing technology has allowed for more fine-grained analysis of neurological phenomena. King and Liberzon (Chapter 4) provide comprehensive coverage of what is known about the impacts of trauma, what are the limits of the data, and where we might expect the field to go based on current research.

In their discussion of a Resource Conservation Conceptualization of retraumatization, Hobfoll and colleagues (Chapter 5) focus on changes in a wide range of resources that can significantly impact the response to trauma. Although this work was initially developed with a focus on losses associated with one specific trauma experience, their contextual view of the intersection of a range of systems provides a strong foundation for understanding retraumatization. In a sense, they demonstrate how the impact of exposure to multiple traumas can create a complex set of feedback loops that exacerbate the initial exposure. Alexander's description (Chapter 8) of the relationship of attachment theory to retraumatization also brings contextual elements to the analysis of the response to repeated traumas. Attachment theory's focus on both the impact of early relationships on the response to trauma and relationship outcomes related to those early experiences enriches our analysis in developing a comprehensive assessment of the client's experience. Courtois (Chapter 7) provides an integrative and thoughtful discussion of a complex set of trauma-related symptoms that are frequently associated with adult trauma that is overlaid on a history of child sexual abuse. The sequelae of multiple trauma experiences such as this can result in a range of difficulties including issues with emotion regulation and interpersonal relationships. This complex symptom presentation can present the therapist with a fundamental dilemma about the necessary basic components of treatment and the temporal ordering of those treatment components.

Developing a comprehensive assessment of the clinical needs of a client who presents for treatment following exposure to repeated trauma experiences is essential for planning effective treatment. In Chapter 6, Bonow and W. Follette take a broad approach to assessment, elaborating on the use of functional analysis as a foundation for assessment in this population. Because of the contextual and flexible process that is an inherent part of a functional analysis, it is particularly relevant to the clinical problems associated with retraumatized clients. Considering variables that range from the intrapersonal to the interpersonal is essential in developing an approach to treatment that may involve a variety of contributing current and historical factors. The examination of contextual variables that range from intimate relationships to cultural influences can enhance a practitioner's case conceptualization, regardless of theoretical orientation.

As the large number of Veterans return from combat in Iraq and Afghanistan, the need for treatment that focuses on retraumatization has become increasingly apparent. There has been an increased awareness of the potential for early trauma experiences to have an impact on how individuals respond to exposure to combat. While the mechanism underlying any increase in vulnerability based on repeated exposure remains unclear, there is a growing body of literature that suggests increased symptomology in those with multiple traumas. In their chapter on multiple combat exposures (Chapter 9), Kuhn and his colleagues explore factors associated with multiple deployments, which has become a more frequent practice in the current war. Examination of proximal and distal outcomes associated with combat exposure has always been complex; however, advances in the assessment of trauma-related symptoms have become more sophisticated, allowing for a more detailed symptom profile across time. Ongoing research that examines individuals prior to deployment, in the battlefield, and at multiple points post-deployment is likely to produce important findings. This longitudinal research is essential for understanding the course of multiple symptoms over time, as well as the factors that predict resilience and recovery. One key issue related to this type of research is that it can lead to the development of programs to better prepare soldiers for combat exposure.

Wartime experiences can also have outcomes that go beyond direct exposure to combat. Moreover, exposure to war-related stressors is not limited to Veterans in the field but can also include civilian and refugee victims. In examining multiple trauma exposures in theater, Iverson and her colleagues (Chapter 10) discuss the clinical issues in those Veterans who are exposed to sexual violence while serving in combat. This is an emerging area of study, and it is fraught with problems, including issues related to reporting the sexual trauma and assessment of treatment priorities. These authors present a compelling argument for the need for more treatment guidelines for our returning Veterans with sexual violence that is concurrent with combat traumatic experiences. In La Bash and Papa's chapter (Chapter 11) on the plight of refugees and civilian casualties, they point out the need to expand our horizons in examining the victims of combat. Life-threatening injuries, loss of family members, resource loss, and sexual victimization are just a few of the problems that represent some of the "collateral damage" of combat.

Even though treatment of Veterans with combat exposure has been long been identified as an important priority, the consideration of treatment for survivors of violence on the home front is relatively new. Interpersonal victimization in the form of child abuse and partner violence has been more recently recognized, relatively speaking. Ghimire and Follette (Chapter 12) provide a comprehensive review of the multiple streams of research that address the particular issues associated with multiple sexual victimization experiences. They examine data on the interaction of the increased risk for substance abuse, particularly alcohol, and risky sex in survivors of child sexual abuse, which has contributed to a more complex set of research questions. Although this relationship has been documented in numerous studies, the interpretation of these findings remains controversial. The primary question at hand is the identification of the underlying mechanism that mediates the relationships between child and adult victimization. However, identifying the mediators and moderations that impact this type of revictimization is complex. A clearer understanding of these factors is essential to the development of effective prevention and treatment programs. Couples violence is one of the many outcomes seen at increased rates in survivors of child abuse. By its very nature, domestic violence is often a multiply occurring event that can occur over several years and frequently occurs in a climate of secrecy and isolation. Lee and Fruzzetti (Chapter 13) provide an interesting discussion of the complex interpersonal dynamics associated with the development and maintenance of violence in couples. For a number of reasons, the development of empirically based treatments for this population has lagged far behind research in other areas of couples research. A key factor is often the question of whether the couple should be treated at all or if rather the problem should be treated in the social and legal domains. Their treatment plan, with its underlying rationale, provides a new and fascinating perspective to consider.

Duckworth, Iezzi, and Shearer (Chapter 14) address the problems associated with disabling physical injuries, an area often not adequately considered in trauma-related psychology. And yet, this research is one of the most important areas for future clinical research, which is at the intersection of medicine and psychology. Frequently, the two disciplines have operated in a parallel fashion, not taking sufficient opportunity to examine the multiplicative impact of interdisciplinary treatment.

We believe that together these chapters provide both theoretical and empirical reviews of the contemporary literature that addresses many of the most current concerns in the area. Batten and Naifeh (Chapter 15) expand on these chapters to provide a stimulating discussion of current controversies in the field and suggestions for future directions. They address a number of issues, including debates about the diagnostic criteria, ranging from the definition of PTEs to the utility of developing a new diagnosis for clients presenting with symptoms not traditionally represented in the PTSD criteria. They also make strong statements about the use of appropriate clinical samples, avoiding an overreliance on college samples or other groups that might be considered "niche" research areas. These concerns represent just a few of the ideas addressed in their thought-provoking piece.

Conceptualizations should be grounded in science. We need to understand etiology of basic trauma and how multiple exposures can lead to exacerbation of symptoms. We need to understand the mechanisms in order to know what treatment is needed. We need to test treatment, and find ways to move beyond traditional diagnostic criteria in designing and implementing treatment. We hope that this text provides some preliminary guidance in answering some of these questions and in suggesting new research directions.

## REFERENCES

Brewin, C. R. (2003). *Posttraumatic stress disorder: Malady or myth?* New Haven, CT: Yale University Press.

Brewin, C. R., Lanius, R. A., Novac, A., Schnyder, U., & Galea, S. (2009). Reformulating PTSD for *DSM V*: Life after Criterion A. *Journal of Traumatic Stress, 22*, 366–373.

McNally, R. J. (2003). Progress and controversy in the study of posttraumatic stress disorder. *Annual Review of Psychology, 54*, 229–252.

Weathers, F. W., & Keane, T. M. (2007). The Criterion A problem revisited: Controversies and challenges in defining and measuring psychological trauma. *Journal of Traumatic Stress, 20*, 917–919.

# Chapter 2

# Cognitive Behavioral Conceptualization of Retraumatization

*Claudia Zayfert*

Traumatic events by their nature are not the kinds of life experiences that most people would like to have. Whether childhood abuse, horrific accidents, interpersonal assaults, or the violence of war, if we could choose our life experiences, most people would likely choose a life free of trauma. Furthermore, we might expect that those who have already experienced such dreadful events would be even more inclined to avoid them. Indeed, the very purpose of fear learning systems is to teach us to avoid future danger. Yet, a repeated finding in the trauma literature is that individuals exposed to trauma are at risk for additional trauma exposure. Such *re-exposure* to trauma is perhaps one of the most perplexing of phenomena in the field of traumatic stress. This is more than just common sense—a vast literature documents that humans are capable of learning fear and avoidance of potentially dangerous stimuli. Posttraumatic stress disorder (PTSD) is understood to be a consequence of such fear learning gone awry. That is, the individual suffering effects of PTSD continues to experience fear and avoidance of trauma-related stimuli well beyond the context when and where such reactions have adaptive value. Even more astounding is that this does not simply happen one or two times beyond the first traumatic event, but rather evidence suggests that for many trauma survivors, it happens repeatedly.

This is a phenomenon of grave importance for those caught up in a wave of trauma, distress, and dysfunction. These individuals are at risk for the serious injury, disease, and death that can result from exposure to many such events.

They are also at risk for serious psychiatric symptoms, life impairment, and self-injury and suicide that can result from any trauma, and is even more likely for those with multiple traumatic experiences. Evidence suggests that repeated trauma exposure, particularly if begun in childhood, puts the survivor at risk for more severe and complex life problems than if only traumatized once (Cloitre et al., 2009). This being the case, helping trauma survivors to avoid further trauma exposure most certainly would mitigate substantial misery and suffering. Yet to formulate a plan to aid trauma survivors in their recovery and avoid further trauma exposure, we must confront two perplexing paradoxes of retraumatization. The first, as highlighted above, is that *initial exposure to trauma does not seem to translate to avoidance learning that lessens the likelihood of subsequent exposure to trauma.*

Identifying victim behaviors that may contribute to risk of exposure is sometimes regarded as "blaming the victim." Whether intended or not, such examinations of the victim's behavior can be equated with assigning the victim with responsibility for the trauma, something that can exacerbate the trauma of the event by magnifying stigma and shame. Yet, identifying those victim behaviors that reduce trauma risk can enhance perceived control and can point to behavior change that might improve future safety. Efforts to enhance percep-tions of control may underlie beliefs about responsibility for traumatic events, which are typically associated with feelings of shame and guilt. This highlights a second paradox in this area of research: *identifying contributory behaviors among victims' behaviors has both potentially harmful and healing effects.*

It is important to recognize that trauma exposure is not always medi-ated by individual behavior. Some retraumatization is simply a function of misfortune. Consider a sexual assault survivor who happened to be in line at the bank the day a pair of thieves walked in, shot the teller, and took her and several other customers hostage, or a survivor of childhood abuse who was a passenger on a bus when it was struck by another vehicle and crashed. Such cases illustrate that not all trauma re-exposure is necessarily etiologically connected. Even so, despite the absence of causal associations among occur-rence of these events, such repeated trauma exposure can have a cumulative effect for the individual who experiences it.

When events are etiologically related, however, there may be additional psychological factors at work. Many who suffer repeated trauma exposure experience the subsequent trauma in the context of situations that might have been avoided or prevented but were not. This might be a serial exposure to the same type of trauma, such as childhood sexual abuse that occurs multiple times by the same perpetrator or by more than one perpetrator. Or, this might be a sequential exposure to different types of trauma, such as when a survivor of childhood sexual abuse experiences intimate partner violence as an adult, or when a combat Veteran is in an alcohol-related car collision. The abuse survivor might have avoided a relationship with a potentially violent partner, or the Veteran might have refrained from drinking before getting behind the wheel of a car. Understanding the role of survivors' cognition and behavior in repeated trauma will enable us to develop ways to train survivors to think and act differently to avoid further trauma. Yet, to do so acknowledges survivors' responsibility for their role in the subsequent trauma. Regardless of the scenarios, when we consider what role the survivors' behavior might have had in subsequent trauma exposure, we risk blaming the victim, which can exacerbate the victim's distress and dysfunction.

It is easy to see why, as an approach to working clinically with trauma survivors, victim blaming is not a constructive stance. Guilt and shame have been identified as being among the most emotionally damaging aftereffects of trauma (Kubany, 1998). Attributions of self-blame for discrete actions (guilt) or, more significantly, as indicative of a global negative view of the self (shame) are widely understood to be a source of emotional pain directly and to interfere with processing fear and grief (Boelen, 2006; Lee, Scragg, & Turner, 2001). If researchers identify evidence that trauma survivors have a role in the occurrence of subsequent traumatic events, this information has the potential to exacerbate guilt and shame. This is confusing information for clinicians to absorb into their work with trauma survivors. On the one hand, there is satisfaction in absolving survivors of the responsibility for horrific events—it often can ease the pain of guilt and shame. On the other hand, identifying behavioral contributants can enhance perceived control and provide targets for behavior change that can enhance future safety and well-being.

Consequently, in developing our collective understanding of the etiology and effects of repeated trauma exposure, we are challenged to develop a conceptualization that is both empirically accurate and clinically constructive for trauma survivors. Understanding the role of survivors' cognition and behavior in repeated trauma will enable us to develop ways to train survivors to think and act differently to avoid further trauma. Accordingly, our goal is to understand trauma survivors' actions within a model that both validates their past choices given the context in which they were made and enables them to alter future ones. This is a delicate balance, though an important one to achieve if future interventions to reduce trauma re-exposure will be taken up by the survivors who need them.

## EFFECTS OF REPEATED TRAUMA EXPOSURE

A growing body of literature documents that the effects of multiple traumatic events on psychological well-being are markedly worse compared to the effects of a single traumatic event. Studies show, for example, that many survivors of sexual assault in adulthood have been previously traumatized in childhood, either in the form of childhood sexual abuse or physical abuse or both (Coid et al., 2001; Maker, Kemmelmeier, & Peterson, 1998). Increasingly, evidence suggests that the experience of multiple traumatic events greatly increases the risk for mental (Suliman et al., 2009) and physical health problems (Campbell, Greeson, Bybee, & Raja, 2008) compared to those who experience a single event, or even a series of one type of event, such as abuse by a single perpetrator or a single military deployment. Those traumatized in both childhood and adulthood tend to be worse off than those who experienced only childhood abuse or only adult sexual assault (Follette, Polusny, Bechtle, & Naugle, 1996). Likewise, among survivors of intimate partner violence, those who experienced abuse by multiple partners account for much of the PTSD, anxiety, depression, and somatic complaints, whereas those who experienced abuse by one partner tend to be no different than those with no history of abuse (Bogat, Levendosky, Theran, von Eye, & Davidson, 2003; Coolidge & Anderson, 2002; Messman-Moore, Long, & Siegfried, 2000). Among war Veterans and survivors of military trauma, those who experienced trauma prior to their military deployment (Cabrera, Hoge, Bliese, Castro, & Messer, 2007) and those who experienced longer deployments (Rona et al., 2007) are at greater risk for PTSD, mood disorders, and other problems.

Existing models for understanding the aftereffects of trauma focus on understanding how trauma leads to the re-experiencing, avoidance, and hyperarousal symptoms of PTSD. The influence of repeated exposure to trauma has not typically been integrated into these models. One exception is in the area of sexual revictimization, where the study of the aftereffects of childhood sexual abuse has focused on sequelae that affect interpersonal functioning and can help to explain the recurrence of sexual trauma in childhood, adolescence, and adulthood. For example, the Traumagenic Dynamics Model of childhood sexual abuse proposed by Finkelhor and Browne (1985) suggests that abuse alters the child's self-concept and worldview in ways that, although adaptive in the context of ongoing abuse, are dysfunctional in coping with the absence of abuse. Finkelhor and Browne discuss four "dynamics" in child sexual abuse—traumatic sexualization, betrayal, stigmatization, and powerlessness—that may influence cognition and behavior in ways that not only affect psychological well-being but also beget further abuse.

In contrast, the study of PTSD as a consequence of traumatic events generally has paid less attention to the repetition of traumatic events in the development and maintenance of psychological symptoms. Considering the strong association between extent of exposure to traumatic events and risk for PTSD and other adverse outcomes (Brewin, Andrews, & Valentine, 2000), this may prove to be a crucial omission. Not only has repeated trauma exposure been linked to more adverse outcomes, but trauma re-exposure may be as a mediator of sex differences in the occurrence of PTSD. Recent findings from a prospective study indicate that sex differences in the prevalence of PTSD in a sample of childhood sexual abuse survivors was largely accounted for by trauma re-exposure in the form of rape or other traumatic events (Koenen & Widom, 2009). However, it is important to note that men with a history of childhood sexual abuse also may be prone to repeat victimization (Tewksbury, 2007).

Repeated trauma may be particularly relevant for military sexual trauma. Women in the U.S. Army and Navy report nearly double the rates of child-hood sexual abuse as reported in the general population (Rosen & Martin, 1996). Female Navy recruits with a history of childhood sexual abuse were 4.8 times more likely to experience a sexual assault while in the military than those who had no history of sexual abuse, even when physical abuse history was controlled (Merrill et al., 1999). Women (Gidycz, Coble, Latham, & Layman, 1993; Roodman & Clum, 2001) and men (Elliott, Mok, & Briere, 2004), however, are equally likely to experience subsequent sexual assaults after childhood sexual abuse.

## COGNITIVE BEHAVIORAL FORMULATIONS

Previous cognitive behavioral formulations of the development and mainte-nance of PTSD are an important starting point in conceptualizing trauma symptomology (Follette & Ruzek, 2006). Although these models have not addressed trauma re-exposure as an outcome of the initial trauma, or as a factor in current psychosocial functioning, they can serve as a foundation for integrating information about multiple traumas. For example, the cogni-tive behavioral model of PTSD proposed by Flack, Litz, and Keane (1998) highlights the importance of fear conditioning and avoidance behaviors in the development and maintenance of the anxiety component of the disorder.

Mowrer's (1947) two-factor model of anxiety has been the foundation of cognitive behavioral models of PTSD. According to Mowrer, two types of con-ditioning, *classical* and *operant*, contribute to fear learning. Initial learning of fear occurs when a neutral stimulus is paired with a fear-inducing stimulus. Subsequently, the neutral stimulus also evokes fear. When the neutral stimu-lus is presented repeatedly without threat of harm, the fear should dissipate. Mowrer proposed that the second factor, operant conditioning, might account for the persistence of fear in the absence of danger. According to Mowrer, the rapid reduction in fear that follows escape from the stimulus reinforces the escape behavior, causing it to persist and increase in frequency. He hypothe-sized that the continuing escape and avoidance of the feared stimulus prevents fear extinction. Thus, according to Mowrer's two-factor model, fear is initially learned via classical conditioning and maintained by operant conditioning. Keane et al. applied this theory to PTSD. After experiencing a traumatic event, patients with PTSD typically avoid objects and situations closely asso-ciated with the event. In addition, as Keane et al. pointed out, many trauma survivors attempt to avoid trauma memories, which has similar results as the behavioral avoidance of real-life stimuli (Keane, Zimering, & Caddell, 1985). They proposed that both behavioral and cognitive avoidance are responsible for the maintenance of fear in PTSD. For example, a survivor of childhood sexual abuse was raped by a man wearing a blue uniform. She coped with her fears by avoiding situations where she might encounter men in blue uniforms (such as bus drivers and policemen) and her memories of the assault. As a result, she failed to learn that neither blue uniforms nor her memories could actually harm her.

Keane and colleagues expanded upon Mowrer's model to account for the wide range of fears that are commonly observed among trauma survivors with PTSD (Flack, Litz, & Keane, 1998). They invoked two fundamental principles of conditioning, higher-order conditioning and stimulus generalization, to account for the expanded range of feared stimuli. Higher-order conditioning occurs when a previously neutral stimulus triggers a conditioned response due to being paired with a conditioned stimulus. For example, after the abuse survivor encountered a bus driver wearing a blue uniform, she became fearful of riding buses, even though buses had no connection to her sexual abuse experience. Stimulus generalization occurs when the trauma survivor becomes fearful of stimuli that resemble the conditioned stimulus, as when the abuse survivor, who initially feared only blue-uniformed men, began to fear all men in uniform.

Although conditioning models have some limitations, they can help to explain many core features of PTSD, such as the wide range of stimuli that trigger trauma memories and the physiological and emotional arousal generated by these stimuli (Brewin & Holmes, 2003). Keane and Barlow (2002) further elaborated upon conditioning models to address their limitations in accounting for individual experiences. They proposed that generalized biological and psychological vulnerabilities might predispose an individual to develop any form of psychopathology after a traumatic experience. They proposed that other factors during development (including early trauma) might increase psychological vulnerability to pathological response to later trauma. Further, in their explanation of fear conditioning that underlies PTSD, they underscored the adaptive function of "true alarms"—the mobilization of physical and cognitive resources as part of the "fight/flight" response that promotes survival during the traumatic event. True alarms are accompanied by intense physical arousal. Keane and Barlow suggested that a variety of stimuli become associated with the experience of a true alarm and as a result develop learned alarms via classical conditioning. Learned alarms, subsequently, are triggered by situations that resemble aspects of the traumatic experience.

Although learned alarms produce the same response as a true alarm, they do so in the absence of objective danger. In the weeks following a traumatic event, many trauma survivors experience learned alarms and other forms of recurring distress in reaction to reminders of the event (North, Smith, McCool, & Lightcap, 1989; Riggs, Rothbaum, & Foa, 1995; Rothbaum, Foa, Riggs, Murdock, & Walsh, 1992). These early posttrauma-learned alarms, however, usually fade over time. Keane and Barlow posit a role for conditioning of other intense emotions, such as shame and guilt, which may be evoked by the same stimuli that evoke fear. In some cases, these emotions may be the predominant reaction learned in association with trauma reminders. Survivors also learn to fear these emotion states due to their aversive nature, which further motivates them to avoid trauma-related stimuli. The emotional numbing of PTSD may represent efforts to avoid their emotions completely. Keane and Barlow emphasize that initial learned alarms are a common reaction to trauma and do not necessarily result in persistent distress associated with PTSD. They propose that other factors, such as a trauma survivor's coping style and resources, and access to social support can influence the persistence of distress. Trauma survivors who are naturally exposed to triggers of learned alarms (such as cues in their environment or through talking about the events with supportive others) in the period after the event may be less prone to experience persistent distress (Wirtz & Harrell, 1987), which helps to explain why most trauma survivors do not develop PTSD. Conditioning models are very helpful in understanding many aspects of PTSD, particularly those related to anxiety. Yet, they do not fully explain nonanxiety symptoms.

Various cognitive models (Chemtob, Roitblat, Hamada, Carlson, & Twentyman, 1988; Ehlers & Clark, 2000; Foa, Steketee, & Rothbaum, 1989) have been developed in an effort to fully explain PTSD symptoms. A common focus of cognitive models is on cognitive processing of traumatic experiences. Cognitive processing is seen as the way in which the trauma survivor makes sense of the event and interprets its meaning about himself or herself and the world. Many cognitive models assume that traumatic events challenge preexisting beliefs about the world and the self (Brewin, Dalgleish, & Joseph, 1996). This is consistent with research indicating that people who engage with their traumatic memory either through writing (Smyth, Hockemeyer, & Tulloch, 2008; van Emmerik, Kamphuis, & Emmelkamp, 2008) or telling a narrative (Neuner et al., 2004) show reductions in stress, whereas those who mentally disconnect from events and inhibit their emotional reactions tend to be at greater risk for developing PTSD (Ozer, Best, Lipsey, & Weiss, 2003). Cognitive models of PTSD presume that processing was incomplete or interrupted, and the individual was left with inaccurate or distorted interpretations about the meaning of the event. Cognitive models suggest that incomplete processing leads to pathological fear. Trauma-related information is presumed to be organized in the mind of the trauma survivor in "fear networks" (Foa & Kozak, 1986; Foa et al., 1989), which are programs to promote survival in the face of life-threatening danger. Fear networks link specific details regarding the event (including stimuli and memories), responses to the event (e.g., behaviors, thoughts, sensations), and meanings and interpretations of the event. Cognitive models presume that incomplete processing results in errors in the fear networks, such that the individual inaccurately associates benign stimuli with danger. Further, avoidance results in a failure to integrate information about safety to correct the errors in the fear network. When fear networks incorrectly link stimuli or contain flawed assumptions, the individual fears safe situations and objects. For example, the fear network of the sexual abuse survivor associated blue uniforms with danger. Thus, blue uniforms activated her fear network, which contains the emotional experience of fear (including heightened arousal) and memories of the rapes, as well as interpretations of the world (e.g., "All men are dangerous"). The survivor experiences the urge to avoid both memories and the actual stimuli (blue uniforms), even though they are not accurate signals of danger.

Avoidance can also be motivated by other emotions, such as anger, guilt, and shame about the events, or about the PTSD symptoms. For example, when disclosure of sexual abuse is met with disbelief, PTSD is more likely to result (Everill & Waller, 1995; Ullman, 1996). Similarly, when Veterans of the Vietnam war experienced negative reactions upon their return, this exacerbated their feelings of shame, which in turn, was related to greater incidence of PTSD (Johnson et al., 1997). Sometimes the individual may have strong emotional reactions to his or her PTSD symptoms, such as when the individual fears that flashbacks are a sign that he or she is "going crazy" or "losing control" or feels ashamed that the symptoms are a sign of weakness. Such secondary reactions can sometimes drive avoidance that maintains the disorder (Ehlers & Steil, 1995).

As indicated above, cognitive behavioral models have primarily focused on explaining how PTSD might develop following a single traumatic experience. Keane and Barlow (2002) extended the discussion of etiology to include a broader array of factors that might contribute to the development of PTSD. In addition to acknowledging the possible role of genetic predisposition, they point to research suggesting that early trauma was a significant risk factor for PTSD among Vietnam combat Veterans (King, King, Foy, & Gudanowski, 1996). Although they underscore the need for more study of the role of early trauma, their discussion primarily focuses on understanding its role in the etiology of PTSD in response to a later event. Increasing evidence suggests, however, that for a subset of trauma survivors, PTSD and trauma re-exposure may become a mutually maintaining pattern of life experiences and responses. A model that addresses the role of trauma re-exposure in PTSD and the role of PTSD in trauma re-exposure may have greater utility for understanding and predicting distress and dysfunction among those with multiple trauma exposures. It is important to consider the range of factors that can lead to repeated trauma exposures and repeated traumatization, and to address the ways in which repeated trauma exposures might exacerbate risk for PTSD and complicate its presentation in terms of associated features and disorders, and in terms of the complexity of belief systems and behaviors that may become self-perpetuating. Figure 2.1 organizes factors that the literature suggests may influence both trauma re-exposure and PTSD into pretrauma, peritraumatic, and posttraumatic factors, and attempts to integrate known moderators and mediators such as social support, cognitive alterations, substance use, and risk behaviors.

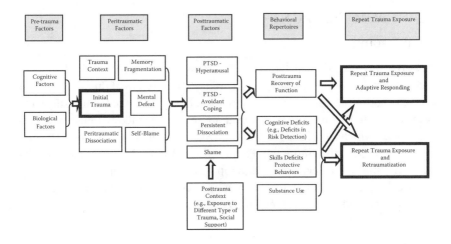

FIGURE 2.1 The direct and indirect influences of pretrauma, peritraumatic, and posttraumatic factors on both trauma re-exposure and retraumatization (PTSD, posttraumatic stress disorder).

## PRETRAUMA FACTORS

Research on the etiology of PTSD has primarily focused on aspects of the traumatic event and immediate and long-term reactions to the event. Recent analyses suggest that pretrauma variables may have a minor role in development of the disorder (Brewin et al., 2000; Ozer et al., 2003). Yet, as Keane and Barlow (2002) point out, the path toward development of PTSD may begin with predisposing biological, psychological, or both vulnerabilities. Research points toward particular background variables, such as low socioeconomic status and family instability, as potentially setting the stage for future adverse reactions to trauma (King, King, Foy, Keane, & Fairbank, 1999). As King et al. suggest, such pretrauma variables may set the stage for later PTSD by depleting the available resources to deal with subsequent events. This is consistent with diathesis-stress models, which conceptualize psychological vulnerabilities as relatively stable individual differences that may not be easily observed but that can interact with stress to result in a disease (Ingram & Price, 2010; McKeever & Huff, 2003). While pretrauma ecological variables appear to have a minor influence on PTSD risk, it is possible that psychological vulnerabilities may be more significant. Research points to the possible role of four cognitive vulnerabilities in the etiology of PTSD: negative attributional style, rumination, anxiety sensitivity, and looming cognitive style (Elwood, Hahn, Olatunji, & Williams, 2009). Whether such pretrauma cognitive vulnerabilities play a role in vulnerability to subsequent trauma independent of PTSD has not been investigated.

## PERITRAUMATIC FACTORS

### Initial Trauma

Research has investigated the role of various aspects of the initial trauma, such as duration, severity, age of onset, and whether physical threat or harm or sexual penetration was involved. Studies of childhood sexual abuse survivors have suggested that more severe sexual abuse is associated with use of avoidant coping, which in turn is related to PTSD symptoms in adulthood (Fortier et al., 2009; Merrill, Guimond, Thomsen, & Milner, 2003). Aspects of the initial trauma that affect sexual development, such as learning to use sex to get affection or to have other needs met, may contribute to future engagement in risky behaviors (Finkelhor & Browne, 1985).

### Trauma Context

The social context of the trauma may be an important factor in risk for adult dysfunction and re-exposure to trauma. Child sexual abuse associated with a known perpetrator and involving more intimate sexual contact has been associated with greater distress in adulthood (Finkelhor & Browne, 1985). When sexual abuse is perpetrated by someone who was previously trusted, the betrayal may contribute to problems with anger and depression and difficulty trusting others. Also, child sexual abuse associated with a known perpetrator and involving more intimate sexual contact has been associated with greater distress in adulthood (Finkelhor & Browne, 1985).

### Peritraumatic Dissociation

Dissociation, including detachment, emotional numbing, and "shutting down" during a traumatic event, has been identified as a strong prospective risk factor for PTSD (Dunmore, Clark, & Ehlers, 2001; Ozer et al., 2003), though it is neither necessary nor sufficient to develop the disorder (Bryant, 2009). Bryant discusses several factors that may account for observed relationships between peritraumatic dissociation and PTSD. These include underlying dissociative tendencies, elevated physiological arousal during the trauma that may precipitate dissociation, negative appraisals of the meaning of dissociation, and the negative relationship of dissociation with intelligence. Some evidence suggests that the primary significance of peritraumatic dissociation lies in its association with *persistent dissociation* that is strongly associated with PTSD. This is consistent with cognitive models of PTSD that posit that avoidance of trauma memories impedes processing and desensitization of related anxiety.

Evidence suggests that dissociation that persists as an ongoing symptom may be a risk factor for subsequent trauma exposure (Banyard, Williams, & Siegel, 2002). Emotional numbing, arguably a form of dissociation, has also been found to predict revictimization in childhood sexual abuse survivors (Ullman, Najdowski, & Filipas, 2009). The fact that peritraumatic dissociation was not highly predictive of PTSD in a review that focused on studies of survivors of single traumatic events suggests that the peritraumatic dissociation may be a phenomenon of relevance primarily to repeated trauma exposure (van der Velden & Wittmann, 2008) and retraumatization. In other words, peritraumatic dissociation following later traumatic events may reflect persistence of dissociation that began with earlier traumas.

## Memory Fragmentation

Dissociation can be problematic for functioning in daily life. Individuals who disconnect from their daily life experiences may find this disrupts their performance of daily activities and their ability to sustain healthy relationships with others. The significance of dissociative tendencies for development of PTSD, however, is thought to lie in its disruption of memory encoding and processing. The assumption is that peritraumatic dissociation may interfere with memory encoding during an event, and subsequent persistent dissociation may impede processing the memory when it is cued. In support of this view, several studies have found that dissociation was related to more disorganized and fragmented trauma narratives in collision and assault survivors (Halligan, Michael, Clark, & Ehlers, 2003; Harvey & Bryant, 1999). Yet, research has yet to clearly establish a link between dissociation, memory fragmentation, and development of PTSD (Giesbrecht, Lynn, Lilienfeld, & Merckelbach, 2008)

## Mental Defeat

The perception of helplessness, powerless, or lack of control during a traumatic experience has been discussed as a significant aspect of the traumatic experience which may lead to development of PTSD. In particular, powerlessness has been discussed as an aspect of child sexual abuse (Finkelhor & Browne, 1985) with significant etiologic implications. Related to this is the cognitive appraisal of "mental defeat" during the traumatic event, which is considered to include and exceed the perception of helplessness. The victim who perceives mental defeat completely gives up, loses the sense of having his or her own will, and may accept that he or she is dying. Mental defeat predicted PTSD in several prospective studies (Dunmore et al., 2001; Kleim, Ehlers, & Glucksman, 2007) and had been associated with poor response to treatment (Ehlers et al., 1998; Stafford et al., 1996). The perception of powerlessness, helplessness, and appraisals of mental defeat may increase in the context of repeated trauma and may have a role in both the risk for psychopathology and trauma re-exposure.

## Self-Blame

Attributions of self-blame during a traumatic experience may also be relevant to the onset of PTSD and risk for further trauma exposure. Longer duration of childhood abuse and older age at onset of abuse were both associated with greater self-blame and greater psychological distress (Zinzow, Seth, Jackson, Niehaus, & Fitzgerald, 2010). A history of multiple victimizations has been associated with self-blame (Breitenbecher, 2006; Filipas & Ullman, 2006), and in prospective research, self-blame at the time of an assault was associated with greater risk for revictimization (Miller, Markman, & Handley, 2007). There is some evidence that suggests that negative social reactions may be at least partially responsible for the relationship between self-blame and PTSD symptoms in sexual assault survivors (Ullman, Townsend, Filipas, & Starzynski, 2007). Self-blame has been associated with psychological symptoms and poor adjustment in women in violent relationships (O'Neill & Kerig, 2000). Ultimately, self-blame at the time of the trauma may translate to shame-proneness over time, which has been associated with poor psychological functioning and risk for PTSD as discussed below.

## POSTTRAUMATIC FACTORS

### Posttraumatic Stress Symptoms

Development of PTSD after an initial traumatic event may be one of the strongest risk factors for exposure to subsequent trauma (Risser, Hetzel-Riggin, Thomsen, & McCanne, 2006). Initial onset of PTSD may account for the greater prevalence of PTSD among women in adulthood. Females appear to be more likely to develop PTSD following childhood abuse experiences (Breslau, Davis, Andreski, Peterson, & Schultz, 1997), and this may account for the greater prevalence in adulthood.

Several studies have demonstrated that PTSD symptoms mediate the relationship between childhood sexual abuse and later adult sexual assaults (Arata, 2000; Messman-Moore et al., 2000). A prospective study of Gulf war Veterans (Orcutt, Erickson, & Wolfe, 2002) found that all three PTSD symptom clusters mediated the effect of Gulf war trauma exposure on subsequent traumatic experiences. In contrast, in their study of childhood sexual abuse survivors using structural equation modeling, Risser et al. (2006) found that although PTSD accounted for a third of the variance in revictimization, hyperarousal symptoms were primarily responsible for the mediating effect of PTSD. However, psychophysiological research suggests that the self-reported hyperarousal of survivors of multiple traumas may not reflect the same physiologic patterns observed in survivors of single traumas (McTeague et al., 2010). McTeague et al. showed that despite self-reported hyperarousal and elevated heart rate reactions, survivors of multiple traumas showed deficits in physiological defensive responding as indicated by lower skin conductance and acoustic startle reactions to aversive imagery.

In addition to elevating risk for subsequent trauma exposure, PTSD following early trauma appears to be the primary risk factor for experiencing retraumatization following a subsequent trauma. Prior trauma exposure alone is not sufficient, rather only those who show a pathological response following the initial trauma appear to be at risk for future PTSD (Breslau, Peterson, & Schultz, 2008). Breslau et al. assert that the preponderance of evidence supports that trauma leads to PTSD among persons with a prior vulnerability, as suggested by neuroticism, family history of psychiatric disorders, or prior history of anxiety or depression. The severity of PTSD and depressive symptoms, however, may be linearly related to the extent of trauma exposure (Suliman et al., 2009).

## Avoidant Coping

Survivors of childhood sexual abuse have been shown to engage in maladaptive coping strategies, such as isolating themselves and making less use of healthier coping strategies such as social support seeking, tension reduction, and problem-focused coping. Experiencing multiple forms of abuse was associated with greater use of disengagement coping strategies (Leitenberg, Greenwald, & Cado, 1992). Adult survivors of sexual assault are more prone to use disengagement and avoidant coping if they had been sexually abused in childhood (Gibson & Leitenberg, 2001).

## Shame

Reid and Sullivan (2009) found that shaming sexual beliefs and behaviors mediated the relationship between sexual victimization in adolescence and later victimization in adulthood. This is consistent with a growing body of research demonstrating that shame is associated with significant risk for psychopathology (Street & Arias, 2001). Individuals prone to feel shame tend to hide from others, create interpersonal distance, and engage in defensiveness and denial as coping strategies (Tangney, Stuewig, & Mashek, 2007). Shame appears to mediate the relationships between prior trauma and avoidant coping in response to subsequent trauma (Gibson & Leitenberg, 2001). Shame has been linked to substance use and abuse (Dearing, Stuewig, & Tangney, 2005; Meehan, O'Connor, Berry, & Weiss, 1996), and shame proneness in early childhood predicted later risky driving and sexual behavior (Tangney & Dearing, 2002). In sum, available data suggest that shame may be a risk factor for both PTSD and subsequent trauma exposure.

## Persistent Dissociation

As indicated above, dissociation may begin during the peritraumatic period but often persists following the trauma. There is evidence that persistent dissociation may be more relevant to the persistence of PTSD than peritraumatic dissociation (Briere, Scott, & Weathers, 2005; Murray, Ehlers, & Mayou, 2002). Persistent dissociation likely entails avoidance of the trauma memory that can impede processing and resolution, and which is consistent with cognitive processing models of PTSD (Bryant, 2007). Persistent dissociation may reflect an avoidant coping pattern associated with repeated trauma exposure. Among sexually assaulted women, those who had also been abused in childhood showed substantially higher levels of dissociation (Cloitre, Scarvalone, & Difede, 1997). Dissociation was found to be predictive of subsequent trauma exposure in a prospective study (Banyard et al., 2002). Several mechanisms have been proposed to explain how dissociation may contribute to subsequent trauma exposure. Dissociation may impair protective behaviors due to decreased awareness of one's surroundings, or it may contribute to the individual appearing confused or distracted, making the person an easy target for victimization (Cloitre et al., 1997). Individuals prone to dissociation may be prone to errors in social cognition that might put them at risk for future victimization (DePrince, 2005). Thus, dissociation may be both a consequence of and precipitant of repeated trauma exposure.

## Social Support

Social support appears to be both a mediator and moderator of the effects of the initial trauma on adjustment and subsequent traumatic events. Positive social support in the aftermath of trauma exposure has been shown to buffer the negative effects of the traumatic experience on long-term adjustment (Muehlenkamp, Walsh, & McDade, 2010). How the support network responds may be crucial; when the support network responds in a validating manner, risk for later psychopathology may be reduced (Ullman, 2003). Negative reactions from the support system may engender stigma and lead to shame, which has been associated with disengagement coping with subsequent adult sexual assault (Gibson & Leitenberg, 2001).

Social support also may be important in preventing subsequent trauma exposure. Receiving less informational and emotional social support and more blame upon disclosure of assault experiences has been associated with revictimization (Mason, Ullman, Long, Long, & Srarzynski, 2009) and data indicate that problem drinking might mediate this relationship (Ullman, Starzynski, Long, Mason, & Long, 2008). Conversely, social support has been associated with reduced risk for subsequent trauma exposure in sexual abuse survivors (Banyard et al., 2002). Overall, evidence suggests that social support can reduce shame and thereby can mitigate the psychological impact of a traumatic experience and reduce revictimization.

## RISK BEHAVIORS

### Cognitive Deficits Leading to Failure of Risk Detection

Research on cognitive factors has primarily focused on understanding the links between sexual abuse and subsequent sexual behavior which may increase risk for both further sexual assaults and contracting sexually transmitted disease. Zurbiggen and Freyd (2004) outline several cognitive mechanisms that may impair decision making in sexual situations and lead to risky sexual behavior. They suggest that sexual abuse can lead to impairments in *consensual sex decision mechanisms, cheater detectors, reality detectors, self-esteem, and to ongoing dissociative behavior.* They hypothesize that such cognitive sequelae of sexual abuse would most likely be the result of trauma that involves betrayal of interpersonal trust. Although there is preliminary support for this hypothesis as it pertains to revictimization (Gobin & Freyd, 2009), this work has not accounted for the potential role of PTSD symptoms in affecting the cognition and behavior of survivors of childhood trauma. Several researchers have implicated PTSD as a mediator of the link between early trauma and subsequent high-risk behavior. Cognitive changes associated with PTSD might affect the survivor's ability to accurately detect danger (Arata, 2000). Moreover, Field, Classen, Butler, Koopman, Zarcone, and Spiegel (2001) found that revictimization tends to amplify the cognitive effects of previous victimization experiences.

### Skills Deficits and Protective Behaviors

Childhood sexual abuse survivors have been found to engage in more promiscuous sexual behavior and multiple sexual relationships (Gidycz et al., 1993). Several studies have shown that the link between childhood sexual abuse and sexual revictimization in adolescence and adulthood was mediated by an increase in risk-taking behaviors (Fargo, 2009; Van Bruggen, Runtz,

& Kadlec, 2006). Researchers have also suggested that PTSD symptoms may result in reductions in protective behaviors (Orcutt et al., 2002). According to this hypothesis, trauma survivors with PTSD experience a high rate of "false alarms" in reaction to nonthreatening stimuli. As a result, emotional arousal no longer cues the self-protective behaviors that help the individual to avoid risky situations or disengage and escape from danger when he or she is faced with it.

## Substance Use

Substance use, abuse, and dependency have been widely discussed as potential pathways through which trauma survivors may be at increased risk for further trauma. Most of this research has focused on sexual abuse and assault. Childhood sexual abuse has been linked to later delinquency behaviors and substance abuse (Merrill et al. 1999) and substance abuse has been shown to lead to promiscuous and high-risk sexual behavior (Gold, Sinclair, & Balge, 1999). Involvement in sexual activity and drug use has been associated with revictimization (Messman-Moore & Long, 2002). Binge drinking has been identified as a risk factor for subsequent rape among sexual assault survivors (McCauley, Calhoun, & Gidycz, 2010).

PTSD may play an important role in substance abuse and risk for repeated trauma. There is evidence supporting the hypothesis that drug abuse is used to "self-medicate" PTSD symptoms (Chilcoat & Breslau, 1998; Reed, Anthony, & Breslau, 2007) and that PTSD and not trauma exposure alone is prospectively related to onset of drug abuse problems (Reed et al., 2007). PTSD and problem drinking both have been associated with repeated victimization (Najdowski & Ullman, 2009), and there is evidence that problem drinking may at least partially mediate the relationship between PTSD symptoms and revictimization (Ullman et al., 2009).

## SUMMARY

Etiological models that consider PTSD as a reaction to a single traumatic event may be unrealistically narrow with regard to the actual experiences of trauma survivors with PTSD, the majority of who report multiple traumatic life experiences. Expansion of these models to understand the recurrence of trauma and traumatic stress reactions in the lives of these individuals may broaden their clinical relevance and lead to more effective interventions for PTSD and for prevention of further trauma. Linear models of causation provide a starting point for understanding the real-world experience of these survivors. However, rather than viewing trauma and PTSD as events and reactions at a single point in time, it is important to begin to see them as part of an iterative process. PTSD following early trauma appears to be one of the strongest risk factors for subsequent trauma. This may be mediated by cognitive changes related to hyperarousal and substance abuse, which impair the individual's ability to detect and respond defensively to threats. Additional trauma escalates the severity of PTSD symptoms, further enhancing risk of subsequent trauma. As suggested by Risser et al. (2006), the complex relationships likely represent reciprocal causal pathways, such that trauma exposure increases PTSD, which increases the likelihood of subsequent trauma exposure and so forth with ballooning effects over time.

## REFERENCES

Arata, C. M. (2000). From child victim to adult victim: A model for predicting sexual revictimization. *Child Maltreatment. Special focus section: Repeat victimization, 5*(1), 28–38.

Banyard, V. L., Williams, L. M., & Siegel, J. A. (2002). Retraumatization among adult women sexually abused in childhood: Exploratory analyses in a prospective study. *Journal of Child Sexual Abuse: Research, Treatment, & Program Innovations for Victims, Survivors, & Offenders, 11*(3), 19–48.

Boelen, P. A. (2006). Cognitive-behavioral therapy for complicated grief: Theoretical underpinnings and case descriptions. *Journal of Loss and Trauma, 11*(1), 1–30.

Bogat, G. A., Levendosky, A. A., Theran, S., von Eye, A., & Davidson, W. S. (2003). Predicting the psychosocial effects of interpersonal partner violence (IPV): How much does a woman's history of IPV matter? *Journal of Interpersonal Violence, 18*(11), 1271–1291.

Breitenbecher, K. H. (2006). The relationships among self-blame, psychological distress, and sexual victimization. *Journal of Interpersonal Violence, 21*(5), 597–611.

Breslau, N., Davis, G. C., Andreski, P., Peterson, E. L., & Schultz, L. R. (1997). Sex differences in posttraumatic stress disorder. *Archives of General Psychiatry, 54*, 1044–1048.

Breslau, N., Peterson, E. L., & Schultz, L. R. (2008). A second look at prior trauma and the posttraumatic stress disorder effects of subsequent trauma: A prospective epidemiological study. *Archives of General Psychiatry, 65*(4), 431–437.

Brewin, C. R., Andrews, B., & Valentine, J. D. (2000). Meta-analysis of risk factors for posttraumatic stress disorder in trauma-exposed adults. *Journal of Consulting and Clinical Psychology, 68*(5), 748–766.

Brewin, C. R., Dalgleish, T. Y., & Joseph, S. (1996). A dual representation theory of posttraumatic stress disorder. *Psychological Review, 103*(670–686).

Brewin, C. R., & Holmes, E. A. (2003). Psychological theories of posttraumatic stress disorder. *Clinical Psychology Review, 23*, 339–376.

Briere, J., Scott, C., & Weathers, F. (2005). Peritraumatic and persistent dissociation in the presumed etiology of PTSD. *The American Journal of Psychiatry, 162*(12), 2295–2301.

Bryant, R. A. (2009). Is peritraumatic dissociation always pathological? In P. F. Dell & J. A. O'Neil (Eds.), *Dissociation and the dissociative disorders: DSM-V and beyond* (pp. 185–196). New York: Routledge.

Bryant, R. A. (2007). Does dissociation further our understanding of PTSD? *Journal of Anxiety Disorders, 21*(2), 183–191.

Cabrera, O. A., Hoge, C. W., Bliese, P. D., Castro, C. A., & Messer, S. C. (2007). Childhood adversity and combat as predictors of depression and post-traumatic stress in deployed troops. *American Journal of Preventive Medicine, 33*(2), 77–82.

Campbell, R., Greeson, M. R., Bybee, D., & Raja, S. (2008). The co-occurrence of childhood sexual abuse, adult sexual assault, intimate partner violence, and sexual harassment: A mediational model of posttraumatic stress disorder and physical health outcomes. *Journal of Consulting and Clinical Psychology, 76*(2), 194–207.

Chemtob, C., Roitblat, H. L., Hamada, R. S., Carlson, J. G., & Twentyman, C. T. (1988). A cognitive action theory of post-traumatic stress disorder. *Journal of Anxiety Disorders, 2*, 253–275.

Chilcoat, H. D., & Breslau, N. (1998). Posttraumatic stress disorder and drug disorders: Testing causal pathways. *Archives of General Psychiatry, 55*(10), 913–917.

Cloitre, M., Scarvalone, P., & Difede, J. (1997). Posttraumatic stress disorder, self- and interpersonal dysfunction among sexually retraumatized women. *Journal of Traumatic Stress, 10*(3), 437–452.

Cloitre, M., Stolbach, B. C., Herman, J. L., van der Kolk, B., Pynoos, R., Wang, J., et al. (2009). A developmental approach to complex PTSD: Childhood and adult cumulative trauma as predictors of symptom complexity. *Journal of Traumatic Stress, 22*(5), 399–408.

Coid, J., Petruckevitch, A., Feder, G., Chung, W.-S., Richardson, J., & Moorey, S. (2001). Relation between childhood sexual and physical abuse and risk of revictimisation in women: A cross-sectional survey. *Lancet, 358*(9280), 450–454.

Coolidge, F. L., & Anderson, L. W. (2002). Personality profiles of women in multiple abusive relationships. *Journal of Family Violence, 17*(2), 117–131.

Dearing, R. L., Stuewig, J., & Tangney, J. P. (2005). On the importance of distinguishing shame from guilt: Relations to problematic alcohol and drug use. *Addictive Behaviors, 30*(7), 1392–1404.

DePrince, A. P. (2005). Social cognition and revictimization risk. *Journal of Trauma & Dissociation, 6*(1), 125–141.

Dunmore, E., Clark, D. M., & Ehlers, A. (2001). A prospective investigation of the role of cognitive factors in persistent posttraumatic stress disorder (PTSD) after physical or sexual assault. *Behaviour Research and Therapy, 39*(9), 1063–1084.

Ehlers, A., & Clark, D. (2000). A cognitive model of posttraumatic stress disorder. *Behaviour Research & Therapy, 38*, 319–345.

Ehlers, A., Clark, D. M., Dunmore, E., Jaycox, L., Meadows, E., & Foa, E. B. (1998). Predicting response to exposure treatment in PTSD: The role of mental defeat and alienation. *Journal of Traumatic Stress, 11*(3), 457–471.

Ehlers, A., & Steil, R. (1995). Maintenance of intrusive memories in posttraumatic stress disorder: A cognitive approach. *Behavioural and Cognitive Psychotherapy, 23*, 217–249.

Elliott, D. M., Mok, D. S., & Briere, J. (2004). Adult sexual assault: Prevalence, symptomatology, and sex differences in the general population. *Journal of Traumatic Stress, 17*(3), 203–211.

Elwood, L. S., Hahn, K. S., Olatunji, B. O., & Williams, N. L. (2009). Cognitive vulnerabilities to the development of PTSD: A review of four vulnerabilities and the proposal of an integrative vulnerability model. *Clinical Psychology Review, 29*(1), 87–100.

Everill, J. T., & Waller, G. (1995). Disclosure of sexual abuse and psychological adjustment in female undergraduates. *Child Abuse and Neglect, 19*(1), 93–100.

Fargo, J. D. (2009). Pathways to adult sexual revictimization: Direct and indirect behavioral risk factors across the lifespan. *Journal of Interpersonal Violence, 24*(11), 1771–1791.

Field, N., Classen, C., Butler, L., Koopman, C., Zarcone, J., & Spiegel, D. (2001). Revictimization and informational processing in women survivors of childhood sexual abuse. *Journal of Anxiety Disorders, 15*(5), 459–469.

Filipas, H. H., & Ullman, S. E. (2006). Child sexual abuse, coping responses, self-blame, posttraumatic stress disorder, and adult sexual revictimization. *Journal of Interpersonal Violence, 21*(5), 652–672.

Finkelhor, D., & Browne, A. (1985). The traumatic impact of child sexual abuse: A conceptualization. *American Journal of Orthopsychiatry, 55*(4), 530–541.

Flack, W. F., Litz, B. T., & Keane, T. M. (1998). Cognitive behavioral treatment of war-zone-related posttraumatic stress disorder. In V. Follette, J. Ruzek, & F. Abueg (Eds.), *Cognitive behavioral therapies for trauma* (pp. 77–99). New York: Guilford Press.

Foa, E., & Kozak, M. (1986). Emotional processing of fear: Exposure to corrective information. *Psychological Bulletin, 99*(1), 20–35.

Foa, E. B., Steketee, G., & Rothbaum, B. O. (1989). Behavioral/cognitive conceptualizations of post-traumatic stress disorder. *Behavior Therapy, 20*, 155–176.

Follette, V. M., Polusny, M. A., Bechtle, A. E., & Naugle, A. E. (1996). Cumulative trauma: The impact of child sexual abuse, adult sexual assault, and spouse abuse. *Journal of Traumatic Stress, 9*(1), 25–35.

Follette, V. M., &. Ruzek, J. I. (Eds.). (2006). *Cognitive behavioral therapies for trauma* (2nd ed.). New York: Guilford Press.

Fortier, M. A., DiLillo, D., Messman-Moore, T. L., Peugh, J., DeNardi, K. A., & Gaffey, K. J. (2009). Severity of child sexual abuse and revictimization: The mediating role of coping and trauma symptoms. *Psychology of Women Quarterly, 33*(3), 308–320.

Gibson, L. E., & Leitenberg, H. (2001). The impact of child sexual abuse and stigma on methods of coping with sexual assault among undergraduate women. *Child Abuse & Neglect, 25*(10), 1343–1361.

Gidycz, C. A., Coble, C. N., Latham, L., & Layman, M. J. (1993). Sexual assault experience in adulthood and prior victimization experiences: A prospective analysis. *Psychology of Women Quarterly, 17*(2), 151–168.

Giesbrecht, T., Lynn, S. J., Lilienfeld, S. O., & Merckelbach, H. (2008). Cognitive processes in dissociation: An analysis of core theoretical assumptions. *Psychological Bulletin, 134*(5), 617–647.

Gobin, R. L., & Freyd, J. J. (2009). Betrayal and revictimization: Preliminary findings. *Psychological Trauma: Theory, Research, Practice, and Policy, 1*(3), 242–257.

Gold, S. R., Sinclair, B. B., & Balge, K. A. (1999). Risk of sexual revictimization: A theoretical model. *Aggression and Violent Behavior, 4*(4), 457–470.

Halligan, S. L., Michael, T., Clark, D. M., & Ehlers, A. (2003). Posttraumatic stress disorder following assault: The role of cognitive processing, trauma memory, and appraisals. *Journal of Consulting and Clinical Psychology, 71*(3), 419–431.

Harvey, A. G., & Bryant, R. A. (1999). A qualitative investigation of the organization of traumatic memories. *British Journal of Clinical Psychology, 38*(4), 401–405.

Ingram, R. E., & Price, J. M. (2010). *Vulnerability to psychopathology: Risk across the lifespan* (2nd ed.). New York: Guilford Press.

Johnson, D. R., Lubin, H., Rosenheck, R., Fontana, A., Southwick, S., & Charney, D. (1997). The impact of homecoming reception on the development of posttraumatic stress disorder: The West Haven Homecoming Stress Scale (WHHSS). *Journal of Traumatic Stress, 10*(2), 259–277.

Keane, T. M., & Barlow, D. H. (2002). Posttraumatic stress disorder. In D. H. Barlow (Ed.), *Anxiety and its disorders: The nature and treatment of anxiety and panic* (2nd ed., pp. 418–521). New York: Guilford Press.

Keane, T. M., Zimering, R. T., & Caddell, J. M. (1985). A behavioral formulation of posttraumatic stress disorder. *The Behavior Therapist, 8*, 9–12.

King, D. W., King, L. A., Foy, D. W., & Gudanowski, D. M. (1996). Prewar factors in combat-related posttraumatic stress disorder: Structural equation modeling with a national sample of female and male Vietnam Veterans. *Journal of Consulting and Clinical Psychology, 64*(3), 520–531.

King, D. W., King, L. A., Foy, D. W., Keane, T. M., & Fairbank, J. A. (1999). Posttraumatic stress disorder in a national sample of female and male Vietnam Veterans: Risk factors, war-zone stressors, and resilience-recovery variables. *Journal of Abnormal Psychology, 108*(1), 164–170.

Kleim, B., Ehlers, A., & Glucksman, E. (2007). Early predictors of chronic post-traumatic stress disorder in assault survivors. *Psychological Medicine, 37*(10), 1457–1467.

Koenen, K. C., & Widom, C. S. (2009). A prospective study of sex differences in the lifetime risk of posttraumatic stress disorder among abused and neglected children grown up. *Journal of Traumatic Stress. Special Issue: Innovations in trauma research methods, 22*(6), 566–574.

Kubany, E. S. (1998) Cognitive therapy for trauma related guilt. In V. Follette, J. Ruzek, & F. Abueg (Eds.), *Cognitive behavioral therapies for trauma* (pp. 124–161). New York: Guilford Press.

Lee, D. A., Scragg, P., & Turner, S. (2001). The role of shame and guilt in traumatic events: A clinical model of shame-based and guilt-based PTSD. *British Journal of Medical Psychology, 74*, 451–466.

Leitenberg, H., Greenwald, E., & Cado, S. (1992). A retrospective study of long-term methods of coping with having been sexually abused during childhood. *Child Abuse & Neglect, 16*, 399–407.

Maker, A. H., Kemmelmeier, M., & Peterson, C. (1998). Long-term psychological consequences in women of witnessing parental physical conflict and experiencing abuse in childhood. *Journal of Interpersonal Violence, 13*(5), 574–589.

Mason, G. E., Ullman, S., Long, S. E., Long, L., & Srarzynski, L. (2009). Social support and risk of sexual assault revictimization. *Journal of Community Psychology, 37*(1), 58–72.

McCauley, J. L., Calhoun, K. S., & Gidycz, C. A. (2010). Binge drinking and rape: A prospective examination of college women with a history of previous sexual victimization. *Journal of Interpersonal Violence, 25*(9), 1655–1668.

McKeever, V. M., & Huff, M. E. (2003). A diathesis-stress model of posttraumatic stress disorder: Ecological, biological, and residual stress pathways. *Review of General Psychology, 7*(3), 237–250.

McTeague, L. M., Lang, P. J., Laplante, M. -C., Cuthbert, B. N., Shumen, J. R., & Bradley, M. M. (2010). Aversive imagery in posttraumatic stress disorder: Trauma recurrence, comorbidity, and physiological reactivity. *Biological Psychiatry, 67*(4), 346–356.

Meehan, W., O'Connor, L. E., Berry, J. W., & Weiss, J. (1996). Guilt, shame, and depression in clients in recovery from addiction. *Journal of Psychoactive Drugs, 28*(2), 125–134.

Merrill, L. L., Guimond, J. M., Thomsen, C. J., & Milner, J. S. (2003). Child sexual abuse and number of sexual partners in young women: The role of abuse severity, coping style, and sexual functioning. *Journal of Consulting and Clinical Psychology, 71*(6), 987–996.

Merrill, L. L., Newell, C. E., Thomsen, C. J., Gold, S. R., Milner, J. S., Koss, M. P., et al. (1999). Childhood abuse and sexual revictimization in a female Navy recruit sample. *Journal of Traumatic Stress, 12*(2), 211–225.

Messman-Moore, T. L., & Long, P. J. (2002). The role of childhood sexual abuse sequelae in the sexual revictimization of women: An empirical review and theoretical reformulation. *Clinical Psychology Review, 23,* 537–571.

Messman-Moore, T. L., Long, P. J., & Siegfried, N. J. (2000). The revictimization of child sexual abuse survivors: An examination of the adjustment of college women with child sexual abuse, adult sexual assault, and adult physical abuse. *Child Maltreatment. Special focus section: Repeat victimization, 5*(1), 18–27.

Miller, A. K., Markman, K. D., & Handley, I. M. (2007). Self-blame among sexual assault victims prospectively predicts revictimization: A perceived sociolegal context model of risk. *Basic and Applied Social Psychology, 29*(2), 129–136.

Mowrer, O. H. (1947). On the dual nature of learning: A reinterpretation of "conditioning" and "problem solving." *Harvard Educational Review, 17,* 102–148.

Muehlenkamp, J. J., Walsh, B. W., & McDade, M. (2010). Preventing non-suicidal self-injury in adolescents: The Signs of Self-Injury Program. *Journal of Youth and Adolescence, 39,* 306–314.

Murray, J., Ehlers, A., & Mayou, R. A. (2002). Dissociation and post-traumatic stress disorder: Two prospective studies of road traffic accident survivors. *British Journal of Psychiatry, 180*(4), 363–368.

Najdowski, C. J., & Ullman, S. E. (2009). Prospective effects of sexual victimization on PTSD and problem drinking. *Addictive Behaviors, 34*(11), 965–968.

Neuner, F., Schauer, M., Karunakara, U., Klaschik, C., Robert, C., & Elbert, T. (2004). Psychological trauma and evidence for enhanced vulnerability for posttraumatic stress disorder through previous trauma among West Nile refugees. *BMC Psychiatry, 4*(34). DOI:10.1186/1471-244X-4-34

North, C. S., Smith, E. M., McCool, R. E., & Lightcap, P. E. (1989). Acute postdisaster coping and adjustment. *Journal of Traumatic Stress, 2*(3), 353–360.

O'Neill, M. L., & Kerig, P. K. (2000). Attributions of self-blame and perceived control as moderators of adjustment in battered women. *Journal of Interpersonal Violence, 15*(10), 1036–1049.

Orcutt, H. K., Erickson, D. J., & Wolfe, J. (2002). A prospective analysis of trauma exposure: The mediating role of PTSD symptomatology. *Journal of Traumatic Stress, 15*(3), 259–266.

Ozer, E. J., Best, S. R., Lipsey, T. L., & Weiss, D. S. (2003). Predictors of posttraumatic stress disorder and symptoms in adults: A meta-analysis. *Psychological Bulletin, 129*(1), 52–73.

Reed, P. L., Anthony, J. C., & Breslau, N. (2007). Incidence of drug problems in young adults exposed to trauma and posttraumatic stress disorder: Do early life experiences and predispositions matter? *Archives of General Psychiatry, 64*(12), 1435–1442.

Reid, J. A., & Sullivan, C. J. (2009). A model of vulnerability for adult sexual victimization: The impact of attachment, child maltreatment, and scarred sexuality. *Violence and Victims, 24*(4), 485–501.

Riggs, D. S., Rothbaum, B. O., & Foa, E. B. (1995). A prospective examination of symptoms of post-traumatic stress disorder in victims of non-sexual assault. *Journal of Interpersonal Violence, 2,* 201–214.

Risser, H. J., Hetzel-Riggin, M. D., Thomsen, C. J., & McCanne, T. R. (2006). PTSD as a mediator of sexual revictimization: The role of reexperiencing, avoidance, and arousal symptoms. *Journal of Traumatic Stress. Special Issue: Dissemination: transforming lives through transforming care, 19*(5), 687–698.

Rona, R. J., Fear, N. T., Hull, L., Greenberg, N., Earnshaw, M., Hotopf, M., et al. (2007). Mental health consequences of overstretch in the UK armed forces: First phase of a cohort study. *BMJ: British Medical Journal, 335*(7620), 603.

Roodman, A. A., & Clum, G. A. (2001). Revictimization rates and method variance: A meta-analysis. *Clinical Psychology Review, 21*(2), 183–204.

Rosen, L. N., & Martin, L. (1996). The measurement of childhood trauma among male and female soldiers in the U.S. Army. *Military Medicine, 161*(6), 342–345.

Rothbaum, B. O., Foa, E. B., Riggs, D. S., Murdock, T., & Walsh, W. (1992). A prospective examination of post-traumatic stress disorder in rape victims. *Journal of Traumatic Stress, 5*, 455–475.

Smyth, J. M., Hockemeyer, J. R., & Tulloch, H. (2008). Expressive writing and post-traumatic stress disorder: Effects on trauma symptoms, mood states, and cortisol reactivity. *British Journal of Health Psychology, 13*(1), 85–93.

Stafford, J., Ehlers, A., Clark, D. M., Winton, E., Jaycox, L., Meadows, E., et al. (1996). *Predicting response to exposure treatment in PTSD: The role of mental defeat and alienation.* Paper presented at the Association for Advancement of Behavior Therapy, New York, NY.

Street, A. E., & Arias, I. (2001). Psychological abuse and posttraumatic stress disorder in battered women: Examining the roles of shame and guilt. *Violence and Victims, 16*(1), 65–78.

Suliman, S., Mkabile, S. G., Fincham, D. S., Ahmed, R., Stein, D. J., & Seedat, S. (2009). Cumulative effect of multiple trauma on symptoms of posttraumatic stress disorder, anxiety, and depression in adolescents. *Comprehensive Psychiatry, 50*(2), 121–127.

Tangney, J. P., & Dearing, R. L. (2002). Shame and guilt. New York: Guilford Press.

Tangney, J. P., Stuewig, J., & Mashek, D. J. (2007). Moral emotions and moral behavior. *Annual Review of Psychology, 58*, 345–372.

Tewksbury, R. (2007). Effects of sexual assaults on men: Physical, mental and sexual consequences. *International Journal of Men's Health, 6*(1), 22–35.

Ullman, S. E. (1996). Correlates and consequences of adult sexual assault disclosure. *Journal of Interpersonal Violence, 11*(4), 554–571.

Ullman, S. E. (2003). Social reactions to child sexual abuse disclosures: A critical review. *Journal of Child Sexual Abuse: Research, Treatment, & Program Innovations for Victims, Survivors, & Offenders, 12*(1), 89–121.

Ullman, S. E., Najdowski, C. J., & Filipas, H. H. (2009). Child sexual abuse, post-traumatic stress disorder, and substance use: Predictors of revictimization in adult sexual assault survivors. *Journal of Child Sexual Abuse: Research, Treatment, & Program Innovations for Victims, Survivors, & Offenders, 18*(4), 367–385.

Ullman, S. E., Starzynski, L. L., Long, S. M., Mason, G. E., & Long, L. M. (2008). Exploring the relationships of women's sexual assault disclosure, social reactions, and problem drinking. *Journal of Interpersonal Violence, 23*(9), 1235–1257.

Ullman, S. E., Townsend, S. M., Filipas, H. H., & Starzynski, L. L. (2007). Structural models of the relations of assault severity, social support, avoidance coping, self-blame, and PTSD among sexual assault survivors. *Psychology of Women Quarterly, 31*(1), 23–37.

Van Bruggen, L. K., Runtz, M. G., & Kadlec, H. (2006). Sexual revictimization: The role of sexual self-esteem and dysfunctional sexual behaviors. *Child Maltreatment, 11*(2), 131–145.

van der Velden, P. G., & Wittmann, L. (2008). The independent predictive value of peritraumatic dissociation for PTSD symptomatology after type I trauma: A systematic review of prospective studies. *Clinical Psychology Review, 28*(6), 1009–1020.

van Emmerik, A. A. P., Kamphuis, J. H., & Emmelkamp, P. M. G. (2008). Treating acute stress disorder and posttraumatic stress disorder with cognitive behavioral therapy or structured writing therapy: A randomized controlled trial. *Psychotherapy and Psychosomatics, 77*(2), 93–100.

Wirtz, P. W., & Harrell, A. V. (1987). Effects of postassault exposure to attack-similar stimuli on long-term recovery of victims. *Journal of Consulting & Clinical Psychology, 55*(1), 10–16.

Zinzow, H., Seth, P., Jackson, J., Niehaus, A., & Fitzgerald, M. (2010). Abuse and parental characteristics, attributions of blame, and psychological adjustment in adult survivors of child sexual abuse. *Journal of Child Sexual Abuse: Research, Treatment, and Program Innovations for Victims, Survivors, & Offenders, 19*(1), 79–98.

# Chapter 3

# A Psychodynamic Conceptualization of Retraumatization

*Harold Kudler*

The past is never dead. It's not even past.

*William Faulkner*

The field of psychological trauma has a long history and is evolving still. This chapter will examine psychological trauma and retraumatization from a psychoanalytic perspective. This, in itself, may challenge some readers. It is not popular to speak in psychoanalytic terms, yet modern concepts and treatments of psychological trauma are inextricably linked with the history of psychoanalysis and psychodynamic psychotherapy. Further, psychodynamic perspectives and practices continue to provide effective, evidence-based treatment (Shedler, 2010). This review may prove helpful to readers regardless of their theoretical or clinical orientation.

For late 19th-century mental health specialists, the study of the mind and its disorders was synonymous with the study of the brain and neuropathology. New technologies facilitated a cascade of neuroscientific discoveries promising to reveal the nature of mental phenomenon and offer new approaches to the management of untreatable conditions. Broca and Wernicke demonstrated that familiar clinical syndromes could be localized within discrete brain regions. Waldeyer built upon the work of Golgi and Ramón y Cajal to propose that the neuron was the functional unit of the central nervous system. It was also an age in which mental disorders were reclassified according to descriptive models. In many ways, it was a time much like our own.

The neurologist Jean-Martin Charcot was a master of the descriptive approach and the founder of modern neurology. He established a neurological clinic at the Salpêtrière Hospital in Paris in 1882, which was the first of its kind in Europe. In the course of his work there, he named and described multiple sclerosis, explicated the pathology of strokes, and lent his name (and those of his coworkers and students, including George Gilles de la Tourette, Pierre Marie, and Joseph Babinski) to a broad range of neurological diseases, syndromes, and signs.

In the course of his 33 years at the Salpêtrière, Charcot took charge of a unit that housed patients who suffered from intermittent disturbances of mental and somatic function that primarily included epilepsy and hysteria. These patients were prone to dramatic, episodic changes in their level of consciousness, behavior, and mentation. This led him to postulate a common neurological basis for hysteria and epilepsy that he called "hystero-epilepsy." Having reframed the age-old concept of hysteria in modern neurological terms, Charcot proceeded to the systematic, neuroscientific study of hysteria.

Charcot and his famous pupil, Pierre Janet, held that most patients who developed hysteria had suffered a severe traumatic event, either physical or mental. They did not believe that traumatic events actually caused hysteria but rather that such experiences could trigger hysteria in those whose brains were already biologically unfit. The contemporary term used to describe such a brain was *degenerate*, which signified that the patient's brain was degenerating biologically. Anyone might be traumatized, but if a person developed hysterical symptoms following that experience, it revealed that their brain had already been degenerate.

Then, as now, the term *degenerate* implied moral as well as biological degeneration. This was a matter of chicken and egg, because weak-brained people were expected to be prone to immoral acts, just as immoral acts were understood to weaken both character and brain. It is hard to blame 19th-century doctors for these beliefs given that half of all patients living in psychiatric hospitals at the time were suffering from neurosyphilis. This made it easy for medical professionals to assume from clinical history, physical examination, and autopsy findings (plus a healthy dose of Victorian morality) that mental disorders were closely linked to bad behavior and bad brains. These considerations matter, because they demonstrate some of the pitfalls associated with reducing all psychiatric findings to biology, of classifying mental disorders in purely descriptive terms, and of confusing mental problems with moral ones.

Our generation is by no means immune to these same mistakes. Although few modern clinicians would describe patients suffering from posttraumatic stress disorder as *degenerates,* many still harbor a deep-seated conviction that such patients must have been fundamentally compromised even before their traumatic experiences, either by their biology or their character, and that this inherent weakness contributed to the traumatic event's pathogenic effect.

FIGURE 3.1  André Brouillet, *Une Leçon Clinique à la Salpêtrière,* 1887. (Reproduced through the courtesy of the National Library of Medicine, http://www.nlm.nih.gov/hmd/emotions/psychosomatic.html.)

The same concern pervades our society, contributing to the stigma associated with reporting postdeployment stress problems, which is probably the most important barrier to access to mental health care among military members and Veterans. Our generation remains on a developmental line with that of our 19th-century predecessors: we claim to apply neuroscience to the classification and treatment of mental disorders because it is a values-neutral empirical science, yet we continue to conflate mental and moral fitness.

Freud entered Charcot's Salpêtrière as a medical student during the winter of 1885 to 1886 on a traveling fellowship from the University of Vienna. He was just under 30 years old at the time. Freud's aim was to learn the advanced principles of neuropathology and clinical neurology being pioneered by Charcot and bring them back to Vienna. He worked closely with Charcot and even translated some of his writings into German. Although his primary interest was neurology, Freud found himself drawn to Charcot's weekly case presentations of hysteria, which demonstrated how hysterical symptoms could (at least temporarily) be manipulated under hypnosis. The dramatic power of those lectures is apparent in Brouillet's famous tableau, "A Clinical Lesson at the Salpêtrière (1887)" (Figure 3.1). The crowd of prominent neurologists depicted includes Gilles de la Tourette (seated in the foreground wearing an apron), Pierre Marie, and Paul Richer. Charcot's equally famous patient, Blanche Wittmann, pictured in a cataleptic state, is flanked by Charcot's assistant, Babinski (who was responsible for hypnotizing the patients), and Charcot. For Charcot, the fact that his patients could be hypnotized only proved that their brains were weak.

While attending these demonstrations, Freud was reminded of a case described to him by his friend and mentor, Josef Breuer. Breuer, several years Freud's senior and an established general physician and neurologist in Vienna, had told Freud about his treatment of a young woman of exceptional intelligence and character who had fallen into severe hysteria in the process of nursing her father through a long and devastating illness. There was no question of the woman who was to become known as Anna O. being degenerate in any way, yet she had become hysterical. Freud tried to tell Charcot about this case and its implications, but Charcot was not interested (Freud, 1925a). When Freud got back to Vienna, he convinced Breuer to write up the case of Anna O. This was to become the first of their *Studies on Hysteria* (1895) to which Freud was to contribute four cases and a chapter on technique.

*Studies on Hysteria* is based on Breuer and Freud's radical notion that "hysterics suffer mainly from reminiscences" (Breuer & Freud, 1895, p. 7). By this, they meant that traumatic experiences and the memories, thoughts, and feelings associated with them were, in themselves, the root cause of hysteria. Breuer and Freud combined ideas about hysterical dissociation already being developed by Charcot and Janet with a new conception of their own, "conversion," thus developing the framework for describing hysterical symptoms still used today. Further, they demonstrated that hysterical symptoms such as paralysis, blindness, amnesia, hallucinations, and trance-states could be systematically eliminated by helping the patient fully remember the traumatic event while also experiencing its full emotional impact (abreaction). This cathartic (purgative) treatment described by Breuer and Freud was the first form of psychoanalysis.

The concept of traumatic neurosis (e.g., railway spine) was already established by the time of the *Studies,* and Breuer and Freud addressed its relation to their new theory of hysteria early in their report:

> *Observations such as these seem to us to establish an analogy between the pathogenesis of common hysteria and that of traumatic neuroses, and to justify an extension of the concept of traumatic hysteria* [emphasis original]. In traumatic neuroses the operative cause of the illness is not the trifling physical injury but the affect of fright—the psychical trauma. In an analogous manner, our investigations reveal, for many, if not for most, hysterical symptoms, precipitating causes which can only be described as psychical traumas. Any experience which calls up distressing affects—such as those of fright, anxiety, shame or physical pain—may operate as a trauma of this kind. (Breuer & Freud, 1895, pp. 5–6)

Breuer and Freud go on to consider that "instead of a single, major trauma … a number of partial traumas [may form] a *group* of provoking causes" (p. 6), thus anticipating the modern concept of cumulative trauma by decades and pointing the way toward an understanding of complex trauma (which is still hotly debated today) and retraumatization. They concluded that "the psychical trauma—or more precisely the memory of the trauma—acts like a foreign body which long after its entry must continue to be regarded as an agent that is still at work" (p. 6). In their view, a traumatic memory could be a discrete vector of pathology, much like a splinter under the skin or a germ within its host. The idea that a memory could, in itself, be pathogenic, was a critical step beyond Charcot and Janet's degeneracy-based theory of hysteria, and marked the beginning of modern medical psychotherapy.

Breuer and Freud agreed that psychological trauma was provoked by overwhelming past events, but they differed decisively on how such memories became pathogenic. One thing alone was clear: the five patients described in the *Studies* were literally haunted by experiences that they could neither fully remember nor forget. Breuer and Freud were close friends and full partners at the start of their efforts, but between the time that their friendly discussions began in the early 1880s and the publication of the *Studies* in 1895, the strain between them became obvious. As they state in their joint preface to the first edition:

> If at some points divergent and indeed contradictory opinions are expressed, this is not to be regarded as evidence of any fluctuation in our views. It arises from the natural and justifiable differences between the opinions of two observers who are agreed upon the facts and their basic reading of them, but who are not invariably at one in their interpretations and conjectures. (Breuer & Freud, 1895, p. xxix)

By the time they produced the second edition in 1908, Breuer and Freud chose to write separate prefaces in which Breuer made it clear that he has retained "no active dealings with the subject," while Freud emphasized that the *Studies* contained "the germs of all that has since been added to the theory of catharsis" but not an understanding of what psychoanalysis had since become.

In writing Breuer's obituary in 1925 (Freud, 1925b), Freud paid homage to his former friend and mentor. In addition to the case history of his first patient, Breuer contributed a theoretical paper to the *Studies*. It is very far from being out of date; on the contrary, it conceals thoughts and suggestions that have even now not been turned to sufficient account.

What follows is an effort to tap Breuer's insights and understand how they differed from Freud's evolving understanding of psychological trauma. Their intellectual differences eventually drove these medical pioneers apart personally and professionally. The key points of debate between them, described in 1895, remain at the heart of modern debate about the nature of psychological trauma and its treatment. They also distinguish the psychodynamic approach to psychological trauma and retraumatization from other theoretical perspectives. Their systematic review may suggest fresh insights and build new and useful bridges between theories, practices, and practitioners.

## THREE KEY CONFLICTS

The underlying conflicts that generated the tension between Breuer and Freud and that continue to divide the field of psychological trauma can be framed as follows:

1. Psychological trauma as a past external event versus an ongoing internal process
2. Psychological trauma as a biological event versus a psychological event
3. Psychological trauma as residing within the patient versus residing within the therapeutic relationship (with implications for the effectiveness and well-being of the therapist)

The means of conceptualization, study, and treatment of survivors of traumatic events follow from one's perspective on these three disputes. Each will be considered in order.

## 1. Psychological Trauma as a Past External Event Versus an Ongoing Internal Process

Is psychological trauma best understood as an encapsulated past experience with the external world or as an ongoing internal process? In the former view, what is traumatic is the event. From this perspective, trauma is firmly rooted in the past, even if it still causes distress in the present. Its clinical manifestations are understood to bear the perceptual imprint of the pathogenic external event as opposed to offering a window into an ongoing adaptive psychological process within which those perceptions are but one element.

The American Psychiatric Association's *Diagnostic and Statistical Manual of Mental Disorders,* 3rd edition (*DSM-III*) (1980) defined a *psychological trauma* solely in terms of a past, external event that was "outside the range of normal human experience" and which would have been "distressing to most people." Psychological trauma was taken to be discrete, objective, and external. *DSM* diagnostic criteria for posttraumatic stress disorder (PTSD) continue to be defined in terms of intrusive recollections and systematic avoidances relevant to a discrete external stressor. More recent editions of the *DSM* have included the A.2 Criterion for PTSD that requires that "the person's response involved intense fear, helplessness, or horror" (APA, 2000). This reflects a significantly different perspective, because it anchors PTSD to a subjective response on the part of the survivor in addition to the experience of an objectively defined external stressor. But note that this subjective response is still framed in the past tense as having happened at the time of the stressful event. Thus, the *DSM* definitions of *trauma* and of *PTSD* remain grounded in the concept of trauma as a discrete past event.

Breuer shared a similar view of psychological trauma. He believed that certain events were pathogenic because the painful traumatic memory of them was stuck in a biopsychological cul-de-sac. His perspective seems to have sprung from the influence of Charcot's application of hypnosis in the treatment of hysterical patients, which was already well known by the time Breuer began his work with Anna O. in 1880 (see, for example, Gamgee, 1878). Breuer was struck by Anna's marked capacity for self-hypnosis and her frequent trance-like states. He came to believe that most patients with hysteria had a tendency to enter alternative mental states that he called "hypnoid states." He suggested that, rather than being a marker of neuropathology, the capacity to enter hypnoid states was relatively common among healthy people. Breuer believed that the tendency to enter hypnoid states increased with practice. He sympathetically explained Anna O.'s strong predisposition to hypnoid states in these terms:

> This girl, who was bubbling over with intellectual vitality, led an extremely monotonous existence in her puritanically-minded family. She embellished her life in a manner which probably influenced her decisively in the direction of her illness, by indulging in systematic day-dreaming, which she described as her "private theatre." While everyone thought she was attending, she was living through fairy tales in her imagination; but she was always on the spot when she was spoken to, so that no one was aware of it. (Breuer & Freud, 1895, p. 22)

Although the tendency to enter hypnoid states might be normal, Breuer believed that trouble could result if a traumatic event occurred while the person happened to be in a hypnoid state. He also suggested that people like Anna who had long practiced going into such states might be preparing fertile soil for the pathogenic implantation of traumatic memories. Robert Kluft, who commented on Breuer's observations, is among many modern theorists and clinicians who might agree with Breuer that a tendency to dissociation is relatively common among normal people but might lay the groundwork for pathological states in the wake of traumatic experiences (Kluft, 2000).

Breuer posited that in normal mental states, stressful memories were actively processed through association with less painful memories, thoughts, and feelings such that they could be progressively managed and assimilated. A memory that entered the brain while it was in a hypnoid state would be filed in a separate register where it would linger in isolation from other memories and mental processes as an unconscious memory. Such unmetabolized memories, while incapable of full expression because of their isolation from normal connectivity, might nonetheless burst out in episodes of anxiety or dysphoria, induce dissociative phenomena, or be expressed through somatic symptoms such as anesthesia, paralysis, tics, mutism, or blindness. It was for this third possibility that Breuer and Freud coined the term *conversion*.

Breuer believed that conversion occurred when excessive nerve activation associated with unmetabolized traumatic memories spilled over from the brain's psychological system into its somatic system to manifest in motor or sensory symptoms. This was a purely biological theory. Freud took a psychological view in understanding conversion as a form of defense by which the mental tension associated with repressed thoughts, feelings, or memories might be partially relieved through symbolic expression as a somatic equivalent. Both men were trying to explain how highly charged mental contents that could not be directly discharged (either because they were stuck in a hypnoid state or because they were actively repressed) might be "converted" into somatic symptoms.

Of note, Roger Pittman and his colleagues suggested that PTSD may result from a misfiling of overwhelming experiences in an alternative and less efficient memory system (Brunet et al., 2008). They reported that the beta-adrenergic blocker propranolol might provide effective treatment under these conditions. If patients were treated with propranolol soon after the original traumatic event or if patients with PTSD were induced to remember the traumatic events and were then treated with propranolol, even extremely stressful events might come to be filed or refiled in more appropriate systems of memory without leading to or maintaining PTSD. Pittman's hypothesis offers a neurophysiology of hypnoid states and of abreaction consistent with Breuer's view of those phenomena.

In Breuer's view, hypnosis offered a mental forceps with which one could probe the hypnoid state and pluck out the traumatic memory. His patient, Anna O., was cured of her symptoms through the systematic application of this method. She went on to become an influential feminist and social pioneer. Breuer did not agree with Freud's theory of hysteria that held that the traumatic memories were pathological in themselves because the traumatized person could not accept such an experience as having happened. Freud held that because hysterical patients refused to remember traumatic events, they banished (repressed) them to an unconscious mental state. Such memories remained highly charged and might seep out in spite of the defense but only in attenuated, disguised forms acceptable to both the pressing unconscious and the repressing defense. Freud termed these *compromise formations* (Freud, 1896). For Freud, hysterical symptoms (and, later, dreams) were compromise formations. Thus, Breuer held that hysterical patients could not process traumatic experiences because they biologically *could not*, while Freud believed that they psychologically *would not*.

Freud began to conceptualize hysteria as the surface expression of an internal dynamic system that existed and operated in real time. Trauma was, for Freud, an ongoing process meant to contain and manage otherwise overwhelming ideas and feelings. Even though this dynamic may have been triggered by a particular past event, it involved much more than that event alone. This system was, in Freud's view, an adaptive one, an idea that fit well with his Darwinian principles. Freud believed that brain and mind must each, at their respective levels, advance the survival of the individual and the species. Freud's insistence that sexually charged events were most likely to lead to hysteria reflected his growing clinical experience and his belief that sexuality was a key driver of survival.

One of the distinguishing principles of psychoanalytic theory is that the symptoms of a mental disorder cannot be equated with its underlying pathology. Instead, they are understood as part of an adaptive effort to solve a problem. For example, many health professionals understand anorexia nervosa as a biological disorder with symptoms involving eating and weight problems that must be reducible to neurological, gastrointestinal, or genetic dysfunction. Psychoanalytically oriented clinicians approach anorexia nervosa as the patient's attempt to manage threatening developmental challenges of adolescence (including separation, individuation, and sexual maturation) by displacing them on to concerns about eating and weight (Bruch, 1978). Oral intake and weight are among the few aspects of life that adolescents can control. By micromanaging what gets into his or her body, the patient with anorexia nervosa can experience a sense of mastery despite the abrupt and mysterious changes he or she is living through. Anorexia can stop puberty in its tracks. By managing what they eat, patients with anorexia nervosa gain a desperately needed sense of control over the boundaries between themselves and others (parents, teachers, and peers). They are often willing to risk their lives to maintain this control. From a psychoanalytic perspective, anorexia is an effort (if a flawed one) to adapt to overwhelming stress.

By the same token, psychoanalytic clinicians do not believe that PTSD can be reduced to the misfiling of a past event. Instead, they hold that the symptoms of PTSD are external signs of an internal struggle for adaptation that can only be understood and addressed as a conflict in the here and now. From the psychoanalytic perspective, trauma cannot simply be extracted from the brain. Once the psychic equilibrium has been disrupted by a traumatic stressor, it is no longer the past event that is the problem: the internal process must be addressed and brought to a new, more adaptive balance.

## 2. Psychological Trauma as a Biological Event Versus a Psychological Event

Many of the theories of psychological trauma prevalent today are, at their roots, biological. As noted, psychoanalysis began at a time when psychiatry rested upon neurobiological principles and descriptive nosologies. We are, for the most part, well past the 19th-century view of psychopathology as a marker for biological (and moral) degeneracy. On the other hand, modern conceptions of psychological trauma and of PTSD often hark back to strikingly similar models. We continue to wonder if trauma might not more easily take hold in some people because of their gender, their peculiar brain structure, their physiology, or their genetics. Because not everyone exposed to a particular stressor develops PTSD, does that mean that those who do go on to meet diagnostic criteria lack a particular neurotransmitter, have burned out a brain component, or are marked by some other biological inadequacy or damage?

Modern medicine is largely founded on the infectious disease model that postulates a specific pathogen, a specific pathology, a specific course, and, hopefully, a specific cure. There is a tendency to consider trauma as if it were an infectious agent that induces discrete pathological changes in somatic structures and processes. We then seek the "antibiotic" that will eradicate the trauma and its pathogenic effects so that the body can return to normal health. This underlying assumption is in operation whether we are offering a drug meant to reset the activity of the amygdala or propose physical manipulations to provide "body therapy." An insistence on the somatic may underlie the retention of the term *Eye Movement Desensitization and Reprocessing* many years after the need for eye movements was disproved. Somatic models helped develop a system of medicine that boasts of being evidence based, yet such models may be misleading when applied to the problem of psychological trauma.

Somatic and psychological premises were clearly in conflict in the *Studies*. Breuer replaced the principle of degeneracy with his concept of hypnoid state but still understood this as a biological phenomenon. At the same time that the *Studies* were being published, Freud was working somewhat frantically on what he called his "Psychology for Neurologists" but which his translator, James Strachey, chose to entitle *Project for a Scientific Psychology* (1895/1950). Freud's original title provides good evidence that his *Project* was an effort to maintain the medical study of psychology within neurology. It may be that Freud's *Project* grew, at least in part, out of his growing concern about whether or not to follow his psychological theories beyond his identification with neurology. By 1895, he had already published important texts on pediatric neurology, coined the term *agnosia,* and predicted the use of cocaine as a topical anesthetic because of its ability to block nerve conduction. Perhaps Freud was also motivated by a wish to maintain peace with Breuer by creating a theory that allowed hysteria to be both biological and psychological at the same time. In any case, his failure to achieve his hoped-for reconciliation of biological and psychological concepts and processes forced him to abandon the *Project*, give up on dualism, and pursue psychoanalysis alone. It was not published during his lifetime.

Although Freud destroyed his own copy of the *Project* and did his best to ensure that the sole surviving copy sent to his friend, Wilhelm Fliess, would also be destroyed (it was not), that did not stop him from interpolating some of its central concepts into his later psychoanalytic writings. For example, Chapter 7 of *The Interpretation of Dreams* (Freud, 1900) contains many of the *Project*'s key ideas about how the brain works in order to explain how dreams might come about through the interplay of psychological and biological processes. Critics suggested that Freud continued to privately harbor a neurobiological agenda throughout his career. For example, Frank Sulloway, who entitled his biographical study *Freud, Biologist of the Mind* (1979), argued that Freud's greatest achievements derived from biology rather than psychology. Sulloway saw the *Project* as a clear statement of Freud's secret and lifelong biological manifesto. Sulloway was not alone in rereading Freud's work in biological terms or in arguing that the shortcomings of 19th-century neurology had created fundamental flaws in psychoanalysis (Crick and Mitchison, 1983; Hobson and McCarley, 1977). Such commentaries were a sign of the times as biological psychiatry consolidated its dominance over psychodynamic psychiatry in the last decades of the 20th century. Eisenberg (1986) described this progression as moving from a brainless psychiatry to a mindless one. Much heat was generated by these arguments, but little light emerged. As pointed out elsewhere,

> It seems neither necessary nor profitable to assume that neuroscience and psychoanalysis are locked in fundamental opposition or even in competition. Further progress must be made in integrating neuroscience and psychoanalysis before a more enlightening common perspective can emerge. (Kudler, 1989, p. 616)

It is, of course, unnecessary and probably foolish to deny that psychological trauma and PTSD exist simultaneously at biological and psychological levels. They can and should be studied and, whenever possible, treated at both levels. By the same token, there are aspects of psychological trauma and PTSD that are most pragmatically addressed at the level of the mind. Freud's entire career became an effort to create a working theory upon which to base effective psychotherapy. He documented his clinical experience in order to test and refine that theory and its technical application. As his case histories demonstrate, Freud could not help but observe that simply abreacting the traumatic memories was insufficient to free his patients from their problems.

Freud struggled with hypnosis and its role in treatment as illustrated in the very first of his cases in the *Studies.* He raised serious questions about the nature and value of hypnosis, including an insightful question about whether it was the hypnotist or the patient who was primarily responsible for inducing the hypnotic state or producing its therapeutic effects. Freud became convinced that, while certain special problems (including acute dissociative and conversion symptoms following acute traumatic shocks) could be successfully treated using abreaction, the problems in living that most people struggle with must be dealt with in a more thorough, iterative process that he called "working through." Sedler (1983) summarized working through in these terms: "Conceived as the labor of the patient, rather than as an analytic technique, working through consists of two phases: recognizing resistances (insight) and overcoming resistances (change)" (p. 72).

Freud provides this clinically based explanation in *Remembering, Repeating and Working Through*:

> For instance, the patient does not say he remembers that he used to be defiant and critical towards his parent's authority; instead he behaves that way to the doctor [transference]. He does not remember how he came to a helpless and hopeless deadlock in his infantile sexual researches; but he produces a mass of confused dreams and associations, complains that he cannot succeed in any-thing and asserts that he is fated never to carry through what he undertakes. He does not remember having been intensely ashamed of certain sexual activities and afraid of their being found out; but he makes it clear that he is ashamed of the treatment on which he is now embarked and tries to keep it secret from everybody. And so on. (Freud, 1914, p. 150)

As Freud learned, getting patients to remember is not always possible and was simply not enough. Most problems have to be worked through from multiple directions, including a thorough review of early development, past psychiatric history, current life issues, current thoughts, affects, dreams, symptoms, and what Freud called *The Psychopathology of Everyday Life* (1901). As will be described in greater detail (below), one of the most power-ful tools available for this work is the patient's transference to the analyst, which revivifies the patient's key past relationships and demonstrates in real time the rules, defensive maneuvers, compromises, expectations, regrets, traumas, grief, wishes, and hopes underlying the patient's relationships, past and present. Transference work provides the raw material and momentum necessary to do psychoanalytic work.

Strangely enough, although Freud moved past abreaction in his work, many clinicians continue to focus on abreaction as central to psychotherapy with trauma survivors. This may reflect the impact of Grinker and Spiegel's landmark work, *Men Under Stress* (1945), that demonstrated the dramatic power of abreaction, whether under the influence of hypnosis or sodium amytal, in alleviating the acute conversion and dissociative symptoms of World War II combat Veterans. Many American physicians who served in the military during World War II came home with tremendous enthusi-asm for abreactive therapy (not unlike the awe inspired among those who had witnessed Charcot's demonstrations). The obvious power of abreaction as practiced in WWII had galvanized academic psychiatry such that many new departments were established at medical schools across the nation in the postwar years. The enthusiasm and optimism resulting from the impressive abreactive cures of World War II thus laid the groundwork for the postwar dominance of psychoanalytic ideas and the present structure of American psychiatry. On the other hand, that enthusiasm may have also sown the seeds of disappointment in psychoanalytic theory and practices, because most of the problems facing American psychiatry proved to be much more complex and more chronic than those World War II posttraumatic dissociations and conversions. Perhaps the lesson to be drawn from this reading of history is that it will take the combined efforts of biological and psychological psychiatry to meet the needs of our patients, posttraumatic and otherwise.

## 3. Psychological Trauma as Residing Within the Patient Versus Residing Within the Therapeutic Relationship (With Implications for the Effectiveness and Well-Being of the Therapist)

Breuer worked under the premise that the psychological trauma behind Anna O.'s mental disorder haunted her precisely because it had been experienced during a hypnoid state. According to his theory, such memories were stored in an encapsulated form inaccessible to the process of mental association by which painful memories were normally detoxified and metabolized. Thus, they rattled around in the brain and popped out in strange forms at odd times and, especially, under stress (at which time the patient was likely to reenter the hypnoid state). In other words, the toxic effects of psychological trauma could be reduced to the problem of a traumatic memory that continued to reside within the patient. This is where the image of trauma as "foreign body" came from and why it made sense to Breuer that the therapist should be able to pluck that memory out by using hypnosis as a mental forceps. Shakespeare's Macbeth requests a similar operation from his wife's physician:

> Canst thou not minister to a mind diseas'd,
> Pluck from the memory a rooted sorrow,
> Raze out the written troubles of the brain,
> And with some sweet oblivious antidote,
> Cleanse the stuff'd bosom of that perilous stuff,
> Which weighs upon the heart?

**Macbeth, V.iii. 40–44**

Abreactive therapy was based on the idea that traumatic memories could be isolated, objectified, and extracted to restore a state of health.

Freud's evolving clinical experience demonstrated that abreaction did not reliably restore health. Even as he wrote up his cases for the *Studies*, he made it clear that his patients required additional interventions. He was also unable to hypnotize a number of patients. These observations led him to look beyond abreaction.

The critical point in the evolution from abreaction to modern psychoanalysis was Freud's discovery of transference. He found that, over time, certain phenomena would creep into the patient's attitudes that interfered with the evolving conversation. These coalesced into stable patterns of relating to the therapist that did not make sense in terms of the available facts and that often threatened to derail the therapy. As his early papers on transference (Freud, 1912a, 1912b, 1913) document, Freud first considered transference a distraction that interfered with the pursuit of unconscious memories and feelings. Over time, he came to understand that by focusing on transference, therapist and patient could open a window on attitudes and concerns, some conscious, some unconscious, which the patient had consistently held toward people in the past and continued to influence relationships in the present.

The most powerful and problematic transferences reflect the patient's most important past relationships. These are usually formative relationships with parents, other caregivers, and siblings, but later life experience could also lay the groundwork for new transference tendencies. Transference is more than a learned way of acting; it is a reenactment of wishes, fears, and defensive patterns inherent in those early relationships. It is not a simple repetition but the final common pathway of a complex and ongoing interaction of past and present interpersonal experiences, beliefs, needs, and fears. Transference patterns can also be reactivated, reworked, and driven to extremes in the wake of traumatic experiences and the personal meanings the patient assigns to them. There is no single *posttraumatic transference*. Preexisting patterns interweave with aspects of the traumatic event or events, their specific meanings, and post-traumatic experiences to create different patterns for different individuals.

To Freud's mind, all transference functions as a resistance to the process of therapy (Freud, 1912a). In other words, the patient enters therapy with the conscious intention of confronting and overcoming a posttraumatic psychological problem, but as these concerns come forward in the therapy, the patient feels increasingly threatened by the therapeutic process. Progress in the therapy becomes associated in the patient's mind with the threatening issues and anxiety that first brought the patient to therapy. This situation calls forth the same defensive strategies that were keeping the posttraumatic conflict in check. Once again, Freud saw counterbalancing forces of mental conflict at work, only now, instead of producing hysterical symptoms, the mind compromised by producing transference.

Freud started with the idea that transference-resistance to psychoanalytic progress needed to be swept out of the way by appeal to the patient's logic or by force of the therapist's authority (including the use of suggestive techniques) so that patient and therapist could get on with the business of finding and abreacting unconscious traumatic memories. The critical breakthrough in Freud's thinking came when he recognized that transference could become the therapy's greatest ally. This was because the nature and intensity of the patient's transference offered important clues about what was being defended against and how those defenses were arrayed. Just as hysterical symptoms bear the stamp of the patient's posttraumatic fears and the defensive forces that oppose them, transference provides invaluable access to unconscious conflict by delivering it fresh and alive right into the office. One can debate the past or the unconscious ad infinitum, but it is hard to dismiss powerful feelings and attitudes that are in the room with you. This is particularly so when the patient sees that these compelling beliefs and feelings are revenants of past relationships rather than realistic appraisals of the therapeutic relationship. Transference can be plumbed in three directions by looking at how these same relationships and attitudes functioned in the past, in the present outside of the therapy, and within the transference. In this way, transference serves as a mental Rosetta Stone with which patient and therapist can bring meaning to otherwise ineffable mental contents, processes, and behaviors. That is why psychoanalysis has become the analysis of transference. As Freud put it,

> It is undeniable that the subjugation of the transference-manifestations provides the greatest difficulties for the psychoanalyst; but it must not be forgotten that they, and they only, render the invaluable service of making the patient's buried and forgotten love-emotions actual and manifest; for in the last resort no one can be slain in absentia or in effigy. (1912a, p. 108)

Psychoanalysis evolved as a technique to precipitate transference. Analysts and patients meet frequently in order to provide opportunities for transference to develop and assert itself. The therapist discloses as little about his or her own history, attitudes, and persona as possible in order to offer the patient a screen upon which to project whatever issues may come forward. The therapist strives to remain neutral to any position the patient might take in order to allow the free play of ideas necessary for transference to take center stage. The couch allows the patient to look away from the therapist so that he or she is free to imagine the therapist's responses (and remain unburdened by any nonverbal response the therapist might make). All of this is orchestrated to provide the maximal opportunity for transference.

Once transferential thoughts and feelings begin to coalesce, the therapist works diligently to help the patient become aware of emerging patterns and themes. Therapist and patient work together to consider the extent to which the patient's transference can be differentiated from reality. This is an iterative process that requires that the patient be sound enough to distinguish external reality from intrapsychic reality (which can be difficult for the best of us). The strength of the transference in the face of conflicting evidence is an intriguing mystery that impels the patient on a mission of self-discovery. This quest drives the therapy. Through systematic exploration, the patient learns about past and present relationships and about the patterns those relationships tend to follow. This sheds light on the sense (often unconscious) the patient has made of his or her life history along with his or her wishes, fears, and compromises. In particular, when a patient's symptoms stem from trauma, the posttraumatic concerns stirred by that trauma are reflected within the transference and become accessible through it. With consistent effort, a strong working relationship and shared dedication to the therapeutic goal, the transference is analyzed, and the patient's problems are worked through.

To review, Breuer's theory held that posttraumatic pathology occurred when traumatic memories became encapsulated within the patient's brain. He saw the problem as residing within the patient and expected that it would be resolved if the therapist could simply extract or ablate the pathogenic agent. The same metaphor remains active in modern theories that hold PTSD to be a discrete biological injury to a brain component, physiological system, or genetic configuration. Freud started out by following Breuer's ideas but came to realize that traumatic memories, thoughts, and concerns and the defenses against them were best identified and grappled with at the interpersonal level through analysis of the transference. This discovery was pragmatic, based on growing clinical experience. For Freud, it became logical and practical to locate and work with posttraumatic mental disorders within the therapeutic relationship.

Freud's advance to the interpersonal level demonstrates that theory and therapy require a two-person field. This idea was later explored by Sullivan (1970), but it sprang from Freud's early work. The therapist cannot simply act upon the patient (as Breuer attempted to do with hypnosis), and the patient is constantly interacting with the therapist. Whatever happens in therapy between a particular patient and therapist is inevitably a unique, collaborative, evolving effort. Also, if analysis of transference is the key to understanding and relieving the patient's problems, then the therapist's internal experiences in working with the patient are essential material for that work.

Because therapy requires inviting and being open to the patient's transference projections, the therapist must allow himself or herself to become exquisitely vulnerable to those projections. None of us are perfect therapists, and even if we were, we would still have personal responses to our patients' transference. Therapists who feel nothing in response to their patients are probably unfit to do psychotherapy. When we offer ourselves as screens upon which the patient may project past relationships and ongoing concerns, we open ourselves to a broad variety of experiences and responses. The therapist faces a difficult task in distinguishing a patient's realistic assessments from his or her neurotic projections. To complicate matters, Freud held that no real distinction could be drawn between transference feelings and real feelings (including transference love) (Freud, 1915). His main point was that it is not only unethical but also impractical for the therapist to respond to the patient's feelings in kind. Because the therapist holds the patient's health and progress as the highest priorities, the therapist must abstain from acting on transference feelings. The pain of projected past relationships, which often flows directly from traumatic experiences within those relationships, is real and immediate even if it is a residue of long past events. This speaks to the truth of Freud's assertion that the unconscious has no sense of time. When a therapist is open to the patient's transference for therapeutic purposes, at least some of that pain will inevitably be borne by the therapist.

By entering the field of the patient's transference, the therapist is prone to respond with countertransference. *Countertransference* has been broadly defined, but for the purpose of this paper, it is a response of the therapist which reflects the therapist's personal history and balance as well as the patient's dynamics. Freud urged therapists to undergo their own analysis in order to keep from acting upon their inevitable countertransference feelings. It is the therapist's responsibility to harness countertransference for therapeutic purposes. First, the therapist explores his or her responses in order to identify them and consider what they might reveal about the patient's transference. Then the therapist works to make that information of practical use to the patient. At all times, the therapist must abstain from acting on his or her own counter-transference. This makes psychoanalytic psychotherapy very demanding work, but it allows countertransference to serve as a powerful therapeutic tool.

When clinicians think of psychological trauma as residing within the patient, their attention and actions center on the patient and not on themselves. When, as Freud suggested, psychological trauma is understood as residing within the therapeutic relationship, the therapist is enjoined to look inward as well. This has important implications for the effectiveness and well-being of the therapist. As noted, psychoanalytic practice, starting with Freud's advice, urges clinicians to seek their therapy in order to assure that their own blind spots and concerns do not interfere with their ability to be available to their patients and to keep their patient's interests clearly separate from and above their own.

These considerations point to a modern problem facing society and the field of psychotherapy. Over the past decade, thousands of new psychotherapists have begun working with hundreds of thousands of new combat Veterans and their family members. In clinical systems that primarily serve military members and Veterans, these therapists carry large caseloads of severely traumatized men and women. Therapists are hearing horrific histories and are becoming immersed in powerful, posttraumatic transferential and counter-transferential fields. Many report significant stress associated with this work. As they put it, they find themselves "taking their patients' problems home with them." This may manifest in the therapist dreading to see one patient or feeling unusually enthusiastic about seeing another. A therapist may be tempted to transgress boundaries with one patient or become withholding with another. The therapist may experience painful, intrusive thoughts, images, feelings, dreams, or other phenomena related to their clinical work. Some may come to doubt their ability to meet their patients' needs, while others become obsessed with feelings of special competence or concerns about being utterly indispensable to their patients. These are but a few of the ways in which transference and countertransference may play out in therapy with trauma survivors.

Most of these new therapists have been trained in disciplines other than psychoanalysis, and many have not had extensive training about transference and countertransference. Some schools of psychotherapy make a point of minimizing or even dismissing consideration of transference and countertransference in favor of emphasizing cognitive, behavioral, and other components of a preferred theory or intervention. Even though countertransference might be mentioned as a conceptual issue, it is not likely to be addressed systematically in course work or in supervision. Psychotherapists who have trained in therapies other than psychoanalysis may not have been encouraged to enter personal psychotherapy to help them focus on these issues. As of this writing, an entire generation of new therapists is immersed in a powerful field of posttraumatic transference and countertransference but lacks the preparation and ongoing support for this mission.

To paraphrase a famous saying of Charcot (as quoted by Freud), "theories are lovely things but they do not prevent the facts from existing" (1893, p. 13). Transference is a universal phenomenon. Whether a therapist chooses to work with transference or not, it will still be present in the therapy, as will countertransference. Clinical experience in doing psychotherapy with trauma survivors demonstrates that therapist responses to such patients are usually poignant and powerful. Without adequate training and personal psychotherapy, inexperienced therapists may be less able to identify or manage their patients' intense posttraumatic transference or their own countertransference. This can create a significant impediment in doing any form of psychotherapy with severely traumatized patients. If ignored or, worse, if acted out, transference and countertransference can derail patient, therapy, and therapist, resulting in therapeutic failure and therapist burnout. This is perhaps the most important implication of conceptualizing psychological trauma as residing within the patient as opposed to understanding it as residing within the therapeutic relationship.

## IMPLICATIONS FOR A PSYCHOANALYTIC THEORY OF RETRAUMATIZATION AND FOR TREATMENT

As I hoped to demonstrate through this historical, theoretical, and technical review, the differences between Breuer and Freud which emerged in the course of writing their 1895 *Studies on Hysteria* have persisted in our ongoing efforts to understand and treat the effects of psychological trauma. But what do they suggest about the concept of *retraumatization*? Their implications are aligned with the three key conceptual conflicts defined above.

### Psychological Trauma as a Past External Event Versus an Ongoing Internal Process

If psychological trauma is understood as an ongoing internal process (as it is in psychoanalysis) rather than static representation of one or more past external events, then trauma is not to be regarded in terms of discrete incidents (or discrete injuries caused by them) taking up residence within the survivor. Rather, each sequential event is understood as but one factor within a more complex, dynamic system—another stone tossed into an already disturbed stream. Sequential traumatic experiences may have cumulative effects, but these will not be simply additive. Their sum effect will be influenced by several factors, including the survivor's achieved developmental stage at the time of each event, the security of his or her attachment to others, the maturity of his or her interpersonal world, the overall strength of the psyche, the state of its dynamic balance and its ability to titrate anxiety, the specific personal meaning of the event, the level of perceived social support, and the level of any ongoing environmental stress. This is by no means an exhaustive list of factors, but it speaks to the complexity necessitated by the psychoanalytic view. It also demonstrates the potential for recovery and further growth implicit within the psychoanalytic perspective. Psychoanalysis is based on the idea that psychological functions are flexibly sub-served by multiple systems, that development is ongoing throughout life, and that adaptation is fundamental to human nature. Within this perspective, there is always the possibility that new balance will be achieved and that further growth will follow.

A great deal has been said about posttraumatic growth in recent years (Tedeschi & Calhoun, 2004). Psychoanalytic theory predicts the capacity for such growth, and psychoanalytic technique was developed specifically to foster it. No treatment can turn a past bad memory into a good memory, much less undo a series of past traumatic events. Some survivors seem to be willing to compromise by trading peace of mind for relative freedom from grief, horror, and fear. Psychoanalysis promotes posttraumatic growth by facilitating the survivor's efforts to achieve a better balance between harsh realities and enduring beliefs, needs, wishes, and fears. Such therapy helps survivors become wiser, which is to say, better adapted and more adaptable.

## Psychological Trauma as a Biological Event Versus a Psychological Event

If trauma is understood as a psychological event rather than a biological one, traumatization is more complex than an infection, a malfunction, or a point lesion. By extension, retraumatization must be more than a relapse or a metastasis. As already suggested, from a psychoanalytic perspective, the effects of one or more traumatic experiences cannot be equal to the sum of its parts. They must be measured in terms of their effects on an evolving, epigenetic developmental process.

It is particularly interesting that the term *epigenetic* has recently become more recognized as the expression of a biological theory of intergenerational transmission of traumatic effects and resiliency by which a traumatic event leads to an enduring alteration in the configuration of the survivor's genetic material that will produce enduring changes within that person and that may also be passed along to any children conceived after the traumatic event (Yehuda & Bierer, 2009). This is quite a leap from the psychoanalyst Eric Erickson's epigenetic theory (Erickson, 1950) that describes how each new stage of development is founded upon the achievements and deficits of past stages. Erickson speaks to the remarkable human potential for new adaptation and new failures of adaptation at each stage and the complex dynamic through which past successes and failures and strengths and weaknesses influence the outcome of successive developmental challenges (including traumatic events). Erickson makes it clear that every time a new developmental stage is reached, there is an opportunity to rework old failures into new successes. As opposed to the new biological epigenetic theory that views traumatic events as becoming encapsulated in discrete, preprogrammed genetic vectors potentially resulting in the transgenerational inheritance of specific, enduring biological alterations, Erickson's psychoanalytic epigenetic theory describes a continuously evolving biopsychosocial dynamic with repeated opportunities for correction of deficits, ongoing growth, and infinite variety within each individual and across generations.

Because of the inherent complexity of dynamic systems and developmental processes (the dimension of time being a fundamental concern of psychoanalytic theory), psychoanalysis cannot reduce repeated traumatic experiences to a set of discrete injuries, each of which is associated with a particular pathological lesion. Instead, each traumatic event is understood as yet another stress on the survivor's developing psychological system. The new trauma may be the final straw that sends a system that was already straining for balance reeling out of control, or it may, instead, promote the adaptation (posttraumatic growth) necessary to restore a stable equilibrium.

Psychoanalytic psychotherapy proceeds by way of the mind rather than the brain. These are not mutually exclusive approaches given that, at some levels, mind and brain are one. This is more than an abstraction because clinical experience demonstrates that biological interventions and psychological interventions often facilitate one another. As Kandel (1979) points out, when you do psychotherapy with a person, you are likely altering the structure and function of that person's brain in discrete and important ways. Biological epigenetic theory suggests that we may be changing that person's genetics as well. But although it is helpful to clarify the difference in their perspectives, it is also important to be clear that biological and psychoanalytic theories of psychological trauma and retraumatization are only abstractions meant to help us conceptualize what must fundamentally be a single process. Kandel follows Wilson (1977) in pointing out that both psychoanalysis and neuroscience function as antidisciplines to the parent discipline of psychiatry. Each provides a theoretical foothold for understanding certain phenomena but cannot or should not be expected to replace or disqualify the other, any more than the theory of relativity could replace or disqualify

Newtonian physics. They are simply different lenses of the scientific instrument. The trick is in knowing when to use the scanning objective and when to use the oil immersion lens.

## Psychological Trauma as Residing Within the Patient Versus Residing Within the Therapeutic Relationship (With Implications for the Effectiveness and Well-Being of the Therapist)

For the psychoanalytically oriented clinician, the enduring effects of retraumatization are not to be mistaken for symptoms and signs of a discrete disorder residing within the patient. Instead, repeated traumatic experiences are to be explored and engaged within the field of the survivor's relationships with others. These include the survivor's past relationships as reported in the therapy, their current relationships outside of the therapy, and in their transference within the therapy. As noted, the psychotherapist's countertransference is often the most important indicator of the patient's maturity, strength, and status of the survivor's interpersonal system. Psychoanalysis is distinguished from other forms of treatment by its emphasis on the therapist's disciplined use of himself or herself as an instrument of therapy.

There is often an intimate relationship between the stage of the survivor's interpersonal development at the time of the first traumatic event and the survivor's current interpersonal valence. In addition, subsequent traumatic experiences may undo past adaptive successes and lead to acute or chronic regression in function. This can seriously undercut previous achievements in intimacy and security.

The psychoanalytic clinician attunes to changes in interpersonal relations as an important indicator of the nature, intensity, and meaning of each traumatic experience and, in particular, remains alert to clues about trauma and retraumatization within transference and countertransference. At the start of their work together, Breuer and Freud shared the view that critical components of traumatic memories were locked within the survivor's unconscious such that they were inaccessible to patient and therapist. Over time, Freud came to understand that "no mortal can keep a secret" (Freud, 1905, p. 215). Even if the patient cannot remember a traumatic event or a series of traumas or has dissociated such memories from the thoughts and affects that originally accompanied them, a focus on transference and countertransference will eventually tease out clues that can lead the patient to deeper understanding, growing acceptance, and new opportunities for growth and development. By the same token, therapists who fail to pay attention to the influence of posttraumatic transference and countertransference on their own thoughts, emotions, relationship with patients, and relationships with others are likely to encounter difficulties in being helpful to patients or maintaining their own well-being.

A 32-year-old male resident in orthopedics presented for treatment with a chief complaint of nightmares and "strange worries which I can't shake." His symptoms began almost immediately after his fiancée died in an accident. Their car had broken down on a broad and busy road, and they decided to wait for assistance in a diner on the opposite side. As they started to cross, a car ran through a stoplight, made a wide left turn, and careened into the young woman. She died instantly, and her body was badly mutilated. The driver, who was intoxicated, was arrested, and his trial was pending. These events occurred 4 months prior to the initial intake appointment.

When asked about the nature of his "strange worries," he explained that since his fiancée's death, he continuously worried about the safety of her belongings that he kept in the apartment they had shared. This anxiety was manageable most days, although sometimes he felt obliged to go home at midday just to be sure that her belongings were still safe. He could not say exactly what might happen to these items (which included an assortment of clothes, CDs, books, photos, and a violin), but if he could not arrange to visit them, his anxiety built to panic levels. He had, in fact, left the operating room on two occasions because of shortness of breath and palpitations. Also, during nights when he was on call at the hospital, he was so overwhelmed by anxiety about the safety of his fiancée's belongings that he sometimes became distracted and short tempered. His fellow residents and attendings had taken notice, and his residency director had directed him to seek psychiatric consultation.

On reviewing his history, the patient clearly met *DSM* criteria for PTSD, but despite his obsessive worries and compulsive behaviors, he did not meet criteria for any other mental disorder and did not have any significant past psychiatric history. On reviewing his family history, he had lost a younger brother to bacterial meningitis when the patient was age 11 and the brother was age 4 years old. He denied any significant problems beyond expectable grief following his brother's death.

The patient was ambivalent about taking medication because of the nature of his work and his need to stay alert. After a discussion of possible side effects, he agreed to a trial of a selective serotonin reuptake inhibitor (SSRI) at a low dose in hopes of reducing his symptoms. When offered choice of a range of psychotherapies, he firmly stated that he wanted "a talking therapy" given that he was far from his family, was living with a great deal of stress, and needed someone he could talk openly with. He and the therapist agreed to a trial of psychoanalytic psychotherapy with twice weekly meetings.

Over the next 6 weeks, the patient reported a good response to treatment. His symptoms were still present but at a lower intensity such that they no longer interfered with his clinical duties. He spoke freely in therapy and displayed a broad knowledge of psychoanalytic concepts and a capacity for self-observation. He seemed to be making steady progress in confronting significant grief which he had, up until the present, "not wanted to feel," even though he reported that not feeling the level of sorrow that he had expected after his fiancée's death had made him "feel like a monster."

Over time, his therapist noted that certain patterns were beginning to emerge within the therapeutic relationship. At the start of the therapy, the patient had made clear and apparently sincere statements about his appreciation for the therapist and his expertise, but the patient was now increasingly critical of the therapist during sessions. He commented about the therapist's level of attention, his ability to "mind the clock properly" at the start and end of sessions, and kept up a running commentary on the therapist's taste in clothes. Within the same session, he would comment that the therapist had been "too passive" and then say the therapist "should not interrupt the way he always did." He made these remarks without any great affect or apparent sense of having contradicted himself. In fact, his manner toward the therapist was, in his own words "tutorial." It became common for the patient to say with a smile, "You're not the perfect therapist but I think you're trainable."

The frequency and intensity of the patient's criticism (and of the patient's emotional intensity associated with these remarks) increased rather suddenly after a particular incident at the start of a session during the second month of therapy. The patient entered the office looking anxious and visibly panting. He flopped into a chair and reported that he was having a hypoglycemic attack. He had had similar symptoms in the past but without any fixed pattern. He assumed that these were hypoglycemic because they always improved after he drank a can of soda. The patient said that he was too weak to go to the soda machine in the clinic lobby and asked the therapist if he would go for him and buy him a can of soda. The patient did not have any change on him and asked the therapist to lay out the money with a promise to pay him back at the start of the next session. The therapist did as asked, and the patient, having sipped his soda, soon felt better and went on with the session.

At the start of the next session, the therapist inquired about the patient's health since their last meeting. The patient said that he had been well and again thanked the therapist for his help. The patient then apologized for not having brought any money with which to repay the therapist. The therapist decided not to make any statement about this other than to note that the patient could bring the money to the next session.

In the weeks that followed this apparently innocuous event, the therapy took a dramatic turn. Despite the fact that the patient was generally free from overriding anxiety at work, was sleeping better, and had regained his previous level of social engagement, the therapeutic relationship seemed to be deteriorating. The patient had become significantly more strident in his criticism of the therapist and was now verbally hammering the therapist in almost every session. He regularly insisted that the therapist spoke when he should not and did not speak when he should. He had no wish to end therapy, as there were still issues about his fiancée that he wanted to work on. In addition, the trial of the driver who had killed her was pending, and the patient felt strongly that he needed to remain in therapy in order to cope with the added stress he anticipated as he thought about testifying in court about his fiancée's death. He had begun once again to have nightmares in which he vividly saw the accident and stood over her disfigured body.

The therapist, for his part, found that he was coming to dread his appointments with the patient. His mind would be on the patient when he'd wake up in the morning. He had found himself obsessing over his choice of ties because of the criticism the patient habitually made about which one he was wearing.

He found himself yawning during sessions (a fact that did not escape the patient's notice or criticism). Matters came to a head three weeks before the trial when the patient insisted that both he and his therapist needed to undergo a consultation in order to "save the therapy." The patient was increasingly anxious during the sessions, even though his PTSD symptoms had decreased significantly and he had successfully completed a preliminary deposition for the court. The therapist was himself feeling very uneasy. Not only did he regret having to see this particular patient, but a sense of insecurity had begun to creep into his interaction with other patients. He decided to seek supervision.

The supervisor, who had worked with this therapist in the past, observed that themes of "being in control" and "doing the right thing" seemed to resonate within the patient's transference and the therapist's countertransference. In reviewing the case with the therapist, the supervisor pointed out that the patient was a lifelong perfectionist who, up until the recent tragedy, had managed to perform at a very high level with considerable grace and very little anxiety. The supervisor suggested that the therapist build upon his recognition of his own gnawing sense of inadequacy (something quite uncharacteristic for the therapist) and the patient's consistent pattern of needing to be (as the patient called it) "best man" by offering an observation to the patient about how important it had become for both of them to "get things right."

The patient found this a very helpful focus. He spoke about his long-standing competitive struggles with peers and even with several teachers. He also noted that he had had lifelong anxiety about "messing things up." For the first time, he told the therapist about the hours of preparation he put in the night before every surgical procedure in order to make sure that "my hands know how to do the operation perfectly even if my head screws up."

The patient went on to tell about how he had always been a good student but how he started pushing himself much harder after his brother's death. He spent a full session telling the story of his brother's death in great detail. The brother had been well that morning but by early evening was desperately ill. It was only at this point that the patient's father, himself a doctor, decided to bundle the whole family in the car and drive to the hospital. The brother died in the patient's lap halfway there. The patient spoke bitterly about his lingering anger at his father who he felt had "simply not tried hard enough" to save the boy. He wondered if his own motivation to become a doctor might have been spurred by a wish to be a better doctor than his father. This led him to wonder if he held himself responsible for his fiancée's death just as he had held his father responsible for his brother's death. The therapist added that this might also clarify why there had been such an emphasis in their sessions on "getting it right."

Over the next several weeks, the patient's criticisms became much fewer and less severe. He reported still greater freedom from anxiety and had begun to date. His PTSD symptoms remained in remission several weeks after discontinuing the SSRI (which the patient still worried might interfere with his ability to take care of patients). He continued therapy and used it constructively as an opportunity to more fully mourn both his fiancée and his brother. He also worked hard to get a better handle on competitive feelings toward his fellow residents which he now saw had isolated him within the team and which might eventually have negative effects on his future career. Of note, for the first time in his life, he found himself able to readily admit to others when he had made a mistake. As he pointed out in a session near the end of his 14 months of twice-a-week therapy, "I don't think I've ever been as confident about my skills as I have since I've learned to admit my mistakes." He completed residency training, married, and has remained symptom free for the past 6 years.

## CONCLUSION

The debate between views first formulated by Josef Breuer and Sigmund Freud at the close of the 19th century persists at the opening of the 21st century. Only the metaphors have changed. On the other hand, time has provided opportunity to reflect on and clarify key differences between their positions. Abreaction of unconscious memories has been set aside in order to better understand how the ongoing effects of trauma are maintained and expressed as the summation of a complex and dynamic system. Instead of seeking the traumatic memory as if it were trapped within the patient's brain or mind, its effects and meaning are sought within the field of the survivor's relationships with others, including past relationships, current relationships outside of the therapy, and transference within the therapy. Rather than attempt to extract or ablate memories or lesions, psychoanalytic clinicians partner with their patients to work the trauma through in the here and now of transference and countertransference.

The personal and intellectual bonds between Breuer and Freud broke down because of their fundamental disagreements. It took Freud 9 years from the time of his work with Charcot to induce Breuer to complete their *Studies on Hysteria*. Perhaps Breuer's hesitancy reflected his realization, conscious or unconscious, that his differences with his young colleague would ultimately drive them apart. Within a few more years, the two men no longer acknowledged one another when they met on the street. If modern workers in the field pioneered by Breuer and Freud also share their theoretical differences, it is no surprise that we often fail to acknowledge one another when we should.

Psychoanalytic theory informs us that our best laid plans are often confounded by unconscious wishes, fears, beliefs, and enduring patterns of relating. Scientific and clinical progress can also be stymied by conflicts between basic assumptions. Hopefully, this review has succeeded in articulating some very old, very persistent debates that, once engaged explicitly and collaboratively, will improve our ability to understand and alleviate the effects of psychological trauma.

## REFERENCES

American Psychiatric Association. (1980). *Diagnostic and statistical manual of mental disorders* (3rd ed.). Washington, DC: Author.

American Psychiatric Association. (2000). *Diagnostic and statistical manual of mental disorders* (4th ed, technical revision). Washington, DC: Author.

Breuer, J., & Freud, S. (1895). *Studies on hysteria*. In J. Strachey, *Standard edition of the complete psychological works of Sigmund Freud* (Vol. 2, pp. 1–319). New York: W.W. Norton.

Brom, D., Kleber, R. J., & Defares, P.B. (1989). Brief psychotherapy for posttraumatic stress disorders. *Journal of Consulting and Clinical Psychology, 57*(5), 607–612.

Bruch, H. (1978). *The Golden Cage: The enigma of anorexia nervosa.* Cambridge, MA: Harvard University Press.

Brunet, A., Orr, S. P., Tremblay, J., Robertson, K., Nader, K., & Pitman, R. K. (2008): Effect of post-retrieval propranolol on psychophysiologic responding during subsequent script-driven traumatic imagery in post-traumatic stress disorder. *Journal of Psychiatric Research, 42*(6), 503–506.

Crick, F., & Mitchison, G. (1983): The function of dream sleep. *Nature, 304,* 111–114.

Eisenberg, L. (1986). Mindlessness and brainlessness in psychiatry. *British Journal of Psychiatry, 148,* 497–508.

Erikson, Erik H. (1950). *Childhood and society.* New York: W.W. Norton.

Freud, S. (1895/1950). *Project for a scientific psychology.* In J. Strachey, *Standard edition of the complete psychological works of Sigmund Freud* (Vol. 1, pp. 281–387). New York: W.W. Norton.

Freud, S. (1896). *Further remarks on the neuro-psychoses of defence.* In J. Strachey, *Standard edition of the complete psychological works of Sigmund Freud* (Vol. 3, pp. 157–186). New York: W.W. Norton.

Freud, S. (1900). *The interpretation of dreams.* In J. Strachey, *Standard edition of the complete psychological works of Sigmund Freud* (Vol. 5, pp. 509–622). New York: W.W. Norton.

Freud, S. (1901). *The psychopathology of everyday life.* In J. Strachey, *Standard edition of the complete psychological works of Sigmund Freud* (Vol. 6, pp. 1–291). New York: W.W. Norton.

Freud, S. (1905). *Fragment of an analysis of a case of hysteria.* In J. Strachey, *Standard edition of the complete psychological works of Sigmund Freud* (Vol. 7, pp. 1–122). New York: W.W. Norton.

Freud, S. (1912a). *The dynamics of transference.* In J. Strachey, *Standard edition of the complete psychological works of Sigmund Freud* (Vol. 12, pp. 97–108). New York: W.W. Norton.

Freud, S. (1912b). *Recommendations to physicians practising psycho-analysis.* In J. Strachey, *Standard edition of the complete psychological works of Sigmund Freud* (Vol. 12, pp. 97–108). New York: W.W. Norton.

Freud, S. (1913). *On beginning the treatment (Further recommendations on the technique of psycho-analysis, II.* In J. Strachey, *Standard edition of the complete psychological works of Sigmund Freud* (Vol. 12, pp. 121–144). New York: W.W. Norton.

Freud, S. (1914). *Remembering, repeating and working through (Further observations on the technique of psycho-analysis, II).* In J. Strachey, *Standard edition of the complete psychological works of Sigmund Freud* (Vol. 12, pp. 145–156). New York: W.W. Norton.

Freud, S. (1915). *Observations on transference-love (Further observations on the technique of psycho-analysis, III).* In J. Strachey, *Standard edition of the complete psychological works of Sigmund Freud* (Vol. 12, pp. 157–171). New York: W.W. Norton.

Freud, S. (1925a). *An autobiographical study.* In J. Strachey, *Standard edition of the complete psychological works of Sigmund Freud* (Vol. 20, pp. 1–74). New York: W.W. Norton.

Freud, S. (1925b). *Josef Breuer, Obituary.* In J. Strachey, *Standard edition of the complete psychological works of Sigmund Freud* (Vol. 19, pp. 279–280). New York: W.W. Norton.

Freud, S. (1893). Charcot. In J. Strachey, *Standard edition of the complete psychological works of Sigmund Freud* (Vol. 3, pp. 7–23). New York: W.W. Norton.

Gamgee, A. (1878). An account of a demonstration on the phenomena of hystero-epilepsy: And on the modification which they undergo under the influence of magnets and solenoids. *British Medical Journal, 2,* 545–548.

Grinker, R. R., & Spiegel, J. P. (1945). *Men under stress.* Philadelphia: The Blakiston Company.

Hobson, J. A., & McCarley, R. W. (1977). The neurobiological origins of psychoanalytic dream theory. *American Journal of Psychiatry, 134,* 1211–1221.

Kandel, E. R. (1979). Psychotherapy and the single synapse. *New England Journal of Medicine, 301,* 1029–1037.

Kluft, R. P. (2000). The psychoanalytic psychotherapy of dissociative identity disorder in the context of trauma therapy. *Psychoanalytic Inquiry, 20,* 259–286.

Kudler, H. (1989). The tension between psychoanalysis and neuroscience. *Psychoanalysis and Contemporary Thought, 12,* 599–617.

Sedler, M. J. (1983). Freud's concept of working through. *Psychoanalytic Quarterly, 52,* 73–98.

Shedler, J. (2010). The efficacy of psychodynamic psychotherapy. *The American Psychologist, 65*(2), 98–109.

Sullivan, H. S. (1970). *The psychiatric interview.* New York: W.W. Norton.

Sulloway, F. (1979). *Freud, biologist of the mind: Beyond the psychoanalytic legend.* New York: Basic Books.

Tedeschi, R. G., & Calhoun, L. G. (2004). Posttraumatic growth: Conceptual foundations and empirical evidence. *Psychological Inquiry, 15*(1), 1–18.

Wilson, E. O. (1977). Biology and the social sciences. *Daedalus, 2,* 127–140.

Yehuda, R., & Bierer, L. M. (2009). The relevance of epigenetics to PTSD: Implications for the *DSM-V. Journal of Traumatic Stress, 22*(5), 427–434.

# Chapter 4

# Neurobiology of Retraumatization

*Anthony P. King and Israel Liberzon*

Epidemiological studies find that one of the strongest risk factors predicting who will develop posttraumatic stress disorder (PTSD) after exposure to a given trauma is whether individuals have experienced other traumas previously in their lifetime (Breslau, Davis, Andreski, & Peterson, 1991; Kessler, Sonnega, Bromet, Hughes, & Nelson, 1995; Koenen et al., 2002). Thus, the phenomenon of retraumatization appears to be of great importance in shaping how people respond to trauma and in predicting the development of PTSD subsequent to trauma. Although the evidence directly investigating retraumatization in humans is currently limited, this chapter will review existing data on the neurobiology of childhood trauma and adult PTSD, which is, in general, consistent with the idea that the experience of trauma may have neurobiological consequences that lead to additional risk upon retraumatization. This chapter will examine existing knowledge about the neurobiology of trauma and the effects of trauma on brain, autonomic nervous system, and neuroendocrine system functions that could underlie the impact of multiple lifetime traumas on PTSD risk. We will review a number of neurobiological systems within which effects of trauma and PTSD have been documented. Human and animal models of the neurobiology of trauma will be reviewed because of the potential all these models have to increase our understanding of how the experience of previous traumas affects responses to subsequent trauma. Trauma and other childhood adversity appear to be associated with particular risk for PTSD; this suggests that childhood trauma could lead to lifelong patterns of reactivity to stress and traumas that might underlie adult PTSD risk. The accumulating neurobiological data in humans is reviewed, with particular emphasis placed on the possible associated childhood trauma exposure to alterations in adult neuroendocrine function, structural alterations in related limbic and cortical brain regions, and differences in functional activity in neurocircuitry implicated in threat detection, emotional regulation, and fear conditioning and extinction. Models of early life adversity in rodents which show lifelong alterations in anxiety behaviors, neuroendocrine responses, and patterns of brain gene expression will also be discussed, with emphasis placed on those mechanisms that potentially serve as mediators or moderators of the relation of early life trauma to PTSD vulnerability. The hypothesis that early life trauma and adversity may lead to lifelong imprinting of brain function and stress responses through neurodevelopmental, and possibly through epigenetic, changes has potentially important implications for understanding the neurobiology of trauma and PTSD.

Psychological trauma is highly prevalent, and the estimates of lifetime exposure of any kind of trauma have ranged from 62% in a nationally representative sample (Kessler et al., 1995) to over 90% in a Detroit-area cohort (Breslau et al., 1991). However, lifetime prevalence of PTSD is much lower, indicating that the majority of trauma-exposed individuals do not develop PTSD, and that mere exposure to a potentially traumatizing event is not sufficient to cause PTSD (Breslau et al., 1991; Kessler et al., 1995; Kulka et al., 1990). Epidemiological studies point toward specific environmental events, particularly early life adversity such as child abuse or other childhood trauma, as risk factors for PTSD (Cabrera, Hoge, Bliese, Castro, & Messer, 2007; Koenen, Moffitt, Poulton, Martin, & Caspi, 2007; Shalev, Peri, Canetti, & Schreiber, 1996; Widom, 1999). A number of other environmental factors, including the nature of the index trauma, previous trauma exposure, age at time of the trauma, and sociodemographic factors such as poverty and social support, all influence risk for PTSD, as do preexisting personal or family histories of depression and anxiety (Breslau et al., 1991; Kessler et al., 1995; Koenen et al., 2002). This suggests that the development of PTSD requires the presence of certain vulnerability factors. Currently, those neurobiological factors that lead to increased vulnerability to PTSD in some and increased resilience in others are not well understood.

In general, psychological trauma can be associated with transient psychological reactions, which can include some of the core intrusive, avoidant, and hyperarousal symptoms of PTSD. For most people, these transient reactions are followed by a period of recovery and a return to baseline functioning; however, for a significant minority, trauma can precipitate the development of PTSD or major depressive disorder (MDD). Even when the experience of trauma does not directly precipitate an immediate psychiatric disorder, it may lead to greater risk for development of psychiatric problems later, perhaps many years later. A developmental perspective of PTSD risk factors could suggest that the experience of trauma in early life could lead to disruptions in neurodevelopmental processes or specific alterations in key neural systems, these disruptions and alterations possibly leading to long-term changes in adult patterns of emotional processing and stress responding that increase vulnerability to PTSD when additional traumas are experienced.

Among the most well-known and enduring theoretical models of psychopathology is the diathesis-stress model, which posits that individual differences in biological and psychological vulnerability (i.e., diathesis) can lead to the expression of psychopathology in the presence of a sufficiently challenging environmental event (i.e., the stressor). Given that the diagnosis of PTSD requires that the individual be exposed to a traumatizing event, the diathesis-stress model is particularly useful in studying this disorder. Although the exact mechanisms that transmit greater PTSD risk are not fully delineated, there is abundant evidence that the experience of psychological trauma can lead to a number of alterations in the psychological functioning of the individual. These alterations may occur along a variety of psychological dimensions, including cognition, emotional regulation, personality and disposition, and intrapersonal and interpersonal functioning. Presumably, alterations in neurobiological and physiological functions underlie these changes in psychological functioning.

## GENETIC FACTORS AND POSTTRAUMATIC STRESS DISORDER VULNERABILITY

There is accumulating evidence that genetic factors contribute to PTSD diathesis. Epidemiological studies suggest that at least some of the risk for PTSD is heritable, and underlying neurobiological differences in stress response systems, all of which can be considered to have genetic predeterminants, may also be important in this context. The genetics of PTSD are likely complex (Burmeister, 1999), involving interactions between multiple genes and between genes and various environmental factors (Koenen, 2007). A crucial step for genetic studies of PTSD will involve determining those phenotype(s) of the disorder that are heritable and the level of that heritability. To our knowledge, PTSD linkage studies have not been performed; however, there is strong evidence of familial aggregation. Family studies indicate that relatives of trauma-exposed persons with PTSD (i.e., probands) have greater risk than trauma-exposed relatives of persons without PTSD. Cambodian refugee children of parents with PTSD have been reported to evidence an approximate fivefold increase in risk for PTSD (Sack, Clarke, & Seeley, 1995), and adult children of Holocaust survivors with PTSD have been reported to evidence higher risk of developing PTSD than children of Holocaust survivors without PTSD (Yehuda, Halligan, & Bierer, 2001). In recent studies of multigenerational Armenian families exposed to the 1988 Spitak earthquake (Bailey et al., 2010; Goenjian et al., 2008), researchers used a quantitative trait variance components approach to evaluate PTSD heritability.

Study findings suggested a high genetic correlation among PTSD, depression, and anxiety symptoms, as well as a unique and substantial degree of heritability for PTSD symptoms, with genetic factors explaining about 40% of the variance in PTSD symptoms. Genetic twin studies using the large Vietnam-Era Twin (VET) registry have found evidence for PTSD heritability (estimates of heritability range from 30% to 40%), suggesting that variance in combat-related PTSD is explained by genetic factors in addition to unique environmental factors (e.g., trauma and other factors) (Chantarujikapong et al., 2001; Koenen et al., 2002; Lurie & Geyer, 1994; McLeod et al., 2001; Segman & Shalev, 2003). Studies also found both shared and unique genetic and environmental risk factors for PTSD, depression, panic disorder, and generalized anxiety disorder (GAD) (Chantarujikapong et al., 2001; Koenen et al., 2008).

There have been only a few molecular genetics association studies of PTSD risk so far, all of which have been candidate gene association studies. Candidate gene studies examine the association of increased frequency of specific genetic variants (such as insertions/deletions, variable number of repeats, or single nucleotide polymorphisms [SNPs]) in genes considered likely candidates to be involved in PTSD pathophysiology. Traditionally, likely candidate genes are selected from genes within genomic regions linked to disease phenotype (e.g., PTSD) in studies of family pedigrees, although as yet there have been no such linkage studies of PTSD. Candidates can also be selected by virtue of the identity of the neurobiological system in which the gene's product is involved, and based on the likely involvement of these biological systems in the disorder of interest. In the case of PTSD, several studies have selected variants in genes in the serotonin, dopamine, neuropeptide, and neuroendocrine systems. Most of the earlier candidate gene studies included very small numbers of subjects (less than 100 cases), and findings from these studies are considered inconclusive. Reports of PTSD association with the dopamine D2 receptor gene (gene symbol *DRD2*) are mixed (Comings, Muhleman, & Gysin, 1996; Gelernter et al., 1999). Initial findings of a positive association between PTSD and the gene for the dopamine transporter (gene symbol *SLC6A3*) have not been replicated (Segman et al., 2002). A negative finding regarding a glucocorticoid receptor gene (gene symbol *NR3C1*) molecular variant was reported (Bachmann et al., 2005), as well as negative findings for SNPs in the gene for brain-derived neurotrophic factor (*BDNF*) (Zhang et al., 2006) and neuropeptide Y (*NPY*) (Lappalainen et al., 2002). An understanding of the interactive influence of genetic and environmental factors on psychological vulnerability is crucial to the understanding of PTSD risk.

Interestingly, recent candidate gene studies involving larger community cohorts (more than 500 subjects) have revealed no main effect of candidate alleles on PTSD risk. These studies have pointed to significant *interactions* between specific gene variants and environmental risk factors beyond those environmental factors specific to the index trauma. This suggests that persons who experience trauma in adulthood, who have a positive history for childhood trauma, and who are carriers of certain genotypes may be at particular risk for PTSD. One of the earliest and best known studies examining Gene × Environment (G × E) interactions that contribute to psychiatric vulnerability is the seminal birth cohort study by Caspi et al. (2003) in which the interaction of serotonin transporter promoter variant 5-HTTLPR short allele with level of childhood stressful life events was found to be associated with increased risk for depression. In an evaluation of PTSD symptoms experienced by a sample of largely impoverished, urban-dwelling African American persons reporting a significant history of lifetime traumatic events, Binder and colleagues (2008) found significant interactions between several SNPs in a gene that encodes a glucocorticoid receptor-associated protein (*FKBP5*) and childhood abuse. Xie et al. (2009) reported intriguing evidence that 5-HTTLPR "short" allele also interacts with childhood trauma to predict adult PTSD risk. This interactive effect of the 5-HTTLPR allele and childhood trauma on PTSD risk has been confirmed by findings from research conducted through our laboratory. Using a case-control cohort of 320 young, urban-dwelling mothers with and without PTSD, we determined that PTSD risk was significantly affected by the interaction of 5-HTTLPR and childhood adversity in the form of sexual abuse, physical abuse, and witnessing violence toward one's mother (King, Seng, & Liberzon, 2010). Interestingly, findings from a recent, small-scale meta-analysis of 5-HTTLPR G × E interaction studies did not support a 5-HTTLPR polymorphism G × E interaction effect on the development of depression. Findings from this meta-analysis would appear to call into question the importance of 5-HTTLPR to psychological vulnerability. However, this important finding is being extensively discussed and debated in the literature, and subsequent more inclusive meta-analyses have provided support for 5-HTTLPR G × E interactions in depression (Karg, Burmeister, Shedden, & Sen, in press; Wankerl, Wust, & Otte, 2010). Although these preliminary findings related to G × E interaction effects are exciting, none of these findings are of sufficient strength to lead to general acceptance. Furthermore, multiple genetic factors may contribute incrementally to PTSD risk, interacting with specific environmental stressors. Findings from studies of survivors of the 2004 Florida hurricane revealed nominally significant interactive effects of the serotonin transporter gene (*SLC6A4*) promoter polymorphism (called 5-HTTLPR), the *RGS2* gene, hurricane-exposure, and social support/crime rate (Amstadter et al., 2009; Kilpatrick et al., 2007) on PTSD diagnosis. The strength of the conclusions that can be drawn from these findings is limited by the limited number of trauma survivors with PTSD included in these studies.

## ENDOPHENOTYPES OF PTSD VULNERABILITY

Figure 4.1 depicts a conceptual framework in which PTSD vulnerability is hypothesized to be influenced by multiple neurobiological traits, which could

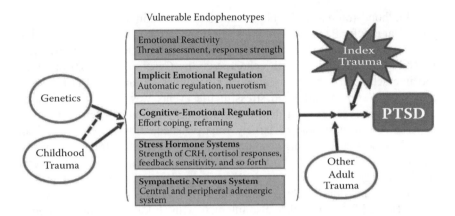

FIGURE 4.1 The influence of genetic factors and childhood trauma on vulnerability endophenotypes and the influence of vulnerability endophenotypes, the index trauma, and other adult traumas on posttraumatic stress disorder (PTSD) risk. A solid line appears from "Genetics" to traits. The dashed line from childhood trauma to genetics represents the interacting influence of genetic and childhood trauma on neural endophenotypes.

play a role in the development of pathophysiological processes that, following trauma exposure, lead to cognitive, affective, and behavioral symptoms of PTSD. Such neurobiological or psychological traits are often referred to as endophenotypes. They are phenotypes (i.e., specific traits) that are under at least partial control of genes, but unlike phenotypes such as hair or eye color, these traits are "internal" and not readily seen. A large number of studies have been conducted over the past three decades using both humans and animals to examine neurobiological endophenotypes associated with PTSD. Human studies have often involved persons with PTSD related to childhood trauma or to various military and civilian traumas. Animal studies have aimed to model the effects of childhood adversity and trauma on PTSD risk. Together, these studies have provided wide-ranging evidence for the role of neuroendocrine stress systems, peripheral psychophysiological systems, and specific brain circuits in the occurrence of PTSD. Thus, multiple endophenotypes may contribute, either incrementally or synergistically, to increased risk for PTSD.

Childhood trauma may be an important causal factor in the expression of these risk endophenotypes, which lead to increased PTSD vulnerability and to development of PTSD upon exposure to subsequent traumas. Evidence suggests that early life experiences have profound effects that endure into adulthood and appear to influence individual differences in responses to threat and stress. Childhood trauma and other adversity can lead to long-term changes in specific neurocircuits that, in turn, cause changes in psychological processes that are associated with PTSD risk. In this manner, the experience of childhood trauma, through changes in neurophysiology, may be a source of vulnerability (i.e., a diathesis) for PTSD. As we discuss below, early trauma could exert neurodevelopmental effects on brain structures that are critical to emotional responding and emotion regulation, including the hippocampus, amygdala, and medial frontal cortex. In Figure 4.1, the relation of genetic factors and childhood trauma to vulnerability endophenotypes and the relation of vulnerability endophenotypes, the index trauma and other adult traumas to PTSD are depicted.

Neural endophenotypes that convey increased PTSD risk are thought to have important genetic contributions. We reviewed the strong epidemiological evidence that genetic factors are involved in PTSD vulnerability (Goldberg, True, Eisen, & Henderson, 1990; Koenen, 2007; Koenen et al., 2008; Segman & Shalev, 2003; True et al., 1993), and the early but accumulating evidence that specific molecular variants in genes such as the serotonin transporter gene and the *FKBP5* gene may be involved in PTSD risk. There is now early but accumulating evidence that some of these same genetic variants can directly influence expression of PTSD risk endophenotypes, presumably by their effects on gene expression and protein functions in neurons. For example, genetic variants could be associated with altered gene expression or altered function of neurotransmitters, receptors, altered functioning of metabolic enzymes controlling neurotransmitter synthesis or breakdown, transporters, or second messenger systems. These genetic variants may also alter neurobiological functioning by affecting the relative strength of specific neurotransmitter circuitry. There is now accumulating evidence that genetic variants in these same classes of molecules have important effects in determining individual differences in emotional processing. A growing number of neuroimaging studies have now demonstrated effects of genetic variants on the amygdala and on ACC, DLPFC, and dmPFC morphology, activity, and functional connectivity, including the gene for serotonin transporter (Hariri & Holmes, 2006; Hariri et al., 2002), tryptophan hydroxylase 2 (*TPH2*), the rate-limiting enzyme for serotonin production (Brown et al., 2005; Canli, Congdon, Gutknecht, Constable, & Lesch, 2005), and catechol-O-meyltransferase (*COMT*), an enzyme involved in synaptic degradation of catecholamines and dopamine (Mobascher et al., 2010; Montag et al., 2008; Weiss et al., 2007). This rapidly expanding and exciting field of neuroimaging of psychological genetics has been well reviewed (Aleman, Swart, & van Rijn, 2008; Brown & Hariri, 2006; Domschke & Dannlowski, 2010; Hariri, Drabant, & Weinberger, 2006; Roffman, Weiss, Goff, Rauch, & Weinberger, 2006).

As will be described in the following sections, all of the specific endophenotypes shown in Figure 4.1 have been linked to PTSD via neuroimaging, psychophysiological, and neuroendocrine studies. Emotional reactivity refers to the strength of emotional responses (e.g., fear or distress) that an individual may have to aversive stimuli. Both animal models and human neuroimaging work have implicated neurocircuitry involving the amygdala and other limbic and paralimbic regions in these responses. Thus, the specific neurobiological endophenotype underlying this psychological process of threat detection could involve differential activation of amygdala circuits by a given emotional stimulus, this activation of amygdala circuits presumably contributing to PTSD vulnerability.

Emotion regulation refers to the psychological processes by which an aversive emotional reaction, once initiated, is modulated or dampened as appropriate for the situation. Psychological processes and negative emotional responses to aversive cues have been associated with PTSD risk and are reflected in temperament and personality traits such as neuroticism and harm avoidance. Both animal studies that use fear extinction models and human neuroimaging research on effortful emotional regulation strategies (i.e., reappraisal, distancing) have implicated neurocircuitry involving structures of the medial wall of prefrontal cortex (i.e., the infralimbic cortex in rodents and the medial prefrontal cortex [mPFC] and dorsal and rostral anterior cingulate cortex [dACC, rACC] in humans). Thus, the neural endophenotypes underlying the capacity for engaging implicit or automatic as well as effortful or volitional forms of emotional regulation could involve the relative strength and functional connections of circuitry involving medial prefrontal structures. Executive processes such as attentional shifting, distraction, and context differentiation, and memory processes such as conditioned fear cue generalization and contextualization of memory are also related to emotional expression and fear conditioning and might reasonably represent additional pathways to PTSD vulnerability.

Stress-responsive autonomic and neuroendocrine systems, such as the sympatho-adrenergic sympathetic nervous system and the limbic–hypothalamic–pituitary–adrenal (LHPA) system are also systems likely to play roles as potential mediators of trauma sensitivity or PTSD risk. Alterations in these systems have been observed in PTSD. Specific functional neural endophenotypes underlying these systems could be affected by exposure to trauma, and these endophenotypes could then contribute to long-term alterations in PTSD risk.

The sympathetic nervous system (SNS) underlies the *fight-or-flight response* and has long been implicated in responses to trauma and the pathology of PTSD. The stress-responsive adrenergic SNS is activated by amygdala and locus ceruleus (the source of central noradrenergic neurons) inputs into brain stem nuclei. These inputs activate descending sympathetic pathways in the spinal cord that innervate multiple organ systems, including the heart, lungs, gut, vasculature, and immune system, leading to the classic sympathetic responses. Given that multiple core symptoms of PTSD involve what appear to be hyperadrenergic states (e.g., physiological and emotional responses to triggers, increased heart rate/tachycardia, increased blood pressure, anxiety, hypervigilance/hyperarousal, exaggerated startle, etc.), the noradrenergic SNS has been a key target of PTSD research (for review, see Krystal & Neumeister, 2009; O'Donnell, Hegadoren, & Coupland, 2004; Southwick et al., 1997).

Increased peripheral SNS activity is well documented in PTSD, with findings of increased blood pressure, heart rate, and skin conductance at baseline and in response to trauma recall having been reported in a large number of studies comparing PTSD patients to normal and psychiatric controls (Orr, Metzger, & Pitman, 2002; Pitman & Orr, 1993; Pitman, Orr, Forgue, de Jong, & Claiborn, 1987; Pitman, Orr, Shalev, Metzger, & Mellman, 1999; Pitman, Orr, & Steketee, 1989; Shalev, Orr, & Pitman, 1992). Furthermore, there is also peripheral neurochemical evidence of increased adrenergic outflow, including increased urinary excretion of catecholamines (i.e., adrenaline and noradrenaline) (deBellis, Baum, Birmaher, & Ryan, 1997; Kosten, Mason, Giller, Ostroff, & Harkness, 1987), increased plasma levels of catecholamines (Blanchard, Kolb, Prins, Gates, & McCoy, 1991), and catecholamine responses in PTSD patients (Liberzon, Abelson, Flagel, Raz, & Young, 1999).

It seems logical that preexisting differences in SNS function could lead to differences in PTSD risk, possibly mediated by differences in peritraumatic responses. Such individual differences in autonomic function could be the result of genetic variation in genes within the SNS. It is also plausible that initial traumatization (including childhood trauma) could lead to enduring alterations in SNS function which could then lead to retraumatization by exposures to subsequent traumas. Retraumatization in the face of repeat trauma exposure might also be a consequence of gene × environment interactions such that persons with certain genotypes could be particularly sensitive to effects of the initial trauma and subsequent traumas. Supporting this hypothesis is the finding in a longitudinal study of trauma survivors suggesting that a higher peritraumatic heart rate (measured in the emergency room) predicted PTSD (Shalev et al., 1998). Furthermore, an intriguing pilot study suggested that peritraumatic treatment of trauma survivors with the beta-adrenergic antagonist (beta-blocker) propranolol in the emergency room may prevent the development of PTSD (Pitman et al., 2002); however, subsequent studies of propranolol use with combat Veterans and burn victims have shown mixed results (Donovan, 2009; McGhee et al., 2009; Nugent et al., 2010; Sharp, Thomas, Rosenberg, Rosenberg, & Meyer, 2010). More research is needed. For example, examining genetic factors and early childhood experiences in the context of a longitudinal study of peritraumatic SNS function and subsequent development of PTSD could shed light on PTSD pathogenesis.

The limbic–hypothalamic–pituitary–adrenal (LHPA) axis is a major stress-responsive neuroendocrine system that is crucial for survival. Like the SNS, the LHPA axis is also activated in response to stressors and traumas in humans and in animals, but with a different time course. While the SNS responds to stressors within seconds, LHPA axis responses peak at about 15 to 30 minutes and usually resolve within 60 to 90 minutes. This system is also strongly implicated in sensitivity of trauma in a large number of studies in humans and animal models. This neuroendocrine axis functions as a hormone cascade, which involves secretion of corticotropin-releasing hormone (CRH) from specialized neurons of the paraventricular nucleus (PVN) of the hypothalamus into the hypophyseal portal circulation, by which CRH travels to the anterior pituitary and binds to specific CRH receptors on the surface of adrenocorticotrope cells. These specialized pituitary cells in turn release another protein hormone, adrenocorticotropic hormone (ACTH) into the peripheral bloodstream. ACTH then travels through the bloodstream to the adrenal gland, where it binds receptors on cells in the adrenal cortex, which leads to synthesis and release of glucocorticoid steroid hormones (cortisol in humans and corticosterone in many animals).

Glucocorticoid hormones have multiple effects on a large number of physiological systems, including glucose utilization and metabolism, lipolysis, immune function, and hemodynamics. They also appear to have important physiological effects on the brain. The receptors for glucocorticoid receptors are nearly ubiquitously expressed in peripheral tissues, as well as cortical and subcortical brain structures (de Kloet & Holsboer, 2005). The widespread actions of cortisol on metabolism and immune function have led many to hypothesize that the stress responsive LHPA axis may mediate the deleterious effects of psychological stress on health (McEwen, 2006). Glucocorticoid effects on the brain are consistent with significant roles for these steroids in shaping behavioral adaptations to changing or challenging environments (de Kloet & Holsboer, 2005; Erickson, Drevets, & Schulkin, 2003).

## ANIMAL MODELS OF CHILDHOOD ADVERSITY AND ADULT TRAUMA: PTSD AND LIMBIC–HYPOTHALAMIC–PITUITARY–ADRENAL (LHPA) AXIS FUNCTION

As mentioned above, early life adversity appears to influence individual differences in predisposition to adult psychopathology, including PTSD and affective disorders (Brown, Bifulco, & Harris, 1987; Cui & Vaillant, 1996; Heim & Nemeroff, 2001; Kendler et al. 1995; Repetti, Taylor, & Seeman, 2002). Models of early life trauma in rodents and primates suggest that manipulation of the early developmental environment can lead to long-term, sometimes lifelong alterations in behavior, brain gene expression, and patterns of stress hormone and neurophysiological responses to stress. Prolonged maternal separation is a well-characterized model of early life adversity that leads to profound changes in neuroendocrine stress responses and behavior (for review, see Sánchez, Ladd, & Plotsky, 2001). The maternal separation model examines the effects of separating neonate rat pups (2 to 14 days old) from their mothers for either 3 hours/day for 10 days (maternal separation), or for only 15 minutes a day ("handled control"). After separation from their pups for 3 hours, rat mothers show decreases in important maternal behaviors, such as pup retrieval, licking, grooming, and nursing, compared to rat mothers not separated from their pups, or those who were separated for only 15 minutes (Huot, Smith, & Plotsky, 1997).

Maternal separation appears to have long-term effects on multiple behavioral and neurobiological systems of the separated rat pups. Behaviorally, rats that are separated from their mothers for 3 hours a day as neonates show increased anxiety-like behaviors, hypervigilance, and development of a depression-like syndrome as adults, including anhedonia and a proclivity for increased ethanol intake. They also show exaggerated and prolonged LHPA axis responses to the mild psychological stressor of an airpuff as adults. Interestingly, these exaggerated LHPA axis responses persist throughout the adult life of the animal. Furthermore, a number of other pronounced neurobiological alterations have now been demonstrated in adult rats that experienced maternal separation as neonates. These include decreased gene expression of glucocorticoid receptors (GRs) in the hippocampus and medial prefrontal cortex. This decrease in brain GR is thought to lead to decreased glucocorticoid feedback sensitivity, and to drive the exaggerated and prolonged corticosterone stress responses, because LHPA axis activation now comes under much reduced inhibitory negative feedback.

Other changes in brain gene expression have also been documented, including increased gene expression of CRH in the amygdala and BNST, increased gene expression of tyrosine hydroxylase (TH, a rate-limiting enzyme in norepinephrine biosynthesis), decreased expression of GABAA receptors (inhibitory neurotransmitters involved in benzodiazepine binding) and decreased expression of alpha-2-adrenergic receptors in the locus ceruleus, and decreased oxytocin receptor binding in the amygdala (Caldji, Diorio, & Meaney, 2000; Caldji, Francis, Sharma, Plotsky, & Meaney, 2000; Cirulli, Alleva, Antonelli, & Aloe, 2000; Francis, Caldji, Champagne, Plotsky, & Meaney, 1999; Huot, Thrivikraman, Meaney, & Plotsky, 2001; Ladd et al., 2000; Liu, Caldji, Sharma, Plotsky, & Meaney, 2000). These findings indicate that early life experiences can lead to lifelong behavioral and neurobiological alterations. It would also appear that differences in responses to stressors and traumas seen in adult rats exposed to neonatal maternal separation may translate to an increase in psychological vulnerability. This may be a valuable model to elucidate the effects of childhood trauma and other adversity on psychological vulnerability in humans.

Even more intriguingly, some of these effects of maternal separation may be due to *epigenetic* imprinting of specific genes leading to altered patterns of brain gene expression. In this instance, these changes refer to long-term, stable (and potentially transmissible) changes in patterns of gene expression that are not transmitted by the classical genetic code (i.e., alterations in the genome) but rather by other forms of systematic alterations in the way the genome is expressed. A detailed discussion of the potential mechanisms of epigenetic imprinting is beyond the scope of the current chapter, but the process involves environment-induced changes in methylation patterns of specific bases on DNA strands and acetylation patterns of histones, the proteins upon which the DNA strands can coil around and which make up the complex structure of chromatin. Increased levels of histone acetylation are thought to "open up" areas of chromatin and increase access of these to transcription factors, leading to increased expression of genes in these areas. In contrast, increased methylation of DNA (and decreased acetylation of histones) is thought to lead to more tightly wound DNA that can effectively silence the expression of genes in these areas of the chromosome. Although the findings are complex, Meaney's group at McGill has found fascinating evidence that maternal licking and grooming leads to alterations in patterns of methylation on specific start sites of the rat GR gene that are primarily active in the hippocampus, leading to decreased binding of specific transcription factors and ultimately decreased GR gene transcription in the hippocampus (Meaney et al., 1996). Even though these observed alterations in animals are admittedly complex, the potential roles for such phenomena in setting up lifelong adaptations to "harsh" versus "nurturing" environmental conditions on gene expression patterns controlling stress responses is intriguing and suggests specific molecular mechanisms by which early life exposures may lead to lifelong patterns of reactivity and perhaps adult psychiatric vulnerability.

In addition to animal models of childhood adversity, several animal models of adult PTSD have been proposed, including exposure to various stressors such as inescapable electric shock (Rau, DeCola, & Fanselow, 2005; Siegmund & Wotjak, 2007; Wakizono et al., 2007), forced swim or underwater exposure (Cohen et al., 2004), and exposure to predators (Adamec, Blundell, & Burton, 2006; Adamec, Muir, Grimes, & Pearcey, 2007), or predator-related cues (Cohen et al., 2007, 2006). These stress exposures in adult rodents lead to an increase in anxiety-like behaviors and, in some cases, exaggerated startle responses, cognitive impairment, enhanced fear conditioning, and reduced social interaction (Cohen et al., 2006; Stam, 2007). Furthermore, some studies reported changes in LHPA axis neuroendocrine responses resembling those observed in patients with PTSD. One such model, the single prolonged stress (SPS) model, developed by our group, results in a number of LHPA neuroendocrine abnormalities that have also been observed in PTSD patients (Liberzon, Krstov, & Young, 1997; Liberzon, López, Flagel, Vázquez, & Young, 1999; Yamamoto et al., 2009), including enhanced glucocorticoid negative feedback. This multiple stress exposure model involves three stages in which rats are sequentially exposed to a 2-hour restraint stress, followed by a 20-minute forced swim (both of which are psychological stressors [i.e., not involving tissue damage] that are potent psychogenic activators of the LHPA axis), and then followed by exposure to ethyl ether until loss of consciousness (which is a pharmacological, neurological activator of the LHPA axis). After the serial stress exposures, the rats are left undisturbed in their home cage for 7 days.

Interestingly, this model of trauma in adult rats is associated with relative sensitization of LHPA axis negative feedback (i.e., increased dexamethasone fast feedback) in response to psychosocial stressors (Liberzon, Krstov, & Young, 1997), and relative increases in GR gene expression in hippocampus

(Liberzon, Abelson et al., 1999). These findings are in stark contrast to the decreased hippocampal GR gene expression seen in adult rats who were exposed to prolonged maternal separation as neonates (Ladd, Huot, Thrivikraman, Nemeroff, & Plotsky, 2004) or who had mothers who exhibited low levels of maternal care ("licking and grooming") (Liu et al., 1997; Meaney et al., 1996). These differential findings between various rodent models of early life adversity and adult trauma are still a matter of intense study, although it is interesting that the SPS model is the only rodent model that has yet shown the pattern of GR feedback hypersensitivity that has been observed in adult human PTSD (as we briefly review below). At least at the level of glucocorticoid negative feedback sensitivity, the maternal separation model appears more similar to the patterns of LHPA axis function found in major depression in humans.

## ALTERED NEUROENDOCRINE HYPOTHALAMIC–PITUITARY–ADRENAL (HPA) AXIS IN CHILDHOOD TRAUMA AND ADULT PTSD IN HUMANS

Potential alterations in the LHPA axis neuroendocrine system in the context of trauma exposure and PTSD have been an area of considerable study over the past 20 years. Although multiple human studies implicated LHPA axis dysregulation in PTSD, and there are theoretical and animal model data supporting the notion that such LHPA axis dysregulation could be related to the central pathophysiology of PTSD, the exact role that LHPA axis dysregulation plays in the development and expression of PTSD symptoms has not been fully elucidated. In trauma-exposed persons and in patients with PTSD, there is now considerable evidence to suggest that hypersensitive feedback inhibition mechanisms are active under specific trauma conditions.

Although fewer studies have been performed, there is evidence of profound alterations in stress hormone responses to social stressors and trauma recall in adult survivors of childhood traumas such as childhood sexual assault. Heim and colleagues (2000) found that women with a history of childhood abuse exhibited greatly increased LHPA axis and autonomic responses to a social stressor (i.e., the Trier Social Stress Test, TSST) compared to women without childhood abuse. The exaggerated responses were particularly robust in women with current symptoms of depression and anxiety. Women with a history of childhood abuse and a current major depression diagnosis exhibited a more than sixfold greater ACTH response to stress than age-matched controls. The authors concluded that the exaggerated LHPA axis and autonomic nervous system responses are a persistent consequence of childhood abuse that may contribute to the diathesis vulnerability for adulthood psychopathological conditions. They further hypothesized that this LHPA and sympathetic hyperreactivity were related to CRH hypersecretion in women with childhood trauma exposure, suggesting that CRH hypersecretion may mediate the effects of childhood trauma on the risk of adult psychopathology in response to stress. However, other studies of individuals with abuse-related PTSD (i.e., PTSD consequent to childhood physical or sexual abuse) which examined cortisol responses to psychosocial stressors have shown more subtle differences in LHPA axis reactivity. A study of 23 women with childhood abuse–related PTSD and 18 matched healthy controls exposed to a 20-minute cognitive challenge (e.g., arithmetic and problem-solving tasks) found elevated cortisol levels before the task was begun (potentially reflecting elevated anticipatory anxiety) but cortisol responses in PTSD patients that were not different than healthy controls (Bremner, Vythilingam, Vermetten, Adil, et al., 2003). Another study exposed women with childhood abuse–related PTSD to personalized trauma scripts and found that PTSD patients had significantly higher cortisol levels before and during script exposure but did not have exaggerated responses to the trauma scripts (Elzinga, Schmahl, Vermetten, van Dyck, & Bremner, 2003). There was, however, a correlation between PTSD symptom severity and cortisol levels during exposure.

There has been mixed evidence that the basal or resting activity of the LHPA axis is altered in adults with PTSD who experienced trauma during adulthood. Several studies have shown evidence of elevated levels of the hormone CRH in the cerebrospinal fluid of PTSD patients, consistent with the notion of increased activation of the system. Higher levels of CRH have been found in cerebrospinal fluid (CSF) in PTSD patients in studies in which lumbar punctures were used to extract CSF from the spinal cord (Baker et al., 1999; Bremner et al., 1997). A more recent study found increased CRH and cortisol levels in CSF over a 6-hour sampling period, with CRH and cortisol levels being correlated (Baker et al., 2005). However, studies further examining downstream effects of CRH-mediated central drive in patients with PTSD have also provided mixed results. Blunted ACTH response to CRH was reported in patients with combat-related PTSD, but only in patients with a comorbid diagnosis of major depressive disorder (MDD) (Smith et al., 1989). One study found women with PTSD (exposed to physical or sexual abuse) had a trend toward higher CRH-induced ACTH and cortisol responses (Rasmusson et al., 2001), but another study of men and women with PTSD related to assault or a motor vehicle accident found no significant differences in basal or total CRH-stimulated ACTH or cortisol responses (Kellner, Yassouridis, Hubner, Baker, & Wiedemann, 2003).

Assessment of peripheral cortisol across the day (i.e., circadian cortisol) in PTSD patients has produced varying results, with studies showing peripheral cortisol levels in PTSD patients to be significantly lower than (Mason, Giller, Kosten, Ostroff, & Podd, 1986; Yehuda et al., 1990, 1995), significantly higher than (Lemieux & Coe, 1995; Maes et al., 1998; Pitman & Orr, 1990), and not different from (Baker et al., 1999; Rasmusson et al., 2001) peripheral cortisol levels evidenced by control subjects. In a large, longitudinal epidemiological study, saliva (Young & Breslau, 2004b) and urine (Young & Breslau, 2004a) cortisol measures were obtained from patients with PTSD, patients with trauma exposure but no PTSD, and healthy controls. PTSD was associated with elevated evening saliva cortisol levels but only in individuals with a comorbid diagnosis of MDD. In contrast, patients with PTSD alone showed normal evening saliva and urine cortisol levels. A negative correlation has been observed between 24-hour urinary cortisol levels and PTSD symptoms in combat Veterans (Baker et al., 1999), but the same study failed to find group differences in circulating cortisol between Veterans with and without a PTSD diagnosis. In a study examining 2,490 Vietnam Veterans, 8:00 A.M. cortisol levels were observed to be significantly lower (by 4%) in PTSD patients compared to healthy controls (Boscarino, 1996). Interestingly, lower awakening cortisol has been associated with current or lifetime PTSD or a past diagnosis of depression in women who were recently diagnosed with breast cancer (Luecken, Dausch, Gulla, Hong, & Compas, 2004). As well, a civilian PTSD group showed substantially reduced cortisol response to awakening (i.e., in the first 60 minutes after awakening) compared to control groups (Wessa, Rohleder, Kirschbaum, & Flor, 2006), and PTSD symptoms were correlated with dampened cortisol response to awakening in active-duty police officers (Neylan et al., 2005). However, another recent report found that cortisol response to awakening did not predict PTSD symptom severity and was only nonsignificantly lower among firefighters with high PTSD risk (Heinrichs et al., 2005). Taken together, these data suggest evidence for some link between PTSD and reduced levels of circulating cortisol, but the nature of that linkage and the clinical relevance of potential group differences in cortisol levels remain unclear.

In addition to the basal level of cortisol output, trauma and PTSD could be associated with altered sensitivity to effects of stress-induced cortisol. Cortisol negative feedback sensitivity can be assessed in humans using the dexamethasone suppression test (DST). The use of this test in patients with major depression revealed that a significant proportion of MDD patients showed substantially blunted dexamethasone suppression, a finding that has greatly stimulated the field of biological psychiatry. Interestingly, the use of the DST in the context of PTSD and trauma exposure has yielded a pattern exactly opposite to that found in MDD. Several studies have shown a significantly greater reduction in ACTH and cortisol in PTSD patients following dexamethasone treatment, suggesting sensitized inhibitory feedback mechanisms in PTSD (Goenjian et al., 1996; Yehuda et al., 1995; Yehuda, Southwick, Krystal, Charney, & Mason, 1993). PTSD patients with early childhood abuse also showed hypersuppression of ACTH following dexamethasone treatment (Newport, Heim, Bonsall, Miller, & Nemeroff, 2004). However, a correlation between DST response and PTSD symptom severity was only reported in some studies (Yehuda, Golier, Halligan, Meaney, & Bierer, 2004; Yehuda et al., 1995). Thus, studies examining differences in circadian cortisol levels have also been inconsistent, although some studies have suggested a potential relationship between low cortisol levels and trauma exposure and with especially high PTSD symptom severity. However, it remains unclear whether the dysregulations documented reflect a consequence of trauma exposure, preexisting alterations that constitute traumatic vulnerability, or a more specific correlate of the disease process.

Only a few studies have examined the effects of psychological challenges on neuroendocrine responses in PTSD patients with adult trauma. Our group observed higher autonomic (i.e., skin conductance and heart rate) and catecholamine responses to white noise and combat-related sounds in Vietnam Veterans with PTSD, but the acute (immediate postexposure) ACTH and cortisol responses to these challenges were not different from that of controls (Liberzon, Abelson, et al., 1999). In a separate study, our group examined acute plasma ACTH responses to trauma-specific (autobiographical trauma script-driven imagery) and nonspecific (International Affective Picture System [IAPS] pictures) aversive emotional stimuli over 20 minutes in patients with Vietnam combat PTSD ($n = 16$), Vietnam combat Veterans without a history of PTSD symptoms ($n = 15$), and noncombat healthy controls ($n = 15$). We found acute plasma ACTH responses to trauma recall but not to other emotional stimuli. Both groups of combat Veterans (with or without PTSD) showed significant acute ACTH responses to the trauma scripts but not to aversive IAPS pictures, suggesting that sensitized HPA axis responses observed in this paradigm were related to trauma exposure rather than PTSD. However, the magnitude of ACTH response was positively correlated with the severity of symptoms in PTSD subjects. In contrast, noncombat-exposed controls did not have ACTH responses to aversive autobiographical scripts or IAPS pictures. Even though the general and trauma-specific aversive challenges elicited strong subjective emotional responses among all participants, acute ACTH responses were seen only to personalized trauma scripts in combat-exposed groups, supporting the notion that the human HPA axis responds to specific psychological stimuli (in this case, memories of personal threat) rather than to general emotional distress.

In summary, these mixed data suggest that existence of abnormalities in circadian cortisol levels in PTSD patients remains equivocal, although there are enough positive results to suggest that in certain conditions, abnormalities may exist. There does seem to be some evidence for a link between PTSD and low 24-hour cortisol levels in some patients, which contrasts with the hypercortisolemia observed among depressed patients. The degree to which changes in cortisol levels might result from trauma exposure rather than PTSD requires further investigation. Whether different circadian levels represent consequences of PTSD or vulnerability factors that are present at the time of trauma and increase the risk of developing PTSD also remains unresolved.

A possibility suggested by animal models is that the psychopathology of PTSD in adults is associated with altered LHPA axis stress responses, and although the available data are limited, there has been some evidence for such differences in adults with PTSD related to childhood abuse (Bremner et al., 2003b; Elzinga et al., 2003). However, a study of combat Veterans with adult trauma found ACTH responses to trauma recall were a function of adult trauma exposure, rather than PTSD status. An additional intriguing possibility suggested by animal models is that the experience of childhood trauma, with or without subsequent psychopathology, may lead to exaggerated LHPA axis stress hormone responses later in life, and these may lead to greater PTSD vulnerability to subsequent trauma. There has been evidence of differences in acute LHPA axis responses to psychosocial stressors and trauma recall in adults with childhood trauma exposures with or without depression compared to non-trauma-exposed adults (Heim et al., 2000).

## IMAGING THE BRAIN: NEUROIMAGING STUDIES OF POSTTRAUMATIC STRESS DISORDER

The last two decades have brought dramatic expansion and improvement in technologies for visualizing the brain and have provided striking insights into our understanding of brain function and the relationships between brain structure and function. These technologies offer the potential for new conceptual frameworks for understanding the normative neurophysiological adaptations to trauma on one hand, and the pathophysiology and symptom generation of trauma-related neuropsychiatric disorders, such as PTSD and depression, on the other. Ultimately, they may also lead to a better understanding of the neurophysiological mechanisms of therapeutic change from psychiatric medications and psychotherapies. There are different brain imaging technologies available today, each of which has its own advantages and limitations. The most basic distinction in neuroimaging is between structural and functional imaging—that is, imaging that gives information about the neuroanatomy and the structure of the brain and imaging that gives information about the function of the brain.

Structural neuroimaging gives information about the morphological features, like relative sizes, densities, and volumes of specific brain structures (e.g., amygdala and hippocampus). Recently developed technologies also allow for study of white matter tract morphology, density, and connections between brain regions (i.e., tractography). Other magnetic resonance imaging (MRI) methods now allow for measurement of the thickness of cortical layers. The initial structural neuroimaging studies of PTSD were performed with computerized tomography (CT), and while CT allowed the initial glimpses of structural neuroanatomy in living persons, the spatial resolution of CT is not particularly high. That and the X-ray radiation exposure associated with CT make it a less desirable option for scientific study of the brain today. The subsequent development of magnetic resonance imaging (MRI) allowed examination of the neuroanatomy of smaller central nervous system (CNS) structures and, in particular, of brain nuclei and other gray matter areas. MRI can visualize structural details of the medial temporal lobe, such as the hippocampal formation, parahippocampal gyrus, and amygdaloid nuclei, and can also detect gross neuropathological abnormalities in the white matter. Structural MRI uses the subtle differences in paramagnetic properties of tissues of differing composition in terms of lipids, proteins, and fluid (e.g., white matter, gray matter, and cerebrospinal fluid) to produce high-resolution images of brain structures. Other recent adaptations of basic MRI technology (diffusion tensor imaging) allow the tracing of white matter tracts in the living brain.

Functional neuroimaging, as the name implies, makes possible depiction of the brain activity while performing different functions. It involves the study of the brain in anatomical space, while the brain carries out particular activities, such as neuronal metabolism, blood flow to different parts of the cerebrum, and neurotransmitter binding. Several different technologies for functional neuroimaging are currently available, and they have been used in the study of emotional processing and regulation, in the study of people exposed to trauma, and in the study of patients with PTSD, depression, and other psychiatric disorders. It is important to recognize that each of these techniques provides different kinds of information about the neuroanatomy and neurophysiology of the brain.

Positron emission tomography (PET) and single photon emission computed tomography (SPECT) involve the administration of minute amounts of radioactively labeled tracer molecules that allow the brain to be imaged using cameras that detect radioactive decay of these tracers within the brain. The kind of information that can be derived from PET or SPECT is determined by the type of physiological activity the radioactive tracer that is used can detect. For example, PET can measure the perfusion in specific brain structures (i.e., regional cerebral blood flow), which is associated with neuronal activity, by labeling people's brains with radioactive water ($[^{15}O]$ $H_2O$). Brain metabolism can be measured with PET using radioactive analogs of glucose (such as 2-flourodeoxyglucose (2-FDG)), which gets picked up by neurons and other brain cells; brain regions that have higher levels of metabolism will have greater levels of radioactivity incorporated. Finally, receptor-binding PET makes use of specific radioactively labeled compounds that specifically bind to neurotransmitter receptors. There are now PET receptor ligands available for a large number of neurotransmitters, including GABAA receptors, mu opioid receptors, dopamine D2 receptors, alpha-2-adrenergic receptors, and others.

In the past decade, functional magnetic resonance imaging (fMRI) has become the most widely used form of functional neuroimaging. fMRI uses the paramagnetic properties of deoxyhemoglobin to mark blood oxygenation changes as an index of neuronal activity. Neuroimaging studies of blood flow and oxygenation and metabolism are sensitive to changes in neuronal activity and are used to visualize the anatomical structures that subserve a particular function. In PTSD, the activation approach provides a natural exploration for studying brain structure–function relationships via symptom provocation, cognitive, or emotional processes.

## STRUCTURAL NEUROIMAGING STUDIES OF CHILDHOOD AND ADULT TRAUMA AND PTSD

Early studies to examine potential abnormalities in brain structure in persons with PTSD used CT in the evaluation of former World War II prisoners of war (POWs). Increased ventricle-to-brain ratio and greater global sulcal widening were associated with sleep disturbances of the former prisoners of war, which suggested that chronic PTSD may be associated with a general loss in brain tissue (Peters, van Kammen, van Kammen, & Neylan, 1990). A number of structural MRI studies have also examined brains of trauma-exposed people and people with PTSD. One study found focal white matter lesions were more common in combat-exposed PTSD patients than in a comparison group of healthy controls (Canive et al., 1997), and another found an increased incidence of a neurodevelopmental abnormality (cavum septum pellucidum) in Veterans with PTSD compared to healthy controls (Myslobodsky et al., 1995).

In the past 15 years, structural neuroimaging studies have focused on two brain regions that have been implicated in trauma and the etiology of PTSD: the hippocampus and the medial frontal cortex. Evidence from animal models and from human functional neuroimaging research implicates medial prefrontal cortex (mPFC) in regulation of emotional responses, including extinction of conditioned fear responses and dampening of neuroendocrine stress responses, as we discuss in greater detail in the following section. In rodent models, for example, the infralimbic region of the prefrontal cortex (analogous to the ventral part of the medial frontal cortex in humans) appears to be involved in dampening of LHPA axis stress responses, lesions of this region lead to exaggerated LHPA axis responses to psychological stressors (Brake, Sullivan, Diorio), and studies from our group and others suggest this region is also involved in dampening of LHPA axis stress responses in humans (King et al., 2009; Pruessner, 2008). The medial frontal cortex also appears to be centrally involved in the maintenance of extinction memory (e.g., extinction recall), a mechanism possibly linked to PTSD development (Milad et al., 2009). Extinction is a psychological process studied in classical fear conditioning (e.g., by pairing a shock with a red light), by which rats learn that a stimulus that has previously been feared is no longer dangerous (e.g., by repeatedly presenting the same red light but without a shock). The process of extinction recall occurs when the first fear conditioned and then extinguished stimulus (i.e., the red light) is presented the next day, and the rat must now "remember" that it is no longer dangerous. Extinction and extinction recall are often invoked as a theoretical foundation for exposure-based therapy for PTSD (such as prolonged exposure therapy and Eye Movement Desensitization and Reprogramming [EMDR]). Fear conditioning requires intact amygdala, whereas the extinction recall appears to require intact mPFC—lesions to the infralimbic cortex have been found to abolish extinction recall (Quirk, Russo, Barron, & Lebron, 2000). Recently, human functional neuroimaging studies have also implicated the ventral mPFC in extinction of conditioned fear responses in humans (Milad et al., 2009; Garfinkel, King, and Liberzon, 2010).

If experiences of trauma could lead to structural and functional alterations in the frontal regions, this could potentially alter a person's capacity for processes such as emotional regulation and extinction recall of conditioned fear, which would have implications for vulnerability to PTSD. There is some evidence of structural alterations in the frontal lobe in PTSD. A study of male combat Veterans with PTSD ($n = 25$) and without PTSD ($n = 25$) matched for age, year, and region of deployment found Veterans with PTSD had reduced cortical thickness in the bilateral superior and middle frontal gyri, left inferior frontal gyrus, and left superior temporal gyrus (Geuze et al., 2008). Another recent study using high-resolution MRI in Vietnam and Gulf war Veterans ($n = 97$) found global cerebral cortical volume, thickness, and area were observed to be smaller in PTSD; in particular, smaller cortical volumes were found in the pars orbitalis of the inferior frontal gyrus, lateral orbitofrontal cortex, superior temporal cortex, and parahippocampal gyrus (Woodward, Schaer, Kaloupek, Cediel, & Eliez, 2009). A 2-year longitudinal MRI study of PTSD in cancer survivors who developed PTSD ($n = 9$) or did not develop PTSD ($n = 67$) using voxel-based morphometry (VBM) found smaller gray matter volume of the right orbitofrontal cortex (OFC) in cancer survivors with PTSD (Hakamata et al., 2007).

Likewise, the hippocampus, a bilateral subcortical structure located in the medial temporal lobe, is implicated in several processes important to PTSD and thus has been an important target of PTSD research. The hippocampus plays important roles in a number of basic brain functions; perhaps the most widely appreciated are memory acquisition and consolidation (Eichenbaum, 2004; Mizuno & Giese, 2005). However, the hippocampus also appears to play an important role in psychophysiological aspects of stress regulation, including dampening of amygdala and neuroendocrine HPA axis fear responses (Jacobson & Sapolsky, 1991; Lathe, 2001; Richter-Levin, 2004; Vertes, 2006). The hippocampus is also a major site of both Type I (mineralocorticoid) and Type II brain glucocorticoid receptors and is an important brain site in stress-response feedback inhibition loops (de Kloet, Karst, & Joels, 2008).

Given the centrality of the hippocampus in two processes important to PTSD—memory and regulation of stress responses—it has been an area of intense interest in neurobiological studies. Animal studies have shown that high cortisol levels can cause specific damage to hippocampal neurons (Sapolsky, 2000), and it has been suggested that severe stressors and trauma could lead to smaller hippocampal volume that, in turn, leads to deficits in hippocampal stress regulation and higher PTSD risk. It had been proposed, therefore, that the smaller hippocampal volume in PTSD may result from trauma-induced excessive cortisol secretion and subsequent neurotoxicity leading to hippocampal damage (Bremner, 1999). Support for this idea in humans comes from studies that have found smaller hippocampal volumes in patients with Cushing's disorder, a disorder characterized by massive increases in circulating cortisol, which appear to be due to cortisol-induced hippocampal atrophy (Starkman, Gebarski, Berent, & Schteingart, 1992; Starkman et al., 1999). Thus, the hypothesis of PTSD resulting from stress-induced "glucocorticoid toxicity damage to the hippocampus" was intuitively appealing and appeared to have good face validity given the effects of very high levels of cortisol on the hippocampus in humans and rodents. However, as discussed in the previous section, the relationship of trauma and PTSD to long-term cortisol levels is far from simple, with some studies even suggesting lower, rather than elevated, levels of cortisol as the long-term effect of trauma. An alternate hypothesis is that decreased hippocampal sizes in PTSD could be unrelated to cortisol secretion and actually predate the development of clinical syndrome. Such preexisting neurobiological abnormality may predispose individuals to develop PTSD.

At the time of writing, there are more than 40 published studies over the past 15 years, comparing the size (volume) of right and left hippocampi among trauma exposed persons with and without PTSD and non-trauma-exposed healthy controls, making the hippocampus probably the most studied brain region in structural imaging studies of PTSD. As will be described in detail below, many of these studies, especially earlier studies, have reported decreased hippocampal volume (ca. 8% to 13% reduction) in subjects with PTSD compared to either trauma-exposed and nonexposed healthy controls. However, a substantial portion of the studies (approximately one in three studies) conducted so far have not found evidence of reduction in hippocampal volume associated with PTSD, calling into question the specificity of this finding in PTSD. Furthermore, there is considerable heterogeneity among the studies in terms of the age of subjects, the age of the trauma exposure, the interval between the trauma and the measurement, the type of trauma exposures, and other potentially confounding factors such as medication use and psychiatric comorbidity, including alcohol and drug dependence. This heterogeneity further complicates meta-analytic studies, and several meta-analyses performed to date have included studies of different trauma types and other confounds (Smith, 2005; Woon & Hedges, 2010),

Several early studies examining hippocampal volume associated with PTSD in military combat Veterans found evidence of smaller hippocampal volume in studies of U.S. military Vietnam combat Veterans (Bremner et al., 1995; Gilbertson et al., 2002; Gurvits et al., 1996; Hedges et al., 2003), U.S. military Gulf war Veterans (Vythilingam et al., 2005), and Croatian combat Veterans (Pavic et al., 2007).

However, several relatively large studies of military Veterans report no differences in hippocampal volumes among combat Veterans with PTSD compared to healthy combat Veterans and civilians, or differences present only in the context of other factors. A study of Vietnam Veterans with PTSD ($n = 18$) compared to healthy civilians ($n = 19$) found no difference in hippocampal volume in PTSD (Schuff et al., 2001), although this study found decreased levels of hippocampal $N$-acetylaspartate and other metabolites in the PTSD subjects. A subsequent larger study (total $n = 104$) by the same researchers also found no differences in hippocampal volumes among four groups of military Veteran subjects: combat Veteran PTSD patients (Vietnam and Gulf wars) with ($n = 28$) and without ($n = 27$) alcohol abuse and Veterans with mixed levels of trauma exposures who were negative for PTSD with ($n = 23$) and without ($n = 26$) alcohol abuse. However, they again found decreased levels of hippocampal $N$-acetylaspartate in the subjects with PTSD (Schuff et al., 2008). Another recent large study of military Veterans (total $n = 99$) using a similar four-group design also found no difference in hippocampal volume in Vietnam and Gulf war combat Veterans with PTSD ($n = 24$) and without PTSD ($n = 20$) without a history of alcohol abuse. Interestingly, they found ~9% reduction in hippocampal volume in combat Veterans with PTSD ($n = 27$) compared to without PTSD ($n = 28$) who also were positive for alcohol abuse or dependence (Woodward et al., 2006). Taken together, these studies suggest both that while hippocampal abnormalities may exist in combat PTSD, volumetric MRI may not be the most sensitive method to study these, and further, PTSD effects may reflect chronicity of illness and interactions with other factors such as alcohol dependence, which could have independent effects on hippocampus via other pharmacological, physiological, and behavioral mechanisms.

Studies of PTSD stemming from adult traumas in civilians have also reported mixed results in terms of hippocampal volume. A Swedish study of civilians with PTSD ($n = 23$) from various traumas (motor vehicle collision, assault, sudden death of loved one, etc.) compared to healthy controls, all without alcohol abuse or dependence, found decreased hippocampal volume in PTSD (Emdad et al., 2006). A study of Dutch police with PTSD ($n = 14$) compared to trauma-exposed police without PTSD ($n = 14$) found a ~10% reduction in bilateral hippocampus in PTSD (Lindauer et al., 2004), and a study of Dutch psychiatric outpatients with PTSD ($n = 18$) and trauma-exposed healthy controls ($n = 14$) also found ~13% reduction in hippocampus in PTSD (Lindauer et al., 2005). However, again, several studies of PTSD from adult civilian traumas report no differences in hippocampal volume. A study of chronic PTSD from the 1988 Ramstein air-show disaster found no differences in hippocampal volume or gray matter density (using anatomical MRI and

VBM analyses, respectively) in traumatized persons with PTSD ($n$ = 15) and matched healthy controls ($n$ = 15) (Jatzko et al., 2006). A study of female intimate partner abuse survivors with PTSD ($n$ = 11) and without PTSD ($n$ = 11) and a matched nonvictimized control group ($n$ = 17) likewise found no differences in hippocampal volumes (Fennema-Notestine, Stein, Kennedy, Archibald, & Jernigan, 2002). A fascinating prospective, longitudinal study was conducted of 37 acutely traumatized survivors recruited in a Jerusalem hospital emergency room and assessed psychiatric diagnostic interview and MRI at 1 week posttrauma and at a 6-month follow-up. Ten subjects (27%) had PTSD at 6 months; however, those with PTSD did not differ from those without PTSD in hippocampal volume (right or left) at either 1 week or 6 months, and there was no reduction in hippocampal volume in the PTSD subjects between 1 week and 6 months (Bonne et al., 2001). The authors concluded that smaller hippocampal volume is not a necessary risk factor for developing PTSD and does not occur within 6 months of expressing the disorder. Furthermore, the findings of this longitudinal study strongly argue against hippocampal "atrophy" related to trauma or PTSD, at least not within 6 months of trauma exposure. It is still possible that a longer time is necessary for the effects of trauma and PTSD to lead to decreased hippocampal size. However, a study of elderly Jewish survivors of the Nazi Holocaust with PTSD ($n$ = 13) and without PTSD ($n$ = 13) and a group of healthy nonexposed Jewish adults ($n$ = 20) did not find differences in hippocampal volumes among any group (Golier et al., 2005), and thus in this study the posttrauma interval was more than 50 years. A study of severe burn victims also found no differences in hippocampal volume in those with PTSD ($n$ = 15) and without PTSD ($n$ = 15), again providing evidence against a PTSD-specific effect on the hippocampus. However, intriguingly, both groups of burn victims had smaller (~12%) hippocampal volume than the nonburned comparison group, presenting the possibility that at least in certain forms of adult trauma, such as severe burns involving widespread tissue damage and severe and chronic pain, reduction in hippocampal volume may not necessarily be a function of PTSD pathophysiology but rather trauma exposure (Winter & Irle, 2004).

As mentioned above, the alternative explanation is that a smaller hippocampus is a preexisting risk factor for PTSD that makes one more likely to develop PTSD following trauma exposure. A study of monozygotic twins discordant for trauma exposure from the Vietnam Era Twin Registry appears to provide evidence for this alternate hypothesis (Gilbertson et al., 2002). It was found that probands with PTSD and their unexposed twins had significantly smaller hippocampal volumes than twin pairs without PTSD. Furthermore, PTSD severity in trauma-exposed Veterans negatively correlated with hippocampal volume. This finding suggests that smaller hippocampal size seems to be an inherited characteristic that increases the likelihood that an individual will develop PTSD in response to trauma exposure, because it is also present in the twins of the PTSD patients who were never exposed to combat trauma, although this is only a single study that requires replication.

Finally, it is also possible that it is necessary to experience trauma during specific developmental phases for it to have effects on the development of the hippocampus and other brain regions. Thus, trauma in childhood or adolescence could interfere with the growth and development of the brain generally, or potentially lead to developmental abnormalities in specific brain regions that may be particularly sensitive to the effects of stress. For example, it could be hypothesized that early life trauma could lead to abnormalities in such brain regions as the hippocampus and frontal cortex, both of which are centrally implicated in regulation of fear and stress responses, and both of which have high levels of glucocorticoid (stress hormone) receptors. Even if such exposure to childhood trauma did not lead to PTSD during childhood, these hypothesized developmental alterations could lead to lifelong changes in brain function, including stress sensitivity and regulation, and thus lead to increased risk for PTSD after exposure to an adult trauma. Similar findings of exaggerated LHPA axis stress responses and dampened capacity for regulation of the stress responses are seen in rodent models of childhood adversity such as maternal separation (Ladd et al., 2000, 2004). Such developmental structural brain alterations could thus provide a neurobiological basis of the *PTSD diathesis* (or neural endophenotype of PTSD vulnerability) created by childhood trauma. It would suggest that childhood traumas could lead to long-term brain alterations that would precede exposure to the index trauma (i.e., the specific trauma that precipitated the PTSD symptoms) and serve as a predisposing factor toward the development of PTSD.

Structural neuroimaging studies of adults with PTSD from childhood trauma, compared to adults with childhood trauma history and no PTSD history and adults without childhood trauma history, have reported smaller hippocampal volume, but again, findings have been mixed, and it is unclear whether hippocampal differences reflect PTSD-specific processes, general developmental sequelae of childhood trauma, or effects due to comorbidity. In the first study to find smaller hippocampus in PTSD, structural MRI was performed on adult psychiatric patients with histories of childhood sexual abuse (Bremner et al., 1997). All PTSD patients were symptomatic at the time of the scan, and most also had comorbid diagnoses of dissociative disorder or depression. The women with childhood sexual abuse history had substantially reduced hippocampal size (~12%) in the left hippocampus compared to healthy controls. Furthermore, smaller hippocampal size was associated with the duration of abuse. The same group reported a subsequent study of women with early childhood sexual abuse and PTSD ($n = 10$), women with abuse without PTSD ($n = 12$), and women without abuse or PTSD ($n = 11$), and found women with childhood abuse and PTSD had 16% smaller hippocampal volumes than women with abuse and no PTSD, and 19% smaller than women with no abuse (Bremner, Vythilingam, Vermetten, Southwick, et al.,

2003). An independent study (Stein, Koverola, Hanna, Torchia, & McClarty, 1997) also found a reduction in left hippocampus in 21 sexually abused (15 of whom had PTSD) compared to nonabused women. Even though the reduction in hippocampal size was smaller (~5%), it was correlated with dissociative symptoms and, to a lesser degree, with PTSD symptoms. However, another study of women (ages 20 to 40) survivors of prepubescent sexual abuse with PTSD ($n = 17$) and without PTSD ($n = 17$) and nonabused comparison group ($n = 17$) did not find differences in hippocampal sizes or in memory performance among any group (Pederson et al., 2004). Smaller hippocampus volumes in subjects with borderline personality disorder and early traumatization have also been found; however, this study also found the association was present irrespective of PTSD diagnosis and traumatic experience (Driessen et al., 2002). Interestingly, some studies also found smaller hippocampal size in adult survivors of child abuse without PTSD, which could also be consistent with the notion that a smaller hippocampus could be a result of development events. A study comparing women with unipolar depression and no childhood abuse history ($n = 11$), depressed women with a history of childhood abuse ($n = 21$), and healthy nonabused controls ($n = 14$) found depressed subjects with childhood abuse had smaller left hippocampal volume than the healthy women (15% smaller) and the nonabused depressed subjects (18% smaller) (Vythilingam et al., 2002). Thus, the decreased hippocampal size appeared to be related to the childhood abuse history rather than major depression, as depressed women without abuse did not have smaller hippocampal size compared to healthy controls. A meta-analysis of the four PTSD-specific studies (three positive and one negative) found evidence for smaller hippocampi in PTSD (Woon & Hedges, 2008); however, given the other evidence of apparent effects on hippocampus from abuse and personality, it is unclear how specific this effect is to PTSD.

Furthermore, studies of relatively large numbers of maltreated children with and without PTSD and nonabused children have not found evidence of smaller hippocampal volume. One study examined structural brain scans in 44 maltreated children and adolescents with PTSD, and 61 matched healthy, nonabused controls. This study showed profound changes in the brains of maltreated children, which were associated with the duration of abuse and the severity of PTSD, including cerebral volume loss and larger ventricular sizes, but no evidence of volumetric differences in hippocampal volume was observed between the children with and without trauma exposure and PTSD. Another study replicated these findings using a sample of 28 children and adolescents with maltreatment-related PTSD and 66 sociodemographically matched healthy subjects (De Bellis et al., 2002). This group recently reported results from a further cohort of 216 children with maltreatment histories ($n = 49$), maltreatment and PTSD ($n = 49$), or no maltreatment ($n = 118$), which again found no significant differences in hippocampal sizes among children with and without maltreatment or PTSD (De Bellis, Hooper, Woolley, & Shenk, 2010).

Taken together, these findings suggest that even with the relatively large number of studies done to date, given the disparities in the findings and the wide array of potentially confounding factors, more data are needed to elucidate the specific effects of PTSD on hippocampal size or, conversely, of hippocampal size on PTSD. Again, additional longitudinal peritraumatic MRI studies of adult trauma and development of PTSD also examining genetic factors and early childhood experiences could shed important light on PTSD pathogenesis.

## FUNCTIONAL NEUROIMAGING OF EMOTIONS IN HEALTH, TRAUMA, AND PTSD CONTEXTS

A large number of studies have now begun to identify brain regions involved in the processing and regulation of emotions (Bechara, Damasio, & Damasio, 2000; Phan, Wager, Taylor, & Liberzon, 2002; Phan, Wager, Taylor, & Liberzon, 2004; Phillips, 2003; Phillips, Drevets, Rauch, & Lane, 2003; Taylor & Liberzon, 2007). Animal experiments and neuropsychological studies in humans have pointed to limbic regions, such as the anterior cingulate cortex, amygdala, and the inferior orbitofrontal and ventromedial frontal cortex, as having a role in the perception, processing, and regulation of emotion (Bechara, Damasio, & Demasio, 2000; Bechara, Tranel, & Damasio, 2000). A large number of studies of amygdala lesions in animals and electrophysiological experiments in animals have demonstrated the central and crucial role of the amygdala in mediating fear conditioning responses, with direct stimulation of the amygdala eliciting dramatic behavioral responses of fear, rage, and aggression in animals (Davis, 1992a, 1992b; LeDoux, 2000, 2003; LeDoux, Cicchetti, Xagoraris, & Romanski, 1990). The amygdala is a small subcortical structure located in the medial temporal cortex. In healthy humans, the amygdala can be activated (i.e., lead to increases in cerebral perfusion) by viewing pictures of aversive visual stimuli and especially by human faces with fearful or angry expressions. (Breiter et al., 1996; Taylor, Liberzon, & Koeppe, 2000). The amygdala is also known to be involved in emotional memories, or memories for aversively motivated learning in animal models (McGaugh, Cahill, & Roozendaal, 1996). Human neuroimaging studies have reported that recall for films with emotional content is correlated with blood flow in the right amygdala (Cahill, 1996; Cahill et al., 1996). However, the role for amygdala in humans seems somewhat more complex than simply being involved in processing aversive or fearful cues, as the amygdala can also be activated in processing positive or pleasant stimuli (Hamann, Ely, Grafton, & Kilts, 1999; Liberzon, Phan, Decker, & Taylor, 2003). This suggests that the amygdala may play a more general role in the evaluation of stimulus salience and stimulus ambiguity (Whalen et al., 1998). Thus, human functional neuro-imaging data suggest that amygdala activation is related to successful recall of emotional stimuli, as well as being centrally involved in fear processing, supporting the idea that amygdala dysfunction or dysregulation could be important in mediating some of the symptoms of PTSD (Liberzon & Phan, 2003; Liberzon & Sripada, 2008; Liberzon et al., 1999; Rauch et al., 2000; Shin, Kosslyn, et al., 1997; Shin, Rauch, & Pitman, 2006)

As we discussed, prefrontal cortex regions such as the inferior orbital cortex, the medial frontal, and the rostral/subgenual anterior cingulate cortex also appear important to emotional experiencing. A large number of human neuroimaging studies have implicated the medial prefrontal cortex and the rostral anterior cingulate in emotional responding (for review, see Phan et al., 2002, 2004; Phillips, 2003; Phillips et al., 2003; Taylor & Liberzon, 2007). There is accumulating evidence from human studies that these medial frontal paralimbic cortical structures are important in the regulation of emotional reactivity (Ochsner, Hughes, Robertson, Cooper, & Gabrieli, 2009; Ochsner et al., 2004; Taylor & Liberzon, 2007; Taylor, Phan, Decker, & Liberzon, 2003) and potentially to neuroendocrine stress responses (King et al., 2009; Pruessner et al., 2008). Lesions to these brain regions cause notable difficulties in impulse control and a loss of the ability to ascertain the appropriate social context for behavior (Bechara, Damasio, et al., 2000; Bechara, Tranel, et al., 2000). The role of these cortical regions is less well understood than that of the amygdala, which may reflect the fact that they appear to mediate emotional dimensions of complex social behavior, for which animal models are not readily available. There is also considerable evidence of dysregulation of these medial frontal regions in PTSD, mainly of decreased functional activity in mPFC during emotional processing (reviewed in Liberzon & Martis, 2006; Liberzon & Phan, 2003; Liberzon & Sripada, 2008), suggesting that trauma may lead to effects on the normal functioning of medial prefrontal cortex (mPFC) that may be important in the development of PTSD symptoms. It is also possible that mPFC dysregulation is a preexisting risk factor unrelated to trauma exposure, or is the result of pathophysiological changes that are the recurrence of PTSD symptoms. Overall, existing evidence highlights the importance of several interconnected brain regions, including the anterior cingulate (ACC), mPFC, insular cortex, and amygdala in the processing and modulation of emotions.

## ALTERATIONS IN FUNCTIONAL NEUROCIRCUITRY ASSOCIATED WITH PTSD AND ADULT AND CHILDHOOD TRAUMA

Functional neuroimaging has the potential to further our understanding of neurocircuitry that is associated with traumatization and PTSD, and in this context, it is important to consider the specific cognitive, emotional, and behavioral contexts in which the traumatized persons and PTSD patients are neuroimaged. Specific types of tasks or probes have been designed to examine or probe different psychological functions and the underlying neuronal circuitry and neurophysiological activity. Functional neuroimaging studies of PTSD patients have utilized a number of activation paradigms that focus on brain regions involved in emotional responses. Researchers have examined potential differences in emotional reactivity and various cognitive and regulatory functions among persons with and without trauma exposure and among persons with and without PTSD. These researchers have employed a variety of paradigms, including "symptom provocation," in which subjects are exposed to trauma memories or trauma-related stimuli, as well as more general probes, such as presentation of generally aversive stimuli (e.g., IAPS) not specifically associated with the person's own trauma.

As discussed, psychophysiological and neuroendocrine studies of symptom provocation in PTSD patients have demonstrated enhanced psychophysiological reactivity to both generic reminders of traumatic experiences, such as battle or combat footage from movies, as well as mental imagery induced by personalized or autobiographical scripts of traumatic events. Such stimuli reliably exaggerated skin conductance and heart rate responses in PTSD patients and enhanced plasma catecholamine secretion (Liberzon, Abelson, et al., 1999; Orr et al., 2002; Pitman et al., 1999), as peripheral markers of altered emotional responses in PTSD patients, suggesting these as face valid paradigms through which the underlying neurocircuitry of emotions can be explored. This chapter thus focuses primarily upon PTSD symptom provocation studies. Functional neuroimaging studies of PTSD related to adult trauma have provided considerable evidence of altered function in limbic (e.g., amygdala) and paralimbic (e.g., OFC, mPFC, insular, temporal polar cortex) cortical regions. In one of the earliest studies, Rauch and colleagues (Rauch & Shin, 1997) used positron emission tomography (PET) with radioactive [$^{15}$O]-labeled water, which measures regional cerebral blood flow (rCBF), in a group of eight PTSD subjects with various traumas using symptom provocation with autobiographical script-driven imagery. This initial, uncontrolled study observed increased rCBF in amygdala, anterior paralimbic (right posterior medial orbitofrontal cortex [OFC]), insular, anterior temporal pole, and medial temporal cortex in response to trauma scripts compared to the control scripts. In a similar study that followed, they compared Vietnam Veterans with PTSD ($n = 7$) to a control group of combat-exposed Vietnam Veterans with no history of PTSD ($n = 7$) to investigate the specificity of emotional processing in PTSD compared to Veterans with similar combat trauma exposures. Combat Veterans with PTSD had increased rCBF in ventral ACC and right amygdala when generating mental images of combat-related pictures, but had decreased rCBF in the ACC in the combat image viewing versus neutral image viewing contrast (Shin, McNally, et al., 1997).

Another study using combat-related pictures and sounds and PET in 10 combat Veterans with and 10 without PTSD revealed decreased blood flow in medial prefrontal cortex (mPFC) (area 25) and other areas in response to traumatic pictures and sounds in PTSD patients, while non-PTSD control subjects activated the anterior cingulate (area 24) to a greater degree than PTSD patients (Bremner, Staib, et al., 1999). Another script-driven imagery and PET study (17 Vietnam Veterans with PTSD and 19 without PTSD) showed rCBF decreases in the medial frontal gyrus for the traumatic versus neutral comparison in the PTSD group. This activity was inversely correlated with rCBF changes in the left amygdala and the right amygdala/periamygdaloid cortex. Only the male combat Veteran subgroup (and not the female nurse Veteran subgroup) showed increased rCBF in left amygdala (Shin et al., 2004).

Researchers who study trauma-related alterations in brain function are often faced with the problem of determining whether brain alterations are due to the pathophysiology of PTSD symptoms, as opposed to the effects of trauma exposure, itself, regardless of PTSD status. To overcome this problem, our group has conducted studies of combat PTSD using three group designs, with combat PTSD patients compared to two healthy control groups: a healthy combat Veteran group with no history of PTSD and a healthy control group with no history of trauma exposure. Thus, contrasts can be made between trauma-exposed and nonexposed groups to determine effects due to trauma exposure (PTSD versus healthy and combat control versus healthy) and which effects are specific to PTSD (PTSD patients versus healthy combat controls). Our group conducted a three-group study (14 combat PTSD subjects, 11 healthy combat Veterans without PTSD, and 11 healthy community subjects without combat exposure) in which subjects were exposed to combat sounds or white noise in two counterbalanced sessions and studied using rCBF with 99mTc- (HMPAO) SPECT. Only the PTSD group showed increased rCBF in the left peri-amygdala region (Liberzon et al., 1999). We subsequently conducted another three-group study in which combat PTSD with Vietnam era Veterans, this time using [$^{15}$O]-labeled water PET, and script-driven imagery of autobiographical events, with 16 combat Veterans with PTSD, 15 healthy combat Veterans (no PTSD), and 14 healthy, age-matched controls. For the traumatic/stressful > neutral scripts, while all subjects deactivated the mPFC and activated the insula in response to the script, PTSD patients deactivated the rostral anterior cingulate cortex (rACC) more than both control groups, who also showed ventromedial PFC (vmPFC) deactivation (Britton, Phan, Taylor, Fig, & Liberzon, 2005).

While much of the neuroimaging data available in traumatized people have involved adults with PTSD from traumas suffered as adults (e.g., combat or sexual assault trauma), there have been several neuroimaging studies involving adults with and without PTSD who were exposed to childhood trauma. Several neuroimaging studies have also been performed in adults with PTSD with a history of childhood traumas, especially childhood sexual abuse.

Early on, Bremner, Narayan, et al. (1999) studied 22 women who experienced childhood sexual abuse (CSA), 10 of whom had current PTSD and 12 without PTSD, using [$^{15}$O] water PET and script-driven imagery. The women with CSA and PTSD showed rCBF increases in posterior cingulate and anterolateral prefrontal cortex (PFC) (superior and middle frontal gyri bilaterally). The PTSD group also showed deactivation in the subcallosal gyrus region of the anterior cingulate (area 25) with a failure of activation in an adjacent portion of the anterior cingulate. Shin et al. (1999) used a similar design in 16 subjects with CSA (8 with PTSD) and found greater increases in rCBF in the orbitofrontal cortex (OFC) and temporal poles and deactivation of the medial prefrontal and left inferior frontal gyrus (Broca's) areas in the PTSD group versus the non-PTSD group in the traumatic versus neutral imagery contrast. Lanius and colleagues reported two studies (Lanius et al., 2001, 2003) where they used a script-driven symptom provocation paradigm and fMRI. The second study also included comparison of nontraumatic negative states (i.e., sadness and anxiety). They reported significantly decreased activations in the ACC in Brodman's area 32 (BA 32) and the thalamus in the PTSD group to both the traumatic and nontraumatic emotional states conditions, suggesting that the earlier neuroimaging findings related to these areas in PTSD may not be specific to traumatic stimuli. In an fMRI study, Lanius et al. (2003) reported that 7 CSA subjects with PTSD and concomitant dissociative responses to symptom provocation by scripts had increased activation in the ACC, mPFC, and several other cortical areas compared to 10 control subjects.

While thus far we had primarily focused on symptom provocation studies in PTSD, a number of other emotional induction and regulation paradigms have been used to probe the neural endophenotypes of PTSD. These studies have been reviewed in a number of previous publications (Liberzon & Martis, 2006; Liberzon & Phan, 2003; Rauch & Shin, 1997; Rauch, Shin, & Phelps, 2006) and include, among others, the presentation of stimuli of faces with emotional expressions such as fear or anger. These presentations generate robust amygdala reactivity in healthy persons, and there are a number of studies that have found heightened amygdala responses to negative (e.g., fearful) emotional face stimuli in PTSD (Bryant et al., 2008; Felmingham et al., 2010; New et al., 2009; Rauch et al., 2000; Shin et al., 2005; Williams et al., 2006). Brain responses to negative words have also been used to probe aversive emotional processing in PTSD, and have found decreased rostral ACC activation during negative words in CSA-related PTSD compared to abused women without PTSD (Bremner et al., 2004). A similar study of combat-related words in Vietnam Veterans with PTSD and without PTSD found a similar deficit in rostral ACC activation in the PTSD group (Shin et al., 2001). Another widely used paradigm for emotional induction is presentation of complex social images with neutral or aversive emotional content. The IAPS developed by Lang and colleagues (Lang, Bradley, & Cuthbert, 1995) is a widely used emotional induction paradigm that has a large number of social and nonsocial photographs containing "neutral" content, such as people engaged in ordinary everyday activities, as well as those containing negative social content, such as photos of crime scenes, war scenes, accidents, surgeries, and so forth. Several studies examined the effects of IAPS pictures in PTSD. Our group performed a $[^{15}O]$ PET study with Vietnam combat Veterans with PTSD ($n = 16$), without PTSD ($n = 15$), and matched healthy community controls ($n = 15$), and found that PTSD patients showed decreased activity in ventral mPFC compared to both control groups while viewing aversive IAPS pictures. Preliminary analysis of data from an ongoing fMRI study of emotional regulation in our group with combat Veterans returning from Iraq and Afghanistan (King & Liberzon, 2010) finds that returning combat Veterans with PTSD ($n = 15$) experienced decreased activity in mPFC and anterior cingulate cortex (ACC) while viewing emotionally aversive IAPS pictures relative to Iraq and Afghanistan combat Veterans without PTSD ($n = 12$), and healthy nonmilitary community controls ($n = 12$).

In summary, symptom provocation studies of PTSD related to adult trauma (e.g., combat exposure) and childhood trauma (e.g., childhood sexual abuse) have yielded interesting and informative results that have related to brain activity, including decreased activity in medial frontal cortical regions (mPFC and rostral and subgenual ACC), and potentially increased or altered activity in other limbic and paralimbic regions (e.g., amygdala and insula) in persons with PTSD. These findings are consistent with a general theoretical model that PTSD is associated with dysregulated neurophysiological responses to potential threat cues and trauma recall. In PTSD, trauma recall or negative emotional cues lead to exaggerated activations of amygdala, insula cortex, and other ventral limbic regions associated with threat and aversive emotional processing, as well as a concomitant hypoactivation of medial frontal cortex structures associated with emotional regulation. However, findings are not always consistent and may be influenced by several methodological issues, including sample size, sample heterogeneity, and varying imaging methods. In particular, the differential effects of childhood trauma versus adult trauma on aspects of emotional induction and regulation are yet to be carefully studied within the same experiment. Ultimately, neuroimaging studies will be designed to study the effects on specific neural endophenotypes of childhood trauma alone and in combination with adult retraumatization, and how these processes affect vulnerability to psychiatric symptoms.

## FUNCTIONAL NEUROANATOMY OF NEUROENDOCRINE STRESS REGULATION IN PERSONS WITH PTSD

Recently, studies have begun to integrate functional neuroanatomical findings related to trauma and PTSD neuroendocrinological findings. This integration might be important to ultimately understand the pathophysiology and etiology of PTSD. We discussed that neurobiological research over the past decades has revealed consistent abnormalities in noradrenergic and LHPA axis stress systems in association with PTSD. It is also becoming clear that stress hormones, such as cortisol, play an important role in cognitive and emotional processes that characterize healthy adjustment as well as psychopathology.

As previously discussed, trauma exposure appears to have long-term and complex impacts on LHPA axis regulation. Early life adversity in rodent models tends to show increased magnitude and length of LHPA axis stress responses, which appears to be due to desensitization of negative feedback (decreased glucocorticoid sensitivity and decreased GR gene expression) (Ladd et al., 2004), whereas a model of adult trauma in rodents shows increased feedback sensitization (i.e., increased glucocorticoid feedback sensitivity and GR expression) (Liberzon, Krstov, & Young, 1997). Evidence that childhood trauma in humans leads to exaggerated LHPA axis responses (ACTH responses to stress) (Heim & Nemeroff, 2001; Heim et al., 2000) and elevated salivary cortisol following personal trauma recall (Elzinga et al., 2003) has also been discussed, as well as evidence that adult trauma (combat deployments) may sensitize glucocorticoid feedback (de Kloet, Vermetten, Bikker et al., 2007; de Kloet, Vermetten, Heijnen et al., 2007; Yehuda, 2003). Modest but rapid ACTH responses are seen to be general trauma cues in combat Veterans with and without PTSD (Liberzon, Abelson, et al., 1999); larger acute (5 minutes) ACTH responses are seen with autobiographical trauma script-driven imagery (Liberzon et al., 2007) but not to highly aversive (but not personally salient) visual stimuli.

Even though limbic structures are clearly implicated in the initiation of LHPA response to challenge, the neural mechanisms by which potentially threatening psychological stimuli activate this system, and the manner in which these systems may be dysregulated in PTSD or other psychiatric disorders are not yet understood. In animals, the neural circuitry through which psychological stimuli (e.g., stressors such as restraint, predator exposure, and conditioned fear) activate the hypothalamus has been partially mapped (Herman, Ostrander, Mueller, & Figueiredo, 2005). LHPA axis activation appears to involve amygdala and bed nucleus of the stria terminalis (Beaulieu, Di Paolo, & Barden, 1986; Saphier & Feldman, 1990), whereas the hippocampus and medial prefrontal cortex (mPFC) are involved in negative modulation (Brake, Sullivan, & Gratton, 2000; Diorio, Viau, & Meaney, 1993) of LHPA axis responses, apparently through multisynaptic projections to regions of hypothalamus peripheral to the PVN (Herman et al., 2005).

Interestingly, human LHPA axis appears to be particularly sensitive to certain forms of psychological stimuli (e.g., novelty, social evaluative threat, lack of control) (Dickerson & Kemeny, 2004) rather than to general distress, and in humans presumably requires considerable processing of social and contextual information. The cortical components of LHPA circuitry that process this information and modulate LHPA axis responses to psychological stimuli in humans have only recently begun to be elucidated, and relationships between brain activity and LHPA axis function have been examined *in vivo* in only a few human studies. Resting plasma or salivary cortisol levels have been linked to amygdala metabolism. Drevets et al. (2002), who used 18F-fluorodeoxyglucose PET, measured regional glucose metabolism in amygdala and hippocampus in patients with familial pure depressive disease, bipolar disorder, and healthy controls. Left amygdala metabolism was increased in the depressed groups relative to the control group, and significantly for understanding effects of cortisol on the brain, amygdala metabolism was also positively correlated with stressed plasma cortisol levels in the depressed groups. This finding may reflect abnormalities in the feedback mechanisms for cortisol possibly mediated by the influence of the amygdala on central stress systems (e.g., corticotropin-releasing hormones).

Several recent studies have examined stress-responsive cortisol levels to brain activation patterns in healthy adults (King & Liberzon, 2009). In an $^{15}O[H_2O]$ PET study of public speaking challenge in social anxiety patients, saliva cortisol responses to speaking stressor were positively correlated to cerebral blood flow (rCBF) in midbrain/hypothalamus, and negatively correlated with dorsal medial PFC (Ahs et al., 2006). In an arterial spin labeling MRI study of mental arithmetic, saliva cortisol responses were linked to increased baseline regional cerebral blood flow (rCBF) in right lateral PFC (Wang et al., 2005). In another recent large study involving healthy subjects and both $^{15}O$ PET blood flow and fMRI and a specialized mental arithmetic task, brain patterns differentiating responders and nonresponders found subjects who had cortisol responses to the stressor also showed relative deactivations in medial frontal areas (anterior cingulate cortex, ACC, and orbitofrontal cortex, OFC) (Pruessner et al., 2008). These studies are consistent with emerging models (Herman et al., 2005) suggesting that activation is driven by emotion processors like amygdala and insula, with inhibitory modulation occurring via medial prefrontal and other paralimbic regions. Because ACTH levels fluctuate more rapidly and in closer temporal proximity to changes in hypothalamic activity, studies examining brain activation associated with peripheral ACTH levels may better illuminate the corticolimbic inputs modulating hypothalamic outputs. A SPECT study in healthy persons found a positive correlation between plasma ACTH levels following sadness induction and rCBF in right insula and left anterior cingulate cortex (Ottowitz et al., 2004).

Recently, neuroimaging studies of LHPA axis function have begun to explore these relationships in traumatized persons with and without PTSD. A resting-state study in PTSD Bonne et al. (2003) compared 11 subjects with PTSD to 17 trauma-exposed subjects without PTSD and 17 nontraumatized healthy controls using 99mTc-HMPAO SPECT 6 months after the trauma. Resting plasma cortisol level in PTSD was negatively correlated with medial temporal lobe rCBF and positively correlated with rCBF in rostral ACC. In a recent [$^{15}O$] PET neuroimaging study of Vietnam combat Veterans with and without PTSD, our group reported links between activity in paralimbic and frontal cortex regions (insula, ACC, parahippocampus, and medial frontal cortex) and plasma cortisol and ACTH levels, using correlational, within-subject analyses (Liberzon et al., 2007). We conducted a [$^{15}$O]H$_2$O PET study of a series of emotional challenges (aversive pictures and autobiographic narratives) in 16 combat PTSD patients, 15 combat controls, and 14 noncombat controls. Plasma ACTH and cortisol were measured 2 minutes before each stimulus presentation and 5 minutes after each scan, thus allowing us to capture dynamic modulation of neural activity in coordination with the HPA axis function in a within-subjects design. Voxel-wise analyses showed ACTH responses covaried with rCBF in rACC and right insula in PTSD patients and rostral anterior cingulate and dmPFC in combat controls. These findings suggest involvement of insula, dmPFC, and rostral anterior cingulate in HPA axis responses to trauma-related stimuli. The prestimulus plasma cortisol level covaried with rCBF in subgenual ACC in PTSD patients and rostral anterior cingulate in combat controls. This suggests that rACC may be a site of modulation by circulating cortisol in trauma-exposed subjects. Differential patterns of covariation between combat Veterans with and without PTSD implicate dmPFC and rostral anterior cingulate as areas of dysregulation of HPA axis responses in PTSD.

Because the LHPA axis appears to have multiple regulatory feedback loops that complicate interpretation of correlational findings, for example, correlation with ACTH levels over time could reveal regions involved in activation of LHPA responses, but such correlations might also result from the activity of coresponsive regulatory regions that actually function to dampen LHPA axis responses. Therefore, we examined patterns of brain activity in combat Veterans who had ACTH responses to trauma recall (responders) and those of combat Veterans who did not have ACTH responses to trauma recall (nonresponders) to find whether or not they had PTSD. In fact, we found that responders had greater activity in right anterior insula, whereas nonresponders had greater activity in a region of rostral ACC/mPFC (BA 32) (King et al., 2009). Interestingly, the region of increased activity in ACTH nonresponders was nearly identical to the region of increased activity in cortisol nonresponders reported in another recent study in healthy subjects (Pruessner et al., 2008).

In summary, it has long been appreciated that exposure to trauma can have effects on personality and behavior, and previous lifetime trauma is among the strongest predictors of PTSD risk. This chapter has reviewed evidence from both naturalistic studies and experimental paradigms that suggest experiences of trauma can be associated with profound changes in the brain and multiple neurobiological systems, including the stress-responsive autonomic and neuroendocrine systems. Thus, the phenomenon of retraumatization is important for understanding the psychology and pathophysiology of PTSD, and here we have reviewed evidence from both animal and human literature that stressors and traumas have an effect on the autonomic and neu-roendocrine systems, in particular, early life stressors and traumas. These data suggest that experience of trauma could lead to long-term adaptations (or maladaptations) in these systems that could contribute to psychiatric risk upon subsequent trauma exposure; traumas experienced in early life may have particularly strong effects due to their influence on development of the brain and neuroendocrine systems. There are also strong individual differences in people's responses to trauma and vulnerability to PTSD. We thus reviewed evidence that at least part of PTSD risk is due to genetic factors, and poten-tially could at least in part reflect genetic differences that lead to underlying differences in these neurobiological systems. Although the genetics of PTSD vulnerability is far from understood, genetic findings of specific variants to date suggest gene × environment interaction between these specific variants and childhood adversity of trauma. It is interesting that the available genetic data indicate an important role for childhood trauma exposure.

## REFERENCES

Adamec, R., Muir, C., Grimes, M., & Pearcey, K. (2007). Involvement of noradrenergic and corticoid receptors in the consolidation of the lasting anxiogenic effects of predator stress. *Behavior and Brain Research, 179,* 192–207.

Adamec, R. E., Blundell, J., & Burton, P. (2006). Relationship of the predatory attack experience to neural plasticity, pCREB expression and neuroendocrine response. *Neuroscience Biobehavioral Review, 30,* 356–375.

Ahs, F., Furmark, T., Michelgard, A., Langstrom, B., Appel, L., Wolf, O. T., … Fredrikson, M. (2006). Hypothalamic blood flow correlates positively with stress-induced cortisol levels in subjects with social anxiety disorder. *Psychosom Med, 68*(6), 859–862.

Aleman, A., Swart, M., & van Rijn, S. (2008). Brain imaging, genetics and emotion. *Biol Psychol, 79*(1), 58–69.

Amstadter, A. B., Koenen, K. C., Ruggiero, K. J., Acierno, R., Galea, S., Kilpatrick, D. G., … Gelernter, J. (2009). Variant in RGS2 moderates posttraumatic stress symptoms following potentially traumatic event exposure. *J Anxiety Disord, 23*(3), 369–373.

Bachmann, A. W., Sedgley, T. L., Jackson, R. V., Gibson, J. N., Young, R. M., & Torpy, D. J. (2005). Glucocorticoid receptor polymorphisms and post-traumatic stress disorder. *Psychoneuroendocrinology, 30*(3), 297–306.

Bailey, J. N., Goenjian, A. K., Noble, E. P., Walling, D. P., Ritchie, T., & Goenjian, H. A. (2010). PTSD and dopaminergic genes, DRD2 and DAT, in multigenerational families exposed to the Spitak earthquake. *Psychiatry Res, 178*(3), 507–510.

Baker, D. G., Ekhator, N. N., Kasckow, J. W., Dashevsky, B., Horn, P. S., Bednarik, L., … Geracioti Jr., T. D. (2005). Higher levels of basal serial CSF cortisol in combat Veterans with posttraumatic stress disorder. *Am J Psychiatry, 162*(5), 992–994.

Baker, D. G., West, S. A., Nicholson, W. E., Ekhator, N. N., Kasckow, J. W., Hill, K. K., … Geracioti Jr., T. D. (1999). Serial CSF corticotropin-releasing hormone levels and adrenocortical activity in combat Veterans with posttraumatic stress disorder. *Am J Psychiatry, 156*(4), 585–588.

Beaulieu, S., Di Paolo, T., & Barden, N. (1986). Control of ACTH secretion by the central nucleus of the amygdala: Implication of the serotoninergic system and its relevance to the glucocorticoid delayed negative feedback mechanism. *Neuroendocrinology, 44*(2), 247–254.

Bechara, A., Damasio, H., & Damasio, A. R. (2000). Emotion, decision making and the orbitofrontal cortex. *Cereb Cortex, 10*(3), 295–307.

Bechara, A., Tranel, D., & Damasio, H. (2000). Characterization of the decision-making deficit of patients with ventromedial prefrontal cortex lesions. *Brain, 123 (Pt 11)*, 2189–2202.

Binder, E. B., Bradley, R. G., Liu, W., Epstein, M. P., Deveau, T. C., Mercer, K. B., ... Ressler, K. J. (2008). Association of FKBP5 polymorphisms and childhood abuse with risk of posttraumatic stress disorder symptoms in adults. *JAMA, 299*(11), 1291–1305.

Blanchard, E. B., Kolb, L. C., Prins, A., Gates, S., & McCoy, G. (1991). Changes in plasma norepinephrine to combat-related stimuli among Vietnam Veterans with post-traumatic stress disorder. *J Nerv Ment Dis, 176*(6), 371–373.

Bonne, O., Brandes, D., Gilboa, A., Gomori, J. M., Shenton, M. E., Pitman, R. K., & Shalev, A. Y. (2001). Longitudinal MRI study of hippocampal volume in trauma survivors with PTSD. *Am J Psychiatry, 158*(8), 1248–1251.

Bonne, O., Gilboa, A., Louzoun, Y., Brandes, D., Yona, I., Lester, H., Barkai, G., Freedman, N., Chisin, R., & Shalev, A. Y. (2003). Resting regional cerebral perfusion in recent post-traumatic stress disorder. *Biological Psychiatry, 54*(10), 1077–1086.

Boscarino, J. A. (1996). Posttraumatic stress disorder, exposure to combat, and lower plasma cortisol among Vietnam Veterans: Findings and clinical implications. *J Consult Clin Psychol, 64*(1), 191–201.

Brake, W. G., Sullivan, R. M., & Gratton, A. (2000). Perinatal distress leads to lateralized medial prefrontal cortical dopamine hypofunction in adult rats. *J Neurosci, 20*(14), 5538–5543.

Bremner, J. D. (1999). Does stress damage the brain? *Biol Psychiatry, 45*(7), 797–805.

Bremner, J. D., Licinio, J., Darnell, A., Krystal, J. H., Owens, M. J., Southwick, S. M., ... Charney, D. S. (1997). Elevated CSF corticotropin-releasing factor concentrations in posttraumatic stress disorder. *Am J Psychiatry, 154*(5), 624–629.

Bremner, J. D., Narayan, M., Staib, L. H., Southwick, S. M., McGlashan, T., & Charney, D. S. (1999). Neural correlates of memories of childhood sexual abuse in women with and without posttraumatic stress disorder. *Am J Psychiatry, 156*(11), 1787–1795.

Bremner, J. D., Randall, P., Scott, T. M., Bronen, R. A., Seibyl, J. P., Southwick, S. M., ... Innis, R. B. (1995). MRI-based measurement of hippocampal volume in patients with combat-related posttraumatic stress disorder. *Am J Psychiatry, 152*(7), 973–981.

Bremner, J. D., Randall, P., Vermetten, E., Staib, L., Bronen, R. A., Mazure, C., ... Charney, D. S. (1997). Magnetic resonance imaging–based measurement of hippo-campal volume in posttraumatic stress disorder related to childhood physical and sexual abuse—A preliminary report. *Biol Psychiatry, 41*(1), 23–32.

Bremner, J. D., Staib, L. H., Kaloupek, D., Southwick, S. M., Soufer, R., & Charney, D. S. (1999). Neural correlates of exposure to traumatic pictures and sound in Vietnam combat Veterans with and without posttraumatic stress disorder: A positron emission tomography study. *Biol Psychiatry, 45*(7), 806–816.

Bremner, J. D., Vermetten, E., Vythilingam, M., Afzal, N., Schmahl, C., Elzing, B., & Charney, D. S. (2004). Neural correlates of the classic color and emotional stroop in women with abuse-related posttraumatic stress disorder. *Biol Psychiatry, 55* (6), 612–620.

Bremner, J. D., Vythilingam, M., Anderson, G., Vermetten, E., McGlashan, T., Heninger, G., Charney, D. S. (2003a). Assessment of the hypothalamic-pituitary-adrenal axis over a 24-hour diurnal period and in response to neuroendocrine challenges in women with and without childhood sexual abuse and posttraumatic stress disorder. *Biol Psychiatry, 54*(7), 710–718.

Bremner, J. D., Vythilingam, M., Vermetten, E., Adil, J., Khan, S., Nazeer, A., ... Charney, D. S. (2003b). Cortisol response to a cognitive stress challenge in posttraumatic stress disorder (PTSD) related to childhood abuse. *Psychoneuroendocrinology, 28*(6), 733–750.

Bremner, J. D., Vythilingam, M., Vermetten, E., Southwick, S. M., McGlashan, T., Nazeer, A., ... Charney, D. S. (2003c). MRI and PET study of deficits in hippocampal structure and function in women with childhood sexual abuse and posttraumatic stress disorder. *Am J Psychiatry, 160*(5), 924–932.

Breiter, H. C., Etcoff, N. L., Whalen, P. J., Kennedy, W. A., Rauch, S. L., Buckner, R. L., ... Rosen, B. R. (1996) Response and habituation of the human amygdala during visual processing of facial expression. *Neuron, 17,* 875–887.

Breslau, N., Davis, G. C., Andreski, P., & Peterson, E. (1991). Traumatic events and posttraumatic stress disorder in an urban population of young adults. *Arch Gen Psychiatry, 48*(3), 216–222.

Britton, J. C., Phan, K. L., Taylor, S. F., Fig, L. M., & Liberzon, I. (2005). Corticolimbic blood flow in posttraumatic stress disorder during script-driven imagery. *Biol Psychiatry, 57*(8), 832–840.

Brown, S. M., & Hariri, A. R. (2006). Neuroimaging studies of serotonin gene polymorphisms: Exploring the interplay of genes, brain, and behavior. *Cogn Affect Behav Neurosci, 6*(1), 44–52.

Brown, S. M., Peet, E., Manuck, S. B., Williamson, D. E., Dahl, R. E., Ferrell, R. E., & Hariri, A. R. (2005). A regulatory variant of the human tryptophan hydroxylase-2 gene biases amygdala reactivity. *Mol Psychiatry, 10*(9), 805, 884–888.

Brown, W. G., Bifulco, A., & Harris, T. O. (1987). Life events, vulnerability and onset of depression: Some refinements. *Br J Psychiatry, 150,* 30–42.

Bryant, R. A., Kemp, A. H., Felmingham, K. L., Liddell, B., Olivieri, G., Peduto, A., ... Williams, L. M. (2008). Enhanced amygdala and medial prefrontal activation during nonconscious processing of fear in posttraumatic stress disorder: An fMRI study. *Hum Brain Mapp, 29*(5), 517–523.

Burmeister, M. (1999). Basic concepts in the study of diseases with complex genetics. *Biol Psychiatry, 45*(5), 522–532.

Cabrera, O. A., Hoge, C. W., Bliese, P. D., Castro, C. A., & Messer, S. C. (2007). Childhood adversity and combat as predictors of depression and post-traumatic stress in deployed troops. *Am J Prev Med, 33*(2), 77–82.

Cahill, L. (1996). Neurobiology of memory for emotional events: Converging evidence from infra-human and human studies. *Cold Spring Harb Symp Quant Biol, 61,* 259–264.

Cahill, L., Haier, R. J., Fallon, J., Alkire, M. T., Tang, C., Keator, D., ... McGaugh, J. L. (1996). Amygdala activity at encoding correlated with long-term, free recall of emotional information. *Proc Natl Acad Sci U S A, 93*(15), 8016–8021.

Caldji, C., Diorio, J., & Meaney, M. (2000). Variations in maternal care in infancy regulate the development of stress reactivity. *Biol Psychiatry, 48*(12), 1164–1174.

Canive, J. M., Lewine, J. D., Orrison, W. W., Jr., Edgar, C. J., Provencal, S. L., Davis, J. T., ... Calais, L. (1997). MRI reveals gross structural abnormalities in PTSD. *Ann N Y Acad Sci, 821,* 512–515.

Canli, T., Congdon, E., Gutknecht, L., Constable, R. T., & Lesch, K. P. (2005). Amygdala responsiveness is modulated by tryptophan hydroxylase-2 gene variation. *J Neural Transm, 112*(11), 1479–1485.

Caspi, A., Sugden, K., Moffitt, T. E., Taylor, A., Craig, I. W., Harrington, H., ... Poulton, R. (2003). Influence of life stress on depression: Moderation by a polymorphism in the 5-HTT gene. *Science, 301*(5631), 386–389.

Chantarujikapong, S. I., Scherrer, J. F., Xian, H., Eisen, S. A., Lyons, M. J., Goldberg, J., & True, W. R. (2001). A twin study of generalized anxiety disorder symptoms, panic disorder symptoms and post-traumatic stress disorder in men. *Psychiatry Res, 103*(2–3), 133–145.

Cirulli, F., Alleva, E., Antonelli, A., & Aloe, L. (2000). NGF expression in the developing rat brain: Effects of maternal separation. *Dev Brain Res, 123*(2), 129–134.

Cohen, H., Kaplan, Z., Matar, M. A., Loewenthal, U., Kozlovsky, N., & Zohar, J. (2006). Anisomycin, a protein synthesis inhibitor, disrupts traumatic memory consolidation and attenuates posttraumatic stress. *Biological Psychiatry, 60*(7), 767–776.

Cohen, H., Kaplan, Z., Matar, M. A., Loewenthal, U., Zohar, J., & Richter-Levin, G. (2007). Long-lasting behavioral effects of juvenile trauma in an animal model of PTSD associated with a failure of the autonomic nervous system to recover. *European Neuropsychopharmacology, 17*, 464–477.

Cohen, H., Zohar, J., Gidron, Y., Matar, M. A., Belkind, D., Loewenthal, U., Kozlovsky, N., & Kaplan, Z. (2006). Blunted HPA axis response to stress influences susceptibility to posttraumatic stress response in rats. *Biological Psychiatry, 59*, 1208–1218.

Cohen, H., Zohar, J., Matar, M. A., Zeev, K., Loewenthal, U., & Richter-Levin, G. (2004). Setting apart the affected: The use of behavioral criteria in animal models of post-traumatic stress disorder. *Neuropsychopharmacology, 29*(11), 1962–1970.

Comings, D. E., Muhleman, D., & Gysin, R. (1996). Dopamine D2 receptor (DRD2) gene and susceptibility to posttraumatic stress disorder: A study and replication. *Biol Psychiatry, 40*(5), 368–372.

Cui, X. J., & Vaillant, G. E. (1996). Antecedents and consequences of negative life events in adulthood: A longitudinal study. *Am J Psychiatry, 153*, 21–26.

Davis, M. (1992a). The role of the amygdala in fear-potentiated startle: Implications for animal models of anxiety. *Trends Pharmacol Sci, 13*(1), 35–41.

Davis, M. (1992b). The role of the amygdala in fear and anxiety. *Annu Rev Neurosci, 15*, 353–375.

DeBellis, M. D., Baum, A. S., Birmaher, B., & Ryan, N. D. (1997). Urinary catecholamine excretion in childhood overanxious and posttraumatic stress disorders. *Ann NY Acad Sci, 821*(1), 451–455.

De Bellis, M. D., Hooper, S. R., Woolley, D. P., & Shenk, C. E. (2010). Demographic, maltreatment, and neurobiological correlates of PTSD symptoms in children and adolescents. *J Pediatr Psychol, 35*(5), 570–577.

De Bellis, M. D., Keshavan, M. S., Shifflett, H., Iyengar, S., Beers, S. R., Hall, J., & Moritz, G. (2002). Brain structures in pediatric maltreatment-related posttraumatic stress disorder: A sociodemographically matched study. *Biol Psychiatry, 52*(11), 1066–1078.

de Kloet, C. S., Vermetten, E., Bikker, A., Meulman, E., Geuze, E., Kavelaars, A., ... Heijnen, C. J. (2007). Leukocyte glucocorticoid receptor expression and immuno-regulation in Veterans with and without post-traumatic stress disorder. *Mol Psychiatry, 12*(5), 443–453.

de Kloet, C. S., Vermetten, E., Heijnen, C. J., Geuze, E., Lentjes, E. G., & Westenberg, H. G. (2007). Enhanced cortisol suppression in response to dexamethasone administration in traumatized Veterans with and without posttraumatic stress disorder. *Psychoneuroendocrinology, 32*(3), 215–226.

de Kloet, E. R., Karst, H., & Joels, M. (2008). Corticosteroid hormones in the central stress response: Quick-and-slow. *Front Neuroendocrinol, 29*(2), 268–272.

de Kloet, J. M., & Holsboer, F. (2005). Stress and the brain: From adaptation to disease. *Nat Rev Neurosci, 6*(6), 463–475.

Dickerson, S. S., & Kemeny, M. E. (2004). Acute stressors and cortisol responses: A theoretical integration and synthesis of laboratory research. *Psychol Bull, 130*, 355–391.

Diorio, D., Viau, V., & Meaney, M. J. (1993). The role of the medial prefrontal cortex (cingulate gyrus) in the regulation of hypothalamic-pituitary-adrenal responses to stress. *J Neurosci, 13*(9), 3839–3847.

Domschke, K., & Dannlowski, U. (2010). Imaging genetics of anxiety disorders. *Neuroimage, 53*(3), 822–831.

Donovan, E. (2009). Propranolol use in the prevention and treatment of posttraumatic stress disorder in military Veterans: Forgetting therapy revisited. *Perspect Biol Med, 53*(1), 61–74.

Drevets, W. C., Price, J. L., Bardgett, M. E., Reich, T., Todd, R. D., & Raichle, M. E. (2002). Glucose metabolism in the amygdala in depression: Relationship to diagnostic subtype and plasma cortisol levels. *Pharmacol Biochem Behav, 71*(3), 431–447.

Driessen, M., Herrmann, J., Stahl, K., Zwaan, M., Meier, S., Hill, A., … Petersen, D. (2000). Magnetic resonance imaging volumes of the hippocampus and the amygdala in women with borderline personality disorder and early traumatization. *Arch Gen Psychiatry, 57*, 1115–1122.

Eichenbaum, H. (2004). Hippocampus: Cognitive processes and neural representations that underlie declarative memory. *Neuron, 44*(1), 109–120.

Elzinga, B. M., Schmahl, C. G., Vermetten, E., van Dyck, R., & Bremner, J. D. (2003). Higher cortisol levels following exposure to traumatic reminders in abuse-related PTSD. *Neuropsychopharmacology, 28*(9), 1656–1665.

Emdad, R., Bonekamp, D., Sondergaard, H. P., Bjorklund, T., Agartz, I., Ingvar, M., … Theorell, T. (2006). Morphometric and psychometric comparisons between non-substance-abusing patients with posttraumatic stress disorder and normal controls. *Psychother Psychosom, 75*(2), 122–132.

Erickson, K., Drevets, W., & Schulkin, J. (2003). Glucocorticoid regulation of diverse cognitive functions in normal and pathological emotional states. *Neurosci Biobehav Rev, 27*, 233–246.

Felmingham, K., Williams, L. M., Kemp, A. H., Liddell, B., Falconer, E., Peduto, A., & Bryant, R. (2010). Neural responses to masked fear faces: Sex differences and trauma exposure in posttraumatic stress disorder. *J Abnorm Psychol, 119*(1), 241–247.

Fennema-Notestine, C., Stein, M. B., Kennedy, C. M., Archibald, S. L., & Jernigan, T. L. (2002). Brain morphometry in female victims of intimate partner violence with and without posttraumatic stress disorder. *Biol Psychiatry, 52*(11), 1089–1101.

Francis, D. D., Caldji, C., Champagne, F., Plotsky, P. M., & Meaney, M. J. (1999). The role of corticotropin-releasing factor—norepinephrine systems in mediating the effects of early experience on the development of behavioral and endocrine responses to stress. *Biol Psychiatry, 46*, 1153–1166.

Garlinkel, S. N., King, A. P., & Liberzon, I. (2010). Neural correlates of fear conditioning and extinction recall in combat Veterans of Iraq and Afghanistan, healthy and with PTSD. Unpublished raw data.

Gelernter, J., Southwick, S., Goodson, S., Morgan, A., Nagy, L., & Charney, D. S. (1999). No association between D2 dopamine receptor (DRD2) "A" system alleles, or DRD2 haplotypes, and posttraumatic stress disorder. *Biol Psychiatry, 45*(5), 620–625.

Geuze, E., Westenberg, H. G., Heinecke, A., de Kloet, C. S., Goebel, R., & Vermetten, E. (2008). Thinner prefrontal cortex in Veterans with posttraumatic stress disorder. *Neuroimage, 41*(3), 675–681.

Gilbertson, M. W., Shenton, M. E., Ciszewski, A., Kasai, K., Lasko, N. B., Orr, S. P., & Pitman, R. K. (2002). Smaller hippocampal volume predicts pathologic vulnerability to psychological trauma. *Nat Neurosci, 5*(11), 1242–1247.

Goenjian, A. K., Noble, E. P., Walling, D. P., Goenjian, H. A., Karayan, I. S., Ritchie, T., & Bailey, J. N. (2008). Heritabilities of symptoms of posttraumatic stress disorder, anxiety, and depression in earthquake exposed Armenian families. *Psychiatr Genet, 18(6),* 261–266.

Goenjian, A. K., Yehuda, R., Pynoos, R. S., Steinberg, A. M., Tashjian, M., Yang, R. K., & Fairbanks, L. A. (1996). Basal cortisol, dexamethasone suppression of cortisol, and MHPG in adolescents after the 1988 earthquake in Armenia. *Am J Psychiatry, 153*(7), 929–934.

Goldberg, J., True, W. R., Eisen, S. A., & Henderson, W. G. (1990). A twin study of the effects of the Vietnam War on posttraumatic stress disorder. *JAMA, 263*(9), 1227–1232.

Golier, J. A., Yehuda, R., De Santi, S., Segal, S., Dolan, S., & de Leon, M. J. (2005). Absence of hippocampal volume differences in survivors of the Nazi Holocaust with and without posttraumatic stress disorder. *Psychiatry Res, 139*(1), 53–64.

Gurvits, T. V., Shenton, M. E., Hokama, H., Ohta, H., Lasko, N. B., Gilbertson, M. W., … Pitman, R. K. (1996). Magnetic resonance imaging study of hippocampal volume in chronic, combat-related posttraumatic stress disorder. *Biol Psychiatry, 40*(11), 1091–1099.

Hakamata, Y., Matsuoka, Y., Inagaki, M., Nagamine, M., Hara, E., Imoto, S., … Uchitomi, Y. (2007). Structure of orbitofrontal cortex and its longitudinal course in cancer-related post-traumatic stress disorder. *Neurosci Res, 59*(4), 383–389.

Hamann, S. B., Ely, T. D., Grafton, S. T., & Kilts, C. D. (1999). Amygdala activity related to enhanced memory for pleasant and aversive stimuli. *Nat Neurosci, 2*(3), 289–293.

Hariri, A. R., Drabant, E. M., & Weinberger, D. R. (2006). Imaging genetics: Perspectives from studies of genetically driven variation in serotonin function and corticolimbic affective processing. *Biol Psychiatry, 59*(10), 888–897.

Hariri, A. R., & Holmes, A. (2006). Genetics of emotional regulation: The role of the serotonin transporter in neural function. *Trends Cogn Sci, 10*(4), 182–191.

Hariri, A. R., Mattay, V. S., Tessitore, A., Kolachana, B., Fera, F., Goldman, D., … Weinberger, D. R. (2002). Serotonin transporter genetic variation and the response of the human amygdala. *Science, 297*(5580), 400–403.

Hedges, D. W., Allen, S., Tate, D. F., Thatcher, G. W., Miller, M. J., Rice, S. A., … Bigler, E. D. (2003). Reduced hippocampal volume in alcohol and substance naive Vietnam combat Veterans with posttraumatic stress disorder. *Cogn Behav Neurol, 16*(4), 219–224.

Heim, C., & Nemeroff, C. B. (2001). The role of childhood trauma in the neurobiology of mood and anxiety disorders: Preclinical and clinical studies. *Biol Psychiatry, 49*(12), 1023–1039.

Heim, C., Newport, D. J., Heit, S., Graham, Y. P., Wilcox, M., Bonsall, R., … Nemeroff, C. B. (2000). Pituitary-adrenal and autonomic responses to stress in women after sexual and physical abuse in childhood. *JAMA, 284*(5), 592–597.

Heinrichs, M., Wagner, D., Schoch, W., Soravia, L. M., Hellhammer, D. H., & Ehlert, U. (2005). Predicting posttraumatic stress symptoms from pretraumatic risk factors: A 2-year prospective follow-up study in firefighters. *Am J Psychiatry, 162*(12), 2276–2286.

Herman, J. P., Ostrander, M. M., Mueller, N. K., & Figueiredo, H. (2005). Limbic system mechanisms of stress regulation: Hypothalamo-pituitary-adrenocortical axis. *Prog Neuropsychopharmacol Biol Psychiatry, 29*(8), 1201–1213.

Huot, R., Smith, M., & Plotsky, P. (1997). Alterations of maternal-infant interaction as a result of maternal separation in Long Evans rats and its behavioral and neuro-endocrine consequences. *Psychoneuroendocrinology, 22*(suppl 2), S173.

Huot, R. L., Thrivikraman, K. V., Meaney, M. J., & Plotsky, P. M. (2001). Development of adult ethanol preference and anxiety as a consequence of neonatal maternal separation in Long Evans rats and reversal with antidepressant treatment. *Psychopharmacology, 158*, 366–373.

Jacobson, L., & Sapolsky, R. (1991). The role of the hippocampus in feedback regulation of the hypothalamic-pituitary-adrenocortical axis. *Endocr Rev, 12*(2), 118–134.

Jatzko, A., Rothenhofer, S., Schmitt, A., Gaser, C., Demirakca, T., Weber-Fahr, W., ... Braus, D. F. (2006). Hippocampal volume in chronic posttraumatic stress disorder (PTSD): MRI study using two different evaluation methods. *J Affect Disord, 94*(1–3), 121–126.

Karg, K., Burmeister, M., Shedden, K., & Sen, S. (in press). The serotonin transporter promoter variant (5-HTTLPR), stress, and depression meta-analysis revisited: Evidence of genetic moderation. *Archives of General Psychiatry*.

Kellner, M., Yassouridis, A., Hubner, R., Baker, D. G., & Wiedemann, K. (2003). Endocrine and cardiovascular responses to corticotropin-releasing hormone in patients with posttraumatic stress disorder: A role for atrial natriuretic peptide? *Neuropsychobiology, 47*(2), 102–108.

Kendler, K. S., Walter, E. E., Neale, M. C., Kessler, R. C., Heath, A. C., & Eaves, J. (1995). The Structure of the genetic and environmental risk factors for six major psychiatric disorders in women: Phobia, generalized anxiety disorder, panic disorder, bulimia, major depression, and alcoholism. *Arch Gen Psychiatry, 52*(5), 374–383.

Kessler, R. C., Sonnega, A., Bromet, E., Hughes, M., & Nelson, C. B. (1995). Posttraumatic stress disorder in the National Comorbidity Survey. *Arch Gen Psychiatry, 52*(12), 1048–1060.

Kilpatrick, D. G., Koenen, K. C., Ruggiero, K. J., Acierno, R., Galea, S., Resnick, H. S., & Gelernter, J. (2007). The serotonin transporter genotype and social support and moderation of posttraumatic stress disorder and depression in hurricane-exposed adults. *Am J Psychiatry, 164*(11), 1693–1699.

King, A. P., Abelson, J. L., Britton, J. C., Phan, K. L., Taylor, S. F., & Liberzon, I. (2009). Medial prefrontal cortex and right insula activity predict plasma ACTH response to trauma recall. *Neuroimage, 47*(3), 872–880.

King, A. P., & Liberzon, I. (2009). Assessing the neuroendocrine stress response in the functional neuroimaging context. *Neuroimage, 47*(3), 1116–1124.

King, A. P., & Liberzon, I. (2010). Neural correlates of effortful and implicit emotional regulation in combat Veterans of Iraq and Afghanistan: Healthy and with PTSD. Unpublished raw data.

King, A. P., Seng, J. S., & Liberzon, I. (2010). Serotonin transporter 5-HTTLPR variant interactive with childhood adversity in association with adult risk for PTSD in women.

Koenen, K. C. (2007). Genetics of posttraumatic stress disorder: Review and recommendations for future studies. *J Trauma Stress, 20*(5), 737–750.

Koenen, K. C., Fu, Q. J., Ertel, K., Lyons, M. J., Eisen, S. A., True, W. R., & Tsuang, M. T. (2008). Common genetic liability to major depression and posttraumatic stress disorder in men. *J Affect Disord, 105*(1–3), 109–115.

Koenen, K. C., Harley, R., Lyons, M. J., Wolfe, J., Simpson, J. C., Goldberg, J., & Tsuang, M. (2002). A twin registry study of familial and individual risk factors for trauma exposure and posttraumatic stress disorder. *J Nerv Ment Dis, 190*(4), 209–218.

Koenen, K. C., Moffitt, T. E., Poulton, R., Martin, J., & Caspi, A. (2007). Early childhood factors associated with the development of post-traumatic stress disorder: Results from a longitudinal birth cohort. *Psychol Med, 37*(2), 181–192.

Kosten, T. R., Mason, J. W., Giller, E. L., Ostroff, R. B., & Harkness, L. (1987). Sustained urinary norepinephrine and epinephrine elevation in post-traumatic stress disorder. *Psychoneuroendocrinology, 12*(1), 13–20.

Lang, P. J., Bradley, M. M., & Cuthbert, B. N. (1995). *International affective picture system (IAPS): Technical manual and affective ratings.* Gainesville, FL: The Center for Research in Psychophysiology, University of Florida.

Lanius, R. A., Williamson, P. C., Densmore, M., Boksman, K., Gupta, M. A., Neufeld, R. W., … Menon, R. S. (2001). Neural correlates of traumatic memories in posttraumatic stress disorder: A functional MRI investigation. *Am J Psychiatry, 158,* 1920–1922.

Lanius, R. A., Williamson, P. C., Hopper, J., Densmore, M., Boksman, K., Gupta, M. A., … Menon, R. S. (2003). Recall of emotional states in posttraumatic stress disorder: An fMRI investigation. *Biol Psychiatry, 53,* 204–210.

Krystal, J. H., & Neumeister, A. (2009). Noradrenergic and serotonergic mechanisms in the neurobiology of posttraumatic stress disorder and resilience. *Brain Res, 1293,* 13–23.

Kulka, R. A., Schlenger, W. E., Fairbanks, J. A., Hough, R. L., Jordan, B. K., Marmar, C. R., & Weiss, D. S. (1990). *Trauma and the Vietnam War generation: Report of findings from the National Vietnam Veterans readjustment study.* New York: Brunner/Mazel.

Ladd, C. O., Huot, R. L., Thrivikraman, K. V., Nemeroff, C. B., Meaney, M. J., & Plotsky, P. M. (2000). Long-term behavioral and neuroendocrine adaptations to adverse early experience. *Prog Brain Res, 122,* 81–103.

Ladd, C. O., Huot, R. L., Thrivikraman, K. V., Nemeroff, C. B., & Plotsky, P. M. (2004). Long-term adaptations in glucocorticoid receptor and mineralocorticoid receptor mRNA and negative feedback on the hypothalamo-pituitary-adrenal axis following neonatal maternal separation. *Biol Psychiatry, 55*(4), 367–375.

Lappalainen, J., Kranzler, H. R., Malison, R., Price, L. H., Van Dyck, C., Rosenheck, R. A., & Gelernter, J. (2002). A functional neuropeptide Y Leu7Pro polymorphism associated with alcohol dependence in a large population sample from the United States. *Arch Gen Psychiatry, 59*(9), 825–831.

Lathe, R. (2001). Hormones and the hippocampus. *J Endocrinol, 169*(2), 205–231.

LeDoux, J. (2003). The emotional brain, fear, and the amygdala. *Cell Mol Neurobiol, 23*(4–5), 727–738.

LeDoux, J. E. (2000). Emotion circuits in the brain. *Annu Rev Neurosci, 23,* 155–184.

LeDoux, J. E., Cicchetti, P., Xagoraris, A., & Romanski, L. M. (1990). The lateral amygdaloid nucleus: Sensory interface of the amygdala in fear conditioning. *J Neurosci, 10*(4), 1062–1069.

Lemieux, A. M., & Coe, C. L. (1995). Abuse-related posttraumatic stress disorder: Evidence for chronic neuroendocrine activation in women. *Psychosom Med, 57*(2), 105–115.

Liberzon, I., Abelson, J. L., Flagel, S. B., Raz, J., & Young, E. A. (1999). Neuroendocrine and psychophysiologic responses in PTSD: A symptom provocation study. *Neuropsychopharmacology, 21*(1), 40–50.

Liberzon, I., King, A. P., Britton, J. C., Phan, K. L., Abelson, J. L., & Taylor, S. F. (2007). Paralimbic and medial prefrontal cortical involvement in neuroendocrine responses to traumatic stimuli. *Am J Psychiatry, 164*(8), 1250–1258.

Liberzon, I., Krstov, M., & Young, E. A. (1997). Stress-restress: Effects on ACTH and fast feedback. *Psychoneuroendocrinology, 22*(6), 443–453.

Liberzon, I., López, J. F., Flagel, S. B., Vázquez, D. M., & Young, E. A. (1999). Differential regulation of hippocampal glucocorticoid receptors mRNA and fast feedback: Relevance to post-traumatic stress disorder. *Journal of Neuroendocrinology, 11*, 11–17.

Liberzon, I., & Martis, B. (2006). Neuroimaging studies of emotional responses in PTSD. *Ann N Y Acad Sci, 1071*, 87–109.

Liberzon, I., & Phan, K. L. (2003). Brain-imaging studies of posttraumatic stress disorder. *CNS Spectr, 8*(9), 641–650.

Liberzon, I., Phan, K. L., Decker, L. R., & Taylor, S. F. (2003). Extended amygdala and emotional salience: A PET activation study of positive and negative affect. *Neuropsychopharmacology, 28*(4), 726–733.

Liberzon, I., & Sripada, C. S. (2008). The functional neuroanatomy of PTSD: A critical review. *Prog Brain Res, 167*, 151–169.

Liberzon, I., Taylor, S. F., Amdur, R., Jung, T. D., Chamberlain, K. R., Minoshima, S., … Fig, L. M. (1999). Brain activation in PTSD in response to trauma-related stimuli. *Biol Psychiatry, 45*(7), 817–826.

Lindauer, R. J., Vlieger, E. J., Jalink, M., Olff, M., Carlier, I. V., Majoie, C. B., … Gersons, B. P. R. (2004). Smaller hippocampal volume in Dutch police officers with posttraumatic stress disorder. *Biol Psychiatry, 56*(5), 356–363.

Lindauer, R. J., Vlieger, E. J., Jalink, M., Olff, M., Carlier, I. V., Majoie, C. B., … Gersons, B. P. R. (2005). Effects of psychotherapy on hippocampal volume in outpatients with post-traumatic stress disorder: A MRI investigation. *Psychol Med, 35*(10), 1421–1431.

Liu, D., Caldji, C., Sharma, S., Plotsky, P. M., & Meaney, M. J. (2000). Influence of neonatal rearing conditions on stress-induced adrenocorticotropin responses and norepinepherine release in the hypothalamic paraventricular nucleus. *J Neuroendocrinol, 12*, 5–12.

Liu, D., Diorio, J., Tannenbaum, B., Caldji, C., Francis, D., Freedman, A., … Meaney, M. J. (1997). Maternal care, hippocampal glucocorticoid receptors, and hypothalamic-pituitary-adrenal responses to stress. *Science, 277*(5332), 1659–1662.

Luecken, L. J., Dausch, B., Gulla, V., Hong, R., & Compas, B. E. (2004). Alterations in morning cortisol associated with PTSD in women with breast cancer. *J Psychosom Res, 56*(1), 13–15.

Lurie, S., & Geyer, P. (1994). Genetic and environmental influences of twins in post-traumatic stress. *Arch Gen Psychiatry, 51*(10), 838–839.

Maes, M., Lin, A., Bonaccorso, S., van Hunsel, F., Van Gastel, A., Delmeire, L., & Scharpé, S. (1998). Increased 24-hour urinary cortisol excretion in patients with post-traumatic stress disorder and patients with major depression, but not in patients with fibromyalgia. *Acta Psychiatr Scand, 98*(4), 328–335.

Mason, J. W., Giller, E. L., Kosten, T. R., Ostroff, R. B., & Podd, L. (1986). Urinary free-cortisol levels in posttraumatic stress disorder patients. *J Nerv Ment Dis, 174*(3), 145–149.

McEwen, B. S., 2006. Sleep deprivation as a neurobiologic and physiologic stressor, allostasis and allostatic load. *Metabolism, 55*, S20–S23.

McGaugh, J. L., Cahill, L., & Roozendaal, B. (1996). Involvement of the amygdala in memory storage: Interaction with other brain systems. *Proc Natl Acad Sci U S A, 93*(24), 13508–13514.

McGhee, L. L., Maani, C. V., Garza, T. H., Desocio, P. A., Gaylord, K. M., & Black, I. H. (2009). The effect of propranolol on posttraumatic stress disorder in burned service members. *J Burn Care Res, 30*(1), 92–97.

McLeod, D. S., Koenen, K. C., Meyer, J. M., Lyons, M. J., Eisen, S., True, W., & Goldberg, J. (2001). Genetic and environmental influences on the relationship among combat exposure, posttraumatic stress disorder symptoms, and alcohol use. *J Trauma Stress, 14*(2), 259–275.

Meaney, M. J., Diorio, J., Francis, D., Widdowson, J., LaPlante, P., Caldji, C., … Plotsky, P. M. (1996). Early environmental regulation of forebrain glucocorticoid receptor gene expression: Implications for adrenocortical responses to stress. *Dev Neurosci, 18*(1–2), 49–72.

Milad, M. R., Pitman, R. K., Ellis, C. B., Gold, A. L., Shin, L. M., Lasko, … Rauch, S. L. (2009). Neural mechanisms of cognitive impairment and aggression in posttraumatic stress disorder and borderline personality disorder. *Biol Psychiatry, 66*(12), 1075–1082.

Mizuno, K., & Giese, K. P. (2005). Hippocampus-dependent memory formation: Do memory type-specific mechanisms exist? *J Pharmacol Sci, 98*(3), 191–197.

Mobascher, A., Brinkmeyer, J., Thiele, H., Toliat, M. R., Steffens, M., Warbrick, T., … Winterer, G. (2010). The val158met polymorphism of human catechol-O-methyltransferase (COMT) affects anterior cingulate cortex activation in response to painful laser stimulation. *Mol Pain, 6*, 32.

Montag, C., Buckholtz, J. W., Hartmann, P., Merz, M., Burk, C., Hennig, J., & Martin, R. (2008). COMT genetic variation affects fear processing: Psychophysiological evidence. *Behav Neurosci, 122*(4), 901–909.

Myslobodsky, M. S., Glicksohn, J., Singer, J., Stern, M., Bar-Ziv, J., Friedland, N., … Bleich, A. (1995). Changes of brain anatomy in patients with posttraumatic stress disorder: A pilot magnetic resonance imaging study. *Psychiatry Res, 58*(3), 259–264.

New, A. S., Fan, J., Murrough, J. W., Liu, X., Liebman, R. E., Guise, K. G., … Charney, D. S. (2009). A functional magnetic resonance imaging study of deliberate emotion regulation in resilience and posttraumatic stress disorder. *Biol Psychiatry, 66*(7), 656–664.

Newport, D. J., Heim, C., Bonsall, R., Miller, A. H., & Nemeroff, C. B. (2004). Pituitary-adrenal responses to standard and low-dose dexamethasone suppression tests in adult survivors of child abuse. *Biol Psychiatry, 55*(1), 10–20.

Neylan, T. C., Brunet, A., Pole, N., Best, S. R., Metzler, T. J., Yehuda, R., & Marmar, C. R. (2005). PTSD symptoms predict waking salivary cortisol levels in police officers. *Psychoneuroendocrinology, 30*(4), 373–381.

Nugent, N. R., Christopher, N. C., Crow, J. P., Browne, L., Ostrowski, S., & Delahanty, D. L. (2010). The efficacy of early propranolol administration at reducing PTSD symptoms in pediatric injury patients: A pilot study. *J Trauma Stress, 23*(2), 282–287.

O'Donnell, T., Hegadoren, K. M., & Coupland, N. C. (2004). Noradrenergic mechanisms in the pathophysiology of post-traumatic stress disorder. *Neuropsychobiology, 50*(4), 273–283.

Ochsner, K. N., Hughes, B., Robertson, E. R., Cooper, J. C., & Gabrieli, J. D. (2009). Neural systems supporting the control of affective and cognitive conflicts. *J Cogn Neurosci, 21*(9), 1842–1855.

Ochsner, K. N., Knierim, K., Ludlow, D. H., Hanelin, J., Ramachandran, T., Glover, G., & Mackey, S. C. (2004). Reflecting upon feelings: An fMRI study of neural systems supporting the attribution of emotion to self and other. *J Cogn Neurosci, 16*(10), 1746–1772.

Orr, S. P., Metzger, L. J., & Pitman, R. K. (2002). Psychophysiology of post-traumatic stress disorder. *Psychiatr Clin North Am, 25*(2), 271–293.

Ottowitz, W. E., Dougherty, D. D., Sirota, A., Niaura, R., Rauch, S. L., & Brown, W. A. (2004). Neural and endocrine correlates of sadness in women: Implications for neural network regulation of HPA activity. *J Neuropsychiatry Clin Neurosci, 16*(4), 446–455.

Pavic, L., Gregurek, R., Rados, M., Brkljacic, B., Brajkovic, L., Simetin-Pavic, I., ... Kalousek, V. (2007). Smaller right hippocampus in war Veterans with posttraumatic stress disorder. *Psychiatry Res, 154*(2), 191–198.

Pederson, C. L., Maurer, S. H., Kaminski, P. L., Zander, K. A., Peters, C. M., Stokes-Crowe, L. A., & Osborn, R. E. (2004). Hippocampal volume and memory performance in a community-based sample of women with posttraumatic stress disorder secondary to child abuse. *J Trauma Stress, 17*(1), 37–40.

Peters, J., van Kammen, D. P., van Kammen, W. B., & Neylan, T. (1990). Sleep disturbance and computerized axial tomographic scan findings in former prisoners of war. *Compr Psychiatry, 31*(6), 535–539.

Phan, K. L., Wager, T., Taylor, S. F., & Liberzon, I. (2002). Functional neuroanatomy of emotion: A meta-analysis of emotion activation studies in PET and fMRI. *Neuroimage, 16*(2), 331–348.

Phan, K. L., Wager, T. D., Taylor, S. F., & Liberzon, I. (2004). Functional neuroimaging studies of human emotions. *CNS Spectr, 9*(4), 258–266.

Phillips, M. L. (2003). Understanding the neurobiology of emotion perception: Implications for psychiatry. *Br J Psychiatry, 182*, 190–192.

Phillips, M. L., Drevets, W. C., Rauch, S. L., & Lane, R. (2003). Neurobiology of emotion perception II: Implications for major psychiatric disorders. *Biol Psychiatry, 54*(5), 515–528.

Pitman, R. K., & Orr, S. P. (1990). Twenty-four hour urinary cortisol and catecholamine excretion in combat-related posttraumatic stress disorder. *Biol Psychiatry, 27*(2), 245–247.

Pitman, R. K., & Orr, S. P. (1993). Psychophysiologic testing for post-traumatic stress disorder: Forensic psychiatric application. *Bull Am Acad Psychiatry Law, 21*(1), 37–52.

Pitman, R. K., Orr, S. P., Forgue, D. F., de Jong, J. B., & Claiborn, J. M. (1987). Psychophysiologic assessment of posttraumatic stress disorder imagery in Vietnam combat Veterans. *Arch Gen Psychiatry, 44*(11), 970–975.

Pitman, R. K., Orr, S. P., Shalev, A. Y., Metzger, L. J., & Mellman, T. A. (1999). Psychophysiological alterations in post-traumatic stress disorder. *Semin Clin Neuropsychiatry, 4*(4), 234–241.

Pitman, R. K., Orr, S. P., & Steketee, G. S. (1989). Psychophysiological investigations of posttraumatic stress disorder imagery. *Psychopharmacol Bull, 25*(3), 426–431.

Pitman, R. K., Sanders, K. M., Zusman, R. M., Healy, A. R., Cheema, F., Lasko, N. B., ... Orr, S. P. (2002). Pilot study of secondary prevention of posttraumatic stress disorder with propranolol. *Biol Psychiatry, 51*(2), 189–192.

Pruessner, J. C., Dedovic, K., Khalili-Mahani, N., Engert, V., Pruessner, M., Buss, C., ... Lupien, S. (2008). Deactivation of the limbic system during acute psychosocial stress: Evidence from positron emission tomography and functional magnetic resonance imaging studies. *Biol Psychiatry, 63*(2), 234–240.

Quirk, G. J., Russo, G. K., Barron, J. L., & Lebron, K. (2000). The role of ventromedial prefrontal cortex in the recovery of extinguished fear. *J Neurosci, 20*(16), 6225–6231.

Rasmusson, A. M., Lipschitz, D. S., Wang, S., Hu, S., Vojvoda, D., Bremner, J. D., ... Charney, D. S. (2001). Increased pituitary and adrenal reactivity in premenopausal women with posttraumatic stress disorder. *Biol Psychiatry, 50*(12), 965–977.

Rau, V., DeCola, J. P., & Fanselow, M. S. (2005). Stress-induced enhancement of fear learning: An animal model of posttraumatic stress disorder. *Neuroscience Biobehavioral Reviews, 29*, 1207–1223.

Rauch, S. L., & Shin, L. M. (1997). Functional neuroimaging studies in posttraumatic stress disorder. *Ann N Y Acad Sci, 821*, 83–98.

Rauch, S. L., Shin, L. M., & Phelps, E. A. (2006). Neurocircuitry models of posttraumatic stress disorder and extinction: Human neuroimaging research—Past, present, and future. *Biol Psychiatry, 60*(4), 376–382.

Rauch, S. L., Whalen, P. J., Shin, L. M., McInerney, S. C., Macklin, M. L., Lasko, N. B., & Pitman, R. K. (2000). Exaggerated amygdala response to masked facial stimuli in posttraumatic stress disorder: A functional MRI study. *Biol Psychiatry, 47*(9), 769–776.

Repetti, R. L., Taylor, S. E., & Seeman, T. E. (2002). Risky families: Family social environments and the mental and physical health of offspring. *Psych Bull, 128*(2), 330–366.

Richter-Levin, G. (2004). The amygdala, the hippocampus, and emotional modulation of memory. *Neuroscientist, 10*(1), 31–39.

Roffman, J. L., Weiss, A. P., Goff, D. C., Rauch, S. L., & Weinberger, D. R. (2006). Neuroimaging-genetic paradigms: A new approach to investigate the pathophysiology and treatment of cognitive deficits in schizophrenia. *Harv Rev Psychiatry, 14*(2), 78–91.

Sack, W. H., Clarke, G. N., & Seeley, J. (1995). Posttraumatic stress disorder across two generations of Cambodian refugees. *J Am Acad Child Adolesc Psychiatry, 34*(9), 1160–1166.

Sánchez, M. M., Ladd, C. O., & Plotsky, P. M. (2001). Early adverse experience as a developmental risk factor for later psychopathology: Evidence from rodent and primate models. *Dev Psychopathol,13*(3), 419–449.

Saphier, D., & Feldman, S. (1990). Iontophoresis of cortisol inhibits responses of identified paraventricular nucleus neurones to sciatic nerve stimulation. *Brain Res, 535*(1), 159–162.

Sapolsky, R. M. (2000). Glucocorticoids and hippocampal atrophy in neuropsychiatric disorders. *Arch Gen Psychiatry, 57*(10), 925–935.

Schuff, N., Neylan, T. C., Fox-Bosetti, S., Lenoci, M., Samuelson, K. W., Studholme, C., ... Weiner, M. W. (2008). Abnormal *N*-acetylaspartate in hippocampus and anterior cingulate in posttraumatic stress disorder. *Psychiatry Res, 162*(2), 147–157.

Schuff, N., Neylan, T. C., Lenoci, M. A., Du, A. T., Weiss, D. S., Marmar, C. R., & Weiner, M. W. (2001). Decreased hippocampal *N*-acetylaspartate in the absence of atrophy in posttraumatic stress disorder. *Biol Psychiatry, 50*(12), 952–959.

Segman, R. H., Cooper-Kazaz, R., Macciardi, F., Goltser, T., Halfon, Y., Dobroborski, T., & Shalev, A. Y. (2002). Association between the dopamine transporter gene and posttraumatic stress disorder. *Mol Psychiatry, 7*(8), 903–907.

Segman, R. H., & Shalev, A. Y. (2003). Genetics of posttraumatic stress disorder. *CNS Spectr, 8*(9), 693–698.

Shalev, A. Y., Orr, S. P., & Pitman, R. K. (1992). Psychophysiologic response during script-driven imagery as an outcome measure in posttraumatic stress disorder. *J Clin Psychiatry, 53*(9), 324–326.

Shalev, A. Y., Peri, T., Canetti, L., & Schreiber, S. (1996). Predictors of PTSD in injured trauma survivors: A prospective study. *Am J Psychiatry, 153*(2), 219–225.

Shalev, A. Y., Sahar, T., Freedman, S., Peri, T., Glick, N., Brandes, D., ... Pitman, R. K. (1998). A prospective study of heart rate response following trauma and the subsequent development of posttraumatic stress disorder. *Arch Gen Psychiatry, 55*(6), 553–559.

Sharp, S., Thomas, C., Rosenberg, L., Rosenberg, M., & Meyer, W., 3rd. (2010). Propranolol does not reduce risk for acute stress disorder in pediatric burn trauma. *J Trauma, 68*(1), 193–197.

Shin, L. M., Kosslyn, S. M., McNally, R. J., Alpert, N. M., Thompson, W. L., Rauch, S. L., ... Pitman, R. K. (1997). Visual imagery and perception in posttraumatic stress disorder. A positron emission tomographic investigation. *Arch Gen Psychiatry, 54*(3), 233–241.

Shin, L. M., McNally, R. J., Kosslyn, S. M., Thompson, W. L., Rauch, S. L., Alpert, N. M., ... Pitman, R. K. (1997). A positron emission tomographic study of symptom provocation in PTSD. *Ann N Y Acad Sci, 821*, 521–523.

Shin, L. M., McNally, R. J., Kosslyn, S. M., Thompson, W. L., Rauch, S. L., Alpert, N. M., ... Pitman, R. K. (1999). Regional cerebral blood flow during script-driven imagery in childhood sexual abuse-related PTSD: A PET investigation. *Am J Psychiatry, 156*, 575–584.

Shin, L. M., Orr, S. P., Carson, M. A., Rauch, S. L., Macklin, M. L., Lasko, N. B., ... Pitman, R. K. (2004). Regional cerebral blood flow in the amygdala and medial prefrontal cortex during traumatic imagery in male and female Vietnam Veterans with PTSD. *Arch Gen Psychiatry, 61*(2), 168–176.

Shin, L. M., Rauch, S. L., & Pitman, R. K. (2006). Amygdala, medial prefrontal cortex, and hippocampal function in PTSD. *Ann N Y Acad Sci, 1071*, 67–79.

Shin, L. M., Whalen, P. J., Pitman, R. K., Bush, G., Macklin, M. L., Lasko, N. B., ... Rauch, S. L. (2001). An fMRI study of anterior cingulate function in posttraumatic stress disorder. *Biol Psychiatry, 50*(12), 932–942.

Shin, L. M., Wright, C. I., Cannistraro, P. A., Wedig, M. M., McMullin, K., Martis, B., ... Rauch, S. L. (2005). A functional magnetic resonance imaging study of amygdala and medial prefrontal cortex responses to overtly presented fearful faces in post-traumatic stress disorder. *Arch Gen Psychiatry, 62*(3), 273–281.

Siegmund, A., & Wotjak, C. T. (2007). A mouse model of posttraumatic stress disorder that distinguishes between conditioned and sensitized fear. *Journal of Psychiatric Research, 41*, 848–860.

Smith, M. A., Davidson, J., Ritchie, J. C., Kudler, H., Lipper, S., Chappell, P., & Nemeroff, C. B. (1989). The corticotropin-releasing hormone test in patients with posttraumatic stress disorder. *Biol Psychiatry, 26*, 349–355.

Smith, M. E. (2005). Bilateral hippocampal volume reduction in adults with post-traumatic stress disorder: A meta-analysis of structural MRI studies. *Hippocampus, 15*(6), 798–807.

Southwick, S. M., Krystal, J. H., Bremner, J. D., Morgan, C. A., 3rd, Nicolaou, A. L., Nagy, L. M., ... Charney, D. S. (1997). Noradrenergic and serotonergic function in posttraumatic stress disorder. *Arch Gen Psychiatry, 54*(8), 749–758.

Stam, R. (2007). PTSD and stress sensitisation: A tale of brain and body. Part 2: Animal models. *Neuroscience and Biobehavioral Review, 31*, 558–584.

Starkman, M. N., Gebarski, S. S., Berent, S., & Schteingart, D. E. (1992). Hippocampal formation volume, memory dysfunction, and cortisol levels in patients with Cushing's syndrome. *Biol Psychiatry, 32*(9), 756–765.

Starkman, M. N., Giordani, B., Gebarski, S. S., Berent, S., Schork, M. A., & Schteingart, D. E. (1999). Decrease in cortisol reverses human hippocampal atrophy following treatment of Cushing's disease. *Biol Psychiatry, 46*(12), 1595–1602.

Stein, M. B., Koverola, C., Hanna, C., Torchia, M. G., & McClarty, B. (1997). Hippocampal volume in women victimized by childhood sexual abuse, *Psych Med, 27*, 951–959.

Taylor, S. F., & Liberzon, I. (2007). Neural correlates of emotion regulation in psychopathology. *Trends Cogn Sci, 11*(10), 413–418.

Taylor S. F., Liberzon, I., Koeppe, R. A. (2000) The effect of graded aversive stimuli on limbic and visual activation. *Neuropsychologia, 38*(10):1415–25.

Taylor, S. F., Phan, K. L., Decker, L. R., & Liberzon, I. (2003). Subjective rating of emotionally salient stimuli modulates neural activity. *Neuroimage, 18*(3), 650–659.

True, W. R., Rice, J., Eisen, S. A., Heath, A. C., Goldberg, J., Lyons, M. J., & Nowak, J. (1993). A twin study of genetic and environmental contributions to liability for posttraumatic stress symptoms. *Arch Gen Psychiatry, 50*(4), 257–264.

Vertes, R. P. (2006). Interactions among the medial prefrontal cortex, hippocampus and midline thalamus in emotional and cognitive processing in the rat. *Neuroscience, 142*(1), 1–20.

Vythilingam, M., Heim, C., Newport, J., Miller, A. H., Anderson, E., Bronen, R., ... Bremner, J. D. (2002). Childhood trauma associated with smaller hippocampal volume in women with major depression. *Am J Psychiatry, 159*(12), 2072–2080.

Vythilingam, M., Luckenbaugh, D. A., Lam, T., Morgan, C. A., 3rd, Lipschitz, D., Charney, D. S., ... Southwick, S. M. (2005). Smaller head of the hippocampus in Gulf War-related posttraumatic stress disorder. *Psychiatry Res, 139*(2), 89–99.

Wakizono, T., Sawamura, T., Shimizu, K., Nibuya, M., Suzuki, G., Toda, H., Hirano, J., Kikuchi, A., Takahashi, Y., & Nomura, S. (2007). Stress vulnerabilities in an animal model of post-traumatic stress disorder. *Physiology and Behavior, 90*(4), 687–695.

Wang, J., Rao, H., Wetmore, G. S., Furlan, P. M., Korczykowski, M., Dinges, D. F., & Detre, J. A. (2005). Perfusion functional MRI reveals cerebral blood flow pattern under psychological stress. *Proc Natl Acad Sci U S A, 102*(49), 17804–17809.

Wankerl, M., Wust, S., & Otte, C. (2010). Current developments and controversies: Does the serotonin transporter gene-linked polymorphic region (5-HTTLPR) modulate the association between stress and depression? *Curr Opin Psychiatry, 23*(6), 582–587.

Weiss, E. M., Stadelmann, E., Kohler, C. G., Brensinger, C. M., Nolan, K. A., Oberacher, H., & Marksteiner, J. (2007). Differential effect of catechol-O-methyltransferase Val158Met genotype on emotional recognition abilities in healthy men and women. *J Int Neuropsychol Soc, 13*(5), 881–887.

Wessa, M., Rohleder, N., Kirschbaum, C., & Flor, H. (2006). Altered cortisol awakening response in posttraumatic stress disorder. *Psychoneuroendocrinology, 31*(2), 209–215.

Whalen, P. J., Rauch, S. L., Etcoff, N. L., McInerney, S. C., Lee, M. B., & Jenike, M. A. (1998). Masked presentations of emotional facial expressions modulate amygdala activity without explicit knowledge. *J Neurosci, 18*(1), 411–418.

Widom, C. S. (1999). Posttraumatic stress disorder in abused and neglected children grown up. *Am J Psychiatry, 156*(8), 1223–1229.

Williams, L. M., Kemp, A. H., Felmingham, K., Barton, M., Olivieri, G., Peduto, A., ... Bryant, R. A. (2006). Trauma modulates amygdala and medial prefrontal responses to consciously attended fear. *Neuroimage, 29*(2), 347–357.

Winter, H., & Irle, E. (2004). Hippocampal volume in adult burn patients with and without posttraumatic stress disorder. *Am J Psychiatry, 161*(12), 2194–2200.

Woodward, S. H., Kaloupek, D. G., Streeter, C. C., Kimble, M. O., Reiss, A. L., Eliez, S., & Arsenault, N. J. (2006). Hippocampal volume, PTSD, and alcoholism in combat Veterans. *Am J Psychiatry, 163*(4), 674–681.

Woodward, S. H., Schaer, M., Kaloupek, D. G., Cediel, L., & Eliez, S. (2009). Smaller global and regional cortical volume in combat-related posttraumatic stress disorder. *Arch Gen Psychiatry, 66*(12), 1373–1382.

Woon, F. L., & Hedges, D. W. (2008). Hippocampal and amygdala volumes in children and adults with childhood maltreatment-related posttraumatic stress disorder: A meta-analysis. *Hippocampus, 18*(8), 729–736.

Woon, F., & Hedges, D. W. (2010). Gender does not moderate hippocampal volume deficits in adults with posttraumatic stress disorder: A meta-analysis. *Hippocampus.* DOI:10.1002/hipo.20746.

Xie, P., Kranzler, H. R., Poling, J., Stein, M. B., Anton, R. F., Brady, K., ... Gelernter, J. (2009). Interactive effect of stressful life events and the serotonin transporter 5-HTTLPR genotype on posttraumatic stress disorder diagnosis in 2 independent populations. *Arch Gen Psychiatry, 66*(11), 1201–1209.

Yamamoto, S., Morinobu, S., Takei, S., Fuchikami, M., Matsuki, A., Yamawaki, S., & Liberzon, I. (2009). Single prolonged stress: Toward an animal model of post-traumatic stress disorder. *Depression and Anxiety, 26*, 1110–1117.

Yehuda, R. (2003). Hypothalamic–pituitary–adrenal alterations in PTSD: Are they relevant to understanding cortisol alterations in cancer? *Brain Behav Immun, 17*(Suppl 1), S73–S83.

Yehuda, R., Golier, J. A., Halligan, S. L., Meaney, M., & Bierer, L. M. (2004). The ACTH response to dexamethasone in PTSD. *Am J Psychiatry, 161*(8), 1397–1403.

Yehuda, R., Halligan, S. L., & Bierer, L. M. (2001). Relationship of parental trauma exposure and PTSD to PTSD, depressive and anxiety disorders in offspring. *J Psychiatr Res, 35*(5), 261–270.

Yehuda, R., Kahana, B., Binder-Brynes, K., Southwick, S. M., Mason, J. W., & Giller, E. L. (1995). Low urinary cortisol excretion in Holocaust survivors with posttraumatic stress disorder. *Am J Psychiatry, 152*(7), 982–986.

Yehuda, R., Southwick, S. M., Krystal, J. M., Charney, D. S., & Mason, J. W. (1993). Enhanced suppression of cortisol following dexamethasone administration in combat Veterans with posttraumatic stress disorder and major depressive disorder. *Am J Psychiatry, 150*, 83–86.

Yehuda, R., Southwick, S. M., Nussbaum, G., Wahby, V., Giller, E. L., Jr., & Mason, J. W. (1990). Low urinary cortisol excretion in patients with posttraumatic stress disorder. *J Nerv Ment Dis, 178*(6), 366–369.

Young, E. A., & Breslau, N. (2004a). Cortisol and catecholamines in posttraumatic stress disorder: An epidemiologic community study. *Arch Gen Psychiatry, 61*(4), 394–401.

Young, E. A., & Breslau, N. (2004b). Saliva cortisol in posttraumatic stress disorder: A community epidemiologic study. *Biol Psychiatry, 56*(3), 205–209.

Zhang, H., Ozbay, F., Lappalainen, J., Kranzler, H. R., van Dyck, C. H., Charney, D. S., & Gelernter, J. (2006). Brain derived neurotrophic factor (BDNF) gene variants and Alzheimer's disease, affective disorders, posttraumatic stress disorder, schizophrenia, and substance dependence. *Am J Med Genet B Neuropsychiatr Genet, 141B*(4), 387–393.

Chapter 5

# Conservation of Resources Theory
## *The Central Role of Resource Loss and Gain in Understanding Retraumatization*

*Jeremiah A. Schumm, Lisa S. Doane, and Stevan E. Hobfoll*

Conservation of Resources (COR) theory is a motivational model of the development and maintenance of stress that focuses on the disproportionate impact of resource loss compared to resource gain (Hobfoll, 1988, 1989, 1998). One central tenet of COR theory, then, is that resource loss is significantly more powerful than resource gain.

Earlier models of stress were focused on the discrepancy between an individual's capacity to cope and the demands of the environment (for example, Lazarus, 1966). These models placed a primary emphasis on the role of appraisal (Lazarus & Folkman, 1984), such that an individual's perception of the incongruity between coping capacity and environmental demands determined whether a situation was interpreted as being stressful. Thus, appraisal rather than the objective nature of events was critical to defining an event as stress.

COR theory was developed in response to weaknesses in earlier models of stress, which focused on perceptions of stressful experiences while deemphasizing the objective nature of loss that contributes to the experience of stress (Lazarus & Folkman, 1984). It is important to underscore that, unlike other stress theories (Lazarus & Folkman, 1984), COR theory incorporates the relevance of appraisal but places less weight on the importance of the individual appraisal to the experience of stress. Rather, COR theory suggests that these appraisals of stressful situations are actually culturally defined as opposed to individual, idiographic appraisals. In other words, the situations that individuals find stressful, the things that are valued, and their behaviors are determined primarily by a shared cultural experience, not an individual interpretation of such. These individual interpretations have only secondary importance.

A significant body of theoretical and empirical work has applied COR theory to our understanding of the responses of individuals and communities to traumatic stress. Further, COR theory provides a useful framework for understanding both the vulnerability toward the experience of and psychological response to future traumatic events. In this chapter, we will present in detail the principles of COR theory and review the literature on the relationship between resource loss and retraumatization. We will also conceptualize and evaluate a range of treatment approaches, often used with multiply traumatized survivors, from a COR theory perspective.

## PRINCIPLES AND COROLLARIES OF CONSERVATION OF RESOURCES (COR) THEORY

COR theory is based on the fundamental notion that individuals naturally strive to obtain, retain, foster, and protect those things (i.e., *resources*) they value, and that which supports both the individual and community. Though there are a wide variety of these resources (and some variability in valued resources across cultures), in general these resources can be categorized as object, condition, personal, and energy resources. *Object* resources include tangible resources that are either necessary for survival or highly valued within a culture, including such things as housing, hygiene needs, food, and transportation. *Condition* resources, including educational or socioeconomic status, marriage, social support, and job security, are valued because they either support survival or bring status that is indirectly related to survival. *Personal* resources, including both personal traits (e.g., self-esteem, self-efficacy) and personal skills (e.g., job skills) are those that are critical to either survival or resiliency. Finally, *energy* resources include those that can be used to directly obtain or exchange for object or condition resources, or for the protection and maintenance of other resources (e.g., money, credit, intelligence).

The COR theory model predicts that psychological stress will occur under the following three conditions: (1) when individuals' resources are threatened with loss, (2) when individuals' resources are actually lost, or (3) when individuals fail to gain sufficient resources following significant resource investment. Thus, loss, threat of loss, or inadequate gain following expenditure of resources in any of the categories described above may result in the experience of stress for an individual. The following principles are central to COR theory.

## Principle 1: Resource Loss Is Disproportionately More Salient Than Resource Gain

COR theory suggests that resource loss is more powerful than resource gain, and, especially in cases of traumatic stress, resource losses occur much more swiftly than do resource gains. When losses occur, they deplete resources to a greater degree than resources are acquired during a period of gain. Further, it is more difficult to prevent resource loss than it is to initiate a resource gain.

## Principle 2: To Protect Against Resource Loss, Recover From Losses, and Gain Additional Resources, One Must Invest Resources

Traumatic events result in significant resource loss. Given that, protecting remaining resources or seeking to recoup lost resources is vital to maintaining a pool of resources. Doing so requires a significant investment of existing resources. This investment of resources can emanate from the self or from resources available to individuals from their environment.

## Principle 3: Although Resource Loss Is More Potent Than Resource Gain, the Salience of Gain Increases Under Situations of Resource Loss

This paradoxical increase in saliency of resource gain is true during any situation of resource loss but is accentuated during traumatic situations. The value placed on gain, even small gains, subsequent to traumatic stress may be quite high and result in such gains being quite powerful to the individual under such circumstances.

These early principles of COR theory have given rise to the following corollaries of the theory, which are also integral to our understanding of reactions to traumatic stressors and offer a way of making specific predictions about how resources will shift over time.

### Corollary 1

Those with greater resources are less vulnerable to resource loss and more capable of orchestrating resource gain. Conversely, those with fewer resources are more vulnerable to resource loss and less capable of resource gain.

The experience of retraumatization often makes demands on a range of resources for survivors and can quickly deplete the resources available to the individual, particularly for those who have fewer resources at the outset. Those with greater resources can afford to lose more and have more resources to invest to stave off further loss, and thus have more protection against the emotional and material consequences of the experience of traumatic stress.

## Corollary 2

Those who lack resources are not only more vulnerable to resource loss, but that initial loss begets future loss.

These losses are referred to as *loss spirals* and are most likely to occur for those who have fewer resources or those for whom earlier losses have depleted their reserve of resources. This is particularly true for repeated traumatic stress, which is likely to lead to an initial significant, swift loss of resources followed by a wave of further strains that attack a weakened state, rendering one's resources further depleted and thus leaving the individual less able to respond at each iteration of the cycle. COR theory further proposes that not only are individuals less able to respond as their resources diminish, this process also increases in momentum as the loss spiral unfolds.

## Corollary 3

Mirroring Corollary 2, those who possess resources are more capable of gain, and that initial resource gain begets further gain. However, because loss is more potent than gain, loss cycles will have a stronger impact than gain cycles.

Gains generally require the investment of major resources to occur, and when gains happen they tend to occur slowly. These gain cycles are referred to as *gain spirals*. However, because resource gain is less potent and moves more slowly than resource loss, this process is more fragile than loss cycles. It is important to note that people are often reluctant to invest resources to initiate a gain cycle, because they are motivated to retain a resource surplus in the event that they may be needed in the future.

## Corollary 4

Those who lack resources are likely to adopt a defensive posture to protect and conserve their resources.

The fourth corollary of COR theory is critical but actually the most understudied. It is quite logical that those with fewer resources would seek to protect the resources they do possess.

## UNDERSTANDING RETRAUMATIZATION
## WITHIN THE CONTEXT OF COR THEORY

Though isolated traumatic events can initiate resource loss, recurrent traumatic events are especially damaging to coping resources. As shown in Figure 5.1, initial trauma sets into motion a chain of resource loss and subsequent risk for additional loss and retraumatization. Because resources travel together like caravans in the desert, initial loss in one resource domain (e.g., social support) directly affects loss in other resource domains (e.g., self-esteem). As a result, resource loss often gains momentum, resulting in ongoing resource loss spirals. These loss spirals, in turn, compound the damaging effects of retraumatization on mental and physical health. By resulting in depletion of important protective factors, this initial cycle of coping resource loss, in turn, creates an opportunity for additional retraumatization to occur. This occurs by individuals, families, and communities becoming depleted of important coping resources that might otherwise help to offset risk factors for additional trauma. Through this process, resource loss sets up individuals, families, and communities for ongoing resource loss spirals and retraumatization. The relationship between ongoing resource loss spirals and retraumatization is bidirectional in that ongoing loss spirals further deplete necessary resources for offsetting the risk for retraumatization. At the same time, retraumatization undermines coping resources, thereby continuing the momentous downward spiral of resource reservoirs. Finally, the processes of resource loss spirals and retraumatization converge, resulting in decreased mental and physical health (see Figure 5.1).

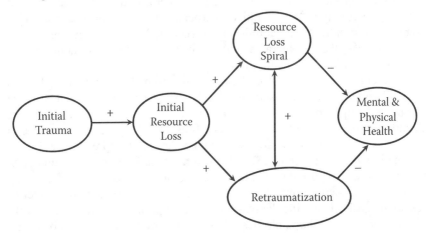

FIGURE 5.1 Model demonstrating how initial trauma and resource loss can lead to cycles of resource loss spirals and retraumatization. These cycles will, in turn, erode mental and physical health.

It is also important to describe the role of resource gains in this process. According to COR theory, resource gains are most critical within the context of resource loss spirals. As such, individuals, families, and communities who have built coping resource reservoirs will be most apt to persevere during periods of resource loss. This suggests that within the context of resource loss spirals and retraumatization, resource gains are important to offset the resource drain that is occurring as a result of ongoing resource loss spirals and retraumatization. A clear example of this is the availability of social support structures to help to offset the damage of ongoing retraumatization. In such situations, the impact of accessibility of helping hands (i.e., instrumental support) or shoulders to cry on (i.e., emotional support) becomes more pronounced.

## Childhood Retraumatization and Resources

Since childhood serves as the foundational structure on which coping resources are built, childhood revictimization is especially damaging to individuals' resources and subsequent adjustment. Revictimization serves to undermine and even prevent growth of the perceptions of the "protective shield," which is largely composed of trust that caregivers, families, organizations, and communities will keep them safe (Pynoos, Steinberg, & Wraith, 1995). Loss in the ability to trust others and to trust institutions is costly, resulting in long-term and widespread loss in other areas of interpersonal resources. For example, studies show that childhood abuse survivors are also at increased risk of experiencing problems with sexual relationships and have more adulthood personality disorders. This suggests that childhood retraumatization creates foundational cracks, particularly in the cognitive-interpersonal domain of resources. This compromises individuals' abilities to garner additional coping resources, thereby leaving them vulnerable to the effects of additional retraumatization throughout childhood and later in life.

Not only does recurrent childhood abuse impede individuals' abilities to build coping resource reservoirs, but it also sensitizes individuals to the detrimental impact of resource loss later in life. In a study of inner-city women, Schumm, Stines, Hobfoll, and Jackson (2006) found that recent increases in resource losses were associated with higher levels of depression and posttraumatic stress disorder (PTSD). However, an interaction was found such that women who reported higher levels of childhood physical abuse frequency were more profoundly impacted by resource loss. Specifically, the effect of resource loss in predicting depression was most pronounced for women with higher levels of childhood physical abuse frequency, while those who experienced low frequencies of childhood physical abuse had less depression in the face of increasing resource loss. These results suggested that childhood abuse served as "kindling" for compounding the detrimental effects of later resource loss. These results suggest that childhood retraumatization can be especially damaging to individuals by depleting them of the resiliency necessary to face the adversity of later loss in psychosocial resources.

## Retraumatization and Coping Resources Across the Life Span

There is clear evidence for the interrelated nature of retraumatization and resource caravans over the life span. In a large sample study of Vietnam Veterans, King, King, Foy, Keane, and Fairbank (1999) utilized a life-span perspective to examine the cumulative effects of trauma and coping resources prior to (e.g., childhood abuse), during (e.g., exposure to atrocities), and following the war (e.g., postwar social support) in predicting PTSD (see Figure 5.2). Separate models for male and female Veterans each indicated that traumatic events and coping resources at each time period were independently predictive of PTSD symptoms. This suggested that coping resources across the life span are important in predicting clinical trauma reactions. These results also showed the importance of considering the effects of traumatic events across the life span in predicting PTSD. Results also demonstrated that higher childhood adversities were related to more traumatic war-zone experiences and less postwar resources to cope with these traumas. In addition, higher degrees of war-zone trauma were associated with less postwar coping resources. Hence, the effects of resources and traumatic experiences in one time period affected coping resources and traumatic experiences of subsequent time periods. These results support the COR theory hypothesis that resource loss spirals can occur over the course of the life span and that retraumatization at various time periods serves to compound the effects of resource loss spirals.

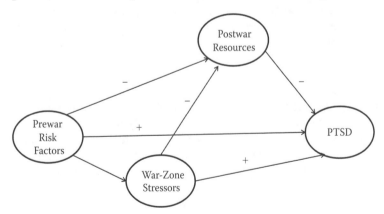

FIGURE 5.2  Model adapted from King, King, Foy, Keane, and Fairbank demonstrating the impact of coping resources and traumatic events over the life span in predicting posttraumatic stress disorder (PTSD). (Adapted from King, D. W., King, L. A., Foy, D. W., Keane, T. M., & Fairbank, J. A., 1999, Posttraumatic Stress Disorder in a National Sample of Male and Female Vietnam Veterans, *Journal of Abnormal Psychology, 108*, 164–170.)

Consistent with the findings of King and colleagues, studies in non-U.S. Veteran samples support the role of retraumatization across the life span in compounding the effects of resource loss spirals. In a sample of Holocaust survivors, Dekel and Hobfoll (2007) studied the role of losses of family members during the Holocaust and resource losses that occurred more recently within the context of ongoing terrorism and missle attack threats within Israel. Results showed that both losing a family member during the Holocaust and recent personal and interpersonal resource loss in the context of terror attacks were associated with general distress and PTSD-related symptoms. These results show that the impact of distal traumatic events can continue to exude negative affects on mental health, while more recent traumatic events can provide the circumstances for additional resource loss and subsequent compounded psychological distress.

In a longitudinal study of women receiving services at a family violence agency, Banyard, Williams, Saunders, and Fitzgerald (2008) found further support for the role of resources over the life-span and retraumatization cycles in predicting psychological maladjustment. Path models were computed to assess the longitudinal relationship between reports of childhood abuse and resources, adulthood abuse and resources, and later psychological trauma symptoms and psychological distress. Results showed that childhood traumatic events were positively associated with other childhood risk factors (i.e., lower childhood resources). A higher number of childhood traumatic events was also associated with lower levels of adulthood resources and a higher number of adulthood traumatic events. This suggests that childhood revictimization led to resource losses in both childhood and adulthood, while also increasing risk for later continued retraumatization. Further lower childhood resources and adulthood resources and higher adulthood retraumatization occurrence were shown to independently predict later psychological trauma symptoms, thereby demonstrating the importance of taking a life-span perspective in assessing retraumatization and resource loss. Finally, the path models revealed that the influence of childhood traumatic experiences on adulthood distress was entirely indirect—that is, childhood traumatic events influenced psychological outcomes via lower childhood and adulthood resource and higher adulthood retraumatization. These results suggest that childhood trauma sets into motion a cascade of resource loss in childhood and into adulthood, while setting victims up for further retraumatization. These results also further highlight the importance of examining retraumatization and coping resource loss across the life span.

## THE EFFECTS OF RETRAUMATIZATION AND COPING RESOURCES ON FAMILIES AND COMMUNITIES

Because individuals are nested within families and within communities (Hobfoll, 1998, 2001), retraumatization does not affect them in isolation. An individual's retraumatization can create splintering of resources for groups (e.g., marriage, family, friendship networks) to which he or she is connected. Likewise, retraumatization of families and communities can drain groups of individuals of collective resources, thereby impacting even those who are not directly exposed to the traumatic events. Consideration of individuals with the context of larger systems is also important because social connections are a conduit by which resources are collectively gained and lost. Therefore, the manner in which individuals are impacted by retraumatization substantially depends upon the collective resources of the larger social network in which they are nested. Individuals who are nested within families and communities with considerable resources are better equipped to cope with the effects of retraumatization. In contrast, those who are set within social systems that lack coping resources are more prone to experience resource loss spirals and severe posttrauma psychological distress reactions. Taken from this perspective, COR theory can be applied to understand the impact of retraumatization on the larger family unit, across generations of families, and within communities.

## Intrafamilial Retraumatization and Coping Resources

Retraumatization that originates from within the family is especially com-promising to coping resources. Retraumatization cycles that are perpetrated by families members create a double-bind for victims. In these environments, victims are in the position of being traumatized by the very individuals whom they would otherwise hope to rely upon for support and cooperation in build-ing coping resources. Rather than working together as a cohesive family unit to build shared resources, intrafamilial perpetrators create resource loss spirals for the victim and for the family unit as a whole.

This scenario of intrafamilial traumatization is an unfortunately common occurrence. For example, lifetime prevalence of intimate partner violence victimization is shown in representative community samples to be 25% for women and 7.6% for men (Tjaden & Thoennes, 2000). Past-year prevalence of intimate partner violence exceeds 60% among clinical samples of individuals with substance use problems (for example, O'Farrell, Murphy, Stephan, Fals-Stewart, & Murphy, 2004; Schumm, O'Farrell, Murphy, & Fals-Stewart, 2009). In addition, childhood sexual abuse of girls is most commonly per-petrated by a family member (Finkelhor, Hotaling, Lewis, & Smith, 1990). Taken together, these results suggest that intrafamilial retraumatization is an unfortunately common experience that compromises the coping resources of victims and their family units.

Violence within families can often become sequential (e.g., partner violence leads to violence toward children; Appel & Holden, 1998), thereby resulting in multiple traumatization within a family unit. In a large-scale study of families, Dixon and colleagues (Dixon, Browne, & Hamilton-Giachristis, 2005; Dixon,

Hamilton-Giachristis, & Browne, 2005) showed that having an adult in the house with violent tendencies increased the chances of children being abused by an odds ratio of 8.66 (766%). From this perspective, retraumatization occurs across individuals within the family unit and works to sequentially drain the family system of shared resources, including the ability to trust each other in maintaining safety within the family structure and the sense that family members can be relied upon as support in the recovery from trauma. There exists a dependency among individuals with regard to their coping resources, and intrafamilial retraumatization works directly against the abilities of family members to utilize the collective resources of their nested family unit.

## Intergenerational Retraumatization and Coping Resources

Not only do coping resources and retraumatization impact individuals and families over the course of their life spans, but the effects of coping resource loss and retraumatization can stretch across generations. This retraumatization can be partially a function of cross-generational contact with the perpetrator. For example, incest perpetrators may victimize not only their children, but assuming their contact with the family unit is ongoing, perpetrators victimize their grandchildren, thereby perpetuating the cycle of incestuous retraumatization. This cycle provides cross-generational momentum to resource loss spirals and results in compounding losses to the original victim, the victim's children, and the entire family unit. In addition, resource loss spirals that are initiated with the original victim may drain the family unit of coping resources that are necessary to protect future generations and prevent intergenerational retraumatization from occurring. Hence, resource loss spirals increase risk for revictimization across family generations. This lack of resources (e.g., low levels of education, low income, lack of social support) can be a partial contributor to those who were abused as children engaging in abusive behaviors toward their own offspring.

Several studies suggest that a lack of resources may partially explain the increased risk for offspring of child abuse survivors to experience abuse themselves. A study by McCloskey and Bailey (2000) found that daughters of sexual abuse surivivors were themselves 3.4 times more likely to be abused than daughters of women who were not sexually abused. This risk compounded nearly sixfold when the sexually abused mother used drugs, such that daughters of sexually abused mothers who used drugs were 23.7 times more likely to be sexually abused versus daughters whose mothers were not sexually abused and did not use drugs. This history of sexual abuse combined with drug use problems is likely to have resulted in resource loss spirals (e.g., loss of social support, loss of self-esteem, economic loss) for the women and their children. The result of this resource loss spiral is an environment devoid of protection for the children and ripe for intergenerational retraumatization.

Dixon and colleagues (Dixon, Browne, & Hamilton-Giachristis, 2005; Dixon, Hamilton-Giachristis, & Browne, 2005) found lower psychosocial resources to partially account for the higher risk of child abuse perpetration by parents who had themselves been abused as children. The study data were drawn from a population cohort of 4,351 children in the United Kingdom, who were then assessed and followed longitudinally as part of a community home health services program. These longitudinal data showed that a parental history of childhood abuse increased the risk of perpetrating abuse by 2.96 (196%). After controlling for the effects of parental childhood abuse, a variety of markers of deficits in psychosocial resources (e.g., parents being under the age of 21, serious financial problems) were associated with increased risk of child abuse perpetration. These results suggest that a lack of coping resources increased the risk for children abuse survivors to themselves engage in childhood abuse toward their own children. In addition, results showed the lower psychological resources partially mediated the impact of parental childhood abuse histories on perpetration of abuse. This suggests that childhood abuse histories directly increased the risk for the continuation of cross-generational childhood abuse, while also lowering psychosocial resources. This resulting resource loss thereby further increased risk for cross-generational retraumatization.

## Community-Level Retraumatization and Coping Resources

Individuals are nested within communities and are, therefore, bound to the collective coping resources held by their larger community systems. Consequently, the impact of retraumatization on the individual is partially dependent upon the levels of coping resources available within the community. Resource-rich communities provide a protective buffer to individuals who experience multiple traumatization, thereby limiting the individual's potential resource loss and resulting damage to physical and psychological health. In contrast, resource-poor communities create collective vulnerabilities for individuals to experience resource loss spirals, which, in turn, compound the damage caused by retraumatization. In this manner, risk and resiliency for an individual who experiences retraumatization are substantially determined by the resources available to the individual within his or her nested community structure.

Following community-wide traumatic events, individuals who are able to maintain coping resources are more likely to show resilience in recovering from trauma. In a large-scale study of New York City residents following the September 11, 2001 terrorist attacks, levels of coping resources (e.g., social support, educational attainment) were found to be an important predictor of recovery from these events (Bonanno, Galea, Bucciarelli, & Vlahov, 2007). In addition to demonstrating the assocation between general coping resource capacity and resiliency, this study also suggested that degree of resource loss following a mass trauma is a key component in determining resiliency. Results showed that levels of income, per se, were not associated with less resiliency. However, those who reported a *loss* of income following the 9/11 attacks were shown to be half as likely to be resilient. These results are consistent with COR theory in showing that the experience of resource loss following mass traumatization is central to understanding how individuals recover from or are impaired by the traumatic experience.

Consistent with these findings, Hobfoll and colleagues (2009) showed that coping resource loss predicts adjustment within the context of mass retraumatization in Israel. This study involved a large nationally representative sample of Jews and Arabs who were followed longitudinally for 1 year. These individuals were assessed during the occurrence of the Second Intifada (2004–2005), which involved ongoing rocket attacks, terrorist acts, and threat of war. Hence, these communities were assessed during periods of community-wide retraumatization. In comparison to Bonanno and colleagues' (2007) sample of New York City residents following the 9/11 attacks, Hobfoll and colleagues found lower proportions of resistance to psychological distress (i.e., displaying minimal PTSD and depression symptoms) in the Israeli sample. These differences may be partially attributable to the effects of chronic retraumatization in lowering resilience, such that New York City residents may have been less exposed to ongoing retraumatization in comparison to the Israeli sample. Consistent with COR theory principles, results from Hobfoll and colleagues showed that greater psychosocial resource loss during this period was found to predict less resistence to psychological distress. Hence, higher resource loss with the context of community-wide retraumatization predicted less resistence to offsetting symptoms of PTSD and depression.

In addition, Hobfoll and colleagues (2009) found results that were consistent with an independent study sample in showing that when exposed to similar levels of ongoing terrorism, Israeli Arabs had less resilience when compared to Israeli Jews (Somer, Maguen, Or-Chen, & Litz, 2009). This result may be explained by Arabs in Israel having less coping resources and experiencing greater coping resource loss due to their minority status (Somer et al., 2009). These results are important, showing that differences in coping resources between communities and cultural groups are important determinants of group differences in adjustment following mass retraumatization. Groups with higher coping resources and who experience less resource loss will collectively be less negatively impacted by retraumatization in comparison with groups who lack coping resources and experience greater resource loss.

## COR THEORY AND INTERVENTIONS FOR RETRAUMATIZATION

### Individually Oriented Interventions

Fortunately, for trauma survivors with PTSD, several psychosocial interventions have strong empirical support and are recommended as first-line treatments by expert organizations (Foa, Keane, Friedman, & Cohen, 2009; Institute of Medicine, 2007). Most of these treatments have a cognitive-behavioral orientation. Though the theoretical rationales underlying these treatments vary (and it is outside the scope of this chapter to review the specific details of the treatments in depth), it is potentially quite useful to conceptualize some of these major treatment approaches within a COR theoretical perspective. We reviewed two of the most widely investigated treatments with strongest empirical support (IOM, 2007): cognitive processing therapy and prolonged exposure therapy.

Cognitive processing therapy (CPT) (Resick & Schnicke, 1996; Resnick, Monson, & Chard, 2008) is primarily a cognitive treatment that includes some behavioral elements. The treatment is designed to modify maladaptive beliefs about safety, trust, power, esteem, and intimacy that have been shifted (or, in cases of early childhood trauma, may have developed in a distorted manner) as a result of the trauma. In a standard CPT protocol, clients will receive education regarding trauma, write an impact statement regarding the effects of the trauma, write a written account of the traumatic event and review it as homework, and engage in cognitive restructuring around distorted trauma-related cognitions that emerge in the impact statement. CPT has demonstrated strong efficacy for the treatment of chronic PTSD in a large-scale randomized clinical trial (Resick, Nishith, Weaver, Astin, & Feuer, 2002). Though this treatment was originally developed to be applied specifically to rape survivors (Resick & Schnicke, 1992, 1996), recent studies have evaluated CPT in a variety of other PTSD populations (sexual abuse survivors: Chard, 2005; Veterans: Monson et al., 2006), and results support its efficacy across groups.

CPT could be conceptualized as a resource-based treatment in several ways. First, the primary technique utilized in the treatment, modifying trauma-related cognitions, is likely to have a direct effect on personal and condition resources. By evaluating and modifying these unhelpful trauma-related beliefs, clients are likely to experience less guilt related to the trauma (and thereby increased self-esteem and self-efficacy). Further, the sheer reduction of PTSD symptoms in treatment is likely to lead to an increase in personal and conditional resources as well, through the impact on improving overall quality of life and interpersonal relationships, reduction of trauma-related guilt, reduction in anxiety, and improvement in mood. We would expect that a client who successfully completed a course of CPT might experience improvements in such vital resources as social support and improved self-esteem.

Prolonged exposure (PE) is also a cognitive-behavioral treatment that is more heavily focused on behaviorally oriented techniques while anticipating cognitive change as a result (Foa, Hembree, & Rothbaum, 2007; Foa & Rothbaum, 1998). A traditional course of PE consists of psychoeducation about reactions to trauma, breathing retraining (a form of relaxation), repeated reliving of the traumatic event (i.e., imaginal exposure), and encouragement to systematically confront feared and avoided trauma-related reminders (i.e., *in vivo* exposure). In PE, patients are provided with the opportunity to counter maladaptive cognitions about the self as incompetent or weak and the world and others as dangerous by directly confronting their fears through the exposure exercises. PE has been studied in numerous clinical trials, and data consistently support its efficacy (e.g., Devilly & Spence, 1999; Foa, Rothbaum, Riggs, & Murdock, 1991; Foa et al., 1999, 2005; Marks, Lovell, Noshirvani, Livanou, & Thrasher, 1998; Tarrier et al., 1999).

Through the process of *in vivo* exposure, an individual is presented with an opportunity to halt the resource losses and loss spirals associated with avoidance. For example, assault survivors (many of whom have been multiply traumatized) often avoid the use of public transportation due to the anxiety they experience while riding. This may result in a loss spiral, in that the initial resource loss results in greater, continued losses by interfering with their social relationships (e.g., if they become overly reliant on others to take them on errands and that person becomes burdened or upset), job performance (if they are unable to get to work on time or reliably), and self-esteem (if they feel incapable of performing well or completing tasks successfully). If, through *in vivo* exposure, that person learns that he or she can ride public transportation and his or her anxiety becomes less severe with time and repetition, the loss spiral may be arrested and these resources may slowly begin to accumulate.

To date, clinical trials examining these individually oriented treatments for PTSD have not specifically examined how change in resources unfolds during treatment. Clearly, one important area of future research lies in prospectively examining resources over the course of treatment for PTSD to evaluate the influence of treatment on resource losses and gains.

## Systems-Based Interventions

Although individually oriented interventions show good empirical support to treating PTSD and other disorders that result from retraumatization (Foa et al., 2009; IOM, 2007), these approaches do not target the broader coping resources that are held by the couples, families, and community systems within which individuals are nested. This is unfortunate, because coping resources are not built and lost in an individual vaccuum. Rather, individuals who experience retraumatization may be buoyed or pulled further down by the collective coping resources shared with their significant others, families, and communities. Therefore, interventions that more broadly target collective coping resources shared across trauma survivors and their networks are more likely to impact the adjustment of those who are directly and indirectly impacted by retraumatization. In addition, instead of requiring the implementation of an intervention across multiple people, systems-based interventions are able to simultaneously target multiple interventions and their shared coping resources. Hence, systems-based interventions are clearly more efficient when retraumatization occurs to entire families and communities.

Following COR theory, collective resources can be categorized for the purpose of developing the strategy of where and how to intervene (Monnier & Hobfoll, 2000). Examples of personal characteristic resources at the levels of the family and the community are pride and cohesion. By increasing and mobilizing collective pride and cohesion, the community can be brought together to increase their collective coping efforts and efficiencies in the wake of recurrent trauma. At the family level, object resources might constitute posessions such as the family home and car, while at the community level, object resources may be things such as roads and industry. Object resources are critical to the short- and long-term coping capabilities of the family and community in coping with retraumatization experiences. Along with personal and object resources, conditional resources such as employment and access to emergency services are important foci for interventions. Finally, energy resources, such as money and fuel, can be targeted at a family or community level. This classification system proposed by COR theory provides a way of organizing and targeting aspects of family- and community-level interventions to address retraumatization.

A series of steps should be taken with intervening at the family and community levels following recurrent trauma. First, the extent of loss should be assessed following each traumatic event (Monnier & Hobfoll, 2000). This might involve estimating the loss in each category of family or community resource (i.e., personal, object, conditional, energy). Second, the availability of resources for coping with the consequences of the loss should be assessed (Monnier & Hobfoll, 2000). For example, it may be important to assess the community-wide availability of mental health professionals to limit clinical reactions to assess the availability of work crews to repair damaged roads. In the context of ongoing, recurrent trauma, this assessment should focus upon the availability of resources that can be employed quickly and used to effectively repair and limit further losses that might occur in the wake of additional traumas. Third, interventions should assess the holistic needs of the family by speaking with each member to understand the scope of the impact of retraumatization on the family unit and to assess the extent of the family unit's collective coping resources. At the community level, interventions should meet with community levels to gain understanding of the community's collective coping resources and need (Monnier & Hobfoll, 2000). In this way, interventions can effectively prioritize targeting the system resources that are most important.

## SUMMARY

COR theory provides researchers and clinicians with a principled approach to conceptualizing the effects of changes in coping resources that occur in conjuction with retraumatization. Coping resources can be categorized as object, conditional, personal, and energy resources. According to COR theory, the impact of coping resource loss is greater than coping resource gain, and initial loss often begets future loss. Hence, initial traumatization and initial coping resource loss often lead to a cycle of additional retraumatization and resource loss spirals, thereby resulting in compromised mental and physical health (see Figure 5.1). COR theory conceptualizes individuals and their coping resources as being nested within larger families and communities. Therefore, resource loss and gains at the level of the individual often mirror those occurring at the larger systematic level of the family and community. COR theory proposes that researchers and clinicians should seek to identify interventions that are aimed at halting resource loss spirals in order to allow individuals, families, and communities to begin to rebuild and recover from the effects of retraumatization.

## AUTHOR NOTE

Support for preparation of this chapter was provided in part by VA Career Development Award CDA-2-019-09S, awarded to Jeremiah A. Schumm, Cincinnati VA Medical Center and University of Cincinnati School of Medicine.

## REFERENCES

Appel, A. E., & Holden, G. W. (1998). The co-occurrence of spouse and physical child abuse: A review and appraisal. *Journal of Family Psychology, 12*, 578–599.

Banyard, V. L., Williams, L. M., Saunders, B. E., & Fitzgerald, M. M. (2008). The complexity of trauma types in the lives of women in families referred for family violence: Multiple mediators of mental health. *American Journal of Orthopsychiatry, 78*, 394–404.

Bonanno, G., Galea, S., Bucciarelli, A., & Vlahov, D. (2007). What predicts psychological resilience after disaster? The role of demographics, resources, and life stress. *Journal of Consulting and Clinical Psychology, 75*, 671–682.

Chard, C. M. (2005). An evaluation of cognitive processing therapy for the treatment of posttraumatic stress disorder related to childhood sexual abuse. *Journal of Consulting and Clinical Psychology, 73*, 965–971.

Dekel, R., & Hobfoll, S. E. (2007). The impact of resource loss on Holocaust survivors facing war and terrorism in Israel. *Aging & Mental Health, 11*, 159–167.

Devilly, G. J., & Spence, S. H. (1999). The relative efficacy and treatment distress of EMDR and a cognitive-behavioral trauma treatment protocol in the amelioration of posttraumatic stress disorder. *Journal of Anxiety Disorders, 13,* 131–157.

Dixon, L., Browne, K., & Hamilton-Giachristis, C. (2005). Risk factors of parents abused as children: A mediational analysis of the intergenerational continuity of child maltreatment (Part I). *Journal of Child Psychology and Psychiatry, 46*, 47–57.

Dixon, L., Hamilton-Giachristis, C., & Browne, K. (2005). Attributions and behaviours of parents abused as children: A mediational analysis of the intergenerational continuinity of child maltreatment (Part II). *Journal of Child Psychology and Psychiatry, 46*, 58–68.

Finkelhor, D., Hotaling, G., Lewis, I. A., & Smith, C. (1990). Sexual abuse in a national survey of adult men and women: Prevalence, characteristics, and risk factors. *Child Abuse and Neglect, 14*, 19–28.

Foa, E. B., Dancu, C. V., Hembree, E. A., Jaycox, L. H., Meadows, E. A., & Street, G. P. (1999). A comparison of exposure therapy, stress inoculation training, and their combination of reducing posttraumatic stress disorder in female assault victims. *Journal of Consulting and Clinical Psychology, 67*, 194–200.

Foa, E. B., Hembree, E. A., Cahill, S. P., Rauch, S. A., Riggs, D. S., Feeny, N. C., & Yadin, E. (2005). Randomized trial of prolonged exposure for PTSD with and without cognitive restructuring: Outcomes at academic and community clinics. *Journal of Consulting and Clinical Psychology, 73*, 953–964.

Foa, E. B., Hembree, E. A., & Rothbaum, B. O. (2007). *Prolonged exposure therapy for PTSD: Emotional processing of traumatic experiences: Therapist guide.* New York: Oxford.

Foa, E. B., & Rothbaum, B. O. (1998). *Treating the trauma of rape: Cognitive-behavioral therapy for PTSD.* New York: Guilford.

Foa, E. B., Rothbaum, B. O., Riggs, D. S., & Murdock, T. B. (1991). Treatment of posttraumatic stress disorder in rape victims: A comparison between cognitive-behavioral procedures and counseling. *Journal of Consulting and Clinical Psychology, 59*, 715–723.

Foa, E., Keane, T., Friedman, M., & Cohen, J. (2009). *Effective treatments for PTSD: Practice guidelines from the International Society for Traumatic Stress Studies.* New York: Guilford.

Hobfoll, S. E. (1988). *The ecology of stress.* New York: Hemisphere.

Hobfoll, S. E. (1989). Conservation of resources theory: A new attempt at conceptualizing stress. *American Psychologist, 44*, 513–544.

Hobfoll, S. (1998). *Stress, culture, and community: The psychology and philosophy of stress.* New York: Plenum.

Hobfoll, S. (2001). The influence of culture, community, and the nested-self in the stress process: Advancing Conservation of Resources theory. *Applied Psychology, 50*, 337–370.

Hobfoll, S., Palmieri, P., Johnson, R., Canetti-Nisim, D., Hall, B., & Galea, S. (2009). Trajectories of resilience, resistance, and distress during ongoing terrorism: The case of Jews and Arabs in Israel. *Journal of Consulting and Clinical Psychology, 77*, 138–148.

Institute of Medicine. (2007). *Treatment of posttraumatic stress disorder: An assessment of the evidence.* Washington, DC: National Academy of Sciences.

King, D. W., King, L. A., Foy, D. W., Keane, T. M., & Fairbank, J. A. (1999). Posttraumatic stress disorder in a national sample of male and female Vietnam Veterans: Risk factors, war-zone stressors, and resilience-recovery variables. *Journal of Abnormal Psychology, 108*, 164–170.

Lazarus, R. S. (1966). *Psychological stress and the coping process.* New York: Springer.

Lazarus, R. S., & Folkman, S. (1984). *Stress, appraisal, and coping.* New York: Springer.

Marks, I., Lovell, K., Noshirvani, H., Livanou, M., & Thrasher, S. (1998). Treatment of posttraumatic stress disorder by exposure and/or cognitive restructuring: A controlled study. *Archives of General Psychiatry, 55*, 317–325.

McCloskey, L. A., & Bailey, J. A. (2000). The intergenerational transmission of risk for child sexual abuse. *Journal of Interpersonal Violence, 15*, 1019–1035.

Monnier, J., & Hobfoll, S. (2000). Conservation of resources in individual and community reactions to traumatic stress. In S. Yehuda & K. McFarlane (Eds.), *International handbook of human response to trauma* (pp. 325–336). New York: Plenum.

Monson, C. M., Schnurr, P. P., Resick, P. A., Friedman, M. J., Young-Xu, Y., & Stevens, S. P. (2006). Cognitive processing therapy for Veterans with posttraumatic stress disorder. *Journal of Consulting and Clinical Psychology, 74*, 898–907.

O'Farrell, T. J., Murphy, C. M., Stephan, S. H., Fals-Stewart, W., & Murphy, M. (2004). Partner violence before and after couples-based alcoholism treatment for male alcoholic patients: The role of treatment involvement and abstinence. *Journal of Consulting and Clinical Psychology, 72*, 202–217.

Pynoos, R. S., Steinberg, A. M., & Wraith, R. (1995). A developmental model of childhood traumatic stress. In D. Cicchetti & D. J. Cohen (Eds.), *Developmental psychopathology: Vol. 2, Risk, disorder, and adaptation* (pp. 72–95). Oxford: Wiley.

Resick, P. A., Monson, C. M., & Chard, K. M. (2008). *Cognitive processing therapy: Veteran/military version*. Washington, DC: Department of Veterans Affairs.

Resick, P. A., Nishith, P., Weaver, T. L., Astin, M. C., & Feuer, C. A. (2002). A comparison of cognitive processing therapy with prolonged exposure and a waiting list condition for the treatment of chronic posttraumatic stress disorder in female rape victims. *Journal of Consulting and Clinical Psychology, 60*, 748–756.

Resick, P. A., & Schnicke, M. K. (1992). Cognitive processing therapy for sexual assault victims. *Journal of Consulting and Clinical Psychology, 60*, 748–756.

Resick, P. A., & Schnicke, M. K. (1996). *Cognitive processing therapy for rape victims*. London: Sage.

Schumm, J. A., O'Farrell, T. J., Murphy, C. M., & Fals-Stewart, W. (2009). Partner violence before and after couple-based alcoholism treatment for female alcoholics. *Journal of Consulting and Clinical Psychology, 77*, 1136–1146.

Schumm, J. A., Stines, L. R., Hobfoll, S. E., & Jackson, A. P. (2006). The double-barrelled burden of child abuse and current stressful experiences on adult women: The kindling effect of early traumatic experiences. *Journal of Traumatic Stress, 18*, 825–836.

Somer, E., Maguen, S., Or-Chen, K., & Litz, B. (2009). Managing terror: Differences between Jews and Arabs in Israel. *International Journal of Psychology, 44*, 138–146.

Tarrier, N., Pilgrim, H., Sommerfield, C., Faragher, B., Reynolds, M., Graham, E. et al. (1999). A randomised trial of cognitive therapy and imaginal exposure in the treatment of chronic post traumatic stress disorder. *Journal of Consulting and Clinical Psychology, 67*, 13–18.

Tjaden, P., & Thoennes, N. (2000). *Extent, nature, and consequences of intimate partner violence: Findings from the National Violence Against Women Survey*. Washington, DC: U.S. Department of Justice.

# Chapter 6

# A Functional Analytic Conceptualization of Retraumatization
## *Implications for Clinical Assessment*

*Jordan T. Bonow and William C. Follette*

In clinical settings, assessment procedures may have a number of uses, particularly in the early stages of therapy. For example, a therapist may use assessment procedures to develop a relationship with a client, increase a client's buy-in, understand the client's vocabulary for describing psychological phenomena, or even demonstrate the necessity of therapeutic services (e.g., to the client's insurance provider). Most importantly, though, all assessment activities should have treatment utility; in other words, they should meaningfully inform treatment in ways that benefit clients (Hayes, Nelson, & Jarrett, 1987). Because the ultimate determination of the adequacy of an assessment is successful treatment, the goals of treatment should serve as the context for a discussion of clinical assessment.

While specifically making recommendations about the treatment of sexually revictimized women, Naugle, Bell, and Polusny (2003) identify two broad goals that are appropriate for the treatment of retraumatized individuals. The first goal is to reduce psychological distress related to retraumatization while improving quality of life. The second goal is to identify and remediate specific risk factors for future retraumatization. Assuming these two overarching treatment goals, this chapter presents a unified approach to the clinical assessment of retraumatized individuals from a functional analytic perspective. This chapter has three broad goals: (1) to clarify terminology used to define

retraumatization as a clinically relevant phenomenon, (2) to broadly describe
the functional analytic approach to clinical assessment, and (3) to highlight
important variables of interest when conducting a functional behavioral
assessment of individuals with a history of retraumatization for the purpose
of improving treatment and reducing the likelihood of further victimization.

## IMPORTANT TERMINOLOGICAL ISSUES

The effective assessment of clients who have been retraumatized can be an
extremely difficult task, and it can be made even more complicated by a lack
of clarity in constructs. The following is intended to clearly define important
terms in order to provide a foundation for the later discussion of the assessment of retraumatized individuals.

At the most foundational level, the construct of *traumatic stress* needs to
be well defined. The *Diagnostic and Statistical Manual of Mental Disorders
(DSM-IV-TR)* (American Psychiatric Association, 2000) provides the current
diagnostic criteria for *posttraumatic stress disorder* (PTSD). These criteria
are being slightly revised and updated in preparation for the upcoming publication of the fifth edition of the *Diagnostic and Statistical Manual of Mental
Disorders (DSM-5)* (see American Psychiatric Association, 2010). Following
directly from their predecessors, the recently proposed *DSM-5* criteria highlight two essential elements of traumatic stress: (1) a previous exposure to a
traumatic event and (2) signs and symptoms representing a number of different
topographical clusters.

Previous exposure to a traumatic event is considered to be any contact with
an event that involves "death or threatened death, actual or threatened serious injury, or actual or threatened sexual violation" (Criterion A) (American
Psychiatric Association, 2010). The signs and symptoms of PTSD are divided
into four categories: intrusion symptoms, avoidance of stimuli associated with
the traumatic event, negative alterations in cognition and mood, and alterations in arousal and reactivity. *DSM* criteria emphasize that these signs and
symptoms must be "associated with the traumatic event(s)," meaning that they
"began after the traumatic event(s)" (American Psychiatric Association, 2010).

While the diagnostic criteria for PTSD are being revised, some have
called for the establishment of a broader trauma-related diagnostic category
of *complex posttraumatic stress disorder* (CPTSD) (Courtois, 2008; see also
Ford & Courtois, 2009). Establishment of a CPTSD diagnostic category would
primarily expand the number and breadth of the possible signs and symptoms
of traumatic stress. Courtois (2008) summarizes Herman's (1992a, 1992b)
initial conceptualization of CPTSD problem areas as including: (1) alterations
in the regulation of affective impulses, (2) alterations in attention and consciousness, (3) alterations in self-perception, (4) alterations in the relationship

to others, (5) somatization and/or medical problems, and (6) alterations in systems of meaning (p. 88).

In some cases, the connections between a trauma history and these broad forms of dysfunction are relatively easy to draw (e.g., relationship problems could develop if a person has difficulty communicating effectively about his or her response to a car accident). In other cases, however, the complexity is so great that functional connections may not be intuitively obvious (e.g., pervasive deficits in emotion regulation do not seem likely to result from the accident). Failure to identify these more complex functional connections could severely limit the utility of treatment. The primary benefit of expanding the definition of traumatic stress to broader problem areas is that it would encourage therapists to identify these more complex connections. By developing a fuller understanding of the sources of a client's psychological suffering and behavioral dysfunction, treatment can be enhanced.

Some caution is warranted when considering such an expansion of the construct of traumatic stress, though. Although many of the problems included in the proposed CPTSD diagnosis are commonly found in individuals with a trauma history, it is important to defend against misattributions. The connection between a client's dysfunction and a documented exposure to a traumatic event should not be assumed, even when the client's problems are included in the topographical definitions of traumatic stress. Especially in complex cases in which the connections between dysfunction and a traumatic event are not immediately clear, it is important for therapists to consider the possibility that a client exhibited dysfunctional patterns of behavior prior to or otherwise apart from the trauma.

The necessity of correctly identifying the functional sequelae of a trauma and the danger in relying on simple attributions and topographical definitions demonstrate the great complexity of the task of assessing individuals with a trauma history. To appropriately navigate this complexity, traumatic stress must be defined in a broad, contextual manner that allows the full impact of a traumatic event to be revealed. This is especially true when an individual experiences multiple traumas or his or her environment contributes to the elaboration and maintenance of psychological symptoms over time in ways that obfuscate the individual's connection to a traumatic event.

It is also important to clarify the term *retraumatization*. Follette and Vijay (2008) define *retraumatization* as "exposure to one or more potentially traumatic events subsequent to an initial exposure to psychological trauma, with the subsequent trauma exposure serving as a reminder of a past psychological trauma and exacerbating the distress that is related to the prior traumatic experiences" (p. 586). Retraumatization should be distinguished from other constructs such as *traumatic stress reactivation* (short-term increases in distress resulting from reminders of past traumas) and *revictimization* (exposure to multiple traumas that have been perpetrated by another person; see Layne et al., 2006, and Follette and Vijay, 2008, for further discussion). As defined, retraumatization can have two different topographical forms. *Serial trauma* is retraumatization involving the same types of trauma (e.g., repeated sexual assaults) (Layne et al., 2006). *Sequential trauma* is retraumatization involving different types of trauma (e.g., combat followed by natural disaster) (Layne et al., 2006).

In summary, this chapter will use the term *retraumatization* to refer to two phenomena: (1) exposure to a new, additional traumatic event subsequent to an initial exposure to a traumatic event; and (2) the psychological process whereby exposure to the additional traumatic event results in the chronic intensification or exacerbation of previous traumatic distress (including the associated behavioral consequences). When discussing the effects of exposure to a traumatic event and retraumatization, *traumatic stress* will be employed in a broad sense, reflecting the wide-ranging negative impact resulting both directly and indirectly from exposure to traumatic events.

## THE FUNCTIONAL ANALYTIC APPROACH TO CLINICAL ASSESSMENT

Before applying it to the specific topic of the assessment of retraumatized individuals, it is necessary to briefly review the foundations of the functional analytic approach to clinical assessment. Unfamiliar readers are encouraged to explore additional resources in the specific areas of (1) the functional analytic approach to PTSD (for example, Follette, Iverson, & Ford, 2009; Follette & Naugle, 2006; Naugle & Follette, 1998), (2) the functional analytic approach to clinical assessment (for example, Follette, Naugle, & Linnerooth, 2000; Haynes & O'Brien, 2000; Kanfer & Saslow, 1969), and (3) the general principles and philosophy underlying the functional analytic approach to behavior (for example, Pierce & Cheney, 2008; Skinner, 1953).

The functional analytic approach involves "the identification of important, controllable, causal functional relationships applicable to a specified set of target behaviors for an individual client" (Haynes & O'Brien, 1990, p. 654). The foundation of the functional analytic approach is the focus on the behavior of individuals and the environmental variables influencing it. Behavior refers to all of the activities in which an individual engages, including thinking, feeling, and physical movement. Behavior does not occur in isolation; it is emitted within a context that involves both the learning history of an individual and the environment in which the individual is currently behaving. Thus, the appropriate unit of analysis in a functional analytic approach is behavior in context (Follette & Naugle, 2006; Follette, Naugle, & Linnerooth, 2000).

The ABCs (antecedents, behaviors, consequences) of behavior provide one useful unit for describing behavior in context (see Ramnero & Torneke, 2008, for an extensive discussion of the use of ABC terminology in a comprehensive approach to therapy). Antecedents (A) refer to the environmental events that precede behavior and make a particular type of behavior more or less likely to occur. These include events that directly elicit behavior (e.g., unconditioned and conditioned stimuli of classical conditioning), set the occasion for behavior to occur (e.g., discriminative stimuli of operant conditioning), and motivate a particular type of behavior (e.g., motivative operations of operant conditioning; see Michael, 1982). Behaviors (B), as noted above, refer to all activities of an individual. Consequences (C) refer to the environmental events that follow behavior and influence whether a particular type of behavior will be likely to occur again. These include events that either increase or decrease the probability of a behavior being emitted again in the future (technically referred to as reinforcers and punishers, respectively). Thus, they lead to the occurrence of B, which further leads to Cs that may reinforce or punish it.

The ABC unit is useful in two ways. First, the ABCs can be used to identify behavioral chains. Chains are sequences of behavior that, while ultimately controlled by environmental events, involve behaviors that build off of each other when (Bs) and (Cs) function as (As) for subsequent behavior (Follette et al., 2009; Linehan, 1993; see also Ferster & Skinner, 1957, for a more technical analysis of behavioral chains). For example, staying at home (B) in order to avoid reminders of a traumatic experience (C) can lead a person to experience depression due to a lack of pleasant activities (a second [C]), which (also functioning as an [A]) leads to excessive eating (B) to regulate one's mood (C) and its negative effects (other [Cs] including physical health problems and negative self-evaluations). The identification of chains can be particularly useful for developing efficient treatment strategies. Promoting changes in the early links of behavioral chains (e.g., preventing patterns of avoidance) can dramatically change their trajectory, resulting in large treatment gains for clients (e.g., elimination of health problems and negative self-evaluations).

Second, the ABCs can be used to identify functional classes of behavior (i.e., behaviors that have the same antecedents and consequences), which typically have much more treatment utility than topographical classes identified by formal properties. Functional classes of behavior are best defined by the environmental consequences influencing the behavior (Follette & Naugle, 2006). Two behaviors that are widely different in form (e.g., crying and laughing) may serve the same function (e.g., distracting from a conversation in a way that prevents an individual from having to admit a mistake) and thus belong in the same functional class. At the same time, two instances of the same topographical behavior (e.g., smiling) may serve completely different functions (e.g., demonstrating pleasure and avoiding feelings of anxiety) and thus belong to two separate functional classes. The functional analytic approach to clinical assessment thus focuses on the identification of functional classes of a client's behavior.

Within this approach, a therapist's task is to manipulate contextual variables in ways that lead a client to engage in more effective functional classes of behavior. Assessment guides and tests the success of these manipulations. Attempting to understand behavior in this way is obviously a complex task.

It would be impossible to identify all of the antecedents and consequences influencing all of the behavior in which an individual engages. Because of this, it is important to keep in mind Haynes and O'Brien's (2000) guideline of focusing on the identification of variables that are important to an individual's clinical presentation. Thus, while it entails a complex task, the functional analytic approach's focus on meaningful variables provides a framework for an efficient approach with many benefits (most of which are directly related to treatment utility).

## BENEFITS OF THE FUNCTIONAL ANALYTIC APPROACH

The most important benefit of the functional analytic approach to the assessment of retraumatized individuals is that it is able to clearly outline the variables that may contribute to traumatic stress. This allows the functional analytic approach to inform treatment in the most effective manner possible. Layne and colleagues (2006) argue that investigating "etiological and maintenance factors" is much more important than identifying "passive markers of risk" for retraumatization (pp. 236–237). According to their definition, passive markers of risk "typically include demographic characteristics, historical events, or preexisting and/or concurrent conditions that contribute to accurate identification of higher risk status but which do not have any demonstrable active influence, either direct or indirect, on targeted outcomes" (Layne et al., 2006, pp. 236–237).

A functional analytic approach agrees with Layne and colleagues' (2006) call to focus on identifying etiological and maintaining factors. However, it further suggests that many variables discussed in the trauma and retraumatization literatures as etiological and maintaining factors may instead be passive markers that do not fully describe the processes leading to traumatic stress. For example, it is known that low socioeconomic status increases risk for retraumatization, but the actual mechanisms that account for this relationship (e.g., higher rates of exposure to potentially traumatic events in low-income areas), though hypothesized, have not been clearly identified (Follette & Vijay, 2008). Another example is the "postwar interpersonal adversities" variable in Layne and colleagues' (2006) "Multiply Mediated Model of Postwar Adjustment" (p. 263). While "interpersonal adversities" suggests some of the mechanisms that might be involved in the generation of traumatic stress following exposure to a conflict, a functional analytic account would require a more in-depth process-related assessment that would better inform treatment. Identifying general interpersonal adversities for a client might suggest a broad social skills training approach. In contrast, a functional understanding of specific, idiographic variables such as a romantic partner who punishes talk about a traumatic event would suggest a more targeted intervention (e.g., couples work that teaches a romantic partner how to more effectively support emotional disclosures).

A closely related benefit of the functional analytic approach is that it is an iterative, self-correcting process (Follette, Naugle, & Linnerooth, 2000). Within this approach, the results and implications of an assessment are treated as a hypothesis that is tested through the implementation of an intervention following from it. If the resulting intervention is not successful, the assessment driving it is considered inaccurate or at least incomplete. In such cases, further assessment is made, and the cycle of assessment and treatment is repeated until successful. In using treatment results to determine the ultimate validity of an assessment, the functional analytic approach clearly promotes (and generally ensures) successful treatment.

Another benefit of the functional analytic approach is that it does not require a full assessment of the origins of traumatic stress. Even though gathering information about a client's history can be useful for a number of reasons (e.g., building rapport, understanding variables that have influenced client behavior in the past), a functional analytic approach primarily focuses on the variables influencing client behavior as it presently occurs. An important implication of this is that therapists do not necessarily need to conduct an intensive gathering of the trauma history of a client that can be both time consuming and unnecessarily distressing to a client. An even more important implication, though, is that the notion of functional autonomy suggests that behaviors that may have initially been emitted for one reason may now occur for a different reason in the current environment.

For example, a client with a history of retraumatization who engaged in substance abuse to manage his or her emotional responding may now be doing so in order to avoid withdrawal symptoms and as part of an addiction process that may also be supported by a dysfunctional social network. At the same time, this substance abuse may actually have begun as part of an attempt to cope with or eliminate intrusive recollections of a previous traumatic event. If a therapist focused on variables highlighting the initial function of the behavior (i.e., avoiding trauma recollections), the therapist may utilize a course of treatment (e.g., exposure to the traumatic event) that will ineffectively treat the client's current substance abuse. Given the substance abuse's current function of avoiding withdrawal symptoms, a treatment strategy that involves focusing on attenuating these symptoms may lead to a more successful course of treatment.

A functional analytic approach also allows clinicians to understand and address the broad distress seen in clients who have been retraumatized. It has been widely documented that PTSD is commonly comorbid with other psychological disorders and dysfunctions. When working within the popular empirically supported treatment (EST) (Chambless & Hollon, 1998; Chambless & Ollendick, 2001) framework, therapists typically apply therapies targeting the alleviation of specific disorders or symptom clusters (e.g., depression, anxiety, and posttraumatic stress). This can lead to a number of difficulties, including needing to determine which type of therapy to apply first, long courses of treatment, and potential resistance to treatments that were developed and empirically supported in samples of individuals with relatively simple presentations (e.g., limited in comorbidity or other major mental illness).

A functional analytic approach provides an alternative with conceptually clear benefits. Because a functional class of behaviors can operate in a wide variety of topographical settings, the large assortment of signs and symptoms of traumatic stress could be the result of a relatively small number of problematic functional classes of behavior. For example, a deficit in the functional class of intimacy building may lead a client with a trauma history to experience difficulty in engaging in a wide variety of relationships (e.g., romantic, familial; see Cordova & Scott, 2001, for a functional analytic approach to intimacy). If this is the case and a therapist can sufficiently identify the problematic functional class, a client's dysfunction can be addressed in a relatively expedient and straightforward manner. The therapist can consistently target a well-specified class of behaviors (e.g., a client's repertoire for intimacy building) for change.

Another clearly identifiable benefit of taking a functional analytic approach is related to its emphasis on constructional therapeutic activities. In the constructional approach, emphasis is placed on building new, functional repertoires based on a person's preexisting, partial repertoires rather than simply eliminating old, dysfunctional ones (Goldiamond, 1974; Hawkins, 1986). As a result, a functional analytic approach may be more likely than other approaches to directly lead to improvements in a client's quality of life (Follette, Linnerooth, & Ruckstuhl, 2001). Moreover, a constructional approach provides an ideal framework for the promotion of resiliency (i.e., the ability of individuals to "maintain relatively stable, healthy levels of psychological and physical functioning" despite exposure to a traumatic event; Bonanno, 2004, p. 20) and the prevention of further trauma exposure. Treatments for traumatic distress are, by definition, reactive (i.e., traumatic distress can only occur after exposure to a traumatic event). Although knowledge regarding resiliency can be successfully applied in a reactive manner, it seems that it would be preferable to apply this knowledge in a more proactive fashion.

A constructional approach would allow for this, especially if the notion of functional classes is fully understood. For example, if a weak social support network is a risk factor for retraumatization and a strong social support network is a contributor to resiliency, a constructional approach will focus on building a client's repertoire for building a strong social support network. Not only will this potentially aid in preventing the development of posttraumatic stress, it could also help prevent further exposure to traumatic events. Even more, the constructional approach would emphasize ways in which factors contributing to resiliency could be promoted prior to any exposure to a traumatic event as part of a prevention program. For example, knowledge regarding the importance of having a strong social support network in functionally reacting to a traumatic event will lead mental health professionals to work with at-risk individuals to help them develop social skills and social supports.

A final benefit of taking a functional analytic approach to retraumatization is that it avoids what is colloquially referred to as "blaming the victim." The functional analytic approach examines the behavior of an individual as it relates to the development of traumatic stress and the occurrence of retraumatization, but it does not reference any intentionality on the part of the traumatized individual which could be interpreted as "blaming" (Follette & Vijay, 2008). From a functional analytic perspective, behavior involves an interaction between an individual and his or her environment. An individual's behavior is a function of environmental variables; thus, an individual can behave in no other way than the way in which he or she behaves. In a therapeutic context, this releases a traumatized individual from culpability for both the occurrence of traumatic events and the development of traumatic stress. Just as a young girl who is unable to protect herself from abuse because she lacks a sufficient repertoire for doing so is not blamed for the occurrence of the abuse, a woman who is victimized because her learning history was insufficient for allowing her to prevent an assault is also not blamed for the occurrence of the assault.

At the same time, the functional analytic approach is extremely respectful and hopeful. From this perspective, there is no "broken" individual who cannot learn new behaviors. Individuals are held "response able" for their behavior, meaning that they are considered able to respond to their environment in more effective ways (Hayes, Strosahl, & Wilson, 1999, p. 103), particularly when provided with a more functional learning history during the course of therapy. Each individual is thus viewed in an idiographic manner that emphasizes building on the skills already present in the individual's repertoire, regardless of the individual's sophistication.

## THE FUNCTIONAL ANALYTIC APPROACH TO CLINICAL ASSESSMENT OF RETRAUMATIZED INDIVIDUALS

With awareness of the importance of the treatment utility of assessment and the two goals of the treatment of retraumatized individuals (reduction of psychological distress, which broadly fits in the category of improving quality of life, and the prevention of future retraumatization), the remainder of this chapter will identify a general approach to assessing individuals with a history of retraumatization. It will discuss the variables and processes that influence traumatic stress in important ways, and some treatment implications related to these variables will be provided. Even though discussion of these implications assumes some familiarity with a variety of treatment approaches and technologies, the body of this manuscript provides references designed to provide access to further understanding of these treatments (e.g., for an overview of a functional analytic behavioral approach to trauma treatment underlying all of the discussed implications, see Follette, Iverson, & Ford, 2009).

## The General Approach

At its core, the functional analytic approach to clinical assessment and intervention involves the strengthening and reduction (increasing and decreasing probability, respectively) of an individual's behaviors. The behaviors targeted for reduction (negative behaviors) coincide with the signs and symptoms of PTSD and CPTSD. The behaviors targeted for strengthening (positive behaviors) are often those that provide access to positive reinforcement and life satisfaction. Traditional measures of these constructs (e.g., clinical interviews, paper questionnaires) may serve as efficient identifiers of appropriate general behavioral targets in therapy. Briere and Spinazzola (2009) provide an excellent overview of evidence-based measures useful for identifying negative behaviors of a wide variety of forms (e.g., PTSD symptomatology, disrupted sense of self, cognitive disturbances, and dissociation). Measures helpful in the identification of positive behaviors include the Pleasant Events Schedule (PES) (MacPhillamy & Lewinsohn, 1982), the Valued Living Questionnaire (VLQ) (Wilson, Sandoz, Kitchens, & Roberts, 2010), and the World Health Organization Quality of Life Scale (WHOQOL) (see WHOQOL Group, 1998).

A typical clinical assessment uses these and similar measures to identify clusters of problem behaviors so that specific treatment technologies can be used to alleviate them. This mechanistic, syndromal approach can be ineffective, because in relying solely on topographical description, it fails to identify the functional relationships between a person's behavior and its antecedents and consequents. Although topographical assessment measures are quite useful in identifying and tracking behaviors of interest, they do not identify the functional relationship between positive behaviors, negative behaviors, and the environmental variables influencing them. For example, if a topographical measure determines that a client exhibits negative behaviors commonly diagnosed as PTSD, this does not mean that those behaviors are the result of a prior trauma. Similarly, if a person is exhibiting positive behavior, this does not mean that the person is optimally functioning in a way that will ameliorate or prevent subsequent development of negative behaviors. All of this suggests that topographical measures can be limited in their ultimate treatment utility. Thus, while initially using the same topographical measures as other approaches to assessment and treatment, the functional analytic approach begins where other approaches end.

The functional analytic approach identifies specific behavioral topographies as belonging to functional classes of behavior that are understood in terms of the ABCs and can be modified by behavioral processes (e.g., reinforcement, punishment, and extinction). As with any behavior, the behavior of an individual experiencing traumatic stress originates from the individual's learning history as it interacts with his or her current environment. The purpose and goal of functional analytic behavioral assessment and treatment are to (1) identify how the client's environment influences his or her behavior, (2) manipulate that environment in ways that will promote the client's engagement in more functional behavior in session, and (3) arrange contingencies such that the modifications in the client's in-session learning history will result in the generalization of a client's in-session gains to the outside environment.

Any client experiencing traumatic stress will certainly be unique (i.e., will have his or her unique individual learning history and current environment). This is particularly important to consider when an individual has been exposed to multiple traumatic events. At the same time, similar functional processes (the identification of which can sometimes be aided by topographical approaches) have been found to be important for many clients with a history of exposure to a traumatic event. Focusing on these common processes during assessment, especially its initial phases, will aid a clinician in efficiently developing a treatment approach. This chapter will discuss these common processes as they relate to individuals who have been retraumatized. Before doing so, though, it is important to consider the potential complexity of traumatic stress and its implications for assessment and treatment.

## The Complexity of Traumatic Stress

A distinction can be made between two general categories of traumatic stress: simple and complex. Simple traumatic stress does not imply that the stress is a simple matter for the client; it only indicates that the client's dysfunction is clearly related to exposure to a traumatic event. Simple traumatic stress primarily involves distress resulting from exposure to a traumatic event (e.g., fear stemming from re-experiencing the event) and behavior following from that distress (e.g., avoidance of trauma reminders). In contrast, complex traumatic stress is indirectly related to exposure to a traumatic event. It involves behavioral chains and functional classes of behavior that are so far removed from the exposure to the traumatic event that the connection between the two is no longer obvious (e.g., general problems in relating with others). An understanding of the processes involved in simple and complex traumatic stress allows for the delineation of a clear strategy for assessing individuals with a history of retraumatization.

As highlighted by Follette and colleagues (2009), Mowrer's (1960) two-factor theory serves as the basis for understanding the development and maintenance of simple traumatic stress. Simple traumatic stress first involves a classical (respondent) conditioning component. A previously neutral stimulus (referred to as a conditioned stimulus, CS) is associated with a naturally evocative stimulus (referred to as an unconditioned stimulus, US) through the learning history of individuals such that the CS comes to have the same function as the US. This means that previously neutral events can come to have important effects on an individual by evoking the same type of behavior that an individual might exhibit in other, more extreme circumstances. Exposure to a traumatic event, which involves an US that automatically elicits aversive fear responses without any specific learning history with regard to that stimulus, can result in the elicitation of similar behavior and aversive experiences by stimuli present during the initial trauma exposure (now functioning as CSs). For example, consider a hypothetical but typical case of a woman traumatized by a date rape. Through classical conditioning processes, a large number of stimuli may come to function as conditioned stimuli eliciting fear and other aspects of the date rape. Walking into the particular restaurant at which the woman dined with her date might elicit a sense of unease or fear in the client. Likewise, specific elements that were present for the client during the rape (e.g., a particular song playing on the radio) may elicit more aversive experiences, including re-experiencing the rape.

The second component of traumatic stress involves an operant conditioning component. When individuals are in the presence of aversive stimuli, behaviors that functionally eliminate those aversive stimuli are negatively reinforced (i.e., the behaviors are more likely to occur again in the future because they removed the aversive stimulus). For example, behavior that leads to the escape or avoidance of aversive fear responding is reinforced and thus likely to be emitted again in similar contexts. Through this process, individuals with a trauma history learn to escape and avoid conditioned stimuli that lead to aversive fear responses. This will prevent the classical conditioning processes of extinction (elimination) of fear responses to CSs that would occur if the client would experience the CS without the US. In other words, the fear-eliciting CSs will continue to function to elicit behaviors involving aversive experiences, because there is no opportunity for the individual to experience a new learning history with regard to those stimuli. In the example of the hypothetical date rape victim, the woman might never agree to eat at the restaurant or might turn off the radio when the song begins to play. This type of behavior will be negatively reinforced because the client escapes or avoids aversive experiences. At the same time, the functional connection between those CSs and the aversive experiences will not be broken (i.e., the restaurant and the song will continue to elicit fear responses).

In some cases, negative reinforcement of the avoidance of aversive CSs is relatively useful. If an individual's life demands and values do not require contact with the conditioned aversive stimuli, then there are no noticeable negative consequences to consistently avoiding those stimuli. In fact, the consequence is that the individual does not have to re-experience the aversive aspects of a trauma exposure, which can easily be viewed as a positive outcome. For example, if the woman in the hypothetical case moves to a different location and never has to have contact with the restaurant again, or the song that was playing on the radio during the rape is unpopular and not commonly played on the radio, the negative consequences of her avoidance of these stimuli will likely be negligible.

However, for individuals with a trauma history, this is often not the case. Even though patterns of behavior maintained by negative reinforcement may prevent an individual with a trauma history from having to contact aversive events, they may also excessively constrain the behavior of that individual. If a client is seeking services from a therapist or similar professional, it is likely that his or her patterns of behavior have become constrained in a dysfunctional manner through classical and operant conditioning processes. For example, through processes of generalization, the date rape may not just be associated with a specific restaurant but a type of restaurant (e.g., all pubs now function to elicit fear responses). If the woman avoids all restaurants of that type, this may limit her options for socializing. It may also limit her access to particular types of food that she enjoys eating. Similar examples related to the song playing during the rape can also be offered (e.g., avoidance of all music by a particular band, not listening to the radio at all, not going to concerts with friends).

Other less obvious but potentially more dysfunctional forms of generalization may also occur, further complicating assessment and treatment of clients with a trauma history. In some cases, clients avoid internal (e.g., emotional, cognitive) experiences associated with the trauma. For example, the woman may avoid dating because the common feeling of anxiety prior to a date is associated with the rape. Moreover, the client can come to avoid stimuli that have no physical similarity to the conditions present during the traumatic experience. According to Relational Frame Theory (RFT) (Hayes, Barnes-Holmes, & Roche, 2001; for a basic overview of RFT and its clinical implications see Blackledge, 2003; Torneke, 2010), individuals can develop arbitrary (i.e., not related to physical characteristics) verbal relations between stimuli. For example, the victim of a sexual assault may have experienced herself as being "helpless" during the assault, resulting in "helpless" taking on a meaning related to her traumatic experience. As a consequence, experiencing "helplessness" in any situation may lead to fear responses similar to those evoked by the original traumatic event. Not only that, the woman may begin to avoid situations she verbally identifies as being "helpless" (e.g., difficult work projects, interpersonal vulnerability), just as she avoids other aversive CSs.

Thus far, this discussion has focused solely on the fear responses and related escape and avoidance behaviors associated with simple traumatic stress. Clients may also exhibit other more complex dysfunctional changes in behavior following a traumatic event. Briere and Spinazzola's (2009) review of the trauma literature reveals that the sequelae of trauma exposure include cognitive disturbance, mood disturbance, somatization, identity disturbance, difficulties in emotion regulation, chronic interpersonal difficulties, dissociation, substance abuse, and dysfunctional tension reduction activities (p. 106). These complex forms of posttraumatic stress typically follow "exposure to severe stressors that (1) are repetitive and prolonged, (2) involve harm or abandonment by caregivers or other ostensibly responsible adults, and (3) occur at developmentally vulnerable times in the victim's life" (Ford & Courtois, 2009, p. 13). Most of these criteria are met in cases in which a person is exposed to multiple traumatic events. As a result, complex sequelae of trauma exposure are extremely important to assess and treat in an individual with a history of retraumatization.

There are a wide variety of potential functional explanations for the development of these complex dysfunctional outcomes of traumatic events. Because of the large variation in clinical presentations involving complex traumatic stress (especially when considering the wide variation in retraumatization an individual client might experience), it is impossible to discuss all possible cases. However, there seem to be commonalities that can be used to guide one's initial assessment and treatment strategies.

Overall, while the distinction between "simple" and "complex" traumatic stress is somewhat arbitrary, it is still useful because it reminds a therapist to consider an important (and perhaps primary) determinant of a client's treatment needs: the breadth of dysfunction he or she exhibits following exposure to a traumatic event. If a traumatic event has had a relatively constrained impact on an individual, the focus of treatment required for a good outcome is significantly more circumscribed than if the traumatic event has had a broad impact on the individual. A clear example of this is that a person who only engages in fear-related responses to a limited set of stimuli (e.g., a particular place) as a result of trauma will likely require therapy of a significantly lesser intensity than an individual who engages in fear responses to a wide variety of stimuli, has difficulty relating to others, abuses multiple substances, and so on.

Thus, as a general rule, increased complexity of dysfunction will require more in-depth assessment and treatment. This suggests a general approach to assessment and treatment that begins at a relatively simple level and becomes more in-depth with clients' exhibitions of greater levels and diversity of dysfunction. There are three progressive levels of assessment that should be examined, especially with increases in a client's level of dysfunction: (1) variables directly related to trauma exposure, (2) variables related to the client's internal environment, and (3) variables related to the client's external environment.

The remainder of this chapter will summarize these levels in order, including some of the important areas to be assessed at the various levels. Although this implies that these levels should be assessed in chronological order, therapists should consider that the following provides guidelines rather than rules. As such, therapists are free to alter this ordering when conducting assessment and treatment, particularly when there are obvious indicators of client dysfunction related to a later level. In addition, it would be impossible to outline all of the areas and variables that could be potentially important to assess at each level. As a result, the levels identify broad goals for assessment (rather than a specific checklist of assessment tasks) and highlight some important variables related to those goals. Furthermore, while most of the levels and specific variables are initially approached in terms of topography, all of them should be recognized as starting points for a functional discussion of the processes important to the assessment and treatment of complex traumatic stress.

There are two final caveats to employing this approach. First, a therapist should not become overwhelmed with attempts to complete a perfect assessment prior to starting treatment. While thorough assessment is important, treatment should not be delayed in order to ensure a full understanding of a client's behavior. The results of treatment will aid a therapist in revising treatment strategies or identifying further treatment targets. Second, therapists should consider that clients who demonstrate complex symptomatology following exposure to a traumatic event may have engaged in ineffective patterns of behavior prior to that event. For example, a client may have exhibited high levels of emotional reactivity and poor relationship skills prior to exposure to a traumatic event (issues such as these may even make individuals more vulnerable to developing traumatic stress). In such a case, the client's patterns of ineffective behavior may have only been exacerbated by exposure to a traumatic event or may even be completely unrelated. Because of this, it is important to assess a client's functioning prior to a trauma. Evidence of dysfunction prior to the trauma, particularly in cases of complex PTSD, is indicative of a need for a more intensive course of assessment and treatment.

## Variables Directly Related to Trauma Exposure

An understanding of Mowrer's two-factor theory leads to a relatively straightforward approach to treating PTSD that focuses on exposure to fear-eliciting CSs with the goal of eliminating the fear responses to those stimuli (see Foa, Hembree, & Rothbaum, 2007, for an overview of exposure therapy for PTSD). Theoretically, exposure therapies work by disrupting the learned association between a traumatic event (a US such as the date rape discussed above) and a stimulus that was connected to that event (a CS such as the restaurant at which the date occurred). This is achieved by having a client repeatedly contact the CS (the restaurant) in the absence of the US (the date rape). During this process, the client habituates to the CS, which functions to extinguish fear responses to that stimulus. As result, a stimulus (the restaurant) no longer functions as a CS (i.e., does not elicit aversive experiences that lead to psychological distress and avoidance). Similar strategies are used when attempted to disrupt arbitrary verbal relations, and the information provided in the present discussion is generally applicable to that approach as well. However, those processes are often explicated using different technical terms (see, for example, Hayes,

Strosahl, & Wilson, 1999; Luoma, Hayes, & Walser, 2007), and, for the sake of simplicity, they are not explicitly discussed here.

The Rescorla-Wagner model of classical conditioning (Rescorla & Wagner, 1972; Wagner & Rescorla, 1972) provides a simple framework for understanding the processes involved in exposure therapy. This framework is centered on the notion of associative strength. Associative strength is a description of how strongly a CS (the restaurant) is related to a US (the date rape); as associative strength increases, a CS comes to function more and more like the US (i.e., the restaurant would function more and more like a sexual assault). Increases in the correlated presentation of the CS and US (e.g., in the length of time they are presented together, in total number of times presented together) lead to an increase in associative strength. In contrast, processes such as extinction reduce associative strength. From this perspective, the association between a US and a CS that is learned during a traumatic experience is unlearned during exposure therapy (i.e., the functional connection between the restaurant and the date rape is eliminated).

Even though subsequent research and clinical application have consistently demonstrated the utility of the concept of associative strength, they have not been completely supportive of all of the initial claims of Rescorla and Wagner. The most important contradictory finding is the demonstration that US and CS associations are not eliminated during the process of extinction (Bouton, 2004). Classically conditioned responses often return after successful exposure therapy, suggesting that extinction (along with other classical conditioning processes) is context dependent (Bouton, 2004). This means that instead of eliminating a US and CS association, exposure therapy creates a new learning history that modifies the contexts in which the learned associations between stimuli affect behavior. For example, the connection between the restaurant and the date rape is not eliminated during exposure therapy. Exposure therapy instead creates a new learning history in which the restaurant has no connection to the date rape.

Given this, the initial level of assessment should be focused on ensuring that exposure therapy creates a learning history that sufficiently overcomes the fear-eliciting functions of conditioned stimuli. This means that a therapist's initial task is to completely assess the variables that function to elicit fear responses so that the therapist can conduct thorough exposure therapy. For clients with a history of retraumatization, many different variables may be important to assess. It can be extremely helpful for the therapist to collect assessment data regarding the traumatic events to which a client has been exposed (e.g., how many events, variety of events). As treatment progresses, it is important for the therapist to continue to assess the function of these variables (i.e., to determine if a client has habituated to a CS, to make sure that CSs no longer elicit fear responses in a variety of circumstances). It is also essential for the therapist to assess variables related to relapse of fear responses. The following provides a more detailed discussion of the variables that may be important to consider during these assessment activities.

## Complete Assessment of Fear-Evoking Stimuli

Of all of the activities at this level of assessment, it is most important to identify as completely as possible the set of stimuli that may have been present when a client was exposed to a traumatic event. All of these stimuli could function as CSs that elicit fear responses in the client. As a result, successful treatment may need to involve successful exposure to all of these stimuli. These stimuli can take a variety of forms, ranging from objects in one's physical environment to unobservable private experiences such as thoughts, feelings, and physiological states. Moreover, stimuli may have acquired fear-eliciting functions through processes of generalization. This expands the number of individual stimuli that could possibly function to elicit fear responses in a client, compounding the assessment activities of a therapist. Furthermore, when an individual has been retraumatized (i.e., exposed to multiple USs), generalization processes can become extremely complex and convoluted, preventing a therapist from identifying how particular stimuli came to function as fear-eliciting stimuli. As a result, when engaging in the assessment process, it is important to remember that a therapist should be driven by the principle of identifying variables that are important to a client's current clinical presentation. This principle provides four important reminders.

First, it is crucial to recognize that the actual function of a particular stimulus is more relevant than one's personal reaction to the stimulus. Even though a therapist (or the general populace) may assume that a specific stimulus should be particularly fear-eliciting (or not), this needs to be empirically tested. Second, there are likely to be many stimuli that were present during a traumatic event that do not function to elicit a client's fear responses (e.g., another passenger in the vehicle during a traumatic car accident, the blue jeans worn by the perpetrator of a sexual assault). It is unnecessary for a therapist to spend an excessive amount of time attempting to identify all of these stimuli. A therapist should conduct a thorough assessment to ensure sufficient exposure procedures, but with individuals with a history of retraumatization, there is a much greater opportunity to engage in excessive assessment activities.

Third, when assessing individuals who have been retraumatized, it may also be useful to identify commonalities among descriptions of traumatic events. As can be understood from the Rescorla-Wagner model, stimuli that were present during multiple traumatic events (e.g., physiological feelings of intoxication) are more likely to function as CSs that consistently elicit fear responses and should be given more attention during assessment and treatment. That does not mean only attending to this subset of stimuli, but it does mean that the most treatment gain in this domain will result from targeting them. Finally, given the goal of preventing further exposure to traumatic events, it is extremely important to consider the role particular fear-eliciting stimuli may serve in a client's future safety. Some stimuli (e.g., weapons) may effectively function as cues signaling danger to the client. If a client is able to successfully respond to these cues (e.g., by leaving the dangerous situation), it may be to the client's benefit to not completely eliminate his or her aversive responses to them. If, however, the client is unable to respond effectively (e.g., is overcome by fear in the presence of the stimuli), it may be of benefit to target these stimuli during exposure therapy.

It is important for a therapist to initially identify CSs to be targeted using exposure therapy, and it is also important that the therapist conduct ongoing assessment of the function of these stimuli during and following exposure (i.e., to test whether or not extinction has actually occurred). Both of these assessment activities can be achieved using the same methods. These methods focus on assessment of client behavior in two different settings: the therapy environment and the client's environment outside of therapy. Therapists have a wide variety of assessment methods available for assessing the function of stimuli as they are presented within the therapy environment (see Foa et al., 2007, for a description of methods commonly used for this purpose). The simplest of these is to ask the client to report his or her level of distress as a stimulus is presented. Therapists can also observe nonverbal behaviors of a client that suggest his or her level of distress (e.g., changes in facial expression). Another method is to directly measure the physiological responses of a client to a stimulus (e.g., heart rate, galvanic skin response; see Watson, Gaind, & Marks, 1972, for a discussion of physiological measurement of habituation). Finally, a therapist can assess the function of the client's other behavior with respect to the stimulus (e.g., avoidance of the stimulus by changing the topic). These methods can be used individually or in combination in order to assess the function of a stimulus.

With regard to the client's environment outside of therapy, therapists are generally forced to rely on a client's report regarding his or her behavior and the fear-evoking (or nonfear-evoking) functions of stimuli. The accuracy of this report may sometimes be questionable, because a client may not be able to sufficiently describe all of these variables, especially if he or she has experienced multiple traumas that lead to frequent experiences of anxiety and fear. Thus, a therapist must work with a client in-session to help him or her better describe his or her behavior and its function. A client may also be assisted in more accurately reporting these variables through the use of prompts and reporting aids (e.g., diary cards). Despite the possibility of inaccurate reporting by a client, this form of assessment should not be overlooked. In fact, it may be the most important form of assessment of client functioning, as it examines whether client's in-session gains during exposure therapy have generalized into meaningful changes in his or her everyday environment.

## Number and Types of Traumatic Events

Follette and Vijay (2008) identify prior exposure to psychological trauma as a potentially important assessment consideration. While noting that, by definition, retraumatization requires some type of previous trauma exposure, these authors emphasize that the importance of considering a client's prior trauma history goes well beyond a simple definitional issue. Research indicates that initial traumatization increases the likelihood of both exposure to a future traumatic event and development of psychological and medical disorders (Follette & Vijay, 2008; see, for example, Follette, Polusny, Bechtel, & Naugle, 1996). There is also evidence that multiple exposures to traumatic events can have a cumulative effect (see, for example, Follette et al., 1996). Overall, "it is hypothesized that responses to traumatic events can impact the way an individual responds to subsequent traumatic events, thus further increasing the risk of future traumatization" (Follette & Vijay, 2008, p. 588).

Although it is obvious that multiple trauma exposures can have an additive effect, it has yet to be determined whether serial (i.e., multiple exposures to the same type of traumatic event) and sequential (i.e., exposure to multiple traumatic events of different types) traumas have differential impacts that are meaningful for clinical work. The following presents some theoretically driven hypotheses regarding possible important differences between these two types of trauma history. These ideas can be used in conjunction with information related to other topics (e.g., associative strength, the breadth of fear-eliciting stimuli) to inform one's assessment and treatment. However, they have not been empirically tested and should thus be used tentatively when one is working with a client.

Serial trauma may lead to particularly strong fear responses to a limited number of stimuli that were present during all of the traumatic events. This may mean that exposure treatments need to be extended well beyond their normal course of time in order for successful habituation and extinction to occur. At the same time, the commonalities among serial traumas may overshadow the importance of other stimuli that were not present during all of the traumas. Focusing on the commonalities and failing to include a specific CS during exposure exercises may leave a client prone to relapse. For example, if a client has experienced repeated sexual assaults, focusing on the commonalities (e.g., that the perpetrator was male, that the assaults all occurred at night) may result in the therapist overlooking an important stimulus (e.g., the scent of a cologne one of the perpetrators was wearing) while preparing for exposure therapy. If the specific scent is contacted by the client following successful exposure to the other stimuli, it may lead the client to experience an acute fear response and a return of fear responses to other CSs (even if those responses were successfully extinguished during exposure therapy). For this reason, it is especially important to identify all of the stimuli that function to elicit fear responses in individuals with a trauma history.

In contrast, individuals with a history of sequential trauma may require less intense levels of exposure therapy to achieve habituation and extinction in relation to specific fear-eliciting stimuli. In addition, it may be important to consider the interaction between different types of trauma when providing exposure therapy following sequential traumas. That the traumas were of different types does not mean that they could not share stimuli that function to elicit fear responding (e.g., loud noises and collapsed buildings in both combat and a natural disaster). Identification of these commonalities can be used to streamline the exposure process. At the same time, it should be considered that sequential trauma may be more difficult to treat with exposure (i.e., exposure treatment may take longer) because of the extended network of stimuli that all elicit fear responses.

### Relapse-Related Processes

It is common for fear responses to CSs to reappear following successful exposure therapy for any anxiety disorder, a phenomenon referred to as "return of fear" (ROF) (Boschen, Neumann, & Waters, 2009, p. 90; see Boschen and colleagues for a more thorough discussion of ROF including some helpful treatment recommendations). There are four types of circumstances that have been found to lead to ROF: spontaneous recovery, renewal, reinstatement, and reacquisition (Boschen, Neumann, & Waters, 2009; Bouton, 2004). Spontaneous recovery occurs when a previously extinguished fear response returns after fear-eliciting stimuli (whether CSs or USs) have not been contacted for a period of time. This type of ROF seems most likely to occur in cases where an individual is being treated for sequential trauma. Although fear responses to a particular CS (e.g., a stimulus associated with a car accident) may have been extinguished during past exposure therapy, they may return as treatment focuses on CSs associated with another trauma (e.g., a sexual assault). This could ultimately lead to a pattern in which exposure therapy is repeated multiple times in response to spontaneous recovery. To prevent this, a therapist should be aware of client responses to all possible CSs that have been identified during prior assessment, regardless of which are currently being targeted during exposure therapy. This will allow a therapist to take measures to prevent spontaneous recovery by conducting booster exposure sessions.

Each of the other three potential sources of ROF leads to additional recommendations. Renewal occurs when a previously extinguished fear response returns when a CS is presented in a context in which exposure did not occur. This source of relapse is especially important to consider when one is solely relying on imaginal exposure in the therapy room. Contacting CSs outside of the therapy environment can lead to a relapse despite great success in the therapy room. The therapist should thus monitor (and potentially program for) client contact with CSs outside of therapeutic environments in order to prevent ROF. Reinstatement occurs when a previously extinguished fear response returns following further exposure to a US (without the CS present). This source of relapse is very pertinent to individuals who have been retraumatized or are at risk for serial retraumatization. A client may begin to exhibit fear responses to a CS that was successfully targeted in previous exposure therapy solely on the basis of contacting a US again. For example, a sexual assault victim's fear response to dark alleys (the location of a previous assault) that was eliminated with exposure therapy may return when the client is assaulted again in an unrelated location (e.g., her home). Thus, therapists should continue to assess for ROF in clients, particularly after additional exposures to traumatic events. Finally, reacquisition occurs when a US and CS are again experienced in conjunction with each other. For example, the sexual assault victim may be assaulted (US) again in the same alley (CS). This is the most obvious possible source of relapse. Similar to reinstatement, a therapist should closely assess a client's reactions to CSs following new instances of trauma in order to be able to curb relapse processes.

Though technically not a relapse or ROF process, topographically similar outcomes (i.e., continued fear responding to CSs following the completion of an exposure therapy protocol) can be observed when inadequate levels of exposure result in a failure to overcome the learned associations between USs and CSs. This may represent a problem of inaccurate assessment of a client's reactions to stimuli during exposure, and it may be indicative of another iatrogenic process. Evidence suggests that many therapists choose alternative therapeutic methods in order to avoid subjecting clients to perceived exacerbations of symptoms during exposure, even when they should be aware of the overall utility of exposure therapy (Becker, Zayfert, & Anderson, 2004). It seems plausible that a similar process may occur when therapists are actually conducting exposure therapy; therapists may stop conducting exposure therapy in the moment as a result of discomfort with subjecting a client to an aversive experience. Given the traumatic nature of PTSD, exposure therapy can be extremely aversive to both the therapist and the client. As a result, therapists who generally focus on alleviating suffering may demonstrate difficulty appropriately conducting exposure when a client is perceived to be suffering unnecessarily.

Inadequate levels of exposure can result in iatrogenic effects for a client. Instead of extinguishing a client's fear responses to a CS, ending an exposure procedure too early (i.e., before habituation has occurred) can function to strengthen the US and CS association and negatively reinforce a client's functional escape behavior. Thus, it is important for therapists to consider their potential role when a client does not appear to be benefitting from the therapy (particularly by assessing their willingness to fully participate in exposure therapy sessions).

## Variables Related to Clients' Internal Environment

If a client exhibits dysfunction beyond simple fear and avoidance patterns or if exposure therapy does not seem to be successful in remediating a client's dysfunction and suffering, it is likely that other, more complex dysfunctional processes are occurring. For example, a client may be engaging in behavior that prevents the extinction of fear responses, or the client may be engaging in patterns of behavior that prevent generalization of treatment gains. A client may also be exhibiting psychological suffering that does not seem to be directly related to the trauma exposure (e.g., depression). Because of this, a therapist should extend the scope of his or her assessment and treatment activities. The second level of assessment of retraumatized individuals should focus on variables that are directly related to the client's internal environment (i.e., the client's private experience of the world including thoughts and feelings). The primary goal at this level of assessment is to identify barriers to the client's successful functioning. Even though these barriers can come in many forms, there are three particular areas that are important to consider: (1) deficits in emotion regulation skills, (2) experiential avoidance, and (3) disruptions in one's sense of self.

## Deficits in Emotion Regulation Skills

It is quite common for clients with traumatic stress to exhibit deficits in their abilities to regulate their own emotional states (Follette, Iverson, & Ford, 2009). For example, a client may become overwhelmed when discussing his or her trauma history, making it difficult to conduct assessment and treatment activities. In contrast, a different client may be able to participate effectively in session but may not generalize gains from therapy sessions to his or her everyday environment by continuing to avoid particular places because he or she becomes easily overwhelmed when not in the therapist's presence. The work of Linehan (1993) has developed a set of skills that can be taught to clients, allowing them to effectively engage their environments. In particular, enacting distress tolerance and emotion regulation skills (Linehan, 1993) can be a particularly effective way to react to distressing events. Thus, a therapist should assess a client's abilities to regulate his or her own emotions, allowing a therapist to address these deficits with direct skills training. While conducting treatment with individuals with a history of retraumatization, therapists should watch for markers indicating that the client has become emotionally dysregulated either outside (e.g., reports of becoming overwhelmed in a stressful situation) or inside (e.g. dissociating when asked about a traumatic experience) of session. Follette and colleagues (2009) and Linehan (1993) offer further guidance for the assessment and training of distress tolerance and emotion regulation skills.

## Experiential Avoidance

Experiential avoidance, a consistent pattern of behaviors involving the avoidance of aversive stimuli, is an important contributor to traumatic stress

(Follette, Iverson, & Ford, 2009). Avoidance can be adaptive in that it can prevent an individual from experiencing distress related to a traumatic event. In contrast, experiential avoidance refers to a pervasive pattern of behavior in which this functional avoidance is generalized to other contexts in a dysfunctional manner (Hayes, Strosahl, & Wilson, 1999). This may explain a wide variety of dysfunctional behaviors in individuals who have been exposed to a traumatic event. For example, Polusny, Rosenthal, Aban, and Follette's (2004) research on sexually victimized adolescents indicated that victimization contributed to greater levels of experiential avoidance, which mediated increased levels of psychological distress. The effects of experiential avoidance can take many different forms. Traumatized individuals may begin to engage in behaviors including substance use and self-injury in order to escape or avoid experiencing aversive thoughts and feelings related to the traumatic events. These same behaviors may begin to be emitted in other contexts involving other aversive stimuli that are unrelated to the trauma. For example, substance abuse may be used to escape relationship stressors or physical pain.

Experiential avoidance represents a functional class of behaviors. As long as the functional class continues to be maintained through negative reinforcement processes, the behaviors will gain strength and may be emitted in an increasingly broad set of circumstances. It is especially interesting to note how this class of behaviors may contribute to further instances of retraumatization. For example, an individual who commonly dissociates when experiencing discomfort may be more likely to be victimized by others as a result of an acute decrease in the ability to assess, avoid, and escape dangerous social situations. Similar effects may be seen if one abuses substances to control private experiences. In addition, an individual's apparent complacency regarding an abusive situation may result from experiential avoidance. For example, a person may not discuss the situation with others (e.g., close friends, a therapist) in order avoid to negative affective experiences. Moreover, a person may actively choose to remain in an abusive environment in order to avoid aversive experiences outside of the environment, whether real or imagined (e.g., acute increases in interpersonal conflict or abuse, difficulty in living independently).

When working with a client with a history of retraumatization, it is important to assess for patterns of experiential avoidance. The primary focus of this evaluation is the identification of patterns that unnecessarily limit his or her activities (e.g., not leaving the house), have directly harmful results (e.g., substance dependence), or otherwise contribute to dysfunctional chains of behavior. This process will identify behaviors that can be directly targeted for change. Overall, strategies for treating experiential avoidance should target increasing a client's acceptance of aversive experiences in the service of his or her more successful functioning (Follette, Iverson, & Ford, 2009; Hayes, Strosahl, & Wilson, 1999). The goal of treatment is not to teach clients acceptance for the sake of acceptance, especially given that some avoidance-driven behaviors can be very functional. A therapist should work with a client to increase his or her willingness to contact aversive experiences that are unavoidable given his or her values (Follette, Iverson, & Ford, 2009; Hayes, Strosahl, & Wilson, 1999). For example, a client who desires to have close relationships must be willing to experience interpersonal vulnerability, and a client who wants to have success in exposure therapy must be willing to interact with fear-eliciting stimuli.

## Sense of Self

There have been extensive discussions of sense of self from a functional analytic perspective (see Hayes, 1984, 1995; Kohlenberg & Tsai, 1991, pp. 125–168; Kohlenberg, Tsai, Kanter, & Parker, 2009; Torneke, 2010, pp. 106–112). From this perspective, one extremely important component of a person's sense of self is the verbal self-concept that can be referred to as the "conceptualized self" (Hayes, 1995, p. 95). The conceptualized self includes perceptions, descriptions, and evaluations of oneself that equate the "I" with some characteristic (e.g., "I am depressed" implies that that the "I" somehow embodies "depression"; see Hayes et al., 2001, for further discussion of relational frames of coordination). Thus, these self statements (or "I" statements) are an important indicator of and contributor to one's sense of self.

An individual's self statements are particularly important because they can influence or direct behavior. Statements identifying one's feelings, goals, needs, wants, and desires can imply how others are to behave with respect to them (see Skinner's, 1957, discussion of verbal mands). In the same way, self statements can function as rules that identify both the form and goals of that individual's activities (see Hayes, Zettle, & Rosenfarb, 1989). In addition to this, self statements can function to elicit emotional responses. Statements such as "I am depressed" can contribute to feelings of depression. Because self statements have such an important function, dysfunctional processes related to them (i.e., disturbances in an individual's sense of self) can have a significant impact on an individual's behavior.

Retraumatized individuals often exhibit and report disruptions in sense of self. One common disruption in this population is a sense of worthlessness (e.g., "I am worthless"). This can have many specific dysfunctional effects. For example, calling oneself "worthless" can lead one to have additional feelings of worthlessness. In addition, this label may constrict one's behavior; identifying oneself as "worthless" can negatively impact one's behavior (e.g., through the form of a rule such as "I'm worthless so I shouldn't even try."). Furthermore, attempts to directly control or suppress thoughts and feelings of worthlessness can actually lead to an increase in their frequency and intensity (Hayes, Strosahl, & Wilson, 1999; Luoma, Hayes, & Walser, 2007). Finally, expressing feelings of worthlessness can directly impact one's interactions with others. This may invite others to treat one as "worthless" (e.g., in an abusive manner). Alternatively, this may result in others attempting to change those feelings (which may, in turn, result in them labeling the traumatized individual as "overdramatic" or "manipulative").

There are many potential sources of disruptions in sense of self. One possible source is a change in a person's overt behavior. According to Bem's (1967, 1972) self-perception theory, one's behavior has an important influence on one's self statements. For example, a man who behaves in a "worthless" manner following exposure to a natural disaster (e.g., does not perform well at work, has feelings of worthlessness) is likely to perceive (i.e., describe and ultimately conceptualize) himself as "worthless."

A second possible source of disruption is the excessive influence of a person's social community on his or her self statements (see "The Social Community" below for additional discussion of the influence of one's social community). Consider a case involving a verbally abusive romantic partner. The abusive partner may provide "descriptions" of the abused partner (e.g., "You're worthless."). If the abusive partner consistently prompts and reinforces the abused partner for ascribing to this quality to himself or herself (e.g., "I'm worthless."), that abused partner may generalize that self-description to a number of contexts. In these cases, an individual is emitting verbal behavior that is under excessive control from the social community. When this occurs, an individual's self statements are not being influenced by other variables (e.g., one's behavior, private experiences, physical stimuli in the environment). Such a context can also lead to a topographically different disruption in sense of self commonly described as feeling as if one does not know who he or she is.

The theoretical model underlying Acceptance and Commitment Therapy (ACT) (Hayes, Strosahl, & Wilson, 1999; see also Luoma, Hayes, & Walser, 2007; Torneke, 2010) suggests yet another alternative: psychological distress resulting from disruptions in one's sense of self primarily results from excessive and inflexible engagement with one's conceptualized self. According to this model, disruptions arise when a person is "cognitively fused" with the content of self statements (Hayes, Strosahl, & Wilson, 1999, p. 72). This means that a person relates to the self statements as if they are literal, true descriptions of the world rather than verbal descriptions that should be believed based on their utility in effectively guiding one's behavior (i.e., the difference between thinking "I am worthless" versus "I am having the thought that I am worthless"; see Hayes, Strosahl, & Wilson, 1999, and Luoma, Hayes, & Walser, 2007, for additional discussions including how cognitive fusion can be the source of other forms of dysfunction).

In assessing and treating retraumatized individuals with disruptions in sense of self, it may be important to identify the source of those disruptions. Different sources of disruption imply a need for different treatment strategies, even though all of the strategies are ultimately focused on increasing the frequency of an individual's engagement in functional overt behavior. Disruptions related to changes in overt behavior suggest a treatment focused on direct behavior change (e.g., contingency management). Disruptions related to interpersonal processes suggest treatment targeted at improving a client's ability to more accurately label his or her experience (e.g., Functional Analytic Psychotherapy, FAP) (Kohlenberg & Tsai, 1991; Tsai et al., 2008). Disruptions related to excessive cognitive fusion suggest treatment targeted at increasing a client's flexibility in relating to "I" statements (e.g., ACT).

The best strategy for making this determination is to carefully observe the content and function of a client's self statements. Disruptions in sense of self resulting from changes in overt behavior are likely to be accompanied by descriptions of those changes. Clients who have difficulty independently labeling their experience are likely to demonstrate such difficulties in session by either reporting an inability to label their experiences or by reporting experiences that are grossly different than what the therapist might expect under the current circumstances. Finally, excessive cognitive fusion can be identified when negative self evaluations function to limit or constrict a person's behavioral repertoires.

## Variables Related to Clients' External Environment

Traumatic stress may be initiated and maintained by variables beyond those found in an individual's internal environment. External variables can impact the client in many ways as they provide the contingencies that set the occasion for and shape behavior. As was suggested in some of the above analyses, an individual's internal environment is influenced by variables in his or her external environment. A focus on external variables is preferable to an analysis of internal variables, because they can be directly observed and manipulated by the therapist (see Hayes & Brownstein, 1986). Thus, the variables in a client's external environment should also be analyzed during assessment, particularly when a client is exhibiting complex forms of traumatic stress (see Follette, Alexander, & Follette, 1991, for an example of the empirical identification of external environmental factors that influence adjustment to and response to treatment of childhood sexual abuse). The role of a client's external environment in the development and maintenance of complex traumatic stress can be extremely complex. However, for the sake of simplicity, these variables can be organized into two broad areas: the client's social community and other contingencies influencing a client's behavior.

As repeatedly mentioned, one important aspect of the functional analytic approach is that it focuses on the identification of variables that are meaningful and manipulable. This latter criterion can be difficult to achieve at the level of the external environment. For example, a therapist does not have the ability to manipulate a client's entire social environment so that it reacts to the client more effectively. The therapist also does not have the resources to directly change other important environmental factors that may contribute to a client's vulnerability to experiencing a trauma; the therapist cannot change the crime rates in a client's neighborhood. In some cases, though, these types of changes are possible on a smaller scale. Family and couples therapy can be used to help a client's social community react to him or her more effectively, and a therapist can coach and aid a client in obtaining social services that will allow him or her to move to a different neighborhood. Despite this, it is generally more beneficial and efficient to work with the client to change his or her behavioral repertoire so that he or she is better able to adapt to his or her environment (particularly as it changes). As a result, this discussion will primarily focus on variables important in shaping more effective client repertoires.

## The Social Community

An individual's social community (referred to in technical behavioral terms as the *verbal community*; Skinner, 1957) includes all of the individuals shaping a person's repertoire for communicating and interacting with others. The social community plays an extremely important role in shaping an individual's behavior throughout his or her life, including contributing to the development and maintenance of traumatic stress. Any social behavior of an individual is controlled by two interacting sources.

The first source is the developmental learning history through which an individual develops a repertoire for relating to others. Skinner (1945) provides an overview of the processes whereby individuals learn how to identify their private experiences in ways that will be effective in the environment. These processes primarily involve the social community reacting to the information available in the current environment (e.g., the events that occurred, the behavior of the individual) and providing cues that help an individual both label his or her experience and, ultimately, behave in socially functional ways (i.e., in ways that prompt the social community to effectively react). If an immediate social community (e.g., parents) does not react to a child in a way reflective of the general social community, the child may not learn to effectively interact in his or her social environment.

Consider a hypothetical case of a boy who is traumatized for many years by the actions of his alcoholic father who physically abused the boy (and the boy's mother) but only while drunk. One possible consequence of this learning history is that the boy will perceive close relationships as a context for unpredictable behavior. This may detrimentally affect his ability to evaluate future relationships. Moreover, the boy may have been affected by the way his mother reacted in the situation. To prevent further abuse, she may have consistently punished the boy's attempts at discussing the effects of the abuse on him (e.g., by ignoring them, by directly telling the boy to not talk about it) while encouraging the boy to appease his father. This may have limited the boy's intimacy-building repertoire, inadvertently hampering his ability to form relationships in adulthood. Consider also a hypothetical case of a young girl who is secretly molested by her grandfather on multiple occasions.

Her grandfather might tell her that he loves her while molesting her, and her parents are also likely to make statements to her that "Grandpa loves you." As a result, a child might not appropriately learn the concept of "love"—the behavior it involves and the conditions under which you might identify love for another person. She might associate "love" with sexual contact, confusion about intimate feelings, or patterns of abuse.

The second source of social behavior is the social contingencies that are directly influencing an individual's behavior in his or her current environment. These contingences are supplied by an individual's immediate social community and can be just as impactful as developmental learning history. An individual is more likely to be prone to the influence of others when he or she is unable to independently label his or her reactions. In the case of traumatic events, an individual lacks a learning history involving the labeling of reactions to those events and is more reliant on (or at the very least has no basis for disagreement with) the social community. When the social community suggests that the individual should be feeling distress of some form, whether directly through verbal statements (e.g., "That must have been so horrible") or indirectly through nonverbal behavior (e.g., crying when talking to the individual), the individual is more likely to label and experience those feelings of distress.

Even though the reactions of the social community can operate in this dysfunctional manner, this discussion should not be taken to imply that social interactions regarding the aversive aspects of traumatic events are always iatrogenic. In fact, traumatic distress can be characterized by feelings of social isolation, which are often a direct result from a lack of appropriate social support. Follette and Naugle (2006) discuss a hypothetical example of this type involving a female sexual assault victim whose husband relates to her in a different dysfunctional manner; he avoids talking to her about the rape and disagrees with her accurate labels of her private experience (e.g., tells her she should not feel ashamed). The same negative reinforcement processes that maintain an individual's avoidance of trauma cues can operate with regard to the family and friends of a traumatized individual who may find it aversive to be reminded of their loved one's trauma experience. This becomes problematic when it prevents an individual from processing the trauma and engaging in more effective patterns of behavior (colloquially referred to as accepting and moving past the trauma).

It is even more problematic, though, when it hampers the continuation of intimacy. For example, the social community's avoidance of interacting with a traumatized individual can prevent that individual from behaving in vulnerable, intimate ways related (e.g., talking about the experience) or unrelated (e.g., sitting in "comfortable silence") to the trauma. An individual's feeling of social isolation can become compounded when the social community behaves in ways that function to actively punish intimacy. For example, many reactions of the social community, often intended to be supportive or helpful (e.g., the husband telling his wife she has no reason to feel ashamed), can make an individual feel as if he or she is not being understood.

When assessing a client's ability to interact with his or her social community, a therapist can rely on many methods. In some cases, a therapist can have direct access to a client's social community (e.g., by having family members or romantic partners attend a therapy session). Observation of the contingencies provided by this community can be beneficial to the therapist. However, as mentioned above, the therapist often cannot observe or directly influence the broader social community. As a result, greater emphasis should be placed on assessing the client's repertoire for effectively behaving in ways he or she values. When conducting such an assessment, a therapist's primary goal should be the identification of social deficits and strengths in a client's current repertoire. Even though a client's developmental history may be important, greater focus should be placed on the client's current level of functioning. Callaghan (2006) outlines an excellent systematic approach for assessing a client's social repertoires in preparation for interpersonally based interventions (e.g., FAP). This approach relies both on semistructured interviews as well as direct observation of the client in therapy sessions.

## Other Contingencies

There are many environmental factors influencing an individual's behavior. Some of these factors may be obvious (e.g., economic gain functioning as a reinforcer, physical limitations preventing engagement in particular kinds of behavior). Others may be less obvious (e.g., nuanced forms of social praise, a long-term history of punishment for variability in one's behavior). Regardless of how easy they are to detect, contingencies in the environment are always influencing the behavior of all people, including clients. Because of this, therapists should always investigate how a client's behavior is influenced by his or her broader environment. A discussion of two examples, contingencies that may reinforce a person for exhibiting traumatic stress and factors that can contribute to a person remaining in a traumatizing environment, will highlight how the broader environment can be included in a functional analytic assessment of an individual with a history of retraumatization.

Some environments directly reinforce a person for dysfunctional behavior. For example, there can be functional reinforcers for malingering. A therapist should certainly be aware of any potential reasons for a client to misrepresent his or her current level of functioning (e.g., release from work requirements, increased social or economic support from others). A functional analytic behavioral approach has the advantage of being nonjudgmental while identifying such functions. Behaviors that could be considered "lying" and "deceiving" are, like any other behavior, merely influenced by functional variables.

A more interesting issue to consider, though, is the potential for other situations in which an individual might be compensated for continuing to have what could be considered "real symptoms." The same contingencies that may cause some to behave in a deceptive manner can also reinforce dysfunction in the form of psychological symptoms. For example, monetary compensation may contribute to an individual's debilitating flashbacks, and escape from spousal abuse can reinforce depressive symptoms. This should not be interpreted as a suggestion that it is in any way the client's intention that he or she continues to behave dysfunctionally following a traumatic event. Just as a client should not be blamed for being traumatized, he or she should not be blamed for behaving "dysfunctionally." The point is that in a functional analytic behavioral approach, all possibilities should be considered. A therapist should investigate any hypotheses related to processes whereby a client's dysfunctional behavior is being maintained by the environment.

A similar (i.e., empirical, nonjudgmental) approach should be taken when clients continue to remain in traumatizing environments. Examples of this are common: an individual is repeatedly victimized by various romantic partners, a person is exposed to combat trauma after choosing to perform another tour of duty, and the list could be extended further. These patterns are also the results of client behavior that is subject to a functional analysis. Many of the issues discussed above are pertinent to this topic. For example, a person retraumatized during combat may choose to remain in the military because of a self-concept related to being a soldier. In addition, experiential avoidance, through a fear of leaving a familiar and predictable situation, may have a similar result (e.g., the soldier may know how to behave in a war zone but struggles when at home with his or her family). Finally, people are likely to return to a social community that supports their struggle or provides intimacy, even if the conditions may be dangerous (e.g., soldiers may relate well to other soldiers but not to civilians who have not experienced the stressors of war). A thorough analysis of those issues may provide a therapist with an opportunity to prevent a client from being retraumatized further.

Other factors should also be explored when attempting to determine why a person continues to remain in a traumatic environment. Changing one's environment can be very difficult, and there may be obvious barriers that prevent a person from leaving an environment where trauma is likely. Examples of such barriers include economic reliance on a particular environment and specific skills deficits. A therapist can assess these barriers relatively directly by asking a client why they continue to remain in the particular environment. This will allow a straightforward treatment plan that involves directly removing the barriers through problem solving and skills coaching.

## CONCLUSION

Traumatic stress can be extremely complex, particularly in circumstances in which retraumatization has occurred. This chapter has outlined a functional analytic approach to assessment that allows a therapist to approach this complexity in a flexible manner. This flexibility of the functional analytic approach can contribute to the effective treatment of individuals with a history of retraumatization in important ways. However, this potential contribution still needs to be evaluated. The approach presented in this chapter largely relies on empirically supported principles and specific research findings, and therapists and researchers in the area of trauma are encouraged to test the actual utility of this approach.

## REFERENCES

American Psychiatric Association. (2000). *Diagnostic and statistical manual of mental disorders* (4th ed.). Washington, DC: Author.

American Psychiatric Association. (2010). *Posttraumatic stress disorder.* Retrieved June 20, 2010, http://www.dsm5.org/ProposedRevisions/Pages/proposedrevision.aspx?rid=165

Becker, C. B., Zayfert, C., & Anderson, E. (2004). A survey of psychologists' attitudes towards and utilization of exposure therapy for PTSD. *Behaviour Research and Therapy, 42,* 277–292.

Bem, D. J. (1967). Self-perception: An alternative interpretation of cognitive dissonance phenomena. *Psychological Review, 74,* 183–200.

Bem, D. J. (1972). Self-perception theory. In L. Berkowitz (Ed.), *Advances in experimental social psychology* (Vol. 6, pp. 1–62). San Diego, CA: Academic Press.

Blackledge, J. T. (2003). An introduction to relational frame theory: Basics and applications. *The Behavior Analyst Today, 3,* 421–433.

Bonanno, G. A. (2004). Loss, trauma, and human resilience: Have we underestimated the human capacity to thrive after extremely aversive events? *American Psychologist, 59,* 20–28.

Boschen, M. J., Neumann, D. L., & Waters, A. M. (2009). Relapse of successfully treated anxiety and fear: Theoretical issues and recommendations for clinical practice. *Australian and New Zealand Journal of Psychiatry, 43,* 89–100.

Bouton, M. E. (2004). Context and behavioral processes in extinction. *Learning and Memory, 11,* 485–494.

Briere, J., & Spinazzola, J. (2009). Assessment of the sequelae of complex trauma. In C. A. Courtois, & J. D. Ford (Eds.), *Treating complex traumatic stress: An evidence-based guide* (pp. 104–123). New York: Guilford Press.

Callaghan, G. M. (2006). The functional idiographic assessment template (FIAT) system: For use with interpersonally-based interventions including functional analytic psychotherapy (FAP) and FAP-enhanced treatments. *The Behavior Analyst Today, 7,* 357–398.

Chambless, D. L., & Hollon, S. D. (1998). Defining empirically supported therapies. *Journal of Clinical and Consulting Psychology, 66,* 7–18.

Chambless, D. L., & Ollendick, T. H. (2001). Empirically supported psychological interventions: Controversies and evidence. *Annual Review of Psychology, 52,* 685–716.

Cordova, J. V., & Scott, R. L. (2001). Intimacy: A behavioral interpretation. *The Behavior Analyst, 24,* 75–86.

Courtois, C. A. (2008). Complex trauma, complex reactions: Assessment and treatment. *Psychological Trauma: Theory, Research, Practice, and Policy*, *8*, 86–100.

Ferster, C. B., & Skinner, B. F. (1957). *Schedules of reinforcement*. New York: Appleton-Century-Crofts.

Foa, E. B., Hembree, E. A., & Rothbaum, B. O. (2007). *Prolonged exposure therapy for PTSD: Emotional processing of traumatic experiences: Therapist guide*. New York: Oxford University Press.

Follette, V. M., Alexander, P. C., & Follette, W. C. (1991). Individual predictors of outcome in group treatment for incest survivors. *Journal of Consulting and Clinical Psychology*, *59*, 150–159.

Follette, V. M., Iverson, K. M., & Ford J. D. (2009). Contextual behavior trauma therapy. In C. A. Courtois, & J. D. Ford (Eds.), *Treating complex traumatic stress: An evidence-based guide* (pp. 264–285). New York: Guilford Press.

Follette, V. M., Polusny, M. A., Bechtle, A. E., & Naugle, A. E. (1996). Cumulative trauma: The impact of child sexual abuse, adult sexual assault, and spouse abuse. *Journal of Traumatic Stress*, *9*, 25–35.

Follette, V. M., & Vijay, A. (2008). Retraumatization. In G. Reyes, J. D. Elhai, & J. D. Ford (Eds.), *Encyclopedia of psychological trauma* (pp. 586–589). Hoboken, NJ: Wiley.

Follette, W. C., Linnerooth, P. J. N., & Ruckstuhl, L. E. (2001). Positive psychology: A clinical behavior analytic perspective. *Journal of Humanistic Psychology*, *41*, 102–134.

Follette, W. C., & Naugle, A. E. (2006). Functional analytic clinical assessment in trauma treatment. In V. M. Follette, & J. I. Ruzek (Eds.), *Cognitive-behavioral therapies for trauma* (2nd ed., pp. 17–33). New York: Guilford Press.

Follette, W. C., Naugle, A. E., & Linnerooth, P. J. N. (2000). Functional alternatives to traditional assessment and diagnosis. In M. J. Dougher (Ed.), *Clinical behavior analysis* (pp. 99–125). Reno, NV: Context Press.

Ford, J. D., & Courtois, C. A. (2009). Defining and understanding complex trauma and complex traumatic stress disorders. In C. A. Courtois & J. D. Ford (Eds.), *Treating complex traumatic stress: An evidence-based guide* (pp. 13–30). New York: Guilford Press.

Goldiamond, I. (1974). Toward a constructional approach to social problems: Ethical and constitutional issues raised by applied behavior analysis. *Behaviorism*, *2*, 1–84.

Hawkins, R. P. (1986). Selection of target behaviors. In R. O. Nelson & S. C. Hayes (Eds.), *Conceptual foundations of behavioral assessment* (pp. 331–385). New York: Guilford Press.

Hayes, S. C. (1984). Making sense of spirituality. *Behaviorism*, *12*, 99–110.

Hayes, S. C. (1995). Knowing selves. *The Behavior Therapist*, *18*, 94–96.

Hayes, S. C., Barnes-Holmes, D., & Roche, B. (Eds.). (2001). *Relational frame theory: A post-Skinnerian account of human language and cognition*. New York: Kluwer Academic/Plenum.

Hayes, S. C., & Brownstein, A. J. (1986). Mentalism, behavior-behavior relations, and a behavior-analytic view of the purpose of science. *The Behavior Analyst*, *9*, 175–190.

Hayes, S. C., Nelson, R. O., & Jarrett, R. B. (1987). The treatment utility of assessment: A functional approach to evaluating assessment quality. *American Psychologist*, *42*, 963–974.

Hayes, S. C., Strosahl, K. D., & Wilson, K. D. (1999). *Acceptance and commitment therapy: An experiential approach to behavior change*. New York: Guilford Press.

Hayes, S. C., Zettle, R. D., and Rosenfarb, I. (1989). Rule-following. In S. C. Hayes (Ed.), *Rule-governed behavior: Cognition, contingencies, and instructional control* (pp. 191–220). Reno, NV: Context Press.

Haynes, S. N., & O'Brien, W. H. (1990). Functional analysis in behavior therapy. *Clinical Psychology Review*, *10*, 649–668.

Haynes, S. N., & O'Brien, W. H. (2000). *Principles and practice of behavioral assessment.* New York: Klewer Academic/Plenum.

Herman, J. L. (1992a). Complex PTSD: A syndrome in survivors of prolonged and repeated trauma. *Journal of Trauma*, *5*, 377–391.

Herman, J. L. (1992b). *Trauma and recovery: The aftermath of violence—From domestic to political terror.* New York: Basic Books.

Kanfer, F. H., & Saslow (1969). Behavioral diagnosis. In C. M. Franks (Ed.), *Behavior therapy: Appraisal and status* (pp. 417–444). New York: McGraw-Hill.

Kohlenberg, R. J., & Tsai, M. (1991). *Functional analytic psychotherapy: A guide for creating intense and curative therapeutic relationships.* New York: Plenum.

Kohlenberg, R. J., Tsai, M., Kanter, J. W., & Parker, C. R. (2009). Self and mindfulness. In M. Tsai, R. J. Kohlenberg, J. W. Kanter, B. Kohlenberg, W. C. Follette, & G. M. Callaghan (Eds.), *A guide to functional analytic psychotherapy: Awareness, courage, love and behaviorism in the therapeutic relationship* (pp. 103–130). New York: Springer.

Layne, C. M., Warren, J. S., Saltzman, W. R., Fulton, J. B., Steinberg, A. M., & Pynoos, R. S. (2006). Contextual influences on posttraumatic adjustment: Retraumatization and the roles of revictimization, posttraumatic adversities and distressing reminders. In L. A. Schein, H. I. Spitz, G. M. Burlingame, P. R. Muskin, & S. Vargo (Eds.), *Psychological effects of catastrophic disasters: Group approaches to treatment* (pp. 235–286). New York: Haworth Press.

Linehan, M. M. (1993). *Cognitive-behavioral treatment of borderline personality disorder.* New York: Guilford Press.

Luoma, J. B., Hayes, S. C., & Walser, R. D. (2007). *Learning ACT: An acceptance and commitment therapy skills-training manual for therapists.* Oakland, CA: New Harbinger.

MacPhillamy, D. J., & Lewinsohn, P. M. (1982). The pleasant events schedule: Studies on reliability, validity, and scale intercorrelation. *Journal of Consulting and Clinical Psychology*, *50*, 363–380.

Michael, J. (1982). Distinguishing between discriminative and motivational functions of stimuli. *Journal of the Experimental Analysis of Behavior*, *37*, 149–155.

Mowrer, O. H. (1960). *Learning theory and behavior.* New York: Wiley.

Naugle, A. E., Bell, K. M., & Polusny, M. A. (2003). Clinical considerations for treating sexually revictimized women. *National Center for PTSD Clinical Quarterly*, *12*, 12–16.

Naugle, A. E., & Follette, W. C. (1998). A functional analysis of trauma symptoms. In V. M. Follette, J. I. Ruzek, & F. R. Abueg (Eds.), *Cognitive-behavioral therapies for trauma* (pp. 48–73). New York: Guilford Press.

Pierce, W. D., & Cheney, C. D. (2008). *Behavior analysis and learning* (4th ed.). New York: Psychology Press.

Polusny, M. A., Rosenthal, M. Z., Aban, I., & Follette, V. M. (2004). Experiential avoidance as a mediator of the effects of adolescent sexual victimization on negative adult outcomes. *Violence and Victims*, *19*, 109–120.

Ramnero, J., & Torneke, N. (2008). *The ABCs of human behavior: Behavioral principles for the practicing clinician.* Oakland, CA: New Harbinger.

Rescorla, R. A., & Wagner, A. R. (1972). A theory of Pavlovian conditioning: Variations in the effectiveness of reinforcement and nonreinforcement. In A. H. Black & W. F. Prokasy (Eds.), *Classical conditioning II: Current research and theory* (pp. 64–69). New York: Appleton-Century-Crofts.

Skinner, B. F. (1945). The operational analysis of psychological terms. *Psychological Review, 52,* 270–277.

Skinner, B. F. (1953). *Science and human behavior.* New York: Free Press.

Skinner, B. F. (1957). *Verbal behavior.* New York: Appleton-Century-Crofts.

Torneke, N. (2010). *Learning RFT: An introduction to relational frame theory and its clinical concepts.* Oakland, CA: New Harbinger.

Tsai, M., Kohlenberg, R. J., Kanter, J. W., Kohlenberg, B., Follette, W. C., & Callaghan, G. M. (2008). *A guide to functional analytic psychotherapy: Awareness, courage, love, and behaviorism.* New York: Springer.

Wagner, A. R., & Rescorla, R. A. (1972). Inhibition in Pavlovian conditioning: Applications of a theory. In R. A. Boakes & M. S. Halliday (Eds.), *Inhibition and learning* (pp. 301–359). London: Academic Press.

Watson, J. P., Gaind, R., & Marks, I. M. (1972). Physiological habituation to continuous phobic simulation. *Behavior Research and Therapy, 10,* 269–278.

WHOQOL Group. (1998). The World Health Organization quality of life assessment (WHOQOL): Development and general psychometric properties. *Social Science and Medicine, 46,* 1569–1585.

Wilson, K. G., Sandoz, E. K., Kitchens, J., & Roberts, M. E. (2010). The Valued Living Questionnaire: Defining and measuring valued action within a behavioral framework. *The Psychological Record, 60,* 249–272.

Chapter 7

# Retraumatization and Complex Traumatic Stress
## *A Treatment Overview*

*Christine A. Courtois*

*Retraumatization*, for the purposes of the current book, is defined as a consequence of multiple exposures to physically or psychologically traumatizing events. As such, it occurs within and across various traumatic event types and experiences; however, in the context of incest or child sexual abuse (CSA) in particular (the type of traumatic event that has received the most investigation), revictimization both in childhood and over the course of adulthood is a depressingly common occurrence. It adds massive insult to the original injury of the sexual abuse and whatever additional family or community factors (including nonbelief and nonintervention) contributed. It confounds the original abuse effects and skews them in the direction of shame, self-hatred, self-blame, self-disgust, and alienation from self and others. It is understandable how a child, and later an adult in such a circumstance, would see himself or herself as the common element and come to believe that the abuse and any subsequent maltreatment were deserved.

A variety of types of revictimization have been identified as associated with the original sexual abuse and its aftermath (Kessler & Bieschke, 1999; Messman-Moore & Long, 2000). Revictimization may be within the original abuse, characterized by repeated episodes and in its initial and long-term aftermath (with both the original abuser and others), or new victimization episodes that occur at the hands of additional abusers (these too may involve repeated episodes with the same primary abuser(s). And, chillingly, these may all intermingle and be further impacted by a lack of assistance and intervention. For females, child sexual abuse history has been found to correlate with later sexual assault and violence by both intimates and strangers in adolescence and adulthood (Wyatt, Guthrie, & Notgrass, 1992) and with violence (sexual, physical, and emotional) in intimate partnerships (Banyard, Williams, & Siegel, 2002; Koenig, Doll, O'Leary & Pequegnat, 2004; Smith et al., 2002; Tjaden & Thoennes, 2000; White, Koss, & Kazdin, 2011). For males, available data suggest that they too have a similar trajectory; however, gender differences have also been identified (Gartner, 1999).

The early literature focused almost exclusively on sexual revictimization, also known as adult sexual victimization (ASV), a focus that has now expanded to incorporate other types of assaults, dangers, risks, and behaviors. For example, child sexual abuse history also correlates with later risk-taking behavior, including substance abuse and other addictive and compulsive behaviors, violence toward self or others, personal disregard, impulsiveness and risk taking, and high-risk and promiscuous sexual behavior with many partners (for some involving prostitution and other employment in the sex industry) that results in sexual damage and disease such as HIV or other sexually transmitted diseases (STDs). Higher rates of self-injury and suicidal ideation, suicide attempts, and suicide completions are found in this population than in the general population (Noll, Horowitz, Bonano, Trickett, & Putnam, 2003). In addition, victims are vulnerable to abuse by caregivers and those in positions of authority, such as clergy, therapist, teacher, and coach either in childhood or adulthood. (Courtois, 2010).

Risk and protective factors have been identified in the *cycle of violence* that includes repetition of victimization across generations, within one nuclear and extended family (*polyabuse*), or focused on one or more individual family members involving multiple perpetrators (*multiple abuse*, both within the family context and outside of it). Etiological models have undergone development and testing. Many variables associated with the original sexual victimization and with its initial aftereffects, including posttraumatic stress disorder (PTSD) along with the availability and success of therapy in the aftermath of the victimization and other restorative relationships, may relate to later risk and vulnerability. Theoretical models are under development and investigation.

The aim of this chapter is twofold: to articulate the problem of *revictimization* as a consequence of incest or sexual abuse in childhood for many victims and survivors and to outline the treatment of those suffering retraumatization. According to Messman and Long (1996), *revictimization* refers to "the experience of both childhood sexual abuse and later sexual or physical abuse as an adult" (p. 297). To this definition, we add other forms of victimization. The definition also expands to encompass cognitions, emotions, and patterns of behavior that can create conditions of risk for revictimization in childhood and adulthood as both a consequence and a risk for reenactment of the original abuse. We wish to make explicitly clear that revictimization is a process that can result from primary experiences of abuse by which the victim is placed at higher than average risk for reabuse, something that is not his or her fault, per se, yet something for which he or she often feels blame. *Retraumatization* is defined here to mean the posttraumatic consequences associated with being revictimized, a compounding of the original traumatization.

The chapter's organization is as follows: It begins with a review of epidemiological data pertaining to the prevalence of child sexual abuse and revictimization and related consequences leading to retraumatization. Types and patterns of revictimization are reviewed next, drawing on data from prospective and retrospective studies. Risk and protective factors are then identified and discussed, again from a review of the available and pertinent literature. The second section of the chapter provides an overview of etiological and theoretical formulations about revictimization. In general, these are multifactorial and ecological formulations that account for the various personal, interpersonal, and sociocultural factors and processes related to revictimization. In the third section, clinical descriptions of distress associated with revictimization and retraumatization are presented, followed by discussion of strategies for assessment, diagnosis, and treatment, all of which are ultimately aimed at interrupting the cycle of violence and revictimization, at emotional and physical safety, and at prevention.

## SCOPE OF THE PROBLEM: EPIDEMIOLOGICAL DATA

The sexual abuse of children occurs at alarmingly high rates, in keeping with all types of childhood victimization. Finkelhor (2008) described children and adolescents as the most victimized segment of the population, something that society has been slow to grasp. According to Finkelhor's research findings, the various forms of victimization that befall children are related to such factors as their smaller size and physical strength; their dependency, accessibility, and lack of power or resources; their lack of physical and psychological maturation—including lack of knowledge, experience, and self-control; a lack of choice and resultant entrapment within community and family settings; and surprisingly weak norms against the criminal victimization of children and a related lack of adequate protection or intervention. Although definitional variability and methodological weaknesses have been impediments to accurate prevalence and incidence estimates of all forms of child abuse and neglect, enough data have accumulated to suggest that they are anything but rare. Concerning sexual abuse, data from large representative samples document an experience of some sort of sexual abuse during childhood in the range of 12% to 17% of girls and 3% to 16% of boys (Putnam, 2003); most authorities consider these to be underestimates. Studies of sexual abuse (and other forms of abuse in childhood) and their consequences have become more sophisticated and methodologically sound over the course of the past 40 years; however, reviews of the field suggest that, among other things, standardization of terms, the representativeness of samples and the use of control groups, the use of other than survey studies of retrospective reports, and other modifications are still needed (Molnar, Buka, & Kessler, 2001; Siegel & Williams, 2001; White, Koss, & Katzin, 2011). In terms of advancements, these researchers note that, whereas most of the early studies were retrospective and correlational, more recent studies are prospective and longitudinal and assess and analyze a range of responses over time using more sophisticated statistical models. A number of meta-analyses and reviews of the research are now available.

## THE AFTEREFFECTS OF CHILD SEXUAL ABUSE

The initial and long-term sequelae of child sexual abuse are well-documented in the empirical literature (recently summarized in Courtois, 2010) and are categorized as follows: emotional and identity difficulties (such as shame, fear, anxiety, depression, self-hatred, alienation); symptoms of posttraumatic stress (such as nightmares, startle response, hypervigilance, emotional shutdown and behavioral stilling associated with fear, and memory disturbance); neurobiological and physiological alterations (such as changed brain development and functioning) that result in developmental disturbances (such as cognitive and learning difficulties, behavioral regressions, accelerations, or expressions of distress); somatic and medical outcomes; problems associated with emotional regulation such as impulsiveness, addiction, substance abuse, self-injurious or risk-taking behavior; avoidance or dissociation; and attachment disturbances and resultant difficulties with security of attachment in relationships in general and in intimate relationships in particular (including problems with sexual functioning).

Many of these aftereffects fit criteria for a variety of psychiatric diagnoses that, if made without attention to their origin, miss the mark and result in treatment that is misdirected. Most often, these aftereffects go unrecognized as to their origin or go untreated at the time of the abuse. From there, some continue and, over time, become chronic (often meeting diagnostic criteria for chronic PTSD). Because these effects of child sexual abuse are evidenced in childhood and persist into adulthood, survivors of child sexual abuse are often diagnosed as evidencing one or more personality disorders, with female sexual abuse survivors most often labeled with borderline personality disorder and male survivors labeled with antisocial personality. These diagnostic labels are applied and treatment undertaken with no attention paid to the antecedent child sexual victimization.

Alternatively, symptoms may go dormant for a period of time during which the individual is asymptomatic and may be extremely well functioning, to reemerge when he or she is triggered in some way by something reminiscent of the original abuse, often by a repeat experience of victimization (of all sorts, but especially sexual assault). Unfortunately, past antecedents to the emergence of once-dormant PTSD symptoms usually go unrecognized by both the individual and others in his or her environment, including the therapist. This lack of connection between past abuse and present-day distress is what causes newly symptomatic individuals to feel as though they are going crazy (or be told this by those around them). All of these reactions may add to the victim's vulnerability to additional abuse by the same abuser and others, in this way contributing to revictimization.

## THE EMPIRICAL STUDY OF REVICTIMIZATION

The problem of sexual revictimization has benefited from the methodological advances in child abuse studies and has undergone parallel development. The data presented here are taken from reviews, critiques, and meta-analyses of information on the revictimization of individuals first sexually abused as children. Messman and Long (1996), in their review of available studies of college, clinical, and community samples documented that women who were sexually abused as children were significantly more likely to experience additional abuse (physical and sexual) as adults as compared to women who had not been so abused: "Results overall suggest that between 16% and 72% of women who experienced sexual abuse as children are likely to be revictimized later in life" (p. 414). They also discussed the compounded effects found as a consequence of revictimization. It is reasonable to conclude that these effects put the individual at additional risk by virtue of the effects of chronic stress (i.e., impaired health status due to immunological impact as well as direct injury; other mishaps and accidents as a result of impaired attention, dissociation, and other stress-related responses).

Muehlenhard, Highby, Lee, Bryan, and Dodrill (1998), Roodman and Clum (2001), and Arata (2002) performed reviews of the empirical revictimization literature and arrived at similar conclusions; however, they also independently noted the methodological limitations of many of the studies and cautioned against overinterpreting findings related to the association between child sexual abuse and adult experiences of abuse without additional longitudinal data.

Breitenbecher (2001) focused her review of the sexual revictimization literature on those empirical investigations that claimed to either have provided support for or refuted the usefulness of the eight theories of sexual revictimization that were available at that time. The eight theories include (1) spurious factors, (2) situational or environmental variables, (3) disturbed interpersonal relationships, (4) cognitive attributions, (5) self-blame and self-esteem, (6) coping skills, (7) perception of threat and trauma-related symptoms, and (8) psychological adjustment. Breitenbecher found some evidence supporting the validity of the reduced threat perception theory but did not find any support for the other seven theories of sexual revictimization.

Rich, Combs-Lane, Resnick, and Kilpatrick (2004) conducted a selective review of nine studies and found support for the phenomenon of revictimization. These researchers concluded that "In each study, women with a history of CSA were significantly more likely than nonvictims to have experienced a subsequent sexual assault. Across these studies, victims of CSA were generally two to three times more likely to have experienced ASA compared with non-CSA-victims" (p. 61) (ASA, adult sexual abuse). In evaluating the methodological strength of the reviewed studies, these authors called for greater methodological tightening, more emphasis on theoretical models to better understand the mechanisms of revictimization, and more consideration of contextual factors that may increase risk or reoccurrence. Although recommendations for improving methodological strength were forwarded, these authors denied any impact of the identified limitations on the overall findings.

More recently, Classen, Palesh, and Aggarwal (2005) completed a review of the empirical literature on sexual revictimization, the literature at the time numbering some 90 studies. They reported that the aggregate research findings document that two of three individuals who are sexually victimized in childhood will be sexually revictimized later in life. They noted that "The occurrence of childhood sexual abuse and its severity are the best documented and researched predictor of sexual revictimization." (p. 103). They also found multiple trauma (i.e., sexual, physical, emotional abuse, and neglect), especially childhood physical abuse, and recency of sexual victimization to be associated with higher risk.

## ETIOLOGICAL FORMULATIONS OF REVICTIMIZATION AND RETRAUMATIZATION

Many vulnerability and protective factors have been noted or hypothesized to account for increased risk of sexual revictimization in the population of adult survivors of previous victimization of all sorts. In this section, we review many such factors using an ecological approach as proposed by Grauerholz (2000) to account for how multiple factors and processes at various levels (personal, interpersonal, sociocultural) are needed for a multidimensional understanding of the issue. She wrote: "The ecological approach assumes that individual behavior can only be understood by taking into account factors at each of these levels—the individual, interpersonal and sociocultural" (p. 6).

### Personal-Level Factors

Aspects of the individual's personal history are understood as shaped by and shaping his or her response to the family and sociocultural environment, and especially to the original victimization. A number of models have been proposed to explain how sexual abuse experience in childhood can result in long-term consequences that, in turn, can cause ongoing vulnerability. These include the secondary elaborations theory of Gelinas (1983) in which vulnerability is understood as due to the secondary elaborations of the untreated effects of the original abuse, a formulation she originally proposed for treating the compounded aftereffects of incest. This and other models (Terr, 1991) also note that the defenses that the child used to cope with the original abuse, especially when repeated and ongoing and involving a known abuser in a position of trust vis-à-vis the child (such as dissociation and motivated forgetting) can become chronic adaptations that can later render the victim powerless and out of touch when in conditions of danger.

The *traumatogenic model* of Finkelhor and Browne (1985) posits four factors associated with child sexual abuse as related to revictimization: traumatic sexualization, betrayal, powerlessness, and stigmatization. These four factors are found in other theoretical formulations such as the *posttraumatic stress model* of Briere (1997), Courtois (1988, 2010), and others, and the *betrayal-trauma model* of Freyd (1995). Other researchers have suggested the *emotional avoidance model* (Polusny & Follette, 1995), the *learning theory* or *learned expectancy model* (Messman & Long, 1996), the *low self-esteem model* (Alexander & Lupfer, 1987); the *social isolation or poor relational skills model* (Kendall-Tackett, Williams, & Finkelhor, 1993); the *developmental model* (Cole & Putnam, 1992); the *developmental/attachment/affect management model* (Alexander, 1992; Cloitre, 1998); the *attribution model* (Spaccarelli & Kim, 1995); the *transactional model* (Spaccarelli, 1994); and the *cumulative trauma model* (Follette, Polusny, Bechtle, & Naugle, 1996); among others. In addition, factors unique to each child, such as the child's temperament, resilience, and ability to withstand or fight traumatic experiences, can play a role in whether he or she is more or less susceptible to later episodes of abuse.

Researchers are also blending these various factors into one model of risk, as in the model proposed by Gold, Sinclair, and Balge (1999), that includes the following personal factors hypothesized to play a mediating role in sexual revictimization: severe psychological symptoms as a consequence of the child sexual abuse, poor coping style, an insecure attachment style, hyperfemininity, delinquent behavior, drug use, and high-risk sexual behavior. Arata (2000) proposed a path model of mediation by self-blame, posttraumatic symptoms, and consensual sexual activity of the relationship between sexual abuse and revictimization. Protective factors such as concerned response, social support, practical support, and effective intervention have also been identified in some investigations but are in need of additional study.

## Interpersonal Level Factors

Among the identified interpersonal-level factors are those associated with the original sexual abuse, including type of sexual contact, especially the more severe and penetrative types, relationship to the perpetrator, degree of betrayal, greater frequency and longer duration of abuse, and use of force. In the general child sexual abuse literature, these factors along with the age of onset of the abuse have been predictive of greater severity of aftereffects (Courtois, 2010). In addition, recent research has been somewhat equivocal about whether abuse that occurs in childhood alone or in both childhood and adolescence or just in adolescence is related to revictimization, and some findings suggest that the recency of experiences of sexual abuse creates greater risk for reabuse (Classen, Palesh, & Aggarwal, 2005). The bottom line is that child sexual abuse, either alone or in combination with child physical and emotional abuse and neglect, is a risk for revictimization. The extent of past victimization and multiple traumas (identified as cumulative trauma) creates a higher likelihood of revictimization (Follette et al., 1996).

Many writers have proposed that abuse must be understood in the context of its occurrence, whether within the family or the broader community. When within the family, patterns of family relationships, dynamics, and parental and family functioning are involved; however, it is not always clear whether family dysfunction is a cause or consequence of child sexual abuse and in many cases it might be both. Attachment researchers and theorists have found that insecure attachment of all types put children increasingly at risk for sexual abuse within or outside of the family, but it is the insecure disorganized or disoriented style that has been found as most damaging to the child and as most related to increased risk of psychopathology over the life span (Alexander, 2009). Neglect and nonresponse on the part of caregivers have also been implicated in creating conditions of increased emotional and social vulnerability.

Factors associated with child sexual abuse paradoxically can lead adolescent and adult victims and survivors to be more sexually active, have more sexual partners, or to engage in high-risk sexual activities, thereby increasing their vulnerability to reabuse or other adverse outcomes such as physical damage and the development of STDs or HIV (Boney-McCoy & Finkelhor, 1995; Ehrensaft et al., 2003). Their attempts to cope with the effects of the past abuse, such as dissociation and the use of alcohol and other substances, create additional conditions of risk, as do other more personal factors such as impaired ability to judge danger, increased dependence on others for personal approval or affirmation, impulsiveness, heightened risk taking, and so on (Ullman, Najdowski, & Filipas, 2009). Other factors such as stigmatization, powerlessness, and low self-esteem may relate to revictimization by causing victims to be unable to resist unwanted sexual contact or to behave assertively with someone stronger and more dominant. Interpersonal effects such as betrayal, alienation, and mistrust of others result in difficulties with relationships that may also play a part in revictimization, especially in conditions of domestic violence and other forms of intimate partner violence (Freyd, 1995; Gobin & Freyd, 2009). Campbell, Greeson, Bybee, & Raja (2008) reported on the co-occurrence of childhood sexual abuse, adult sexual assault, inti-mate partner violence, and sexual harassment and found four predominant patterns of women's lifetime experiences of violence co-occurrence. They also found that PTSD played a meditational role between violence and later physi-cal health symptomatology. From their findings, they suggested that for one subgroup of women, sexual revictimization was but one component of their lifetime victimization and that future research should include more compre-hensive assessments of physical, sexual, and emotional abuse across the entire life span and expand on the investigation of factors in the sociocultural context.

## Sociocultural-Level Factors

Race, ethnicity, cultural issues, and socioeconomic status (SES) may also be implicated factors that require additional research attention. Available data suggest that revictimization is highest in samples of African American women followed by Caucasian women, Latinas, and Asian American women (Urquiza and Goodlin-Jones, 1994). Recent writings stress how economic status and means, and cultural, ethnic, and spiritual and religious beliefs, traditions, and mandates often lead to greater vulnerability of females and children to more powerful and dominant members of the community. These factors relate to how society and particular cultures attend to issues of victim-ization of its members, especially its less powerful members, namely women and children (male and female). The sociocultural environment may actually be conducive to the sexual abuse of these members and may not provide assistance when abuse surfaces or is disclosed. Moreover, the tendency has been to blame the victim for his or her own abuse, a circumstance that has the effect of further alienating the abused and enabling and even empower-ing the perpetrators. When help is not forthcoming and episodes of abuse are ignored and then occur repeatedly, victims internalize shame and self-blame. In this way, we can see how a cycle of violence and abuse is supported and how victims can come to feel hopeless and in despair of anything changing. Social attitudes have changed in the past 30 years, yet much more needs to be done for victims to be assured of responses that do not further traumatize them. Many social disadvantages such as poverty, lack of education, home-lessness, lack of financial independence, are related to creating additional conditions of vulnerability.

## Correlates of Sexual Revictimization

In their extensive literature review, Classen et al. (2005) identified the following as correlates of sexual revictimization: (a) marital status, with risk differing for women depending upon their marital status; (b) greater distress as a consequence of the original abuse and other victimizations; (c) psychiatric disorders, especially depression, PTSD and other anxiety disorders, dissociative disorders, and alcohol or other substance abuse, and severe mental illness such as schizophrenia, schizoaffective, or bipolar disorder, and certain personality disorders, especially borderline personality in women and antisocial personality in men; (d) difficulties with affect regulation; (e) difficulties with information processing; (f) negative schema regarding self and others; (g) behavioral factors such as interpersonal problems, social functioning, sexual behaviors and functioning, and disclosure and its consequences (especially when negative and unhelpful); (h) shame, blame, and powerlessness; and (i) coping, especially the greater use of avoidance strategies. It should be noted that these correlates are not mutually exclusive as many interact with one another. Because they are so interwoven, it is not always possible to know if these are causes or consequences of abuse. Finally, it stands to reason that these correlates would be related to other forms of victimization besides only the sexual but that this assertion requires additional investigation.

## Theoretical Models

Several recent theoretical models have sought to incorporate and expand upon those that were previously available. Based on their own and other research findings, Maker, Kemmelmeier, & Peterson (2001) suggested a *specificity model of trauma* that holds that child sexual abuse alone is a risk factor that places women on a developmental trajectory for sexual revictimization over time. In their research study, they focused on comorbid childhood stressors and peer sexual abuse as separate risk factors that require additional investigation to better understand the relationships between varying childhood traumas, later sexual assault, and other psychosocial aftereffects.

Lynn, Pintar, Fite, Ecklund, and Stafford (2004) proposed a *social-narrative* model of revictimization based on three major explanatory themes originally proposed in Sandberg, Lynn, and Green (1994): (a) the search for mastery and meaning, (b) dysfunctional learning, and (c) cognitive defenses. They discussed these themes from a wide variety of theoretical orientations (i.e., Freudian analytic, object relations, psychodynamic, learning and cognitive-behavioral, attachment/developmental, dissociation, and posttraumatic) and proposed that the experience of sexual abuse puts the child at odds with his or her social surroundings that, by and large, do not acknowledge the occurrence of abuse. They refer to the extreme discrepancy between the victim's personal narrative and the shared social narratives as a form of *social incoherence*, resembling features of cognitive dissonance and double-bind theories that put the child's experiences at odds with the narrative of the larger social context. These theorists view dissociation as an adaptation to ongoing social incoherence, that is, the ongoing discrepancy between experienced personal events (child sexual abuse and later revictimization) and social context. In this model, the dysfunction leading to revictimization is located more in the social environment than in the victim, thus working against victim blaming. The goal of intervention is to help the victim to understand the social context that supports abuse and to make cognitive and behavioral changes that increase safety-in-the-world and, as desired, to work to change the larger social context that supports abuse perpetration.

Marx, Heidt, and Gold (2005) reviewed the available empirical literature and found the findings inconclusive and offering little support for available theories of sexual revictimization, possibly due to the deficiencies in methodology discussed earlier. They developed and proposed a *speculative model*, "a parsimonious, testable and comprehensive model of sexual revictimization specifying CSA survivors are at risk for sexual revictimization in adulthood. This theoretical model will also explain how and why individual differences occur as well as how these differences produce increased vulnerability" (p. 75). Based on learning and fear theory in humans and animals, they hypothesized that uncontrollable and unpredictable experiences of child sexual abuse elicit a set of conditioned and unconditioned emotional responses characterized by fear and arousal that, when exhibited in social situations, signal vulnerability to potential perpetrators. This incorporative theory highlights learned behavior that can later put the individual at risk and suggests points of therapeutic intervention. It has potential to increase understanding of paradoxical dimensions of revictimization (i.e., how attempts at self-regulation and fear management and avoidance may put the individual at future risk). Like other theoretical models, it is in need of additional development and testing, in general and as pertains to treatment. We now discuss clinical distress associated with revictimization and treatment strategies and approaches directed at its alleviation.

## CLINICAL DISTRESS ASSOCIATED WITH REVICTIMIZATION AND TREATMENT

Meta-analyses of research on the aftereffects of CSA and other childhood trauma document many additional symptoms having to do with the developmental impact of abuse (especially when chronic and in the context of other parental and familial dysfunction) that are above and beyond those associated with *classic PTSD* as defined in the current *Diagnostic and Statistical Manual of Mental Disorders (DSM-IV-TR)* (American Psychiatric Association, 2000). Herman (1992) proposed a new diagnosis of Complex Posttraumatic Stress Disorder/Disorders of Extreme Stress Not Otherwise Specified (CPTSD/DESNOS) to account for and organize these symptoms. This diagnostic conceptualization was listed as an associated feature of PTSD in the *DSM-IV-TR* and is currently under consideration as a freestanding diagnosis in *DSM-5*. The criteria categories for CPTSD/DESNOS resemble those described above as potentially related to revictimization: (1) alterations in the ability to regulate affect; (2) alterations in attention or consciousness; (3) alterations in self-perception; (4) alterations in perception of the perpetrator; (5) alterations in relations with others (specifically including revictimization); (6) somatization; and (7) alterations in systems of meaning.

Victims of child sexual abuse, especially when it occurs within the family, have often been subjected to what Courtois and Ford (2009) defined as "*complex psychological trauma* involving traumatic stressors that (1) are repetitive or prolonged; (2) involve direct harm and/or neglect and abandonment by caregivers or ostensibly responsible adults; (3) occur at developmentally vulnerable times in the victim's life, such as early childhood; and (4) have great potential to compromise severely a child's development" (p. 1). Trauma of this type can also occur in adulthood in response to multiple or cumulative trauma, often superimposed upon childhood trauma effects. The aftereffects of such exposure across the life span are equally complex and match the formulation proposed by Herman. Courtois and Ford conceptualized them as *complex traumatic stress disorders* that can be understood as compounded posttraumatic responses having to do with layered or cumulative trauma that occurs and recurs over long spans of time usually beginning in childhood.

The complex trauma formulation has significant utility to the understanding of the myriad and varied aftereffects of child sexual abuse and later revictimization and to their treatment. Complex traumatic stress disorders may result in the classic triad of symptoms found in standard PTSD, namely, re-experiencing, avoidance, and physiological hyperarousal, and meet criteria for the diagnosis, but additional symptoms spanning all five axes of the *DSM* diagnostic system are also common and additional diagnoses may apply. A sampling of core problems that might require treatment (and that might contribute to subsequent trauma exposure and risk) include affect dysregulation, dissociation, impaired self-concept and self-development, somatic disturbances, insecure and unstable patterns of attachment, relational problems, spiritual/existential issues and personal meaning-making, in addition to other associated features such as depression, anxiety, and numerous other comorbidities.

As a result of this complexity, these symptoms may be difficult to accurately conceptualize, diagnose, and treat. The complex traumatic stress formulation and the CPTSD diagnosis offer an overarching and parsimonious conceptualization for the identification, understanding, and organization of symptoms in the context of their abuse etiology. It further assists in understanding that, for some clients, PTSD symptoms are evident in an ongoing way (chronic presentation), yet for others they emerge periodically, usually in response to a trigger of some sort, but may remain dormant for years and even decades (periodic or delayed presentation). However they play out, long-term mental health difficulties can be identified as both effects and vulnerability factors. They render the original victim susceptible to repeat episodes of harm and thus need to be addressed in the treatment. This formulation neatly fits with the one presented by Gelinas in 1983, that these are the secondary elaborations of the original untreated effects of abuse.

What then might be the consequences of repeat episodes of revictimization and retraumatization on top of the childhood trauma? Many clinicians have noted a compounding of the already complex trauma reactions (Kluft, 1990). Preliminary studies have identified those persons with layered or cumulative episodes of trauma to incur a heightened risk of lifetime (chronic) PTSD and to have more mental health diagnoses as compared to nonvictims (Arata, 1999), to have more dissociation and to endorse more symptoms of dissociative identity disorder (DID), and to experience trauma-specific symptoms at a frequency that is consistent with the frequency of reported victimization experiences (Follette et al., 1996). As the therapist begins to learn the full extent of the client's traumatization, he or she must work from an understanding of the commonality of prior and ongoing victimization and be emotionally prepared to hear details and to help the client to take action. Obviously, the therapist must take care not to be judgmental and instead to work with the client to understand his or her idiosyncratic vulnerability. Individualized safety planning and protective interventions can then be built on this base of subjective understanding. Exposure to multiple victimizations may affect the rate of recovery (or even its possibility). Multiple experiences of trauma (including those that are recent) impact the client's presentation for treatment, ongoing mental health, and the efficacy and duration of current and future treatment.

## Assessment and Treatment

Elsewhere, I have discussed treatment for complex trauma and its reactions (Courtois, 1999, 2004) as a sequenced and hierarchical three-phase model originally based on Herman's model (Herman, 1992, 1997). This model has as its goals the development of skills for safety, life stabilization, self-management developed within the context of a relationally attuned and responsive treatment, along with the identification and treatment of the primary effects of the trauma and how these have played out over time. This model has approximately 25 years of development, based largely upon clinical application, observation, modification, and consensus. Many variations or "hybrid" models of treatment that combine or sequence strategies in different ways for the complex client have been developed, some of which have empirical support or are now under empirical testing (see Cloitre, 1998; Cloitre, Cohen, & Koenen, 2006; Cloitre et al., 2010; Ford & Russo, 2006). Some models focus on specific problem areas associated with complex trauma including substance abuse, self-injury, safety, and chronic mental illness.

At the root of this treatment is the question of whether an individual can truly recover if he or she is in a condition of ongoing danger. The treatment model discussed here is predicated on a foundation of safety from further abuse (to and from self and others to whatever degree the client can control this and with recognition that exposure to experiences of trauma or victimization occur on a random basis and thus not be totally avoided or guaranteed to not occur), a first order of business in the model proposed by Herman (1992). A victim would be assumed to have a difficult time recovering if faced with almost certain repeat abuse and traumatization. Yet, while the client remains in ongoing danger, strong defenses and coping skills are needed and should not be approached or dismantled in treatment until the client is in a relative condition of safety. Achieving this overarching goal may take a long time and enormous effort in some cases, as is typical of the treatment of domestic violence.

## Goals of Treatment for Symptoms of Posttraumatic Stress Disorder (PTSD) and Complex Trauma

A number of general treatment goals for the symptoms of PTSD have been identified. These include (1) increasing personal stability; (2) restoring self-esteem; (3) restoring psychological safety and trust; (4) reducing severity of PTSD and other symptoms by reducing trauma intrusions and re-experiencing, decreasing numbing and avoidance strategies, and reducing levels of hyperarousal in order to reestablish the normal stress response; (5) deconditioning anxiety or fear and providing ongoing desensitization; (6) treating comorbid problems; (7) maintaining or improving adaptive functioning; (8) restoring social relations and reconnecting with others; and (9) preventing relapse but planning for its recurrence.

The treatment of complex trauma may include all of these goals and much more. The developmental or attachment deficits that complex trauma clients experience require additional treatment focus; thus, treatment goals are more extensive than those directed solely to the symptoms of PTSD and are geared to work on the seven symptom categories of CPTSD/DESNOS along with the developmental difficulties. These goals include (1) identifying and treating developmental deficits through direct education and skill building; (2) providing an attuned and responsive treatment relationship as both a deliberate treatment intervention and a secure base for the client's self-exploration; (3) developing and restoring access to and identification of emotions and the capacity for and tolerance of emotional expression; (4) recognizing emotional dysregulation and teaching skills for increased regulation and self-management; (5) restoring attachment security and moving the client's attachment style from insecure to "earned secure"; (6) restoring the capacity to trust others; (7) preventing reenactments of the trauma and revictimization of self and others through direct teaching and skill building, a goal especially pertinent to those who have been repeatedly traumatized; (8) processing core emotions besides fear and anxiety (i.e., shame, self-loathing, self-disgust, anger and rage, grief and sadness, powerlessness, and so on); and (9) identifying dissociative processes and the dissociative sequestering of emotion and information. Related to this goal, encouraging personality integration and integration of information that has been split off; (10) identifying trauma-related cognitions and providing information to challenge and modify them; (11) restoring a positive identity and a sense of self-worth and pride; (12) processing the dynamics of betrayal-trauma as needed and processing ambivalent attachment to abusive and nonprotective caregivers; (13) processing trauma to the point of resolution in order to develop personal authority over the remembering process and the traumatic memories; (14) restoring or developing attention to physical and health status; and (15) supporting the client's consideration of existential issues and personal meaning-making.

In addition, goals might be determined to address highly individualized client concerns (i.e., address a specific sexual problem or improve sexual functioning; develop a strategy for safely visiting with formerly abusive family members; develop a plan for parent skill training; develop a workplace plan; help write a letter of confrontation—to be sent or not; plan a family intervention, etc.) and changed according to phase and treatment focus in which they are implemented. The therapist should not be surprised that the achievement of a goal or the resolution of an issue might lead to the emergence of other concerns that were previously not in evidence or dormant (for example, the achievement of sobriety might lead to the emergence of intrusive memories of abuse that the client may or may not have been previously aware of; smoking cessation might lead to an increase in the use of dissociation; the death of a perpetrator might lead to the emergence of previously unacknowledged feelings and memories).

In the treatment of revictimized clients with compounded reactions, the therapist must also expect to encounter mixed attachment patterns with regard to perpetrators, especially those in close relation to the client. Such ambivalent attachments can be disconcerting to the therapist who, at various points in the treatment, may hear differences in reactions to the perpetrator and others ranging from love to hate and all emotions in between. Therapists are well-advised to expect such reactions and to not scapegoat the perpetrator to the client. Rather, they should be prepared to explore the mixed emotions and to understand them as part of the trauma bonding that has been identified in many types of victimization involving primary caregivers and significant others and the victim. Clients often have great shame and confusion about these mixed patterns of attachment and benefit when the therapist can help them to explore and resolve them.

## Treatment Strategies

In recent years, treatment for patients with the "classic" form of PTSD has emphasized the use of cognitive behavioral interventions (CBTs), including prolonged exposure (PE) and cognitive restructuring (CR) techniques, for which empirical support has been increasingly reported (Foa, Keane, Friedman, & Cohen, 2008). The findings in support of the effectiveness of these techniques in ameliorating the often refractory symptoms of PTSD are fairly consistent; however, the wholesale application of CBT techniques to patients with complex traumatic stress disorders and those reacting to recent episodes of revictimization in particular (even those who clearly meet the criteria for PTSD) is often problematic if applied too early in the process, because some of the problems described in the previous paragraph can resurface, namely, the penetration of needed defenses and too direct opening of the trauma. Techniques of this sort have their place in the treatment of compounded complex trauma, but are to be applied later rather than sooner in the process as described in more detail below. These techniques are most effective when applied after the client has achieved safety, has been free of the traumatic circumstances (including episodes of revictimization), and has developed improved self-esteem and skills in emotional regulation, self-assertion, and in the recognition and avoidance of danger.

## Assessment: General Approach

Strategies and instruments for the assessment of traumatized individuals are relatively recent developments. The recommended approach is to initially inquire about trauma as part of the standard psychosocial assessment conducted at the beginning of treatment. From the point of intake, the therapist should include questions having to do with possible victimization in the individual's past and current life and, when these are identified, about posttraumatic or dissociative symptomatology. Obviously, from our discussion here, it is important to obtain as thorough a history of trauma across the life span as possible, including all forms of child and adolescent abuse and neglect, significant attachment disturbances and disturbed modes of family functioning, and episodes of abuse or other forms of trauma (including combat, community violence, and natural or human-designed disasters). However, the clinician cannot assume that asking about trauma will result in disclosure, especially early on and before the development of a basic degree of trust.

Whether the therapist is asking questions about trauma in an initial assessment or later, several principles guide the process. The individual must be approached with respect and with the understanding that asking about trauma can be difficult, painful, and shame or disgust evoking, as can its disclosure (especially current or multiple traumas or any type that carries additional shame and stigma). The issue of empowerment of the individual is also important. The therapist must convey an attitude of openness and must ask questions from a supportively neutral position.

Inquiry about and discussion of trauma details can cause the spontaneous emergence of symptoms. The therapist should be aware ahead of time and be prepared to respond in a preventative way, with titration or even cessation of the inquiry if the client becomes dissociative or hyperaroused in the session or if any decompensation occurs. Being sensitive to this range of possible responses conveys several important messages: that the emotional content associated with traumatization can be overwhelming and that the therapist recognizes this and gives the individual's safety and welfare precedence over the story. Specialized assessment might need to be repeated at different points in treatment, because posttraumatic and dissociative symptoms might only emerge gradually, often after enough safety has been established, in both outside life and in the treatment relationship.

For detailed discussion of the assessment of complex traumatic stress disorders, see articles by Briere and Spinnazola (2005, 2009) and Brown (2009), and the book on assessment of PTSD by Wilson and Keane (2004). Specialized approaches and instruments are also now available for assessment of dissociative symptoms and the dissociative disorders (DDs), described in the recently published handbook by Dell and O'Neill (2009) and by Loewenstein (1991).

The more comprehensive the assessment, hopefully the more the therapist gains an understanding of the individual's symptom picture, defensive and self-structure, use of dissociation and other avoidance strategies, capacity for emotional self-regulation, functional competence, attachment style (and Inner Working Model), and relational ability. In terms of multiple traumatic experiences, the therapist will also want to determine the individual's awareness of situations of danger and capacity for self-assertion and self-protection. The therapist should additionally assess the individual's strengths and resources, so as not to suggest or join a perception of being a "helpless victim," to whatever extent multiple traumas come to light. Whenever possible, the therapist wants to call upon and reinforce the individual's strengths as a means of empowering, to encourage growth rather than regression and an agency-based identity.

## Treatment Meta-Model: Sequenced, Phased, Progressive Treatment

The consensus-based meta-model most in use in the contemporary treatment of complex trauma involves a sequence of three or more phases of treatment that are organized to hierarchically and progressively develop a variety of essential life skills and to address specific issues (Courtois, 1999). The sequencing of treatment was determined due to several factors, among them, the large number of symptoms and diagnoses that are often initially confusing for therapist and client alike; the chaos of the client's life and presentation for treatment (including the crisis presentation in the aftermath of an episode of revictimization); the client's lack of effective strategies for emotional regulation that, by association, impact other aspects of self and life management; and major relational disturbances (including mistrust) that get projected onto the therapist that create difficulties in the development of the treatment alliance. A sequenced model with specific tasks-by-phase assists the therapist in organizing the treatment beginning with a primary emphasis on safety, stabilization, education, and life skills. It also helps in introducing the client to structure and order in the psychotherapy as a counter to the dysregulation that is so often evident.

The model does not prescribe or mandate that particular interventions be used with every client; rather, it serves as a general template that emphasizes safety and security, affect identification and regulation, and relational stability as core foundations of treatment. Moreover, by virtue of the therapist's responsiveness and attunement to the client's story and emotions, it works against the use of avoidance and dissociation. It also emphasizes resiliency, posttraumatic growth, and the ability to function in the world, and seeks to halt the ongoing decline that is so often a legacy of chronic PTSD, complex trauma, and especially ongoing and repeated traumatization. Where repeated episodes of trauma have been the norm, it emphasizes the ability to protect and defend oneself against further victimization. Although the treatment model is described as a linear process, it is better described as a recursive spiral because it tends to move back and forth between phases and issues. Treatment usually proceeds in starts and stops, and clients can be expected to advance and relapse as they progress. Clients can be taught that recovery and healing are processes that occur over time with the application of knowledge and skills acquired during the course of the treatment. The model is also modified according to the specific issues that emerge during the initial assessment and later and according to the client's capacities and defenses, and such internal and external resources as ego strength, an available and stable support network, safety from additional victimization, financial and insurance resources, and so forth.

The primary phases and tasks of treatment are as follows.

## Phase 1: Pretreatment Issues, Treatment Frame, Safety, Alliance Building, Education, Affect Regulation, Stabilization, Skill Building, Self-Care, and Support

This is likely to be the longest stage of the treatment and the most important to its success. It includes pretreatment issues such as the development of motivation, informed consent regarding client rights and responsibilities, and education about what psychotherapy is about, the "rules of treatment," along with suggestions for how to engage successfully. It also begins the development of the treatment relationship, in a way that allows a collaborative alliance to build over time. Some clients never move beyond this stage and benefit from what it provides, namely, ongoing support and general life improvement.

The primary emphasis of phase 1 is personal safety in addition to education, life stabilization, emotional and self-regulation in addition to other skill building, and the development of social relationships and support. *Safety* is defined broadly and involves real and perceived injury and threats to self, and to and from others. Many clients (especially those who have been chronically retraumatized) may have no concept of what it means to be safe and may not believe they can ever achieve safety from external harm. From its inception, treatment must be geared to the modification of such erroneous but trauma-related cognitions and beliefs about self and others, and to the teaching of skills in risk and threat assessment, and the initiating of safety planning. The therapist assists the client to gain control over impulsive behavior, self-destructive thoughts and behaviors, dangerous interpersonal situations, addictions, ongoing avoidance and dissociation, and intense affect discharges that can result in retraumatization, and seeks to replace them with personal safety planning. Safety planning is more than a time-limited safety contract. It involves the development of a plan for achieving and maintaining safety from harm over time and does not have an expiration date. Clients are expected to assist in developing the plan and in implementing it throughout the treatment. In addition, because these clients so often use dissociation and avoidance as a means of coping, the therapist must counter these strategies and teach alternatives that raise the client's level of awareness and ability to remain "present" and further to behave assertively when feeling triggered or threatened in some way.

Client education is an integral component of this stage. It is used to demystify the process of psychotherapy and to teach about trauma, post-traumatic reactions, and secondary elaborations, including the risk of additional victimization. Quite paradoxically, many traumatized individuals know nothing about trauma, may not label what happened to them as traumatic, and have little or no understanding that their symptoms and their ongoing vulnerability may be related to their past experiences. Education about trauma and its impact including PTSD and complex trauma is therefore important and may effectively help a client to understand his or her reactions and to develop increased self-esteem and self-compassion and to counter the shame and self-disgust that are so common. Clients must also receive specific education about the negative consequences of avoidance when overused as a coping mechanism.

In addition to imparting new knowledge, education is the foundation for teaching specific skills that cover many domains: the identification and regulation of emotional states; personal mindfulness; self-care; and life skills such as assertiveness, coping, problem-solving, social skills, decision making, and so on. Education and skill building are ongoing and offered throughout the treatment process. The client must be motivated to change and must actively practice what is taught. Affect-regulation is perhaps the most important skill that the client needs to learn.

Self-care and mind–body issues are related to all of the topics discussed in this section but need a focus in their own right. Many of these clients are alienated from themselves (their minds as well as their bodies) and their general well-being and quality of life. The literature on aftereffects of trauma (especially chronic trauma of the sort discussed in this chapter) suggests that they are also at high health risk. Their bodies may be literally under siege from the inside due to the ongoing stress load associated with PTSD and related hyperarousal. Moreover, as part of their self-alienation, many clients are at war with their bodies because they blame their bodies for what happened to them or for being the repository and reminder of aftereffects; consequently, they ignore their bodies, are neglectful, (or avoidant) regarding wellness and medical concerns, may be phobic about medical care and medical personnel, and due to these concerns, put themselves at unnecessary medical risk. As these issues are identified, the therapist may need to actively engage around issues of general self-care, preventive medicine, and actual treatment. Additionally, the client may need to be re-embodied, that is, encouraged in paying attention to his or her bodily responses and their relation to emotional states. Treatment approaches that are "whole person" and that address issues of the body and mind under chronic stress have been developed in recent years especially for this population (Fisher & Ogden, 2009; Ogden Minton, & Pain, 2006; Rothschild, 2000).

Psychopharmacology is another treatment for the related physical and psychological symptoms. Combined psychopharmacology and psychotherapy are recommended for the treatment of PTSD in general, a recommendation that extends to complex trauma patients. Guidelines for the medical management of PTSD can be found in Opler, Grennan, & Ford (2009) and in Foa, Keane, Friedman, & Cohen (2008), especially the chapter on psychopharmacology by Friedman, Davidson, & Stein (2008).

Relations with others (including with the therapist) and building support networks are also crucial issues of this stage. As discussed earlier, mistrust due to interpersonal betrayal is a major relational hallmark of many complex trauma clients. Social and relational deficits and problems have long been identified as a legacy of abuse trauma, a recognition that has been given additional emphasis in the past two decades by attachment researchers. The insecure disoriented style is most associated with chronic childhood abuse trauma in a family and results in children and later adults whose attachment styles reflect what they learned in their relationships with primary caretakers: those who were exposed to the most abusive and disorganized of family backgrounds often develop disorganized or dissociative attachment styles (i.e., those involving shifting states of identity, emotional lability, shifting relationships with others, self-injury as a means of self-soothing, etc.). Clinicians must work directly with these various styles while providing a secure relational base within the treatment from which to acquire more interpersonal skills, including the ability to negotiate relationships and to develop intimacy with others while maintaining safety. Over time, it is hoped that the relationship with the therapist may be so influential that it allows the client to develop an "earned secure" attachment style, one that is considerably healthier and more flexible in supporting the client in self and relational development.

Attention to the traumatic experiences and events occurs throughout phase 1 but is deliberately kept at an intellectual and cognitive, didactic, and educational level, to the degree possible. Phase 1 does not specifically focus on trauma processing and resolution, although much of the work described above relates to traumatic antecedents either directly or indirectly. The client is educated about trauma, short- and long-term posttraumatic responses, conditions, and disorders, and the developmental adaptations and deformations found to be associated with chronic and complex forms of trauma, and how these can lead to ongoing vulnerability. Attachment and trauma-based cognitions and beliefs are constantly attended to, and the therapist looks for opportunities to identify them and provide trauma-referenced corrective information. Changing abuse and trauma-related cognitions is nothing short of a paradigm shift for the client and can begin the challenging of negative self-perception that so often underlies depression and other associated reactions, sometimes to such a degree that the client can become less symptomatic with cognitive interventions of this sort.

Some clients remain in phase 1 throughout their treatment (or alternatively, engage in phases 1 and 3, as described by Gold, 2000) and do not engage in the formal trauma resolution work of phase 2. This can occur for a variety of reasons, among them, personal motivation, limited financial and other resources, other life circumstances that make trauma resolution work unfeasible, such as age, illness, and other factors that impede the client's ability to tolerate the additional stress involved in facing and processing the trauma. Whatever the circumstance, clients who have successfully engaged in phase 1 (and additionally in phase 3 work, when possible) will have gained valuable knowledge and skills that are designed to improve their lives. Treatment gains and trajectories vary and some clients remain in phase 1 because they specifically benefit from the ongoing support provided by the therapist.

## Phase 2: Deconditioning, Mourning, Resolution, and Integration of the Trauma

Other factors not interfering with proceeding to phase 2, the client's ongoing symptoms become the basis for determining whether more directed work with the trauma is needed. If the client remains symptomatic and is willing to work more directly on the trauma, treatment proceeds to phase 2. Many times, this shift occurs rather seamlessly from the more cognitive work in phase 1, as the client begins to experience more feelings while discussing trauma-related material. Connecting affectively with the trauma story and the trauma-based cognitions and behaviors within the context of a supportive relationship is a major focus of trauma processing (Fosha, 2003; Paivio & Pascuale-Leone, 2010).

Phase 2 utilizes exposure and narrative-based techniques to directly address issues related to the trauma (the objective trauma story including description of how it occurred, where, with whom, and so forth, along with the subjective reactions that occurred at the time and afterwards) and relies on the client utilizing the increased self-regulatory skills developed in phase 1 without resorting to maladaptive defenses. At the present time, gradual as opposed to prolonged exposure and associated desensitization conducted imaginally, verbally, or in writing seem to be the choice most therapists make, although this might change as more technical developments occur.

Whatever exposure or narrative technique is selected, its pace and intensity must match the client's capacity and be calibrated so as to not overwhelm. It is now recognized that clients have windows of emotional tolerance and therapists should strive to titrate their strategies to this window. Per Briere (2002), if the window is "undershot," the client will not have enough emotion stimulated to make any change; if "overshot," the client will experience overly strong emotion and respond by becoming symptomatic. This sometimes involves a return to maladaptive means of coping (such as self-injury, addictive or compulsive behavior, increased depression and anxiety, revictimization, and so on) that may require moving back to phase 1 work to allow restabilization before moving back to phase 2 in a more titrated way.

When desensitization strategies are employed, clients are taught to achieve and observe different responses to the trauma story in order to break the association between particular emotions and the trauma. This disparity allows the client to know that he or she can have a memory of the trauma that does not result in the same posttraumatic feelings and reactions that were formerly conditioned. Harvey (2000) described trauma processing as a means for the client to achieve personal authority over traumatic memories. As the traumatic memories become deconditioned, they begin to resemble memories of other life events and lose their ability to trigger the client into re-experiencing, shutdown, or hyperarousal responses, those most classically associated with PTSD. Equally important is the therapist's ability to "stay with" the client, that is, to hear the story and its associated emotion in some detail, to emotionally resonate with the client, to titrate the affect as needed (coregulation that allows more self-regulation), and to provide safety via attachment security. In this stage, the therapist must be prepared to be more available to the client because the processing may cause considerable distress and be quite disorienting until deconditioning takes place.

Whether the processing is formalized and utilizes a specialized approach or technique (e.g., Eye Movement Desensitization and Reprocessing, EMDR [Shapiro, 2001], imaginal rescripting [Smucker & Niederee, 1995], narrative telling and writing [Pennebaker, 2000], sensorimotor approaches [Fisher & Ogden, 2009; Ogden et al., 2006; Rothschild, 2000]) or occurs more spontaneously as the client comes to understand more about past events and their impact, other issues requiring therapeutic attention also surface. For example, strong feelings of shame and rage may emerge along with grief and mourning for all that was lost. Phase 2 work involves processing whatever emotions emerge to the point of some resolution, in order for symptoms to diminish. During this stage, the client may choose to undertake specific actions to resolve relationships with abusers or others. These might involve such actions as disclosures and discussions, boundary development, separation from or reconnection with others, all from a position of increased awareness and understanding and increased assertiveness as well as self-regulatory skills.

### Phase 3: Self and Relational Development and Enhanced Daily Living

Although phase 3 is envisioned as the culmination of the previous work, it may also be fraught with difficulty for some trauma survivors (particularly those who were repeatedly revictimized) who have never had the opportunity for a life that is in the range of normal. Phase 3 therefore might be a time when the client, building upon the awareness developed earlier, more directly identifies the dysfunction and pathology of the past as he or she continues to attempt to move beyond its influence. Phase 3 frequently involves work on unresolved developmental deficits and fixations and continued fine-tuning of self-regulatory skills developed in earlier phases of treatment. Some of the issues most in evidence in this phase are the development of trustworthy and restitutive relationships, increased capacity for intimacy and sexual functioning, parenting, career and other life decisions, and ongoing decisions and discussions with abusive others.

As noted earlier, the intensity and duration of the treatment differs substantially between clients. Some (those most revictimized and those most damaged) require treatment for years or even decades. Others may complete treatment in 6 to 12 months. The initial focus of safety, affect regulation, and skills development is designed to give all who enter treatment a set of functional life skills.

In recent years, many variations or "hybrid" models of treatment that combine or sequence strategies in different ways for the complex client have been developed, some of which are now available in treatment manuals. Some have empirical support or are now being empirically tested (see Cloitre, 1998; Cloitre, Cohen, & Koenen, 2006; Ford & Russo, 2006). Some models specialize in specific problem areas associated with complex trauma, including substance abuse, self-injury, safety, and chronic mental illness. Development efforts of this sort can be expected to continue as the field evolves.

## SUMMARY

This chapter has reviewed the problem of retraumatization in the aftermath of incest and child sexual abuse. Numerous theoretical models and factors ranging from those that are individual to those involving family, community, and society which create additional risk for the victimized were also reviewed. The variety of symptoms experienced and expressed by clients who have been multiply revictimized have been categorized within the diagnostic conceptualization of complex PTSD in order to assist in their understanding and treatment. A sequenced, organized, and progressive meta-model of treatment was described by which these clients can be treated and restored to a life of improved functioning and safety from additional harm and trauma.

## REFERENCES

Alexander, P. C. (1992). Application of attachment theory to the study of sexual abuse. *Journal of Consulting and Clinical Psychology, 60,* 2, 185–195.

Alexander, P. C., & Lupfer, S. L. (1987). Family characteristics and long-term consequences associated with sexual abuse. *Archives of Sexual Behavior, 16,* 235–245.

Alexander, P. C. (2009). Childhood trauma, attachment, and abuse by multiple partners. *Psychological Trauma: Theory, Research, Practice, and Policy, 1,* 1, 78–88.

American Psychiatric Association. (2000). *Diagnostic and statistical manual of mental disorders–text revision.* (4th ed. Rev.). Washington, DC: Author.

Arata, C. M. (1999). Repeated sexual victimization and mental disorders in women. *Journal of Child Sexual Abuse, 7,* 3, 1–17.

Arata, C. M. (2000 February). From child victim to adult victim: A model for predicting sexual revictimization. *Child Maltreatment, 5,* 1, 28–38.

Arata, C. M. (2002). Child sexual abuse and sexual revictimization. *Clinical Psychology: Science and Practice, 9,* 135–164.

Banyard, V. L., Williams, L. M., & Siegel, J. A. (2002) Retraumatization among adult women sexual abused in childhood: Exploratory analyses in a prospective study. *Journal of Child Sexual Abuse, 11,* 3, 19–48.

Boney-McCoy, S., & Finkelhor, D. (1995). Prior victimization: A risk factor for child sexual abuse and for PTSD-related symptomatology among sexually abused youth. *Child Abuse and Neglect, 19,* 1401–1421.

Breitenbecher, K. H. (2001). Sexual revictimization among women: A review of the literature focusing on empirical investigations. *Aggression and Violent Behavior, 6,* 415–432.

Briere, J. (1997). *Psychological assessment of adult posttraumatic states.* Washington, DC: American Psychological Association.

Briere, J. (2002). Treating adult survivors of severe childhood abuse and neglect: Further development of an integrative model. In J. E. B. Myers, L. Berliner, J. Briere, T. Reid, & C. Jenny (Eds.). *The APSAC handbook on child maltreatment* (2nd ed., pp. 175–203). Newbury Park, CA: Sage.

Briere, J., & Spinazzola, J. (2005). Phenomenological and psychological assessment of complex posttraumatic states. *Journal of Traumatic Stress, 18* (5), 401–412.

Briere, J., & Spinazzola, J. (2009). Assessment of the sequelae of complex trauma: Evidence-based measures. In C. A. Courtois & J. D. Ford, *Treating complex traumatic stress disorders: An evidence-based guide* (pp. 104–123). New York: Guilford Press.

Brown, D. (2009). Assessment of attachment. In C. A. Courtois. & J. D. Ford (Eds.), *Treating complex traumatic stress disorders: An evidence-based guide* (pp. 124–143). New York: Guilford Press.

Campbell, R., Greeson, M. R., Bybee, D., & Raja, S. (2008). The co-occurrence of childhood sexual abuse, adult sexual assault, intimate partner violence, and sexual harassment: A mediational model of posttraumatic stress disorder and physical health outcomes. *Journal of Consulting and Clinical Psychology, 76,* 194–207.

Classen, C. C., Palesh, O. G., & Aggarwal, R. (2005). Sexual revictimization: A review of the empirical literature. *Trauma, Violence, & Abuse 6,* 103–129.

Cloitre, M. (1998) Sexual revictimization: Risk factors and prevention. In V. M. Follette, J. I. Ruzek, & F. R. Abueg (Eds.). *Cognitive-behavioral therapies for trauma* (pp. 278–305). New York: Guilford Press.

Cloitre, M., Cohen, L. R., & Koenen, K. C. (2006). *Treating survivors of childhood abuse: Psychotherapy for the interrupted life.* New York: Guilford Press.

Cloitre, M., Scarvalone, P., & Defede, J. (1997). Posttraumatic stress disorder, self- and interpersonal dysfunction among sexually re-traumatized women. *Journal of Traumatic Stress, 10,* 3, 437–452.

Cloitre, M., Stovall-McLough, K. C., Nooner, K., Zorbas, P., & Cherry, S., Jackson, C., Gan, W., & Petkova, E. (2010). Treatment for PTSD related to childhood abuse: A randomized controlled trial. *American Journal of Psychiatry, 167,* 915–924.

Cole, P. M., & Putnam, F. W. (1992). Effect of incest on self and social functioning: A developmental psychopathology perspective. *Journal of Consulting and Clinical Psychology, 60*(2), 174–184.

Courtois, C. A. (1988). *Healing the incest wound: Adult survivors in therapy.* New York: W.W. Norton.

Courtois, C. A. (1999). *Recollections of sexual abuse: Treatment principles and guidelines.* New York: W.W. Norton.

Courtois, C. A. (2004). Complex trauma, complex reactions: Assessment and treatment. *Psychotherapy: Theory, Research, Practice, and Training, 41,* 412–425.

Courtois, C. A. (2010). *Healing the incest wound: Adult survivors in therapy* (2nd ed.). New York: W.W. Norton.

Courtois, C. A., & Ford, J. D. (Eds.). (2009). *Treating complex traumatic stress disorders: An evidence-based guide.* New York: Guilford Press.

Dell, P. F., & O'Neill, J. A. (2009). *Dissociation and the dissociative disorders: DSM-V and beyond.* New York: Routledge.

Ehrensaft, M. K., Cohen, P., Brown, J., Smailes, E., Chen, H., & Johnson, J. G. (2003). Intergenerational transmission of partner violence: A 20-year prospective study. *Journal of Consulting and Clinical Psychology, 71,* 741–753.

Finkelhor, D. (2008). *Childhood victimization: Violence, crime, and abuse in the lives of young people.* New York: Oxford University Press.

Finkelhor, D., & Browne, A. (1985). The traumatic impact of child sexual abuse: A conceptualization. *American Journal of Orthopsychiatry, 55,* 530–541.

Fisher, J., & Ogden, P. (2009) Sensorimotor psychotherapy. In C. A. Courtois & J. D. Ford (Eds.), *Treating complex traumatic stress disorders: An evidence-based guide* (pp. 312–328). New York: Guilford Press.

Foa, E. B., Keane, T. M., Friedman, M. J., & Cohen, J. A. (Eds.). (2008). *Effective treatments for PTSD: Practice guidelines from the International Society for Traumatic Stress Studies* (2nd ed.). New York: Guilford Press.

Follette, V. M., Polusny, M. A., Bechtle, A. E., and Naugle, A. E. (1996). Cumulative trauma: The impact of child sexual abuse, adult sexual assault, and spouse abuse. *Journal of Traumatic Stress, 9*(1), 25–35.

Ford, J. D., & Russo, E. (2006). A trauma-focused, present-centered, emotional self-regulation approach to integrated treatment for post-traumatic stress and addiction: Trauma Adaptive Recovery Group Education and Therapy (TARGET). *American Journal of Psychotherapy, 60,* 335–355.

Fosha, D. (2000). *The transforming power of affect: A model for accelerated change.* New York: Basic Behavioral Science.

Freyd, J. J. (1995). *Betrayal-trauma: The logic of forgetting childhood abuse.* Boston: Harvard University Press.

Freyd, J. J. (1996). *Betrayal trauma: The logic of forgetting childhood abuse.* Cambridge, MA: Harvard University Press.

Friedman, M. J., Davidson, J. R. T., & Stein, D. J. (2008). Psychopharmacotherapy for adults. In E. B. Foa, T. M. Keane, M. J. Friedman, & J. A. Cohen (Eds.), *Effective treatments for PTSD: Practice guidelines from the International Society for Traumatic Stress Studies* (2nd ed., pp. 245–278). New York: Guilford Press.

Gartner, R. B. (1999). *Betrayed as boys: Psychodynamic treatment of sexually abused men.* New York: Guilford Press.

Gelinas, D. (1983). The persistent negative effects of incest. *Psychiatry, 46,* 312–332.

Gobin, R., & Freyd, J. (2009). Betrayal and revictimization: Preliminary findings. *Psychological Trauma: Theory, Research, Practice, and Policy, 1*(3), 242–258.

Gold, S. N. (2000). *Not trauma alone: Therapy for child abuse survivors in family and social context.* Philadelphia: Brunner-Routledge/Taylor & Francis.

Gold, S. R., Sinclair, B. B., & Balge, K. A. (1999). Risk of sexual revictimization: A theoretical model. *Aggression and Violent Behavior, 4*(4), 457–470.

Grauerholz, L. (2000, February). An ecological approach to understanding sexual revictimization: Linking personal, interpersonal, and sociocultural factors and processes. *Child Maltreatment, 5,* 1, 5–17.

Harvey, M. (2000). In the aftermath of sexual abuse: Making and remaking meaning in narratives of trauma and recovery. *Narrative Inquiry, 10,* 291–311.

Herman, J. L. (1992). *Trauma and recovery: The aftermath of violence—from domestic to political terror.* New York: Basic Books.

Herman, J. L. (1997). *Trauma and recovery: The aftermath of violence—from domestic to political terror* (2nd ed.). New York: Basic Books.

Kendall-Tacket, K., Williams, L., & Finkelhor, D. (1993). Impact of sexual abuse on children: A review and synthesis of recent empirical studies. *Psychological Bulletin, 113,* 164–180.

Kessler, B. L., & Bieschke, K. J. (1999). A retrospective analysis of shame, dissociation, and adult victimization in survivors of childhood sexual abuse. *Journal of Counseling Psychology, 46*(3), 335–341.

Kluft, R. P. (1990). Incest and subsequent revictimization: The case of therapist–patient sexual exploitation, with a description of the sitting duck syndrome. In R. P. Kluft (Ed.), *Incest-related syndromes of adult psychopathology* (pp. 263–287). Washington, DC: American Psychiatric Association.

Koenig, L. J., Doll, L. S., O'Leary, A., & Pequegnat, W. (Eds.). (2004). *From child sexual abuse to adult sexual risk: Trauma, revictimization, and intervention.* Washington, DC: American Psychological Association.

Loewenstein, R. J. (1991, September). An office mental status examination for complex chronic dissociative symptoms and multiple personality disorder. *The Psychiatric Clinics of North America, 14*(3), 567–604.

Lynn, S. J., Pintar, J., Fite, R., Ecklund, K., & Stafford, J. (2004).Toward a social-narrative model of revictimization. In L. J. Koenig, L. S. Doll, A. O'Leary, & W. Pequegnat, W. (Eds.), *From child sexual abuse to adult sexual risk: Trauma, revictimization, and intervention* (pp. 159–180). Washington, DC: American Psychological Association.

Maker, A. H., Kemmelmeier, M., & Peterson, C. (2001). Child sexual abuse, peer sexual abuse, and sexual assault in adulthood: A multi-risk model of revictimization. *Journal of Traumatic Stress, 14*(2), 351–368.

Marx, B. P., Heidt, J. M., & Gold, S. D. (2005). Perceived uncontrollability and unpredictability, self-regulation, and sexual revictimization. *Review of General Psychology, 9*(1), 67–90.

Messman, T. L., & Long, P. J. (1996). Child sexual abuse and its relationship to revictimization in adult women: A review. *Clinical Psychology Review, 16*, 397–420.

Messman-Moore, T. L., & Long, P. J. (2000). Child sexual abuse and revictimization in the form of adult sexual abuse, adult physical abuse, and adult psychological maltreatment. *Journal of Interpersonal Violence, 15*, 489–502.

Molnar, B. E., Buka, S. L., & Kessler, R. C. (2001). Child sexual abuse and subsequent psychopathology: Results from the National Comorbidity Survey. *American Journal of Public Health, 91*, 753–760.

Muehlenhard, C. L., Highby, B. J., Lee, R. S., Bryan, T. S., & Dodrill, W. A. (1998). The sexual revictimization of women and men sexually abused as children: A review of the literature. *Annual Review of Sex Research, 9*, 177–223.

Noll, J. G., Horowitz, L. A., Bonanno, G., Trickett, P. K., & Putnam, F. W. (2003). Revictimization and self-harm in females who experienced childhood sexual abuse. *Journal of Abnormal Psychology, 18*, 1452–1471.

Ogden, P., Minton, K., & Pain, C. (2006). *Trauma and the body: A sensorimotor approach to psychotherapy*. New York: Norton.

Opler, L. A., Grennan, M. S., & Ford, J. D. (2009). Pharmacotherapy. In C. A. Courtois & J. D. Ford (Eds.). *Treating complex traumatic stress disorders: An evidence-based guide* (pp. 333–349). New York: Guilford Press.

Paivio, S. C., & Pascual-Leone, A. (2010). *Emotion focused therapy for complex trauma: An integrative approach*. Washington, DC: American Psychological Association.

Pennebaker, J. W. (2000). The *effects of traumatic disclosure on physical and mental health*. In J. Violante & D. Paton (Eds.), Posttraumatic stress intervention (pp. 97–114). Springfield, IL: Charles C. Thomas.

Polusny, M. M., & Follette, V. M. (1995). Long-term correlates of child sexual abuse: Theory and review of the empirical literature. *Applied and Preventive Psychology, 4*, 143–166.

Putnam, F. W. (2003, March). Ten-year research update review: Child sexual abuse. *Journal of the American Academy of Child and Adolescent Psychiatry, 42*(3), 269–278.

Rich, C. L., Combs-Lane, A. M., Resnick, H. S., & Kilpatrick, D. G. (2004). Child sexual abuse and adult sexual revictimization. In L. J. Koenig, L. S. Doll, A. O'Leary, & W. Pequegnat (Eds.), *From child sexual abuse to adult sexual risk: Trauma, revictimization, and intervention* (pp. 29–68). Washington, DC: American Psychological Association.

Roodman, A. A., & Clum, G. A. (2001). Victimization rates and method variance: A meta-analysis. *Journal of Traumatic Stress, 21*, 183–204.

Rothschild, B. (2000). *The body remembers: The psychophysiology of trauma and trauma treatment*. New York: W. W. Norton.

Sandberg, D., Lynn, S. J., & Green, J. (1994). Sexual abuse and revictimization: Mastery, dysfunctional learning, and dissociation. In S. J. Lynn & J. Rhue (Eds.), *Dissociation: Clinical and theoretical perspectives* (pp. 242–267). New York: Guilford Press.

Shapiro, F. (Ed.) 2001. *Eye movement desensitization and reprocessing (EMDR): Basic principles, protocols, and procedures.* New York: Guilford Press.

Smith, P. H., Thornton, G. E., DeVellis, R., Earp, J., & Coker, A. L. (2002). A population-based study of the prevalence and distinctiveness of battering, physical assault, and sexual assault in intimate relationships. *Violence Against Women, 8,* 1208–1232.

Smucker, M. R., & Niederee, J. (1995). Treating incest-related PTSD and pathogenic schemas through imaginal exposure and rescripting. *Cognitive and Behavioral Practice, 2,* 63–92.

Spaccarelli, S. (1994). Stress, appraisal, and coping in child sexual abuse: A theoretical and empirical review. *Psychological Bulletin, 116,* 340–362.

Spaccarelli, S., & Kim, S. (September 1995). Resilience criteria and factors associated with resilience in sexually abused girls. *Child Abuse & Neglect, 19*(9), 1171–1182.

Terr. L. (1991). Childhood traumas: An outline and overview. *American Journal of Psychiatry, 148,* 10–20.

Tjaden, P. T. N., & Thoennes, N. (2000). Extent, Nature, and Consequences of Intimate Partner Violence: Findings from the National Violence Against Women Survey Retrieved March 2, 2009, from http://www.ncjrs.gov/pdffiles1/nij/181867.pdf

Ullman, S. E., Najdowski, C. J., & Filipas, H. H. (2009). Child sexual abuse, post-traumatic stress disorder, and substance use: Predictors of revictimization in adult sexual assault survivors. *Journal of Child Sexual Abuse, 18*(4), 367–385.

Urquiza, A. J., & Goodlin-Jones, B. L. (1994). Child sexual abuse and adult revictimization with women of color. *Violence and Victims, 9*(3), 223–232.

White, J. W., Koss, M. P., & Kazdin, A. E. (2011). *Violence against women and children: Consensus, critical analysis and emergent priorities. Volume 1: Mapping the terrain.* Washington, DC: American Psychological Association.

Widom, C. S., Czaja, S. J., & Dutton, M. A. (2008). Childhood victimization and lifetime revictimization. *Child Abuse and Neglect, 32,* 785–796.

Wilson, J. P., & Keane. T. M. (2004). *Assessing psychological trauma and PTSD* (2nd ed.). New York: Guilford Press.

Wyatt, G. E., Guthrie, D., & Notgrass, C. M. (1992). Differential effects of women's child sexual abuse and subsequent sexual revictimization. *Journal of Consulting and Clinical Psychology, 60*(2), 167–173.

Chapter 8

# Retraumatization and Revictimization
## *An Attachment Perspective*

*Pamela C. Alexander*

*Retraumatization* has been defined as "one's reaction to a traumatic exposure that is colored, intensified, amplified, or shaped by one's reactions and
adaptational style to previous traumatic experiences" (Danieli, 2010, p. 195).
Although the exposure may not be inherently traumatic but may only carry
reminders of the original traumatic event or relationship, retraumatization typically refers to the reemergence of symptoms previously experienced as a result
of the trauma. Attachment theory brings an added dimension to this notion
by framing trauma and adaptation to trauma within the context of close relationships. Early attachment relationships can either compensate for the initial
experience of trauma, thus protecting the individual from retraumatization,
or can exacerbate the initial experience of trauma, thus greatly increasing an
abuse survivor's risk for retraumatization. Furthermore, a new exposure not
only to a traumatic event, but also to a new relationship that approximates
the initial attachment relationship can act as a trigger for similar emotional
reactions and similar behavioral responses to the new relationship. Thus, the
individual may be at risk not only for emotional re-experiencing but also for
actual revictimization. In fact, research suggests that child abuse and neglect
(most of which occurs within the context of attachment relationships) leads to
increased risk of interpersonal violence (physical and sexual assault or abuse,
kidnapping or stalking) but not to increased risk of general traumas, crime
victimization, or witnessing traumatic events (Widom, Czaja, & Dutton, 2008),

suggesting the interpersonal specificity of revictimization. This chapter will describe how attachment theory can explain both the process of emotional re-experiencing as well as the behavioral interactional patterns of abuse survivors which increase their risk for this revictimization and retraumatization.

The frame for this chapter is developmental psychopathology. In other words, the timing of the traumatic experiences is significant, as is the developmental trajectory of effects, with different outcomes expected at different developmental stages. Also important is the developmental trajectory of relationships, with the effect of traumatization and insecure attachment necessarily limiting and defining the potential pool of subsequent relationships and the potential pool of affective and behavioral responses to subsequent traumas. Given that trauma that occurs within the context of close interpersonal relationships is much more deleterious in its outcomes (Trickett, Reiffman, Horowitz, & Putnam, 1997), attachment relationships are particularly relevant contexts for evaluating the impact of trauma experiences. Therefore, this chapter will begin with a description of attachment theory, including specific attachment categories in childhood and adulthood and a brief overview of neurobiological studies demonstrating the long-term effects of disrupted attachment and maltreatment. The chapter will then proceed to a review of literature on peer victimization, dating violence victimization, and victimization by an intimate partner in adulthood, highlighting research on the association of each of these topics with insecure attachment. The frequent use of observational research, multiple informants, and longitudinal designs by attachment researchers provides support for the validity of their findings. Finally, just as insecure attachment can exacerbate the effects of abuse, a supportive attachment relationship can protect against the occurrence of abuse or overcome its impact. Therefore, awareness of attachment processes can facilitate the development of effective trauma prevention and intervention efforts.

## ATTACHMENT THEORY

Attachment is assumed to be a biologically based bond that assures the child's proximity to the caregiver, particularly during periods of perceived danger and fear (Bowlby, 1969/1982). An essential premise of attachment theory is that the human infant is literally unable to survive without access to some sort of protective caregiver. Abandonment or even the attachment figure's careless inattention in the face of danger are realistically the biggest threats that an infant can experience—traumatizing by any definition of the term. Perhaps that is why the effects of neglect appear to be more significant than the effects of abuse (Hildyard & Wolfe, 2002). Therefore, a child will develop all sorts of strategies, including distortions of affect and cognition, if necessary, to avoid the very real traumatization of this lack of access to the attachment figure.

The initial role of the caregiver is to help the infant regulate his or her affective states by paying attention to the child's facial expressions (Schore, 2000). When a mother or other caregiver reflects or mirrors her child's emotional state (thus labeling the child's experience), but then displays a different emotional state by soothing the child (thus modeling the mastery of her own emotions while effectively regulating her child's emotions), the child comes to understand his or her own feelings, to develop control of these feelings, and to recognize that his or her emotional state is distinct from that of the mother's. This process has been referred to as reflective functioning (Fonagy, 1999; Fonagy, Target, & Gergely, 2000), and it is this parental ability to reflect on the child's internal mental states that accounts for the transmission of secure attachment and sensitive parenting (Slade, Grienenberger, Bernbach, Levy, & Locker, 2005). This caregiver attachment behavior also has a direct impact upon the development of those areas of the brain (e.g., the rostral limbic system) most responsible for processing emotional information and for regulating affect (Schore, 2000). Therefore, sensitive parenting has implications for the management of any type of trauma or stressful experience.

In addition to a model of affect regulation, attachment theory is a model of cognition, consisting of unconscious internal working models that encode these patterns of affect regulation (Schore, 2000). Since the human child cannot *not* be attached, these internal working models establish the most effective behavioral strategies for maintaining access to the attachment figure; they are also the basis of expectations about intimate relationships. Moreover, it is proposed that the child internalizes both sides of the attachment relationship (Sroufe & Fleeson, 1986). Therefore, the child may model the attachment figure's behavior and may also elicit from others similar reactions to that of the original attachment figure by displaying behaviors that were enacted in the initial attachment relationship.

Three organized attachment strategies (secure, avoidant, and anxious or ambivalent) were first identified by Mary Ainsworth (Ainsworth, Blehar, Waters, & Wall, 1978) in her classification of children's behavior in a separation-reunion paradigm (the "Strange Situation"). This classification of attachment strategies has been validated with extensive observations of the parent–child interactions in the home. In addition, a disorganized attachment strategy was later identified by researchers who noted that the three organized classifications did not adequately describe the behavior of certain children in the Strange Situation. The function of these behavior patterns is readily observable when one remembers that the goal of the child is to maintain access to a caregiver who, because of his or her own past experiences or current stresses, may or may not be adequately available to the child during situations of threat. The adult counterparts to these attachment categories, while not directly comparable to the child's attachment pattern, are reflections of the adult's current state of mind regarding attachment. They are assessed by means of discourse analysis of Mary Main's Adult Attachment Interview

(AAI) (Main & Goldwyn, 1998); as such, the AAI does not assess the content of the individual's story but instead how the adult tells his or her story. The continuity of adult attachment with the child's behavior is demonstrated both through longitudinal research following children from 12 months of age (in the Strange Situation) to more than 20 years of age (cf., Fraley, 2002; Waters, Merrick, Treboux, Crowell, & Albersheim, 2000) as well as research demonstrating that the parent's state of mind with respect to attachment (even prior to the birth of the child) predicts the child's later behavior in the Strange Situation (van IJzendoorn, 1995; Ward & Carlson, 1995). As will be described further, the child's attachment behaviors and internal working models also have direct implications for his or her eventual risk of later victimization and traumatization. In the interest of space, both the child and adult's behavior will be described together.

> *Secure attachment* is associated with the parent's ability to respond appropriately to soothe the child when needed and to provide a secure base, from which the child returns rapidly to play and exploration of the environment. Because the secure child is confident that the parent will be available and responsive as necessary, the child feels free to engage in play without undue attention to monitoring the parent's whereabouts. In other words, the secure child does not need to distort either affect or cognition to maintain access to the parent; the secure child instead asks for support or reassurance when needed. By internalizing the parent's relatively effective regulation of the child's affect, the securely attached child learns to self-soothe and develops positive expectations of himself or herself and others. The adult counterpart to this secure attachment is called *secure/autonomous attachment*. It is characterized on the AAI by a coherent, collaborative narrative with an apparently objective access to both positive and negative memories, and by a valuing of attachment relationships (Main, 2000). Secure adults are self-confident, trusting, and comfortable with closeness (Collins & Read, 1990; Feeney & Noller, 1990; Hazan & Shaver, 1987; Main & Goldwyn, 1984), although because of their lack of defensiveness, they may be uniquely vulnerable to psychopathic individuals (Crittenden, 1994).
> In *avoidant attachment*, the parent is cold and rejecting precisely when the child is distressed or needy. As a result, the child learns to suppress the negative affect that appears to drive the parent away (Izard & Kobak, 1991). Although this organized insecure strategy allows the child to maintain connection with the parent, the child's compulsive self-reliance occurs at the expense of the child's ability to recognize and thus to modulate his or her own negative affect, as manifest in marked physiological arousal in situations of stress (Spangler & Grossmann, 1993). The avoidant child's defensive focus on the environment and away from the rejecting parent does not appear to inhibit the child's

competence at play but his or her negative expectations of others does appear to diminish the quality of interactions with peers (McElwain, Cox, Burchinal, & Macfie, 2003). The adult counterpart to avoidant attachment is called *dismissing attachment*. Like the avoidant child, the dismissing adult presents as "more normal than normal" (Crittenden, Partridge, & Claussen, 1991), exhibits increased physiological arousal when asked about parental rejection and separation (Dozier & Kobak, 1992), and is likely to be described as hostile by peers (Kobak & Sceery, 1988). He or she also tends to minimize the significance of early attachment relationships and describes little overt distress while covertly exhibiting hostility, loneliness, and anxiety (Bartholomew & Horowitz, 1991; Kobak & Sceery, 1988; Main & Goldwyn, 1984).

In *anxious/ambivalent attachment*, another organized albeit insecure strategy, the parent is inconsistently available, combining a pattern of neglect with direct interference in the child's play (Cassidy & Berlin, 1994). Because of this ongoing threat of abandonment, the child maintains access to the inconsistent parent by heightening negative affect in order to elicit a reaction. Unfortunately, while this strategy is effective at attracting attention in the moment, it also generates the parent's aversion and avoidance of the child. Thus, this strategy leads to an even greater need for the child to alternate fussy, angry, and demanding behaviors with coy, clinging, and guilt-inducing behaviors when the parent retreats from the onslaught (Crittenden, 1997; Moran & Pederson, 1998). As a result, the anxious or ambivalent child is not easily soothed and unable to use the parent as a secure base (Main, 2000), sees himself or herself as incompetent and helpless, is inhibited in interacting with peers and the environment, and may emphasize immaturity in order to elicit attention (Cassidy & Berlin, 1994). In relationships with peers and teachers, this child hyperactivates attachment needs, has low self-efficacy, and is babied but disliked (Main, 2000). The adult counterpart of this attachment pattern is called *preoccupied* because the individual is characterized by either a passive or angry preoccupation with the parent or other attachment figures (Main & Goldwyn, 1998). Preoccupied adults use coercive behaviors (including clinging, dependency, and jealousy) to increase their proximity to the attachment figure, inevitably leading to rejection that heightens their fears of abandonment (Allen, Stein, Fonagy, Fultz, & Target, 2005; Cassidy & Berlin, 1994).

Finally, *disorganized/disoriented attachment*, prevalent among abused samples of children (Carlson, Cicchetti, Barnett, & Braunwald, 1989), is characterized in the Strange Situation by the child's contradictory approach-avoidant behavior, dazed expressions, and apprehension on the parent's return (Main & Solomon, 1986, 1990). Disorganized attachment is unrelated to temperament, constitutional variables, or gender (van IJzendoorn, Schuengel, & Bakermans-Kranenburg, 1999).

According to Liotti (1992), the disorganized child inadvertently elicits anxiety in the parent with an unresolved history of loss or trauma. In essence, the child's very presence is retraumatizing to the parent whose own existence as a child appeared to elicit abuse and neglect from the parent's caregiver. The parent responds to this retraumatization by relying inappropriately upon the child to reduce the parent's own anxiety. This parental role reversal signals to the child that the parent is obviously not in control (another dangerous situation for a young child) and is accompanied by the parent's frightening (abusive) or frightened behavior (Main & Hesse, 1990). However, what any child will necessarily do during a situation of threat or danger is to look for protection from the attachment figure. The disorganized child thus finds himself or herself in the paradoxical situation of needing to seek comfort from the very attachment figure who is the source of fear. This "fright without solution" (Main, 1995) predisposes the child to dissociation in adulthood (Ogawa, Sroufe, Weinfield, Carlson, & Egeland, 1997). In fact, in an interview study of 112 incest survivors, what best distinguished the 8 women who had been diagnosed with dissociative identity disorder from the rest of the sample was their characterization of their very abusive fathers as also their primary attachment figures (Anderson & Alexander, 1996). These women had to find a way to separate their view of their father as extremely dangerous from their view of him as their only source of protection. The specificity of this connection between dissociation and attachment was also demonstrated in an emotional Stroop test in which high and low dissociators differed only with regard to stimuli reflecting attachment-related anxiety and not with regard to either general anxiety or neutral stimuli (Loos & Alexander, 2001).

In the preschool years, the disorganized child appears to try to control the parent who is the source of the child's unintegrated fears by engaging in either punitive behavior in reaction to hostile and intrusive parental behavior, or caregiving behavior in reaction to helpless and passive parental behavior (Lyons-Ruth, Lyubchik, Wolfe, & Bronfman, 2002; Solomon, George, & DeJong, 1995). Not surprisingly, the disorganized child exhibits high rates of internalizing and externalizing behavior and major deficiencies in affect regulation (Lyons-Ruth, Easterbrooks, & Cibelli, 1997). The adult counterpart to disorganized attachment in childhood is *unresolved attachment*, classified as such on the AAI when the adult displays lapses in reasoning or dissociated ideas or memories precisely when asked to speak about any experiences of trauma or loss (Main & Goldwyn, 1998). These individuals tend to be socially inhibited and unassertive, lack a sense of personal agency, and are more likely to exhibit self-defeating and borderline tendencies (Alexander et al., 1998; Bartholomew & Horowitz, 1991). In fact, Wagner and Linehan (1997) have noted that even more important than a history of abuse or neglect in women with borderline personality disorder, is their experience of an invalidating family environment. In other words, as children, their caregiver failed to relate to them as having an independent mind, leading the child to internalize the parent's feeling of rage or view of the child as frightening or unmanageable (Fonagy, 1999). Needless to say, unresolved individuals are more likely to be characterized by psychiatric disorders in general (Fonagy et al., 1996).

## Neurobiological Effects of Attachment and Trauma

Neurobiological studies based on animal models and maltreated humans have demonstrated the long-term and sometimes irreversible effects of both attachment behavior and maltreatment on the developing brain. In a review of this research, Putnam (2005) noted that rats experiencing prolonged maternal separation exhibit significantly increased plasma adrenocorticotropic hormone (ACTH) and corticosterone responses to subsequent stressors. Furthermore, long-term individual differences in stress reactivity in rats are due in part to normal variations and experimentally induced variations in maternal behavior (Francis & Meaney, 1999). Suomi (1996) compared the behavior of peer-reared monkeys with mother-reared monkeys and found the former to exhibit greater HPA-axis reactivity in addition to disrupted behavior. Research with maltreated human populations has similarly indicated that a child abuse history can permanently result in greater HPA-axis reactivity in response to subsequent victimization or even to laboratory stressors (Putnam, 2005). Finally, MRI research has demonstrated brain atrophy in maltreated as compared to nonmaltreated children which was correlated with the extent of posttraumatic stress disorder (PTSD) symptoms and dissociation (De Bellis et al., 1999). As mentioned previously, the closer the relationship between the abused child and the perpetrator, the greater is the degree of long-term dysfunction (Trickett et al., 1997); therefore, the analogies between the HPA-reactivity found in animal models of attachment disruption and the HPA-reactivity of maltreated persons are striking.

## PEER VICTIMIZATION IN CHILDHOOD AND ADOLESCENCE

One important stage in the developmental trajectory of retraumatization is children's victimization by and aggression toward peers. There are several reasons for considering victimization and aggression together. First, while some children are pure bullies and others are pure victims (Woods & White, 2005), a small but significant group can be classified as both aggressors and victims or "bully/victims" (Crick & Bigbee, 1998; Woods & White, 2005). Relatedly, for some children, aggressive behavior may lead to victimization by peers (Ostrov, 2008; van Hoof, Raaijmakers, van Beek, Hale, & Aleva, 2008). Another reason for considering aggressors and victims together is that both aggressors and victims are likely to be rebuffed by the larger peer group. As a consequence, they both experience problems associated with peer rejection, such as depression and anxiety (Irons & Gilbert, 2005; Shields & Cicchetti, 2001). Finally, because of this social rejection by the larger peer group, aggressors and victims may be more likely to end up interacting with each other by default (Perry, Kusel, & Perry, 1988). Therefore, both their intentional and de facto interaction with each other is relevant to understanding the dynamics of their behavior. Consequently, the following review will be framed in terms of both constructs, making distinctions where they exist.

Aggression toward and victimization by same-age peers in school is not uncommon with estimates for extreme victimization ranging from 10% to 25% of children and adolescents (Perry et al., 1988; Storch & Masia-Warner, 2004; Woods & White, 2005). Crick and Bigbee (1998) have argued (and subsequent researchers have agreed) that relational aggression, referring to the hurtful manipulation of peer or friendship relationships, should be included in any consideration of aggression and victimization. Although relational aggression is more prevalent than overt or physical aggression (Woods & White, 2005), it, like emotional abuse, is no less damaging in its effects. For example, both overt aggression and relational aggression result in peer rejection, loneliness, depression, physiological symptoms, and social avoidance (Crick & Bigbee, 1998; Storch, Brassard, & Masia-Warner, 2003). Although there are no apparent age or sex differences in overall rates of victimization (Perry et al., 1988; Shields & Cicchetti, 2001), boys are more likely to engage in and be victimized by overt or physical aggression, and girls are more likely to be involved in relational aggression (Casas et al., 2006; Crick & Bigbee, 1998; Storch et al., 2003). Interestingly, nearly 85% of victimization experienced in adolescence is perpetrated by members of the same sex (Gallup, O'Brien, White, & Wilson, 2009). Furthermore, researchers have noted a stable propensity to be victimized (Perry et al., 1988; Sweeting, Young, West, & Der, 2006).

Both aggression and victimization by peers are clearly associated with a history of child maltreatment and exposure to domestic violence (Bowes et al., 2009; Duncan, 1999; Holt, Kantor, & Finkelhor, 2009; Mohr, 2006). Moreover, the type of maltreatment experienced appears to be important, with histories of physical abuse or sexual abuse more common among aggressive children and histories of neglect more common among children who exhibit social withdrawal, social rejection, and feelings of incompetence suggestive of potential victimization (Finzi, Ram, Har-Even, Shnit, & Weizman, 2001; Shields & Cicchetti, 2001). In general, maltreatment history predicts physical aggression in boys and relational aggression in girls, physical abuse leads to physical aggression, and child sexual abuse (CSA) leads to relational aggression for girls only (Cullerton-Sen et al., 2008).

## Impact of Peer Victimization

The notion that peer victimization is experienced as retraumatization can be readily inferred from the symptoms associated with it. The most obvious sequela of peer victimization is emotion dysregulation. Both overt and relational victimization result in physiological symptoms in boys and girls (Storch et al., 2003). This emotion dysregulation is not only a mediator between initial maltreatment history and later aggression (Cullerton-Sen et al., 2008; Shields & Cicchetti, 2001), but also between relational victimization by peers and subsequent relational and physical aggression toward others (Sullivan, Farrell, & Kliewer, 2006). Because both relational aggression and physical aggression lead to even more victimization (Kochenderfer-Ladd, 2003; Leadbetter & Hoglund, 2006; Ostrov, 2008), the stage is set for a vicious cycle of aggression and victimization and retraumatization. Emotion dysregulation resulting from peer victimization also manifests itself in internalizing problems, including depression, loneliness, and anxiety (Erdur-Baker, 2009; Gladstone, Parker, & Malhi, 2006; van Hoof et al., 2008). Depression appears to be particularly associated with an experience of relational victimization (McLaughlin, Hatzenbuehler, & Hilt, 2009), perhaps through its impact on reducing an individual's ability to identify perpetrators or to avoid risk (Breslau, Davis, Peterson, & Schultz, 1997). Therefore, understanding the initial attachment dynamics that contribute to this form of retraumatization and revictimization is essential in developing interventions to prevent it.

## Attachment and Peer Victimization

Attachment-based research has focused for some time on exploring the observed connection between maltreatment history and peer aggression or victimization. One of the first longitudinal research studies to explore the relationship between attachment security and peer victimization was conducted by Troy and Sroufe (1987). They classified children's attachment category in the Strange Situation at ages 12 and 18 months and then assigned these children at ages 4 to 5 years old to same-sex play dyads in order to examine all possible combinations of attachment history. Three blind independent judges observed these play pairs in seven 15-minute sessions and found patterns of physical and emotional aggression and victimization in 5 of the 14 dyads. All victimizers had previously been categorized as avoidant, and all victims had previously been categorized as insecurely attached (either avoidant or anxious or ambivalent). Interestingly, securely attached children were never in a victimizing relationship, whether or not the play partner was avoidant, either making the interaction as positive for themselves as possible or simply not engaging in the relationship. In rare instances in which the secure child's play partner attempted to intimidate him or her, the secure child responded with just enough force early in the relationship to dissuade the other child from bullying any further. On the other hand, the authors noted that victims appeared to have an active role in maintaining the pattern. For example, in one dyad, the victim made 119 attempts over the course of the play sessions to initiate a friendly interaction with the aggressive play partner even though only 19 attempts were responded to favorably. Troy and Sroufe (1987) concluded that avoidant children's early experience of rejection and abuse had been internalized into the roles of victimizer and victim. Conversely, anxious or ambivalent children's history of interacting with an inconsistent caregiver appeared to encourage them to continue to make attempts to engage with a play partner, albeit ineffectively. Finally, although this study was conducted prior to the development of the disorganized attachment category, it is likely that at least some of the avoidant children would actually have been classified as disorganized, including perhaps a play pair of girls who switched the direction of victimization several times with the result that each girl was both a victim and a victimizer (i.e., bully/victims).

As stated previously, securely attached children may also experience abuse, albeit not typically by their primary attachment figure. Because of this attachment relationship, however, the child is protected from the types of interactions with other children that could lead to retraumatization and revictimization. For example, security of attachment to fathers is associated with lower levels of aggression (Booth-LaForce et al., 2006), higher levels of attachment to peers and social self-efficacy (Coleman, 2003), more effective reasoning and peer conflict resolution (Steele & Steele, 2005), and lower levels of rejection and victimization, based on peer nomination (Rubin et al., 2004). The mother-child attachment relationship is also important in fostering social competence in boys and reducing the risk for internalizing problems in girls (Rubin et al., 2004). Finally, in a sample of 140 adolescents, secure attachment was inversely related to submissive behavior, depression, and anxiety (Irons & Gilbert, 2005). The authors concluded that secure attachment protected adolescents from seeing their environment as a competitive, threatening place.

The impact of avoidant attachment on subsequent aggression and victimization in peer relationships has been demonstrated in a number of studies. For example, in the National Institute of Child Health and Human Development (NICHD) study of Early Child Care, attachment security was assessed at 15 months and 36 months and children's interactions with a same-sex friend were observed at 36 months. In an analysis of these data, McElwain et al. (2003) found that avoidant attachment was associated with instrumental aggression during play. In a comparison of secure and dismissing (avoidant) adolescents who had been assessed on the AAI, Dykas, Ziv, and Cassidy (2008) found that the dismissing adolescents were more likely to be perceived as aggressive and to be victimized by peers, pointing once again to the frequent connection between aggression and victimization. Moreover, dismissing girls were more likely to be neglected than were secure girls—another type of traumatization that was not observed among boys, presumably because boys tend to interact in larger groups than do girls.

As described previously, the anxious or ambivalent child has a parent who is highly inconsistent, alternating inattention and neglect with overinvolvement. Ladd and Kochenderfer-Ladd (1998) videotaped the interactions of 197 kindergartners and their caregivers in their homes; both low parental responsiveness and high intrusive demandingness were associated with peer victimization in boys and girls. Anxious or ambivalent attachment has been associated with decreased levels of self-assertion (McElwain et al., 2003), a dynamic that frequently results in social exclusion (Fox & Boulton, 2006). Finzi et al. (2001) similarly argued that the experience of parental neglect frequently observed in anxious or ambivalent children puts them at risk for social rejection and feelings of incompetence. In other words, the behaviors of passivity alternating with heightened attention seeking are an attempt to head off the anticipated neglect by the other person. Unfortunately, these behaviors are experienced as highly annoying by peers, leading them to either actively avoid or harass the anxious or ambivalent child. Either reaction will be experienced by the anxious or ambivalent child as a reenactment of the original attachment relationship.

Finally, disorganized attachment is not only particularly germane to a history of childhood trauma but is also particularly relevant to a discussion of bully/victims. McElwain et al. (2003) found that disorganized attachment was associated with more controlling behavior in 3-year-old children than that found in any other attachment category, but only with friends, suggesting that aggression and victimization among disorganized children may be most likely in close relationships. Both disorganized children and bully/victims exhibit the highest levels of affect dysregulation (Woods & White, 2005; van IJzendoorn et al., 1999), suggesting the role of emotion dysregulation as a mediator between parental maltreatment and later aggression or victimization. Bully/victims are both anxious as bullies and provocative as victims (Guerin & Hennessy, 2002), a characterization that would apply equally well to disorganized children.

In conclusion, peer victimization leads to many symptoms and behaviors that contribute to a trajectory of retraumatization and revictimization. For example, peer victimization leads to disrupted concentration at school and poor school engagement (Boulton, Trueman, & Murray, 2008; Hoglund, 2007), narrowing a child's or adolescent's potential pool of social contacts. Relational aggression both precedes and follows from sexual risk-taking in females (Gallup et al., 2009; Leenaars, Dane, & Marini, 2008), a behavior obviously connected with subsequent risk for sexual revictimization. Finally, peer victimization has been found to lead to increased alcohol and drug use (Sullivan et al., 2006), social rejection (Andreou, 2001; Perry et al., 1988; Storch et al., 2003), and dating violence and peer sexual harassment (Espelage & Holt, 2007). The following section will focus on retraumatization and revictimization at this next developmental stage.

## DATING VIOLENCE

Involvement in an abusive dating relationship has been associated with a history of child maltreatment (Wolfe, Wekerle, Scott, & Straatman, 2004). Based on the reports of both males and females, a bidirectional pattern of dating violence predominates (Straus, 2008; Wolfe, Scott, Wekerle, & Pittman, 2001). The fact that the violence is mutual in no way mitigates its significance. Mutually violent dating relationships are significantly more violent (leading to more injury), are characterized by reciprocal violent behavior in that the average amount of violence perpetrated equals the average amount of violence received, are associated with the greatest acceptance of dating violence, and are not generally characterized by motivations of self-defense or retaliation (Gray & Foshee, 1997; Sharpe & Taylor, 1999). Therefore, as with peer victimization, distinctions between perpetration and victimization are not always clear.

A new dating relationship is a significant milestone in the developmental trajectory of retraumatization and revictimization because it typically represents the first opportunity for a close attachment relationship outside of one's family. Therefore, patterns of interactions consistent with initial internal working models of intimate relationships can be expected. For example, in a study of heterosexual dating couples, Rapoza and Baker (2008) found that anxious attachment predicted young men's physical violence and that childhood abuse by the opposite-gender parent predicted victimization for both males and females, suggesting the specificity of attachment relationships with parents in increasing the risk for victimization. Anxiety surrounding attachment may also lead to counterproductive strategies to regulate this affect, not only failing to relieve the anxiety but also setting the stage for actual revictimization. Two ineffective strategies frequently observed among insecurely attached or previously traumatized adolescents are substance abuse and sexual risk-taking. These behavior patterns are certainly not exclusive to adolescent or dating relationships but will be described here because this developmental stage is when they commonly make their first appearance.

## Attachment, Substance Abuse, and Revictimization

Researchers have found that victims of sexual assault and other kinds of trauma frequently misuse substances in an attempt to self-medicate (McCauley et al., 2009). Furthermore, prospective studies have found that substance abuse mediated the relationship between initial PTSD symptoms and subsequent rape or other violence experiences occurring during the follow-up period (Hedtke et al., 2008; Messman-Moore, Ward, & Brown, 2009). The nature of this vicious cycle was also demonstrated by a prospective study finding that alcohol use led to incapacitated rape, leading to even greater alcohol use (Kaysen, Neighbors, Martell, Fossos, & Larimer, 2006).

Many studies have demonstrated the connection between a history of insecure attachment and substance abuse. For example, physical or emotional abuse was mediated by insecure attachment in the prediction of polysubstance use (Hodson, Newcomb, Locke, & Goodyear, 2006). Moreover, just as the neurobiological research reviewed earlier indicated that early attachment relationships can impact HPA-reactivity to subsequent stress, measures of childhood neglect by mothers have been found to predict plasma ACTH levels of abstinent but addicted patients (Gerra et al., 2008), suggesting a persistent effect of poor parent–child attachment on HPA axis function and increasing the risk for substance abuse. Thus, both early attachment experiences and early maltreatment may increase the risk for revictimization through their effects on substance abuse associated with affect dysregulation in response to stress.

## Attachment, Trauma, and Sexual Risk Taking

A substantial body of research indicates that a history of child sexual abuse (CSA) is associated with sexual risk taking in both men and women (e.g., Cinq-Mars, Wright, Cyr, & McDuff, 2003). Much of this sexual risk taking associated with a history of CSA is mediated by substance abuse (Smith, Davis, & Fricker-Elhai, 2004). What attachment theory contributes to this research is the notion that not just the initial trauma but also the context of the attachment relationship at the time of the trauma can explain risky sexual behavior in adolescents and young adults. For example, that fearful attachment (associated with unresolved trauma) leads to multiple sex partners (Ciesla, Roberts, & Hewitt, 2004) is consistent with the previously described research on the sequelae of CSA. Moreover, when a history of CSA is associated with avoidance (more common among dismissing individuals), the outcomes appear to be sexual problems and fewer partners (Merrill, Guimond, Thomson, & Milner, 2003). When the CSA is associated with self-destructive coping (more common among preoccupied individuals), the outcome is an increased number of sexual partners. Preoccupied attachment assessed in a sample of adolescents on the AAI has similarly been associated with sexual risk taking (Kobak, Zajac, & Smith, 2009). Therefore, sexual risk taking may serve the function of attempting to achieve or maintain the intimacy of a new attachment relationship. Unfortunately, the result is frequently revictimization (Arata, 2000).

## INTIMATE PARTNER VIOLENCE

Involvement in an abusive intimate relationship in adulthood is clearly related to a childhood history of exposure to violence (Ehrensaft et al., 2003; Kwong, Bartholomew, Henderson, & Trinke, 2003). For example, a history of CSA or adolescent rape has been found to increase the odds of experiencing and perpetrating intimate partner violence (IPV) by 9 and 13 times, respectively (Feerick, Haugaard, & Hien, 2002). Although even securely attached individuals may find themselves in an abusive relationship (Bookwala, 2002), a secure attachment to a nonabusive parent appears to protect survivors of childhood trauma from subsequent symptoms and revictimization (Reinert & Edwards, 2009; Siegel, 2000). Conversely, insecure attachment and a poor relationship with a parent increase one's risk for victimization by one's partner (Cleveland, Herrera, & Stuewig, 2003; Higginbotham, Ketring, Hibbert, Wright & Guarino, 2007). For example, Feerick et al. (2002) found that the odds of victimization by a partner were six times higher for women who were insecure in their attachment to a primary caregiver in childhood. The following sections describe interpersonal dynamics that are particularly pertinent to individuals of different attachment categories.

## Intimate Partner Violence (IPV) and Dismissing Attachment

The specific dynamics of finding or tolerating an abusive partner are determined in large part by the internal working models that developed out of the initial parent–child attachment relationship. For example, the dynamics of avoidant or dismissing attachment generally involve control of one's own and one's partner's behavior and expressions of emotion (Babcock, Jacobson, Gottman, & Yerington, 2000; Smallbone & Dadds, 2001). In an analysis of 10,500 AAIs, dismissing attachment was prevalent among individuals diagnosed with antisocial personality disorder (Bakermans-Kranenburg & van IJzendoorn, 2009). Dismissing attachment has been found to substantially increase the relationship between a history of neglect and subsequent violent victimization, perhaps by limiting these individuals' opportunities to learn more self-protective strategies when faced with personal threat (Irwin, 1999). The implication of avoidant attachment for revictimization may be inferred from the avoidant child's willingness to suppress negative affect in order to maintain a relationship with a dismissing caregiver. Similarly, on the basis of facial electromyography, women who experienced abuse by someone close were significantly more likely to show less of a startle response while viewing pictures of men threatening women and to show more mimicry of happy faces and less mimicry of angry faces than did women who were either abused by someone not close or not abused at all (Reichmann-Decker, DePrince, & McIntosh, 2009). Although this study did not explicitly assess the attachment orientation of the participants, the suppression of negative affect observed in the high betrayal group parallels the suppression of negative affect typically observed in avoidant children (Izard & Kobak, 1991) and suggests a comparable strategy to maintain a relationship with the attachment figure. Unfortunately, this strategy as well as the alexithymia associated with avoidant attachment (De Rick & Vanheule, 2006) could interfere with an individual's awareness of her actual risk within the relationship.

## IPV and Preoccupied Attachment

Preoccupied attachment suggests an intensity of involvement and anxiety resulting from the perceived unavailability of the attachment figure. Consistent with their heightened expression of negative affect, preoccupied individuals are much more likely than individuals from other attachment categories to respond to a partner's perceived withdrawal with aggression (Babcock et al., 2000; Bookwala, 2002), and to engage in bidirectional violence (Bookwala & Zdaniuk, 1998). The basis for this aggression is, as one would expect with the anxious or ambivalent child, a strategy for maintaining connection with an inconsistent and easily distracted attachment figure. For example, in a diary study, when compared with either secure or dismissing individuals, preoccupied individuals reported greater intimacy, more self-disclosure, more positive emotions, and more positive views of their partners during high-conflict interactions, thus appearing to associate conflict and expression of anger specifically with increased intimacy (Pietromonaco & Barrett, 1997). In a laboratory study, Fishtein, Pietromonaco, and Barrett (1999) found that preoccupied individuals experienced intimate conflict as highly reinforcing and not something to be avoided or reduced. Similarly, Morgan and Pietromonaco (1994) found that preoccupied individuals reported more positive emotion and passion in high-conflict romantic relationships. Consequently, although preoccupied women may be more likely to separate from an abusive partner (Henderson, Bartholomew, & Dutton, 1997; Shurman & Rodriguez, 2006), they are also more likely to continue their emotional and sexual involvement with that partner following the separation (Henderson et al., 1997; Kirkpatrick & Hazan, 1994). They are also more likely to fail to follow through with protection orders (Roberts, Wolfer, & Mele, 2008; Zoellner et al., 2000) and to minimize the abuse they have experienced (Alexander, Tracy, Radek, & Koverola, 2009). In other words, they remain preoccupied with their current attachment relationship even in the face of physical assault. Their risk for revictimization or continued victimization is thus significant.

## IPV and Unresolved Attachment

As mentioned previously, unresolved childhood trauma leads to psychopathology and major lapses in affect regulation (Bakermans-Kranenburg & van IJzendoorn, 2009; Cole-Detke & Kobak, 1998; Creasey, 2002). One manifestation of this affect dysregulation is borderline personality disorder (Alexander et al., 1998; Fonagy et al., 1996), a diagnosis associated with risk for physical or sexual assault in adulthood (Zanarini et al., 1999). Another manifestation of the affect dysregulation arising from unresolved attachment is dissociation (Ogawa et al., 1997). Zurbriggen and Freyd (2004) have found increased dissociation among CSA survivors who were abused by caregivers, thus suggesting that the betrayal by an attachment figure was a primary predictor of the impact of the abuse. This dissociation contributes to revictimization by interfering with an individual's attention to danger cues, making it difficult for the individual to differentiate between threatening and nonthreatening information (Noll, Horowitz, Bonanno, Trickett, & Putnam, 2003; Sandberg, Matorin, & Lynn, 1999; Woller, 2005). Furthermore, dissociation has been empirically associated on an emotional Stroop test using attachment-related stimuli with a perception of oneself as essentially bad (Loos & Alexander, 2001). Dissociation may also interfere with reality assessments and with "cheater detector" mechanisms that are used to assess how trustworthy someone is, may lead to dissociated sexual behaviors, and may interfere with the ability to make consensual decisions regarding sex (Zurbriggen & Freyd, 2004). Therefore, in all these ways, an unresolved dissociative individual will be at increased risk for abuse by a partner.

Finally, unresolved attachment may take different forms (Lyons-Ruth, Yellin, Melnick, & Atwood, 2003) based on the type of parenting experienced—either "hostile" (rejecting, negative-intrusive, and role confusing) or "helpless" (fearful, withdrawing, and inhibited). Even though a mix of these hostile and helpless characteristics is frequently observed (Lyons-Ruth, Bronfman, & Atwood, 1999), distinctions between them suggest different dynamics in the risk for revictimization and retraumatization. Namely, memories of hostile parenting are associated with a history of physical abuse or witnessed violence, identification with an aggressive or devalued attachment figure, and a minimization of vulnerability (Lyons-Ruth, Dutra, Schuder, & Bianchi, 2006; Lyons-Ruth, Yellin, Melnick, & Atwood, 2005). Conversely, memories of helpless parenting are associated with a history of sexual abuse or parental loss, pervasive fearfulness and helplessness, and sometimes identification with a victimized attachment figure. These helpless behaviors are also highly predictive of dissociation and borderline features in adulthood (Dutra & Lyons-Ruth, 2005; Lyons-Ruth, Holmes, & Hennighausen, 2005). Although no research on the relevance of these hostile or helpless states of mind to revictimization has yet been conducted, it could be hypothesized that hostile characteristics are associated either with the perpetration of violence or with revictimization within the context of bidirectional violence, and that helpless characteristics are associated with unidirectional victimization and with the failure or inability to leave an abusive relationship.

## IPV by Multiple Partners

Another form of revictimization that is rarely studied but is quite common is IPV by multiple partners. Surveys have found that 27% to 59% of victims experience this type of retraumatization, leading to significantly more negative mental health outcomes than typically observed in women who were abused in only one relationship in adulthood (Alexander, 2009). In a sample of 93 victims of IPV (Alexander, 2009), 56% reported abuse by a previous partner, exhibited substantially more problems with affect regulation, and were significantly more likely to have been sexually abused and to have witnessed IPV in childhood. Their responses on the AAI, rated by blind independent judges, suggested different developmental pathways to this type of retraumatization, including parent–child role reversal, unresolved attachment with regard to childhood trauma, and affect dysregulation that might have preceded as well as followed their retraumatization. Finally, in a sample of 400 couples in which the men were court-ordered to batterer treatment (Alexander, 2007a), the female partners who self-reported a history of abuse by multiple partners were significantly more likely to have been sexually abused, physically abused, and to have witnessed IPV in childhood. They were also more likely to be preoccupied in their attachment. Importantly, the women were no more likely to describe their partners as violent, even though the men described themselves as more antisocial and more violent both inside and outside the relationship. Thus, it appears that women with a history of abuse by multiple partners may tend to minimize the risk of violence, even when associating with significantly more violent men.

## Couple Attachment Dynamics

It is important to remember that IPV occurs within the context of an ongoing relationship and occurs within the context of the couple's mutual attachment dynamics. Even before the occurrence of any abuse within a relationship, there is some evidence that individuals may choose their partners on the basis of internal working models of attachment relationships. For example, couples are significantly likely to be concordant in their histories of childhood trauma (Alexander, 2007b; Musser & Alexander, 2007) and recollections of parenting (Lustenberger et al., 2008). Moreover, individuals who are unresolved in their attachment are significantly more likely to have partners who are similarly unresolved (van IJzendoorn & Bakermans-Kranenburg, 1996). Patterns of mate selection have also been observed with regard to other behaviors and personality traits frequently associated with a history of trauma and insecure attachment, such as substance use (Low, Cui, & Merikangas, 2007) and antisocial behavior (Galbaud du Fort, Boothroyd, Bland, Newman, & Kakuma, 2002). As mentioned previously, these pairings may also have been facilitated by the individuals' respective experiences of social rejection by their larger peer groups. Therefore, by intention or default, partnering with a less desirable mate increases the risk for revictimization and retraumatization. Furthermore, certain types of attachment pairings appear to be particularly vulnerable to IPV (Bookwala, 2002; Doumas, Pearson, Elgin, & McKinley, 2008). Based on ratings of couples' interpersonal behaviors in a conflict situation, both men and women who were unresolved showed more domineering behavior than either dismissing or preoccupied men and women (Creasey, 2002). In fact, the presence of negative conflict management behavior, especially controlling behavior, was particularly prominent in the interactions of couples in which both were unresolved, as indicated in some cases by well over 200 instances of negative behavior in 15 minutes. Therefore, both partners' individual attachment histories as well as the interaction of their histories predict the perpetration of IPV and each partner's risk for victimization and traumatization.

## Help-Seeking and Social Support

One final attachment-related context that may affect either the initial risk for revictimization or the likelihood of escaping an abusive relationship is one's ability to enlist help and support from others outside the relationship. Because of securely attached individuals' positive experiences with supportive attachment figures, they are more likely to seek and receive social support when stressed (Bachman & Bippus, 2005; DeFronzo, Panzarella, & Butler, 2001; Mikulincer & Shaver, 2009; Ognibene & Collins, 1998), suggesting that they will be more able to escape an abusive relationship. Although research suggests that a dismissing individual is less likely to seek social support, especially under conditions of stress (Collins & Feeney, 2000; DeFronzo et al., 2001; Larose and Bernier, 2001; Ognibene & Collins, 1998), this individual may be pragmatic in seeking tangible resources, although not emotional resources, from whomever is available. Therefore, social support may play a role for dismissing individuals, albeit to a lesser degree than for securely attached individuals.

Although the interpersonal dependency observed in preoccupied individuals would imply that they would seek social support, the evidence is mixed. Preoccupied individuals appear to experience such intense stress that they have little hope of getting sufficient support, resulting in dissatisfaction with support received and even a lack of actual help-seeking (Bachman & Bippus, 2005; Larose & Bernier, 2001). In a sample of women who had experienced childhood maltreatment by parents, preoccupied women had significantly lower expectations of receiving social support than did securely attached women, with the expectations of dismissing women falling between those of preoccupied women and securely attached women (Cloitre, Stovall-McClough, Zorbas, & Charuvastra, 2008). Ognibene and Collins (1998) noted that preoccupied individuals may seek social support in response to stress but report receiving less support from family. It is also possible that preoccupied individuals may defer either to their partner's active attempts to isolate them from others or to their partner's more subtle disapproval of friends or family who would help them to escape the violence. Alexander, Radek, and Koverola (2003) found that abused women who were preoccupied in their attachment were likely to cite their satisfaction with their current level of social support as a reason for remaining in the abusive relationship, suggesting that they may have been worried about receiving adequate support from others if they should leave their partner. Finally, given their distrust of others, individuals who are unresolved are less likely to seek social support and more likely to distance themselves from others (Ognibene & Collins, 1998). This increased isolation from others outside their marriage could interfere on a tangible level with their ability to escape the violence. Therefore, attachment dynamics not only alter an individual's risk for revictimization by an intimate partner but also affect that individual's ability to escape a relationship once violence has ensued.

## SPECIAL ISSUES

This chapter has provided a brief overview of attachment theory and how its assumptions and findings are useful in explaining retraumatization and revictimization in three specific contexts—namely, in children's and adolescents' interactions with peers, in dating relationships, and in intimate partner relationships in adulthood. Other developmental stages are also pertinent to issues of retraumatization because of the triggers of early trauma and attachment relationships. These include the transition to parenthood in which the presence of a dependent child may be experienced as an occasion for re-experiencing traumatic reactions associated with early trauma. A traumatic childbirth may be especially challenging for women with a prior history of abuse or loss (Soderquist, Wijma, & Wijma, 2004). Another developmental stage that has received far too little attention is old age. Adult children will react to their aging or dying parents as a function of their attachment relationships with their parents, which may or may not have been resolved (Shemmings, 2006). Furthermore, childhood experiences of trauma as well as disrupted attachments with one's own child may contribute to the re-experiencing of traumatic stress reactions that may be associated with the onset of dementia, the use of restraints in nursing homes, or dependence upon an abusive or neglectful adult child.

## CONCLUSIONS

In conclusion, this chapter has described how attachment strategies developed in childhood to maintain connection with a caregiver have important implications for an individual's subsequent risk for trauma and victimization and for the management of affect related to subsequent stress and trauma. Although this chapter has emphasized the importance of developmental trajectories, the contexts of current attachment relationships and current stressors will always moderate the effects of childhood trauma and early insecure attachment on the risk for retraumatization and revictimization. Having a close friend in childhood or adolescence can compensate for the effects of being bullied (Storch & Masia-Warner, 2004), and having a supportive partner has repeatedly been demonstrated to counteract the effects of a history of child maltreatment or insecure attachment on one's current functioning (Cohn, Silver, Cowan, Cowan, & Pearson, 1992; Dickstein, Seifer, & Albus, 2009). Therefore, current attachment relationships (including those with a therapist) can provide the resilience needed by a trauma survivor to avoid retraumatization. Describing therapeutic interventions from an attachment perspective is beyond the scope of this chapter. However, therapists using an attachment perspective work in many different ways to help reestablish secure attachment relationships (between a parent and child or between intimate partners); to facilitate the development of reflective functioning; to help individuals recognize, manage, and resolve negative affect associated with past trauma or loss; and to alter internal working models of intimate relationships. The therapeutic relationship thus allows individuals to explore their environment (their relationships as well as their own thoughts, perceptions, emotions, and memories) from the safety of a secure base.

## REFERENCES

Ainsworth, M. D. S., Blehar, M., Waters, E., & Wall, S. (1978). *Patterns of attachment.* Hillsdale, NJ: Erlbaum.

Alexander, P. C., Anderson, C. L., Brand, B., Schaeffer, C., Grelling, B. Z., & Kretz, L. (1998). Adult attachment and long-term effects in survivors of incest. *Child Abuse & Neglect, 22*, 45–81.

Alexander, P. C. (2007a, July). Childhood trauma and battered women's abuse by multiple partners. Paper presented at the annual meeting of the International Family Violence Research Conference, Portsmouth, NH.

Alexander, P. C. (2007b, November). Dual trauma parents and their risk for abusive parenting. Paper presented at the annual meeting of the International Society for Traumatic Stress Studies, Baltimore, MD.

Alexander, P. C. (2009). Childhood trauma, attachment, and abuse by multiple partners. *Psychological Trauma, 1*, 78–88.

Alexander, P. C., Radek, M., & Koverola, C. (2003, July). Predicting stage of change in battered women. Paper presented at the annual meeting of the International Family Violence Research Conference, Portsmouth, NH.

Alexander, P. C., Tracy, A., Radek, M., & Koverola, C. (2009). Predicting stages of change in battered women. *Journal of Interpersonal Violence, 24*, 1652–1672.

Allen, J. G., Stein, H., Fonagy, P., Fultz, J., & Target, M. (2005). Rethinking adult attachment: A study of expert consensus, *Bulletin of the Menninger Clinic, 69*, 59–80.

Anderson, C. L., & Alexander, P. C. (1996). The relationship between attachment and dissociation in adult survivors of incest. *Psychiatry, 59*, 240–254.

Andreou, E. (2001). Bully/victim problems and their association with coping behavior in conflictual peer interactions among school-age children. *Educational Psychology, 21*, 59–66.

Arata, C. M. (2000). From child victim to adult victim: A model for predicting sexual revictimization. *Child Maltreatment, 5*, 28–38.

Babcock, J. C., Jacobson, N. S., Gottman, J. M., & Yerington, T. P. (2000). Attachment, emotional regulation, and the function of marital violence: Differences between secure, preoccupied, and dismissing violent and nonviolent husbands. *Journal of Family Violence, 15*, 391–409.

Bachman, G. F., & Bippus, A. M. (2005). Evaluations of supportive messages provided by friends and romantic partners: An attachment theory approach. *Communication Reports, 18*, 85–94.

Bakermans-Kranenburg, M. J., & van IJzendoorn, M. H. (2009). The first 10,000 adult attachment interviews: Distributions of adult attachment representations in clinical and non-clinical groups. *Attachment & Human Development, 11*, 223–263.

Bartholomew, K., & Horowitz, L. M. (1991). Attachment styles among young adults: A test of a four-category model. *Journal of Personality and Social Psychology, 61*, 226–244.

Bookwala, J. (2002). The role of own and perceived partner attachment in relationship aggression. *Journal of Interpersonal Violence, 17*, 84–100.

Bookwala, J., & Zdaniuk, B. (1998). Adult attachment styles and aggressive behavior within dating relationships. *Journal of Social & Personal Relationships, 15*, 175–190.

Booth-LaForce, C., Oh, W., Kim, A. H., Rubin, K. H., Rose-Krasnor, L. & Burgess, K. (2006). Attachment, self-worth, and peer-group functioning in middle childhood. *Attachment & Human Development, 8*, 309–325.

Boulton, M. J., Trueman, M., & Murray, L. (2008). Associations between peer victimization, fear of future victimization and disrupted concentration on class work among junior school pupils. *British Journal of Educational Psychology, 78*, 473–489.

Bowes, L., Arseneault, L., Maughan, B., Taylor, A., Caspi, A., & Moffitt, T. E. (2009). School, neighborhood, and family factors are associated with children's bullying involvement: A nationally representative longitudinal study. *Journal of the American Academy of Child & Adolescent Psychiatry, 48*, 545–553.

Bowlby, J. (1969/1982). *Attachment and loss: Vol. 1. Attachment.* New York: Basic Books.

Breslau, N., Davis, G. C., Peterson, E. L., & Schultz, L. (1997). Psychiatric sequelae of PTSD in women. *Archives of General Psychiatry, 54*, 81–87.

Carlson, V., Cicchetti, D., Barnett, D., & Braunwald, K. (1989). Disorganized/disoriented attachment relationships in maltreated infants. *Developmental Psychology, 25*, 525–531.

Casas, J. F., Weigel, S. M., Crick, N. R., Ostrov, J. M., Woods, K. E., Jansen Yeh, A., & Huddleston-Casas, C. A. (2006). Early parenting and children's relational and physical aggression in the preschool and home contexts. *Applied Developmental Psychology, 27*, 209–227.

Cassidy, J., & Berlin, L. J. (1994). The insecure/ambivalent pattern of attachment: Theory and research. *Child Development, 65*, 971–981.

Ciesla, J. A., Roberts, J. E., & Hewitt, R. G. (2004). Adult attachment land high-risk sexual behavior among HIV-positive patients. *Journal of Applied Social Psychology, 34*, 108–124.

Cinq-Mars, C., Wright, J., Cyr, M., & McDuff, P. (2003). Sexual at-risk behaviors of sexually abused adolescent girls. *Journal of Child Sexual Abuse, 12*, 2–18.

Cleveland, H. H., Herrera, V. M., & Stuewig, J. (2003). Abusive males and abused females in adolescent relationships: Risk factor similarity and dissimilarity and the role of relationship seriousness. *Journal of Family Violence, 18*, 325–339.

Cloitre, M., Stovall-McClough, C., Zorbas, P., & Charuvastra, A. (2008). Attachment organization, emotion regulation, and expectations of support in a clinical sample of women with childhood abuse histories. *Journal of Traumatic Stress, 21*, 282–289.

Cohn, D. A., Silver, D. H., Cowan, C. P., Cowan, P. A., & Pearson, J. (1992). Working models of childhood attachment and couple relationships. *Journal of Family Issues, 13*, 432–449.

Cole-Detke, H., & Kobak, R. (1998). The effects of multiple abuse in interpersonal relationships: An attachment perspective. *Journal of Aggression, Maltreatment, & Trauma, 2*, 189–205.

Coleman, P. K. (2003). Perceptions of parent-child attachment, social self-efficacy, and peer relationships in middle childhood. *Infant and Child Development, 12*, 351–368.

Collins, N. L., & Feeney, B. C. (2000). A safe haven: An attachment theory perspective on support seeking and caregiving in intimate relationships. *Journal of Personality & Social Psychology, 78*, 1053–1073.

Collins, N. L., & Read, S. J. (1990). Adult attachment, working models, and relationship quality in dating couples. *Journal of Personality and Social Psychology, 58*, 644–663.

Creasey, G. (2002). Associations between working models of attachment and conflict management behavior in romantic couples. *Journal of Counseling Psychology, 49*, 365–375.

Crick, N. R., & Bigbee, M. A. (1998). Relational and overt forms of peer victimization: A multi-informant approach. *Journal of Consulting and Clinical Psychology, 66*, 337–347.

Crittenden, P. M. (1994, October). *Trauma: Effects on memory systems, internal representational models, and behavior.* Paper presented at the Rochester Symposium on Developmental Psychopathology, Rochester, NY.

Crittenden, P. M. (1997). Toward an integrative theory of trauma: A dynamic-maturation approach. In D. Cicchetti & S. L. Toth (Eds.), *Developmental perspectives on trauma: Theory, research, and intervention* (pp. 33–84). Rochester, NY: University of Rochester Press.

Crittenden, P. M., Partridge, M. F., & Claussen, A. H. (1991). Family patterns of relationship in normative and dysfunctional families. *Development and Psychopathology, 3*, 491–512.

Cullerton-Sen, C. Cassidy, A. R., Murray-Close, D., Cicchetti, D., Crick, N. R., & Rogosch, F. A. (2008). Childhood maltreatment and the development of relational and physical aggression: the importance of a gender-informed approach. *Child Development, 79*, 1736–1751.

Danieli, Y. (2010). Fundamentals of working with (re)traumatized populations. In G. H. Brenner, D. H. Bush, & J. Moses (Eds.), *Creating spiritual and psychological resilience: Integrating care in disaster relief work* (pp. 195–210). New York: Routledge/Taylor & Francis.

De Bellis, M. D., Keshava, M. S., Clark, D. B., Casey, B. J., Giedd, J. N., Boring, A. M., ... Ryan, N. D. (1999). Developmental traumatology: Part II. Brain development. *Biological Psychiatry, 45*, 1271–1284.

DeFronzo, R., Panzarella, C., & Butler, A. C. (2001). Attachment, support seeking, and adaptive inferential feedback: Implications for psychological health. *Cognitive & Behavioral Practice, 8*, 48–52.

De Rick, A., & Vanheule, S. (2006). The relationship between perceived parenting, adult attachment style and alexithymia in alcoholic inpatients. *Addictive Behaviors, 31*, 1265–1270.

Dickstein, S., Seifer, R., & Albus, K. E. (2009). Maternal adult attachment representations across relationship domains and infant outcomes: The importance of family and couple functioning. *Attachment & Human Development, 11*, 5–27.

Doumas, D. M., Pearson, C. L., Elgin, J. E., & McKinley, L. L. (2008). Adult attachment as a risk factor for intimate partner violence: The "mispairing" of partners' attachment styles. *Journal of Interpersonal Violence, 23*, 616–634.

Dozier, M., & Kobak, R. (1992). Psychophysiology in attachment interviews: Converging evidence for deactivating strategies. *Child Development, 63*, 1473–1480.

Duncan, R. D. (1999). Maltreatment by parents and peers: The relationship between child abuse, bully victimization, and psychological distress. *Child Maltreatment, 4*, 45–55.

Dutra, L., & Lyons-Ruth, K. (April 2005). Maltreatment, maternal and child psychopathology, and quality of early care as predictors of adolescent dissociation. Paper presented at the biennial meeting of the Society for Research in Child Development, Atlanta, GA.

Dykas, M. J., Ziv, Y., & Cassidy, J. (2008). Attachment and peer relations in adolescence. *Attachment & Human Development, 10*, 123–141.

Ehrensaft, M. K., Cohen, P., Brown, J., Smailes, E., Chen, H., & Johnson, J. G. (2003). Intergenerational transmission of partner violence: A 20-year prospective study. *Journal of Consulting and Clinical Psychology, 71*, 741–753.

Erdur-Baker, O. (2009). Peer victimization, rumination, and problem solving as risk contributors to adolescents' depressive symptoms. *Journal of Psychology: Interdisciplinary and Applied, 143*, 78–90.

Espelage, D. L., & Holt, M. K. (2007). Dating violence and sexual harassment across the bully-victim continuum among middle and high school students. *Journal of Youth and Adolescence, 36*, 799–811.

Feeney, J. A., & Noller, P. (1990). Attachment style as a predictor of adult romantic relationships. *Journal of Personality and Social Psychology, 58*, 281–291.

Feerick, M. M., Haugaard, J. J., & Hien, D. A. (2002). Child maltreatment and adulthood violence: The contribution of attachment and drug abuse. *Child Maltreatment, 7*, 226–240.

Finzi, R., Ram, A., Har-Even, D., Shnit, D., & Weizman, A. (2001). Attachment styles and aggression in physically abused and neglected children. *Journal of Youth and Adolescence, 30*, 769–786.

Fishtein, J., Pietromonaco, P. R., & Barrett, L. (1999). The contribution of attachment style and relationship conflict to the complexity of relationship knowledge. *Social Cognition, 17*, 228–244.

Fonagy, P. (1999). Male perpetrators of violence against women: An attachment theory perspective. *Journal of Applied Psychoanalytic Studies, 1*, 7–27.

Fonagy, P., Leigh, T., Steele, M., Steele, H., Kennedy, R., Mattoon, G., … Gerber, A. (1996). The relation of attachment status, psychiatric classification, and response to psychotherapy. *Journal of Consulting & Clinical Psychology, 64*, 22–31.

Fonagy, P., Target, M., & Gergely, G. (2000). Attachment and borderline personality disorder: A theory and some evidence. *Psychiatric Clinics of North America, 23*, 103–122.

Fox, C. L., & Boulton, M. J. (2006). Longitudinal associations between submissive/nonassertive social behavior and different types of peer victimization. *Violence and Victims, 21*, 383–400.

Fraley, R. C. (2002). Attachment stability from infancy to adulthood: Meta-analysis and dynamic modeling of developmental mechanisms. *Personality and Social Psychology Review*, *6*, 123–151.

Francis, D., & Meaney, M. (1999). Maternal care and the development of stress responses. *Current Opinion in Neurobiology*, *9*, 128–134.

Galbaud du Fort, G., Boothroyd, L. J., Bland, R. C., Newman, S. C., & Kakuma, R. (2002). Spouse similarity for antisocial behavior in the general population. *Psychological Medicine*, *32*, 1407–1416.

Gallup, A. C., O'Brien, D. T., White, D. D., & Wilson, D. S. (2009). Peer victimization in adolescence has different effects on the sexual behavior of male and female college students. *Personality and Individual Differences, 46*, 611–615.

Gerra, G., Leonardi, C., Cortese, E., Zaimovic, A., Dell'Agnello, G., Manfredini, M., Somaini, L., ... Donnini, C. (2008). Adrenocorticotropic hormone and cortisol plasma levels directly correlate with childhood neglect and depression measures in addicted patients. *Addiction Biology, 13*, 95–104.

Gladstone, G. L., Parker, G. B., & Malhi, G. S. (2006). Do bullied children become anxious and depressed adults?: A cross-sectional investigation of the correlates of bullying and anxious depression. *Journal of Nervous and Mental Disease, 194*, 201–208.

Gray, H. M., & Foshee, V. (1997). Adolescent dating violence: Differences between one-sided and mutually violent profiles. *Journal of Interpersonal Violence, 12*, 126–141.

Guerin, S., & Hennessy, E. (2002). *Aggression and bullying*. Oxford: Blackwell.

Hazan, C., & Shaver, P. (1987). Romantic love conceptualized as an attachment process. *Journal of Personality and Social Psychology*, *52*, 511–524.

Hedtke, K. A., Ruggiero, K. J., Fitzgerald, M. M., Zinzow, H. M., Saunders, B. E., Resnick, H. S., & Kilpatrick D. G. (2008). A longitudinal investigation of interpersonal violence in relation to mental health and substance use. *Journal of Consulting and Clinical Psychology*, *76*, 633–647.

Henderson, A. J. Z., Bartholomew, K., & Dutton, D. G. (1997). He loves me; he loves me not: Attachment and separation resolution of abused women. *Journal of Family Violence, 12*, 169–191.

Higginbotham, B. J., Ketring, S. A., Hibbert, J., Wright, D. W., & Guarino, A. (2007). Relationship religiosity, adult attachment styles, and courtship violence experienced by females. *Journal of Family Violence, 22*, 55–62.

Hodson, C., Newcomb, M. D., Locke, T. R., & Goodyear, R. K. (2006). Childhood adversity, poly-substance use, and disordered eating in adolescent Latinas: Mediated and indirect paths in a community sample. *Child Abuse & Neglect, 30*, 1017–1036.

Hoglund, W. L. G. (2007). School functioning in early adolescence: Gender-linked responses to peer victimization. *Journal of Educational Psychology, 99*, 683–699.

Holt, M. K., Kantor, G. K., & Finkelhor, D. (2009). Hidden forms of victimization in elementary students involved in bullying. *School Psychology Review, 36*, 345–360.

Irons, C., & Gilbert, P. (2005). Evolved mechanisms in adolescent anxiety and depression symptoms: The role of the attachment and social rank systems. *Journal of Adolescence, 28*, 325–341.

Irwin, H. J. (1999). Violent and nonviolent revictimization of women abused in childhood. *Journal of Interpersonal Violence, 14*, 1095–1110.

Izard, C., & Kobak, R. (1991). Emotion system functioning and emotion regulation In J. Garber & K. Dodge (Eds.), *The development of affect regulation* (pp. 303–321). Cambridge: Cambridge University Press.

Kaysen, D., Neighbors, C., Martell, J., Fossos, N., & Larimer, M. E. (2006). Incapacitated rape and alcohol use: A prospective analysis. *Addictive Behaviors, 31*, 1820–1832.

Kirkpatrick, L. A., & Hazan, C. (1994). Attachment styles and close relationships: A four-year prospective study. *Personal Relationships, 1*, 123–142.

Kobak, R. R., & Sceery, A. (1988). Attachment in late adolescence: Working models, affect regulation, and representations of self and others. *Child Development, 59*, 135–146.

Kobak, R., Zajac, K., & Smith, C. (2009). Adolescent attachment and trajectories of hostile-impulsive behavior: Implications for the development of personality disorders. *Development and Psychopathology, 21*, 839–851.

Kochenderfer-Ladd, B. (2003). Identification of aggressive and asocial victims and the stability of their peer victimization. *Merrill-Palmer Quarterly, 49*, 401–425.

Kwong, M. J., Bartholomew, K., Henderson, A. J. Z., & Trinke, S. (2003). The intergenerational transmission of relationship violence. *Journal of Family Psychology, 17*, 288–301.

Ladd, G. W., & Kochenderfer Ladd, B. K. (1998). Parenting behaviors and parent-child relationships: Correlates of peer victimization in kindergarten? *Developmental Psychology, 34*, 1450–1458.

Larose, S., & Bernier, A. (2001). Social support processes: Mediators of attachment state of mind and adjustment in late adolescence. *Attachment & Human Development, 3*, 96–120.

Leadbetter, B. J., & Hoglund, W. L. G. (2006). The effects of peer victimization and physical aggression on changes in internalizing from first to third grade. *Child Development, 80*, 843–859.

Leenaars, L. S., Dane, A. V., & Marini, Z. A. (2008). Evolutionary perspective on indirect victimization in adolescence: The role of attractiveness, dating and sexual behavior. *Aggressive Behavior, 34*, 404–415.

Liotti, G. (1992). Disorganized/disoriented attachment in the etiology of the dissociative disorders. *Dissociation, 5*, 196–204.

Loos, M. E., & Alexander, P. C. (2001). Dissociation and the processing of threat related information: An attachment theory perspective on maintenance factors in dissociative pathology. *Maltrattamento e abuse all'infanzia, 3*, 61–83.

Low, N., Cui, L., & Merikangas, K. R. (2007). Spousal concordance for substance use and anxiety disorders. *Journal of Psychiatric Research, 41*, 942–951.

Lustenberger, Y., Fenton, B. T., Rothen, S., Vandeleur, C. L., Gamma, F., Matthey, M.–L., … Preisig, M. (2008). Spouse similarity in recollections of parenting received: A study in a nonclinical sample. *Swiss Journal of Psychology, 67*, 165–176.

Lyons-Ruth, K., Bronfman, E., & Atwood, G. (1999). A relational diathesis model of hostile-helpless states of mind: Expressions in mother-infant interaction. In J. Solomon & C. George (Eds.), *Attachment disorganization* (pp. 33–70). New York: Guilford Press.

Lyons-Ruth, K., Dutra, L., Schuder, M. R., & Bianchi, I. (2006). From infant attachment disorganization to adult dissociation: Relational adaptations or traumatic experiences? *Psychiatric Clinics of North America, 29*, 63–86.

Lyons-Ruth, K., Easterbrooks, M. A., & Cibelli, C. D. (1997). Infant attachment strategies, infant mental lag, and maternal depressive symptoms: Predictors of internalizing and externalizing problems at age 7. *Developmental Psychology, 33*, 681–692.

Lyons-Ruth, K., Holmes, B., & Hennighausen, K. (2005, April). Prospective longitudinal predictors of borderline and conduct symptoms in late adolescence: The early caregiving context. Paper presented at the Biennial Meeting of the Society for Research in Child Development. Atlanta, GA.

Lyons-Ruth, K., Lyubchik, A., Wolfe, R., & Bronfman, E. (2002). Parental depression and child attachment: Hostile and helpless profiles of parent and child behavior among families at risk. In S. H. Goodman & I. H. Gotlib (Eds.), *Children of depressed parents: Mechanisms of risk and implications for treatment* (pp. 89–120). Washington, DC: American Psychological Association.

Lyons-Ruth, K., Yellin, C., Melnick, S., & Atwood, G. (2003). Childhood experiences of trauma and loss have different relations to maternal unresolved and Hostile-Helpless states of mind on the AAI. *Attachment & Human Development, 5*, 330–352.

Lyons-Ruth, K., Yellin, C., Melnick, S., & Atwood, G. (2005). Expanding the concept of unresolved mental states: Hostile/Helpless states of mind on the Adult Attachment Interview are associated with disrupted mother-infant communication and infant disorganization. *Development and Psychopathology, 17*, 1–23.

Main, M. (1995). Recent studies in attachment: Overview, with selected implications for clinical work. In S. Goldberg, R. Muir, & J. Kerr (Eds.), *Attachment theory: Social, developmental and clinical perspectives* (pp. 407–474). Hillsdale, NJ: Analytic Press.

Main, M. (2000). The organized categories of infant, child, and adult attachment: Flexible vs. inflexible attention under attachment-related stress. *Journal of the American Psychoanalytic Association, 48*, 1055–1096.

Main, M., & Goldwyn, R. (1984). Predicting rejection of her infant from mother's representation of her own experience: Implications for the abused-abusing intergenerational cycle. *Child Abuse & Neglect, 8*, 203–217.

Main, M., & Goldwyn, R. (1998). *Adult attachment scoring and classification system.* Version 6.3. Unpublished manuscript, University of California at Berkeley.

Main, M., & Hesse, E. (1990). Parents' unresolved traumatic experiences are related to infant disorganized attachment status: Is frightened and/or frightening parental behavior the linking mechanism? In M. T. Greenberg, D. Cicchetti, & E. M. Cummings (Eds.), *Attachment in the preschool years* (pp. 161–182). Chicago: University of Chicago Press.

Main, M., & Solomon, J. (1986). Discovery of a new, insecure-disorganized/disoriented attachment pattern. In T. B. Brazelton & M. W. Yogman (Eds.), *Affective development in infancy* (pp. 95–124). Norwood, NJ: Ablex.

Main, M., & Solomon, J. (1990). Procedures for identifying infants as disorganized/disoriented during the Ainsworth strange situation. In M. T. Greenberg, D. Cicchetti, & E. M. Cummings (Eds.), *Attachment in the preschool years* (pp. 121–160). Chicago: University of Chicago Press.

McCauley, J. L., Amstadter, A. B., Danielson, C. K., Ruggiero, K. J., Kilpatrick, D. G., & Resnick, H. S. (2009). Mental health and rape history in relation to non-medical use of prescription drugs in a national sample of women. *Addictive Behaviors, 34*, 641–648.

McElwain, N. L., Cox, M. J., Burchinal, M. R., & Macfie, J. (2003). Differentiating among insecure mother-infant attachment classifications: A focus on child-friend interaction and exploration during solitary play at 36 months. *Attachment & Human Development, 5*, 136–164.

McLaughlin, K. A., Hatzenbuehler, M. L., & Hilt, L. M. (2009). Emotion dysregulation as a mechanism linking peer victimization to internalizing symptoms in adolescents. *Journal of Consulting and Clinical Psychology, 77*, 894–904.

Merrill, L. L., Guimond, J. M., Thomsen, C. J., & Milner, J. S. (2003). Child sexual abuse and number of sexual partners in young women: The role of abuse severity, coping style, and sexual functioning. *Journal of Consulting and Clinical Psychology, 71*, 987–996.

Messman-Moore, T. L., Ward, R. M., & Brown, A. L. (2009). Substance use and PTSD symptoms impact the likelihood of rape and revictimization in college women. *Journal of Interpersonal Violence, 24,* 499–521.

Mikulincer, M., & Shaver, P. R. (2009). An attachment and behavioral systems perspective on social support. *Journal of Social and Personal Relationships, 26,* 7–19.

Mohr, A. (2006). Family variables associated with peer victimization: Does family violence enhance the probability of being victimized by peers? *Swiss Journal of Psychology, 65,* 107–116.

Moran, G., & Pederson, D. R. (1998). Proneness to distress and ambivalent relationships. *Infant Behavior and Development, 21,* 493–503.

Morgan, H. J., & Pietromonaco, P. R. (1994, August). *Traumatic bonding: A natural function of attachment in unnatural circumstances.* Poster presented at the 102nd Annual Convention of the American Psychological Association, Los Angeles, CA.

Musser, P., & Alexander, P. C. (2007, November). Dual trauma couples and intimate partner violence. Paper presented at the annual meeting of the International Society for Traumatic Stress Studies, Baltimore, MD.

Noll, J. G., Horowitz, L. A., Bonanno, G. A., Trickett, P. K., & Putnam, F. W. (2003). Revictimization and self-harm in females who experienced childhood sexual abuse: Results from a prospective study. *Journal of Interpersonal Violence, 18,* 1452–1471.

Ogawa, J., Sroufe, A., Weinfield, N., Carlson, E., & Egeland, B. (1997). Development and the fragmented self: Longitudinal study of dissociative symptomatology in a non-clinical sample. *Development and Psychopathology, 9,* 855–879.

Ognibene, T. C., & Collins, N. L. (1998). Adult attachment styles, perceived social support and coping strategies. *Journal of Social and Personal Relationships, 15,* 323–345.

Ostrov, J. M. (2008). Forms of aggression and peer victimization during early childhood: A short-term longitudinal study. *Journal of Abnormal Child Psychology, 36,* 311–322.

Perry, D. G., Kusel, S. J., & Perry, L. C. (1988). Victims of peer aggression. *Developmental Psychology, 24,* 807–814.

Pietromonaco, P. R., & Barrett, L. (1997). Working models of attachment and daily social interactions. *Journal of Personality and Social Psychology, 73,* 1409–1423.

Putnam, F. W. (2005). The developmental neurobiology of disrupted attachment: Lessons from animal models and child abuse research. In L. J. Berlin, Y. Ziv, L. Amaya-Jackson, & M. T. Greenberg (Eds.), *Enhancing early attachments: Theory, research, intervention, and policy* (pp. 79–99). New York: Guilford Press.

Rapoza, K. A., & Baker, A. T. (2008). Attachment style, alcohol, and childhood experience of abuse: An analysis of physical violence in dating couples. *Violence and Victims, 23,* 52–65.

Reichmann-Decker, A., DePrince, A. P., & McIntosh, D. N. (2009). Affective responsiveness, betrayal, and childhood abuse. *Journal of Trauma & Dissociation, 10,* 276–296.

Reinert, D. F., & Edwards, C. E. (2009). Childhood physical and verbal mistreatment, psychological symptoms, and substance use: Sex differences and the moderating role of attachment. *Journal of Family Violence, 24,* 589–596.

Roberts, J. C., Wolfer, L., & Mele, M. (2008). Why victims of intimate partner violence withdraw protection orders. *Journal of Family Violence, 23,* 369–375.

Rubin, K. H., Dwyer, K. M., Booth-LaForce, C., Kim, A. H., Burgess, K. B., & Rose-Krasnor, L. (2004). Attachment, friendship, and psychosocial functioning in early adolescence. *Journal of Early Adolescence, 24,* 326–356.

Sandberg, D. A., Matorin, A. I., & Lynn, S. J. (1999). Dissociation, posttraumatic symptomatology, and sexual revictimization: A prospective examination of mediator and moderator effects. *Journal of Traumatic Stress, 12,* 127–138.

Schore, A. N. (2000). Attachment and the regulation of the right brain. *Attachment & Human Development, 2*, 23–47.

Sharpe, D., & Taylor, J. K. (1999). An examination of variables from a social-developmental model to explain physical and psychological dating violence. *Canadian Journal of Behavioural Science, 31*, 165–175.

Shemmings, D. (2006). Using adult attachment theory to differentiate adult children's internal working models of later life filial relationships. *Journal of Aging Studies, 20*, 177–191.

Shields, A., & Cicchetti, D. (2001). Parental maltreatment and emotion dysregulation as risk factors for bullying and victimization in middle childhood. *Journal of Clinical Child Psychology, 30*, 349–363.

Shurman, L. A., & Rodriguez, C. M. (2006). Cognitive-affective predictors of women's readiness to end domestic violence relationships. *Journal of Interpersonal Violence, 21*, 1417–1439.

Siegel, J. A. (2000). Aggressive behavior among women sexually abused as children. *Violence & Victims, 15,* 235–255.

Slade, A., Grienenberger, J., Bernbach, E., Levy, D., & Locker, A. (2005). Maternal reflective functioning, attachment, and the transmission gap: A preliminary study. *Attachment & Human Development, 7*, 283–298.

Smallbone, S. W., & Dadds, M. R. (2001). Further evidence for a relationship between attachment insecurity and coercive sexual behavior in nonoffenders. *Journal of Interpersonal Violence, 16*, 22–35.

Smith, D. W., Davis, J. L., & Fricker-Elhai, A. E. (2004). How does trauma beget trauma? Cognitions about risk in women with abuse histories. *Child Maltreatment, 9*, 292–303.

Soderquist, J., Wijma, K., & Wijma, B. (2004). Traumatic stress in late pregnancy. *Journal of Anxiety Disorders, 18*, 127–142.

Solomon, J., George, C., & De Jong, A. (1995). Children classified as controlling at age six: Evidence of disorganized representational strategies and aggression at home and at school. *Development and Psychopathology, 7*, 447–463.

Spangler, G., & Grossmann, K. E. (1993). Biobehavioral organization in securely and insecurely attached infants. *Child Development, 64*, 1439–1450.

Sroufe, L. A., & Fleeson, J. (1986). Attachment and the construction of relationships. In W. Hartup & Z. Rubin (Eds.), *Relationships and development* (pp. 51–71). New York: Cambridge University Press.

Steele, H., & Steele, M. (2005). Understanding and resolving emotional conflict: The London parent-child project. In K. E. Grossmann, K. Grossmann, & E. Waters (Eds.), *Attachment from infancy to adulthood: The major longitudinal studies* (pp. 137–164). New York: Guilford.

Storch, E. A., Brassard, M. R., & Masia-Warner, C. L. (2003). The relationship of peer victimization to social anxiety and loneliness in adolescence. *Child Study Journal, 33*, 1–18.

Storch, E. A., & Masia-Warner, C. (2004). The relationship of peer victimization to social anxiety and loneliness in adolescent females. *Journal of Adolescence, 27*, 351–362.

Straus, M. A. (2008). Dominance and symmetry in partner violence by male and female university students in 32 nations. *Children and Youth Services Review, 30*, 252–275.

Sullivan, T. N., Farrell, A. D., & Kliewer, W. (2006). Peer victimization in early adolescence: Association between physical and relational victimization and drug use, aggression, and delinquent behaviors among urban middle school students. *Development and Psychopathology, 18*, 119–137.

Suomi, S. J. (1996). Effects of differential early social experience on biological and behavioral development of rhesus monkeys. *European Neuropsychopharmacology*, 6, S4/52.

Sweeting, H., Young, R., West, P., & Der, G. (2006). Peer victimization and depression in early-mid adolescence: A longitudinal study. *British Journal of Educational Psychology*, 76, 577–594.

Trickett, P. K., Reiffman, A., Horowitz, L. A., & Putnam, F. W. (1997). Characteristics of sexual abuse trauma and the prediction of developmental outcomes. In D. Cicchetti & S. L. Toth (Eds.), *The Rochester Symposium on Developmental Psychopathology: Vol. VIII. The effects of trauma on the developmental process* (pp. 289–314). Rochester, NY: University of Rochester Press.

Troy, M., & Sroufe, L. A. (1987). Victimization among preschoolers: Role of attachment relationship history. *Journal of the American Academy of Child and Adolescent Psychiatry, 26,* 166–172.

Van Hoof, A., Raaijmakers, Q. A. W., van Beek, Y., Hale, W. W., & Aleva, L. (2008). A multi-mediation model on the relations of bullying, victimization, identity, and family with adolescent depressive symptoms. *Journal of Youth and Adolescence, 37,* 772–782.

van IJzendoorn, M. (1995). Adult attachment representations, parental responsiveness, and infant attachment: A meta-analysis on the predictive validity of the Adult Attachment Interview. *Psychological Bulletin, 117,* 387–403.

van IJzendoorn, M. H., & Bakermans-Kranenburg, M. J. (1996). Attachment representations in mothers, fathers, adolescents, and clinical groups: A meta-analytic search for normative data. *Journal of Consulting and Clinical Psychology, 64,* 8–21.

van IJzendoorn, M. H., Schuengel, C., & Bakermans-Kranenburg, M. J. (1999). Disorganized attachment in early childhood: Meta-analysis of precursors, concomitants, and sequelae. *Development and Psychopathology, 11,* 225–249.

Wagner, A. W., & Linehan, M. M. (1997). Biosocial perspective on the relationship of childhood sexual abuse, suicidal behavior, and borderline personality disorder. In M. C. Zanarini (Ed.), *Role of sexual abuse in the etiology of borderline personality disorder* (pp. 203–223). Washington, DC: American Psychiatric Press.

Ward, M. J., & Carlson, E. A. (1995). Associations among adult attachment representations, maternal sensitivity, and infant-mother attachment in a sample of adolescent mothers, *Child Development, 66,* 69–79.

Waters, E., Merrick, S., Treboux, D., Crowell, J., & Albersheim, L. (2000). Attachment security in infancy and early adulthood: A twenty-year longitudinal study. *Child Development, 71,* 684–689.

Widom, C. P., Czaja, S. J., & Dutton, M. A. (2008). Childhood victimization and lifetime revictimization. *Child Abuse & Neglect, 32,* 785–796.

Wolfe, D. A., Scott, K., Wekerle, C., & Pittman, A. -L. (2001). Child maltreatment: risk of adjustment problems and dating violence in adolescence. *Journal of the American Academy of Child and Adolescent Psychiatry, 40,* 282–289.

Wolfe, D. A., Wekerle, C., Scott, K., & Straatman, A. -L. (2004). Predicting abuse in adolescent dating relationships over 1 year: The role of child maltreatment and trauma. *Journal of Abnormal Psychology, 113,* 406–415.

Woller, W. (2005). Trauma repetition and revictimization following physical and sexual abuse. *Fortschritte der Neurologie, Psychiatrie, 73,* 83–90.

Woods, S., & White, E. (2005). The association between bullying behavior, arousal levels and behavior problems. *Journal of Adolescence, 28,* 381–395.

Zanarini, M. C., Frankenburg, F. R., Reich, D. B., Marino, M. F., Haynes, M. C., & Gunderson, J. G. (1999). Violence in the lives of adult borderline patients. *Journal of Nervous & Mental Disease, 187,* 65–71.

Zoellner, L. A., Feeny, N. C., Alvarez, J., Watlington, C., O'Neill, M. L., Zager, R., & Foa, E. B. (2000). Factors associated with completion of the restraining order process in female victims of partner violence. *Journal of Interpersonal Violence, 15,* 1081–1099.

Zurbriggen, E. L., & Freyd, J. J. (2004). The link between child sexual abuse and risky sexual behavior: The role of dissociative tendencies, information-processing effects, and consensual sex decision mechanisms. In L. J. Koenig, L. S. Doll, A. O'Leary, & W. Pequegnat (Eds.), *From child sexual abuse to adult sexual risk: Trauma, revictimization, and intervention* (pp. 135–157). Washington, DC: American Psychological Association.

# Chapter 9

# Multiple Experiences of Combat Trauma

*Eric Kuhn, Julia E. Hoffman, and Josef I. Ruzek*

Among the most salient hazards of military service is the risk of being deployed to a war zone. Service members deployed in a war zone endure protracted separation from home, extremely stressful environments, and potentially, multiple exposures to a host of combat traumas, which can have lasting negative effects on psychological, psychosocial, and physical functioning. In this chapter, we explore a variety of factors that put individuals at risk of experiencing one or more combat traumas and the resultant psychological sequelae. Features of war-zone deployments that increase risk of exposure to combat trauma—and, consequently, retraumatization—are reviewed. We also offer possible explanations for the relationship between combat trauma and retraumatization. The long-term psychological adjustment difficulties that can result from experiencing multiple combat traumas as well as effective assessment tools, treatments, and possible prevention techniques for these difficulties are summarized. Finally, several special topics are presented, such as the increasing role of women in combat and the effects of combat trauma exposure on nonmilitary professionals working in war zones.

## EPIDEMIOLOGICAL DATA PERTAINING TO COMBAT TRAUMA EXPOSURE

Exposure to combat trauma has been estimated to occur in about 6.4% of men and less than 1% of women in the general population (Kessler, Sonnega,

Bromet, Hughes, & Nelson, 1995). Obviously, the rate of exposure to combat trauma is much higher among those who serve in the military during times of war and are deployed to a war zone. Yet not everyone who is deployed to a war zone will be exposed to combat trauma. For example, during the Vietnam war, it has been estimated that only 15% to 50% of all service members who were in theater were exposed to combat (see Dohrenwend et al., 2006). This is also true for the Iraq and Afghanistan wars, with 65.1% of Operation Iraqi Freedom (OIF) and 46% of Operation Enduring Freedom (OEF) deployed service members reporting any combat experience (Hoge et al., 2004). In fact, there is evidence suggesting that being deployed to a war zone and not experiencing combat is associated with *lower* rates of posttraumatic stress disorder (PTSD) (Smith et al., 2008a) and depression (Wells et al., 2010) than found in service members who are not deployed. This has been explained as the "healthy warrior effect" that hypothesizes that the most fit, able, psychologically healthy individuals are deployed while those falling short of this are not deployed (Wilson et al., 2009).

## Defining *Combat Trauma*

Combat trauma exposure can include a variety of extremely stressful experiences that typically involve serious threat of bodily injury or death. Exposure could include traditional direct combat stressors encountered when attacking or defending strategic positions during which lives are threatened by a variety of lethal weapons (e.g., small arms, mortars, rockets, grenades, etc.). Combat trauma exposure could also occur during operations to seek out and destroy enemy targets when fighters encounter a multitude of defensive weapons (e.g., land mines, trip wires) without directly confronting the enemy. The aftermath of combat can also be traumatic because service members may witness horrific, grotesque scenes, including seeing dismembered and burned bodies and wide-scale destruction. Combatants may be required to attend to the wounded and dying and collect and dispose of the bodies of the enemy and their fallen comrades.

In war, killing the enemy is often required to meet strategic objectives. About half of the Vietnam and Iraq war combat Veterans report taking enemy life (Laufer, Gallops, & Frey-Wouters, 1984; Hoge et al., 2004). The psychological impact of killing during war can exact a heavy toll (Maguen et al. 2009).

Aside from these experiences, recent wars have presented a number of novel, nontraditional combat experiences. The Vietnam, Iraq, and Afghanistan wars have been characterized as "wars without fronts," where, at times, distinguishing between the enemy and innocent civilians is impossible (Dohrenwend et al., 2006). A major feature of these types of conflicts is a guerilla-style warfare in which an inferior force employs nonconventional means to demoralize and weaken the fighting spirit of a superior force. For example, in OEF/OIF, suicide bombings and improvised explosive devices (IEDs) are the weapons of choice of the enemy and cause many casualties of U.S. and coalition forces.

However, violence is not exclusively a tool to further strategic objectives; it can also be a calculated or impulsive expression of extreme frustration or anger, a means to exact revenge, or seem entirely senseless. For Vietnam Veterans, reports of witnessing or participating in atrocities or extraordinary abusive violence (e.g., mutilations, killing civilians) were fairly common (Laufer et al., 1984), and involvement in these types of acts is associated with PTSD (King, King, Foy, & Gudanowski, 1996), even after accounting for traditional combat exposure (Beckham, Feldman, & Kirby, 1998). Perpetrating atrocities or abusive violence appears to be related to the amount of traditional combat exposure and not preexisting antisocial tendencies (King et al., 1996).

In addition to the intentional casualties combatants exact and receive, unintentional injury and loss of life abound in war zones, which may be just as psychologically damaging. Service members may mistakenly fire on friendly troops believing them to be the enemy (i.e., "friendly fire") or be required to kill civilian noncombatants who threaten security (e.g., run a checkpoint). Civilians may be used by the enemy as human shields to protect high-value targets, or otherwise are caught in the crossfire of war (i.e., "collateral damage").

Other forms of trauma that would not necessarily be considered combat-related also occur at high rates in war zones. These include accidents, such as motor vehicle accidents (e.g., Humvee rollovers, helicopter or plane crashes), weapon or equipment malfunction (e.g., untimely ordnance explosion), falls, electrocutions, and fires. It is beyond the scope of this chapter to enumerate an exhaustive list of all of the potential traumas that could be experienced in the war zone. Instead, this sample of common war-zone traumas serves to highlight the vast range of such traumas and the enormous potential for retraumatization when serving in a war zone.

## PSYCHOLOGICAL IMPACT OF COMBAT TRAUMA EXPOSURE

During or shortly after combat trauma, service members may experience acute stress reactions, which the U.S. military has classified as combat and operational stress reactions (COSRs). COSRs include physical, emotional, cognitive, and behavioral responses such as depression, fatigue, anxiety, anger, somatic complaints, decreased concentration/memory, and hyperarousal. COSR is not considered a psychiatric disorder but a normal reaction to extreme stress that is expected to be short lived. When COSR is severe, impairs ability to uphold duties, or persists for longer than a few days, it would be classified as a combat and operational stress injury (Adler, Castro, & McGurk, 2009b)

It has long been recognized that being exposed to combat trauma can have lasting psychological effects (Weathers, Litz, & Keane, 1995). Yet despite this long acknowledgement, a trauma-specific disorder did not appear in the psychiatric nomenclature until 1980, with the inclusion of PTSD in the *Diagnostic and Statistical Manual of Mental Disorders* (Third Edition) (*DSM-III*) (APA, 1980). This was largely due to the advocacy efforts of Vietnam combat Veterans who continued to struggle to readjust many years after their war-zone service (Weather, Litz, & Keane, 1995). In *DSM-IV-TR* (APA, 2000), a PTSD diagnosis requires the following criteria. First, the person must be exposed to a trauma involving threat of death or serious injury to self or others during which one responds with intense fear, helplessness, or horror (Criterion A). Second, the traumatic event is persistently re-experienced in various ways, including intrusive memories, flashbacks, nightmares, and psychological or physical distress upon exposure to trauma reminders (Criterion B). Third, the trauma survivor avoids trauma reminders, such as situations, conversations, and thoughts of the trauma, and experiences emotional numbing including feeling distant or cut off from others, feeling less pleasure in previously enjoyed activities, and having restricted range of affect (Criterion C). Fourth, the person has persistent symptoms of increased arousal (i.e., hyperarousal), including sleep problems, concentration difficulties, elevated anger, hypervigilance, and excessive startle reactions (Criterion D). Fifth, the symptoms included above must be present for more than 1 month (Criterion E) and must cause clinically significant distress or impairment in functioning (Criterion F).

Of those exposed to combat trauma, approximately 10% to 30% will develop PTSD. Rates of PTSD differ depending on the war. For example, rates of PTSD in Vietnam Veterans range 18% to 30% for lifetime and 9% to 15% for current (Dohwenrend et al., 2006; Kulka et al., 1990). Estimated rates of PTSD in Gulf war Veterans have been found to be lower (e.g., 10.1%; Kang, Natelson, Mahan, Lee, & Murphy, 2003)—ostensibly from the short duration of that conflict and resultant lower level of traumatic exposure. Whereas in Iraq Veterans, estimates (e.g., 18%, Hoge et al., 2004) fall closer to those found in Vietnam Veterans than Gulf war Veterans, rates for OEF Veterans (e.g., 12%, Hoge et al., 2004) appear closer to those of Gulf war Veterans, although with the recent escalation of violence in Afghanistan, one would expect the gap between OEF and OIF to narrow.

## PSYCHOLOGICAL, NEUROPSYCHOLOGICAL, AND PHYSICAL COMORBIDITIES

Exposure to combat trauma can lead to a variety of medical, psychological, and functional consequences. Literature specifically delineating the relationship between comorbidities and retraumatization is lacking. However, it is possible to draw some inferences in this domain because increased trauma exposure is directly related to incidence and severity of PTSD, and more severe PTSD comes with more comorbidities of various kinds.

Combat exposure increases the risk of psychological problems, including guilt (e.g., Beckham, Feldman, & Kirby, 1998); anger and violence (e.g., Novaco & Chemtob, 2002; Beckham et al., 1998); depression (e.g., Dedert et al., 2009); substance misuse (Prigerson, Maciejewski, & Rosenheck, 2002; Sareen et al., 2007); sleep problems including nightmares, sleep onset insomnia, and disrupted sleep maintenance (Neylan et al., 1998); and personality disorders (e.g., Axelrod, Morgan, & Southwick, 2005). In general, deployment to a war zone alone does not appear to increase suicide risk (Kang & Bullman, 2009). However, subgroups of war-zone deployed Veterans show increased suicide risk. For example, Vietnam Veterans with PTSD were seven times more likely to commit suicide compared to the U.S. population (Bullman & Kang 1994), and wounded combat Veterans were also at higher risk of suicide (Bullman & Kang 1996). OEF/OIF Veterans who had served on active duty or had a mental disorder were at increased risk of suicide than the general population (Kang & Bullman, 2009).

Combat exposure has also been linked to nonclinical unhealthy behaviors such as risk-taking behaviors (Killgore et al., 2008) and aggressive or risky driving (Fear et al., 2008). Increased exposure to combat trauma has been associated with functional and social problems as well, including incarceration (e.g., Yager, Laufer, & Gallops, 1984), unemployment and job loss, divorce and separation, and spousal abuse (McCarroll et al., 2000; Prigerson et al., 2002).

Finally, there are various neuropsychological issues associated with exposure to combat trauma including increased incidence of traumatic brain injuries (Vasterling et al., 2009) and cognitive functioning changes (Marx et al., 2009; Vasterling et al., 2006). Interestingly, Marx and colleagues (2009) found that higher levels of combat intensity during deployment were related to more efficient cognitive reaction time. Although Vasterling et al. (2006) identified the same effect with regard to reaction time, their study indicated that combat resulted in relative deficits in attention, learning, memory, and reaction time. It should be noted that these findings are specific to combat exposure rather than PTSD, which is known to impede cognitive performance in a number of ways (Vasterling et al., 2002). This may be due to the nervous system's tendency to become oversensitive and dysregulated when exposed to severe stressors (e.g., Orr et al., 2003).

In addition to impaired cognitive functioning, increased and repeated exposure to traumatic events, including combat trauma, is associated with poor physical health (Friedman & Schnurr, 1995; Green & Kimerling, 2004; Resnick, Acierno, & Kilpatrick, 1997; Schnurr & Jankowski, 1999). A growing literature indicates that combat exposure is linked to specific medical malfunctions, including coronary artery disease (Sibai, Armenian, & Alam, 1989; Kubzansky, Koenen, Spiro, Vokonas, & Sparrow, 2007), immune functioning (Segerstrom & Miller, 2004), and other systemic medical illnesses (e.g. Taft, Stern, King, & King, 1999). Trauma exposure is also related to health-care utilization: trauma-exposed individuals use more medical services than non-trauma-exposed controls (see Walker, Newman, & Koss, 2004).

## ETIOLOGICAL FORMULATIONS AND THEORETICAL MODELS

The extent of retraumatization and PTSD is a function of combat trauma exposure, which is directly related to several war-zone deployment factors, including length and number of deployments, as well as branch of service and types of combat traumas experienced (e.g., being a prisoner of war [POW]). Below, each of these factors is reviewed. Following this is a review of the various ways retraumatization can occur in the context of combat trauma exposure. Last, possible explanations for the relationship between combat trauma and retraumatization are offered. First, however, literature is reviewed on the long-recognized relationship between increasing levels of exposure to combat trauma (i.e., intensity of trauma and extent of retraumatization) and increasing rates of PTSD (i.e., the dose-response relationship), as this is a major link through which deployment factors operate on psychological outcomes.

### Dose-Response Relationship

It is well established that frequency and intensity of combat exposure are associated with various mental health problems, most commonly PTSD (e.g., Helzer, Robins, & McEvoy, 1987; Hoge et al., 2004; Kang et al., 2003; Kessler et al., 1995). One of the earliest studies to demonstrate this was the National Vietnam Veterans Readjustment Study (NVVRS) (Kulka et al., 1990), which examined a representative sample of 1,200 Vietnam Veterans. The dose-response relationship was found to be quite strong, and a recent re-examination of these data linking them to military records, historical accounts, diagnostic histories, Minnesota Multiphasic Personality Inventory (MMPI) validity scales, and compensation data found that this relationship was actually stronger than originally reported (Dohrenwend et al., 2006). Other studies of Vietnam Veterans have confirmed this finding, with many suggesting that dose of exposure is the most potent risk factor for PTSD (e.g., Boscarino, 1995; Buydens-Branchey, Noumair, & Branchey, 1990). This relationship has also been evidenced among Gulf war Veterans (Kang et al., 2003) and OEF/OIF Veterans (Baker et al., 2009; Schell & Marshall, 2008).

### Length of War-Zone Deployments

If increased combat exposure predicts psychological difficulties as reviewed above, it follows that prolonged war-zone deployments would increase risk of retraumatization and, consequently, problematic outcomes. Consistent with this reasoning, Buydens-Branchey and colleagues (1990) found a significant relationship between duration of combat exposure and prevalence and persistence of PTSD with all of the participants exposed to combat for more than one year having PTSD. The relationship between deployment length and postdeployment difficulties has also been demonstrated with OEF/OIF (Schell & Marshall, 2008) and the Gulf war Veterans (Kang et al., 2003). Given the relatively short stressor exposure during the Gulf war, as compared to wars before and since, it is notable that the dose-response relationship was still apparent.

While no absolute war-zone deployment length threshold has been identified, Rona, Fear, and Hull (2007) determined that UK service members who were deployed to Iraq for 13 months or more within a 3-year period were more likely to have PTSD than those with shorter deployments. Shen, Arkes, and Pilgrim (2009) found that sailors deployed for longer than 180 days were more likely to screen positive for PTSD compared to those deployed for less time. Similarly, Vietnam Veterans from New Zealand deployed for more than 19 months had an increased incidence of PTSD than those with shorter deployments (Vincent, Chamberlain, & Long, 1994).

## Branch of Service

There are various factors that influence duration of deployments, one of which is branch of service. In fact, relationships between extent of combat exposure, duration of deployment, and branch of service are not entirely independent. Deployment length varies based on job function, operational tempo, and other considerations. The Air Force tends to have the shortest deployments (4 to 6 months), followed by the Marines (approximately 7 months), and the Army (1 year). Frequency of deployment and time between deployments is also dependent upon service, job function, and rank. It is therefore unsurprising that Baker et al. (2009) found a relationship between branch of service, combat exposure, and incidence of PTSD. Specifically, this study found that Veterans of the Army and Marines were exposed to more potentially traumatic events and were more than twice as likely to screen positive for PTSD as were their Navy counterparts.

## Number of War-Zone Deployments

Being deployed multiple times contributes to retraumatization and can be most easily seen in Veterans who have served in different war zones. U.S. military service members who served only in the Gulf war were less likely to have PTSD than those who also had served in Vietnam (McCarroll, Fagan, Hermsen, & Ursano, 1997). This is consistent with a finding by Wolfe, Erickson, Sharkansky, King, and King (1999), in which Gulf war Veterans with previous combat experience had higher rates of PTSD than those without previous experience.

The sustained concurrent wars in Iraq and Afghanistan require that many service members complete multiple deployments. Approximately 37%

of service members deployed to OEF/OIF have been deployed at least twice to these combat theaters (Litz & Schlenger, 2009). As the number of tours increases, the likelihood of exposure to combat trauma increases, as does the possibility of deleterious psychological and functional effects. Polusny et al. (2009) assessed the impact of prior deployments in OEF/OIF National Guard and Reserve (NGR) soldiers 1 month before their next deployment. Not surprisingly, soldiers who had completed previous deployments reported more PTSD, depressive, and somatic symptoms than those deploying for the first time. The third report by the Mental Health Advisory Team (MHAT-III, 2006), which focused on active-duty personnel, also found that those with prior deployments to Iraq had increased PTSD during the later deployment and lower perceived support from their units. Killgore, Stetz, Castro, and Hoge (2006), however, found that soldiers with previous combat deployments to Iraq preparing to reenter combat reported decreased psychological distress but increased somatic symptoms. They speculated that this may indicate a tendency to repress affective symptoms and express distress as somatic complaints instead.

## Retraumatization in Prisoners of War

Retraumatization is a virtual certainty for those who are held as a POW and studies of Vietnam War POWs have shown a strong dose-response relationship between this traumatic stressor and increased rates of PTSD (Ursano, Boydstrun, & Wheatley, 1981). Many POWs report chronic repeated trauma including psychological intimidation, severe physical abuse, starvation, diseases due to malnutrition, unprotected exposure to elements, overcrowding and unsanitary conditions, witnessing of torture and executions, constant threats of death and torture, forced marches, and solitary confinement (Sutker, Allain, & Winstead, 1993). In a study of World War II survivors, Sutker and colleagues (1993) found that those who had been a POW had significantly higher rates of current PTSD compared with controls who had been exposed to severe combat but had never been a POW (70% and 18%, respectively). POWs also had significantly higher lifetime rates of PTSD than controls (78% and 29%, respectively). This has also been found in studies of POWs in the Pacific theater during World War II (Goldstein, van Kammen, Shelly, Miller, & van Kammen, 1987) and the Korean War (Sutker, Winstead, Galina, & Allain, 1991).

## Retraumatization and Combat Trauma Exposure

For some, combat trauma exposure may be the first of a series of traumatic events, whereas for others, it may be the second, third, fourth, and so on. Retraumatization can occur in various ways: if a service member experiences childhood or premilitary trauma (T1), the combat trauma (T2) may be retraumatizing; multiple combat traumas can occur (T1, T2, and so on) with later traumas considered retraumatization; combat trauma can occur (T1), and postmilitary traumatic events (T2) can be retraumatizing. In what follows, each of these possible sequences of retraumatization is reviewed.

Premilitary traumatic experiences can include physical or sexual assault, child abuse, natural disasters, and other extreme stressors. Exposure to traumatic stressors prior to military service is common. Dedert and colleagues (2009) found that 67% of Veterans whose service began in or after 2001 had experienced at least one potential traumatic stressor prior to service. Some have argued that this exposure is minimally relevant because clinical outcomes such as PTSD are linked to combat experiences and are not strongly associated with premilitary variables (Green, Grace, Lindy, Gleser, & Leonard, 1990). However, many studies have found that preservice variables can impact both the amount of exposure to potentially traumatic events and the psychological consequences of combat exposure (see King et al., 1996; Riddle et al., 2007).

Although not necessarily traumatic, Cabrera, Hoge, Bliese, and Castro (2007) outlined six adverse experiences that children may experience that may have problematic psychological consequences: (1) exposure to a mentally ill person in the home, (2) exposure to an alcoholic adult in the home, (3) sexual abuse, (4) physical abuse, (5) psychological abuse, and (6) violence directed against the respondent's mother. Various studies have confirmed the high prevalence of these adverse childhood experiences among Veterans and the interaction between these childhood experiences and combat exposure leading to more psychological difficulties than combat exposure without this history (Bremner, Southwick, Johnson, Yehuda, & Charney, 1993; Cabrera et al., 2007; Iversen et al., 2008). Childhood adversity and trauma are also linked to higher rates of combat exposure. King and colleagues (1996) proposed that early adversity may impact individuals in two ways: they are more likely to have negative psychological consequences from any given traumatic exposure, and they are more likely to be exposed to combat trauma.

Childhood abuse is a significant issue in the Veteran population. Zaidi and Foy (1994) found that 45% of Vietnam Veterans with PTSD experienced severe physical abuse during childhood. Lapp et al. (2005) found that 60% of male Veterans with combat-related PTSD in a psychiatric inpatient unit reported childhood physical abuse and 41% reported childhood sexual abuse. Childhood physical abuse is related to more severe PTSD, depression, and alcohol use in Veterans (Bremner et al., 1993; Clancy et al., 2006). This has also been observed in Gulf war Veterans (Engel et al., 1993). In Veterans who served after September 11, 2001, childhood physical assault and accidents and disasters predicted increased likelihood of PTSD after controlling for combat exposure and demographic covariates (Dedert et al., 2009).

In cases where combat trauma is the second (or later) traumatic experience, evidence suggests that more deleterious psychological consequences can be expected. Previous trauma has been associated with higher rates of

PTSD in the military (Riddle et al., 2007). In the NVVRS, previous trauma history, including accidents, assaults, and natural disasters, predicted PTSD directly and interacted with war-zone stressor levels in Veterans with high combat exposure to exacerbate PTSD symptoms (King et al., 1996). Bremner and colleagues (1993) had similar findings of premilitary traumatic events having a negative impact on psychiatric casualties. Prior assault appears to be a particularly problematic premilitary factor in the development of PTSD. Assault includes both physical/violent and sexual assault (forced sexual relations). OEF and OIF Veterans who experienced assault prior to deployment had twice the rate of first-onset PTSD symptoms compared to those with no assault history (Smith et al., 2008b). The prevalence and type of assault differed by gender, but the increased likelihood of PTSD following combat exposure was nearly identical.

Combat trauma can be experienced multiple times (T1, T2, etc.), both within a single deployment and over the course of multiple deployments. Prior combat trauma increases the risk of PTSD (Polusny et al., 2009). This increased risk may be related to the dose-response relationship: more combat exposure is associated with higher rates of PTSD (Kulka et al., 1990). A possibly confounding variable is the Healthy Warrior Effect (Wilson et al. 2009), which suggests that those who return for multiple deployments are more physically and mentally hardy than those who do not, because struggling individuals may never be deployed due to lack of fitness or may be discharged during or after a challenging deployment. Symptoms may go unrecognized if limited or no functional impairment is present or criteria for deciding fitness for deployment is adjusted depending on availability of able bodies during periods of low recruitment and high engagement.

In light of what has already been reviewed, previous exposure to combat trauma would be expected to increase problems upon combat retraumatization. In line with this, Solomon (1990) found that Israeli combat Veterans who experienced acute stress reactions in their initial deployment were more likely to experience stress reactions in subsequent deployments than Veterans without such previous reactions. In this case, we can infer that prior combat trauma negatively affected the individual's later experience of combat. However, it may not always operate in this manner. As discussed below, under some circumstances (e.g., mortuary work in war zone), successfully managing previous trauma may inoculate individuals against the impact of subsequent exposures.

In some cases, combat trauma (T1) is followed by postdeployment retraumatizing events (T2). Orcutt, Erickson, and Wolfe (2002) argued that combat exposure may increase the risk of future trauma exposure, but that this effect may be mediated by development of PTSD, increased risk taking, motor vehicle accidents, or aggressive driving. Past combat trauma may also make individuals more likely to enter combat-related occupations or volunteer for deployment to combat areas (Breslau, Davis, & Andreski, 1995; Orcutt et al., 2002). Dedert and colleagues (2009) studied Veterans whose service began in

2001 or later and found that 29% had been exposed to potentially traumatic events postservice. Lapp et al. (2005) found that 93% of male Veterans on a psychiatric inpatient unit for combat-related PTSD had experienced adult physical assault, 20% adulthood sexual assault, and 46% either physical or sexual assault within the past year.

This is especially problematic, because the postdeployment factors that have been associated with chronic PTSD, depression, and substance abuse include low social support, negative homecoming experiences, poor coping, and posttraumatic life events (Boscarino, 1995; Engdahl, Dikel, Eberly, & Blank, 1997; Green et al., 1990; Johnson, 1997; King, King, Fairbank, Keane, & Adams, 1998; Solomon, Mikulincer, & Avitzur, 1988; Solomon, Mikulincer, & Habershaim, 1990). Although social support has been generally viewed as a protective factor (Brewin, Andrews, & Valentine, 2000; King et al., 1998; Ozer, Best, Lipsey, & Weiss, 2003; Sutker, Davis, Uddo, & Ditta, 1995) that is even more important in postwar military than in civilian populations (Brewin, Andrews, & Valentine, 2000), there is evidence that soldiers exposed to high rates of combat and grotesque death are less likely to discuss their experiences with others and, subsequently, have fewer social supports (Green et al., 1990). This subgroup of service members is also more likely to experience negative life events after deployment (Green et al., 1990).

## Potential Explanations for Retraumatization in Combat Veterans

There are a number of possible reasons that could better help explain retraumatization in combat Veterans, including the development of problems after combat trauma exposure leading to increased risk of subsequent traumas. Some problems increase risk of interpersonal violence. For example, substance use disorders and anger problems can be associated with increased likelihood of violence perpetration and exposure to assault. For example, Veterans may come into contact with dangerous individuals when procuring illicit drugs. Some behaviors associated with PTSD (e.g., improper firearm storage, carrying of weapons) may be associated with increased likelihood of injury when violence occurs. Increased exposure to combat trauma has been associated with functional and social problems that include incarceration (e.g., Yager et al., 1984) and spousal abuse (McCarroll et al., 2000; Prigerson et al., 2002). These problems are associated with increased risk of exposure to assault.

PTSD symptoms and other posttrauma problems also increase risk for accidental injury and death (Dresher, Rosen, Burling, & Foy, 2003). Aggressive driving is associated with PTSD (Kuhn, Drescher, Ruzek, & Rosen, 2010) and can lead to motor vehicle accidents. Untreated comorbid substance use disorders may increase accident risk. Veterans with combat-related PTSD may have particular difficulties with sleep which may cause accidents while driving or operating equipment. Vasterling et al. (2006) reported that combat resulted in relative deficits in attention, learning, memory, and reaction time; these and a range of trauma-related symptoms (e.g., concentration difficulties, thought intrusions, panic reactions, dissociative phenomena) may place individuals at risk for motor vehicle and other accidents.

Problems associated with PTSD also are likely to affect the course of coping with exposure to subsequent traumas. For example, social support, including within military units, is a predictor of response to traumatic events (Polusny et al., 2009) that is likely to be diminished in those with PTSD. Combat Veterans with PTSD often experience difficulties in relationships with family and friends and decreased involvement in recreational activities. For example, combat Veterans with PTSD have more problems with intimacy, sociability, self-disclosure and expressiveness, physical aggression, and overall relationship adjustment and were more likely to be separated or divorced, have lower educational qualifications and income, and be unemployed than combat Veterans without PTSD symptoms (Carroll, Rueger, Foy, & Donahoe, 1985; Roberts et al., 1982; Vincent et al., 1994).

When individuals with PTSD are exposed to a new potentially traumatic event, difficulties in recruitment of social support, emotional avoidance coping, and inability to manage physiological arousal are likely to impair coping ability. Similarly, individuals with PTSD are commonly troubled by negative trauma-related cognitions. Strongly held negative beliefs may interact with new experiences and increase the likelihood that they will be appraised in negative ways. For example, a Veteran who believes that the world is an extremely dangerous place and that he cannot effectively protect himself may react to a civilian event in ways that increase sense of fear and maintain a sense of ongoing threat. Similarly, a person who believes himself responsible for a previous trauma may be more likely to blame himself in new circumstances.

## CLINICAL DESCRIPTION OF TRAUMA-SPECIFIC DISTRESS

As mentioned above, exposure to combat trauma can produce both acute and lasting negative psychological effects, with PTSD being among the most common lasting mental health conditions. However, PTSD is not the only disorder that commonly results from combat trauma. Major depression, substance use disorders, and other anxiety disorders are also common in service members who have experienced combat traumas. Veterans with combat-related PTSD may have particular difficulties with sleep, possibly because of chronically disturbed sleep during deployment. Likewise, while living in a war zone, being constantly on guard for threat may be adaptive, but chronic problems with hypervigilance and excessive safety behaviors can persist long after deployment. It is also important for survival in a war zone to perform tasks with the utmost accuracy and precision and to maintain control over all elements of one's surroundings. However, overcontrol and expectations of perfectionism, especially of others, can create a host of psychosocial problems if they persist beyond deployment.

Combat Veterans may also experience chronic functional impairments that include difficulties in relationships with family and friends, increased interpersonal violence, problems with work and major role obligations, and decreased involvement in recreational activities. For example, Vietnam combat Veterans with PTSD symptoms had more problems with intimacy and sociability than did combat Veterans without PTSD symptoms (Roberts et al., 1982). They also had more problems in intimate relationships with self-disclosure and expressiveness, physical aggression, and overall relationship adjustment (Carroll et al., 1985). Israeli combat Veterans with PTSD had poorer employment, family, sexual, and social functioning than did their counterparts without PTSD (Solomon & Mikulincer, 1987). The NVVRS documented similar psychosocial functioning impairments of Veterans with PTSD, including problems with marital and family adjustment, employment functioning, and violence (Jordan et al., 1992; Kulka et al., 1990; Zatzick et al., 1997a, 1997b). Similarly, having PTSD related to demographic indices of social adjustment such as being separated or divorced, lower educational qualifications and income, and unemployment (Vincent, Chamberlain, & Long, 1994).

## ASSESSMENT, DIAGNOSIS, AND PROGNOSIS IN CONTEXT OF COMBAT TRAUMA EXPOSURE

As mentioned above, participating in combat can expose one to a vast array of extremely stressful events. Furthermore, while different combat environments can share many common experiences, the weaponry and battle tactics typically evolve to suit the demands of the specific combat setting so that each war zone presents its own unique combat experiences. For example, during the Gulf war and early in OIF there was a threat of biological and chemical weapons. In OIF, and more recently in OEF, suicide bombs and IEDs are common. Therefore, combat trauma exposure measures developed for one conflict may need modification to be suitable for use with service members of other conflicts, or the same conflict as it evolves over time.

### Assessing Combat and Noncombat Trauma

Comprehensive self-report measures of trauma often include an item about combat trauma or war-zone exposure (see Norris & Hamblen, 2004). In order to obtain more detailed information about particular combat traumas and important dimensions of these traumas, such as frequency, intensity, and duration, a specific combat trauma measure is required. One of the most widely used measures of traditional combat experiences is the Combat Exposure Scale (CES) (Keane, Fairbank, Caddell, Zimering, Taylor, & Mora, 1989). This 7-item self-report measure inquires about combat situations, such as firing rounds at the enemy and being on dangerous duty. A total score classifies combat exposure into five categories of intensity ranging from "light" to "heavy." The CES is easily and quickly administered and scored, making it useful in both research and clinical settings. Again, if one is interested in measuring nontraditional combat or other war-zone-specific traumatic and nontraumatic stressors, additional items may need to be included or other measures may need to be sought. A recently developed promising self-report measure for this purpose is the Deployment Risk and Resilience Inventory (DRRI), which assesses 14 war-zone stressors and important predeployment (e.g., childhood adversity) and postdeployment stressors (e.g., homecoming experiences) related to problematic readjustment (King, King, Vogt, Knight, & Sampler, 2006).

Given that noncombat traumas occurring both before and after combat can affect responses from combat, a thorough assessment of these should also be undertaken. A number of very good self-report trauma screens exist that can be used for this purpose. Notable among these is the Trauma History Screen (THS) (Carlson et al., in press) because it captures details about specific trauma exposures (e.g., count, age of occurrence, intensity and duration of distress) that other screens do not assess.

## Assessing PTSD and Comorbid Conditions

Fundamentally, assessment and diagnosis of PTSD is little different for the multiply traumatized Veteran than for individuals who have experienced a single traumatic event. After deployment to a war zone, it is important to rapidly and effectively identify service members who are experiencing combat-related PTSD. It is also necessary to rescreen at a later time point (for example, 3 months or later postdeployment), as studies have consistently shown that rates of positive screens actually increase in the months following return (Bliese, Wright, Adler, Thomas, & Hoge, 2007; Milliken, Auchterlonie, & Hoge, 2007; Wolfe et al. 1999). For this purpose, the U.S. military has adopted the Primary Care PTSD screen (PC-PTSD) (Prins et al., 2004) in its required postdeployment health screening programs, and it is also being used by Veterans Affairs (VA) to identify Veterans with PTSD. This 4-item screen includes a yes–no question each about re-experiencing, avoidance, hyperarousal, and numbing symptoms of PTSD. Three or more yes responses is considered a positive screen with this cut-score providing acceptable sensitivity (0.78), specificity (0.87), and diagnostic utility (0.85) compared to a PTSD diagnosis based on structured clinical interview.

To diagnose combat-related PTSD and other mental health conditions that may be present, a structured clinical interview can be very helpful. For the diagnosis of PTSD, the Clinician-Administered PTSD Scale (CAPS) (Blake et al. 1995) is an excellent option among existing interviews because it has been widely used, it has strong psychometric properties, and it captures the frequency and intensity of symptoms (Weathers, Keane, & Davidson, 2001). For other common conditions (major depression, anxiety disorders, and substance use disorders), the Structured Clinical Interview for *DSM-IV* (First, Spitzer, Gibbon, & Williams, 1995) can be particularly helpful.

A number of validated self-report measures of PTSD are also available (see Keane, Street, & Stafford 2004 for a review). One of the most widely used is the PTSD Checklist (PCL), which has a specific version for individuals who have experienced military-related trauma (PCL—Military [M]). The PCL-M includes 17 items based on the *DSM-IV* symptoms of PTSD, and respondents are asked to rate how much they were bothered by each item in the past month using a 5-point scale ranging from 1 ("not at all") to 5 ("extremely"). It can be scored in several ways, including a total sum score (range 17 to 85) and separate subscores for Criteria B, C, and D of PTSD. The PCL-M is useful in monitoring PTSD symptoms during treatment, and for clinical purposes, a cut score of 50 provides good sensitivity and specificity for a PTSD diagnosis in Veterans (Weather, Litz, Herman, Huska, & Keane, 1993).

## PREVENTION AND TREATMENT

### Primary Prevention

In terms of prevention, the most obvious, and idealistic, primary prevention strategy for combat trauma and retraumatization and psychological consequences is for nations to cease engaging in warfare. Unfortunately, this seems unlikely to occur, so current primary prevention efforts instead focus on mitigating the psychological impact of combat traumas. According to the *DSM*, it is not just objective exposure to a traumatic event that determines if an event is traumatic; there must also be a subjective perception that the experience was traumatic. Therefore, if potentially traumatic combat events are unavoidable, then altering reactions to and perception of them may reduce risk of PTSD.

While not labeled as such, military selection, training, and preparation for combat can be considered a form of primary prevention, although not directly targeted at preventing mental health problems but instead maintaining performance during deployment. Initial selection into the military involves evaluations of mental fitness. Likewise, decisions about who will and will not deploy are based on mental fitness, which has been used to explain the healthy warrior effect and may prevent retraumatization in service members who are expressing symptoms of PTSD from previous combat or civilian traumas. Preparedness for combat duty has been found to predict reactions to combat exposure, with those feeling most prepared showing less of a negative reaction than those who do not feel adequately prepared.

For example, feeling unprepared or too inexperienced for work in theater is strongly associated with subsequent PTSD (Iversen, 2008). This could be due to further decreased feelings of control or an increased estimation of threat to autonomy at the time of trauma. There is evidence that both of these possibilities are associated with PTSD (Baum & Fleming, 1993; Ehlers & Clark, 2000). A specific example of these issues was provided by McCarroll, Ursano, Fullerton, and Lundy (1995) who found that for American soldiers working in a mortuary during the Persian Gulf war, those without prior mortuary experience and those who did not volunteer for the task had significantly higher rates of PTSD from exposure to dead bodies. This phenomenon appears to impact rates of depression as well: Wells et al. (2010) found that individuals who were exposed to combat were less likely to have an onset of depression if they had been trained for combat exposure as opposed to those who were underprepared. This lack of perceived readiness may also explain the findings that suggest that sailors deployed on shore missions have higher rates of PTSD (Shen et al., 2009).

Furthermore, Basoglu and colleagues (1997, 2005) demonstrated with war, torture, and natural disaster survivors, that perceived control and predictability during a traumatic event relates to PTSD risk. In fact, torture survivors who were prepared to endure torture had less psychological consequences during and after the torture (Basoglu et al, 1997). These findings have been replicated in UK service members who served in Iraq with perceived ill-preparedness for deployment experiences being linked to PTSD (Iversen et al., 2008).

In OEF/OIF, National Guard and Reservists (NGR) are playing a more central role than ever before due to a need to supplement active forces. Individuals who enlisted with the expectation that their service would consist of 1 weekend per month and 2 weeks per year have been deployed—in some cases multiple times—to war zones. NGR troops represent nearly half of the combat brigades in Iraq; compare this to the 8,700 NGR deployed to the Vietnam war (Polusny et al., 2009). NGR troops of all eras have increased rates of postdeployment problems compared to active duty troops (MHAT II, 2005; Milliken et al., 2007; Wolfe et al., 1999). These problems may increase over time: Milliken and colleagues (2007) found that 6 months after deployment the rates of PTSD and depression more than doubled among NGR troops from an assessment given immediately upon return.

The explanation for this increased suffering among NGR troops is somewhat unclear. It is possible that NGR are not as thoroughly trained for combat as described above. Browne et al. (2007) noted that reservists from the United Kingdom were older and of higher rank than regular forces and had more family problems at home that made deployment more challenging and, subsequently, PTSD more likely. Browne et al. (2007) also found that these reservists were exposed to more traumatic experiences than regular forces. However, PTSD symptoms seemed to be more associated with problems at home than problems encountered in Iraq.

Explicit forms of primary prevention include providing psychoeducation and stress inoculation training (SIT) (Meichenbaum & Novaco, 1985) to service members before they are deployed (Baker & Armfield, 1996). SIT prepares individuals to more effectively manage stressful events. Whealin, Ruzek, and Southwick (2008), based on cognitive behavioral theory and research, proposed that preparation efforts for potentially traumatic events, including combat, should consider targeting several cognitive and behavioral mechanisms that relate to posttrauma difficulties. Included among these are increasing perceptions of control and self-efficacy, for example, through graduated exposure to internal and external stimuli associated with actual combat trauma exposure to decrease the novelty and unexpectedness of these experiences. They also propose preemptively targeting negative appraisals, especially those that commonly arise in combatants (e.g., self-blame for deaths of buddies). To reduce peritraumatic physiological and emotional arousal during combat exposure, they recommend training in stress management skills (e.g., diaphragmatic breathing). Last, service members preparing for combat should be taught ways to reduce maladaptive coping (e.g., avoidant coping) and enhance adaptive coping (e.g., using social support, active problem solving) following combat exposure.

## Secondary Prevention

Because PTSD is likely to place Veterans at risk for additional trauma exposure upon return to civilian life, prevention of retraumatization should involve both prevention and treatment of PTSD and related problems (e.g., substance misuse and depression). Secondary prevention strategies target at-risk populations, such as service members who have recently been exposed to combat trauma or returned from a war-zone deployment. The military has a long tradition of intervening immediately after combat missions using unit-based group psychological debriefing (Adler, Castro, & McGurk, 2009). Typically during debriefing, a structure group discussion reviewing the stressful event is conducted with encouragement of sharing thoughts and emotions with the group. Service members are reassured that their reactions are common and normal given what they have experienced. While these programs are widely used, there has been little research of their efficacy. An exception to this is Battlemind, an early intervention for service members exposed to combat (Adler, Bliese, McGurk, Hoge, & Castro, 2009). Battlemind is designed to help combatants make a successful transition from the war zone by translating their existing military training and skills (e.g., mental toughness, ability to overcome challenges) to facilitate meeting the challenges of readjustment. In a recent randomized controlled trial, Battlemind was found to perform better than standard postdeployment stress education at reducing later symptoms of posttraumatic stress, depression, and sleep problems in OIF soldiers with high levels of combat exposure (Adler et al., 2009a).

## Tertiary Prevention

Tertiary prevention efforts are designed to treat those service members expressing mental health difficulties from their combat traumas. Effective psychotherapies for combat-related PTSD exist, including exposure therapy, cognitive behavior therapy, and eye movement desensitization and reprocessing therapy (Bradley, Greene, Russ, Dutra, & Westen, 2005). Two exposure/CBT variants, prolonged exposure (PE) therapy and cognitive processing therapy (CPT), have been shown to be effective in treating both female and male Veterans with PTSD (Schnurr et al., 2007; Monson et al., 2006). These therapies are recommended as first-line treatments for PTSD (Veterans Health Administration [VHA], 2003), with nationwide clinician training efforts underway to make them available to all Veterans with PTSD being treated in VA hospitals. PE and CPT address PTSD symptoms by focusing primarily on a specific trauma, possibly of many, that currently causes the most distress and disturbance in functioning. However, both also allow clients to address additional traumas that may be unresolved, making them well suited for the multiply traumatized Veteran. As mentioned earlier, PTSD partially mediated the relationship between combat trauma and later trauma (Orcutt et al., 2002), suggesting that effectively treating combat-related PTSD may have an additional benefit of reducing risk of retraumatization.

To reduce additional psychological issues and possibly risk of retraumatization, it is also important to address common comorbid problems, such as substance use disorders, anger, and other risky behaviors (e.g., improper firearm storage, aggressive driving, and suicidal behaviors) that may contribute to additional trauma exposures. Untreated comorbid substance use disorders may increase retraumatization risk through impaired decision making, increased accident risk, disinhibition and violence, and contact with dangerous individuals when procuring illicit drugs. Seeking Safety is an evidence-based manualized group therapy for substance use and PTSD comorbidity that has shown promising results with Veterans (for example, Desai, Harpaz-Rotem, Najavits, & Rosenheck, 2008). Likewise, extreme, explosive anger can produce disproportionate and inappropriate responses to provoking situations leading to interpersonal violence resulting in physical, financial, and legal consequences. Fortunately, CBT treatments for comorbid anger have been shown to be helpful and effective with combat Veterans with PTSD (e.g., Chemtob, Novaco, Hamada, & Gross, 1997; Morland et al., 2010).

Effective medications are also available for combat-related PTSD. The Veterans Affairs (VA)/Department of Defense (DoD) Clinical Practice Guidelines for management of PTSD recommend the selective serotonin reuptake inhibitors (SSRIs) as providing significant benefit and should be considered a first-line treatment agent (VHA, 2003). Other types of antidepressants, including the tricyclic antidepressants (TCAs) and monoamine oxidase inhibitors (MAOIs) are second-line treatments that have demonstrated some benefit. Other medications can be used to augment treatment for specific PTSD symptoms as well. For example, Prazosin has been used successfully to target posttraumatic nightmares. Notably, although antianxiety medications such as benzodiazepines address acute stress, they are not beneficial and are possibly harmful to use long term due to their potential impact on emotion regulation and cognition, and their addictive properties. Polypharmacy—prescribing multiple medications at once—frequently occurs in clinical practice, but it is not recommended due to a lack of evidence supporting efficacy of this approach.

Unlike during previous conflicts that relied upon a draft (e.g., during Vietnam) or were short lived (e.g., Gulf war), the current conflicts in Iraq and Afghanistan are burdening a limited number of service members with multiple deployments to sustain the protracted operations. This presents new challenges for mental health providers treating service personnel with PTSD who may be facing redeployment and possible retraumatization. Service members, too, may be confronting challenges and concerns related to treatment, including worry that treatment could reduce their ability to fight effectively and may put them at higher risk of retraumatization. Unfortunately, research is unavailable to offer direction to clinicians about expected outcomes of those successfully treated and redeployed, and to service members concerned about losing PTSD symptoms (e.g., hypervigilence) that they may see as adaptive in a war zone.

## SPECIAL ISSUES

### Increasing Role of Women in Combat

American women have been involved in combat operations for every U.S. military conflict since the Revolutionary War (Goldstein, 2001), but the extent of their involvement has changed dramatically over time (Street, Vogt, & Dutra, 2009). As recently as the Vietnam war, enlistment for women was capped at 2%, promotion opportunities for women were limited, and women served primarily in administrative or medical roles (Murdoch et al., 2006). By contrast, in the Gulf war, women made up approximately 11% of the total military, and less than half were in administrative and medical roles (Murdoch et al., 2006). Instead, many women provided critical support to combat missions (e.g., military police). Since the Gulf war, restrictions related to the positions that women can hold during combat have eased, and now 90% of positions—almost all except for any direct combat positions—are open to women (Donegan, 1996). In OEF and OIF, women represent approximately 14% of deployed service members (Department of Defense, 2008, as cited in Street et al., 2009).

Regulations still preclude women from holding direct combat positions, but this has not prevented women from experiencing combat traumas. Carney and colleagues (2003) found that the percentage of male and female Gulf war Veterans who had experienced at least one combat trauma was approximately equal. However, in the current conflicts, which are characterized by urban guerrilla warfare and hidden enemies, the lack of a clearly defined frontline makes the traditional distinction between direct combat and indirect combat roles less meaningful. Recent studies have shown that women serving in OEF and OIF experience less combat on average than their male counterparts (MHAT-IV, 2006; Rona et al., 2007; Tolin & Foa, 2006), but trauma exposure is still substantial (MHAT-IV, 2006).

Most research on retraumatization in combat Veterans has been on men. This may be a shortcoming because women are differentially affected by certain types of traumas both outside as well as inside the military (e.g., sexual assault; see Chapter 10 on combat and military sexual trauma). Factors of retraumatization may be different as well. For example, having only recently been accepted in combat-related roles, women may be reluctant to admit problems following a combat trauma because they feel they need to prove themselves as capable as men and, therefore, may risk retraumatization before adequately recovering.

## Combat Trauma and Military Medical Personnel

Military medical professionals are required in war zones to help wounded service members. These medical professionals are not only exposed to the dangers of the war zone, but as required by their roles, to the horrific physical injuries and suffering of wounded and dying service members, enemies, and civilians. The psychological consequences of these experiences have received very little study. The scant existing research suggests that military medical personnel experience the same psychological ill effects of war (e.g., PTSD and depression) as do other service members (for example, Grieger et al., 2007).

However, it remains unresolved if medical role-specific war-zone experiences (e.g., exposure to the severely wounded or dead) heighten risk for problematic psychological outcomes. Kolkow and colleagues (2007) found that, like with other deployed service members, threat of personal harm (both direct and perceived) predicted PTSD, but exposure to wounded and dead patients did not. However, Jones and colleagues (2008) found that in UK armed forces personnel deployed to Iraq, those with medical roles had more psychological distress (but not PTSD), multiple physical symptoms, and fatigue (for men but not women) than did other deployed personnel. In this case, traumatic medical experiences (e.g., saw personnel wounded or killed) were associated with worse psychological distress. They found that poorer group cohesion and preparation were also linked to poorer psychological health.

Increasingly included among teams of deployed military medical personnel are mental health specialists who deliver early intervention to service members suffering psychological injuries of battle. Unfortunately, the extant literature does not specifically address how these professionals fare following deployment. It is reasonable to suspect that exposure to the dangers of the war zone would have similar ill effects on these individuals as they do on other deployed medical service members; although having the training and skills to address the psychological effects of trauma perhaps would moderate this impact.

## Secondary Traumatization of Family Members of Combat Trauma Survivors

The effects of combat trauma, in particular PTSD, can spread beyond the afflicted Veteran to those close to him or her. This has been termed *secondary traumatization*. Secondary traumatization has been documented in spouses of combat Veterans with PTSD, with these spouses reporting more distress and worse psychological functioning than spouses of combat Veterans without PTSD (Jordan et al. 1992; Waysman, Mikulincer, Solomon, & Weisenberg, 1993). It appears that specific PTSD symptoms, namely anger and emotional numbing or withdrawal, are especially problematic in these intimate relationships (Galovski & Lyons, 2004).

Unfortunately, spouses of combat Veterans with PTSD are not the only family members who are impacted by secondary traumatization—their children can also be affected. These children have been found to have impaired relationships with their combat Veteran father and have problems with aggression, relating to peers, academic performance, and emotion regulation, and are more likely to receive psychiatric treatment (Galovski & Lyons, 2004). Here again, PTSD symptoms appear to be mediating this relationship between combat trauma and

Given these findings, the question arises of whether secondary traumatization predisposes one for PTSD following retraumatization. Although the research in this area is scant, there is some evidence suggesting that this may be the case.

## Combat Trauma and Other Professionals in War Zones

Aside from deployed service members, various other nonindigenous professionals live and work in war zones. These include U.S. government civilian employees (e.g., State Department employees) and private civilian contractors, many of whom are ex-military who serve as security guards for private companies or the U.S. government. They also fill logistic roles (e.g., food and fuel supply) that were formerly filled by military personnel. Not surprisingly, in wars without fronts, contractors are exposed to many of the same combat traumas as are military service personnel and, consequently, sustain similar lasting psychological injuries (Feinstein & Botes, 2009)

Another group of civilians typically found in war zones are journalists. It is common for war journalists to experience combat trauma and retraumatization (Feinstein & Nicolson, 2005). In fact, Feinstein, Owen, and Blair (2002) interviewed 28 war journalists, and all reported being shot at numerous times with some reporting being wounded or having close colleagues killed. The lifetime rate of PTSD in war journalists (28.6%) is similar, if not higher, to that found in combat Veterans (Feinstein et al., 2002). It is important to recognize that unlike service members, civilian contractors and war journalists do not receive the same degree of prewar-zone preparation and training, and support and assistance following exposure to combat trauma.

## SUMMARY AND FUTURE DIRECTIONS

Unlike many trauma survivor populations, combat Veterans almost always find themselves subject to multiple traumatic events. War deployment means daily risk of exposure to a wide range of potentially traumatizing experiences, and combatants are expected to perform in the face of repeated exposures. Perhaps because of the number of trauma exposures, as well as the nature and intensity of those exposures, combat Veterans are at increased risk of development of PTSD compared to many other survivor groups.

It is important that rates of exposure in the war zone are managed when possible, with periods of rest and return to safe circumstances made available. Such approaches will be limited due to the nature of military deployments, however. Therefore, prevention of retraumatization in Veterans includes two important goals. First, because Veterans who have returned to civilian status are at increased risk of additional civilian trauma exposures, treatment must address risk factors for additional traumatization. In addition to reducing PTSD symptoms, clinicians should work with Veterans to address substance abuse, suicidal ideation, problems with anger and violence, problem driving behavior, high-risk sexual behavior, maladaptive weapon storage, lack of social support, and other high-risk behaviors. Most treatment research trials assess PTSD symptoms but do not measure these behaviors to evaluate the impact of treatment on these important outcomes. And, there are few investigations of methods that attempt to directly change these behaviors. Nonetheless, clinicians should assess these problem areas and include relevant treatment components to target them.

A second and more ambitious approach to prevention of multiple trauma exposure and retraumatization involves preparation that reduces exposure to a potentially traumatic event that will result in psychological traumatization. That is, retraumatization might be reduced if active-duty personnel can be more effectively trained beforehand to cope with potential traumas. As noted above, there may be ways of accomplishing this objective, but research is needed in this virtually overlooked area.

# REFERENCES

Adler, A. B., Bliese, P. D., McGurk, D., Hoge, C. W., & Castro, C. A. (2009a). Battlemind debriefing and battlemind training as early interventions with soldiers returning from Iraq: Randomization by platoon. *Journal of Consulting and Clinical Psychology, 77*, 928–940.

Adler, A. B., Castro, C. A., & McGurk, D. (2009b). Time-driven battlemind psychological debriefing: A group-level early intervention in combat. *Military Medicine, 174*, 21–28.

Adler, A. B., Huffman, A. H., Bliese, P. D., & Castro, C. A. (2005). The impact of deployment length and experience on the well-being of male and female soldiers. *Journal of Occupational Health Psychology, 10*, 121–137.

American Psychiatric Association. (1980). *Diagnostic and statistical manual of mental disorders* (3rd ed.). Washington, DC: Author.

American Psychiatric Association. (2000). *Diagnostic and statistical manual of mental disorders* (4th ed., text revision). Washington, DC: Author.

Axelrod, S. R., Morgan, C. A., & Southwick, S. M. (2005). Symptoms of posttraumatic stress disorder and borderline personality disorder in Veterans of Operation Desert Storm. *American Journal of Psychiatry, 16*, 270–275.

Baker, D. G., Heppner, P., Afari, N., Nunnink, S., Kilmer, M. Simmons, A., ... Bosse, B. (2009). Trauma exposure, branch of service, and physical injury in relation to mental health among U.S. Veterans returning from Iraq and Afghanistan. *Military Medicine, 174*, 773–778.

Baker, M. S., & Armfield, F. (1996). Preventing post-traumatic stress disorders in military medical personnel. *Military Medicine, 161*, 262–264.

Basoglu, M., Livanou, M., Crnobaric, C., Franciskovic, T., Suljic, E. Duric, D., & Vranseic, M. (2005). Psychiatric and cognitive effects of war in former Yugoslavia: Association of lack of redress for trauma and posttraumatic stress reactions. *Journal of the American Medical Association, 294*, 580–590.

Basoglu, M., Mineka, S., Parker, M., Aker, T., Livanou, M., & Gok, S. (1997). Psychological preparedness for trauma as a protective factor in survivors of torture. *Psychological Medicine, 27*, 1421–1433.

Baum, A., & Fleming, I. (1993). Implications of psychological research on stress and technological accidents. *American Psychologist, 48*, 665–672.

Beckham, J. C., Feldman, M. E., & Kirby, A. C. (1998). Atrocities exposure in Vietnam combat Veterans with chronic posttraumatic stress disorder: Relationship to combat exposure, symptom severity, guilt, and interpersonal violence. *Journal of Traumatic Stress, 11*, 777–785.

Blake, D. D., Weathers, F. W., Nagy, L. M., Kaloupek, D. G., Gusman, F. D., Charney, D. S., & Keane, T. M. (1995). The development of a clinician-administered PTSD scale. *Journal of Traumatic Stress, 8*, 75–90.

Bliese, P. D., Wright, K. M., Adler, A. B., Thomas, J. L., & Hoge, C. W. (2007). Timing of postcombat mental health assessments. *Psychological Services, 4*, 141–148.

Boscarino, J. A. (1995). Post-traumatic stress and associated disorders among Vietnam Veterans: The significance of combat exposure and social support. *Journal of Traumatic Stress, 8*, 317–336.

Bradley, R., Greene, J., Russ, E., Dutra, L., & Westen, D. (2005). A multidimensional meta-analysis of psychotherapy for PTSD. *American Journal of Psychiatry, 16*, 214–227.

Bremner, J. D., Southwick, S. M., Johnson, D. R., Yehuda, R., & Charney, D. S. (1993). Childhood physical abuse and combat-related posttraumatic stress disorder in Vietnam Veterans. *American Journal of Psychiatry, 150*, 235–239.

Breslau, N., Davis, G. C., & Andreski, P. (1995). Risk factors for PTSD-related traumatic events: A prospective analysis, *American Journal of Psychiatry, 152*, 529–535.

Brewin, C. R., Andrews, B., & Valentine, J. D. (2000). Meta-analysis of risk factors for posttraumatic stress disorder in trauma exposed adults. *Journal of Consulting and Clinical Psychology, 68*, 748–766.

Browne, T., Hull, L., Horn, O., Jones, M., Murply, D., Fear, N. T., … Hotopf, M. (2007). Explanations for the increase in mental health problems in UK reserve forces who have served in Iraq. *British Journal of Psychiatry, 190*, 484–489.

Bullman, T. A., & Kang, H. K. (1994). Posttraumatic stress disorder and the risk of traumatic deaths among Vietnam Veterans. *Journal of Mental Disorders, 182*, 604–610.

Bullman, T. A., & Kang, H. K. (1996). The risk of suicide among wounded Vietnam Veterans. *American Journal of Public Health, 86*, 662–667.

Buydens-Branchey, L., Noumair, D., & Branchey, M. (1990). Duration and intensity of combat exposure and posttraumatic stress disorder in Vietnam Veterans. *Journal of Nervous and Mental Disease, 178*, 582–587.

Cabrera, O. A., Hoge, C. W., Bliese, P. D., & Castro, C. A. (2007). Childhood adversity and combat as predictors of depression and post-traumatic stress in deployed troops. *American Journal of Preventive Medicine, 33*, 77–82.

Carlson, E. B., Smith, S. R., Palmieri, P. A., Dalenberg, C., Ruzek, J. I., Kimerling, R., … Spain, D. A. (in press). Development and validation of a brief self-report measure of trauma exposure: The trauma history screen. *Psychological Assessment*.

Carney, C. P., Sampson, T. R., Voelker, M., Woolson, R., Thorne, P., & Doebbeling, B. N. (2003). Women in the Gulf War: Combat experience, exposures, and subsequent health care use. *Military Medicine, 168*, 654–661.

Carroll, E. M., Rueger, D. B., Foy, D. W., & Donahoe, C. P. (1985). Vietnam combat Veterans with posttraumatic stress disorder: Analysis of marital and cohabiting adjustment. *Journal of Abnormal Psychology, 94*, 329–337.

Chemtob, C. M., Novaco, R. W., Hamada, R. S., & Gross, D. M. (1997). Cognitive-behavioral treatment for severe anger in posttraumatic stress disorder. *Journal of Consulting and Clinical Psychology, 65*, 184–189.

Clancy, C. P., Graybeal, A., Tompson, W. P., Badgett, K. S., Feldman, M. E., Calhoun, P. S., … Beckham, J. C. (2006). Lifetime trauma exposure in Veterans with military-related posttraumatic stress disorder: Association with current symptomatology. *Journal of Clinical Psychiatry, 67*, 1346–1353.

Dedert, E. A., Green, K. T., Calhoun, P. S., Yoash-Gantz, R., Taber, K. H., Mumford, M. M., …
Beckham, J. C. (2009). Association of trauma exposure with psychiatric morbidity in
military Veterans who have served since September 11, 2001. *Journal of Psychiatric
Research, 43*, 830–836.

Desai, R. A., Harpaz-Rotem, I., Najavits, L. M., & Rosenheck, R. A. (2008). Impact of the
Seeking Safety program on clinical outcomes among homeless female Veterans with
psychiatric disorders. *Psychiatric Services, 59*, 996–1003.

Dohrenwend, B. P., Turner, J. B., Turse, N. A., Adams, B. G., Koenen, K. C., & Marshall, R.
(2006). The psychological risks of Vietnam for U.S. Veterans: A revisit with new data
and methods. *Science, 313*, 979–982.

Donegan, C. (1996). New military culture: Do women, blacks, and homosexuals get fair
treatment? *CQ Researcher, 6*, 361–384.

Drescher, K. D., Rosen, C. S., Burling, T. A., & Foy, D. W. (2003). Causes of death among
male Veterans who received residential treatment for PTSD. *Journal of Traumatic
Stress, 16*, 535–543.

Ehlers, A., & Clark, D. M. (2000). A cognitive model of posttraumatic stress disorder.
*Behavior Research and Therapy, 38*, 319–345.

Engdahl, B. E., Dikel, T. N., Eberly, R. E., & Blank, A. S. (1997). Posttraumatic stress
disorder in a community group of former prisoners of war: A normative response to
severe trauma. *American Journal of Psychiatry, 154*, 1576–1581.

Engel, C. J., Engel, A., Campbell, S., McFall, M. E., Russo, J., & Katon, W. (1993).
Posttraumatic stress disorder symptoms and precombat sexual and physical abuse
in Desert Storm Veterans. *Journal of Nervous and Mental Disease, 181*, 683–688.

Fear, N. T., Iversen, A. C., Chatterjee, A., Jones, M., Greenberg, N., Hull, L., … Wessely, S.
(2008). Risky driving among regular armed forces personnel from the United
Kingdom. *American Journal of Preventive Medicine, 35*, 230–236.

Feinstein, A., & Botes, M. (2009). The psychological health of contractors working in war
zones. *Journal of Traumatic Stress, 22*, 102–105.

Feinstein, A., & Nicolson, D. (2005). Embedded journalists in the Iraq war: Are they at
greater psychological risk? *Journal of Traumatic Stress, 18*, 129–132.

Feinstein, A., Owen, J., & Blair, N. (2002). A hazardous profession: War, journalists, and
psychopathology. *American Journal of Psychiatry, 159*, 1570–1575.

First, M. B., Spitzer, R. L., Gibbon, M., & Williams, J. B. W. (1995). *Structured clinical
interview for DSM-IV axis I Disorders—Patient edition (SCID-I/P, version 2.0)*. New
York: Biometrics Research Department, New York State Psychiatric Institute.

Friedman, M. J., & Schnurr, P. P. (1995). The relationship between trauma, posttraumatic
stress disorder, and physical health. In M. J. Friedman, D. S. Charney, & A. Y. Deutch
(Eds.), *Neurobiological and clinical consequences of stress: From normal adaptation to post-traumatic stress disorder* (pp. 507–524). Philadelphia: Raven.

Galovski, T., & Lyons, J. A. (2004). Psychological sequelae of combat violence: A review
of the impact of PTSD on Veteran's family and possible interventions. *Aggression
and Violent Behavior, 9*, 477–501.

Goldstein, G., van Kammen, W., Shelly, C., Miller, D. J., & van Kammen, D. P. (1987).
Survivors of imprisonment in the Pacific theater during World War II. *American
Journal of Psychiatry, 144*, 1210–1213.

Goldstein, J. (2001). *War and gender: How gender shapes the war system and vice versa*.
Cambridge: Cambridge University Press.

Green, B. L., & Kimerling, R. (2004). Trauma, PTSD, and health status. In P. P. Schurr
& B. L. Green (Eds.), *Physical health consequences of exposure to extreme stress*
(pp. 13–42). Washington DC: American Psychological Association.

Green, B. L., Grace M. C., Lindy J. D., Gleser, G. C., & Leonard, A. (1990). Risk factors for PTSD and other diagnoses in a general sample of Vietnam Veterans. *American Journal of Psychiatry, 147,* 729–733.

Helzer, J. E., Robins, L. N., & McEvoy, L. (1987). Post-traumatic stress disorder in the general population: Findings of the Epidemiologic Catchment Area survey. *New England Journal of Medicine,* 317, 1630–1634.

Hoge, C. W., Auchterlonie, J. L., & Milliken, C. S. (2006). Mental health problems, use of mental health services, and attrition from military service after returning from deployment to Iraq or Afghanistan. *JAMA, 295*(9), 1023–1032.

Hoge, C. W., Castro, C. A., Messer, S. C., McGurk, D., Cotting, D. I., & Koffman, R. L. (2004). Combat duty in Iraq and Afghanistan, mental health problems, and barriers to care. *New England Journal of Medicine,* 351, 13–22.

Iversen, A. C., Fear, N. T., Ehlers, A., Hacker Hughes, J., Hull, J., Earnshaw, M., … Hotopf, M. (2008). Risk factors for post-traumatic stress disorder among UK armed forces personnel. *Psychological Medicine, 38,* 511–522.

Johnson, D. R., Lubin, H., Rosenheck, R., Fontana, A., Southwick, S., & Charney, D. (1997). The impact of the homecoming reception on the development of post-traumatic stress disorder. The West Haven Homecoming Stress Scale (WHHSS). *Journal of Traumatic Stress, 10,* 259–277.

Jordan, K., Marmar, C. R., Fairbank, J. A., Schlenger, W. E., Kulka, R. A., Hough, R. L., & Weiss, D. S. (1992). Problems in the families of male Vietnam Veterans with posttraumatic stress disorders. *Journal of Consulting and Clinical Psychology, 60,* 916–926.

Kang, H. K., & Bullman, T. A. (2009). Is there an epidemic of suicides among current and former U.S. military personnel? *Annals of Epidemiology, 19,* 757–760.

Kang, H. K., Natelson, B. H., Mahan, C. M., Lee, K. Y., & Murphy, F. M. (2003). Posttraumatic stress disorder and chronic fatigue-like illness among Gulf War Veterans: A population-based survey of 30,000 Veterans. *American Journal of Epidemiology, 157,* 141–148.

Keane, T., Fairbank, J., Caddell, J., Zimering, R., Taylor, K., & Mora, C. (1989). Clinical evaluation of a measure to assess combat exposure. *Psychological Assessment, 1,* 53–55.

Keane, T. M., Street, A. E., & Stafford, J. (2004). The assessment of military-related PTSD. In J. P. Wilson & T. M. Keane (Eds.), *Assessing psychological trauma and PTSD* (2nd ed., pp. 262–285). New York: Guilford Press.

Kessler, R. C., Sonnega, A., Bromet, E., Hughes, M., & Nelson, C. B. (1995). Posttraumatic stress disorder in the National Comorbidity Survey. *Archives of General Psychiatry, 52,* 1048–1060.

Killgore, W. D., Cotting, D. I., Thomas, J. L., Cox, A. L., McGurk, D., Vo, A. H., … Hoge, C. W. (2008). Post-combat invincibility: Violent combat experiences are associated with increased risk-taking propensity following deployment. *Journal of Psychiatric Research, 42,* 1112–1121.

Killgore, W. D., Stetz, M. C., Castro, C. A., & Hoge, C. W. (2006). The effects of prior combat experience on the expression of somatic and affective symptoms in deploying soldiers. *Journal of Psychosomatic Research, 60,* 379–385.

King, D. W., King, L. A., Foy, D. W., & Gudanowski, D. M. (1996). Prewar factors in combat-related posttraumatic stress disorder: Structural equation modeling with a national sample of female and male Vietnam Veterans. *Journal of Consulting and Clinical Psychology, 64,* 520–531.

King, L. A., King, D. W., Fairbank, J. A., Keane, T. M., & Adams, G. A. (1998). Resilience-recovery factors in post-traumatic stress disorder among female and male Vietnam Veterans: Hardiness, postwar social support, and additional life events. *Journal of Personality and Social Psychology, 74*, 420–434.

King, L. A., King, D. W., Vogt, D., Knight, J., & Sampler, R. (2006). Deployment Risk and Resilience Inventory: A collection of measures for studying deployment-related experiences of military personnel and Veterans. *Military Psychology, 18*(2), 89–120.

Koenen, K. C., Moffitt, T. E., Poulton, R., Martin, J., & Caspi, A. (2007). Early childhood factors associated with the development of post-traumatic stress disorder: Results from a longitudinal birth cohort. *Psychological Medicine, 37,* 181–192.

Kolkow, T. T., Spira, J. L., Morse, J. S., & Grieger, T. A. (2007). Post-traumatic stress disorder and depression in health care providers returning from deployment to Iraq and Afghanistan. *Military Medicine, 172*, 451–455.

Kubzansky, L. D., Koenen, K. C., Spiro, A. III, Vokonas, P. S., & Sparrow, D. (2007). Perspective study of posttraumatic stress disorder symptoms and coronary heart disease in the normative aging study. *Archives of General Psychiatry, 64,* 109–116.

Kuhn, E. L., Drescher, K. D., Ruzek, J. I., & Rosen, C. R. (2010). Aggressive and unsafe driving in male Veterans receiving residential treatment for PTSD. *Journal of Traumatic Stress, 23*(3), 399–402.

Kulka, R. A., Schlenger, W. E., Fairbank, J. A., Hough, R. L., Jordan, B. K., Marmar, C. R., ... Grady, D. A. (1990). *Trauma and the Vietnam War generation.* New York: Brunner/ Mazel.

Lapp, K. G., Bosworth, H. B., Strauss, J. L., Stechuchak, K. M., Horner, R. D., Calhoun, P. S., ... Butterfield, M. I. (2005). Lifetime sexual and physical victimization among male Veterans with combat-related post-traumatic stress disorder. *Military Medicine, 170,* 787–790.

Laufer, R. S., Gallops, M. S., & Frey-Wouters, E. (1984). War stress and trauma: The Vietnam Veteran experience. *Journal of Health and Social Behavior, 25,* 65–85.

Litz, B. T., & Schlenger, W. E. (2009, Winter). PTSD in service members and new Veterans of the Iraq and Afghanistan wars: A bibliography and critique. *PTSD Research Quarterly, 20,* 1–8.

MacDonald, C., Chamberlain, K., Long, N., & Flett, R. (1999). Posttraumatic stress disorder and interpersonal functioning in Vietnam War Veterans: A mediation model. *Journal of Traumatic Stress, 12,* 701–707.

Maguen, S., Metzler, T. J., Litz, B. T., Seal, K. H., Knight, S. J., & Marmar, C. R. (2009). The impact of killing in war on mental health symptoms and related functioning. *Journal of Traumatic Stress, 22,* 435–443.

Marx, B. P., Brailey, K., Proctor, S. P., MacDonald, H. Z., Graefe, A. C., Amoroso, P., ... Vasterling, J. (2009). Association of time since deployment, combat intensity, and posttraumatic stress symptoms with neuropsychological outcomes following Iraq War deployment. *Archives of General Psychiatry, 66,* 996–1004.

McCarroll, J. E., Fagan, J. G., Hermsen, J. M., & Ursano, R. J. (1997). Posttraumatic stress disorder in the U.S. Army Vietnam Veterans who served in the Persian Gulf War, *Journal of Nervous and Mental Disease, 185,* 682–685.

McCarroll, J. E., Ursano, R. J., Fullerton, C. S., & Lundy, A. (1995). Anticipatory stress of handling human remains from the Persian Gulf War: Predictors of intrusion and avoidance. *Journal of Nervous and Mental Disease, 183,* 698–703.

Meichenbaum, D., & Novaco, R. (1985). Stress inoculation: A preventive approach. *Issues in Mental Health Nursing, 7,* 419–435.

Milliken, C. S., Auchterlonie, J. L., & Hoge, C. W. (2007). Longitudinal assessment of mental health problems among active and reserve component soldiers returning from the Iraq war. *Journal of the American Medical Association, 2989,* 2141–2148.

Monson, C. M., Schnurr, P. P., Resick, P. A., Friedman, M. J., Young-Xu, Y., & Stevens, S. P. (2006). Cognitive processing therapy for Veterans with military-related posttraumatic stress disorder. *Journal of Consulting and Clinical Psychology, 74,* 898–907.

Morland, L. A., Greene, C. J., Rosen, C. S., Foy, D., Reilly, P., Shore, J., ... Frueh, B. C. (2010). Telemedicine for anger management therapy in a rural population of combat Veterans with posttraumatic stress disorder: A randomized noninferiority trial. *Journal of Clinical Psychiatry, 71*(7), 855–863.

Murdoch, M., Bradley, A., Mather, S. H., Klein, R. E., Turner, C. L., & Yano, E. M. (2006). Women and war: What physicians should know. *Journal of General Internal Medicine, 21,* S5–S10.

Neylan, T. C., Marmar, C. R., Metzler, T. J., Weiss, D. S., Zatzick, D. F., Delucchi, K. L. et al. (1998). Sleep disturbances in the Vietnam generation: Findings from a nationally representative sample of male Vietnam Veterans. *American Journal of Psychiatry, 155*(7), 929–933.

Norris, F. H., & Hamblen, J. L. (2004). Standardized self-report measures of civilian trauma and PTSD. In J. P. Wilson & T. M. Keane (Eds.), *Assessing psychological trauma and PTSD* (2nd ed., pp. 63–102). New York: Guilford Press.

Novaco, R. W., & Chemtob, C. M. (2002). Anger and combat-related posttraumatic stress disorder. *Journal of Traumatic Stress, 15,* 123–132.

Orcutt, H. K., Erickson, D. J., & Wolfe, J. (2002). A prospective analysis of trauma exposure: The mediating role of PTSD symptomatology. *Journal of Traumatic Stress, 15,* 259–266.

Orr, S. P., Metzger, L. J., Lasko, N. B., Macklin, M. L., Hu, F. B., Shalev, A. Y., & Pitman, R. K. (2003). Harvard/Veterans Affairs Post-traumatic Stress Disorder Twin Study Investigators. Physiologic responses to sudden, loud tones in monozygotic twins discordant for combat exposure: Association with posttraumatic stress disorder. *Archives of General Psychiatry, 60,* 283–288.

Ozer, E. J., Best, S. R., Lipsey, T. L., & Weiss, D. S. (2003). Predictors of posttraumatic stress disorder and symptoms of adults: A meta-analysis. *Psychological Bulletin, 129,* 52–73.

Polusny, M. A., Erbes, C. R., Arbisi, P. A., Thuras, P., Kehle, S. M., Rath, M., ... Duffy, C. (2009). Impact of prior Operation Enduring Freedom/Operation Iraqi Freedom combat duty on mental health in a predeployment cohort of National Guard Soldiers. *Military Medicine, 174,* 353–357.

Prigerson, H. G., Maciejewski, P. K., & Rosenheck, R. A. (2002). Population attributable fractions of psychiatric disorders and behavioral outcomes associated with combat exposure among US men. *American Journal of Public Health, 92,* 59–63.

Prins, A., Ouimette, P. C., Kimerling, R., Thrailkill, A., Cameron, R., Shaw, J., ... Sheik, J. (2004). The Primary Care PTSD Screen (PC-PTSD): Development, operating characteristics and clinical utility. *Primary Care Psychiatry, 9,* 9–14.

Resnick, H. S., Acierno, R., & Kilpatrick, D. G. (1997). Health impact of interpersonal violence. Section II: Medical and mental health outcomes. *Behavioral Medicine, 23*(2), 65–78.

Riddle, J. R., Smith, T. C., Smith, B., Corbeil, T. E., Engel, C. C., Wells, T. S., ... Blazer, D. (2007). Millennium cohort: The 2001–2003 baseline prevalence of mental disorders in the U.S. military. *Journal of Clinical Epidemiology, 60,* 192–201.

Roberts, W. R., Penk, W. E., Gearing, M. L., Robinowitz, R., Dolan, M. P., & Patterson, E. T. (1982). Interpersonal problems of Vietnam combat Veterans with symptoms of post-traumatic stress disorder. *Journal of Abnormal Psychology, 91*, 444–450.

Rona, R. J., Fear, N. T., Hull, L., Greenberg, N., Earnshaw, M., Hotopf, M., & Wessely, S. (2007). Mental health consequences of overstretch in the UK armed forces: First phase cohort study. *British Medical Journal, 335*, 603–609.

Sareen, J., Cox, B. J., Afifi, T. O., Stein, M. B., Belik, S. L., Meadows, G., & Asmundson, G. J. (2007). Combat and peacekeeping operations in relation to prevalence of mental disorders and perceived need for mental health care: Findings from a large representative sample of military personnel. *Archives of General Psychiatry, 64*, 843–852.

Schell, T. L., & Marshall, G. N. (2008). Survey of individuals previously deployed for OEF/OIF. In T. Tanielian & L. H. Jaycox (Eds.), *Invisible wounds of war: Psychological and cognitive injuries, their consequences, and services to assist recovery* (pp. 87–115). Santa Monica, CA: RAND Center for Military Health Policy Research.

Schnurr, P. P., & Jankowski, M. K. (1999). Physical health and post-traumatic stress disorder: Review and synthesis. *Seminars in Clinical Neuropsychiatry, 4*, 295–304.

Schnurr, P. P., Friedman, M. J., Engel, C. C., Foa, E. B., Shea, M. T., Chow, B. K., … Bernardy, N. (2007). Cognitive behavioral therapy for posttraumatic stress disorder in women: A randomized controlled trial. *Journal of the American Medical Association, 297*, 820–830.

Segerstrom, S. C., & Miller, G. E. (2004). Psychological stress and the human immune system: A meta-analytic study of 30 years of inquiry. *Psychological Bulletin, 130*, 601–630.

Shen, Y., Arkes, J., & Pilgrim, J. (2009). The effects of deployment intensity on post-traumatic stress disorder: 2002–2006. *Military Medicine, 174*, 217–223.

Sibai, A., Armenian, H., & Alam, S. (1989). Wartime determinants of arteriographically confirmed coronary artery disease in Beirut. *American Journal of Epidemiology, 130*, 623–631.

Smith, T. C., Ryan, M. A. K., Wingard, D. L., Slymen, D. J., Sallis, J. F., & Kritz-Silverstein, D. (2008a). New onset and persistent symptoms of post-traumatic stress disorder self-reported after deployment and combat exposures: Prospective population based US military cohort study. *British Medical Journal, 336*, 366–371.

Smith, T. C., Wingard, D. L., Ryan, M. A. K., Kritz-Silverstein, D., Slymen, D. J., & Sallis, J. F. (2008b). Prior assault and Posttraumatic Stress Disorder after combat deployment. *Epidemiology, 19*(3), 505–512.

Solomon, Z. (1990). Back to the front: Recurrent exposure to combat stress and reactivation of posttraumatic stress disorder. In M. E. Wolf (Ed.), *Post-traumatic stress disorder: Etiology, phenomenology, and treatment* (pp. 114–124). Washington, DC: American Psychiatric Press.

Solomon, Z., & Mikulincer, M. (1987). Combat stress reactions, posttraumatic stress disorder, and social adjustment: A study of Israeli soldiers. *Journal of Nervous and Mental Disease, 175*, 277–284.

Solomon, Z., Mikulincer, M., & Avitzur, E. (1988). Coping, locus of control, social support, and combat-related post-traumatic stress disorder. *Journal of Personality and Social Psychology, 55*, 279–285.

Solomon, Z., Mikulincer, M., & Habershaim, N. (1990). Life events, coping strategies, social resources, and somatic complaints among combat stress reaction casualties. *British Journal of Medical Psychology, 63*, 137–148.

Street, A. E., Vogt, D., & Dutra, L. (2009). A new generation of women Veterans: Stressors faced by women deployed to Iraq and Afghanistan. *Psychology Review, 29,* 685–694.

Sutker, P. B., Allain, A. N., & Winstead, D. K. (1993). Psychopathology and psychiatric diagnoses of World War II Pacific theater prisoner of war survivors and combat Veterans. *American Journal of Psychiatry, 150,* 240–245.

Sutker, P. B., Davis, J. M., Uddo, M., & Ditta, S. R. (1995). Assessment of psychological distress in Persian Gulf troops: Ethnicity and gender comparisons. *Journal of Personality Assessment, 64,* 415–427.

Sutker, P. B., Winstead, D. K., Galina, Z. H., & Allain, A. N. (1991). Cognitive deficits and psychopathology among former prisoners of war and combat Veterans of the Korean conflict. *American Journal of Psychiatry, 148,* 67–72.

Taft, C. T., Stern, A. S., King, L. A., & King, D. W. (1999). Modeling physical health and functional health status: The role of combat exposure, posttraumatic stress disorder, and personal resource attributes. *Journal of Traumatic Stress, 12,* 3–23.

Tolin, D. F., & Foa, E. B. (2006). Sex differences in trauma and posttraumatic stress disorder: A quantitative review of 25 years of research. *Psychological Bulletin, 132,* 959–992.

U.S. Army Surgeon General (January 2005). *Report: Operation Iraqi Freedom (OIF-II) Mental Health Advisory Team (MHAT-II).* Washington DC: U.S. Government Printing Office.

U.S. Army Surgeon General (May 2006). *Report: Operation Iraqi Freedom 04–06 Mental Health Advisory Team III (MHAT-III).* Washington DC: U.S. Government Printing Office.

U.S. Army Surgeon General (November 2006). *Report from Operation Iraqi Freedom 05–07 Mental Health Advisory Team III (MHAT-IV).* Washington DC: U.S. Government Printing Office.

Vasterling, J. J., Duke, L. M., Brailey, K., Constans, J. I., Allain, A. N., & Sutker, P. B. (2002). Attention, learning and memory performances and intellectual resources in Vietnam Veterans: PTSD and no disorder comparisons. *Neuropsychology, 16,* 5–14.

Vasterling, J. J., Proctor, S. P., Amoroso, P., Kane, R., Heeren, T., & White, R. F. (2006). Neuropsychological outcomes of army personnel following deployment to the Iraq War. *Journal of the American Medical Association, 296,* 519–529.

Vasterling, J. J., Verfaellie, M., & Sullivan, K. D. (2009). Mild traumatic brain injury and posttraumatic stress disorder in returning Veterans: Perspectives from cognitive neuroscience. *Clinical Psychology Review, 29*(8), 674–684.

Veterans Health Administration. (2003). Management of posttraumatic stress (Office of Quality and Performance Publication #10Q-CPG/PTSD-04). Washington, DC: Veterans Administration, Department of Defense Clinical Practice Guideline Working Group; 2003. Available at: http://www.oqp.med.va.gov/cpg/PTSD/PTSD_ Base.htm. Accessed March 21, 2007.

Vincent, C., Chamberlain, K., & Long, N. (1994). Relation of military service variables to posttraumatic stress disorder in New Zealand Vietnam War Veterans. *Military Medicine, 159,* 322–326.

Walker, E., Newman, E., & Koss, M. P. (2004). Costs and health utilization associated with traumatic experiences. In P. S. Schnurr & B. L. Green (Eds.) *Physical Health Consequences of Exposure to Extreme Stress* (pp. 43–71). Washington DC: American Psychological Press.

Waysman, M., Mikulincer, M., Solomon, Z., & Weisenberg, M. (1993). Secondary traumatization among wives of posttraumatic combat Veterans: A family typology. *Journal of Family Psychology, 7,* 104–118.

Weathers, F. W., Keane, T. M., & Davidson, J. R. T. (2001). Clinician-administered PTSD scale: A review of the first ten years of research. *Depression and Anxiety, 13(3)*, 132–156.

Weathers, F., Litz, B., Herman, D., Huska, J., & Keane, T. (October 1993). *The PTSD Checklist (PCL): Reliability, Validity, and Diagnostic Utility.* Paper presented at the the Annual Convention of the International Society for Traumatic Stress Studies. San Antonio, TX.

Weathers, F. W., Litz, B. T., & Keane, T. M. (1995). Military trauma. In J. R. Freedy & S. E. Hobfoll (Eds.), *Traumatic stress: From theory to practice* (pp. 103–128). New York: Plenum Press.

Wells, T. S., LeardMann, C. A., Fortuna, S. O., Smith, B., Smith, T. C., Ryan, M. A. K., … Blazer, D. (2010). A prospective study of depression following combat deployment in support of the wars in Iraq and Afghanistan. *America Journal of Public Health, 100*, 90–99.

Whealin, J. M., Ruzek, J. I., & Southwick, S. (2008). Cognitive behavioral theory and preparation for professionals at risk for trauma exposure. *Trauma, Violence & Abuse, 9(2)*, 100–113.

Wilson, J., Jones, M., Fear, N. T., Hull, L., Hotopf, M., Wessely, S., & Rona, R. J. (2009). Is previous psychological health associated with the likelihood of Iraq War deployment? An investigation of the "healthy warrior effect." *American Journal of Epidemiology, 169*, 1362–1369.

Wolfe, J., Erickson, D. J., Sharkansky, E. J., King, D. W., & King, L. A. (1999). Course and predictors of post-traumatic stress disorder among Gulf War Veterans: A prospective analysis. *Journal of Consulting and Clinical Psychology, 67*, 520–528.

Yager, T., Laufer, R., & Gallops, M. (1984). Some problems associated with war experience in men of the Vietnam generation. *Archives of General Psychiatry, 41*, 327–333.

Zaidi, L. Y., & Foy, D. W. (1994). Childhood abuse experiences and combat-related PTSD. *Journal of Traumatic Stress, 7*, 33–42.

Zatzick, D. F., Marmar, C. R., Weiss, D. S., Browner, W. S., Metzler, T. J., Golding, J. M., … Wells, K. B. (1997a). Posttraumatic stress disorder and functioning and quality of life outcomes in a nationally representative sample of male Vietnam Veterans. *American Journal of Psychiatry, 154*, 1690–1695.

Zatzick, D. F., Weiss, D. S., Marmar, C. R., Metzler, T. J., Wells, K. B., Golding, J. M., … Browner, W. S. (1997b). Post-traumatic stress disorder and functioning and quality of life outcomes in female Vietnam Veterans. *Military Medicine, 162*, 661–665.

Chapter 10

# Dual Combat and Sexual Trauma During Military Service

*Katherine M. Iverson, Candice M. Monson, and Amy E. Street*

Combat deployment is one of the most stressful and dangerous experiences associated with serving in the military. The U.S. military has been engaged in combat operations in Afghanistan, Iraq, and neighboring countries in service of Operation Enduring Freedom (OEF) and Operation Iraqi Freedom (OIF). These deployments are marked by intense urban combat, persistent risk of improvised explosive devices (IEDs) and roadside bombs, multiple and prolonged tours, and the omnipresent threat involved in differentiating ally from enemy combatant in these settings. Many deployed OEF/OIF Veterans report multiple exposures to combat trauma, which may lead to substantial physical and mental injuries as well as reductions in quality of life (Hoge, Auchterlonie, & Milliken, 2006; Hoge & Castro, 2006; Milliken, Auchterlonie, & Hoge, 2007; Schnurr, Lunney, Bovin, & Marx, 2009).

Of course, combat experiences are not the only traumatic events that service members may encounter. Unfortunately, experiences of sexual harassment and sexual assault during military service, referred to as *military sexual trauma* within the Department of Veterans Affairs (VA), are all-too-common stressors for both male and female service members. Although the occurrence of sexual trauma during peacetime military service has been well documented, the phenomenon of sexual trauma during war-zone deployments has received increased attention in recent years. Not surprisingly, experiences of sexual harassment and sexual assault during military service are associated with substantial negative effects on mental and physical health (Butterfield, McIntyre,

Stechuchak, Nanda, & Bastien, 1998; Kimerling et al., 2010; Murdoch, Pryor, Polusny, & Gackstetter, 2007; Skinner et al., 2000). Although little empirical work has examined this question directly, those Veterans who have experienced both combat and sexual trauma as part of their military service are likely to be facing particularly deleterious effects. For such Veterans, these two potentially traumatic exposures must be considered in tandem, because while each type of exposure alone is robustly associated with posttraumatic stress sequelae, together they may have a synergistic effect in contributing to deleterious health outcomes among Veterans.

This chapter provides an overview of issues that the survivors of both combat and sexual trauma face, emphasizing both distal and proximal factors contributing to physical and mental health consequences. We begin with an overview of the prevalence of combat trauma and sexual trauma during military service with a focus on their role in the etiology and exacerbation of health problems including posttraumatic stress disorder (PTSD). With rare exception (e.g., Fontana, Litz, & Rosenheck, 2000), the prevalence and consequences of combat trauma and sexual trauma during military service have been examined separately.

## COMBAT TRAUMA AND ITS SEQUELAE

Only in the last 20 years have researchers conducted methodologically rigorous epidemiological studies of combat trauma and its mental health effects of PTSD and other forms of psychological distress. Although a brief overview of combat trauma and health effects follows, readers are referred to Chapter 9 of this volume for a more comprehensive review of combat trauma and its aftereffects. The combat stress literature demonstrates the clear toll of combat exposure on Veterans' mental health. In terms of Vietnam Veterans, 15% of males and 9% of females serving in the Vietnam theater met full diagnostic criteria for PTSD 15 years after the war had ended, documenting the long-term psychological effects of combat exposure (Kulka et al., 1990). These rates were five to ten times higher than Vietnam Veteran era and civilian counterparts. Similarly, prevalence estimates of PTSD among Veterans deployed in service of Gulf war I were significantly higher than the prevalence of PTSD in the non-Gulf war I comparable Veterans, 10.1% compared with 4.2%, respectively (Kang, Natelson, Mahan, Lee, & Murphy, 2003).

There has been unprecedented attention in recent years on the combat experiences of Veterans serving in Iraq and Afghanistan. OEF/OIF Veterans report significant exposure to combat trauma, with 46% of OEF soldiers and between 67% and 70% of OIF service members reporting at least one combat experience (Hoge et al., 2006; Milliken et al., 2007). Accordingly, it is not surprising that a growing number of studies have revealed that many service members and Veterans struggle with mental health problems following deployment, particularly PTSD, depression, anxiety, and substance abuse (Hoge et al., 2006; Milliken et al., 2007; Smith et al., 2008a; Tanielian & Jaycox, 2008; Wells et al., 2010). Negative health consequences are not limited to mental health. Among those deployed in support of OEF/OIF, PTSD is not only common but is associated with poorer physical health, even after controlling for physical injuries sustained during combat (Hoge, Terhakopian, Castro, Messer, & Engel, 2007). Moreover, such combat-related mental health problems contribute strongly to distress in interpersonal relationships and reductions in quality of life (Milliken et al., 2007; Schnurr et al., 2009).

## SEXUAL TRAUMA DURING MILITARY SERVICE AND ITS SEQUELAE

Sexual trauma during military service has received increasing attention over the past two decades, and data from several large-scale studies document that sexual trauma is a far too common experience during men's and women's military service (e.g., Kimerling, Gima, Smith, Street, & Frayne, 2007; Lipari, Cook, Rock, & Matos, 2008; Street, Stafford, Mahan & Hendricks, 2008). At one end of the sexual trauma stressor continuum are experiences of sexual harassment. Sexual harassment refers to unwanted experiences of a sexual nature within the workplace (EEOC, 1999). These are experiences that contribute to an intimidating, hostile, or offensive work environment (e.g., unwanted sexual advances; repeated, offensive comments about a person's body or sexual activities; the display of pornographic or other sexually demeaning material). A severe form of sexual harassment involves coerced sexual activity, either required as a condition of employment or used as the basis of employment-related decisions. This coercion can take many forms, including threats of punishment (e.g., lowered performance evaluations) or promises of rewards (e.g., better/safer job assignments). At the most severe end of the sexual trauma stressor continuum is sexual assault, or experiences of unwanted physical sexual contact ranging from unwanted touching to attempted or completed rape. Experiences of sexual assault involve coercion, either through the abuse of authority (as with the sexual harassment examples provided above) or by using physical force or situations in which the victim is incapable (e.g., by intoxication or illness) of consenting to sexual activity.

Although the prevalence of these experiences differs across studies due to variations in samples and measurement, available data suggest that sexual trauma experiences occur at alarming frequency among active duty military forces. In the 2006 Department of Defense (DoD) Workplace and Gender Relations Survey (Lipari et al., 2008), the annual prevalence of experiencing offensive sexual behaviors (e.g., being told repeated offensive sexual stories or jokes) was 52% among military women and 29% among military men. In terms of more severe sexual trauma experiences, the prevalence of sexually coercive experiences (e.g., feeling threatened with punishment or retaliation for not being sexually cooperative, believing better assignments or treatment were implied in exchange for sexual cooperation) were 9% and 3%, respectively, for military women and men, while the annual prevalence rate of sexual assault was estimated to be 6.8% for women and 1.8% for men.

Rates of sexual harassment and assault are similarly high in the Reserve components of the Armed Forces. In a representative sample of former Reservists, Street and her colleagues (2008) found that 60% of women and 27% of men had experienced sexual harassment, and 13.1% of women and 1.6% of men had experienced sexual assault during their military service.

Consistent with epidemiological studies of military men and women, high rates of sexual trauma are also found among VA health-care users. In a national sample of female Veterans who use VA outpatient care, 55% reported experiencing sexual harassment and 23% reported experiencing sexual assault during military service (Skinner et al., 2000). All VA patients are briefly screened for a history of sexually traumatic experiences during their military service by a health-care provider. Data from all VA patients indicate that 21.5% of women and 1% of men have disclosed experiences of sexual trauma during military service to a VA health-care provider (Kimerling et al., 2007).

Less is known about the prevalence of sexual trauma among troops deployed to a war zone. Two examinations of sexual trauma during military service have been conducted among men and women deployed during Gulf war I. In one study of deployed women, 66% reported verbal sexual harassment, 33% reported physical sexual harassment, and 7% reported sexual assault during deployment (Wolfe et al., 1998). Research from another sample of Gulf war I deployed personnel indicated that 24% of women and 0.6% of men reported sexual harassment, and 3% of women and 0.2% of men reported sexual assault during deployment (Kang, Dalager, Mahan, & Ishii, 2005). Even though these rates appear comparable with or lower than rates of sexual trauma reported among nondeployed troops, these rates are still striking given the focus only on the deployment time period and the relatively short duration of Gulf war I.

Investigations are currently underway to examine rates of sexual trauma among OEF/OIF Veterans, though only a small amount of empirical data exist on the topic. In the first national study of military sexual trauma screening among OEF/OIF VA health-care users (Kimerling et al., 2010), 15.1% of women and 0.7% of men reported having experienced sexual trauma during their military service to a VA health-care provider, slightly lower than the rates reported among all VA health-care users (Kimerling et al., 2007).

However, a slightly different picture emerges from the 2006 DoD Workplace and Gender Relations Survey, which included a small subsample of individuals who had been recently deployed. Results indicated that 9% of women and 2% of men who had been deployed in the prior year reported that they had been sexually assaulted (Lipari et al., 2008). These rates were in contrast to rates of 6% of women and 2% of men who were not deployed, suggesting that women may be more likely to experience sexual assault while deployed, whereas the rates appear equivalent for men regardless of deployment status.

As can be seen from these data, as in the civilian literature, the prevalence of sexual trauma during military service is consistently higher among women. However, unlike the civilian world, within the military there is a disproportionate ratio of men to women. Accordingly, while a larger proportion of women experience sexual trauma during their military service, the ratio of men to women results in large absolute numbers of both women and men who have experienced sexual trauma (Street et al., 2008). Sexual trauma in the military cannot be considered only a women's issue.

The rates of sexual trauma experienced during military service are of particular concern given the associations between these experiences and negative mental and physical health outcomes. Women and men who report a history of sexual trauma during military service are significantly more likely than those who did not to be diagnosed with mental health conditions (Kimerling et al., 2008, 2010). PTSD is the most prevalent mental health condition observed among Veterans who have experienced sexual harassment or assault during military service. Several studies utilizing cross-sectional designs have shown a strong association between sexual trauma during service in the military and PTSD symptoms or diagnosis (Kang et al., 2005; Kimerling et al., 2007; Street, Gradus, Stafford, & Kelly, 2007; Street et al., 2008), and at least one study has documented a prospective relationship between sexual trauma and PTSD symptoms in military service members (Shipherd, Pineles, Gradus, & Resick, 2009). Along with PTSD, depression, other anxiety disorders, and substance use disorders are associated with sexual harassment and assault during service in the military even after adjusting for demographics, health-care use, and military service characteristics (Kimerling et al., 2010). Sexual trauma during military service is also associated with poor self-image, feelings of loneliness and isolation, and suicide (Kimerling et al., 2007; Skinner et al., 2000). Given the substantial mental health consequences of sexual trauma endured during military service, it is not surprising that such experiences are associated with difficulties in occupational and financial readjustment following discharge from the military (Sadler, Booth, Nielson, & Doebbeling, 2000; Skinner et al., 2000).

Problems with physical health are also well documented in survivors of sexual trauma during military service. These sexual trauma survivors report more adverse health behaviors, including smoking and lack of exercise (Frayne, Skinner, Sullivan, & Freund, 2003). Among VA health-care users, sexual trauma during military service is associated with medical conditions like obesity, hypertension, liver disease, pulmonary disease, and respiratory disorders (Frayne et al., 1999; Kimerling et al., 2007; Skinner et al., 2000). Studies have also found associations with reproductive conditions, including pregnancy complications and endometriosis (Frayne et al., 1999), similar to findings in research on sexual assault conducted with civilian samples.

## DUAL COMBAT AND SEXUAL TRAUMA EXPOSURE AND ITS SEQUELAE

There is a paucity of research on the prevalence and sequelae of experiencing both sexual assault and combat trauma while serving in the military. Although there are several studies underway that will document the rates and health consequences of dual combat trauma and sexual trauma among current service members, existing research with earlier cohorts provides some information about the frequency of dual combat and sexual trauma and suggests that the health effects may be compounded when both traumas are experienced.

In a cross-sectional survey of 4,918 men and women seeking VA disability entitlements for PTSD, Murdoch, Polusny, Hodges, and O'Brien (2004) found that a substantial proportion of combat Veterans reported sexual trauma during military service or postservice sexual assault. Among male combat Veterans, 3.7% reported sexual trauma during military service, and 4.1% reported postservice sexual assault. Among female Veterans, 62.9% reported sexual assault during the military, and 47.1% reported postservice sexual assault. These rates of sexual trauma during military service among Veterans are quite high when placed in the context of prevalence rates of sexual assault in community samples and the general population of VA health-care users (Kimerling et al., 2007; Tjaden & Thoennes, 2000). Murdoch and her colleagues (2004) found that the prevalence of sexual assault was approximately five to nine times higher than that reported by males in the general population and three to 10 times higher than that reported by females in the general population. These data suggest that sexual trauma during military service, as well as postservice sexual assault, is a frequent experience among combat Veterans seeking VA disability entitlements for PTSD.

Although combat exposure is strongly associated with PTSD, at least one study suggests that sexual trauma during a war-zone deployment is predictive of PTSD for both men and women above and beyond the effects of combat exposure. Kang and his colleagues (2005) examined the impact of reported sexual trauma during Gulf war I deployment on the risk of PTSD following the war using data collected in a population-based health survey of 30,000 Gulf war I era Veterans. A total of 1,381 Gulf war I Veterans with current PTSD were compared with 10,060 Gulf war I Veteran controls without PTSD for self-reported sexual trauma and combat exposure. The results indicated that sexual trauma experienced during deployment was a significant predictor of PTSD even after controlling for relatively severe levels of combat exposure. This study also found a dose-response relationship between sexual trauma levels (i.e., no sexual trauma, sexual harassment only, sexual assault only, sexual harassment and assault) and the odds of having a PTSD diagnosis in both men and women.

There are data from a cross-sectional study suggesting that combat exposure may increase the odds of experiencing sexual trauma during military service. In a sample of 1,307 male and 197 female Somali peacekeepers, Fontana et al. (2000) found that experiencing sexual harassment mediated the association between women's combat exposure and PTSD symptoms and independently contributed to men's PTSD symptom severity. The authors suggest that this finding may be because occasions of sexual harassment or assault may be associated with the relaxation of military discipline in combat situations. Furthermore, for both men and women, severity of PTSD symptoms was associated with exposure to combat directly and indirectly through fear and sexual harassment. Although additional research employing longitudinal methods is needed to replicate these findings, it is possible that experiencing one form of trauma may increase the risk for the other while in the military through the presence of PTSD symptoms.

Although we are not aware of research examining the specific psychological, neuropsychological, and physical comorbidities associated with dual combat and sexual trauma, a number of studies lead us to speculate that this dual trauma has substantial aftereffects in each domain. For example, combat deployment confers risk for traumatic brain injury, particularly mild traumatic brain injury (mTBI) (Hoge et al., 2008). A recent study found that 88% of combat-related TBIs involved exposure to explosions, such as IEDs, mortar fire, mines, and rocket-propelled grenades (Galarneau, Woodruff, Dye, Mohrele, & Wade, 2008). Raskin (1997) compared the neuropsychological functioning of a community sample of women who had experienced mTBI only, sexual assault only, both sexual assault and mTBI, and a normal control group. Findings indicated that compared with the normal control subjects, women with mTBI only demonstrated deficits in working memory, and those with sexual assault only demonstrated deficits in executive functioning. Those with both mTBI and sexual assault demonstrated the greatest number of neuropsychological deficits, including greater deficits in working memory, executive functioning, and learning compared to the three other groups. Interestingly, symptoms of anxiety, depression, and PTSD were found in all three clinical groups, but these symptoms did not correlate with the neuropsychological test performance scores that differentiated the groups. Thus, individuals with mTBI and sexual assault appear to demonstrate both the deficits associated with the mTBI group and those associated with the sexual assault group, as well as unique deficits in learning and memory functioning. Although this research suggests that combat Veterans who experienced mTBI and sexual trauma during military service may experience more neuropsychological symptoms, this notion has yet to be subjected to empirical examination in a sample of service members or Veterans who have experienced dual combat-related mTBI and sexual assault.

## RISK FACTORS ASSOCIATED WITH DUAL COMBAT AND SEXUAL TRAUMA DURING MILITARY SERVICE

Because the study of dual combat and sexual trauma exposure during military service is still in the early stages, there are no well-developed theoretical models that conceptualize risk factors for experiencing these traumatic events or risk factors for developing PTSD and other mental health problems subsequent to dual combat and sexual trauma exposure. However, in the absence of established theoretical models identifying those at risk for dual combat and sexual trauma exposure and associated health consequences, researchers and clinicians can draw on several lines of research to shed light on premilitary and service-related vulnerability factors. This review highlights risk factors associated with sexual trauma in the military to a greater extent than those associated with combat exposure alone given that conceptual issues related to repeated combat exposure and its health effects are discussed in Chapter 9.

### Premilitary Vulnerability Factors

#### Prior Traumatic Experiences as Risk Factors

A significant proportion of individuals who enlist for military service report extensive and complex childhood trauma histories. A survey of male VA patients who had served in the military since September 11, 2001, revealed that 45% reported childhood physical abuse and 19% reported childhood sexual abuse (Dedert et al., 2009). A recent review of the prevalence of trauma exposures among women found approximately 35% experience childhood physical abuse, and between 27% and 49% experience childhood sexual abuse (Zinzow, Grubaugh, Monnier, Suffoletta-Maierle, & Frueh, 2007). A substantial proportion of service members have also experienced neglect and witnessed parental domestic violence during critical periods of socioemotional development (Keane, Marshall, & Taft, 2006; Rosen & Martin, 1996). All of these forms of child maltreatment serve as robust risk factors for sexual assault more generally in adulthood (Classen, Palesh, Aggarwall, 2005), and in fact, these experiences appear to be particularly common among women who experience sexual trauma during their military service (Rosen & Martin, 1996; Sadler, Booth, Cook, & Doebbeling, 2003). Childhood exposure to multiple or prolonged traumatic events, including abusive and chaotic home environments, plays a significant role in problems in emotional development (Fairbank, Putnam, & Harris, 2007). These traumatic experiences, combined with the invalidating home environments in which they occur, are postulated to set off a chain of events leading to subsequent or repeated trauma exposure in later life for some.

There are several other risk factors associated with childhood maltreatment experiences that may increase the likelihood of experiencing these traumatic events and developing mental health problems subsequent to dual combat and sexual trauma during military service. Service members who grow up in abusive and neglectful home environments are more likely to have lower income levels (Sameroff, 1998), lower educational achievement, and younger age at the time of enlistment (Green, Grace, Lindy, Glesser, & Leonard, 1990; True, Goldberg, & Eisen, 1988), which, in turn, increase risk for combat and sexual trauma exposures (Green et al., 1990; Sadler, Booth, Cook, Torner, & Doebbeling, 2001; Sadler et al., 2000). Additionally, these demographic variables are known risk factors for the development of PTSD following exposure to traumatic events (Brewin, Andrews, & Valentine, 2000).

Studies demonstrate that childhood traumatic experiences are generally associated with PTSD in Veteran samples (for example, King, King, Foy, & Gudanowski, 1996; Schnurr, Lunney, & Sengupta, 2004). However, at least one study of male and female Gulf war I Veterans found sex differences in the association between prior trauma and combat-related PTSD. Engel and colleagues (1993) found that precombat childhood or adult abuse was associated with more combat-related PTSD symptoms in women. This relationship was not found for men; men with and without prior abuse had equivalent combat-related PTSD symptom severity. These sex differences were maintained even after controlling for combat exposure and precombat psychiatric history.

Specific to the current wars in Iraq and Afghanistan, Smith and his colleagues (2008b) conducted an investigation of military service members in the Millennium Cohort Study to examine the relation between prior assault (in childhood, adulthood, or both) and new onset of PTSD symptoms following a war-zone deployment in male and female service members. They found a substantial proportion of combat-exposed women (30%) and men (10%) reported interpersonal assaults prior to deployment in service of OEF/OIF. Men and women who reported a prior assault had more than twice the odds of new-onset PTSD symptoms after combat deployment. These findings indicate that prior assault increases the risk of new onset PTSD and persistence of PTSD among combat-exposed service members.

## Other Clinical Characteristics as Risk Factors

Several other premilitary characteristics are associated with increased likelihood of PTSD. In particular, studies have shown that preexisting psychiatric disorders, including depression, anxiety, early conduct problems, and antisocial personality disorder, may confer vulnerability for PTSD in Veterans (Keane et al., 2006; King et al., 1996; Schnurr, Friedman, & Rosenburg, 1993). Personality characteristics, such as proclivity toward negative emotionality, have been shown to influence individual cognitions, self-concept, and worldviews, all of which may relate directly or indirectly to the development of PTSD (Miller, 2004).

## Trauma-Related Factors

### Military Contextual Factors

There are several aspects of the military environment that may contribute to risk for experiencing sexual trauma and the subsequent development of PTSD. Literature on sexual violence in the workplace has documented that work environments that are male-dominated and composed of large power differentials between organizational levels, characteristics that are representative of the military environment, are associated with increased rates of on-the-job sexual harassment and assault (DeFleur, 1985; Llies, Hauserman, Schwochau, & Stibal, 2003). Organizational-level power differentials may be even more pronounced for women in the military relative to men given women's minority status. In addition, tolerance of sexual harassment by military leaders is associated with elevated risk for sexual trauma. Sadler and her colleagues (2003) found that risk for rape in the military environment increased substantially when ranking officers allowed or initiated sexually demeaning gestures or comments toward female soldiers, even after controlling for prior victimization and demographic variables.

### The War-Zone Deployment Environment

Service members are exposed to a number of diffuse stressors in the context of war-zone deployments that may contribute to the development of PTSD subsequent to dual combat and sexual trauma during military service exposure. Studies show that service members report greater work-related stress than civilians, and in turn, such stress is associated with increased vulnerability to psychological problems (Pflanz & Sonnek, 2002). Since the beginning of the wars in Iraq and Afghanistan, the operation tempo has resulted in frequent deployments that are lengthy in duration and often extended; service members have little time for readjustment between their deployments. Although combat exposures have received the most attention in the literature, research shows that the stressful living and working conditions surrounding traumatic stress exposure likely exacerbate distress for dual trauma survivors (King, King, Gudanowski, & Vrevren, 1995). For example, lack of privacy, poor living conditions, long hours, heavy workloads, limited sleep, and unpredictable schedules are common experiences among those deployed. As a result of such stressful environmental situations, individuals may not have the emotional and physical resources needed to cope with and process their combat and sexual traumas, thereby contributing to an increased risk for PTSD.

Another factor that may exacerbate distress among dual combat and sexual trauma survivors is that sexual trauma experienced during a combat deployment may be more distressing than similar experiences occurring in peacetime settings (Street, Vogt, & Dutra, 2009). Sexual harassment and assault experiences in the military, which are often perpetrated by fellow service members, may be experienced as extreme betrayals of trust. This dynamic is likely to be exacerbated in the context of a combat deployment in which service members are responsible for each others' well-being. Traumas that are perpetrated by those expected to protect or to have another's best interest in mind can be particularly damaging to one's psychological well-being (Freyd, 1996). Veterans may struggle profoundly with feelings of self-blame, finding ways to blame themselves for what happened (i.e., "I must have done something to provoke it" or "Maybe I am gay and that is why he assaulted me") rather than conceiving of betrayal at the hands of a fellow service member. Of all of the threats that military personnel have been trained to deal with during deployment, they do not expect to experience harm from a fellow service member. Being a victim can also conflict with the identity that is ingrained into service members during their military training—being strong, tough, and physically powerful. These ideals can become deeply embedded in the self-identity of military personnel. Experiences of sexual trauma may therefore shatter their assumptions about themselves, as well as their beliefs about others.

Sexual trauma during military service typically occurs where the service member works and lives. Victims of sexual trauma may have to continue to interact with their perpetrators, perhaps even working side-by-side, contributing to a dynamic in which it feels as if there is no escape from an unsafe situation. This dynamic may be exacerbated in the context of combat operations because of the additive effect of multiple types of trauma exposure and stressors. Such fear and anxiety may lead individuals to be in a state of constant alert, interfering with sleep, appetite, and concentration, which can add to standard deployment stressors.

Victims of sexual harassment and assault may also avoid reporting or disclosing the events, either out of fear of retaliation from the perpetrator or others or because of concerns that their disclosure may interfere with unit cohesion and therefore the success of the unit's mission. As a result, victims of sexual trauma may lack social support from their leadership or peers. This lack of social support may be compounded by the victim's loss of predeployment support systems. During deployment, service members are in reduced contact with their families and friends and so may be less able to turn to others outside of their units for support in coping with stressful or traumatic experiences. Accordingly, victims of dual combat and sexual trauma may lack both military and nonmilitary sources of social support, a consistent predictor of poorer recovery following trauma exposure (Brewin et al., 2000).

## Injury and Perceived Threat

Another characteristic of the stressor that confers greater likelihood of posttraumatic stress problems is injury as a result of traumatization. Individuals who experience injury as a consequence of combat exposure or sexual assault are at higher risk for PTSD than those who are not injured (Brewin et al., 2000). In addition to injury and frequency of combat and sexual trauma exposure, Kelly and Vogt (2009) astutely point out the important role of perceived threat during traumatic events. Perceived threat refers to the fear of harm that a service member may experience in the war zone or during a sexual assault experience, including threat or fear of attack, entrapment, injury, and death (King, King, Vogt, Knight, & Samper, 2006; Vogt & Tanner, 2007). Perceived threat also encompasses fear of harm for other unit members, including friends, leaders, and other military personnel (King et al., 2006). Perceived threat is associated with an array of mental and physical health problems following deployment and has been shown to mediate the effect of combat on PTSD in Veterans (King et al., 2006; Vogt & Tanner, 2007).

## CLINICAL DESCRIPTION OF THE SEQUELAE ASSOCIATED WITH DUAL COMBAT AND SEXUAL TRAUMA

The mental health symptoms commonly observed in trauma-exposed combat Veterans are discussed in detail in Chapter 9, and the common presentation observed in sexually traumatized individuals is presented in greater detail in Chapter 12. Therefore, the focus here is more on the clinical presentations of individuals who have experienced sexual harassment or sexual assault during military service. When conceptualizing the clinical presentations of dual combat and sexual trauma survivors, it is important to remember that combat and sexual trauma are independently the two types of traumatic stressors with the highest conditional risk for PTSD (Kessler, Sonnega, Bromet, Hughes, & Nelson, 1995), with evidence suggesting that sexual trauma is more strongly associated with PTSD than combat. Although either exposure alone may lead to PTSD and other traumatic stress-related problems, dual exposure to these traumas appears to lead to more severe symptoms of PTSD, as well as other mental health symptoms (Bolton, Litz, Britt, Adler, & Roemer, 2001; Street et al., 2009).

Although PTSD is the mental health condition most closely associated with experiences of sexual harassment and assault during military service, evidence suggests that sexual trauma survivors experience heterogeneous mental health problems (Bell & Reardon, 2011; Street, Kimerling, Bell, & Pavao, 2011). A recent study of all Veterans using VA health care found that Veterans who reported sexual trauma during military service as part of the VA's universal screening program were at a threefold increased risk for receiving a mental health diagnosis as compared with those who did not report such experiences (Kimerling et al., 2007). Depression, anxiety disorders, substance use disorders, dissociative disorders, eating disorders, bipolar disorder, suicidal ideation and behavior, personality disorder characteristics, and somatization are common mental health correlates of sexual trauma during military service (Frayne et al., 1999; Kimerling et al., 2007; Street et al., 2007, 2008).

Similar to survivors of sexual assault in other contexts, survivors of sexual trauma during military service may experience interpersonal difficulties and have difficulties trusting themselves or others, exhibit emotion regulation deficits, display problems with asserting and maintaining appropriate interpersonal boundaries, and report sexual dysfunction (Polusny, Dickinson, Murdoch, & Thuras, 2008; Street, Gradus, Stafford, & Kelly, 2007; Vogt, Pless, King, & King, 2005; Wolfe et al., 1998). In addition, although many combat trauma survivors without a history of sexual trauma struggle with issues related to power and control, in our clinical experience, survivors of dual combat and sexual trauma seem to be more prone to have extreme difficulties with hierarchies, systems, and institutions, as well as interpersonal interactions in which one person has power over another, such as employee–employer or client–therapist relationships. Clinicians may find it takes longer to establish a working alliance with dual combat and sexual trauma survivors. After being betrayed by a trusted ally, it may be exceedingly difficult for survivors to trust others, even after an individual has repeatedly shown himself or herself to be relatively trustworthy (Street et al., 2011). Similarly, concerns related to safety are often exacerbated among clients with dual combat and sexual trauma relative to other trauma survivors. It is common for these clients to describe nightmares about both their sexual trauma experiences and combat missions that revolve around themes related to power and control, as well as safety and self-protection.

## ASSESSMENT OF DUAL COMBAT TRAUMA AND SEXUAL TRAUMA DURING MILITARY SERVICE

In light of the data reviewed earlier on prevalence and associated health consequences, it is imperative that Veterans be screened for the range and extent of military-related exposures, including combat trauma and sexual trauma. Given that a large absolute number of male Veterans have experienced sexual trauma during their military service and that female Veterans are experiencing combat trauma at higher rates than ever before, it is important to assess for a wide range of military-related exposures without preconceived notions. However, assessment of both combat and sexual trauma experiences requires sensitivity to different gender-based experiences in trauma exposure and trauma-related symptom presentations. Because a detailed discussion of assessment issues related to combat exposure and its mental health sequelae is provided in Chapter 9 of this volume, we will not present recommendations for assessing combat trauma here.

## Assessment of Sexual Trauma During Military Service

When initiating a discussion about experiences of sexual trauma during military service, it is often helpful to introduce the topic with a statement that normalizes the ensuing questions. For example, clinicians may introduce the line of inquiry by stating: "I ask all of the Veterans I see about certain types of negative experiences they may have experienced while serving in the military. Such experiences are common and can be hard to talk about, so I find it best to just ask directly," or "Many of the Veterans I work with have had upsetting experiences while serving in the military that still bother them today. I'd like to ask you about whether or not you have had some of these experiences."

Several psychometrically validated self-report measures can be used to assess sexual trauma experiences, including those that occur during military service (see Chapter 12 for a more thorough review). The VA health-care system uses the following questions to facilitate universal assessment of sexual trauma experiences during military service. "While you were in the military: Did you receive uninvited and unwanted sexual attention, such as touching or cornering, pressure for sexual favors, or verbal remarks?" (sexual harassment) "Did someone ever use force or the threat of force to have sexual contact with you?" (sexual assault).

Alternatively, clinicians can weave questions about sexual trauma experienced during military service into their standard assessments related to sexual and physical victimization experiences and relationship history. Using behaviorally anchored and descriptive questions, the clinician can inquire: "During your deployment did you experience any unwanted sexual attention or experiences?" "During your deployment did anyone touch you in a sexual way or have you touch them in a sexual way that made you uncomfortable?" "Did you have any other sexual experience that made you feel uncomfortable that I haven't asked about?" Querying about objective behaviors is preferable to questions that contain jargon or emotionally laden terms such as *rape, sexual assault,* or *sexual harassment,* because some Veterans may not have yet labeled their experiences with these terms. It is important to identify sexual trauma survivors even if they have not labeled their experiences as assault or harassment, as they are still likely to experience significant distress related to these traumatic experiences (Harned, 2004).

Similar to the assessment process with other types of sexually traumatized individuals, the manner in which clinicians respond to both positive and negative responses is important, particularly in regard to rapport building and the validity of information collected. For positive endorsements, the therapist should provide support and validation for the disclosure (e.g., "I'm sorry that happened to you. No one deserves to be hurt like that. I'm glad you were willing to share this information with me. Experiences like the one(s) you described can be even more difficult during a deployment."). Done well, disclosing experiences of sexual trauma during military service can be a therapeutic and healing experience for the Veteran. It is also important to remember that some survivors may initially respond "No" when asked about their sexual trauma experiences, either due to stigma, shame, or a perceived need for secrecy. Even if a provider suspects the Veteran has a history of sexual trauma during his or her military service, it is important to respect his or her decision not to disclose. Responding sensitively while providing education about sexual trauma conveys that the provider cares about the topic and takes the issue seriously. This approach leaves the door open for later disclosure (Street et al., 2011).

Following disclosure of sexual trauma, clinicians should engage in additional information gathering about the experience(s) while remaining sensitive to what the Veteran is ready to disclose during the assessment phase. It is important to allow the Veteran to control the pacing of disclosure and the level of detail he or she is willing to provide. The clinician should aim to obtain an understanding of the Veteran's response at the time of the sexual trauma, reactions in the immediate aftermath, and current reactions. In addition, it is important to gather information about the context within which the experiences occurred (e.g., when during the deployment the sexual trauma occurred, the overlap or intersection between the sexual trauma and combat trauma and other deployment-related stressors), to assess for the general attitude toward sexual assault and harassment in the Veteran's unit, and to assess for others' responses to the trauma at the time. Such details can inform clinician interventions, targeting any current struggles with self-blame, trust, or intimacy (Street et al., 2011). It is also important to ask about any prior or subsequent traumatic experiences in order to elucidate how the sexual trauma and combat experiences fit into the larger context of the Veteran's life, including the reinforcement of preexisting core beliefs about themselves, others, and the world. Using clarifying questions and reflective listening, the clinician can help the Veteran begin to make sense of the experiences and to appreciate how the effects of sexual trauma experienced during military service may interact with the effects of the combat trauma.

## PREVENTION AND TREATMENT OF DUAL COMBAT AND SEXUAL TRAUMA

### Prevention

#### Primary Prevention

Theoretically, the military could extrapolate from the research on risk factors for PTSD subsequent to combat trauma and sexual assault during military service to screen out individuals who appear to be vulnerable to trauma exposure and developing PTSD as a primary prevention strategy. For example, some might argue for excluding service members from combat deployments who have a prior trauma history. However, a major problem with this argument is that the research to date does not predictably translate into the identification of specific individuals who will develop PTSD after trauma exposure. Moreover, posttrauma variables, which are not measurable prior to trauma exposure, are relatively more important in predicting who will later have PTSD (Brewin et al., 2000). Accordingly, these prevention methods are not feasible and, further, would unfairly discriminate against a large number of potential service members.

As opposed to screening out those individuals who may be vulnerable to trauma exposure and posttraumatic stress problems, it seems more ethical and effective to modify military culture to decrease factors that may promote sexual assault perpetration. For instance, in light of research documenting that leadership tolerance for inappropriate sexual behavior is a strong predictor of sexual assault (Sadler et al., 2003), military leadership should adopt a no-tolerance attitude toward sexual harassment and assault of any sort. Similarly, investigations of sexual trauma allegations and strong punishments need to be actively pursued. Additionally, research from the civilian literature demonstrates that sexual assault risk reduction programs can promote changes in attitudinal variables associated with sexual assault (i.e., rape myth acceptance; Breitenbecher, 2000). Because it is unclear whether changes in attitudes translate into reductions in sexual victimization perpetration, it is important to conduct such research in high-risk populations such as military samples.

In response to the pressing need to eliminate sexual assault experienced by service members, the DoD has taken important steps to tackle this issue. Specifically, the DoD's Sexual Assault Prevention and Response Office has developed extensive primary prevention strategies to address sexual harassment and assault tailored to the military context and values, including training for basic trainees and new commanders, social marketing campaigns to increase awareness of sexual trauma, and partnering with key federal agencies and civilian experts (Department of Defense, 2009).

### Secondary Prevention

Secondary preventive measures, or efforts to reduce the development of PTSD and related disorders following trauma exposure, have included psychoeducation, stress inoculation, and psychological debriefing approaches among service members (Friedman, Schnurr, & McDonagh-Coyle, 1994). Unfortunately, these strategies have had minimal success (Feldner, Monson, & Friedman, 2007). Psychological first aid (e.g., Litz & Gray, 2004; Ruzek, 2006) represents a new cognitive-behavioral approach to secondary prevention that holds promise for military and other trauma-exposed populations. Psychological first aid does not foster disclosure of traumatic events, but instead emphasizes survivor education about stress reactions, normalization, promotion of health-seeking behaviors, encouragement of enjoyable activities and positive coping strategies, and garnering social support in the acute aftermath of combat and other forms of trauma.

It is also important to develop and evaluate mechanisms to foster resilience within service members' military and home environments to promote recovery after exposure. Although this chapter focused on risk factors associated with poor health subsequent to combat and sexual trauma, it is also important to better understand the question: Why are some individuals *resilient* following exposure to combat and sexual assault, while others develop PTSD and other disorders in the aftermath of similar events? Such research is essential to guide program development to foster resilience among all Veterans, particularly those at risk for PTSD, and to identify the unique resiliency factors that may be associated with recovery from dual combat and sexual trauma exposure in the military. For instance, programs need to be developed and evaluated to enhance social support and modify social reactions to military traumas. Given that poor social support is a robust risk factor for PTSD subsequent to both combat and sexual trauma (e.g., Keane, Scott, Chavoya, Lamparski, & Fairbank, 1985; Ullman, 1999), and social support facilitates recovery following trauma (Griffith & Vaitkus, 1999), this is an important target for secondary prevention. Interventions aimed at enhancing social support among service members, as well as increasing access to peer support and mental health professionals within the military environment, may help reduce the long-term negative effects of dual combat and sexual trauma during the military. Such interventions could break down barriers to disclosure and recovery by reducing stigma, social isolation, and other obstacles to treatment and support seeking.

## General Principles for Treatment

Although psychotropic medication for symptom management may be indicated for some Veterans with dual combat and sexual trauma (Institute of Medicine, 2008), the focus of this section is on general principles for psychotherapy. The space limitations of this chapter preclude an in-depth discussion of the specifics of clinical care for this population; however, we highlight several therapy strategies and principles that are applicable to the mental health treatment of survivors of dual combat and sexual trauma during the military.

### Empirically Supported Treatments for Posttraumatic Stress Disorder (PTSD)

Although there has not yet been a treatment outcome study focusing on decreasing psychological distress resulting specifically from dual combat and sexual trauma during the military, cognitive-behavioral therapies have been developed for and validated on survivors of both combat and sexual traumas (for a review, see Iverson, Lester, & Resick, 2011). Because PTSD is the most common and severe presentation observed among dual combat and sexual assault survivors, first-line treatments should be trauma focused and include the emotional processing of both types of traumatic events. For some clients, emotional processing of the events alone will provide significant symptom relief. However, many survivors of dual combat and sexual trauma survivors require the acquisition of cognitive and emotional skills to further reduce symptoms and more effectively attain one's life goals.

Prolonged Exposure (PE) (Foa, Hembree & Rothbaum, 2007) and Cognitive Processing Therapy (CPT) (Resick, Monson, & Chard, 2008) are two empirically supported interventions that were originally developed to treat PTSD and its comorbid symptoms among civilian sexual assault survivors. CPT has subsequently been validated with male and female survivors of combat and sexual trauma during the military (Monson et al., 2006), and PE has been applied to women Veterans with a range of trauma experiences (Schnurr et al., 2007). CPT is a primarily cognitive therapy for PTSD that consists of cognitive restructuring strategies to challenge maladaptive beliefs related to the traumatic experiences and their consequences. The inclusion of cognitive therapy techniques allows the client to address during therapy emotional reactions beyond fear that may be interfering with recovery from PTSD, including humiliation, shame, and anger (Resick et al., 2008). In PE, the therapist assists the client in systematically and repeatedly revisiting the traumatic memory through imaginal exposures to allow emotional processing of the trauma memory; and the repeated confrontation of situations and other stimuli reminiscent of the trauma while in an objectively safe situation until the associated fear and anxiety decrease through *in vivo* exposure strategies.

Clinicians working with dual combat and sexual trauma survivors should be mindful of the Veteran's potential for retraumatization. Rates of physical and sexual revictimization are high among survivors of sexual trauma during military service, even for personnel not in contact with their sexual assault perpetrator (Sadler et al., 2001). An alarming 71% of women report experiencing sexual or physical assault since separating from the military (Sadler et al., 2000). Moreover, childhood trauma has been shown to be directly associated with trauma exposure among male and female Veterans following military service (King, King, Foy, Keane, & Fairbank, 1999).

Mental health symptoms, and PTSD in particular, may contribute to individuals' risk for revictimization (Classen et al., 2005; Messman-Moore & Long, 2003). Many of the symptoms of distress (i.e., numbing and depression) and behaviors (i.e., experiential avoidance) that survivors might engage in to avoid uncomfortable memories and feelings associated with their traumas, unfortunately, may leave them more vulnerable to subsequent trauma. For example, excessive substance use, inattention to internal sensations and emotions, and dissociation are believed to increase risk for retraumatization (Cloitre & Rosenburg, 2006; Follette, Iverson, & Ford,

2009). Providers working with dual combat and sexual trauma survivors may be able to help reduce clients' risk for retraumatization by treating their mental health symptoms. Preliminary evidence suggests that reducing PTSD and depression symptoms in interpersonal trauma survivors also reduces their likelihood of future victimization (Iverson et al., 2011). Additional research is needed to determine whether such findings generalize to dual combat and sexual trauma survivors.

## Other Intervention Strategies

In some cases, clients with dual combat and sexual trauma are unwilling or unable to receive these trauma-focused PTSD treatments. For example, clients may have difficulty engaging in CPT or PE without escaping, either emotionally or by dropping out of therapy. They are often terrified that they will never be able to overcome the distress they feel when they remember the combat and sexual trauma experiences. Therefore, other symptom-focused interventions, including stress and anger management skills, emotion regulation skills, and assertiveness skills, can also play an important role in the treatment of dual combat and sexual trauma survivors. The following skills training techniques can be useful precursors for clients whose use of adaptive coping strategies should be strengthened before beginning a course of trauma-focused therapy or in response to residual symptoms following treatment.

Seeking Safety (Najavits, 2002) and Dialectical Behavior Therapy (DBT) (Linehan, 1993) are two examples of skills-based interventions that may be effective for Veterans who have experienced dual combat and sexual trauma. Seeking Safety, a cognitive-behavioral treatment for comorbid PTSD and substance use disorders, has demonstrated effectiveness with civilian survivors of sexual assault (Najavits, Weiss, Shaw, & Muenz, 1998) and feasibility with women Veterans (Desai, Harpaz-Rotem, Najavits, & Rosenheck, 2008). DBT has been successfully adapted for Veterans with chronic trauma-related disorders, including PTSD subsequent to combat or sexual trauma (Spoont, Sayer, Thuras, Erbes, & Winston, 2003). Both Seeking Safety and DBT warrant additional research with dual combat and sexual trauma populations. There is also empirical support for Cognitive Behavioral Conjoint Therapy for PTSD, a disorder-specific conjoint intervention with the simultaneous goals of enhancing relationship satisfaction and improving PTSD symptoms in cases of dual combat and sexual trauma survivors and their partners (Monson & Fredman, under contract).

## Common Themes and Issues

Regardless of the specific treatment strategies adopted, several themes are often prominent in the treatment of dual combat and sexual trauma survivors. Many Veterans have not talked to anyone else about their experiences or may have received negative reactions from others when discussing their traumas. Psychoeducation about the impact of combat and sexual trauma and efforts to normalize emotions and other reactions can be extremely powerful interventions in their own right. Particularly in the case of sexual trauma, the betrayal of assault from a fellow service member can lead survivors to struggle with trust, safety, intimacy, and other core features of interpersonal relations. As a result, many dual survivors experience difficulties "letting their guard down" emotionally and physically, leading to difficulties being close with anyone, resulting in loneliness, hopelessness, and depression. For instance, it is common for clients to describe satisfying relationships with intimate partners prior to deployments in which dual combat and sexual trauma occurred, but upon returning home they struggle with feeling anxious, angry, or numb around their partners. In an attempt to minimize these aversive states, they may emotionally or physically disengage from the relationship. Yet, most clients state that they value intimate relationships. Working with clients to identify and modify these behavior patterns through therapeutic strategies such as values clarification (e.g., Follette et al., 2009), experiential exercises to reduce numbness, and scheduling pleasant events with their partner can help restore intimacy.

As noted earlier, given the power differentials inherent in military life in general, and particularly those inherent in sexual trauma experiences during military service, themes related to power and control in relationships are common. Many combat and sexual trauma survivors have strong reactions to situations where one individual has power over another, such as in employee–employer or client–therapist relationships (Street et al., 2011). Dual trauma clients are more likely to approach treatment and the therapist from a position of intense mistrust born of their dual combat and sexual trauma experiences and may be quite difficult to engage in a therapeutic relationship. Providing validation and normalization of the client's difficulties with power and control can help to reduce the client's mistrust and ambivalence about the therapeutic relationship and therapy. Similarly, dual combat and sexual trauma survivors may question their general ability to accurately judge others' intentions or trustworthiness or their own ability to make effective decisions given the occurrence of the combat and sexual traumas. Thus, the context of therapy provides an opportunity for the client to build a trusting therapeutic relationship within which the client can become increasingly able to work through his or her issues related to power, control, and trust.

Self-blame and guilt are two additional characteristics associated with dual combat and sexual trauma. Clients may blame themselves for a fellow service member's death or injury during a combat situation. They may believe they should have responded differently to prevent it or undermine their decision making during the event (i.e., "If I hadn't agreed to switch Humvees with him then he'd still be alive") and attempt to mentally "undo" the event from ever occurring ("If only I hadn't gone for a walk that night, I wouldn't have been raped"). Socratic questioning can be useful to help clients identify these patterns of thinking, explore other potential interpretations, and make room for different emotional experiences. In addition to promoting more balanced thinking, this process promotes acceptance of the primary emotions (i.e., grief, disappointment, sadness, and so forth) elicited by the combat and sexual trauma memories.

In addition to addressing prominent interpersonal and intrapersonal themes, when doing trauma-focused psychotherapy, it is often necessary to focus on both the combat and sexual assault scenes in order to have adequate processing of the traumas, because there may be less generalization across the different types of trauma than there might be when focusing on combat or sexual trauma alone. Although all traumas often lead to disruptions in the themes mentioned above, there may be more and different current situations avoided and in need of *in vivo* exposures in the case of PE. Likewise, there may need to be imaginal exposures specific to the combat and sexual trauma memories. Cognitive interventions pinpointed at particular parts of each type of traumatic memory will likely be necessary.

Although rewarding, providing psychotherapy to survivors of dual combat and sexual trauma can be challenging, not only in terms of the skill and sensitivity it requires, but also in terms of the emotional impact it can have on the therapist. Providers engaging in therapy with this population should engage in consistent self-care, be mindful of the limits of their competency, and be willing to refer and seek consultation as needed.

## SPECIAL ISSUES

### Sexual War Crimes

Although sexual harassment and assault are commonly perpetrated by fellow service members, it is also important to recognize that sexual harassment and assault can also be perpetrated by enemy combatants as a weapon of war (i.e., acts of sexual torture, rape of prisoners of war). There is a lack of research on the issue of sexual war crimes experienced by OEF/OIF service members and Veterans; however, research from survivors of other wars documents the negative effects of sexual torture as a war strategy (Basoglu, 2009).

### VA Services for Survivors of Sexual Trauma During Military Service

Clinicians treating Veterans should be aware that since 1992, the Veterans Health Administration has been developing programs to monitor military sexual trauma screening and treatment, provide staff with training on sexual trauma-related issues, and engage in outreach to Veterans. All Veterans seen in VA are asked whether they experienced sexual trauma during their military service, and all treatment for physical and mental health conditions related to these experiences is free for both men and women. These services are unique within VA, because free care for sexual trauma-related conditions does not require a VA disability rating or proof that the sexual trauma occurred. Every VA facility has a designated "Military Sexual Trauma Coordinator" who serves as a contact person for sexual trauma-related issues and can help Veterans find and access VA services and programs. Each VA facility has providers knowledgeable about treatment for the aftereffects of sexual trauma during military service, and many have specialized outpatient mental health services focusing on sexual trauma. Nationwide, there are programs that offer specialized sexual trauma treatment in residential or inpatient settings for Veterans who need more intense treatment and support. This treatment option may be useful to bring to the attention of clients with dual combat and sexual trauma. However, some Veterans may choose not to seek care from the VA, despite the specialized services available. Therefore, VA treatment can be discussed as a treatment option as opposed to an expectation.

## FUTURE DIRECTIONS

This review of the literature on combat and sexual trauma prevalence and associated health consequences highlights many areas in need of investigation. First, there is a need to document the prevalence of dual combat and sexual assault exposures, as well as quantify their specific and combined health effects. We were unable to identify a single study in our review that set out to specifically examine the occurrence of both combat trauma and sexual trauma among OEF/OIF Veterans. Such research is necessary to clarify the scope of the problem and inform policy in this area. Additionally, systematic research has not yet described the specific combat and sexual trauma experiences of men and women deployed in service of OEF/OIF. In particular, research is needed to replicate existing research that suggests combat exposure may increase the risk of experiencing sexual trauma during the military (Fontana et al., 2000). Such investigations should examine potential gender differences in the prevalence and consequences of both types of trauma exposures. It is likely that the prevalence estimates and health consequences will be affected by the unique experiences of the wars in Iraq and Afghanistan, including extended and multiple deployments, stressful war-zone conditions, and heavy reliance on Reservist service members. Finally, longitudinal research identifying risk and resiliency factors in military settings will guide prevention and early intervention programs for service members (Street et al., 2009).

## CONCLUSION

As the wars in Iraq and Afghanistan continue, it is essential to meet the mental health needs of dual combat and sexual trauma survivors. Historically, many male and female Veterans have endured both forms of trauma yet suffered in silence because there was little acknowledgement of sexual harassment and sexual assault during military service up until the last two decades. While awareness of this specific form of retraumatization is growing, treatments had not yet been fully developed to address symptoms of PTSD and comorbid conditions subsequent to dual exposure to these two traumas. With the newest cohort of Veterans continuing to return from deployments in support of OEF/OIF, clinicians have the opportunity to identify service members and Veterans who are dual combat and sexual trauma survivors and provide them with effective treatment before the mental health consequences of these experiences become chronic and pernicious. As highlighted in this chapter and elsewhere (Bell & Reardon, 2011; Street et al., 2011), effective strategies for assessment and treatment are available, and these resources can help clinicians address the mental health needs of dual combat and sexual trauma during the military.

## REFERENCES

Basoglu, M. (2009). A multivariate contextual analysis of torture and cruel, inhuman, and degrading treatments: Implications for an evidence-based definition of torture. *American Journal of Orthopsychiatry, 79,* 135–145.

Bell, M. E., & Reardon, A. (2011). Experiences of sexual harassment and sexual assault in the military among OEF/OIF Veterans: Implications for healthcare providers. *Social Work in Healthcare, 50,* 34–50.

Bolton, E. E., Litz, B. T., Britt, T. W., Adler, A., & Roemer, L. (2001). Reports of prior exposure to potentially traumatic events and PTSD in troops poised for deployment. *Journal of Traumatic Stress, 14,* 249–256.

Breitenbecher, K. H. (2000). Sexual assault on college campuses: Is an ounce of prevention enough? *Applied and Preventative Psychology, 9,* 23–52.

Brewin, C. R., Andrews, B., & Valentine, J. D. (2000). Meta-analysis of risk factors for post-traumatic stress disorder in trauma-exposed adults. *Journal of Consulting and Clinical Psychology, 68,* 748–766.

Butterfield, M. I., McIntyre, L. M., Stechuchak, K. M., Nanda, K., & Bastian, L. A. (1998). Mental disorder symptoms in Veteran women: Impact of physical and sexual assault. *Journal of the American Medical Women's Association, 53,* 198–200.

Classen, C. C., Palesh, O. G., & Aggarwal, R. (2005). Sexual revictimization: A review of the empirical literature. *Trauma, Violence, & Abuse, 6,* 103–129.

Cloitre, M., & Rosenberg, A. (2006). Sexual revictimization: Risk factors and prevention. In V. M. Follette & J. I. Ruzek (Eds.), *Cognitive-behavioral therapies for trauma* (2nd ed., pp. 321–361). New York: Guilford Press.

Dedert, E. A., Green, K. T., Calhoun, P. S., Yoash-Gantz, R., Taber, K. H., Mumford, M. M., … Beckham, J. C. (2009). Association of trauma exposure with psychiatric morbidity in military Veterans who have served since September 11, 2001. *Journal of Psychiatric Research, 43*, 830–836.

DeFleur, L. B. (1985). Organizational and ideological barriers to sex integration in military groups. *Work and Occupations, 12,* 206–228.

Department of Defense. (2009). Report of the Defense Task Force on Sexual Assault in the Military Services. Washington, DC: Government Printing Office.

Desai, R. A., Harpaz-Rotem, I., Najavits, L. M., & Rosenheck, R. A. (2008). Impact of the Seeking Safety program on clinical outcomes among homeless female Veterans with psychiatric disorders. *Psychiatric Services, 59,* 996–1003

U.S. Equal Employment Opportunity Commission (EEOC). (1999). Policy Guidance on Current Issues of Sexual Harassment. Retrieved April 13, 2010, from http://www.eeoc.gov

Engel, C. J., Engel, A., Campbell, S., McFall, M. E., Russo, J., & Katon, W. (1993). Posttraumatic stress disorder symptoms and precombat sexual and physical abuse in Desert Storm Veterans. *Journal of Nervous and Mental Disease, 181,* 683–688.

Fairbank, J. A., Putnam, F. W., & Harris, W. W. (2007). The prevalence and impact of child traumatic stress. In M. J. Friedman, T. M. Keane, & P. A. Resick (Eds.), *Handbook of PTSD: Science and practice* (pp. 229–251). New York: Guilford Press.

Feldner, M. T., Monson, C. M., & Friedman, M. J. (2007). A critical analysis of approaches to targeted PTSD prevention: Current status and theoretically-derived future directions. *Behavior Modification, 31,* 80–116.

Foa, E. B., Hembree, E. A., & Rothbaum, B. O. (2007). *Prolonged exposure therapy for PTSD: Emotional processing of traumatic experiences.* New York: Oxford University Press.

Follete, V. M., Iverson, K. M., & Ford, J. (2009). Contextual behavioral treatment for complex PTSD. In C. Courtois and J. D. Ford (Eds.), *Treating complex traumatic stress disorders: An evidence-based clinician's guide* (pp. 264–285). New York: Guilford Press.

Fontana, A., Litz, B., & Rosenheck, R. (2000). Impact of combat and sexual harassment on the severity of posttraumatic stress disorder among men and women peacekeepers in Somalia. *Journal of Nervous and Mental Diseases, 188,* 163–169.

Frayne, S. M., Skinner, K. M., Sullivan, L. M., & Freund, K. M. (2003). Sexual assault while in the military: Violence as a predictor of cardiac risk? *Violence and Victims, 18,* 219–225.

Frayne, S. M., Skinner, K., Sullivan, L., Tripp, T., Hankin, C., Kressin, N., & Miller, D. (1999). Medical profile of women VA outpatients who report a history of sexual assault while in the military. *Women's Health, 8*(6), 835–845.

Freyd, J. J. (1996). *Betrayal trauma: The logic of forgetting childhood abuse.* Cambridge, MA: Harvard University Press.

Friedman, M. J., Schnurr, P. P., & McDonagh-Coyle, A. (1994). Post-traumatic stress disorder in the military Veteran. *Psychiatric Clinics of North America, 17,* 265–277.

Garlarneau, M. R., Woodruff, S. I., Dye, J. L., Mohrele, C. R., & Wade, A. L. (2008). Traumatic brain injury Operation Iraqi Freedom: Findings from the United States Navy–Marine Corps Combat Trauma Registry. *Journal of Neurosurgery, 108,* 950–957.

Green, B. L., Grace, M. C., Lindy, J. D., Gleser, G. C., & Leonard, A. (1990). Risk factors for PTSD and other diagnoses in a general sample of Vietnam Veterans. *American Journal of Psychiatry, 147,* 729–733.

Griffith, J., & Vaitkus, M. (1999). Relating cohesion to stress, strain, disintegration, and performance: An organizing framework. *Military Psychology, 11*, 27–55

Harned, M. S. (2004). Does it matter what you call it? The relationship between labeling unwanted sexual experiences and distress. *Journal of Consulting and Clinical Psychology, 72*, 1090–1099.

Hoge, C. W., Auchterlonie, J. L., & Milliken, C. S. (2006). Mental health problems, use of mental health services, and attrition from military service after returning from deployment from Iraq or Afghanistan. *Journal of the American Medical Association, 295*, 1023–1032.

Hoge, C. W., & Castro, C. (2006). Post-traumatic stress disorder in the UK and US forces deployed to Iraq. *Lancet, 368,* 837.

Hoge, C. W., McGurk, D., Thomas, J. L., Cox, A. L., Engel, C. C., & Castro, C. A. (2008). Mild traumatic brain injury in U.S. soldiers returning from Iraq. *New England Journal of Medicine, 358,* 453–463.

Hoge, C. W., Terhakopian, A., Castro, C. A., Messer, S. C., & Engel, C. C. (2007). Association of posttraumatic stress disorder with somatic symptoms, health care visits, and absenteeism among Iraq war Veterans. *The American Journal of Psychiatry, 164,* 150–153.

Institute of Medicine. (2008). *Treatment of posttraumatic stress disorder: An assessment of the evidence.* Washington, DC: National Academies Press.

Iverson, K. M., Gradus, J. L., Resick, P. A., Suvak, M. K., Smith K. F., & Monson, C. M. (2011, February 21). Cognitive-behavioral therapy for PTSD and depression symptoms reduces risk for future intimate partner violence among interpersonal trauma survivors. *Journal of Consulting and Clinical Psychology.* Advance online publication, DOI: 10.1037/a0022512.

Iverson, K. M., Lester, K., & Resick, P. A. (2011). Psychosocial treatments. In D. M. Benedek & G. H. Wynn (Eds.), *Clinical manual for the management of PTSD* (pp. 157–203). Washington, DC: American Psychiatric Publishing.

Kang, H., Dalager, N., Mahan, C., & Ishii, E. (2005). The role of sexual assault on the risk of PTSD among Gulf War Veterans. *Annals of Epidemiology, 15*, 191–195.

Kang, H. K., Natelson, B. H., Mahan, C. M., Lee, K. Y., & Murphy, F. M. (2003). Posttraumatic stress disorder and chronic fatigue-like illness among Gulf War Veterans: A population-based survey of 30,000 Veterans. *American Journal of Epidemiology, 157*, 141–148.

Keane, T. M., Marshall, R. P., & Taft, C. (2006). Posttraumatic stress disorder: Etiology, epidemiology, and treatment outcome. *Annual Review of Clinical Psychology, 2*, 161–197.

Keane, T. M., Scott, W. O., Chavoya, G. A., Lamparski, D. M., & Fairbank, J. A. (1985). Social support in Vietnam Veterans with posttraumatic stress disorder: A comparative analysis. *Journal of Consulting and Clinical Psychology, 53,* 95–102.

Kelly, M. M., & Vogt, D. S. (2009). Military stress: Effects of acute, chronic and traumatic stress on mental and physical health. In A. M. Freeman, B. A. Moore, & A. Freeman (Eds.), *Living and surviving in harm's way: A psychological treatment handbook for pre- and post-deployment of military personnel* (pp. 85–106). New York: Routledge.

Kessler, R. C., Sonnega, A., Bromet, E., Hughes, M., & Nelson, C. B. (1995). Posttraumatic stress disorder in the National Comorbidity Survey. *Archives of General Psychiatry, 52,* 1048–1060.

Kimerling, R., Gima, K., Smith, M. W., Street, A., & Frayne, S. (2007). The Veterans' Health Administration and military sexual trauma. *American Journal of Public Health, 97*, 2160–2166.

Kimerling, R., Street, A. E., Gima, K., & Smith, M. W. (2008). Evaluation of universal screening for military-related sexual trauma. *Psychiatric Services, 59*, 635–640.

Kimerling, R., Street, A. E., Pavao, J., Smith, M. W., Cronkite, R. C., Holmes, T. H., & Frayne, S. M. (2010). Military-related sexual trauma among VHA patients returning from Afghanistan and Iraq. *American Journal of Public Health, 100*(8), 1409–1412.

King, D. W., King, L. A., Foy, D. W., & Gudanowski, D. M. (1996). Prewar factors in combat-related posttraumatic stress disorder: Structural equation modeling with a national sample of female and male Vietnam Veterans. *Journal of Consulting and Clinical Psychology, 64*, 520–531.

King, D. W., King, L. A., Foy, D. W., Keane, T. M., & Fairbank, J. A. (1999). Posttraumatic stress disorder in a national sample of female and male Vietnam Veterans: Risk factors, war zone stressors, and resilience-recovery variables. *Journal of Abnormal Psychology, 108,* 164–170.

King, D. W., King, L. A., Gudanowski, D. M., & Vrevren, D. L. (1995). Alternative representations of war zone stressors: Relationships to posttraumatic stress disorder in male and female Vietnam Veterans. *Journal of Abnormal Psychology, 104,* 184–196.

King, L. A., King, D. W., Vogt, D. S., Knight, J., & Samper, R. E. (2006). Deployment risk and resilience inventory: A collection of measures for studying deployment-related experiences of military personnel and Veterans. *Military Psychology, 18,* 89–120.

Kulka, R. A., Schlenger, W. E., Fairbank, J. A., Hough, R. L., Jordan, B. K., Marmar, C. R., … Grady, D. A. (1990). *Trauma and the Vietnam War Generation*. New York: Brunner/Mazel.

Linehan, M. M. (1993). *Skills training manual for treating borderline personality disorder*. New York: Guilford Press.

Lipari, R. N., Cook, P. J., Rock, L. M., & Matos, K. (2008). *2006 gender relations survey of active duty members*. Arlington, VA: Department of Defense Manpower Data Center.

Litz, B. T., & Gray, M. J. (2004). Early intervention for trauma in adults: A framework for first aid and secondary prevention. In B. Litz (Ed.), *Early intervention for trauma and traumatic loss* (pp. 87–111). New York: Guilford Press.

Llies, R., Hauserman, N., Schwochau, S., & Stibal, J. (2003). Reported incidence rates of work-related sexual harassment in the United States: Using meta-analysis to explain reported rate disparities. *Personnel Psychology, 56,* 607–631.

Messman-Moore, T. L., & Long, P. J. (2003). The role of childhood sexual abuse sequelae in the sexual revictimization of women: An empirical review and theoretical reformulation. *Clinical Psychology Review, 23,* 537–571.

Miller, M. W. (2004). Personality and the development and expression of PTSD. *National Center for PTSD Clinical Quarterly, 15,* 1–3.

Milliken, C. S., Auchterlonie, J. L., & Hoge, C. W. (2007). Longitudinal assessment of mental health problems among active and reserve component soldiers returning from the Iraq war. *Journal of the American Medical Association, 298,* 2141–2148.

Monson, C. M., & Fredman, S. J. (under contract). *Cognitive-behavioral conjoint therapy for posttraumatic stress disorder: Therapist's manual*. New York: Guilford.

Monson, C. M., Schnurr, P. P., Resick, P. A., Friedman, M. J., Young-Xu, Y., & Stevens, S. P. (2006). Cognitive processing therapy for Veterans with military-related posttraumatic stress disorder. *Journal of Consulting and Clinical Psychology, 74,* 898–907.

Murdoch, M., Polusny, M. A., Hodges, J., & O'Brien, N. (2004). Prevalence of in-service and post-service sexual assault among combat and noncombat Veterans applying for Department of Veterans Affairs posttraumatic stress disorder disability benefits. *Military Medicine, 169,* 392–395.

Murdoch, M., Pryor, J. B., Polusny, M. A., & Gackstetter, G. D. (2007). Functioning and psychiatric symptoms among military men and women exposed to sexual stressors. *Military Medicine, 172,* 718–725.

Najavits, L. M. (2002). *Seeking safety: A treatment manual for PTSD and substance abuse.* New York: Guilford Press.

Najavits, L. M., Weiss, R. D., Shaw, S. R., & Muenz, L. R. (1998). "Seeking safety": Outcome of a new cognitive-behavioral psychotherapy for women with posttraumatic stress disorder and substance dependence. *Journal of Traumatic Stress, 11,* 437–456.

Pflanz, S., & Sonnek, S. (2002). Occupational stress and psychiatric illness in the military: Investigation of the relationship between occupational stress and mental illness among military mental health patients. *Military Medicine, 167,* 887–892.

Polusny, M. A., Dickinson, K. A., Murdoch, M., & Thuras, P. (2008). The role of cumulative sexual trauma and difficulties identifying feelings in understanding female Veterans' physical health outcomes. *General Hospital Psychiatry, 30,* 162–170.

Raskin, S. A. (1997). The relationship between sexual abuse and mild traumatic brain injury. *Brain Injury, 11,* 587–604.

Resick, P. A., Galovski, T. E., O'Brien Uhlmansiek, M., Scher, C. D., Clum, G. A., & Young-Xu, Y. (2008). A randomized clinical trial to dismantle components of cognitive processing therapy for posttraumatic stress disorder in female victims of interpersonal violence. *Journal of Consulting and Clinical Psychology, 76,* 243–258.

Resick, P. A., Monson, C. M., & Chard, K. M. (2008). *Cognitive processing therapy: Veteran/military version.* Washington, DC: Department of Veterans Affairs.

Rosen, L. N., & Martin, L. (1996). The measurement of childhood trauma among male and female soldiers in the US army. *Military Medicine, 161,* 342–345.

Ruzek, J. A. (2006). Bringing cognitive-behavioral psychology to bear on early intervention with trauma survivors: Accident, assault, war, disaster, mass violence, and terrorism. In V. M. Follette & J. I. Ruzek (Eds.), *Cognitive-behavioral therapies for trauma* (2nd ed., pp. 433–462). New York: Guilford Press.

Sadler, A. G., Booth, B. M., Cook, B. L., & Doebbeling, B. N. (2003). Factors associated with women's risk of rape in the military environment. *American Journal of Industrial Medicine, 43,* 262–273.

Sadler, A. G., Booth, B. M., Cook, B. L., Torner, J. C., & Doebbeling, B. N. (2001). The military environment: Risk factors for women's non-fatal assaults. *Journal of Occupational & Environmental Medicine, 43,* 325–334.

Sadler, A. G., Booth, B. M., Nielson, D., & Doebbling, B. N. (2000). Health related consequences of physical and sexual violence: Women in the military. *Obstetrics & Gynecology, 96,* 473–480.

Sameroff, A. J. (1998). Environmental risk factors in infancy. *Pediatrics, 102,* 1287–1292.

Schnurr, P. P., Friedman, M. J., Engel, C. C., Foa, E. B., Shea, M. T., Chow, B. K., … Bernardy, N. (2007). Cognitive behavioral therapy for posttraumatic stress disorder in women: A randomized controlled trial. *Journal of the American Medical Association, 297,* 820–830.

Schnurr, P. P., Friedman, M. J., & Rosenburg, S. D. (1993). Premilitary MMPI scores as predictors of combat-related PTSD symptoms. *American Journal of Psychiatry, 150,* 479–483.

Schnurr, P. P., Lunney, C. A., Bovin, M. J., & Marx, B. P. (2009). Posttraumatic stress disorder and quality of life: Extension of findings to Veterans of the wars in Iraq and Afghanistan. *Clinical Psychology Review, 29,* 727–735.

Schnurr, P. P., Lunney, C. A., & Sengupta, A. (2004) Risk factors for the development versus maintenance of posttraumatic stress disorder. *Journal of Traumatic Stress, 17,* 85–95.

Shipherd, J. C., Pineles, S. L., Gradus, J. L., & Resick, P. A. (2009). Sexual harassment in the Marines, posttraumatic stress symptoms and perceived health: Evidence for sex differences. *Journal of Traumatic Stress, 22,* 3–10.

Skinner, K. M., Kressin, N., Frayne, S., Tripp, T. J., Hankin, C. S., Miller, D. R., & Sullivan, L. M. (2000). The prevalence of military sexual assault among female Veterans Administration outpatients. *Journal of Interpersonal Violence, 15,* 291–310.

Smith, T. C., Ryan, M. A. K., Wingard, D. L., Slymen, D. J., Sallis, J. F., & Kritz-Silverstein, D. (2008a). New onset and persistent symptoms of post-traumatic stress disorder self-reported after deployment and combat exposures: Prospective population based US military cohort study. *British Medical Journal, 336,* 366–371.

Smith, T. C., Wingard, D. L., Ryan, M. A. K., Kritz-Silverstein, D., Slymen, D. J., & Sallis, J. F. (2008b). Prior assault and Posttraumatic Stress Disorder after combat deployment. *Epidemiology, 19*(3), 505–512.

Spoont, M. R., Sayer, N. A., Thuras, P., Erbes, C., & Winston, E. (2003). Adaptation of Dialectical Behavior Therapy by a VA Medical Center. *Psychiatric Services, 54,* 627–629.

Street, A. E., Gradus, G. J., Stafford, J., & Kelly, K. (2007). Gender differences in experiences of sexual harassment: Data from a male-dominated environment. *Journal of Consulting and Clinical Psychology, 75,* 464–474.

Street, A. E., Kimerling, R., Bell, M. E., & Pavao, J. (2011). Sexual harassment and sexual assault during military service. In J. Ruzek, P. Schnurr, J. Vasterling, & M. Friedman (Eds.), *Veterans of the global war on terror* (pp. 131–150). Washington, DC: American Psychological Association Press.

Street, A., Stafford, J., Mahan, C., & Hendricks, A. M. (2008). Sexual harassment and assault experienced by reservists during military service: Prevalence and health correlates. *Journal of Rehabilitation Research & Development, 45,* 409–420.

Street, A. E., Vogt, D., & Dutra, L. (2009). A new generation of women Veterans: Stressors faced by women deployed to Iraq and Afghanistan. *Clinical Psychology Review, 29,* 685–694.

Tanielian, T., & Jaycox, L. H. (2008). *Invisible wounds of war: Psychological and cognitive injuries, their consequences, and services to assist recovery.* Santa Monica, CA: RAND Corporation.

Tjaden, P., & Thoennes, N. (2000). *Extent, nature, and consequences of intimate partner violence: Findings from the National Violence Against Women Survey.* Washington DC: Department of Justice.

True, W. R., Goldberg, J., & Eisen, S. A. (1988). Stress symptomatology among Vietnam Veterans: Analysis of the Veterans Administration survey of Veterans, II. *American Journal of Epidemiology, 128,* 85–92.

Ullman, S. E. (1999). Social support and recovery from sexual assault: A review. *Aggression and Violent Behavior, 4,* 343–358.

Vogt, D. S., Pless, A. P., King, L. A., & King, D. W. (2005). Deployment stressors, gender, and mental health outcomes among Gulf War I Veterans. *Journal of Traumatic Stress, 18,* 272–284.

Vogt, D. S., & Tanner, L. R. (2007). Risk and resilience factors for posttraumatic stress symptomatology in Gulf War I Veterans. *Journal of Traumatic Stress, 20,* 27–38.

Wells, T. S., LeardMann, C. A., Fortuna, S. O., Smith, B., Smith, T. C., Ryan, M. A. K., ... Blazer, D. (2010). A prospective study of depression following combat deployment in support of the wars in Iraq and Afghanistan. *America Journal of Public Health, 100*, 90–99.

Wolfe, J., Sharkansky, E. J., Read, J. P., Dawson, R., Martin, J. A., & Ouimette, P. C. (1998). Sexual harassment and assault as predictors of PTSD symptomatology among U.S. female Persian Gulf War military personnel. *Journal of Interpersonal Violence, 13*, 40–57.

Zinzow, H. M., Grubaugh, A. L., Monnier, J., Suffoletta-Maierle, S., & Frueh, B. C. Trauma among female Veterans: A critical review. *Trauma Violence & Abuse, 8,* 384–400.

Chapter 11

# Multiple Traumas in Civilian Casualties of Organized Political Violence

*Anthony Papa and Heidi La Bash*

Civilians' experience of organized political violence (OPV) can vary widely depending upon the political context in which it occurs. Conventional warfare, state-sponsored terrorism, and political terrorism by non-nation-state entities can be associated with different potentially traumatic events (PTEs). For example, conventional warfare often entails the close proximity of noncombatants to military action focused on establishing control over defined areas and institutions. Stressors most commonly associated with conventional warfare include loss of life; lack of access to basic needs such as food, water, shelter, and health care; as well as destruction of personal property, infrastructure, and means for livelihood. Terrorism practiced by nation-states is mainly utilized to achieve foreign policy goals or to maintain domestic control and often entails imprisonment and torture but can also include intimidation and exile, among other tactics. To the extent that these forms of violence necessitate that civilians seek shelter outside of their country of origin, fleeing civilians are conferred refugee status. Refugee status comes with its own broad set of acute and chronic stressors. In this chapter, we will review the epidemiological evidence for postviolence disruption, review these disparate potential traumas, provide a theoretical frame to conceptualize the impact of these events, and discuss the assessment and treatment of civilians exposed to OPV.

## EPIDEMIOLOGICAL DATA PERTAINING TO TRAUMA

In 2008, of a total Iraqi population of approximately 28,950,000 (2009 estimate; www.cia.gov/library/publications/the-world-factbook/geos/iz.html), the
UN High Commissioner on Refugees reported 2,647,300 internally displaced
persons and 1,742,400 registered refugees sheltering in neighboring countries,
of which (for areas with statistics available) approximately 38% were under the
age of 18. In Somalia (population estimated at 9,800,000 in 2009; www.cia.
gov/library/publications/the-world-factbook/geos/so.html), the United Nations
estimated 1.3 million persons were internally displaced by the ongoing conflict
between the transitional government and Islamic fundamentalist insurgents.
In addition, 3.5 million were in need of humanitarian assistance due to flood,
drought, and escalating food and fuel costs exacerbated by scorched-earth war
tactics. Internationally, the United Nations estimates that 42 million people
were forcibly displaced as of 2009 (http://www.unhcr.org/4a2fd52412d.html),
including 5.2 million refugees, 827,000 pending asylum seekers, and 26 million
internally displaced persons. Of these, one third lived in camps, only 25 million
of which received UN protection or assistance.

Due to the nature of OPV, systematic, large-scale epidemiological research
is often precluded by difficulties in gaining access to target populations
because of ongoing violence, disruption of civil organization, governmental
interference, and difficulties accessing remote areas. The epidemiological
data that exist on the mental health consequences of exposure to war trauma
for civilians is sparse, often relying on limited assessment of nonrepresen-
tative samples (de Jong et al., 2001), inadequately validated translations of
measures, and use of measures that do not capture the full range of potential
experiences or mental health responses (Hollifield et al., 2002). In addition,
cross-conflict comparisons often compare survivors whose current living situation and ongoing level of threat differ dramatically, allowing only the broad-
est view of the consequences of OPV.

A notable exception to the relative dearth of systematic research about
the mental health effects of OPV has been the Balkan conflicts in the 1990s.
Intense United Nations involvement, and relatively easy access for Western
researchers, has resulted in numerous studies of the mental health impact of
the dissolution of the communist republic of Yugoslavia. The dismantling of
Yugoslavia entailed a series of protracted ethnic clashes that included ethnic
cleansings and organized rape campaigns, which have resulted in war crimes
trials that have continued into 2011. Unsurprisingly, a number of studies have
documented the continuing deleterious long-term impact of displacement
on the mental and physical health of both refugees and nonrefugees of the
Yugoslav and Kosovar wars. Eytan et al. (2004) found diagnostic levels of
posttraumatic stress disorder (PTSD) to be 23.5% in repatriated Kosovar refugees two and a half years after the conflict's end. Other estimates of PTSD
prevalence in the former Yugoslav republics, conducted at different time

frames after conflicts and targeting different histories of displacement, show similar levels of PTSD diagnosis in nonpatient samples (e.g., Ahern et al., 2004 [14.1%]; Basoglu et al., 2005 [22%]; Cardozo, Vergara, Agani, & Gotway, 2000 [17.1%]; Mollica et al., 1999 [26.3%]; Toscani et al., 2007 [25.5%]); with combat exposure, near-death experiences, witnessing murder, forced separation from family, and unnatural death of family member increasing the odds of developing PTSD four to eight times (Eytan et al., 2004). Eytan and colleagues also found that PTSD prevalence increased based on level of exposure to OPV, with the odds ratios increasing 1.5 for one to two PTEs (11% of sample), 7.3 for three to four PTEs (33.4%), 16.2 for five to six (25.3%), 47.7 for seven to eight (16.8%), and 79.5 for nine or more (8.1%). Similarly, in a survey conducted in Kosovo immediately after the end of hostilities, Cardozo and colleagues (2000) found that 66% reported exposure to combat, 61.6% being close to death, 48.9% torture or abuse, 26.4% the murder of family or friend, and 4.4% rape. Overall, 39% reported experiencing 4 to 7 PTEs, 27% reported 8 to 11, and 12% reported more than 11. Increases in PTSD were linearly related to the number of PTEs reported, strongly suggesting that cumulative exposure and retraumatization play a significant role in these prevalence rates.

Similarly, a meta-analysis of the studies published by 1999 on refugee and nonrefugee persons in the former Yugoslavia republics found displacement to be one of the strongest risk factors for ongoing mental health difficulties (Porter & Haslam, 2001). Subsequently, Schmidt, Kravic, and Ehlert (2008) found that while refugees initially have the most negative adjustment, refugees had more positive adjustment than internally displaced persons (IDPs) 10 years later (10% of refugees meeting criteria for PTSD versus 73% of IDPs). This level was similar to nondisplaced persons (NDPs) (15% meeting criteria for PTSD), even though NDPs reported significantly less exposure to war PTEs. This result is consistent with a large-scale meta-analysis of the long-term adjustment of refugees from conflicts around the world (Porter & Haslam, 2005), which found that IDPs had significantly poorer outcomes than refugees, refugees that were repatriated fared worse than those permanently resettled in host countries, and those resettled refugees who had greater economic opportunity and freedom to engage in their own cultural practices fared best (see also Porter, 2007), though maintenance of high levels of cultural practice may be associated with decreased acculturation and worse outcomes over time (e.g., Marshall, Schell, Elliott, Berthold, & Chun, 2005). These studies appear to support a diathesis-stress model of traumatization in which residual stress from exposure to PTEs can be potentiated by ecological stressors such as lack of economic opportunity or acculturation difficulties for refugee status (see McKeever & Huff, 2003).

Looking across cultures, multiple studies agree that the toll of OPV on mental health can be high. For example, de Jong et al. (2001) randomly selected persons in Algeria, Cambodia, Ethiopia, and Gaza who were all exposed to war or resettlement to participate in a psychiatric diagnostic assessment (see also de Jong, Komproe, & Van Ommeren, 2003). Although they found significant differences in the PTSD prevalence between countries (37.4% in Algeria, 28.4% in Cambodia, 17.8% in Gaza, and 5.8% in Ethiopia) and between gender by country (in Cambodia and Algeria, women had higher rates; in Gaza, men had more), overall rates of individuals meeting criteria for PTSD diagnosis were high (e.g., in Algeria, about 80% endorsed re-experiencing symptoms, 52% avoidance/numbing, and 71% hyperarousal; in Gaza, the numbers were 73%, 59%, and 38%, respectively). Mood (about 23% in Algeria, 12% in Cambodia, 9% in Gaza, and 5% in Ethiopia) and somatoform disorders (about 8% in Algeria, 2% in Cambodia, 5% in Gaza, and 3% in Ethiopia) prevalence also varied by country. A number of factors may account for the difference in prevalence rates of PTSD between countries, including recentness of events, differential exposure to violence, and chronicity of conflicts. At the time of the de Jong and colleagues study, Algerian participants were experiencing ongoing terrorist attacks; participants from Cambodia suffered from the Pol Pot era, the Vietnamese invasion, and ongoing strife that lasted until UN intervention in the early 1990s; and the Gaza strip had been exposed to chronic sporadic violence that mainly entailed male combatants for decades. The effects of intensity of exposure across cultures are supported by Steel et al.'s (2009) meta-analysis of 161 articles of studies looking at IDPs, refugees, and NDPs. They found that PTSD incidence was associated with cumulative exposure to potentially traumatic events, time since conflict, and the conflict's overall level of political terror or violence as assessed by Amnesty International and U.S. State Department reports, again suggesting that residual stress from intense or accumulative exposure is associated with PTSD prevalence.

In terms of other risk factors associated with increases in residual stress unique to OPV, torture has received a significant amount of attention and has been strongly linked to increased PTSD symptoms in a number of studies (see Silove, Steel, & Watters, 2000; Steel et al., 2009). Spurred partially by the organized rape campaigns during the Balkan and Rwandan conflicts, the effects of war rape have begun to be systematically studied and have also been strongly linked with increases in PTSD symptoms (e.g., Johnson et al., 2008; Kozaric-Kovacic, Folnegovic-Smalc, Skrinjaric, Szajnberg, & Marusic, 1995; Mollica, Lavelle, & Knoun, 1986; Tankink & Richters, 2007). In addition to direct exposure to violence, refugees, IDPs, and NDPs face a number of other unique ecological stressors that may further interact with violence-related risk factors. These unique stressors include continued threat and insecurity, marginalization in either the country of origin or in host countries, prolonged detention, acculturation stress, lack of access to socioeconomic opportunities, poor access to health care, and loss or destruction of community, culture, and other social resources (see Porter & Haslam, 2005; Silove, Sinnerbrink, Field, Manicavasagar, & Steel, 1997; Silove et al., 2000). These stressors may be salient for IDPs and NDPs who remain in high conflict areas or are the focus of terrorism. These stressors are likely to be equally salient for externally displaced persons (EDPs) who either fled or were forced into exile, leaving behind family, community, and belongings, and who may be facing long-term exile and resettlement, or possible repatriation based on prevailing political policy (e.g., Porter & Haslam, 2005).

Finally, general PTSD risk factors are also salient for civilian populations affected by OPV (for example, Ozer, Best, Lipsey, & Weiss, 2003). These general risk factors include previous mental health status; previous exposure to traumatic event(s); levels of exposure; perceived life threat; postevent demands and stressors; social support; individual differences in resilience; and other static individual differences such as female gender, younger age, lower IQ, lower levels of education, lower socioeconomic status (SES), and minority status. Given the potential for chronic, multiple exposure to PTEs, all of these factors can be particularly salient for people harmed by OPV. Examining de Jong and colleagues' (2001) results, previous mental health status increased risk of developing PTSD from 0.03 to 5.2 times, levels of exposure increased risk 2 to 7.9 times, postevent demands and stressors such as poor living conditions in camps increased risk 2 to 33.7 times, unresolved health issues increased risk 1.4 to 3.3 times, and higher levels of daily hassles increased risk 1.7 to 2.3 times. In Porter and Haslam's (2005) meta-analysis of pre- and postdisplacement factors associated with PTSD development in EDP and IPD populations, they found that female gender was associated with poorer outcomes, while higher education and predisplacement SES were protective. However, unlike the results of Ozer et al. (2003) and Brewin, Andrews, and Valentine (2000), older age was found to be associated with worse outcomes when faced with significant material loss, loss of social status and community, and acculturation pressures further highlighting the role of ecological factors in traumatization in these populations.

## ETIOLOGICAL FORMULATIONS AND THEORETICAL MODELS OF RETRAUMATIZATION

A theoretical account of civilian response to war must account for the heterogeneous nature of the potential stressors, the loss of instrumental and social resources including home, culture, possessions, means to support self and family, social standing, social support availability, and the political contexts and cultural meanings in which these events occur. In terms of the effects of political environment, Khmer Rouge marginalization and genocide of specific ethnic groups in Cambodia likely had a strong impact on perceptions of controllability, expectations of the future, and meaning making for targeted groups. In each case, the effects of persecution are magnified by the destruction of communities, that destruction being similar to that found in the context of large-scale natural disasters (Hobfoll, 2002; Norris & Kaniasty, 1996).

For example, Nepalese persecution of the Lhotshampa minority has resulted in the displacement of a large segment of the population, of which approximately 90,000 remain in refugee camps in Nepal and possibly 30,000 in India in 2010 despite major resettlement initiatives (www.unhcr.org/cgi-bin/texis/vtx/page?page=49e487646; UNHCR, 2009). Refugees in these situations face significant ecological stressors and social resource loss that differ depending on if displacement means living in a refugee camp across an international border or acculturating to far-away resettlement. Other stressors in refugee camps that can be associated with retraumatization in these populations include ongoing exposure to violence; loss of freedom; lack of essentials such as adequate food, water, and health care; questions about legal status; and forced repatriation, all of which can have a significant impact on the ability to cope with the experience of trauma (Hondius, van Willigen, Kleijn, & van der Ploeg, 2000; Michultka, Blanchard, & Kalous, 1998; Miller et al., 2002). Refugees seeking political asylum and permanent resettlement in other, often more developed countries, face discrimination, language barriers, significant acculturation pressures, loss of social status and supports, financial need, and so forth (see Miller et al., 2002). For example, Iraqi refugees in neighboring countries face rampant inflation but, in many cases, are barred from seeking employment (Laipson, 2009).

In addition to macro factors such as heterogeneity of events, culture, and political climate, and individual factors, such as exposure and reexposure to death and the threat of death, injury, and disability, the interpersonal nature of some of these events must also be considered. For example, Tutsi-directed violence during the Rwandan civil war included targeting specific individuals in communities, systematic discrimination, torture, and rape. Norris et al. (2002) suggested that in the context of large-scale events, long-term mental health consequences can be minimized if the disaster does not take on more symbolic meanings of human neglect or maliciousness. Moreover, the cultural implications of specific types of OPV may differ from situation to situation (e.g., rape as a tool of OPV, such as that perpetrated in the conflicts in Rwanda, Bosnia, and Darfur) (Kozaric-Kovacic et al., 1995; Mollica et al., 1986).

## Posttraumatic Stress Disorder (PTSD) in Context

Theoretical accounts of the development of PTSD differentially emphasize the role of specific cognitions and cognitive processing, memory encoding and retrieval (both in terms of encoding processes as well as in terms of autobiographical memory), conditioning or learning, or dysregulation of emotion (see Brewin & Holmes, 2003; Dalgleish, 2004; Rubin, Berntsen, & Bohni, 2008 for reviews). Cognitive factors related to PTSD development revolve around individuals' efforts to reconcile the reality of their experiences, actions, or reactions to a traumatic event or events, and their beliefs about how the world should be and how individuals should interact (see Dalgleish, 2004). From this view, PTSD develops when a person is unable to reconcile the realities of events with their established belief systems. This disconnection between event realities and established belief systems serves to undermine individuals' sense of who they are in the world and in relation to others. This undermined sense of self is reflected in changes in goal setting related to diminished self-efficacy, negative self-attributions ("I am weak"), and emotional and behavioral responses to events as a result of attributions such as, "the world is dangerous," " I am helpless," and "I am a bad person." These give rise to associated emotional responses such as shame, guilt, fear, and anger that reflect unresolved threat to the integrity of one's sense of self or the experience of change in one's self (Dunmore, Clark, & Ehlers, 1999; Ehlers, Maercker, & Boos, 2000). Benight and Bandura (2004) suggest that PTSD may develop as a result of exposure to PTEs as mediated by the experience's effect on self-efficacy and esteem as a result of diathesis-driven reductions in agentic control of one's environment and one's reactions. What's more, there is accumulating evidence that PTSD-related alterations in self-efficacy and self-esteem are associated with further accumulation of resource losses and re-exposures to PTEs and serve to create a cycle of maladaptation to trauma (e.g., Schumm, Stines, Hobfoll, & Jackson, 2005; Walter, Horsey, Palmieri, & Hobfoll, 2010). This suggests that the ebb and flow of PTSD symptom intensity seen in initial incidence, recovery, and retraumatization would be directly related to the effect of ecological diathesis, residual stress, and biological dispositions on the individuals' sense of agency. Clearly, the magnitude of political violence has the potential to overwhelm individuals' sense of self and positive self-illusions of the predictability, controllability, and justice in the world (Taylor & Brown, 1988). Supporting this idea that self-efficacy may mediate PTSD symptoms development is research that suggests the relationship of political violence to psychological outcomes is moderated by expectancies. Basoglu and colleagues (Basoglu, Paker, Özmen, Tasdemir, & Sahin, 1994; Basoglu et al., 1997) found that in Turkish political opposition members, psychological preparedness for torture blunted the impact of torture; survivors of torture who were psychologically prepared showed much lower levels of PTSD symptoms than did other survivors of torture in Turkey. Benight et al. (2000) found that subjective appraisals of coping self-efficacy were negatively related to PTSD symptoms after the Oklahoma City bombing.

Memory theories propose that trauma memories are subject to different levels of encoding and retrieval. It is the linking of associational memory networks and the integration of these memories in autobiographical memory that account for PTSD-related re-experiencing and dissociative symptoms as well as subsequent hyperarousal and avoidance symptoms (Foa & Rothbaum, 1998). Other research suggests that trauma memories, like autobiographical memory in general, are constructive and are influenced by current attributions, attitudes, beliefs, affective states, and personality (Rubin et al., 2008). This is particularly intriguing as autobiographical memory is proposed to be (a) the mechanism in which the continuity of the self is experienced and (b) motivated by beliefs and expectations based on individual learning histories within cultural and social contexts (Conway, 2005; Conway, Wang, Hanyu, & Haque, 2005) and thus would be the source for self-attributions of efficacy in specific situations. In this vein, autobiographical memory reflects the relative differences in independence and interdependence expected from individuals from individualistic versus collectivist cultures (Conway et al., 2005).

Culturally based role expectations, norms for the appropriate expression of distress, and expectations about how social interactions influence the meaning given to different PTEs can have a marked impact on the development and maintenance of PTSD symptoms (e.g., somatic versus psychological expression; de Jong & Van Ommeren, 2002; Draguns, 1986; see Jobson, 2009 for a review). Thus, events that are consistent with one's expectation for one's self or events that are culturally or collectively accepted may have less impact on esteem or efficacy for the individual. For example, Bachar, Canetti, Bonne, Denour, & Shalev (1997) and Levav (1989) in comparing the adjustment of parents and children of Israelis who died randomly due to a car accident to those who died during combat, found that war bereavement was associated with higher well-being in both groups. Just as the emotion of *amae* is thought to reflect the strong collectivist basis of Japanese culture (Niiya, Ellsworth, & Yamaguchi, 2006), in Russia, pessimism and sadness are socially motivated emotional modes of functioning that are thought to protect against an uncertain world (Chentsova-Dutton, 2010). These culturally bound worldviews, often formalized as religious beliefs, can impact responses to OPV (Johnson & Thompson, 2008). For example, Buddhist beliefs around the roles of suffering and fate in the maintenance of the self and in the process of reincarnation have been found to serve a protective function for Burmese and Cambodian refugees (Allden et al., 1996; Chueng, 1994).

## The Role of Culture

Maintaining social status and social connections has profound implications for our sense of self (e.g., Chen, Boucher, & Tapias, 2006; Leary, Tambor, Terdal, & Downs, 1995), our emotional reactions to events (e.g., MacDonald & Leary, 2005), and our ability to cope with stress (e.g., Hobfoll, 2002; Moos & Holahan, 2003). Given the far-reaching effects of OPV on the interpersonal and cultural inputs that serve to maintain the self, we suggest that the link between the experience of PTEs and development of PTSD is at least partially mediated by the effect of these events on the individual's ability to maintain a socially derived sense of self, as reflected in a sense of control and purpose in the social environment. Accumulating research suggests that the self is experienced as the sum of self-attributions, meanings, goals, emotional experiences, self-regulatory strategies, and behavioral responses evoked when relating to others in specific contexts (see Chen et al., 2006). This research suggests that relational selves differ in elaboration and accessibility between individuals and serve as important touchstones for the experience of continuity of the self as an efficacious agent in the world (see Brown & Rafaeli, 2007; Chen et al., 2006). Within this frame, external displacement, exile, and resettlement may doubly burden those struggling with the personal consequences for OPV. Displacement entails loss of the social-cultural base for the maintenance of the self in the face of adversity. Displacement represents the loss of cultural frames for meaning making and functioning and may require that the individual function in a new culture that ascribes potentially incompatible meanings and normative response expectations (Aroche & Coello, 2004) and, thereby, magnifies feelings of marginalization. This is particularly salient for a theory of relational selves that hypothesizes that the self consists of associative networks of if–then contingencies that reflect social learning specific to a particular person or group(s) of people. Thus, reinforcement from satisfying these contingencies is likely to be achieved only within these specific social contexts (Chen et al., 2006).

Bereavement research suggests that those persons who are most resilient are those who are best able to maintain social engagement and daily routines (see Bonanno, 2009, for a review). There is also evidence that maintaining social engagement and daily routines may be related to decreased incidence of PTSD symptoms (Cohen & Eid, 2007; Pat-Horenczyk, Schiff, & Doppelt, 2006). This suggests that resiliency is related to either a multiplicity of social roles and relational selves that allow for a broader range of emotion, regulation, and response to the challenges of OPV, or is related to more developed general or global relational selves that allow these persons to maintain stability and functioning in the face of adversity (i.e., Brown & Rafaeli, 2007). Thus, those events that narrow access to social resources tied to identity maintenance, those individuals with relational selves attached to specific persons or social roles, and those with poorly developed general and global relational selves would result in the narrowest range of responses available to cope with environmental challenges. In these situations, as a result of nonreinforcement and possible extinction of relationally associated, goal-directed responding, individuals would be at highest risk for developing PTSD.

The link between social resources, identity maintenance, and coping with threat is consistent with Conservation of Resources (COR) models (e.g., Hobfoll, 2002; Moos & Holahan, 2003) in which loss of individual (e.g., internal locus of control, self-esteem, self-efficacy, and socioeconomic status) and social resources (e.g., availability of support and diversity of support resources) during the experience and aftermath of PTEs shape attributions, responding, and the experience of stress. The impact of resource loss in OPV cannot be understated given the association of OPV not only with high prevalence of trauma in the form of injuries, threat to life, and loss of life but also with widespread damage to property, and serious and ongoing financial problems for individuals and communities. Supporting this assertion is research that links these specific losses to the most deleterious mental health consequences as a result of natural and manmade disasters (Norris et al., 2002).

Thus, based on COR models, research on relational selves, and social cognitive theory, a key factor in determining the effects of PTEs on adjustment is the availability of social resources and the social context in which individuals accumulate and lose resources. Community support not only mitigates the effects of OPV by disseminating information and resources to help individuals meet basic needs, but also by reducing isolation, normalizing suffering, and promoting healing disclosures (e.g., Kaniasty & Norris, 2004). However, the impact of loss of extended social network ties may be moderated by culture. Research suggests that the centrality of the relational aspects of self-concept may vary dramatically by culture (e.g., Cross, Gore, & Morris, 2003; English & Chen, 2007; Markus & Kitamaya, 1991; Mesquita & Walker, 2003; Rhee, Uleman, Lee, & Roman, 1995). For example, East Asian cultures generally are marked by an overriding focus on maintaining relationships and relative status within communities rather than maintenance of global self-concepts such as are generally found in Western cultures. Thus, depending on the cultural context, large-scale loss of community may be especially likely to undermine well-being and magnify the impact of stressor events.

## Effects of Cumulative Trauma in Organized Political Violence (OPV)

Research indicates that individuals with previous exposure to PTEs tend to be more reactive to exposure to subsequent traumas (see Brewin et al., 2000; Ozer et al. 2003), and there may be a cumulative effect of traumatization as a result of previous trauma exposure as well as the experience of PTSD symptoms (Breslau, Chilcoat, Kessler, & Davis, 1999; Follette, Polusny, Bechtle, & Naugle, 1996; McCauley, Kern, Kolodner, Dill, & Schroeder, 1997). People exposed to OPV often face cumulative stressors associated with continuing armed conflict, deterioration of social and civil structures and organizations, extended periods of external or internal displacement, social and economic marginalization, exile, acculturation, and repatriation. As a result, retraumatization is common (e.g., Schwarz-Langer, Deighton, Jerg-Bretzke, Weisker, & Traue, 2006). Research with Southeast Asian survivors of OPV suggests a dose effect relationship between level of exposure to violence and subsequent PTSD symptoms (Mollica et al, 1998; Mollica, McInes, Poole, & Tor, 1998). These findings have been supported by a number of other studies of OPV in a number of other cultures (see Johnson & Thompson, 2008). In a large study of Israeli adolescents, greater exposure to terrorism was associated with more PTSD symptoms and greater functional impairment (Pat-Horenczyk et al., 2006). Looking across armed conflicts in Central America, increases in PTSD were associated with level of exposure to war-related violence in terms of both frequency and intensity of experience (Michultka, Blanchard, & Kalous, 1998). For Iraqi civilians who were potentially exposed to both warfare and chemical weapons attacks during the Iran–Iraq War in the 1980s, it was found that the effects of exposure to both stressors were multiplicative compared to warfare exposure alone in terms of odds of lifetime PTSD diagnosis (5% versus 19%), depression (2% versus 7%), or some other anxiety (2 versus 15%) (Hashemian et al., 2006).

However, a one-to-one correspondence between exposure and symptoms does not always occur. Shalev and Freedman (2005) found that levels of exposure to terrorism in the general Israeli population did not affect the rate of symptoms following exposure to a subsequent traumatic event, raising the possibility that the effects of retraumatization in this political and cultural context may be related to some other factor such as preexisting mental health difficulties (see Brewin et al., 2000 and Ozer et al. 2003). For example, during the Gulf war, Israeli individuals with preexisting depressive mood in the context of war or SCUD attacks were at greater risk of clinical depression (Hobfoll, Lomranz, Eyal, Bridges, & Tzemach, 1989; Lomranz, Hobfoll, Johnson, Eyal, & Zemach, 1994). Holocaust survivors reported stronger feelings of panic, fear, stress, and depression symptoms than other Israeli individuals impacted by the Gulf war. This increased intensity of symptoms experienced by Holocaust survivors has been attributed, in part, to parallels between World War II and the Gulf war, which include similarities such as the threat of poisonous gas, the targeting of unarmed civilians, and the challenge of living with the actions of a totalitarian state (Solomon, 1995). In a clinical sample of refugees displaced to the United States after conflicts in Bosnia, Somalia, Vietnam, Laos, and Cambodia, televised exposure to the events of September 11, 2001, was associated with a significant spike in symptom levels and functional difficulties in the months after the attacks, particularly in those from the more recent conflicts in Bosnia and Somalia (Kinzie, Boehnlein, Riley, & Sparr, 2002). A related and crucial moderator between exposure and symptoms to consider is the stress and social isolation related to displacement and exile, which has been found to be associated with increased levels of PTSD, comorbid depression, and maladjustment across many different cultural groups and conflicts (e.g., Hondius et al., 2000; Michultka et al., 1998; Miller et al., 2002; Silove et al., 2010).

## CLINICAL DESCRIPTION OF TRAUMA-SPECIFIC DISTRESS

The diagnostic validity of a Western-established diagnosis when applied across cultural lines has been frequently criticized (e.g., Bracken, Giller, & Summerfield, 1995; Kleinman, 1977). In particular, it has been suggested that rigid application of *Diagnostic and Statistical Manual of Mental Disorders* (*DSM*) PTSD diagnostic criteria has the potential to decontextualize and distort the experiences of refugees by assigning Western assumptions to the meaning and effects of these experiences or by overlooking other culture-specific pathologies or response patterns (Muecke, 1992; Nicholl & Thompson, 1994; Shrestha et al., 1998; Silove, 1999). However, there is evidence of some commonality in symptom expression across some cultures that would support the utility of the *DSM* PTSD diagnosis (e.g., Carlson & Rosser-Hogan, 1994; Cheung, 1994). As reviewed above, multiple studies of PTSD prevalence in OPV-torn regions have found that incidence of PTSD symptom reports increases with increases in exposure to known PTSD risk factors. In addition, several studies have found comparable PTSD factor structures across different cultural groups (e.g., Marshall, 2004; Norris, Perilla, & Murphy, 2001). However, others have had more mixed results. One example is the finding of a unique *aroused-intrusion* factor in a sample of Central and West African refugees (Rasmussen, Smith, & Keller, 2007). Even though some studies suggest some level of commonality in symptom expression across some cultural groups, identifying similar symptoms cross-culturally does not guarantee that the symptoms have the same meaning as in Western cultures (Bracken et al., 1995; Kleinman, 1977). For example, in a recent study that employed a sample of persons from Algeria, Ethiopia, and Palestine, de Jong, Komproe, Spinazzola, van der Kolk, and Van Ommeren (2005) examined the factor structure of the Structured Interview for Disorders of Extreme Stress (SIDES), an interview designed to assess the symptoms of Disorders of Extreme Stress Not Otherwise Specified (DESNOS), and determined that Western-derived theoretical concepts underlying DESNOS were not representative across cultures. This result was attributed to significant cultural differences in response to questions about suicide, amnesia, attributions of events to external causes, understandings of guilt and shame, different standards for social desirability, and even conceptualization of time.

   Cross-cultural differences in factor structures and response to measurement suggest that conclusions about the endorsement of PTSD symptoms should be made with caution. Trauma-specific distress may take many forms based on the culture. Taking a qualitative ethnographic approach, Pedersen, Tremblay, Errázuriz, and Gamarra (2008) found that Quechua speakers, who were disproportionally affected by violence in the 1980s and 1990s between Peruvian government and Shining Path forces, described their reactions to PTE exposure in terms of *llaki* (head, stomach, and body pains) and *piensamientuwan* (worrying memories), as well as collective emotional distress and helplessness termed *nakary*. These symptoms mirror those of PTSD, and the collectivist and somatic elements of these symptom descriptions highlight the importance of cultural frames for understanding and treating Quechua speakers. Cambodian refugees in the United States also exhibit high levels of PTSD symptoms (e.g., Carlson & Rosser-Hogan, 1994; de Jong et al., 2001; Sack, Seeley,

& Clarke, 1997) with comorbid panic disorder (Hinton et al., 2000; Hinton, Pollack, Pich, Fama, & Balrlow, 2005), and sleep paralysis (e.g., Hinton, Pich, Chhean, Pollack, & McNally, 2005; Hinton, Pollack, Pich, Fama, & Barlow, 2005). However, these Western symptom classifications overlap significantly with the Cambodian experience of *khsaoy beh daung* (weak heart) (see Hinton, Hinton, Um, Chea, & Sak, 2002). *Khsaoy beh daung* is conceptualized as worry about results of future emotional shocks after the experience of a PTE resulting in weakness, "low body energy," loss of energy in the extremities, and heart palpitations. In this condition, if the person is emotionally surprised, shocked, or overwhelmed, it is thought to cause heart stoppages. This results in a pattern of monitoring interceptive cues, anxiety, and functional impairment similar to panic disorder, and a pattern of avoidance of trauma-related triggers similar to PTSD.

## ASSESSMENT, DIAGNOSIS, AND PROGNOSIS IN THE CONTEXT OF SPECIFIC TRAUMA

The assessment of a person who has experienced OPV shares many of the same elements as an intake with any other client (e.g., review of chief complaints, psychiatric history, family history, psychosocial functioning, current stressors) (Sadock & Sadock, 2003). However, there are a number of factors that a clinician must be aware of that are often associated with OPV that revolve around the nature of PTEs, associated secondary stressors, and culture.

### OPV-Related PTEs and Secondary Stressors

In terms of evaluating *DSM* Criterion A stressors, survivors of OPV typically experience a range of intense emotional, physical, and economic hardships. As previously noted, this may include witnessing or experiencing death, murder, life threats, kidnappings and other "disappearances," deliberate food shortages, and human rights violations (Ehntholt & Yule, 2006). Those who are displaced to refugee camps, after a likely arduous and dangerous escape, face conditions that can be primitive and overcrowded, with a lack of appropriate nutrition, water, sanitation, and access to health care. Secondary stressors for those who are resettled or seek asylum include marginalization and discrimination that, along with unresolved legal status, separation from family, and retelling experiences to immigration officials, can exacerbate depression and PTSD symptoms (e.g., Davis & Davis, 2006; Ekblad & Jaranson, 2004; Heptinstall, Sethna, & Taylor, 2004; Laban, Gernaat, Komproe, van der Tweel, & de Jong, 2005; Sack, Clarke, & Seeley, 1996; Silove, 1999; Socialstyrelsen, 1997).

## Culture

Given the potential influence of culture on meaning, experience, and response to PTEs, a broadminded stance is required in understanding individuals' experiences, interpersonal expectations of the assessor, and how they may differ from implicit ethnocentric biases of the assessor related to ideas of illness, health, and normality (Marsella, Friedman, & Spain, 1996). For example, in Western cultures, silence is often viewed as a means to avoid or repress a traumatic event or to demonstrate resistance to therapy. Yet, silence has been found to serve as a positive coping mechanism in Sudanese refugee rape survivors (Tankink & Richters, 2007). In this instance, the stance of the mental health-care provider would play a pivotal role in the successful assessment of the refugee.

Drozdek and Wilson (2004) suggest that assessors create an environment of mutual respect, trust, and safety with transparency, predictability, and calmness. This is especially important as the client may also have limited exposure to people from the assessor's home country or to mental health providers in general, have little idea of what to expect from the interaction, and may be distrustful of those in authoritative positions given previous persecution (Drozdek & Wilson, 2007; Tankink & Richters, 2007). For example, Hussain and Bhushan (2009) found that, compared to concerns about physical survival or deprivation uncertainty, Tibetan refugees' concerns about cultural survival were most strongly correlated with PTSD symptoms. This means that the assessor must obtain a rudimentary level of knowledge about the refugee's culture and ethnicity. However, it is important to note that there may be significant variability in individual response due to regional and familial differences, and individual differences in acculturation (Marsella et al., 1996). Finally, it is advisable to ask about native healing practices, as the person's expectations for assessment and subsequent intervention may be based on these frames.

The lack of extensive cultural knowledge may not necessarily undermine assessment as long as the provider allows the client to take the lead in interpreting cultural-related issues (Drozdek, 2007). This entails assessing how culture informs the individual's general understanding of the PTE and the distress and coping responses employed in response to the PTE (Wilson, 2007). As previously noted, culture provides the reference point for how individuals experience themselves and how they relate to others. For Western cultures, identity tends to revolve around individual experiences and focus on the individual self. More interdependent cultures use the larger group as a reference point, focusing on a communal self. For many, the important unit for defining self is the family, and any individual trauma experiences are not conceptualized apart from the experience of a family. In addition, many cultures prohibit the sharing of troubles outside the family, which may necessitate including family members in the assessment process more directly. Thus, familial expectations can greatly impact the individual's response, recovery, and decision to seek treatment after psychological trauma (Kastrup & Arcel, 2004).

It is also likely that physical symptoms will be presented as a primary concern. Although somatic complaints can be cultural idioms of distress, medical problems are common among survivors of OPV, including high rates of diabetes and hypertension, as well as secondary to physical harm endured as a consequence of OPV (Kinzie, 2007). Thus, medical consults are critical and may also assist in building credibility with the client (Kinzie, Wilson, Friedman, & Lindy, 2001). However, diagnosis of a physical disorder does not preclude the possibility of physical symptoms being exacerbated by psychological distress.

In terms of assessing for culture-specific responses to trauma or comorbidities, Appendix I of the current *DSM*, entitled "Outline for Cultural Formulation and Glossary of Culture-Bound Syndromes," serves as a useful guide in identifying culturally relevant factors (APA, 2000). These factors include societal influences on the client's self-concept, the cultural identity of the client, cultural explanations for the illness, and cultural influences on levels of functioning and psychosocial environment (APA, 2000). Draguns (1986) outlines domains that can be influenced by cultural norms that can impact a client's experience of trauma, including (1) stressors, (2) experience, (3) response, (4) explanation, (5) residues (i.e., awareness and comfort with their psychological responses), (6) coping, (7) help seeking, and (8) outcome. In order to understand the cultural context of the refugee's individual experiences, symptom expression, and related behaviors, Kleinman (1977) suggests that clinicians ask what the person thinks the illness does, how the illness works, how severe the illness is, what the course of the illness is likely to be, and what types of treatment should be employed. In working with adolescent and child refugees, important questions to answer revolve around how their relationships have changed with caretakers prior to, during, and after their flight, and what might account for those changes (Adam & van Essen, 2004). For families, important questions to answer revolve around the differences in family responsibilities between homeland and exile, the current state of legal residency, changes or instability in residence within the country of exile, and the family's involvement in crimes of war (Adam & van Essen, 2004).

Another challenge of any multicultural assessment is language. It is important to clarify the client's preferred language, especially if an interpreter is needed and available (Aroche & Coello, 2004). The use of interpreters does not immediately result in culturally appropriate, sensitive, and relevant care (Weine, 2001). It is important to consider the issues of privacy and ethnicity, political party, dialect, and gender in selecting an interpreter (Ehntholt & Yule, 2006), as well as the facility of the interpreter in the nuances of psychological language (McFarlane, 2004). Clinicians are directed to a number of good resources for working with interpreters in psychotherapy (see Bot & Wadensjö, 2004; d'Ardenne, Ruaro, Cestari, Fakhioury, & Priebe, 2007;

Farooq, Fear, & Oyebode, 1997; Faust & Drickey, 1986; Raval & Smith, 2003; Schulz, Huber, & Resick, 2006, Tribe & Ravel, 2003).

## Assessment Instruments

In addition to the psychosocial interview, structured or semistructured clinical interviews, such as the Clinician Administered PTSD Scale (Blake et al., 1996), have been used with refugee populations (e.g., Hinton, Pich, Chhean, Safren, & Pollack, 2006; Malekzai et al., 1996). Other structured interviews include the Structured Clinical Interview for *DSM-III-R* (Spitzer, Williams, & Gibbon, 1992), Allodi Trauma Scale (Allodi, 1985), the Composite International Diagnostic Interview (Kessler et al., 1998), and the Levonn Cartoon-based Interview for Assessing Children's Distress Symptoms (Richters, Martinez, & Valla, 1990). Although these assessment instruments are considered to be psychometrically sound and are in frequent use, the cultural validity of these standardized measures of posttrauma reactions and symptomatology has not been clearly established (see de Jong et al.'s, 2005, validation trial of the SIDEs reviewed above). Self-report assessment measures are also often utilized but are limited in that many standard self-report PTSD measures are not available in a range of native languages and have not been validated in regard to the relevant social norms or the range of experiences found in survivors of OPV (de Jong & Van Ommeren, 2002). Hollifield et al. (2002) conducted a review of instruments used to measure trauma and health status in refugees and found only four instruments that were well described in the literature. These four instruments are the Harvard Trauma Questionnaire (Mollica, Caspi-Yavin, Bollini, & Truong, 1992), the Resettlement Stressor Scale (Clarke, Sack, & Goff, 1993), the War Trauma Scale (Clarke et al., 1993), and the Post Migration Living Difficulties Scale (Silove, Steel, McGorry, & Mohan, 1998). As Hollifield et al.'s (2002) review reveals, the majority of instruments used to assess refugee trauma and health status should be used with caution. Guidelines for adapting standardized instruments for across cultures are available (e.g., de Jong & Van Ommeren, 2002; Van Ommeren et al., 1999).

# PREVENTION AND TREATMENT

## Prevention

Prevention of war, persecution, terrorism, and genocide is a political issue. Prevention of secondary stressors for those exposed to OPV involves addressing significant legal and logistical barriers to seeking asylum; provision of adequate shelter, food, health care, sanitation, financial resources, and economic opportunity; addressing acculturation and discrimination concerns;

aiding with reuniting families; and providing safety. All of these possible prevention efforts are dependent on domestic and foreign policy of countries of origin as well as host countries. Given the complexities of nation-state relations and vested interests in established policies, change leading to reduction in secondary stressors for those exposed to OPV often involves the intervention of members of the international community and multinational organizations (see Silove et al., 2000). Implementing programs and services that help create stability, facilitate faster recovery, and reduce risk of further psychological distress requires distribution of often limited resources, significant contributions from developed nations, and exercising limitations on the sovereign rights of nations.

## Treatment

For victims of OPV, treatment planning and implementation entail a few unique elements. For example, it is particularly important to be sensitive to extratherapy events that may impact treatment. Media reports on political violence at home, negative coverage of immigration policies in their host country, and interviews with immigration officials can trigger distress, negatively influence attributions about safety and security in the host country, impact an individual's sense of acculturation, marginalization, and belonging in the host country, as well as impact the individual's feelings about health care and ongoing psychotherapy (Aroche & Coello, 2004; Kinzie, 2007). This is particularly important as it is likely that deficits in instrumental and social resources may be key presenting complaints. Referrals may be needed to help gain access to medical treatment, housing, employment programs, language classes, and information about legal status. Directed assistance in accessing resources can greatly impact the refugee's ability to access services, sense of stability, and willingness to participate in the therapeutic relationship.

### Psychosocial Interventions

Choosing appropriate interventions can be difficult. Most of the literature on psychosocial treatments for OPV populations is based on case studies (Nicholl & Thompson, 2004). However, there are a handful of controlled studies that suggest that cognitive behavioral therapy approaches can be effective in reducing PTSD symptoms in torture survivors (Basoglu, 1998), adult refugees (Hinton, Hofmann, Pollack, & Otto, 2009; Paunovic & Ost, 2001), and adolescent refugees (e.g., Onyut et al., 2005). Complicating this is the need to balance a patient's beliefs in traditional healing while incorporating best practices (Wilson, 2007). Some have reported that incorporation of traditional healing practices typically does no harm to the client and can facilitate the client's recovery (e.g., Bracken et al., 1995), while others have reported that these healing practices impede recovery (e.g., Boehnlein & Kinzie, 1992).

In terms of specific interventions, cognitive therapy has been found to be effective in reducing PTSD symptoms in civilians in Northern Ireland (Duffy, Gillespie, & Clark, 2007) and in reducing PTSD and somatoform symptoms in Bosnian refugees when combined with emotional regulation skills training (Kruse, Joksimovic, Cavka, Wöller, & Schmitz, 2009). Paunovic and Öst (2001) compared cognitive therapy and prolonged exposure therapy in a sample of mixed-nationality refugees living in Sweden. Both therapies were found to be effective in reducing PTSD symptoms (see also case studies by Basoglu & Aker, 1996; Basoglu, Ekblad, Bäärnheilm, & Livanou, 2004; Schulz, Marovic-Johnson, & Huber, 2006; and Schwarz-Langer et al., 2006; examining the effects of prolonged exposure therapy). Otto et al. (2003) combined prolonged exposure with cognitive restructuring and a selective serotonin reuptake inhibitor and found that the combination of medication and exposure therapy with cognitive restructuring was more effective than medication alone in a sample of Cambodian refugees. In a multiple baseline, case series study of a treatment protocol designed to address comorbid PTSD and panic disorder in Cambodian refugees, researchers found that a combination of relaxation, interceptive exposure, imaginal exposure, and cognitive restructuring framed within Cambodian and Buddhist norms was successful in reducing panic attacks and flashbacks (Hinton, Pich, Chhean, Safren, & Pollack, 2006).

Other exposure-based therapies have also received limited empirical support to date. Eye Movement Desensitization and Reprocessing has been found to be effective with refugee children in two studies (e.g., Oras, Ezpeleta, & Ahmad, 2004; Weine, Kulenovic, Pavkovic, & Gibbons, 1998). Cognitive Processing Therapy, which combines elements of cognitive restructuring and written exposure, has shown initial efficacy in treating refugees from Bosnia and Afghanistan (Schulz, Resick, Huber, & Griffin, 2006). Especially promising is Narrative Exposure Therapy (NET). NET entails creating a detailed, narrative biography of the individual, with a particular focus on reliving the events until habituation occurs. The goal is to process memories of the events and integrate those memories into individuals' autobiography. NET has been found to reduce PTSD and depression symptoms in a group of African refugee children (Onyut et al., 2005), in Sri Lankan refugees (Catani et al., 2009), in a mixed nationality sample of refugees (Neuner, Schauer, Klaschik, Karunakara, & Elbert, 2004; Nuener et al., 2009), and in political detainees over the age of 60 (Bichescu, Neuner, Schauer, & Elbert, 2007). When administered by trained lay counselors, the combination of NET and general supportive therapy was also effective in reducing PTSD symptoms in adult Rwandan and Somalian refugees living in a refugee settlement (Neuner et al., 2008).

Basoglu (1998) proposed that for torture victims, prolonged exposure should be provided in a stepped model similar to that proposed by Grey and Young (2008) for refugees and by Courtois (see Chapter 7 of this book) for complex PTSD and retraumatization. This stepped model entails relationship building, establishment of trust, and psychoeducation in stage 1, moving into active, symptom focusing intervention in stage 2, and social reintegration in stage 3. Schwarz-Langer and colleagues (2006) suggest a similar four-step model that includes addressing safety and security concerns in and out of the consulting room, promoting self-control through addressing medical issues and relaxation training, using cognitive and exposure techniques to address symptoms of PTSD, depression, and grief, and finally, social integration.

Group therapy has also been found to be effective in treating posttraumatic distress in refugees (e.g., Bolton et al., 2003, 2007; Drozdek, 1997; Ehntholt, Smith, & Yule, 2005). Some have advocated that group treatments are best for refugees who have broadly had similar experiences (e.g., Yule, 2000). It has also been suggested that group interventions may be appropriate for more interdependent cultures (Ekblad & Jaranson, 2004) or for cultures where discussion of traumas is taboo. It is possible that these group interventions would need to be structured as social events, emphasizing social interactions while providing psychoeducation on acculturation and mental illness (Kinzie, Boehnlein, Sack, & Danieli, 1998). Again, there is limited research to guide these types of decisions. If group approaches are used, it is important to negotiate these activities with local leaders in order to facilitate mutual respect and maintain credibility as a provider in the refugee community (Shah, 2007).

## Psychopharmacology

Psychopharmacological intervention for OPV has been an increasing topic of research. Kinzie and Leung (1989) found a combination of Clonidine and Imipramine improved depression symptoms in a sample of Cambodian refugees who suffered from chronic PTSD and major depression. Boynton, Bentley, Strachan, Barbato, and Raskind (2009) found preliminary support for the use of Prazosin in reducing trauma-related nightmares and overall levels of PTSD within a sample of severely traumatized refugee patients. Smajkic et al. (2001) found that although PTSD diagnostic criteria were still met, Sertraline and Paroxetine produced statistically significant improvement in PTSD, depression symptoms, and overall functioning in a sample of Bosnian refugees (see also Schwarz-Langer, Deighton, Jerg-Bretzke, Weisker, & Traue, 2006, for summary of comprehensive psychopharmacological treatment with persons from the former Yugoslavia).

Although some have found success with psychopharmacology, others have questioned its usefulness in multicultural settings given that biological differences in ethnic groups may affect the metabolism of some drugs (e.g., DeMartino, Mollica, & Wilk, 1995; Lin, Poland, & Nakasaki, 1993). In addition, other aspects of a culture, including diet and use of traditional healing drugs, can impact drug response (e.g., Branch, Salih, & Homeida, 1978). Moreover, cultural barriers may limit effectiveness. Kinzie and

Friedman (2004) stress that the success of pharmacological treatments with refugees may be limited by noninvolvement of families in treatment planning, unfamiliarity with standard prescription regimens and medication, lack of health insurance, and limited income. Kinzie and colleagues provide specific guidelines to help facilitate successful use of psychopharmological treatment in OPV populations, including (1) using medicine early in treatment as it can provide rapid relief, (2) provision of hope, (3) keeping medication plans simple, and (4) preparing the client for the possibility of long-term treatment, as PTSD and severe depression in refugees are often long lasting and require a long course of treatment (Kinzie, 2007; Kinzie & Friedman, 2004).

## PSYCHOLOGICAL AND PHYSICAL COMORBIDITIES

There is considerable variation in primary presentation and comorbidity across cultures. In general, these tend to fall into the broad categories of comorbid depression, anxiety, and somatization disorders. As noted above, de Jong, Komproe, and Van Ommeren (2003), assessing lifetime *DSM-IV* mood anxiety, somatoform or PTSD disorders in Algeria, Cambodia, Ethiopia, and Palestine, found that PTSD symptoms were most prevalent in Algeria, Ethiopia, and Palestine. In Cambodia, other anxiety disorders were more prevalent. In terms of comorbidity, mood disorders ranged from 23% in Algeria, 13% in Cambodia and Palestine, to 5% in Ethiopia. Somatoform disorders were most prevalent in Islamic countries. Similarly, Laban et al. (2005) found similar levels of somatoform disorders (9.2%) among Iraqi refugees living in the Netherlands, in whom levels of PTSD (36.7%), anxiety (22.4%), and depression (34.7%) were also high. However, high rates of somatization are not limited to Islamic cultures. Hinton and colleagues (2006), working with Cambodian refugees in the United States, suggest that anxiety disorders in this population tend to be related to somatization that manifests as anxiety rather than as a somatoform disorder (see discussions of *khsaoy beh daung* above and also *hwa-byung* in Korean populations below), a pattern also seen in Senegalese survivors of OPV (Tang & Fox, 2001). In general, comorbid anxiety symptoms are high across cultures after exposure to PTEs, which includes simple phobias, generalized anxiety disorder, agoraphobia, and social phobia as well as high levels of comorbid depression in Latin American, Balkan, Cambodian, Afghan, Iraqi, Tamil, Tibetan, and Bhutanese samples, among others (for example, Crescenzi et al., 2002; Eisenman, Gelberg, Liu, & Shapiro, 2003; Hashemian et al., 2006; Marshall, Schell, Elliott, Berthold, Chun, 2005; Michultka, Blanchard, & Kalous, 1998; Miller et al., 2002; Sabin, Cardozo, Nackerud, Kaiser, & Varese, 2003; Salama, Spiegel, Van Dyke, Phelps, & Wilkinson, 2000; Scholte et al., 2004; Silove et al., 1998; Van Ommeren et al., 2001).

In addition to differential patterns of comorbidities of *DSM*-defined disorders, there may be comorbid culture-bound symptoms or variations of symptoms. For example, in Korea, *hwa-byung* is proposed to be a culturally bound response that includes anxiety and depression, fear of impending death, dysphoria, insomnia, feelings of helplessness, resentfulness, and guilt. This culture-bound response is highly comorbid with Major Depression and Somatization Disorder (Park, Kim, Schwartz-Barcott, & Kim, 2002; Roberts, Han, & Weed, 2006). It is thought to occur when an individual's expression of emotions in response to adversity would undermine social harmony. *Dhat*, the preoccupation with semen loss, fatigue, weakness, stomach pains, anxiety and depression, is a culturally bound response manifested by individuals living in India and nearby countries in response to stress (Ranjith & Mohan, 2006).

Physical comorbidities and increased mortality are also high as a result of OPV (Murray, King, Lopez, Tomijima, & Krug, 2002), especially among survivors of torture (e.g., Tol et al., 2007). Functional difficulties, quality of life impediments, and disability are common across conflicts and cultures (e.g., Cardazo et al., 2000; Eisenman et al., 2003; Mollica et al., 1999; Toscani et al., 2007). For survivors of torture, chronic pain is a common issue that can exacerbate PTSD symptoms (Carlsson, Olsen, Mortensen, & Kastrup, 2006; Olsen et al., 2007; Thomsen, Eriksen, & Smidt-Nielsen, 2000). Injury or dismemberment can be a direct result of OPV-related violence or disease but can also occur as a result of damage to infrastructure or refugee camp conditions that impede access to basic needs (e.g., adequate nutrition, clean water, sanitation, and heath care; Salama et al., 2008; Toscani et al., 2007; Willis & Levy, 2000). Increased incidence of tuberculosis, measles, hepatitis B, malaria, cancer, AIDS, and other sexually transmitted diseases are all associated with conflict areas (Ghobarah, Huth, & Russett, 2004; Pedersen, 2002)

## SPECIAL ISSUES

In the preceding sections of this chapter we have given a broad overview of the many different PTEs associated with different types of political violence and the political and cultural issues that may influence assessment, diagnosis, and treatment of OPV-related PTSD in what is necessarily a multinational, multicultural population. Another important issue is the role of individual nation-states in creating immigration and asylum policies that can be a source for retraumatization and exacerbation of existing symptoms for individuals (e.g., Silove, Steel, & Watters, 2000) as a result of a general tightening of these policies in developed nations since September 11, 2001 (see Steel, Mares, Newman, Blick, & Dudley, 2004). Given the importance of legal status, immigration processes, and humanitarian assistance by host countries in affecting overall mental health status, working with refugees and those seeking asylum requires a working understanding of the complicated, confusing, stressful, and oftentimes dehumanizing legal processes that can require reliving aspects of their exposure and flight from OPV, impacting a refugee's sense of security, safety, and belonging.

## CONCLUSION

Research into the consequences of OPV against civilians is complicated by the many manifestations of violence found in the many different political and cultural contexts in which such violence occurs. To provide a common ground to conceptualize traumatization and retraumatization across cultures and across OPV-related stressors, we sketched out a preliminary diathesis-stress framework that focuses on changes in the agentic and relational aspects of the self, framed by the cultural milieu, as critical factors in PTSD development. However, much of the work summarized in this chapter is limited in scope, this limitation in the scope of the work being a function of the practical limitations imposed on research by the very nature of OPV and perhaps of the long periods of relative stability and security that characterize life in most developed nations. Either way, researchers with access to stable funding and institutional support have conducted very little systematic research in this area, despite the continuing experience of OPV in the world at large. In developed countries, the experience of OPV is most often limited to military personnel. Concordantly, significantly more resources have been invested in the prevention and treatment of OPV-related mental health difficulties in active-duty service members and Veterans. Providing care for war Veterans is a matter of social justice. We suggest that the obligations of citizens and researchers in developed nations do not end with the care of military service members. Providing care for civilian populations affected by use of military force or affected by foreign policies that support regimes that engage in domestic terrorism is also a matter of social justice. Mental health professionals, in their roles as citizens, researchers, and care providers, are charged with advocating for policies that reduce harm to civilian populations, reduce the potential for retraumatization in refugees and asylum seekers, and increase efforts aimed at assessing and treating people who are in need of care as a result of OPV.

## REFERENCES

Adam, H., & van Essen, J. (2004). In-between: Adolescent refugees in exile. In J. P. Wilson & B. Drožðek (Eds.), *Broken spirits: The treatment of traumatized asylum seekers, refugees, war and torture victims.* (pp. 520–546). New York: Brunner-Routledge.

Ager, A. (1993). *Mental Health Issues In Refugee Populations: A Review.* Cambridge, MA: Harvard Center for the Study of Culture and Medicine.

Ahern, J., Galea, S., Fernandez, W. G., Koci, B., Waldman, R., & Vlahov, D. (2004). Gender, social support, and posttraumatic stress in postwar Kosovo. *The Journal of Nervous and Mental Disease, 192*, 762.

Allden, K., Poole, C., Chantavanich, S., Ohmar, K., Aung, N. N., & Mollica, R. F. (1996). Burmese political dissidents in Thailand: Trauma and survival among young adults in exile. *American Journal of Public Health, 86*, 1561–1569.

Allodi, F. (1985). Physical and psychiatric effects of torture: Canadian study. In E. Stover & E. O. Nightingale (Eds.), *The breaking of bodies and minds: Torture, psychiatric abuses and the health professions* (pp. 66–78). New York: Freeman.

American Psychiatric Association. (2000). *Diagnostic and statistical manual of mental disorders (DSM-IV-TR)* (4th ed.). Washington, DC: Author.

Aroche, J., & Coello, M. J. (2004). Ethnocultural considerations in the treatment of refugees and asylum seekers. In J. P. Wilson & B. Drožđek (Eds.), *Broken spirits: The treatment of traumatized asylum seekers, refugees, war and torture victims.* (pp. 53–80). New York: Brunner-Routledge.

Bachar, E., Canetti, L., Bonne, O., Kaplan De-Nour, A., & Shalev, A. Y. (1997). Psychological well-being and ratings of psychiatric symptoms in Israeli bereaved adolescents: Differential effect of war vs. accident related bereavement. *Journal of Nervous and Mental Diseases, 185*, 402–406.

Başoğlu, M. (1998). Behavioral and cognitive treatment of survivors of torture. In J. M. Jaranson & M. Pokin (Eds.), *Caring for victims of torture* (pp. 131). Washington, DC: American Psychiatric Press.

Başoğlu, M., & Aker, T. (1996) Cognitive-behavioural treatment of torture survivors: A case study. *Torture, 6*, 61–65.

Başoğlu, M., Ekblad, S., Bäärnhielm, S., & Livanou, M. (2004) Cognitive-behavioral treatment of tortured asylum seekers: A case study. *Journal of Anxiety Disorders, 18*, 357–369.

Başoğlu, M., Livanou, M., Crnobarić, C., Frančišković, T., Suljić, E., ... Vranešić, M. (2005). Psychiatric and cognitive effects of war in former Yugoslavia: Association of lack of redress for trauma and posttraumatic stress reactions. *JAMA, 294*, 580.

Başoğlu, M., Mineka, S., Paker, M., Aker, T., Livanou, M., & Gök, S. (1997). Psychological preparedness for trauma as a protective factor in survivors of torture. *Psychological Medicine: A Journal of Research in Psychiatry and the Allied Sciences, 27*, 1421–1433.

Başoğlu, M., Paker, M., Özmen, E., Tasdemir, Ö., & Sahin, D. (1994). Factors related to long-term traumatic stress responses in survivors of torture in Turkey. *JAMA, 272*, 357–363.

Benight, C. C., & Bandura, A. (2004). Social cognitive theory of posttraumatic recovery: The role of perceived self-effcacy. *Behaviour Research and Therapy, 42*, 1129–1148.

Benight, C. C., Freyaldenhoven, R. W., Hughes, J., Ruiz, J. M., Zoschke, T. A., & Lovallo, W. R. (2000). Coping self-efficacy and psychological distress following the Oklahoma City bombing. *Journal of Applied Social Psychology, 30*(7), 1331–1344.

Bichescu, D., Neuner, F., Schauer, M., & Elbert, T. (2007). Narrative exposure therapy for political imprisonment-related chronic posttraumatic stress disorder and depression. *Behaviour Research and Therapy, 45*, 2212–2220.

Blake, D., Weathers, F., Nagy, L., Kaloupek, D., Klauminzer, G., Charney, D., & Keane, T. (1996). *Clinician-administered PTSD scale (CAPS).* Boston: National Center for PTSD, Boston VA Medical Center.

Boehnlein, J. K., & Kinzie, J. D. (1992). DSM diagnosis of posttraumatic stress disorder and cultural sensitivity: A response. *Journal of Nervous and Mental Disease, 180*, 597.

Bolton, P., Bass, J., Betancourt, T., Speelman, L., Onyango, G., Clougherty, K. F., ... Verdeli, H. (2007). Interventions for depression symptoms among adolescent survivors of war and displacement in Northern Uganda: A randomized controlled trial. *JAMA, 298*, 519.

Bolton, P., Bass, J., Neugebauer, R., Verdeli, H., Clougherty, K. F., Wickramaratne, P., ... Weissman, M. (2003). Group interpersonal psychotherapy for depression in rural Uganda: A randomized controlled trial. *JAMA, 289*, 3117.

Bonanno, G. A. (2009). *The other side of sadness*. New York: Basic Books.

Bot, H., & Wadensjö, C. (2004). The presence of a third party: A dialogical view on interpreter-assisted treatment. In J. P. Wilson, & B. Drožđek (Eds.), *Broken spirits: The treatment of traumatized asylum seekers, refugees, war and torture victims*. (pp. 355–378). New York: Brunner-Routledge.

Boynton, L., Bentley, J., Strachan, E., Barbato, A., & Raskind, M. (2009). Preliminary findings concerning the use of prazosin for the treatment of posttraumatic nightmares in a refugee population. *Journal of Psychiatric Practice, 15*, 454–459.

Bracken, P. J., Giller, J. E., & Summerfield, D. (1995). Psychological responses to war and atrocity: The limitations of current concepts. *Social Science & Medicine, 40*, 1073–1082.

Branch, R. A., Salih, S. Y., & Homeida, M. (1978). Racial differences in drug metabolizing ability: A study with antipyrine in the Sudan. *Clinical Pharmacology and Therapeutics, 24*, 283–286.

Breslau, N., Chilcoat, H. D., Kessler, R. C., & Davis, G. C. (1999). Previous exposure to trauma and PTSD effects of subsequent trauma: Results from the Detroit Area Survey of Trauma. *The American Journal of Psychiatry, 156*, 902–907.

Brewin, C. R., Andrews, B., & Valentine, J. D. (2000). Meta-analysis of risk factors for posttraumatic stress disorder in trauma-exposed adults. *Journal of Consulting and Clinical Psychology, 68*, 748–766.

Brewin, C. R., & Holmes, E. A. (2003). Psychological theories of posttraumatic stress disorder. *Clinical Psychology Review, 23*, 339–376.

Brown, G., & Rafaeli, E. (2007). Components of self-complexity as buffers for depressed mood. *Journal of Cognitive Psychotherapy, 21*, 310–333.

Cardozo, B. L., Vergara, A., Agani, F., & Gotway, C. A. (2000). Mental health, social functioning, and attitudes of Kosovar Albanians following the war in Kosovo. *JAMA, 284*, 569–577.

Carlson, E. B., & Rosser-Hogan, R. (1994). Cross-cultural response to trauma: A study of traumatic experiences and posttraumatic symptoms in Cambodian refugees. *Journal of Traumatic Stress, 7*, 43–58.

Carlsson, J. M., Olsen, D. R., Mortensen, E. L., & Kastrup, M. (2006). Mental health and health-related quality of life: A 10-year follow-up of tortured refugees. *Journal of Nervous and Mental Disorders, 194*, 725–731.

Catani, C., Kohiladevy, M., Ruf, M., Schauer, E., Elbert, T., & Neuner, F. (2009). Treating children traumatized by war and tsunami: A comparison between exposure therapy and meditation-relaxation in North-East Sri Lanka. *BMC Psychiatry, 9*, 22.

Chen, S., Boucher, H. C., & Tapias, M. P. (2006). The relational self revealed: Integrative conceptualization and implications for interpersonal life. *Psychological Bulletin, 132*, 151–179.

Chentsova-Dutton, Y. (2010, January 28). *Interdependence of Evolutionary and Cultural Influences on Emotions.* Presented at the Emotion Preconference of the 2010 Society for Personality and Social Psychology Annual Meeting Las Vegas, NV.

Cheung, P. (1994). Posttraumatic stress disorder among Cambodian refugees in New Zealand. *International Journal of Social Psychiatry, 40,* 17–26.

Clarke, G., Sack, W. H., & Goff, B. (1993). Three forms of stress in Cambodian adolescent refugees. *Journal of Abnormal Child Psychology, 21,* 65–77.

Cohen, M., & Eid, J. (2007). The effect of constant threat of terror on Israeli Jewish and Arab adolescents. *Anxiety, Stress & Coping: An International Journal, 20,* 47–60.

Conway, M. A. (2005). Memory and the self. *Journal of Memory and Language, 53,* 594–628.

Conway, M. A., Wang, Q., Hanyu, K., & Haque, S. (2005). A cross-cultural investigation of autobiographical memory: On the universality and cultural variation of the reminiscence bump. *Journal of Cross-Cultural Psychology, 36,* 739–749.

Crescenzi, A., Ketzer, E., Van Ommeren, M., Phuntsok, K., Komproe, I., & de Jong, J. T. V. M. (2002). Effect of political imprisonment and trauma history on recent Tibetan refugees in India. *Journal of Traumatic Stress, 15,* 369–375.

Cross, S. E., Gore, J. S., & Morris, M. L. (2003). The relational-interdependent self-construal, self-concept consistency, and well-being. *Journal of Personality and Social Psychology, 85,* 933–944.

d'Ardenne, P., Ruaro, L., Cestari, L., Fakhioury, W., & Priebe, S. (2007). Does interpreter-mediated CBT with traumatised refugee people work? A comparison of patient outcomes in East London. *Behavioural & Cognitive Psychotherapy, 35,* 293–301.

Dalgleish, T. (2004). Cognitive approaches to posttraumatic stress disorder: The evolution of multirepresentational theorizing. *Psychological Bulletin, 130*(2), 228–260.

Davis, R. M., & Davis, H. (2006). PTSD symptom changes in refugees: PTSD symptom changes after immigration: A preliminary follow-up study in refugees. *Torture, 16*(1), 10–19.

de Jong, J., & Van Ommeren, M. (2002). Toward a culture-informed epidemiology: Combining qualitative and quantitative research in transcultural contexts. *Transcultural Psychiatry, 39,* 422.

de Jong, J. T. V. M., Komproe, I. H., & Van Ommeren, M. (2003). Common mental disorders in postconflict settings. *The Lancet, 361,* 2128–2130.

de Jong, J. T. V. M., Komproe, I. H., Spinazzola, J., van der Kolk, B. A., & Van Ommeren, M. H. (2005). DESNOS in three postconflict settings: Assessing cross-cultural construct equivalence. *Journal of Traumatic Stress, 18,* 13–21.

de Jong, J. T. V. M., Komproe, I. H., Van Ommeren, M., El Masri, M., Araya, M., Khaled, N., … Somasundaram, D. (2001). Lifetime events and posttraumatic stress disorder in 4 postconflict settings. *JAMA, 286,* 555.

DeMartino, R., Mollica, R. F., & Wilk, V. (1995). Monoamine oxidase inhibitors in post-traumatic stress disorder: Promise and problems in Indochinese survivors of trauma. *Journal of Nervous and Mental Disease, 183,* 510–515.

Draguns, J. G. (1986). Culture and psychopathology: What is known about their relationship? *Australian Journal of Psychology, 38,* 329.

Draguns, J. G. (1996). Humanly universal and culturally distinctive. In P. B. Pedersen, J. G. Draguns, W. J. Lonner, & J. E. Trimble (Eds.), *Counseling across cultures* (4th ed., pp. 1–20). Thousand Oaks, CA: Sage.

Drozdek, B. (1997). Follow-up study of concentration camp survivors from Bosnia-Herzegovina: Three years later. *The Journal of nervous and mental disease, 185,* 690.

Drozdek, B. (2007). The rebirth of contextual thinking in psychotraumatology. In B. Drozdek & J. P. Wilson (Eds.), *Voices of trauma: Treating psychological trauma across cultures* (pp. 1–26). New York: Springer.

Drozdek, B., & Wilson, J. P. (2007). *Voices of trauma: Treating psychological trauma across cultures*. New York: Springer.

Duffy, M., Gillespie, K., & Clark, D. M. (2007). Post-traumatic stress disorder in the context of terrorism and other civil conflict in northern Ireland: Randomised controlled trial. *British Medical Journal, 334*, 1147.

Dunmore, E., Clark, D. M., & Ehlers, A. (1999). Cognitive factors involved in the onset and maintenance of posttraumatic stress disorder (PTSD) after physical or sexual assault. *Behaviour Research and Therapy, 37*, 809–829.

Ehlers, A., Maercker, A., & Boos, A. (2000). Posttraumatic stress disorder following political imprisonment: The role of mental defeat, alienation, and perceived permanent change. *Journal of Abnormal Psychology, 109*, 45–55.

Ehntholt, K. A., Smith, P. A., & Yule, W. (2005). School-based cognitive-behavioural therapy group intervention for refugee children who have experienced war-related trauma. *Clinical Child Psychology and Psychiatry, 10*(2), 235.

Ehntholt, K. A., & Yule, W. (2006). Practitioner review: Assessment and treatment of refugee children and adolescents who have experienced war-related trauma. *Journal of Child Psychology and Psychiatry, 47*, 1197–1210.

Eisenman, D. P., Gelberg, L., Liu, H., & Shapiro, M. F. (2003). Mental health and health-related quality of life among adult Latino primary care patients living in the United States with previous exposure to political violence. *JAMA, 290*, 627–634.

Ekblad, S., & Jaranson, J. M. (2004). Psychosocial rehabilitation. In J. P. Wilson & B. Drozdek (Eds.), *Broken spirits: The treatment of traumatized asylum seekers, refugees, war and torture victims.* (pp. 609–636). New York: Brunner-Routledge.

English, T., & Chen, S. (2007). Culture and self-concept stability: Consistency across and within contexts among Asian Americans and European Americans. *Journal of Personality and Social Psychology, 93*, 478–490.

Eytan, A., Gex-Fabry, M., Toscani, L., Deroo, L., Loutan, L., & Bovier, P. A. (2004). Determinants of postconflict symptoms in Albanian Kosovars. *The Journal of Nervous and Mental Disease, 192*, 664–671.

Farooq, S., Fear, C., & Oyebode, F. (1997). An investigation of the adequacy of psychiatric interviews conducted through an interpreter. *Psychiatric Bulletin, 21*, 209–213.

Faust, S., & Drickey, R. (1986). Working with interpreters. *Journal of Family Practice, 22*, 131–138.

Foa, E. B., & Rothbaum, B. O. (1998). *Treating the trauma of rape: Cognitive-behavioral therapy for PTSD.* New York: Guilford Press.

Follette, V. M., Polusny, M. A., Bechtle, A. E., & Naugle, A. E. (1996). Cumulative trauma: The impact of child sexual abuse, adult sexual assault, and spouse abuse. *Journal of Traumatic Stress, 9*, 25–35.

Ghobarah, H. A., Huth, P., & Russett, B. (2004). The post-war public health effects of civil conflict. *Social Science & Medicine, 59*, 869–884.

Grey, N., & Young, K. (2008). Cognitive behaviour therapy with refugees and asylum seekers experiencing traumatic stress symptoms. *Behavioural and Cognitive Psychotherapy, 36*, 3–19.

Hashemian, F., Khoshnood, K., Desai, M. M., Falahati, F., Kasl, S., & Southwick, S. (2006). Anxiety, depression, and posttraumatic stress in Iranian survivors of chemical warfare. *JAMA, 296*, 560–566.

Heptinstall, E., Sethna, V., & Taylor, E. (2004). PTSD and depression in refugee children. *European Child & Adolescent Psychiatry, 13*, 373–380.

Hinton, D., Ba, P., Peou, S., & Um, K. (2000). Panic disorder among Cambodian refugees attending a psychiatric clinic: Prevalence and subtypes. *General Hospital Psychiatry, 22*, 437–444.

Hinton, D., Hinton, S., Um, K., Chea, A., & Sak, S. (2002). The Khmer "Weak Heart" syndrome: Fear of death from palpitations. *Transcultural Psychiatry, 39*(3), 323–344.

Hinton, D. E., Hofmann, S. G., Pollack, M. H., & Otto, M. W. (2009). Mechanisms of efficacy of CBT for Cambodian refugees with PTSD: Improvement in emotion regulation and orthostatic blood pressure response. *CNS Neuroscience & Therapeutics, 15*, 255–263.

Hinton, D. E., Pich, V., Chhean, D., Pollack, M. H., & McNally, R. J. (2005). Sleep paralysis among Cambodian refugees: Association with PTSD diagnosis and severity. *Depression and Anxiety, 22*, 47–51.

Hinton, D. E., Pich, V., Chhean, D., Safren, S. A., & Pollack, M. H. (2006). Somatic-focused therapy for traumatized refugees: Treating posttraumatic stress disorder and comorbid neck-focused panic attacks among Cambodian refugees. *Psychotherapy: Theory, Research, Practice, Training, 43*, 491–505.

Hinton, D. E., Pollack, M. H., Pich, V., Fama, J. M., & Barlow, D. H. (2005). Orthostatically induced panic attacks among Cambodian refugees: Flashbacks, catastrophic cognitions, and associated psychopathology. *Cognitive and Behavioral Practice, 12*, 301–311.

Hobfoll, S. E. (2002). Social and psychological resources and adaptation. *Review of General Psychology, 6*, 307–324.

Hobfoll, S. E., Lomranz, J., Eyal, N., Bridges, A., & Tzemach, M. (1989). Pulse of a nation: Depressive mood reactions of Israelis to the Israel–Lebanon War. *Journal of Personality and Social Psychology, 56*, 1002–1012.

Hollifield, M., Warner, T. D., Lian, N., Krakow, B., Jenkins, J. H., Kesler, J., … Westermeyer, J. (2002). Measuring trauma and health status in refugees: A critical review. *JAMA, 288*(5), 611–621.

Hondius, A. J. K., van Willigen, L. H. M., Kleijn, W. C., & van der Ploeg, H. M. (2000). Health problems among Latin-American and Middle-Eastern refugees in the Netherlands: Relations with violence exposure and ongoing sociopsychological strain. *Journal of Traumatic Stress, 13*, 619–634.

Hussain, D., & Bhushan, B. (2009). Development and validation of the Refugee Trauma Experience Inventory. *Psychological Trauma: Theory, Research, Practice, and Policy, 1*, 107–117.

Jobson, L. (2009). Drawing current posttraumatic stress disorder models into the cultural sphere: The development of the "threat to the conceptual self" model. *Clinical Psychology Review, 29*(4), 368–381.

Jobson, L., & O'Kearney, R. (2008). Cultural differences in personal identity in post-traumatic stress disorder. *British Journal of Clinical Psychology, 47*, 95–109.

Johnson, H., & Thompson, A. (2008). The development and maintenance of post-traumatic stress disorder (PTSD) in civilian adult survivors of war trauma and torture: A review. *Clinical Psychology Review, 28*, 36–47.

Johnson, K., Asher, J., Rosborough, S., Raja, A., Panjabi, R., Beadling, C., & Lawry, L. (2008). Association of combatant status and sexual violence with health and mental health outcomes in postconflict Liberia. *JAMA, 300*, 676–690.

Kaniasty, K., & Norris, F. H. (2004). Social support in the aftermath of disasters, catas-
trophes, and acts of terrorism: Altruistic, overwhelmed, uncertain, antagonistic, and
patriotic communities. In R. Ursano, A. Norwood, & C. Fullerton (Eds.), *Bioterrorism:
Psychological and public health interventions* (pp. 200–229). Cambridge: Cambridge
University Press.

Kastrup, M., & Arcel, L. (2004). Gender specific treatment. In J. P. Wilson & B. Drozdek
(Eds.), *Broken spirits: The treatment of traumatized asylum seekers, refugees, war
and torture victims* (pp. 547–571). New York: Brunner-Routledge.

Kessler, R. C., Wittchen, H. -U., Abelson, J. M., McGonagle, K. A., Schwarz, N., Kendler,
K. S., ... Zhao, S. (1998). Methodological studies of the Composite International
Diagnostic Interview (CIDI) in the US National Comorbidity Survey. *International
Journal of Methods in Psychiatric Research, 7*, 33–55.

Kinzie, J. D. (2007). Combined psychosocial and pharmacological treatment of traumatized refugees. In J. P. Wilson & C. S. -K. Tang (Eds.), *Cross-cultural assessment of
psychological trauma and PTSD* (pp. 359–370). New York: Springer.

Kinzie, J. D., Boehnlein, J. K., Riley, C., & Sparr, L. (2002). The effects of September 11
on traumatized refugees: Reactivation of posttraumatic stress disorder. *Journal of
Nervous and Mental Disease, 190*, 437–441.

Kinzie, J. D., Boehnlein, J., Sack, W. H., & Danieli, Y. (1998). The effects of massive trauma
on Cambodian parents and children. In *International handbook of multigenerational
legacies of trauma* (pp. 211–224). New York: Plenum Press.

Kinzie, J. D., & Friedman, M. J. (2004). Psychopharmacology for refugee and asylum-seeker
patients. In J. P. Wilson & B. Drozdek (Eds.), *Broken spirits: The treatment of
traumatized asylum seekers, refugees, war and torture victims* (pp. 579–600). New
York: Brunner-Routledge.

Kinzie, J. D., & Leung, P. (1989). Clonidine in Cambodian patients with posttraumatic
stress disorder. *Journal of Nervous and Mental Disease, 177*, 546–550.

Kinzie, J. D., Wilson, J. P., Friedman, M. J., & Lindy, J. D. (2001). Cross-cultural treatment
of PTSD. In N. Zador, J. P. Wilson, M. J. Friedman, & J. D. Lundy (Eds.), *Treating
psychological trauma and PTSD* (pp. 255–277). New York: Guilford.

Kleinman, A. M. (1977). Depression, somatization and the new cross-cultural psychiatry.
*Social Science & Medicine, 11*, 3–10.

Kozaric-Kovacic, D., Folnegovic-Smalc, V., Skrinjaric, J., Szajnberg, N. M., & Marusic,
A. (1995). Rape, torture, and traumatization of Bosnian and Croatian women:
Psychological sequelae. *American Journal of Orthopsychiatry, 65*, 428–433.

Kruse, J., Joksimovic, L., Cavka, M., Wöller, W., & Schmitz, N. (2009). Effects of trauma-
focused psychotherapy upon war refugees. *Journal of Traumatic Stress, 22*, 585–592.

Laban, C. J., Gernaat, H., Komproe, I. H., van der Tweel, I., & de Jong, J. (2005).
Postmigration living problems and common psychiatric disorders in Iraqi asylum
seekers in the Netherlands. *Journal of Nervous and Mental Disease, 193*, 825–832.

Laipson, E. (2009, March 31). The Iraqi refugee crisis in regional context: Testimony to the
Senate Foreign Relations Committee Subcommittee on the Middle East and South Asia.
Available at http://foreign.senate.gov/testimony/2009/LaipsonTestimony090331pp.pdf.
Accessed March 10, 2010.

Leary, M. R., Tambor, E. S., Terdal, S. K., & Downs, D. L. (1995). Self-esteem as an
interpersonal monitor: The sociometer hypothesis. *Journal of Personality and Social
Psychology, 68*, 518–530.

Levav, I. (1989). Second thoughts on the lethal aftermath of a loss. *Omega 2*, 81–90.

Lin, K. M., Poland, R. E., & Nakasaki, G. (1993). *Psychopharmacology and psychobiology
of ethnicity*. Washington, DC: American Psychiatric Press.

Lomranz, J., Hobfoll, S. E., Johnson, R., Eyal, N., & Zemach, M. (1994). A nation's response to attack: Israelis' depressive reactions to the Gulf War. *Journal of Traumatic Stress, 7*, 59–73.

MacDonald, G., & Leary, M. R. (2005). Why does social exclusion hurt? The relationship between social and physical pain. *Psychological Bulletin, 131*, 202–223.

Malekzai, A., Niazi, J. M., Paige, S. R., Hendricks, S. E., Fitzpatrick, D., Leuschen, M. P., & Milliment, C. R. (1996). Modification of CAPS-1 for diagnosis of PTSD in Afghan refugees. *Journal of Traumatic Stress, 9*, 891–893.

Markus, H., & Kitayama, S. (1991). Culture and the self: Implications for cognition, emotion, and motivation. *Psychological Review, 98*, 224–253.

Marsella, A. J., Friedman, M. J., & Spain, E. H. (1996). Ethnocultural aspects of PTSD: An overview of issues and research directions. In A. J. Marsella, M. J. Friedman, E. T. Gerrity, & R. M. Scurfield (Eds.), *Ethnocultural aspects of posttraumatic stress disorder: Issues, research, and clinical applications.* (pp. 105–130). Washington, DC: American Psychiatric Association.

Marshall, G. N. (2004). Posttraumatic stress disorder symptom checklist: Factor structure and English–Spanish measurement invariance. *Journal of Traumatic Stress, 17*, 223–230.

Marshall, G. N., Schell, T. L., Elliott, M. N., Berthold, S. M., & Chun, C. A. (2005). Mental health of Cambodian refugees 2 decades after resettlement in the United States. *JAMA, 294*, 571–579.

McCauley, J., Kern, D. E., Kolodner, K., Dill, L., & Schroeder, A. F. (1997). Clinical characteristics of women with a history of childhood abuse: Unhealed wounds. *JAMA, 277*, 1362–1368.

McFarlane, A. C. (2004). Assessing PTSD and comorbidity: Issues in differential diagnosis. In J. P. Wilson & B. Drozdek (Eds.), *Broken spirits: The treatment of traumatized asylum seekers, refugees, war and torture victims.* (pp. 81–104). New York: Brunner-Routledge.

McKeever, V. M., & Huff, M. E. (2003). A diathesis-stress model of posttraumatic stress disorder: Ecological, biological, and residual stress pathways. *Review of General Psychology, 7*, 237–250.

Mesquita, B., & Walker, R. (2003). Cultural differences in emotions: A context for interpreting emotional experiences. *Behaviour Research and Therapy, 41*, 777–793.

Michultka, D., Blanchard, E. B., & Kalous, T. (1998). Responses to civilian war experiences: Predictors of psychological functioning and coping. *Journal of Traumatic Stress, 11*, 571–577.

Miller, K. E., Weine, S. M., Ramic, A., Brkic, N., Bjedic, Z. D., Smajkic, A., … Worthington, G. (2002). The relative contribution of war experiences and exile-related stressors to levels of psychological distress among Bosnian refugees. *Journal of Traumatic Stress, 15*, 377–387.

Mollica, R., Lavelle, J., & Khoun, F. (1986). Khmer widows at highest risk. Paper presented at the Cambodian Mental Health Conference, "A Day to Explore Issues and Alternative Approaches to Care," New York.

Mollica, R. F., Caspi-Yavin, Y., Bollini, P., & Truong, T. (1992). The Harvard Trauma Questionnaire: Validating a cross-cultural instrument for measuring torture, trauma, and posttraumatic stress disorder in Indochinese refugees. *Journal of Nervous and Mental Disease, 180*, 111–116.

Mollica, R. F., McInnes, K., Pham, T., Smith Fawzi, M. C., Murphy, E., & Lin, L. (1998). The dose-effect relationships between torture and psychiatric symptoms in Vietnamese ex-political detainees and a comparison group. *Journal of Nervous and Mental Disease, 186*, 543–555.

Mollica, R. F., McInnes, K., Poole, C., & Tor, S. (1998). Dose-effect relationships of trauma to symptoms of depression and post-traumatic stress disorder among Cambodian survivors of mass violence. *British Journal of Psychiatry, 173*, 482–488.

Mollica, R. F., McInnes, K., Sarajlic, N., Lavelle, J., Sarajlic, I., & Massagli, M. P. (1999). Disability associated with psychiatric comorbidity and health status in Bosnian refugees living in Croatia. *JAMA, 282*, 433–439.

Moos, R. H., & Holahan, C. J. (2003). Dispositional and contextual perspectives on coping: Toward an integrative framework. *Journal of Clinical Psychology, 59*, 1387–1403.

Muecke, M. A. (1992). New paradigms for refugee health problems. *Social Science & Medicine, 35*, 515–523.

Murray, C. J. L., King, G., Lopez, A. D., Tomijima, N., & Krug, E. G. (2002). Armed conflict as a public health problem. *British Medical Journal, 324*, 346–349.

Neuner, F., Kurrecj, S., Ruf, M., Odenwad, M., Elbert, T., & Schauer, M. (2009). Can asylum-seekers with posttraumatic stress disorder be successfully treated? A randomized controlled pilot study. *Cognitive Behaviour Therapy*, Published online October 8, 2009.

Neuner, F., Onyut, P. L., Ertl, V., Odenwald, M., Schauer, E., & Elbert, T. (2008). Treatment of posttraumatic stress disorder by trained lay counselors in an African refugee settlement: a randomized controlled trial. *Journal of Consulting and Clinical Psychology, 76*, 686–694.

Neuner, F., Schauer, M., Klaschik, C., Karunakara, U., & Elbert, T. (2004). A comparison of narrative exposure therapy, supportive counseling, and psychoeducation for treating posttraumatic stress disorder in an African refugee settlement. *Journal of Consulting and Clinical Psychology, 72*, 579–587.

Nicholl, C., & Thompson, A. (2004). The psychological treatment of Post Traumatic Stress Disorder (PTSD) in adult refugees: A review of the current state of psychological therapies. *Journal of Mental Health, 13*, 351–362.

Niiya, Y., Ellsworth, P. C., & Yamaguchi, S. (2006). Amae in Japan and the United States: An exploration of a "culturally unique" emotion. *Emotion, 6*, 279–295.

Norris, F. H., Friedman, M. J., Watson, P. J., Byrne, C. M., Diaz, E., & Kaniasty, K. (2002). 60,000 disaster victims speak: Part I. An empirical review of the empirical literature, 1981–2001. *Psychiatry: Interpersonal & Biological Processes, 65*, 207–239.

Norris, F. H., & Kaniasty, K. (1996). Received and perceived social support in times of stress: A test of the social support deterioration deterrence model. *Journal of Personality and Social Psychology, 71*, 498–511.

Norris, F. H., Perilla, J. L., & Murphy, A. D. (2001). Postdisaster stress in the United States and Mexico: A cross-cultural test of the multicriterion conceptual model of post-traumatic stress disorder. *Journal of Abnormal Psychology, 110*, 553–563.

Olsen, D. R., Montgomery, E., Bojholm, S., & Foldspang, A. (2007). Prevalence of pain in the head, back and feet in refugees previously exposed to torture: A ten-year follow-up study. *Disability Rehabilitation, 29*, 163–171.

Onyut, L. P., Neuner, F., Schauer, E., Ertl, V., Odenwald, M., Schauer, M., et al. (2005). Narrative Exposure Therapy as a treatment for child war survivors with posttraumatic stress disorder: Two case reports and a pilot study in an African refugee settlement. *BMC Psychiatry, 5*, 7.

Oras, R., Ezpeleta, S. C., & Ahmad, A. (2004). Treatment of traumatized refugee children with eye movement desensitization and reprocessing in a psychodynamic context. *Nordic Journal of Psychiatry, 58*, 199–203.

Otto, M. W., Hinton, D., Korbly, N. B., Chea, A., Ba, P., Gershuny, B. S., & Pollack, M. H. (2003). Treatment of pharmacotherapy-refractory posttraumatic stress disorder among Cambodian refugees: A pilot study of combination treatment with cognitive-behavior therapy vs sertraline alone. *Behaviour Research and Therapy, 41*, 1271–1276.

Ozer, E. J., Best, S. R., Lipsey, T. L., & Weiss, D. S. (2003). Predictors of posttraumatic stress disorder and symptoms in adults: A meta-analysis. *Psychological Bulletin, 129*, 52–73.

*Park, Y. J., Kim, H. S., Schwartz-Barcott, D., & Kim* J. W. (2002). The conceptual structure of Hwa-Byung in middle-aged Korean women. *Health Care for Women International, 23*, 389–397.

Pat-Horenczyk, R., Schiff, M., & Doppelt, O. (2006). Maintaining routine despite ongoing exposure to terrorism: A healthy strategy for adolescents? *Journal of Adolescent Health, 39*, 199–205.

Paunovic, N., & Ost, L. -G. (2001). Cognitive-behavior therapy vs exposure therapy in the treatment of PTSD in refugees. *Behaviour Research and Therapy, 39*, 1183–1197.

Pedersen, D. (2002). Political violence, ethnic conflict and contemporary wars: Broad implications for health and social well-being. *Social Science & Medicine, 55*, 175–190.

Pedersen, D., Tremblay, J., Errázuriz, C., & Gamarra, J. (2008). The sequelae of political violence: Assessing trauma, suffering and dislocation in the Peruvian highlands. *Social Science & Medicine, 67*, 205–217.

Pierce, T., & Lydon, J. (1998). Priming relational schemas: Effects of contextually activated and chronically accessible interpersonal expectations on responses to a stressful event. *Journal of Personality and Social Psychology, 75*, 1441–1448.

Porter, M. (2007). Global evidence for a biopsychosocial understanding of refugee adaptation. *Transcultural Psychiatry, 44*, 418–439.

Porter, M., & Haslam, N. (2001). Forced displacement in Yugoslavia: A meta-analysis of psychological consequences and their moderators. *Journal of Traumatic Stress, 14*, 817–834.

Porter, M., & Haslam, N. (2005). Predisplacement and postdisplacement factors associated with mental health of refugees and internally displaced persons: A meta-analysis. *JAMA, 294*, 602–612.

Ranjith, G., & Mohan, R. (2006). Dhat syndrome as a functional somatic syndrome: Developing a sociosomatic model. *Psychiatry, 69*, 142–150.

Rasmussen, A., Smith, H., & Keller, A. S. (2007). Factor structure of PTSD symptoms among west and central African refugees. *Journal of Traumatic Stress, 20*, 271–280.

Raval, H., & Smith, J. A. (2003). Therapists' experience of working with language interpreters. *International Journal of Mental Health, 32*, 6–31.

Rhee, E., Uleman, J. S., Lee, H. K., & Roman, R. J. (1995). Spontaneous self-descriptions and ethnic identities in individualistic and collectivistic cultures. *Journal of Personality and Social Psychology, 69*, 142–152.

Richters, J. E., Martinez, P., & Valla, J. P. (1990). *Levonn: A cartoon-based structured interview for assessing young children's distress symptoms.* Washington, DC: National Institute for Mental Health.

Roberts, M. E., Han, K. H., & Weed, N. C. (2006). Development of a scale to assess hwa-byung, a Korean culture bound syndrome, using the Korean MMPI-2. *Transcultural Psychiatry, 43,* 383–400.

Rubin, D. C., Berntsen, D., & Bohni, M. K. (2008). A memory-based model of post-traumatic stress disorder: Evaluating basic assumptions underlying the PTSD diagnosis. *Psychological Review, 115*(4), 985–1011.

Sabin, M., Cardozo, B. L., Nackerud, L., Kaiser, R., & Varese, L. (2003). Factors associated with poor mental health among Guatemalan refugees living in Mexico 20 years after civil conflict. *JAMA, 209*, 635–642.

Sack, W. H., Clarke, G. N., & Seeley, J. (1996). Multiple forms of stress in Cambodian adolescent refugees. *Child Development, 67*(1), 107–116.

Sack, W. H., Seeley, J. R., & Clarke, G. N. (1997). Does PTSD transcend cultural barriers? A study from the Khmer Adolescent refugee project. *Journal of the American Academy of Child & Adolescent Psychiatry, 36*, 49–54.

Sadock, B. J., & Sadock, V. A. (2003). *Synopsis of psychiatry.* Baltimore: Lippincott.

Salama, P., Spiegel, P., Van Dyke, M., Phelps, L., & Wilkinson, C. (2008). Mental health and nutritional status among the adult Serbian minority in Kosovo. *JAMA, 284*, 578–584.

Schmidt, M., Kravic, N., & Ehlert, U. (2008). Adjustment to trauma exposure in refugee, displaced, and non-displaced Bosnian women. *Archives of Women's Mental Health, 11*, 269–276.

Scholte, W. F., Olff, M., Ventevogel, P., de Vries, G., Jansveld, E., Lopes Cardozo, B., & Gotway Crawford, C. A. (2004). Mental health symptoms following war and repression in Eastern Afghanistan. *JAMA, 292*, 585–593.

Schulz, P. M., Huber, L. C., & Resick, P. A. (2006). Practical adaptations of cognitive processing therapy with Bosnian refugees: Implications for adapting practice to a multicultural clientele. *Cognitive and Behavioral Practice, 13*, 310–321.

Schulz, P. M., Resick, P. A., Huber, L. C., & Griffin, M. G. (2006). The effectiveness of cognitive processing therapy for PTSD with refugees in a community setting. *Cognitive and Behavioral Practice, 13*, 322–331.

Schumm, J. A., Stines, L. R., Hobfoll, S. E., & Jackson, A. P. (2005). The double-barreled burden of child abuse and current stressful circumstances on adult women: The kindling effect of early traumatic experience. *Journal of Traumatic Stress, 18,* 467–476.

Schwarz-Langer, G., Deighton, R. R., Jerg-Bretzke, L., Weisker, I., & Traue, H. C. (2006). Psychiatric treatment for extremely traumatized civil war refugees from former Yugoslavia. Possibilities and limitations of integrating psychotherapy and medication. *Torture, 16,* 69–80.

Shah, S. A. (2007). Ethnomedical best practices for international psychosocial efforts in disaster and trauma. In J. P. Wilson & C. S. Tang (Eds.), *Cross-cultural assessment of psychological trauma and PTSD* (pp. 51–64). New York: Springer.

Shalev, A. Y., & Freedman, S. (2005). PTSD following terrorist attacks: A prospective evaluation. *American Journal of Psychiatry, 162*, 1188–1191.

Shrestha, N. M., Sharma, B., Van Ommeren, M., Regmi, S., Makaju, R., Komproe, I., ... de Jong, J. T. V. M. (1998). Impact of torture on refugees displaced within the developing world: Symptomatology among Bhutanese refugees in Nepal. *JAMA, 280*, 443–448.

Silove, D. (1999). The psychosocial effects of torture, mass human rights violations, and refugee trauma: Toward an integrated conceptual framework. *Journal of Nervous and Mental Disease, 187*, 200–207.

Silove, D., Sinnerbrink, I., Field, A., Manicavasagar, V., & Steel, Z. (1997). Anxiety, depression and PTSD in asylum-seekers: Associations with pre-migration trauma and post-migration stressors. *British Journal of Psychiatry, 170*, 351–357.

Silove, D., Steel, Z., McGorry, P., & Mohan, P. (1998). Trauma exposure, postmigration stressors, and symptoms of anxiety, depression and post-traumatic stress in Tamil asylum-seekers: Comparison with refugees and immigrants. *Acta Psychiatrica Scandinavica, 97*, 175–181.

Silove, D., Steel, Z., & Watters, C. (2000). Policies of deterrence and the mental health of asylum seekers. *JAMA, 284*, 604–611.

Simich, L., Hamilton, H., & Baya, B. K. (2006). Mental distress, economic hardship and expectations of life in Canada among Sudanese newcomers. *Transcultural Psychiatry, 43*, 418–444.

Smajkic, A., Weine, S., Djuric-Bijedic, Z., Lewis, J., Pavkovic, I., & Boskailo, E. (2001). Sertraline, Paroxetine, and Venlafaxine in refugee posttraumatic stress disorder with depression symptoms. *Journal of Traumatic Stress, 14*, 445–452.

Socialstyrelsen—National Swedish Board of Health and Welfare. (1997). *Public Health Report 1997*. Stockholm.

Solomon, Z. (1995). The effect of prior stressful experience on coping with war trauma and captivity. *Psychological Medicine: A Journal of Research in Psychiatry and the Allied Sciences, 25*, 1289–1294.

Spitzer, R. L., Williams, J. B., & Gibbon, M. (1992). The Structured Clinical Interview for DSM-III-R (SCID): history, validation, and description. *Archives of General Psychiatry, 49*, 624–629.

Steel, Z., Chey, T., Silove, D., Marnane, C., Bryant, R. A., & van Ommeren, M. (2009). Association of torture and other potentially traumatic events with mental health outcomes among populations exposed to mass conflict and displacement: A systematic review and meta-analysis. *JAMA, 302*, 537–549.

Steel, Z., Mares, S., Newman, L., Blick, B., & Dudley, M. (2004). The politics of asylum and immigration detention: Advocacy, ethics, and the professional role of the therapist. In J. P. Wilson & B. Drožđek (Eds.), *Broken spirits: The treatment of traumatized asylum seekers, refugees, war and torture victims.* (pp. 659–687). New York: Brunner-Routledge.

Tang, S. S., & Fox, S. H. (2001). Traumatic experiences and the mental health of Senegalese refugees. *Journal of Nervous and Mental Disease, 189*, 507–512.

Tankink, M., & Richters, A. (2007). Giving voice to silence: Silence as coping strategy of refugee women from South Sudan who experienced sexual violence in the context of war. In B. Drozdek & J. P. Wilson (Eds.), *Voices of trauma: Treating psychological trauma across cultures* (pp. 191–210). New York: Springer.

Taylor, S. E., & Brown, J. D. (1988). Illusion and well-being: A social psychological perspective on mental health. *Psychological Bulletin, 103*, 193–210.

Thomsen, A. B., Eriksen, J., & Smidt-Nielsen, K. (2000). Chronic pain in torture survivors. *Forensic Science International, 108*, 155–163.

Tol, W. A., Komproe, I. H., Thapa, S. B., Jordans, M. J. D., Sharma, B. & de Jong, J. T. V. M. (2007). Disability associated with psychiatric symptoms among torture survivors in rural Nepal. *Journal of Nervous & Mental Disease, 195*, 463–469.

Toscani, L., DeRoo, L. A., Eytan, A., Gex-Fabry, M., Avramovski, V., Loutan, L., & Bovier, P. (2007). Health status of returnees to Kosovo: Do living conditions during asylum make a difference? *Public Health, 121*, 34–44.

Tribe, R., & Ravel, H. (2003). *Working with interpreters in mental health.* New York: Routledge.

United Nations High Commissioner for Refugees. (2009, June 16). 2008 Global trends: Refugees, asylum-seekers, returnees, internally displaced and stateless persons. Available at http://www.unhcr.org/4a375c426.html. Accessed March 3, 2010.

Van Ommeren, M., de Jong, J. T. V. M., Sharma, B., Komproe, I., Thapa, S., & Cardeña, E. (2001). Psychiatric disorders among tortured Bhutanese refugees in Nepal. *Archives of General Psychiatry, 8*, 475–482.

Van Ommeren, M., Sharma, B., Thapa, S., Makaju, R., Prasain, D., Bhattarai, R., et al. (1999). Preparing instruments for transcultural research: use of the translation monitoring form with Nepali-speaking Bhutanese refugees. *Transcultural Psychiatry, 36*, 285–301.

Walter, K. H., Horsey, K. J., Palmieri, P. A., & Hobfoll, S. E. (2010). The role of protective self-cognitions in the relationship between childhood trauma and later resource loss. *Journal of Traumatic Stress, 23,* 264–273.

Weine, S. (2001). From war zone to contact zone: Culture and refugee mental health services. *JAMA, 285,* 1214.

Weine, S. M., Kulenovic, A. D., Pavkovic, I., & Gibbons, R. (1998). Testimony psychotherapy in Bosnian refugees: A pilot study. *American Journal of Psychiatry, 155,* 1720–1726.

Willis, B. M., & Levy, B. S. (2000). Recognizing the public health impact of genocide. *JAMA, 284,* 612–614.

Wilson, J. P. (2007). The lens of culture: Theoretical and conceptual perspectives in the assessment of psychological trauma and PTSD. In J. P. Wilson & C. S. Tang (Eds.), *Cross-cultural assessment of psychological trauma and PTSD* (pp. 3–30). New York: Springer.

Wilson, J. P., & Drozdek, B. (2004). Uncovering: Trauma Focused Treatment Techniques with Asylum Seekers. In J.P Wilson & B. Drozdek (Eds.), *Broken spirits: The treatment of traumatized asylum seekers, refugees, war and torture victims,* (pp. 243–276). New York: Brunner-Routledge.

Yule, W. (2000). Emanuel Miller Lecture: From pogroms to "ethnic cleansing": Meeting the needs of war affected children. *Journal of Child Psychology and Psychiatry and Allied Disciplines, 41,* 695–702.

Chapter 12

# Revictimization
## *Experiences Related to Child, Adolescent, and Adult Sexual Trauma*

*Devika Ghimire and Victoria M. Follette*

Sexual revictimization, defined as the experience of repeated occurrences of sexual victimization among those with a preexisting history of sexual trauma (Follette & Vijay, 2008), is serious and pervasive problem. Although there is a significant range in the victimization rates reported in the literature, many studies suggest that one out of every eight women experiences sexual victimization at some point in her life. Moreover, 67% of women with histories of sexual victimization report one or more additional experiences of sexual victimization (Cloitre, Cohen, & Koenen, 2006; Cloitre & Rosenberg, 2006). Identification of the mechanisms associated with increased risk for revictimization is crucial to the development of effective prevention and treatment protocols. Additionally, the psychological sequelae associated with revictimization may be somewhat different than what is observed in individuals with one episode of abuse.

There is a large literature on the long-term correlates of child sexual abuse (CSA), with research suggesting that survivors report a range of psychological difficulties, including posttraumatic stress disorder (PTSD), depression, anxiety, and substance use disorders (Beitchman, Zucker, Hood, Da Costa, & Akman, 1991; Jumper, 1995; Paolucci, Genuis, & Violato, 2001; Polusny & Follette, 1995). Sexual victimization and rape during adolescence and adulthood can also result in similar types of psychological difficulties (e.g., Boudreaux, Kilpatrick, Resnick, Best, & Saunders, 1998; Breslau et al., 1998; Kessler, Sonnega, Bromet, Hughes, & Nelson, 1995). Deficits in interpersonal functioning, emotional regulation, and risk recognition have been observed in survivors of CSA, adolescent sexual abuse, and adult rape; however, the findings in these areas are less conclusive. Additionally, it is important to note that data on multiple victimization experiences suggest that the effects of trauma can be cumulative such that individuals with revictimization histories have increased rates of trauma symptoms (Casey & Nurius, 2005; Cloitre, Scarvalone, & Difede, 1997; Follette, Polusny, Bechtle, & Naugle, 1996; Kilpatrick, Acierno, Resnick, Saunders, & Best, 1997; Kimerling, Alvarez, Pavao, Kaminski, & Baumrind, 2007; Messman-Moore, Long, & Siegfried, 2000).

In this chapter, we will highlight the problem of sexual revictimization in adolescents and adults with preexisting histories of child, adolescent, and adult sexual trauma. Specific data pertaining to prevalence rates and a review of some relevant clinical variables implicated as risk factors and clinical distress in this population will be presented. In doing so, the problem of revictimization will be addressed using a contextual behavioral approach, with a particular focus on the process of experiential avoidance (Follette, Palm, & Rasmussen-Hall, 2004). Consistent with our behavioral theory, we will discuss the use of a functional approach to classifying behaviors that are associated with revictimization. Subsequently, we will address a number of applied issues including assessment, prevention, and treatment. Finally, the chapter will present recommendations for future directions related to the problem of sexual revictimization.

## A CONTEXTUAL APPROACH TO UNDERSTANDING REVICTIMIZATION

The process of classification, as a central task of science, is important to consider when examining the factors associated with any analysis of human behavior. The primary classification system in the field of psychopathology is based on syndromes, with a focus on signs and symptoms in order to identify disorders with a known etiology, course, and response to treatment (Foulds, 1971; Hayes, Wilson, Gifford, Follette, & Strosahl, 1996). With regard to traumatic stress and sexual revictimization, PTSD is considered one of the most prevalent problems observed. The identification of PTSD as a risk factor for sexual revictimization should not be discounted, but focusing on PTSD exclusively can be limiting for a number of reasons. The problems associated with revictimization extend beyond PTSD; high rates of comorbidity have been shown to exist between PTSD and other psychiatric conditions, with as much as 80% of those diagnosed with PTSD found to have comorbid conditions

(Breslau et al., 1991). Additionally, the literature examining individual differences indicates diversity in the trajectories of posttrauma symptoms over time (Bonanno, 2004, 2005). Some individuals demonstrate chronically elevated levels of PTSD for years after the event; however, many individuals will quickly return to baseline levels of functioning. Another group of individuals will be slower in the return to baseline after a period of acute symptomology. Finally, there is a pattern of a delayed emergence of symptoms, in which individuals experience subthreshold PTSD that gradually worsens over time (Bonanno, Rennicke, & Dekel, 2005; Buckley, Blanchard, & Hickling, 1996). Thus, the literature indicates that even with what would be considered a homogeneous group of individuals based on a diagnostic category, pathways differ in terms of symptom onset and recovery.

Classification is important, for purposes of both research and clinical effectiveness; however, it can be argued that the problems with syndromal classification necessitate alternative methods of categorizing outcomes related to revictimization. In classifying problematic behaviors, Hayes et al. (1996) suggest a functional approach to classification in which behaviors or sets of behaviors are organized by the functional processes hypothesized to generate and maintain them, rather than the topography. Notably, a functional classification approach is theoretically driven at least at the basic level and differs from the atheoretical goals of the syndromal system of classification. Experiential avoidance is one functional process that can be used to conceptualize the problems proposed as pathways to revictimization. Experiential avoidance is characterized by instances in which an individual is unwilling to experience or contact particular private experiences including bodily sensations, emotions, thoughts, memories, and behavioral tendencies (Acceptance and Commitment Therapy, ACT) (Hayes et al., 1996). Clinically, this is evidenced as attempts to avoid or escape private events in a psychologically inflexible manner, even in contexts that necessitate alternative strategies. Avoidance of internal experiences has been implicated in a variety of psychological disorders, including depression, anxiety, panic disorder, and borderline personality disorder (Hayes et al., 2004b). Experiential avoidance is also thought to play a central role in the psychological difficulties associated a history of abuse (Follette, Palm, & Rasmussen-Hall, 2004; Pistorello, Follette, & Hayes, 2000, Polusny & Follette, 1995).

Experiential avoidance is particularly helpful in facilitating the organization of potential outcomes of trauma understood diagnostically as complex posttraumatic stress disorder (CPTSD) (Follette, Iverson, & Ford, 2009). There is some suggestion that trauma that is chronic, repeated, and typically interpersonal in nature results in symptoms that go beyond what is traditionally labeled as PTSD. The constellation of symptoms associated with revictimization, which can include marked alteration in self-perception, attention and consciousness, affective regulation, and interpersonal disruptions, have been described as complex posttraumatic stress disorder (Courtois, 2008; Herman,

1992b). A basic premise often discussed in relation to complex PTSD is the idea that chronic abuse affects the normative developmental processes leading to marked alterations that are not captured by the traditional PTSD diagnosis. Even though the elaboration of complex PTSD has been controversial (Lewis & Grenyer, 2009), and represents yet another syndromal approach to the problem, the identification of this construct has had important implications in treatment development. We would suggest that the wide range of symptoms associated with multiple victimization experiences and related to CPTSD can be explained by the functional process of experiential avoidance. Moreover, experiential avoidance is particularly useful in facilitating the understanding of the risk for revictimization.

## PREVALENCE OF SEXUAL REVICTIMIZATION

In examining the prevalence data related to sexual revictimization, it is important to note that the rates reported have a considerable range across studies, and this has resulted in a number of controversies about the actual rate of sexual victimization in the population. Some of this variability can be accounted for by methodologies that have varied significantly across time and research groups. Additionally, the stigma associated with sexual victimization may well explain some reporting differences. Although the exact rates of each type of sexual victimization are not yet precisely documented, a review of the literature provides general indications of the prevalence of sexual victimization. Numerous studies conducted in the last 30 years indicate that approximately 25% of individuals experience sexual abuse during childhood (Briere & Elliott, 2003; Finkelhor, 1994; Pereda, Guilera, Forns, & Gomez-Benito, 2009). Rates of sexual revictimization within this subset have shown that women with CSA were six times more likely to be sexually victimized by a current intimate partner and 11 times more likely to be sexually victimized by a nonintimate partner, compared to those without a history of CSA (Desai, Arias, Thompson, & Basile, 2002). When considering rape as a form of sexual revictimization, Messman-Moore and Brown (2004) found that women with a history of CSA are twice as likely to experience rape compared to women without a history of CSA, after controlling for child physical and emotional abuse, and family functioning. High rates of revictimization are also supported by the findings of a meta-analysis, with 15% to 79% of women with a CSA history reporting they were raped as adults (Roodman & Clum, 2001). These authors reported an effect size of 0.59, suggesting a moderate relationship between CSA and sexual revictimization in adulthood. In discussing the discrepancy in the prevalence rates observed, they reported that the most significant finding concerned the variability in the definition of abuse, with greater effect sizes being observed with more restrictive definitions of abuse. Overall, these findings indicate a reliable relationship between CSA and sexual revictimization.

Sexual assault during adolescence and adulthood occurs at fairly high rate. Surveys conducted primarily with college women report that between 15% and 20% of the population has experienced rape during adolescence or adulthood (Kahn, Jackson, Kully, Badger, & Halvorsen, 2003; Littleton & Radecki Breitkopf, 2006; Schwartz & Leggett, 1999). In terms of revictimization in this population, prior rape history is a strong risk factor for subsequent sexual revictimization. Compared to women without a history of prior rape, those with such histories are at 2 to 4.5 times greater risk for experiencing future sexual assaults (Gidycz, Hanson, & Layman, 1995; Humphrey & White, 2000). Some data suggest that adolescent sexual victimization, even more than CSA, places a woman at greatest risk for revictimization as an adult (Gidycz, Coble, Lathman, & Layman, 1993; Humphrey & White, 2000; Rich, Gidycz, Warkentin, Loh, & Weiland, 2005). Thus, the data make it clear that early sexual assault increases a woman's risk for later sexual victimization. However, identifying psychological mediators and moderators of this phenomenon will provide information that can help to identify prevention and treatment strategies.

## SEXUAL REVICTIMIZATION IN MALES

The empirical data related to sexual victimization in men are limited in quality and quantity. CSA is a significant problem among males despite lower prevalence rates reported in males compared to females (Merrill, Thomsen, Gold, & Milner, 2001; Urquiza & Keating, 1990). Briere and Elliott (2003), in a national study including a random sample of 1,442 participants, found that 14.2% of males reported experiences in childhood that met criteria for CSA. A study examining the long-term impact of sexual abuse in 17 male and 59 female CSA survivors revealed that male participants reported poorer social adjustment compared to female participants (Seidner, Calhoun, & Kilpatrick, 1985). Cloitre, Tardiff, Marzuk, Leon, and Portera (2001) studied both revictimization and perpetration among men with child physical and sexual abuse histories. Compared to those without child abuse histories, those with child abuse histories were five times more likely to both experience victimization and perpetrate interpersonal violence. When revictimization was examined alone, rather than in combination with perpetration, rates among child abuse survivors were still two and a half times greater compared to nonabused males. In a nationally representative sample of both males and females, Desai, Arias, Thompson, and Basile (2002) conducted a large study to explore the relationship between childhood physical and sexual abuse and risk for revictimization in both men and women. In men, childhood victimization increased the risk for victimization in adulthood; however, this increased risk was not present in their intimate partner relationships. There was also increased risk for revictimization in women; however, this risk included increased risk from partners. These studies have provided some important data, but it is clear that there is a need for more research on men who have experienced victimization of all types.


# RISK FACTORS

## Posttraumatic Stress Disorder (PTSD)

PTSD has been established as the most common diagnostic reaction to child sexual abuse (Rowan, Foy, Rodriguez, & Ryan, 1994; Saunders, Villeponteaux, Lipovsky, Kilpatrick, & Veronen, 1992). Not all survivors of CSA will develop PTSD, but it appears that trauma symptoms are one factor that may predispose individuals to vulnerability for later victimization. Moreover, comparisons between revictimized survivors and their nonrevictimized counterparts demonstrate higher rates of PTSD in the revictimized group (Arata, 1999a, 1999b; Koverola, Proulx, Battle, & Hanna, 1996; Messman-Moore, Long, & Siegfried, 2000; Noll, Horowitz, Bonanno, Trickett, & Putnam, 2003; Wilson, Calhoun, & Bernat, 1999). For example, Arata (1999a, 1999b) found that in comparing women with no history of sexual victimization, adult sexual victimization only, and both CSA and adult sexual victimization, the women with both types of trauma demonstrated the greatest levels of PTSD (both current and lifetime diagnosis).

PTSD has been observed as a risk factor for revictimization in survivors of CSA, but the exact mechanism of this relationship is unclear. In a follow-up to her earlier study, Arata (2000) found that higher levels of posttraumatic symptoms mediated the relationship between CSA and revictimization. In a study of college students, Sandberg, Matorin, and Lynn (1999) found that posttraumatic symptomatology moderated but did not mediate the relationship between previous victimization (CSA or adolescent sexual victimization) and subsequent victimization over a period of 10 weeks. However, as the authors note in their discussion, 10 weeks is a rather limited follow period, and assessment of trauma history was limited. However, in other longitudinal studies, there is stronger evidence indicating that PTSD mediates the relationship between CSA and revictimization (Acierno, Resnick, Kilpatrick, Saunders, & Best, 1999; Arata, 2000; Messman-Moore, Brown, & Koelsch, 2005; Ullman, Nadjowski, & Filipas, 2009). In the National Women's Study (Acierno et al., 1999), in which 3,006 women, ages 18 to 34, were followed for a period of 2 years, prior victimization and PTSD both significantly increased the risk of experiencing a new rape. Results from that study also supported the meditational link between PTSD and sexual revictimization. Despite the limitations inherent in all studies that examine these phenomena, the evidence clearly suggests that PTSD symptomatology following CSA may serve as a risk factor for revictimization.

To better understand the relationship of PTSD and sexual revictimization, some researchers have separated the phenomenon of PTSD into its different symptom clusters. Risser, Hetzel-Riggin, Thomsen, and McCanne (2006) studied 1,449 college students and found that PTSD was a significant mediator of the relationship between CSA and adult sexual assault. However, when the three symptoms clusters defining PTSD (reexperiencing, avoidance, and hyperarousal) were examined individually, only the hyperarousal cluster of PTSD appeared to mediate the relationship between CSA and revictimization. The authors of this study suggested that experiencing high levels of arousal consistently, in a context where high arousal is not useful, can somewhat paradoxically impair one's ability to detect risk. In a related area of research, Ullman, Nadjowski, and Filipas (2009) conducted a longitudinal study of 555 participants over the course of 1 year and found CSA survivors were likely to have more symptoms of PTSD following adult sexual assault than those without a prior history of victimization. These authors reported that when testing re-experiencing, avoidance, arousal, and numbing in relation to revictimization, only numbing symptoms directly predicted revictimization. It is conceivable that numbing, while being considered a symptom of PTSD, may in fact represent a coping mechanism contributing to increased risk. Additional research in this area is required to determine how particular symptom clusters within PTSD may directly predict sexual revictimization.

Studies have also investigated the role of PTSD and sexual revictimization in the context of other behavioral variables. For example, in the study mentioned above, Ullman, Nadjowski, and Filipas (2009) found that the effects of certain clusters of PTSD (re-experiencing, avoidance, and hyperarousal) predicted problem drinking that then predicted later victimization. The authors considered their findings to be in support of the self-medication theory of drinking in trauma survivors. Messman-Moore, Brown, and Koelsch (2005) examined *self-dysfunction* that they described as referring to a variety of difficulties such as intrusive experiences, defensive avoidance, dissociation, impaired self-reference, dysfunctional sexual behavior, sexual concerns, and tension-reducing behavior. The authors specified that this symptom pattern, measured with the Trauma and Self scales of the Trauma Symptoms Inventory (TSI) (Briere, 1995), reflects a range of problems often associated with CPTSD. The results of this longitudinal study indicated that the effect of posttraumatic symptoms on sexual revictimization during the follow-up period was indirect and mediated by self-dysfunction. It should be noted that CSA was defined as abusive experiences prior to age 17 and thus included adolescent sexual victimization as well.

The research examining individuals with histories of adolescent or adult sexual victimization in relation to PTSD and sexual revictimization has a number of limitations. Some studies implicating PTSD as a risk factor in sexual revictimization (for example, Sandberg et al., 1999) have combined experiences of adolescent sexual victimization with CSA in the determination of initial trauma history. Moreover, many of these studies do not have comparison groups that would clarify the findings. Given the data, PTSD appears to be a significant and consistent predictor of sexual revictimization. At the same time, other mechanisms, possibly dysfunctional coping behaviors, seem to play an essential role in explaining the relationship between PTSD and revictimization.

## Alcohol Use

Data clearly suggest that a history of sexual victimization, in childhood or beyond, is associated with increased substance use and abuse in adolescence and adulthood (see, for review, Humphrey & White, 2000; Sartor, Agrawal, McCutcheon, Duncan, & Lynskey, 2008). Alcohol use, in turn, has been identified as a risk factor in sexual assaults, particularly in the case of college women (Abbey & McAuslan, 2004; Abbey et al., 2002; Testa, Livingston, VanZile-Tamsen, & Frone, 2003). Given these findings, the role of alcohol in sexual revictimization is worthy of additional attention. By conducting a retrospective survey of 1,887 women who were Navy recruits, Merrill and colleagues (1999) examined the effects of CSA and alcohol use on adult rape. Women who had experienced CSA were 4.8 times more likely to have experienced adult rape. However, the effects of alcohol use on adult rape appeared to be independent of the effects of the CSA. Messman-Moore and Long (2002) also found similar results in a sample of 300 community women studied retrospectively. Compared to those without CSA histories, CSA survivors were more likely to report rape, and coerced intercourse, and to meet criteria for substance use disorders. In this study, both CSA and substance-related disorders were predictive of adult sexual victimization, without any significant interactions between these risk factors.

In a study of 372 college women followed for 2 months, researchers found that sexual assault occurred at a fairly high rate (22.6%) during the study (Gidycz, Loh, Lobo, Rich, Lynn, & Pashdag, 2007). In women who were previously victimized, increase in risk for sexual revictimization was found to be associated with higher rates of alcohol use. In discussing their findings, the authors suggest that the relationship between victimization and alcohol use is complex. However, there is some evidence that alcohol may moderate between past victimization and later revictimization. McCauley, Calhoun, and Gidycz (2010) examined a sample of 228 college women reporting at least one experience of unwanted attempted or completed sexual assault in adolescence or adulthood. Prior levels of binge drinking predicted subsequent binge drinking which predicted alcohol-involved rape. It should be noted that this sample only included women with previous sexual assault, and findings are somewhat limited by the lack of a comparison group.

Research indicates a complex set of findings when PTSD is introduced into the relationship between CSA, alcohol use, and revictimization.

Messman-Moore, Ward, and Brown (2009) evaluated a sample of adult survivors of child abuse, which included physical or emotional abuse in addition to CSA. They found that posttraumatic stress symptoms predicted both substance use and rape, with substance use mediating the relationship between PTSD symptomatology and rape. These results are similar to those mentioned previously in the study by Ulman, Nadjoswki, and Filipas (2009). Messman-Moore, Brown, and Koelsch (2005) observed a similar pattern of relations, with alcohol use mediating the relationship between PTSD and revictimization in CSA survivors. Overall, longitudinal studies suggest the role of substance use as a problem that frequently occurs in response to trauma-related symptoms, particularly among those with histories of CSA.

Alcohol use may pose a risk for sexual revictimization for a number of reasons, and research conducted in laboratory settings provides some insight regarding this matter. Testa, VanZile-Tamsen, Livingston, and Buddie (2006) conducted two studies to examine the impact of alcohol consumption on vulnerability to sexual assault using a type of vignette methodology. In the first study, they recruited women from bars who were measured as having either a high or low breath alcohol level. Those with higher alcohol levels perceived less risk in the situation and were more passive in their responses. In a follow-up study, they conducted their research in the laboratory in order to provide more stringent controls. There were three groups in the study: a placebo control, no alcohol control, and the alcohol condition. The findings were similar to those in the first study; however, even after serious aggression, the women in the alcohol group were only likely to use polite resistance. Together, the studies provide clear evidence for alterations in risk perception related to alcohol exposure. In another line of research, incapacitation or unconsciousness as a result of substance use has been identified as a noteworthy problem in sexual victimization (Kilpatrick, Resnick, Ruggiero, Conoscenti, & McCauley, 2007). Abbey, McAuslan, and Ross (1998) found that when both men and women consumed alcohol, men were more likely to interpret friendly behaviors in women as an indication of sexual interest.

The research indicates associations between early victimization, alcohol use, and revictimization, but the specific nature of the relationship varies across studies. It is likely that differences in samples, assessment methods, and research design all contribute to the variable findings. Whether alcohol use is an independent risk factor for adult sexual victimization remains unclear. However, there is strong evidence that alcohol is frequently a factor in assault in adolescent and college samples. Misuse is related to initial victimization and revictimization experiences. Findings suggest that alcohol use may increase risk by decreasing the capability to recognize and resist risk, and may also increase the chances of being perceived as sexually interested. At even greater levels, alcohol may completely inhibit one's ability to verbally or physically resist sexual advances.

## Risky Sexual Behavior

The role of high-risk sexual behavior in relation to revictimization has also been explored. Even though the data provide some evidence for risky sex as a mediator of CSA and revictimization, the relation is multifaceted. In a retrospective study of college women, Van Bruggen, Runtz, and Kadlec (2006) found that sexual self-esteem, sexual concerns, and high-risk sexual behaviors partially mediated the relationship between child abuse (CSA and another forms of maltreatment) and sexual revictimization after the age of 14. Fargo (2009), in a cross-sectional sample composed primarily of African American women (88%), found a relationship between child sexual abuse and adolescent sexual victimization which was mediated by risk-taking behavior in adolescence. The author also reported that the relationship between child sexual abuse and risky sexual behavior was predicted by a number of factors, including problematic alcohol use and frequent use of alcohol before sexual activity. These retrospective studies indicate that risky sexual behaviors may partially explain the relation between prior victimization and subsequent sexual victimization.

In a longitudinal study by Fergusson, Horwood, and Lynskey (1997), the researchers followed over 500 women in New Zealand from birth to 18 years of age. Women with histories of CSA, especially CSA with intercourse, had significantly higher rates of sexual assault after the age of 16 than those without a history of CSA. Women with a history of CSA also had consensual sexual activity at an earlier age, higher rates of teenage pregnancy, more sexual partners, and higher rates of unprotected intercourse and sexually transmitted diseases. The authors reported that these variables, sometimes labeled as "risky sex," were involved in a causal chain that linked CSA to later sexual revictimization. The mechanism that would explain this relationship is unclear; however, researchers suggest that social and contextual variables may be related to the increased risk for all types of victimization.

In a study that examined related factors, Krahe, Scheinberger-Olwig, Waizenhofer, and Kolpin (1999) reported that women who reported CSA were more likely to report unwanted sexual experiences in adolescence. This study was conducted in Germany with 281 adolescent women. The authors suggested that survivors of CSA had significantly higher numbers of sexual partners, and this factor partially explained the increased risk for later sexual revictimization. In a large-scale study of adolescent health, Raghavan, Bogart, Elliott, Vestal, and Schuster (2004) followed 7,545 young women from 1995 to 1996. They conducted a complex multivariate analysis and found that alcohol and emotional distress both predicted revictimization. However, in the full model, only "risky sex," which was defined as engaging in early sexual relations and genital touching within a romantic relationship, was found to predict revictimization during the 1-year follow-up period. Testa, Hoffman, and Livingston (2010) reported higher levels of risky sexual behaviors, including number of sexual partners and casual sexual encounters, among college students who were sexually victimized during adolescence. High-risk behaviors in college students, which included alcohol use in addition to risky sexual behaviors, partially mediated the relationship between victimization in adolescence and revictimization in the first year of college.

Because both risky sex and alcohol use have been implicated as risk factors in revictimization, studying these variables together is particularly important. Schacht et al. (2010) examined alcohol intoxication and sexual abuse history as risk factors for sexual risk taking in a laboratory setting. Participants were randomly assigned to consume varied levels of alcoholic drinks, or nonalcoholic drinks, after which sexual arousal was induced by the use of brief erotic films. Participants read and responded to a written vignette, and risky sex was measured as the self-reported likelihood of engaging in unprotected sexual behaviors which were further subgrouped based on condom use, oral sex, genital contact, and unprotected intercourse. Women with CSA histories reported significantly lower likelihood of condom use but also reported less likelihood of unprotected intercourse, compared to women with adult sexual abuse (ASA) histories or women without sexual abuse (NSA) histories. Intoxicated women, compared to sober women, also reported greater likelihood of risky sex. Compared to intoxicated ASA and NSA women and sober CSA women, intoxicated CSA women reported greater likelihood of unprotected oral sex and less likelihood of condom use. This study suggests that the timing of abuse may play a role in revictimization, with alcohol use being particularly problematic for revictimization in women with CSA histories.

The research presented here indicates that a number of factors associated with sexual victimization in childhood or adolescence, including early onset sexual activity, increased sexual activity, and greater number of sexual partners, predicts revictimization. Although the very nature of these acts would likely increase the chances of encounters with perpetrators and of being revictimized, the underlying mechanism is less clear. In a longitudinal study of community women, they reported the use of sex to reduce negative affect (depression, anxiety), and this mediated the relationship between CSA and adolescent sexual assault (Orcutt, Cooper, & Garcia; 2005). Thus, it appears that early victimization may result in negative affect that would lead to a range of activities that would facilitate experiential avoidance. This avoidance combined with a lack of effective interpersonal skills may combine to create the increased risk for revictimization that has been observed across studies.

## Risk Recognition

One concern that has been related to the issue of risky sexual behavior and revictimization is deficiencies in risk recognition. Of course, the inability to recognize potential danger or risky situations can occur outside of the context of engaging in risky sexual behavior. Almost all the research in this area has utilized some form of a vignette methodology (Marx & Gross, 1995), in which participants are presented with an audiotape of a date rape. A gradual increase in risk is characteristic of the sexual advances in the vignettes as they progress from verbal appeals to coercion. Risk recognition is captured by measuring the response latency, or the length of time taken by participants to determine whether the perpetrator should stop from making further sexual advances.

Wilson, Calhoun, and Bernat (1999) conducted a study using the audio-taped date rape vignette methodology to compare the response latencies between nonvictimized women, women with a single incident of adolescent or adult victimization, women with multiple adolescent and adult victimization histories, and revictimized women with a history of CSA. Revictimized women, in comparison to single-incident victims or nonvictims, displayed significantly longer latencies for risk recognition. Women with a history of multiple victimizations waited until the situation was at the highest risk level before responding. Specifically, revictimized women waited until or after verbal threats by the perpetrator, and adamant refusals by the victim were displayed, to indicate that the perpetrator should refrain from making further sexual advances. It is plausible that revictimized women may not only take longer to recognize risk but may also take longer to respond effectively to that risk.

Marx, Calhoun, Wilson, and Meyerson (2001) conducted a longitudinal study following adolescent and adult women with histories of child sexual abuse for a period of 8 weeks. Women who experienced revictimization in the form of rape, compared to nonrevictimized women, displayed poorer risk recognition skills. It should be noted that these results did not generalize to revictimization including other forms of unwanted sexual activities. Using the same methodology, Soler-Baillo, Marx, and Sloan (2005) replicated previous findings indicating significantly longer response latencies among women with a history of sexual victimization (after the age of 14) compared to women without any history of sexual victimization. Additionally, there were physiological differences in responding. The authors suggest that differing responses to threat cues may interfere with the ability to effectively deal with threat situations. Taken together with the results showing longer latencies in identifying risk among survivors, the authors believe that recognition of risk during ambiguous interactions may be particularly critical to risk recognition. The study of risk recognition among survivors of sexual victimization and revictimization is still somewhat limited, in the number of studies and the methodology used. However, findings indicate the need for additional research in this area. Moreover, there is a need to study how alcohol use may intersect with risk recognition tasks.

## EXPERIENTIAL AVOIDANCE

Sexual revictimization is marked by the presence of topographically varied behaviors and seemingly complex symptom profiles, which may well be accounted for by the core psychological process of experiential avoidance. Experiential avoidance is described as an individual's unwillingness to experience negatively evaluated private experiences including thoughts, emotions, memories, and bodily reactions along with attempts to alter or avoid them (Hayes et al., 1996). More recently, the term has evolved to include psychological inflexibility which refers to the chronic use of experiential avoidance in response to psychological distress, even when doing so is destructive. Several studies have documented higher levels of experiential avoidance in survivors of CSA and ASA (Batten, Follette, & Aban, 2001; Marx & Sloan, 2002; Polusny, Rosenthal, Aban, & Follette, 2004; Rosenthal, Rasmussen-Hall, Palm, Batten, & Follette, 2005). PTSD, implicated as a major risk factor and outcome in revictimization, is known for symptoms of intrusion and arousal (*DSM-IV-TR*; American Psychiatric Association, 2000) which, among some survivors of trauma, are reported as a disturbance and an indication of "going crazy" (Shipherd, Beck, Hamblen, & Freeman, 2000). Survivors of repeated victimization may also experience a variety of aversive private experiences associated with the trauma, including thoughts (e.g., "I am a bad person") and emotions (e.g., fear, anger, shame) that they may then attempt to reduce, alleviate, or numb by the use of avoidance coping strategies (Follette, Iverson, & Ford, 2009). Avoidance coping strategies provide short-term relief, as experienced in the immediate reduction or suppression of distressing experiences, and are maintained by negative reinforcement (Hayes et al., 1996; Polusny & Follette, 1995). Generalized and chronic use of experiential avoidance, in contexts other than when it may have been adaptive in coping with the trauma, is believed to result in problems, including continuing distress (Polusny & Follette, 1995; Wagner & Linehan, 2006). Such maintenance of distress has been supported in a sample of undergraduate women, in which experiential avoidance mediated the relationship between CSA and psychological distress (Rosenthal et al., 2005).

Cognitive and emotional suppression, strategies to control and avoid thoughts and emotions, respectively, are forms of experiential avoidance that survivors may engage in to manage trauma-related distress. Experiential avoidance is shown to be highly correlated with the use of suppression (Hayes et al., 2004b). Suppression as a coping strategy may seem effective intuitively, but experimental research has proved otherwise. Research indicates that suppression of thoughts leads to a paradoxical increase in the thoughts being avoided, at least in the long term (Clark, Ball, & Pape, 1991; Wegner & Schneider, 2003; Wenzlaff & Wegner, 2000). Shipherd & Beck (1999) examined suppression of thoughts among survivors of sexual assault with and without PTSD. Participants with PTSD reported a rebound in the frequency of rape-related thoughts after deliberately suppressing their thoughts compared to participants without PTSD who did not experience such a rebound effect. Emotional suppression involving the avoidance of emotional experiencing is also known to be problematic, because it is associated with poor psychological health (John & Gross, 2004; Gross & John, 2003). Overall, the research on suppression indicates that its use as a coping strategy among trauma survivors may only facilitate the maintenance of trauma-related symptoms. The continued use of suppression to manage trauma-related distress, which continues to be maintained, could also place individuals at risk for revictimization. A recent study examined prior sexual victimization, negative mood states, *in vivo* suppression, and cognitive resource usage as predictors of poor risk recognition and less effective defensive actions when presented with sexual assault vignettes (Walsh, 2009). Although sexual victimization history, mood state, and their interaction did not impact risk recognition, *in vivo* emotional suppression and cognitive resource usage predicted delays in risk recognition.

In addition to cognitive and emotional suppression strategies, individuals may engage in overt behavioral avoidance strategies that could lead to risk for revictimization. Studies have shown that those suffering from PTSD may use alcohol to reduce PTSD symptoms (Epstein, Saunders, Kilpatrick, & Resnick, 1998). Coffey and colleagues (2002) conducted a study among participants with PTSD in which intrusive memories were found to increase cravings for alcohol and drugs compared to cues that were more neutral. Overall, it appears that maintenance of trauma symptoms may increase alcohol consumption, which may be used as a coping strategy to avoid painful experiences. Alcohol use to reduce tension or anxiety is consistent with the tension-reduction hypothesis that has received much attention historically and cross-culturally (see Young, Oei, & Knight, 2006). Risky sex, which has also been implicated in revictimization, can be conceptualized as a behavioral form of experiential avoidance. Results from one study have shown that the level of generalized experiential avoidance interacts with the extent of CSA history to predict high-risk sexual behavior (Batten et al., 2001). Briere and Elliott (1994) theorize that sexual arousal and positive sexual attention can offer temporary relief of trauma-related distress by providing experiences that are more pleasurable or incompatible with distress. It is possible that survivors' attitudes and behaviors related to sex may be indicators of avoidance of private experiences associated with sexual victimization, which may seem obvious in their interactions with potential perpetrators. At the same time, it seems likely that individuals at risk for revictimization may use engagement in sex in order to avoid other private experiences, thus placing them at risk. The use of varied forms of behaviors such as suppression, alcohol use, and risky sex, may not only share a common function of experiential avoidance but may also lead to common outcomes relevant to the risk for revictimization.

## PREVENTION

Prevention work that targets high-risk populations, including those with prior histories of victimization, is an important developing area of research.

A variety of prevention programs designed to reduce sexual assault risk have been implemented (Anderson & Whiston, 2005; Breitenbecher & Gidycz, 1998; Hanson & Gidycz, 1993; Rothman & Silverman, 2007). The majority of the early literature indicated that prevention programs aimed at reducing risk of sexual assaults suggests that while these programs are somewhat helpful for women with no prior history of victimization, there is less demonstrated success among those with prior histories of sexual victimization.

In an effort to gain a better understanding of the differences between revictimized and nonrevictimized groups, Yeater and O'Donohue (2002) evaluated responses of college women to an information-based sexual assault prevention. The researcher assessed differences in knowledge regarding rape myths and facts, risk factors and risk perception, and response strategies using a vignette method. Sexually revictimized women were not significantly different in time required for learning the material presented compared to those without any prior sexual victimization or those with single victimization experiences. Further analyses showed that women with a revictimization history, compared to nonvictimized women, demonstrated even greater knowledge and ability to discriminate risk in date rape situations. These results suggest that revictimized women display adequate knowledge and recognition of risk upon training, at least under laboratory conditions. It is possible that the lack of success of training programs with previously victimized individuals could be occurring because of the difficulties previously victimized women have in specifically applying or acting on the knowledge gained.

One promising prevention program for college students was developed by Marx, Calhoun, Wilson, and Meyerson (2001). In the two-session module, they emphasized factual knowledge and understanding of social forces fostering assaults while also teaching practical strategies for preventing unwanted sexual experiences and altering dating behaviors. Effective risk recognition was delivered through the use of varied methods including education, discussion, use of videotapes, and modeling. Evaluations of the program conducted after 2 months did not show differences between the intervention group and the control group with regard to general rates of revictimization. However, when rates of rape were examined, approximately 30% in the control group reported rape compared to 12% in the experimental condition. It is possible that the nature of the prevention program, which covered a variety of delivery methods, including behavioral participation in the form of discussions and modeling, acted as a better teaching tool for previously victimized women.

In addition to examining the effects of participating in a sexual assault risk reduction program on general revictimization rates, Mouilso, Calhoun, and Gidycz (2010) evaluated the impact of a program on reports of psychological distress. The researchers evaluated 450 women with histories of attempted or completed rape prior to participation in the study. Participants were randomized to either the prevention program or the control group. The

4-month follow-up analyses showed that women in the intervention group had reduced rates of revictimization (41.5%) compared to the control group (58.5%). When the two groups of revictimized participants were compared, the intervention group reported greater reduction in psychological distress and PTSD symptoms, even after controlling for the frequency of revictimization. The frequency and severity of victimization, self-blame, and use of avoidance coping explained a significant amount of the variance in distress following revictimization. This study provides insight into the factors contributing to distress in response to revictimization and also highlights another important area of study in the field of prevention. In particular, this study helps us to understand prevention programs not only in the context of reducing risk of revictimization but also in terms of preventing psychological difficulties after the occurrence of revictimization.

## ACT: A Contextual Behavioral Treatment

Acceptance and Commitment Therapy (ACT) (Hayes, Strosahl, & Wilson, 1999) is a contextual behavior therapy, derived from both traditional behavior-analytic and cognitive-behavioral approaches, and is well suited to clients with a history of multiple victimizations. Because of the primary emphasis on the function rather than the topography of behaviors, ACT is particularly effective in addressing the range of behavioral repertoires likely to be present in sexual revictimization. An overarching goal of the intervention is to undermine experiential avoidance, which the literature suggests may explain the variability observed in trauma-related problems. Additionally, ACT encourages psychological flexibility, by emphasizing contact with the present moment and behavioral activation, in the service of the client's chosen values. For a comprehensive discussion of both the theory and the intervention, see Hayes et al. (1999) and Hayes and Strosahl (2005). In treating clients with a history of sexual victimization and revictimization, the treatment model is most suited for those with pervasive difficulties related to experiential avoidance, including a variety of difficulties that extend beyond straightforward symptoms of PTSD. For individuals presenting primarily with PTSD, research indicates that two forms of exposure therapies may be effective (Resick, Nishith, & Astin, 1996). Proper assessment of difficulties is crucial for selecting clients who will benefit from the treatment as well as implementation of particular treatment components.

## ASSESSMENT

A functional analysis is a useful assessment tool that can be used initially and throughout the course of trauma treatment, particularly when complex problems complicate client conceptualization. A functional analysis, when carried out appropriately, allows for a thorough analysis of variables that could be critical in understanding the relationship between behaviors, their antecedent conditions, and maintaining effects (Follette & Naugle, 2006). For purposes of this population, a functional analysis can serve the useful function of identifying not only the symptoms that are present but most importantly, underlying processes to be targeted in treatment, including but not limited to experiential avoidance. A thorough discussion on functional analysis can be found in Chapter 6 of this volume.

Supplementing a functional analysis, a thorough assessment is informed by the measuring of various processes related to experiential avoidance. As a self-report measure, the Acceptance and Action Questionnaire (AAQ) (Bond & Bunce, 2003; Hayes et al., 2004) is useful in capturing experiential avoidance including behavioral avoidance, emotion-focused inaction, as well as emotional acceptance and action. Any of the three earlier versions of the AAQ—a 9-item single-factor scale (Hayes et al., 2004), a 16-item single-factor scale (Hayes et al., 2004), and another 16-item two-factor scale (Bond & Bunce, 2003)—may be used. A more recent nine-item measure of experiential avoidance (AAQ-II) (Bond et al., submitted) is currently being used in most outcome research related to ACT. In order to measure specific strategies used to control unpleasant or unwanted thoughts, the Thought Control Questionnaire (TCQ) (Wells & Davies, 1994) serves as an appropriate assessment tool. Mindfulness can be measured using the Kentucky Inventory of Mindfulness Skills (KIMS) (Baer, Smith, & Cochran, 2004) or the Mindfulness Attention Awareness Scale (MAAS) (Brown & Ryan, 2003). Another useful instrument is the Valued Living Questionnaire (VLQ) (Wilson, & Groom, 2002), a 20-item instrument that measures 10 domains of valued living including family, marriage/couples/intimate relations, parenting, friendship, work, education, recreation, spirituality, citizenship, and physical self-care.

## TREATMENT COMPONENTS

### Acceptance and Mindfulness

*Acceptance*

Clinically, we frequently work with survivors of sexual victimization who report a life dominated by avoidance of both public and private experiences that are trauma related. In order to get away from the "pain," clients may describe engaging in various behaviors such as drinking, self-harm, dissociation, and risky sex. Underlying this range of behaviors is usually painful emotional content, such as sadness, shame, and fear, which the person attempts to escape. Despite responding to problems in the manner described above, it is often the case that when presenting to treatment these "painful" private experiences are still viewed as problems that need to be reduced and eliminated. In light of these private experiences that are not responsive to active change strategies, clients have to come to a realization of the futility of their attempts to manipulate and control private events. Through detailed exploration of previously internally focused change strategies, and commonplace metaphors, this result can be achieved where their behaviors are seen not only as intensifying difficulties, in the long term, but also leading to a sense of "suffering" that extends beyond the original pain. Problematic behaviors are thus understood as being maintained and reinforced by these control strategies.

Teaching clients alternatives to control strategies, including acceptance or willingness to experience private experiences, is a primary focus of ACT. Rather than engaging in experiential avoidance, clients are encouraged to approach and contact previously avoided events. In doing so, ACT utilizes *mindfulness*, which traditionally has been conceptualized as nonjudgmental awareness of, and contact with, the present moment (Kabat-Zinn, 1990). For example, when feelings of fear related to trauma surface, acceptance would involve bringing awareness to the presence of that fear and exploring how it actually feels to have that fear, without attempts to escape it. The same approach can be used for a variety of other response dimensions, such as memories, thoughts, and urges to act. Practicing mindfulness provides opportunities for the clients to observe and experience private events, including thoughts and emotions as part of the present moment, that do not require change. Ultimately, though, mindfulness facilitates emotional experiencing while reducing experiential avoidance.

Because the client with a history of sexual victimization may struggle with experiences of self-blame, shame, and hopelessness, care needs to be taken to ensure that the individual recognizes their previous strategies as being problematic, and in need of change, rather than the self. Normalization of the client's efforts in the context of the trauma history serves to understand rather than judge clients for their efforts to cope with their experiences. Acceptance, although ultimately helpful, may seem especially frightening and counterintuitive to many. Consider the individual who has a lengthy history, possibly starting early in development, of consistent attempts to regulate emotions through some form of avoidance. Limited understanding of the self including knowledge and awareness of emotions may be observed. In such cases, the therapy may need to be supplemented by a focus on skills training around these issues. A discussion of emotions may have to start at a very basic level with a focus on the physical, behavioral, and cognitive components of various emotional experiences.

## Cognitive Defusion

It is part of the general human experience to hold tightly to the belief in the importance of thoughts. People often cling to the believability of thoughts as representing some literal truth, and we describe this attachment as "fusion" with the phenomena of our thoughts. High levels of fusion with thoughts prevent contact with the present moment and results in inflexible behavioral repertoires. This is especially problematic when we consider thoughts that may be associated with a history of victimization. Consider a survivor of trauma who consistently struggles with thoughts such as "I am a bad person" or "There must be something wrong with me to deserve these abusive experiences." In situations in which risk of sexual revictimization may be detectable in the environment, including behaviors of potential perpetrators, the individual fused with thoughts of self-blame may fail to attend to "problems" in the environment or respond effectively. In order to address the cognitive entanglement often observed among clients, clients are encouraged to participate in mindfulness and to notice a thought as a thought rather than the literal truth. Use of mindfulness in relation to thoughts is sometimes difficult to comprehend and often requires clarification. On the one hand, ACT attempts to increase awareness of having certain thoughts rather than attempts to change their nature or content. At the same time, the treatment distances individuals from their believability in their thoughts and challenges the client's belief of the control of thoughts on behaviors. We especially work with clients to help them to come in contact with the thought that they can have a painful history and pursue their valued life goals without having to change thoughts and feelings.

## Self as Context

Another area in which we observe psychological difficulties after sexual victimization is that of self-concept. For many individuals, self-concept is tied to life experiences as well as one's stories about those experiences. In some survivors, we notice a tendency to define their lives as "an abused person" with expected limitations on what can be experienced or achieved in life. Sometimes what is observed is an exhaustive sense of struggle to make sense of the abuse with the hope that doing so will somehow improve one's self-concept. In yet other individuals, we may notice rigid ways of interpersonal relatedness irrespective of context. In ACT, the focus is on developing a continuous sense of self that transcends thoughts, feelings, history, roles, and related constructs. The goal of ACT is to move the client toward a stable sense of self that allows the psychological flexibility to engage in effective behaviors that are consistent with valued goals. Rather than remained fused to the story of "an abused person" determining the life experiences of an individual, the client is helped to develop a sense of self that is capable of engaging life in a vital way. Mindfulness, as used throughout ACT, is also used in helping clients to remain in contact with that stable sense of self.

## Behavior Change and Committed Action Based on Values

In the case of many survivors with histories of sexual trauma and psychological difficulties, behaviors tend to be driven by avoidance based on negatively evaluated private experiences. Client presentations may be highlighted by narrow repertoires of behaviors. It is important to validate the client in that some of these behaviors may have served some survival mechanism at one time (or at least have seemed to do so). For example, dissociation during sexual relations may have helped to distance from the pain of the experience. However, in working toward a goal of emotional intimacy with a caring partner, dissociation during sexual relations may no longer be useful.

Other problems associated with revictimization such as alcohol use and risky sex generally are not consistent with clients' valued life goals. A lack of contact with the present moment can result in disengagement from life, limiting opportunities for more positive experiences. In terms of revictimization, this is relevant because the escape strategies used may place individuals at risk for additional revictimization, At the same time, for the person who has lived a life of avoidance without contacting meaningful valued experiences, stepping in new directions may seem uncomfortable and dangerous.

Care should be taken to highlight that while acceptance is indicated in the case of internal experiences, taking behavioral control in potentially dangerous situations is totally appropriate. Part of the work of therapy is to determine the appropriate repertoire for different situations. For example, difficulties establishing external control may be evident, as in the case with someone who is not able to create boundaries in situations that are potentially risky. It is absolutely important to communicate that letting go of the control of thoughts and feelings does not imply letting go of engaging in behaviors that are effective in creating safety. In fact, we would argue that being able to remain fully aware and present of current surroundings will facilitate the use of appropriate behaviors to maintain safety. Additional work around these issues is often useful, including the use of exercises in which the client can imagine strategies for dealing with difficult scenarios.

In addition to awareness, flexibility, and openness to being exposed to previously avoided events, the development of new response functions is an integral part of ACT. Values-based living is introduced as an alternate path, one guided by meaning in life, versus one guided by avoidance of difficult private experiences. As the topic of the values is explored, it is helpful to consider values across a variety of domains, such as family, friends, health, leisure, career, romantic relationships, spirituality, and other domains the client may identify. Determination of specific goals related to different values as well as behaviors indicative of working toward valued directions are important aspects in the approach. Effective behaviors that move the client toward a more vital life and that involve strategies for safety are generally primary in relation to values and are particularly relevant when considering revictimization. An ACT approach can be especially useful in this population in that we work to create a collaborative therapeutic relationship that involved client identification of values. Many of our clients have come from patriarchal or other controlling environments and thus are very compliant with regard to complying with external demands. Helping them to develop a sense of identity and life goals that are self-determined is central to the therapy.

## FUTURE DIRECTIONS

The literature clearly shows disproportionately high rates of sexual revictimization in survivors of prior sexual victimization and the associated problems of substance use and misuse, psychological difficulties, and high-risk sexual behavior are well documented. However, the behavioral repertoires associated with revictimization are varied and complex. Researchers have examined a number of relevant mediators and moderators in an effort to understand the relationship between prior and subsequent victimization. At the same time, only a few studies have included characteristics one would hope to see in well-designed research, including large sample sizes, representative samples, appropriate control groups, definitional clarity of constructs, longitudinal designs, and varied forms of assessment. We are increasingly interested in the idea that initial sexual victimization does not directly lead to sexual revictimization, but rather can be explained by underlying psychological processes. Research on mediators and moderators, along with psychological processes, allows one to focus on particular features of an individual's repertoire that are relevant to the risk for sexual revictimization. We want to emphasize that this focus does not imply blaming individuals for additional experiences of sexual victimization. Rather, such work focuses on individual behaviors that are malleable more immediately, if identified, with the purpose of safety in mind. Finally, although beyond the scope of the discussion in this chapter, we hope that research on sexual revictimization emphasizes focus on factors associated with perpetration, including the sociocultural factors that influence attitudes related to aggression and assault.

## REFERENCES

Abbey, A., & McAuslan, P. (2004). A longitudinal examination of college men's perpetration of sexual assault. *Journal of Consulting and Clinical Psychology, 72,* 747–756.

Abbey, A. McAuslan, P., & Ross, L. T. (1998). Sexual assault perpetration by college men: The role of alcohol, misperception of sexual intent, and sexual beliefs and experiences. *Journal of Social and Clinical Psychology, 17,* 167–195.

Abbey, A., Zawacki, T., Buck, P. O., Testa, M., Parks, K., Norris, J., ... Martell, J. (2002). How does alcohol contribute to sexual assault? Explanations from laboratory and survey data. *Alcoholism: Clinical and Experimental Research, 26,* 575–581.

Acierno, R., Resnick, H., Kilpatrick, D., Saunders, B., & Best, C. (1999). Risk factors for rape, physical assault, and PTSD in women: Examination of differential multivariate relationships. *Journal of Anxiety Disorders, 13*(6), 541–564.

American Psychiatric Association. (2000). *Diagnostic and statistical manual of mental disorders* (revised 4th ed.). Washington, DC: Author.

Anderson, L. A., & Whiston, S. C. (2005). Sexual assault education programs: A meta-analytic examination of their effectiveness. *Psychology of Women Quarterly, 29,* 374–388.

Arata, C. M. (1999a). Coping with rape: The roles of prior sexual abuse and attributions of blame. *Journal of Interpersonal Violence, 14,* 62–78.

Arata, C. M. (1999b). Repeated sexual victimization and mental disorders in women. *Journal of Child Sexual Abuse, 7,* 1–17.

Arata, C. M. (2000). From child to adult victim: A model for predicting sexual revictimization. *Child Maltreatment, 5,* 28–38.

Baer, R. A., Smith, G. T., & Cochran, K. B. (2004). Assessment of mindfulness by self-report. The Kentucky Inventory of Mindfulness Skills. *Assessment, 11,* 191–206.

Batten, S. V., Follette, V. M., & Aban, I. B. (2001). Experiential avoidance and high-risk sexual behavior in survivors of child sexual abuse. *Journal of Child Sexual Abuse, 10,* 101–120.

Beitchman, J., Zucker, K., Hood, J., Da Costa, G., & Akman, D. (1991). A review of the short-term effects of child sexual abuse. *Child Abuse & Neglect, 15,* 537–556.

Bonanno, G. A. (2004). Loss, trauma, and human resilience: Have we underestimated the human capacity to thrive after extremely aversive events? *American Psychologist, 59,* 20–28.

Bonanno, G. A. (2005). Resilience in the face of potential trauma. *Current Directions in Psychological Science, 14,* 135–138.

Bonanno, G. A., Rennicke, C., & Dekel, S. (2005). Self-enhancement among high-exposure survivors of the September 11th terrorist attack: Resilience or social maladjustment? *Journal of Personality and Social Psychology, 88,* 984–998.

Bond, F. W., & Bunce, D (2003). The role of acceptance and job control in mental health, job satisfaction, and work performance. *Journal of Applied Psychology, 88,* 1057–1067.

Bond, F. W., Hayes, S. C., Baer, R. A., Carpenter, K. M., Orcutt, H. K., Waltz, T., & Zettle, R. D. *Acceptance and Action Questionnaire—II.* (Submitted).

Boudreaux, E. D., Kilpatrick, D. G., Resnick, H. S., Best, C. L., & Saunders, B. E. (1998). Criminal victimization, post-traumatic stress disorder, and comorbid psychopathology among a community sample of women. *Journal of Traumatic Stress, 11,* 665–678.

Breitenbecher, K. H., & Gidycz, C. A. (1998). Empirical evaluation of a program designed to reduce the risk of multiple sexual victimization. *Journal of Interpersonal Violence, 13,* 472–488.

Breslau, N., Davis, G. C., Andreski, P., & Peterson, E. (1991). Traumatic events and post-traumatic stress disorder in an urban population of young adults. *Archives of General Psychiatry, 48,* 216–222.

Breslau, N., Kessler, R. C., Chilcoat, H. D., Schultz, L. R., Davis, G. C., & Andreski, P. (1998). Trauma and posttraumatic stress disorder in the community: The 1996 Detroit Area Survey of Trauma. *Archives of General Psychiatry, 55,* 626–632.

Briere, J. (1995). *Trauma Symptom Inventory (TSI).* Odessa, FL: Psychological Assessment Resources.

Briere, J. N., & Elliott, D. M. (1994). Immediate and long-term impacts of child sexual abuse. *Sexual Abuse of Children, 4,* 54–69.

Briere, J. N., & Elliott, D. M. (2003). Prevalence and symptomatic sequelae of self-reported childhood physical and sexual abuse in a general population sample of men and women. *Child Abuse & Neglect: The International Journal, 27,* 1205–1222.

Brown, K. W., & Ryan, R. M. (2003). The benefits of being present: Mindfulness and its role in psychological well-being. *Journal of Personality and Social Psychology, 84,* 822–848.

Buckley, T. C., Blanchard, E. B., & Hickling, E. J. (1996). A prospective examination of delayed onset PTSD secondary to motor vehicle accidents. *Journal of Abnormal Psychology, 105,* 617–625.

Casey, E. A., & Nurius, P. S. (2005). Trauma exposure and sexual revictimization risk: Comparisons across single, multiple incident, and multiple perpetrator victimizations. *Violence Against Women,* 11(4), 505–530.

Clark, D. M., Ball, S., & Pape, D. (1991). An experimental investigation of thought suppression. *Behavior Research and Therapy, 29,* 253–257.

Cloitre, M., Cohen, L. R., & Koenen, K. C. (2006). *Treating survivors of childhood abuse: Psychotherapy for the interrupted life.* New York: Guilford Press.

Cloitre, M., & Rosenberg, A. (2006). Sexual revictimization: Risk factors and prevention. In V. M. Follette J. I. Ruzek (Eds.), *Cognitive-behavioral therapies for trauma* (pp. 321–361). New York: Guilford Press.

Cloitre, M., Scarvalone, P., & Difede, J. (1997). Posttraumatic Stress Disorder, self- and interpersonal dysfunction among sexually retraumatized women. *Journal of Traumatic Stress, 10,* 437–451.

Cloitre, M., Tardiff, K., Marzuk, P. M., Leon, A. C., & Portera, L. (2001). Consequences of childhood abuse among male psychiatric inpatients: Dual roles as victims and perpetrators. *Journal of Traumatic Stress, 14,* 47–62.

Coffey, S. F., Saladin, M. E., Drobes, D. J., Brady, K. T., Dansky, B. S., & Kilpatrick, D. G. (2002). Trauma and substance cue reactivity in individuals with comorbid posttraumatic stress disorder and cocaine or alcohol dependence. *Drug and Alcohol Dependence, 65*(2), 115–127.

Courtois, C. (2004). Complex trauma, complex reactions: Assessment and treatment. *Psychotherapy Theory, Research, Practice, Training, 41,* 412–425.

Desai, S., Arias, I., Thompson, M. P., & Basile, K.C. (2002). Childhood victimization and subsequent adult revictimization assessed in a nationally representative sample of women and men. *Violence and Victims, 17*(6), 639–653.

Epstein, J. N., Saunders, B. E., Kilpatrick, D. G., & Resnick, H. S. (1998). PTSD as a mediator between childhood rape and alcohol use in adult women. *Child Abuse and Neglect, 22,* 223–234.

Fargo, J. D. (2009). Pathways to adult sexual revictimization: Direct and indirect behavioral risk factors across the lifespan. *Journal of Interpersonal Violence, 24,* 1771–1791.

Fergusson, D. M., Horwood, L. J., & Lynskey, M. T. (1997). Childhood sexual abuse, adolescent sexual behaviors and sexual revictimization. *Child Abuse and Neglect, 21,* 789–803.

Finkelhor, D. (1994). Current information on the scope and nature of child sexual abuse. *The Future of Children, 4*(2), 31–53.

Follette, V. M., Iverson, K. M., & Ford, J. (2009). Contextual behavioral trauma therapy. In C. A. Courtois & J. D. Ford (Eds.), *Treating complex traumatic stress disorders* (pp. 264–287). New York: Guilford Press.

Follette, V., Palm, K., & Rasmussen-Hall, M. (2004). Mindfulness and acceptance in the treatment of sexual abuse survivors. In S. C. Hayes, V. M. Follette, & M. Linehan (Eds.), *Mindfulness and acceptance.* New York: Guilford Press.

Follette, V. M., Polusny, M. A., Bechtle, A., & Naugle, A. (1996). Cumulative trauma: Impact of child sexual abuse, sexual assault, and spouse abuse. *Journal of Traumatic Stress, 9,* 25–35.

Follette, V. M., & Vijay, A. (2008). Retraumatization. In G. Reyes, J. D. Elhai, & J. D. Ford (Eds.), *Encyclopedia of psychological trauma* (pp. 586–589). Hoboken, NJ: Wiley.

Follette, W. C., & Houts, A. C. (1996). Models of scientific progress and the role of theory in taxonomy development: A case study of the *DSM. Journal of Consulting and Clinical Psychology, 64,* 1120–1132.

Follette, W. C., & Naugle, A. E. (2006). Functional analytic clinical assessment in trauma treatment. In V. M. Follette & J. I. Ruzek (Eds.), *Cognitive-behavioral therapies for trauma* (2nd ed., pp. 17–33). New York: Guilford Press.

Foulds, G. A. (1971). Personality deviance and personal symptomatology. *Psychological Medicine, 3,* 222–233.

Gidycz, C. A., Coble, C. N., Latham, L., & Layman, M. J. (1993). Sexual assault experience in adulthood and prior victimization experiences: A prospective analysis. *Psychology of Women Quarterly, 17*(2), 151–168.

Gidycz, C. A., Hanson, K., & Layman, M. J. (1995). A prospective analysis of the relationship among sexual assault experiences: An extension of previous findings. *Psychology of Women Quarterly, 19,* 124–131.

Gidycz, C. A., Loh, C., Lobo, T., Rich, C., Lynn, S. J., & Pashdag, J. (2007). Reciprocal relations among alcohol use, risk perception, and sexual victimization: A prospective analysis. *Journal of American College Health, 56,* 5–14.

Gross, J. J., & John, O. P. (2003). Individual differences in two emotion regulation processes: Implications for affect, relationships, and well-being. *Journal of Personality and Social Psychology, 85,* 348–362.

Hanson, K. A., & Gidycz, C. A. (1993). An evaluation of a sexual assault prevention program. *Journal of Consulting and Clinical Psychology, 61,* 1046–1052.

Hayes, S. C., Missett, R., Roget, N., Padilla, M., Kohlenberg, B. S., Fisher, G., et al. (2004a). The impact of acceptance and commitment training and multicultural training on the stigmatizing attitudes and professional burnout of substance abuse counselors. *Behavior Therapy.*

Hayes, S. C., & Strosahl, K. D. (Eds.). (2005). *A practical guide to acceptance and commitment therapy.* New York: Springer Science.

Hayes, S. C., Strosahl, K., & Wilson, K. G. (1999). *Acceptance and commitment therapy: An experiential approach to behavior change.* New York: Guilford Press.

Hayes, S. C., Strosahl, K. D., Wilson, K. G., Bissett, R. T., Pistorello, J., Toarmino, D., … McCurry, S. M. (2004b). Measuring experiential avoidance: A preliminary test of a working model. *Psychological Record, 54,* 553–578.

Hayes, S. C., Wilson, K., Gifford, E. V., Follette, V. M., & Strosahl, K. (1996). Experiential avoidance and behavioral disorders: A functional dimensional approach to diagnosis and treatment. *Journal of Consulting and Clinical Psychology, 64,* 1152–1168.

Herman, J. L. (1992b). Complex PTSD: A syndrome in survivors of prolonged and repeated trauma. *Journal of Traumatic Stress, 5,* 377–391.

Humphrey, J. A., & White, J. W. (2000). Women's vulnerability to sexual assault from adolescence to young adulthood. *Journal of Adolescent Health, 27,* 419–424.

John, O. P., & Gross, J. J. (2004). Healthy and unhealthy emotion regulation: Personality processes, individual differences, and life-span development. *Journal of Personality, 72,* 1301–1333.

Jumper, S. (1995). A meta-analysis of the relationship of child sexual abuse to adult psychological adjustment. *Child Abuse & Neglect, 19,* 715–728.

Kabat-Zinn, J. (1990). *Full catastrophe living: Using the wisdom of your body and mind to face stress, pain and illness.* New York: Dell.

Kahn, A. S., Jackson, J., Kully, C., Badger, K., & Halvorsen, J. (2003). Calling it rape. *Psychology of Women Quarterly, 27,* 233–242.

Krahe, B., Scheinberger-Olwig, R., Waizenhofer, E., & Kolpin, S. (1999). Childhood sexual abuse and revictimization in adolescence. *Child Abuse and Neglect, 23,* 383–394.

Kessler, R. C., Sonnega, A., Bromet, E., Hughes, M., & Nelson, C. B. (1995). Posttraumatic stress disorder in the National Comorbidity Survey. *Archives of General Psychiatry, 52,* 1048–1060.

Kilpatrick, D. G., Acierno, R., Resnick, H. S., Saunders, B. E., & Best, C. L. (1997). A two year longitudinal analysis of the relationship between violent assault and alcohol and drug use in women. *Journal of Consulting and Clinical Psychology, 65*(5), 834–847.

Kilpatrick, D. G., Resnick, H. S., Ruggiero, K., Conoscenti, L. M., & McCauley, J. (2007). Drug facilitated, incapacitated, and forcible rape: A national study (NIJ 219181). Washington, DC: U.S. Department of Justice.

Kimerling, R., Alvarez, J., Pavao, J., Kaminski, A., & Baumrind, N. (2007). Epidemiology and consequences of women's revictimization. *Women's Health Issues, 17,* 101–106.

Koverola, C., Proulx, J., Battle, P., & Hanna, C. (1996). Family functioning as predictors of distress in revictimized sexual abuse survivors. *Journal of Interpersonal Violence, 11,* 263–280.

Lewis, K. L., & Grenyer, B. F. S. (2009). Borderline personality or complex posttraumatic stress disorder? An update on the controversy. *Harvard Review of Psychiatry, 17*(5), 322–328.

Littleton, H., & Radecki Breitkopf, C. (2006). Coping with the experience of rape. *Psychology of Women Quarterly,* 30, 106–116.

Marx, B. P., Calhoun, K. S., Wilson, A. E., & Meyerson, L. A. (2001). Sexual revictimization prevention: An outcome evaluation. *Journal of Consulting and Clinical Psychology, 69*(1) 25–32.

Marx, B. P., & Gross, A. M. (1995). An analysis of two contextual variables. *Behavior Modification, 19,* 451–463.

Marx, B. P., & Sloan, D. M. (2002). The role of emotion in the psychological functioning of adult survivors of childhood sexual abuse. *Behavior Therapy, 33,* 563–577.

McCauley, J. L., Calhoun, K. S., & Gidycz, C. A. (2010). Binge drinking and rape: A prospective examination of college women with a history of previous sexual victimization. *Journal of Interpersonal Violence, 25*(9), 1655–1668.

Merrill, L. L., Newell, C. E., Thomsen, C. J., Gold, S. R., Milner, J. S., Koss, M. P., & Rosswork, S. G. (1999). Childhood abuse and sexual revictimization in a female Navy recruit sample. *Journal of Traumatic Stress, 12*(2), 211–225.

Merrill, L. L., Thomsen, C. J., Gold, S. R., & Milner, J. S. (2001). Childhood abuse and premilitary sexual assault in male Navy recruits. *Journal of Consulting and Clinical Psychology, 69,* 252–261.

Messman-Moore, T., & Brown, A. L. (2004). Child maltreatment and perceived family environment as risk factors for adult rape: Is child sexual abuse the most salient experience? *Child Abuse & Neglect, 28,* 1019–1034.

Messman-Moore, T. L., Brown, A. L., & Koelsch, L. E. (2005). Posttraumatic symptoms and self-dysfunction as consequences and predictors of sexual revictimization. *Journal of Traumatic Stress, 18,* 253–261.

Messman-Moore, T. L., & Long, P. J. (2002). Alcohol and substance use disorders as predictors of child to adult sexual revictimization in a sample of community women. *Violence and Victims, 17,* 319–340.

Messman-Moore, T. L., Long, P. J., & Siegfried, N. J. (2000). The revictimization of child sexual abuse survivors: An examination of the adjustment of college women with child sexual abuse, adult sexual assault, and adult physical abuse. *Child Maltreatment, 5*(1), 18–27.

Messman-Moore, T. L., Ward, R. M., & Brown, A. L. (2009). Substance use and PTSD symptoms impact the likelihood of rape and revictimization in college women. *Journal of Interpersonal Violence, 24,* 499–521.

Mouilso, E. R., Calhoun, K. S., & Gidycz, C. A. (2010). Effects of participation in a sexual assault risk reduction program on psychological distress following revictimization. *Journal of Interpersonal Violence.* DOI: 10.1177/0886260510365862

Noll, J. G., Horowitz, L. A., Bonanno, G. A., Trickett, P. K., & Putnam, F. W. (2003). Revictimization and self-harm in females who experienced childhood sexual abuse. *Journal of Interpersonal Violence, 18,* 1452–1471.

Orcutt, H. K., Cooper, M. L., & Garcia, M. (2005). Use of sexual intercourse to reduce negative affect as a prospective mediator of sexual revictimization. *Journal of Traumatic Stress, 18,* 729–739.

Paolucci, E. O., Genuis, M. L., & Violato, C. (2001). A meta-analysis of the published research on the effects of child sexual abuse. *Journal of Psychology, 135*(1), 17–36.

Pereda, N., Guilera, G., Forns, M., & Gomez-Benito, J. (2009). The international epidemiology of child sexual abuse: A continuation of Finkelhor (1994), *Child Abuse & Neglect 33,* 331–342.

Pistorello, J., Follette, V. M., & Hayes, S. C. (2000). Long-term correlates of childhood sexual abuse: A behavior analytic perspective. In M. J. Dougher (Ed.), *Clinical behavior analysis* (pp. 75–98). Reno, NV: Context.

Polusny, M. A., & Follette, V. M. (1995). The long term correlates of child sexual abuse: Theory and review of the empirical literature. *Applied and Preventive Psychology, 4,* 143–166.

Polusny, M. A., Rosenthal, M. Z., Aban, I., & Follette, V. M. (2004). Experiential avoidance as a mediator of the effects of adolescent sexual victimization on negative adult outcomes. *Violence and Victims, 19,* 109–120.

Raghavan, R., Bogart, L. M., Elliott, M. N., Vestal, K. D., & Schuster, M. A. (2004). Sexual victimization among a national probability sample of adolescent women. *Perspectives on Sexual and Reproductive Health, 36,* 225–232.

Resick, P. A., Nishith, P., & Astin, M. C. (November 1996). Results of an outcome study comparing cognitive processing therapy and prolonged exposure. In P. Resick (Chair), *Treating sexual assault/sexual abuse pathology: Recent findings.* Symposium conducted at the meeting of the Association for Advancement of Behavior Therapy, New York.

Rich, C. L., Gidycz, C. A., Warkentin, J. B., Loh, C., & Weiland, P. (2005). Child and adolescent abuse and subsequent victimization: A prospective study. *Child Abuse and Neglect: The International Journal, 29,* 1373–1394.

Risser, H. J., Hetzel-Riggin, M. D., Thomsen, C. J., & McCanne, T. R. (2006). PTSD as a mediator of sexual revictimization: The role of reexperiencing, avoidance, and arousal symptoms. *Journal of Traumatic Stress, 19,* 687–698.

Roodman, A. A., & Clum, G. A. (2001). Revictimization rates and method variance: A meta-analysis. *Clinical Psychology Review, 21,* 183–204.

Rosenthal, M. Z., Rasmussen-Hall, M. L., Palm, K., Batten, S. V., & Follette, V. M. (2005). Chronic avoidance helps explain the relationship between severity of childhood sexual abuse and psychological distress in adulthood. *Journal of Child Sexual Abuse, 14,* 25–41.

Rothman, E., & Silverman, J. (2007). The effect of a college sexual assault prevention program on first-year students' victimization rates. *Journal of American College Health, 55*(5), 283–290.

Rowan, A. B., Foy, D. W., Rodriguez, N., & Ryan, S. (1994). Posttraumatic stress disorder in a clinical sample of adults sexually abused as children. *Child Abuse and Neglect, 18*, 51–61.

Sandberg, D. A., Matorin, A. I., & Lynn, S. J. (1999). Dissociation, posttraumatic symptomatology, and sexual revictimization: A prospective examination of mediator and moderator effects. *Journal of Traumatic Stress, 12*, 127–138.

Sartor, C. E., Agrawal, A., McCutcheon, V. V., Duncan, A. E., & Lynskey, M. T. (2008). Disentangling the complex association between childhood sexual abuse and alcohol-related problems: A review of methodological issues and approaches. *Journal of Studies on Alcohol and Drugs, 69*(5), 718–727.

Saunders, B. E., Villeponteaux, L. A., Lipovsky, J. A., Kilpatrick, D. G., & Veronen, L. J. (1992). Child sexual assault as a risk factor for mental disorders among women: A community survey. *Journal of Interpersonal Violence, 7*(2), 189–204.

Schacht, R. L., George, W. H., Davis, K. C., Heiman, J. R., Norris, J., Stoner, S. A., & Kajumulo, K. F. (2010). Sexual abuse history, alcohol intoxication, and women's sexual risk behavior. *Archives of Sexual Behavior, 39*, 898–906.

Schwartz, M. D., & Leggett, M. S. (1999). Bad dates or emotional trauma? The aftermath of campus sexual assault. *Violence Against Women, 5*(3), 251–271.

Seidner, A. S., Calhoun, K. S., & Kilpatrick, D. G. (1985). Childhood and/or adolescent sexual experiences: Predicting variability in subsequent adjustment. Paper presented at the annual meeting of the American Psychological Association, Los Angeles, CA.

Shipherd, J. C., & Beck, J. G. (1999). The effects of suppressing trauma-related thoughts in women with rape-related posttraumatic stress disorder, *Behaviour Research and Therapy, 37*, 99–112.

Shipherd, J. C., Beck, J. G., Hamblen, J. L., & Freeman, J. B. (2000). Assessment and treatment of PTSD in motor vehicle accident survivors. In L. VandeCreek (Ed.), *Innovations in clinical practice: A source book* (Vol. 18, pp. 135–152). Sarasota, FL: Professional Resource Press.

Soler-Baillo, J. M., Marx, B. P., & Sloan, D. M. (2005). The psychophysiological correlates of risk recognition in victims of sexual assault. *Behaviour Research and Therapy, 43*, 169–181.

Testa, M., Hoffman, J. H., & Livingston, J. A. (2010). Alcohol and sexual risk behaviors as mediators of the sexual victimization–revictimization relationship. *Journal of Consulting and Clinical Psychology, 78*, 249–259.

Testa, M., Livingston, J. A., Vanzile-Tamsen, C., & Frone, M. R. (2003). The role of women's substance use in vulnerability to forcible and incapacitated rape. *Journal of Studies on Alcohol, 64*, 756–764.

Testa, M., VanZile-Tamsen, C., Livingston, J. A., & Buddie, A. (2006). The role of women's alcohol consumption in managing sexual intimacy and sexual safety motives. *Journal of Studies on Alcohol, 67*, 665–674.

Ullman, S. E., Najdowski, C. J., & Filipas, H. H. (2009). Child sexual abuse, post-traumatic stress disorder, and substance use: Predictors of revictimization in adult sexual assault survivors. *Journal of Child Sexual Abuse, 18*, 367–385.

Urquiza, A., & Keating, L. M. (1990). The prevalence of sexual victimization of males. In Hunter, M. (Ed.), *The sexually abused male*. Lexington, MA: Lexington Books.

Van Bruggen, L. K., Runtz, M. G., & Kadlec, H. (2006). Sexual revictimization: The role of sexual self-esteem and dysfunctional sexual behaviors. *Child Maltreatment, 11,* 131–145.

Wagner, A. W., & Linehan, M. M. (2006). Applications of dialectical behavior therapy to PTSD and related problems. In V. M. Follette & J. I. Ruzek (Eds.), *Cognitive-behavioral therapies for trauma* (pp. 117–145). New York: Guilford Press.

Wegner, D. M., & Schneider, D. J. (2003). The white bear story. *Psychological Inquiry, 14,* 326–329.

Wells, A., & Davies, M. I. (1994). *Attention and emotion: A clinical perspective.* Hillsdale, NJ: Erlbaum.

Wenzlaff, R. M., & Wegner, D. M. (2000). Thought suppression. In S. T. Fiske (Ed.), *Annual review of psychology* (Vol. 51, pp. 59–91). Palo Alto, CA: Annual Reviews.

Wilson, A., Calhoun, K. S., & Bernat, J. A. (1999). Risk recognition and trauma-related symptoms among sexually re-victimized women. *Journal of Consulting and Clinical Psychology, 67,* 705–710.

Wilson, K. G., & Groom, J. (2002). *The Valued Living Questionnaire.* Available from the first author at the Department of Psychology, University of Mississippi.

Yeater, E. A., & O'Donohue, W. (2002). Sexual revictimization: The relationship among knowledge, risk perception and ability to respond to high-risk situations. *Journal of Interpersonal Violence, 17*(11), 1135–1144.

Young, R. M., Oei, T. P., & Knight, R. S. (1990). The tension reduction hypothesis revisited: An alcohol expectancy perspective. *British Journal of Addiction, 85*(1), 31–40.

# Chapter 13

# Multiple Experiences of Domestic Violence and Associated Relationship Features

*Alan E. Fruzzetti and Jung eun Lee*

Domestic violence occurs when a partner, or ex-partner, in an intimate relationship, attempts to harm or control another person with sexual abuse, stalking, emotional and psychological abuse, or physical abuse or aggression (Tjaden & Thoennes, 2000). Many different terms are used to describe these domestic violence–related behaviors in a couple, including marital or domestic violence, dating violence, battering, spouse or partner abuse, domestic abuse, partner aggression, and intimate partner violence. Researchers employ different definitions of the phenomena of partner abuse or domestic violence, which results in inconsistent prevalence estimates and makes it difficult to compare across studies. In this chapter, various terms will be used interchangeably to describe "domestic violence." We will include physical and sexual violence or aggression, threats of physical and sexual violence or aggression (including physical control), and psychological and emotional abuse that occur in the context of current or prior physical or sexual violence, and we will discuss research and intervention programs for any of these problems. Consequently, we will *not* include in our focus more ordinary verbal aggression that occurs in relationships that have no history of physical or sexual aggression or violence.

Domestic violence is a serious problem, with 4.8 million victims annually in the United States, according to the U.S. Department of Justice (2000). Their estimate includes only physically or sexually abused women. This is a low estimate of the broader phenomena of domestic abuse, because the prevalence of domestic violence is much higher when psychological abuse is included in the estimate. The impact of domestic violence is significant: being a victim of various kinds of abuse from a partner contributes to a significant loss in the quality of life across multiple domains. Victims often suffer from a variety of physical, psychological, and sexual problems as a result of domestic violence, and victims are more vulnerable to further violence in their future relationships.

Although there is a growing awareness of prevention and intervention strategies for domestic violence victims, retraumatization has not received enough attention from researchers and clinicians. There are a few studies exploring the links between childhood abuse (especially sexual abuse) experiences and subsequent domestic violence. However, most of these studies simply have looked for a correlation between child sexual abuse and adult domestic violence. Not many studies have been done exploring the role of more general child abuse, including witnessing domestic violence, or being a victim of adult domestic violence on future victimization. Mechanisms of retraumatization regarding domestic violence have not been identified. Understanding diverse patterns and mechanisms of retraumatization is important to help identify protective and risk factors and to develop effective intervention and prevention strategies. This chapter will explore retraumatization processes related to domestic violence, review extant prevention programs, and suggest integrated assessment and intervention strategies. We will begin the chapter with a review of three factors that evidence suggests result in an increased risk of domestic violence: abuse during childhood, witnessing domestic violence as a child, and earlier domestic violence experiences.

## RISK FACTORS FOR RETRAUMATIZATION OF DOMESTIC VIOLENCE

### Physical and Sexual Abuse During Childhood

*Risk of Becoming a Victim of Domestic Violence*

Physical and sexual abuse during childhood can have long-term negative effects on victims. Adult women who were victimized as children report feeling less self-confident and more depressed, anxious, fearful, angry, hostile, and lonely than women who were not victimized (Harper & Arias, 2009). They also engaged in more self-destructive behaviors, substance abuse, and problematic sexual behaviors. In the long term, they are more likely to have chronic depression, experience elder abuse, and have problems related to trauma misdiagnosed as dementia or mental illness (Allers, Benjack, & Allers, 1992).

Negative consequences resulting from childhood abuse increase the likelihood of becoming a victim of various types of violence in adulthood (Irwin, 1999). Specifically, women abused as children are at increased risk of physical (24.2% to 51.4%) or psychological abuse (62% to 70.8%) during adulthood

(Noll, Horowitz, Bonanno, Trickett, & Putnam, 2003) compared to adults without any childhood abuse history. It has been reported that a disproportional number of victims of domestic violence are also survivors of childhood sexual abuse (e.g., Koopman et al., 2005). Alexander (2009) reported that multiple relationship traumatizations as an adult (abuse experiences by more than one partner) were not associated with factors such as education, income, employment status, ethnicity, relationship status, number of children, or residence in a shelter. Rather, childhood trauma experiences (including childhood sexual abuse and witnessing violence between parents) appeared to be a predictor associated with an increased risk, at least two to three times, for subsequent multiple victimizations in adulthood. Therefore, a history of physical or sexual trauma in childhood can be a distal contributor to multiple subsequent retraumatization experiences including domestic violence.

### Risk of Becoming a Perpetrator of Domestic Violence

Men who experience early physical or sexual abuse or child maltreatment in a home setting with domestic violence are more likely to become perpetrators of domestic violence in adulthood. Because these men learned early on that aggression can be used to manage interpersonal conflicts, they view their use of violence against their partners as legitimate (Salisbury, Henning, & Holdford, 2009). Unfortunately, there are no data about whether abuse during childhood increases the risk for subsequently perpetrating domestic violence as a teen or adult.

## Witnessing Domestic Violence as a Child

### Risk of Becoming a Victim of Domestic Violence

The second factor that increases the risk of becoming an adult victim of domestic violence is witnessing abuse between one's parents while still a child. In fact, some researchers have reported that witnessing interparental violence is a more consistent predictor of becoming a domestic violence victim later on than a history of child abuse (e.g., Gottman & Rushe, 1995). It is estimated that 3.3 million to 10 million children in the United States between the ages of 3 and 17 are exposed to violence between their parents each year (Straus, 1991). When looking at women victims who go to shelters to get services, at least 70% of those battered women have children who accompany them (Jaffe, Wolfe, & Wilson, 1990), and 72% of those children have witnessed violence (Markward, 1997). Although these children may not be fully aware that abuse happens (Peled, 1993), they report elevated levels of anger, fear, terror, confusion, guilt, shame, hopelessness, helplessness, general psychological distress, and lower levels of social adjustment than those who did not (Ericksen

& Henderson, 1992; Henning, Leitenberg, Coffey, Turner, & Bennett, 1996). These difficulties may contribute to retraumatization when these children grow into adulthood (Kalmuss, 1984). For example, 131 college women who witnessed domestic violence as children later experienced more sexual and physical abuse in their adulthood than did women who had not witnessed domestic violence. In addition, there was more violence and adult sexual abuse in their dating relationships (Maker, Kemmelmeier, & Peterson, 1998).

### Risk of Becoming a Perpetrator of Domestic Violence

One of the biggest risk factors for men becoming abusive toward their female partners is having witnessed father-to-mother violence in their families of origin (Guterman and Lee, 2005; Heyman & Smith, 2002). Children who witness domestic violence between their parents often see violence as a normal, effective, and socially acceptable way to resolve conflict, and report a much higher threshold at which they consider aggression problematic (Campbell & Lewandowski, 1997). When violence is frequent in their family of origin, children may learn an accepting attitude toward the use of aggression (Bandura, 1973). Aggression is normative in their experience. This may explain why children who witness aggression between parents have a higher risk of assaulting their siblings, their parents, and their own intimate partners, and are more likely to commit violent crimes outside their families (Alexander, 2009).

## Prior Domestic Violence Experiences as a Victim

### Risk of Serial Victimization From More Than One Partner

Experiencing domestic violence with one partner is a marker for increased risk of subsequent or recurring partner abuse. For example, Alexander (2009) surveyed 93 abused women and found that 56% of them reported that their previous intimate partners were also abusive. Cattaneo and Goodman (2005) reported that 19% to 44% of previously battered women continued to experience abuse over the course of 3 years with subsequent partners. However, repeated victimization from multiple partners has just started getting attention, and there have not been enough studies to establish prevalence rates. It is also not yet clear what other specific risk factors might be relevant.

### Risk of Ongoing Abuse From the Same Partner

Adult domestic violence victims' ongoing vulnerability to further abuse with the same partner has been well reported. However, the rates of re-abuse vary depending on which definitions and research methods are employed. For example, it is likely that using new arrest records from police data results in lower (and likely misleading) prevalence rates. In contrast, using data that include physical, sexual, and psychological abuse results in much higher prevalence rates. Bcause of this variation among studies, the rate of re-abuse by the same violent partner ranges enormously from 1.6% (Ford & Regoli, 1992) to 93% (Jacobson, Gottman, Gortner, Berns, & Shortt, 1996). Nevertheless, there is a consensus among researchers that abused women have increased vulnerability to further domestic violence by the same violent partner. Cattaneo and Goodman (2005) reviewed risk factors for re-abuse and suggested three levels of analysis (or, types of moderator variables): individual-, relationship-, and system-level variables. With individual-level variables, the perpetrator's ethnicity and abuse history in his childhood and the victim's age are not found to predict re-abuse. On the other hand, the victim's socioeconomic status (SES) is negatively associated with re-abuse, which indicates that lower SES victims are more likely to be re-abused than higher SES counterparts. This may be because more resources are available to leave the abuser and get safe for high SES victims, and may reflect greater losses potentially incurred for higher SES perpetrators (e.g., employment, social status, that could be threatened with incarceration). The amount of time the couple has lived together was a significant negative predictor of re-abuse among the interpersonal-level variables. Staying in a long-term relationship could be related to less frequent re-abuse because of relationship investment. However, this only applied to women with higher SES. Having children with the perpetrator increased by a factor of four the reports of re-abuse. Minimal prosecution and the type of treatment for perpetrators are important predictor variables at the system level. This is because victims are reluctant to report re-abuse to the police when their partners already have been arrested and are in treatment (Taylor, Davis, & Maxwell, 2001). This suggests significant limitations in the effectiveness of the criminal justice system in deterring revictimization from the same perpetrator over time.

Thus, from previous literature, it is clear that there are two more vulnerable populations for domestic violence revictimization or retraumatization: women who suffered abuse as children and women previously victimized by domestic violence. Although there are not many studies that address mechanisms of domestic violence retraumatization, the effects of the initial episode of abuse on the victims' cognition and a variety of behaviors are known to increase the risk of further traumatization (Davies & Frawley, 1994). More details about the putative cognitive and emotional impairment mechanisms will now be provided.

## MECHANISMS OF RETRAUMATIZATION FOR DOMESTIC VIOLENCE

### Interpersonal Problems

One of most salient possible mechanisms of retraumatization concerns the interpersonal problems children or adult victims develop. Abused children typically grow up in distressed families. Family distress is a general term that reflects a variety of processes, including higher rates of parent neglect, less family cohesion, greater conflict, increased chaos, poorer emotion socialization, problematic meta-emotional climate, increased invalidation of children's experiences, parenting deficits, and so on. Children often are not treated appropriately in these environments in part because parents are emotionally unavailable and unable to provide protection (Lieberman & Pawl, 1988). Thus, child abuse typically reflects not just the index behavior (one or more episodes) that is defined as abusive, but also a host of other nonabusive but nevertheless potentially damaging processes. In research, then, "child abuse" reflects not only specific abusive behaviors, but also is a proxy for these often chronically problematic family processes. As a result of all of these, children may show higher levels of aggression, passivity, withdrawal, somatic symptoms, anxiety, depression, and suicidal gestures (Browne & Finkelhor, 1986), which would, in turn, contribute to problems developing healthy interpersonal relationships. These children also are more likely to experience significant interpersonal betrayal and have difficulty trusting others (e.g., Alexander & Warner, 2003). Therefore, child victims develop negative and sometimes illogical (overgeneralized) beliefs or schemas (e.g., that abuse is acceptable, or that abuse is the only way to connect with a partner) and carry those problematic interpersonal schemas into their adulthood (Grauerholz, 2000).

These maladaptive beliefs may be associated with various emotions, other cognitions, and behaviors that contribute to subsequent retraumatization and other negative outcomes. For example, women who experienced childhood sexual abuse reported that their view of others as hostile and controlling generalized to their current relationship, even when it was a nonviolent one (Cloitre, Cohen, & Scarvalone, 2002).

Adult women victims also experience more interpersonal problems after being exposed to partner aggression and violence. Abusive partners, in addition to being overtly physically or sexually violent, also invalidate victims' experiences, including their emotions, self-determination, safety needs, wants, beliefs or opinions, and actions. Victims are frequently punished either overtly or subtly. *Invalidation* is communicating rejection, criticism, contempt, illegitimacy, or disregard for the other's experiences and behaviors. In a chronically invalidating environment such as this, victims develop increased sensitivity, vulnerability, and high levels of negative emotion, including sadness, fear, anxiety, and shame (Fruzzetti & Worrall, 2010; Iverson, Shenk, & Fruzzetti, 2009). Even women who get out of abusive relationships continue to experience high levels of negative emotions and have difficulty asking for or receiving social support. Inaccurate expression of emotions and wants can lead to interpersonal problems and isolation, along with individual distress and psychopathology (Fruzzetti & Iverson, 2006; Fruzzetti & Worrall, 2010). For example, 52 women who were domestic violence victims reported greater relationship problems compared to nonvictimized women in a control group.

They showed significantly higher interpersonal problems, social avoidance, nonassertive, and overly nurturing characteristics (Classen, Field, Koopman, Nevill-Manning, & Spiegel, 2001).

Theoretically, both psychodynamic theory and social learning theory provide support for the idea that experiencing violence in childhood can affect negatively a person's interpersonal functioning. Psychodynamic approaches assume that early childhood trauma can impair one's sense of self, which distorts healthy ways of relating to others (Davies & Frawley, 1994; Herman, 1994). Subsequently, women may repeat the violent relationship they developed in their childhood. Social learning theory suggests that learning contributes in a variety of ways to the increased risk of subsequent violence for abused children or those witnessing violence between parents. Early victims are likely to understand (and experience) aggression, sexuality, and intimacy very differently than children without an abuse history. They can learn violence as a way to relate to others, achieve desired outcomes, resolve conflict, and communicate. Their parents' conflict pattern may have modeled violence for them, possibly both as a means of conflict resolution and as a pathway to intimacy. Children can thus learn maladaptive behaviors, beliefs, and attitudes about domestic violence, and their physiological reactions to aggression and violence can change as well. Child victims of domestic violence may become less sensitive to violence and accept violence as a valid conflict-resolving or communication strategy. At the same time, they fail to learn alternative, adaptive behaviors to resolve or manage conflict. Hence, they may be more likely to use (or tolerate) aggression and antisocial responses as a way of coping in relationships and may rationalize the use of violence (Campbell & Levendosky, 1997).

## Individual Psychological Distress and Psychopathology

Both child and adult survivors of various forms of trauma subsequently demonstrate higher rates of depression, anxiety, substance use, and other forms of individual distress and psychopathology. These trauma-related outcomes can have a number of effects that increase vulnerability to subsequent revictimization: (1) individual distress may decrease a woman's ability to discriminate more safe from less safe potential partners; (2) lowered self-esteem associated with these kinds of problems may increase the likelihood that a woman may affiliate with more dangerous, or simply less well-matched, potential partners; (3) these same factors may make it more difficult for women previously victimized to get out of new relationships as they become abusive; (4) individual distress and psychopathology puts strain on relationships and negatively affects partners; and (5) individual distress and psychopathology impair work and social functioning, making women more dependent on partners, increasing the power differential between them.

## Hypersensitization

Both children and adults who experienced direct or indirect abuse are sensitized to victimization and are more likely to remember abusive experiences later. In other words, a history of exposure to extreme stress can make a person more vulnerable to experiencing psychological distress when he or she has stressful events later in life (Bremner, Southwick, & Charney, 1995). This vulnerability to trauma symptoms is called *hypersensitization* (Post, Weiss, & Smith, 1995). The process of hypersensitization begins with the original abuse experiences and the problems that are initiated by the original abuse. As similarly stressful life events are experienced, victims become progressively more sensitive to these events and respond with increased distress (McFarlane & Yehuda, 1996). These recent life events and stressful experiences can be associated with specific trauma-related problems (e.g., posttraumatic stress disorder [PTSD]), including anxiety, dissociation, re-experiencing, avoidance, hypervigilance, sexual problems, and sleep disturbance (Classen, Nevo, Koopman, Nevill-Manning, Gore-Felton, Rose, & Spiegel, 2002). Of course, even absent PTSD, significant impairment and suffering can result.

Hypersensitivity has been examined using bio/physiological tools. Studies of child sexual abuse survivors have revealed hormonal disruptions and dysregulation of the hypothalamic–pituitary–adrenal (HPA) axis (DeBellis et al., 2002). In a study examining adult sexual abuse victims who underwent medical forensic exams, victims evidenced immune functioning consistent with sensitization (Groer, Thomas, Evans, Helton, & Weldon, 2006). Woods et al. (2005) developed a bio-psycho-immunologic model to explain how domestic violence affects women's physical condition, especially their immune systems. An African American sample of domestic violence victims showed more physical pain symptoms as a result of immune system functioning impairment compared to nonabused women. Hence, abuse experiences can change victims' immune systems, which can lead to increased mental health as well as physical health problems. This physical and mental sensitization, in turn, makes the victim more vulnerable to similar episodes later.

## Problems Regulating Emotion

Abuse can directly contribute to emotion regulation problems, because it promotes chronic arousal that reduces the ability to regulate emotion (Cloitre, 1998). After experiencing traumatic events, victims have enormous emotional arousal and psychological distress. For example, shame is a common emotion experienced in response to childhood abuse (especially sexual abuse) and domestic violence in adulthood. When a victim feels shame, this emotion makes the individual more vulnerable in general (Wurmser, 1987) but also more likely to withdraw socially and fail to discuss the incident, because social withdrawal is associated with shame. This withdrawal interrupts both the needed emotional healing (reduced shame via exposure and support) and effective problem solving to achieve safety (which often requires both emotional and instrumental support). To relieve emotional distress, some victims instead use problematic emotion regulation strategies, including dissociation, depression, substance use, or self-harm behaviors. Dissociation is a prominent avoidant behavior that functions to "protect" victims from psychological suffering. There is evidence that women with a childhood sexual abuse history tend to dissociate more than women without such a history (Goodwin, Cheeves, & Connell, 1988). Dissociation also alters the cognitive framework of a person's reality and increases one's vulnerability to subsequent violence (Braun, 1988).

From both learning and emotional development perspectives, early abuse can contribute to failure to learn effective emotion regulation skills. In abusive environments, children have poor models for managing negative emotions (Cloitre, 1998). Children may not learn how to interpret accurately or modulate their emotions, how to appraise potentially dangerous situations accurately, and how to engage fight-or-flight reactions effectively. Consequently, emotion regulation problems may interfere with good problem solving and decision making, resulting in victims making poor choices about potential intimate partners (e.g., high arousal could interfere with making accurate discriminations around subtle cues about safety and other factors). Similarly, high emotional arousal and dysregulation contribute to a lack of cognitive and emotive skills to understand or cope with violent situations, and can increase the risk of retraumatization (Dietrich, 2007; Iverson et al., 2009). Sadly and paradoxically, being an early victim makes subsequent victimization more likely.

## TREATMENT AND PREVENTION

There have been a few studies of couple interventions successfully treating victims of trauma. Most of them are skills focused, putting emphasis on improving communication, problem solving, coping, and mutual support (Riggs, 2000). However, the literature on the use of couple therapy with domestic violence is still lacking, and there are few empirical examinations of the efficacy of such interventions. Nevertheless, it is helpful to look at current treatment programs and their targets or strategies when developing treatments to prevent domestic violence retraumatization. Interventions for domestic violence address both batterers and victims, which will be considered separately below.

### Intervention for Batterers

There are few empirically supported programs for batterers. Based on a meta-analytic review of 22 studies examining treatment for abusers, current interventions do not have much empirical support for reducing recidivism: one thorough meta-analysis reported effect sizes only from 0.18 to 0.25 (Babcock, Green, & Robbie, 2004). Many of the most common treatments for batterers show few effects when evaluated in a rigorous way (e.g., utilize measures of recidivism beyond the self-report of the batterer, evaluate his behavior after criminal penalty threats end). The most common evidence-based intervention approach is based on a cognitive-behavioral conceptualization of battering behavior. Cognitive-behavioral models assume that abuse-supporting beliefs, lack of behavioral self-control, and poor relationship skills are important causes of abuse. The main interventions were developed by Sonkin, Martin, and Walker (1985), and the program typically includes anger management training, skill development, cognitive restructuring (in particular around attitudes toward women, power, and control), relaxation training, and assertiveness training. This approach emphasizes altering functional aspects of behavior. The most popular batterer treatment program is focused on anger management, although evidence for its effectiveness is quite weak. Anger management, of course, focuses on poor regulation of anger as the primary factor in domestic violence (Gondolf, 1985).

In addition, there are several conjoint treatment programs developed to decrease battering. Most are psychoeducation programs, also loosely based on a cognitive-behavioral approach. Conjoint treatments are somewhat controversial. Critics point out that when the main treatment target is relationship improvement, which involves changes that both partners can make, this may imply that the victim of domestic violence (typically the female partner) is responsible for being battered (i.e., if she changes her behavior, she will not be battered). On the other hand, advocates of this approach note that many couples conceptualize aggression in their relationship as sometimes involving bilateral violence, and that many couples seek treatment for battering expecting and desiring to be treated conjointly. The treatments described in Table 13.1 are the most common conjoint treatments. Among them, only Domestic Violence Focused Couples Treatment (DVFCT) and Physical Aggression Couples Treatment (PACT) have empirical support to date.

## Intervention for Victims

Not only are there few treatment programs that focus on victims, but those that do focus on victims often address only key practical or instrumental outcomes (e.g., housing, medical attention) and pay less attention to victims' emotional well-being. Clearly, instrumental outcomes are very important and provide a basis for later addressing emotional outcomes. But, because the emotional consequences of domestic violence are severe and often linger even after the violence stops, targeting psychological health and well-being is also essential.

## TABLE 13.1 Programs to Decrease Male-to-Female Violence

| Treatment Title | Citation | Treatment Summary |
| --- | --- | --- |
| CBT Program | Dunford (2000) | Cognitive restructuring, empathy enhancement, communication skills, anger modification, and skills teaching for 26 weeks |
| Couples Abuse Prevention Program (CAPP) | LaTaillade, Epstein, & Werlinich (2006) | Focusing on enhancing the quality of the couple relationship and reducing risk factors; psychoeducation about abusive behavior and its negative consequences |
| Domestic Violence Focused Couples Treatment (DVFCT) | Stith, McCollum, Rosen, Locke, & Goldberg (2005) | Psychoeducation to develop a vision of a healthy relationship, communication skills, and dealing with relapse to remove any type of violence between partners, and help couples to improve relationship qualities |
| Physical Aggression Couples Treatment (PACT) | Heyman & Schlee (2003) | Psychoeducation about violence patterns and alternatives to increase awareness of one's responsibility about using violence; anger management, effective communication, and conflict problem-solving skill training to decrease and eventually reduce violent behaviors |

HOPE (Helping to Overcome PTSD with Empowerment) (Johnson & Zlotnick, 2006) and Dialectical Behavior Therapy (DBT) (Iverson, Shenk, & Fruzzetti, 2009) are representative treatments that have been developed specifically to treat emotional difficulties of domestic violence victims. HOPE is a treatment aimed at the psychological suffering women victims have, centered around PTSD-related problems. The primary goal of HOPE is to decrease PTSD-related problems, depression, loss of resources, and degree of social impairment and to increase victims' effective use of community resources. Thus, HOPE primarily addresses the cognitive, behavioral, and interpersonal dysfunction associated with PTSD. It also encourages collaboration with shelter staff, incorporates individual goals into treatment, and prioritizes immediate safety needs and empowerment. Participants who received HOPE reported high satisfaction with treatment and showed significant decreases in PTSD and depression severity, less social impairment and resource loss, as well as a significant increase in the effective use of resources (Johnson & Zlotnick, 2006).

One DBT program for domestic violence is a 12-week program that focuses on improving skills related to emotion regulation. DBT was originally developed to treat borderline personality disorder using emotion regulation and mindfulness skills (Linehan, 1993a, 1993b). From a DBT perspective,

emotion regulation problems are a common consequence of domestic violence and influence women's abilities to manage other skill domains in their
lives. Thus, there are four treatment foci (Iverson et al., 2009): (1) teaching
skills (mindfulness, emotion regulation, distress tolerance, self-validation,
and interpersonal effectiveness); (2) skills generalization to problem areas
of life; (3) motivation to use skillful behaviors as alternatives to maladaptive behaviors that they may be utilizing (e.g., withdrawal, substance use);
and (4) reducing or eliminating problematic barriers to improvement coming
from their social and family environments (Fruzzetti et al., 2009; Fruzzetti
& Iverson, 2004, 2006). Women who participated in this program reported
significant reductions in depression, hopelessness, and general psychiatric distress, and significantly increases in social adjustment (Iverson et al., 2009).

Emotion-Focused Couple Therapy (EFT) is one of very few treatments
with evidence for treating trauma in couples. This approach was originally
developed for couples with ordinary relationship distress and enjoys empirical support for that. EFT is designed to increase an individual's sense of
emotional connection by reprocessing a partner's emotional responses and
changing their interaction pattern. It was modified to treat couples where one
or both partners are traumatized by abuse, violent crime, and natural disasters,
and has been shown to be effective (Johnson & Williams-Keeler, 1998).
The treatment is relatively short term, with intervention ranging from 12 to
20 sessions. It consists of stabilization, building self and relational capacities,
and integration. Stabilization includes assessment, identification of couple's
interaction patterns, and underlying emotions. When a couple becomes stable
and ready for the next steps of treatment, development of capacities to handle
traumatic experiences follows. In an integration process, couples learn alternative ways of coping and practice new interaction patterns. After completion
of the EFT process, the goal is for a couple to be able to work on solutions
to their trauma-related issues, including anniversary dates and reminders of
previous trauma experiences (e.g., Riggs, 2000).

## Couple Interventions as an Adjunct to Individual Treatment

Women who have experienced childhood abuse or adult domestic violence
have been reported to suffer significantly (Waysman, Mikulincer, Solomon,
& Weisenberg, 1993). Interpersonal or relationship difficulties are one afteref-
fect with enduring painful consequences. For example, women with a history
of childhood sexual abuse are not as satisfied with their adult intimate relationships (Fleming, Mullen, Sibthorpe, & Bammer, 1999), have more difficulty trusting their partners (DiLillo & Long, 1999), and report more sexual
problems (Mullen, Martin, Anderson, & Romans, 1994) than women without
any childhood sexual abuse history. Their male partners also report more relationship difficulties, reporting that their relationship satisfaction level is lower

and that there is a higher level of general distress due to caring for victimized partners (Nelson & Wampler, 2000). Partners also feel hopeless and helpless about their relationship and report more general relationship problems (Riggs, Byrne, Weathers, & Litz, 1998), higher levels of hostility (Carroll, Rueger, Foy, & Donahoe, 1985), less self-disclosure and intimacy (Roberts et al., 1982), and more sexual disinterest (Litz, Keane, Fisher, Marx, & Monaco, 1992). It is obvious that the experience of trauma has the potential to harm later intimate relationships and negatively affect both partners. Moreover, the soothing, love, acceptance, and validation that can be found or developed in healthy intimate partnerships could provide a vehicle to aid in the successful resolution (and management) of the sequelae of traumatic experiences that burden one partner. Therefore, couple interventions are a logical way to treat distress coming from one partner's trauma history, either as an adjunct to individual treatment or as a comprehensive mode of treatment. These may take a variety of forms, which now will be discussed.

## Roles for One Partner in Couple Interventions for the Other Partner's Trauma

### Psychoeducation

With appropriate psychoeducation, partners of victims may develop a better understanding of victims' trauma, behaviors related to their trauma experiences, and the aftereffects of trauma. In addition, understanding the impact of trauma, both directly and indirectly, on their relationship helps partners understand their conflict and other relationship patterns more fully. Psychoeducation also offers skills to improve the quality of the relationship in general, including communication, problem solving, effective response skills, emotion regulation, and other strategies (Riggs, 2000; Waysman et al., 1993). An overview of psychoeducational topics is presented in Table 13.2.

### Functional Support

Couple interventions have been reported to be a useful tool to aid in recovery from traumatic events. For example, rape victims expressed fewer somatic symptoms and enhanced perceptions of health by getting higher levels of social support (Kimerling & Calhoun, 1994). After getting enough social support, victims showed increased general well-being (Acitelli & Antonucci, 1994) and marital satisfaction (Julien & Markman, 1991). A partner can be a great source of social support (Fruzzetti & Worrall, 2010), perhaps boosting the victim's individual treatment (even when the partner is not directly involved in treatment). One partner can encourage and support the other partner with a trauma history to engage actively in individual treatment (including attending regularly, doing homework, or practicing skills to decrease target problems). For example, when a victim partner wants to skip the session (perhaps part of a pattern of avoidance), acknowledging that partner's difficulties as well as reminding him or her of the target of getting treatment (leading to trauma resolution) may provide a kind of cheerleading that helps reduce missed sessions or even dropout. Providing instrumental assistance, such as giving a ride to the clinic, providing child care, and doing errands for the partner can be helpful, as can minimizing demands during difficult treatment periods. These kinds of assistance can help the victim to engage in and complete individual treatment and increase treatment effectiveness.

### Active Assistance

It was reported that partner support can be an effective resource for trauma survivors, helping to decrease problems associated with traumatic experiences (e.g., Davidson, Hughes, Blazer, & George, 1991). A partner can help with problem solving and even provide coaching that is consistent with treatment targets and skills. For example, when a victimized partner is having a flashback, he or she can ask for emotional support or coaching (including reminders of what to do to manage the situation more effectively) from the other partner. A partner can legitimize the victim's experiences (validate emotions, wants, thoughts, beliefs, and sensations). The victimized partner can use the security of the current relationship and active support from the other partner to attempt difficult new steps (e.g., *in vivo* or imaginal exposure interventions). Having that kind of support is likely to help to regulate arousal, improve safety, and facilitate outcomes. One of the most common emotions child abuse or domestic violence victims have is shame. They feel ashamed about what happened to them and try to hide or withdraw. Victims often feel sadness about the situation, a sense of grief and loss, anger toward perpetrators and others, as well as a pervasive sense of disempowerment. Partners can help them sort out their emotions and respond in accepting, soothing, and validating ways that help reduce negative emotions associated with, and overgeneralized from their traumatic experiences. With a partner's help, victims may be able to function more adaptively more quickly and decrease destructive behaviors such as social withdrawal, self-invalidating responses, or even aggressive or self-destructive behaviors.

## ASSESSMENT AND INTERVENTION

### Assessment

Assessment begins by identifying the trauma history of the survivor. In addition, the impact of the trauma on the couple's current relationship and conflicts needs to be clarified. Strengths that a couple has, such as closeness or intimacy, can be helpful in facilitating the treatment process. As treatment targets are developed, assessment should be specific, allowing for the development of a detailed treatment target hierarchy, including safety targets, trauma targets, and other quality of life and relationship targets (Fruzzetti & Fantozzi, 2008). The basic tools for assessment are questionnaires, daily diary cards or self-monitoring forms, individual and conjoint interviews, or recorded (or observed) samples of the couple's conversations and interactions (Fruzzetti & Jacobson, 1990).

## Questionnaires

There are standardized questionnaires available for trauma victims. The Childhood Trauma Questionnaire (CTQ) is a 28-item self-report with five subscales, including physical, sexual, emotional abuse, physical neglect, and emotional neglect in childhood (Bernstein, & Fink, 1998). The Impact of Events Scale, Revised (IES-R) can be useful to assess victims' distress related to traumatic events. It is a quick self-report measure, and more than half of its items correspond to *Diagnostic and statistical manual of mental disorders* (fourth edition) (*DSM-IV*) (APA, 1994) criteria for PTSD (Weiss & Marmar, 1996). In addition, the Trauma Symptom Inventory (TSI) provides a child/adulthood interpersonal trauma history with 100 items addressing a variety of trauma-related problems (Briere, Elliott, & Harris, 2009).

It is essential to get a thorough sense of relationship aggression in both the current relationship and in previous relationships. The Revised Conflict Tactics Scale (CTS-2) (Straus, Hamby, Boney-McCoy, & Sugarman, 1996) identifies specific behaviors (type and frequency) that each partner engages in when in relational conflict. It includes subcategories of physical, psychological, and sexual violence. In cases in which one of the partners has multiple traumatic experiences, the CTS-2 can be used to begin to assess both previous and current relationship aggression and violence, typically followed up with interviews of the partners separately. In addition, other versions of the CTS allow for detailed assessment of childhood abuse experiences.

Unfortunately, there is no measure for the impact of previous trauma on a victim's current relationship. However, the Dyadic Adjustment Scale (DAS) (Spanier, 1976) is a common measure of global relationship distress, discrepancies between individuals' descriptions of relationship problems, and areas of agreement and conflict (Spanier, 1976). The Couple Satisfaction Index (CSI) has excellent psychometric properties and also measures relationship satisfaction and quality. The CSI includes 32 items (Rogge & Funk, 2007), although shorter versions are also reliable. The Personal Assessment of Intimacy in Relationships (PAIR) provides couple's current perceived and expected relationship patterns around closeness and intimacy, and includes subscales assessing different domains of intimate relationship functioning, including social, sexual, intellectual, recreational, and emotional intimacy (Schaefer & Olson, 2007).

The Difficulties in Emotion Regulation Scale (DERS) can be useful to measure emotion regulation strategies, including both more adaptive and functional strategies and more maladaptive and destructive ones. Childhood abuse or domestic violence victims have reported significant difficulties regulating their emotions. Assessing victims' emotion regulation patterns can be helpful in treating problematic or dysfunctional behaviors that function to manage emotions.

In addition, assessment of depression and a variety of other forms of psychological distress, including suicidality, is essential. Using a quick screening tool such as the Beck Depression Inventory (Beck, 1979) or an omnibus assessment tool such as the Brief Symptom Inventory or Symptom Checklist–90 (Derogatis) can provide a quick screening that can be followed up in an interview.

## Recorded Interaction or Conversation Samples

Recorded samples of partners interacting around real topics offer an opportunity to see a couple's communication patterns. They allow the therapist to evaluate accurate (versus inaccurate) expression, validating (versus invalidating) responses, negative escalation and its triggers, and a variety of other targets that are easier to observe directly than assess in other ways (Fruzzetti & Fantozzi, 2008; Fruzzetti & Jacobson, 1992).

Couples can engage in ordinary conversation around any topics that illustrate their communication patterns. It may be useful to get samples of how partners interact around both problems in the relationship (e.g., each partner could pick one problem topic for discussion) and more neutral or positive topics and situations, as well as how they interact around partners expressing distress of any kind, and in particular, how they interact around trauma-related topics. Recording the conversations has the benefits of allowing the therapist to leave the room and thereby reduce whatever influence or demand characteristics he or she might bring to the situation, and allows the therapist to watch the conversations more than once to identify possible patterns, to "code" the interactions, and even to get consultation. Moreover, the therapist could use parts of the recording in-session as feedback in later sessions. However, recording is not always possible. In such cases, the therapist may simply move out of the line of sight of the partners and observe their conversation, without interruption.

It is important to have guidelines available to interpret partner behaviors during observed (or recorded) interactions. For example, while watching the couple's conversation, the therapist must evaluate what each partner is doing according to some criteria or along certain dimensions. Given the important roles of accurate expression and validating (and invalidating) responses, these particular responses may be useful to rate (cf. Fruzzetti, Santisteban, & Hoffman, 2007, for examples of how to identify and rate validating and invalidating responses).

## Interviews

Victims' intimate relationship histories need to be clarified to understand previous relationships, their qualities, and their impact on current relationships. Both separate and conjoint interviews are required. Individual interviews allow the therapist to develop rapport with each partner and to assess the current relationship for aggression and violence directly and confidentially, if necessary. The presence of an abusive partner can inhibit the victim and result in missed information concerning any type of abuse or fears of abuse, and other sensitive topics (Fruzzetti & Jacobson, 1992). In this interview, the therapist is also able to get individual history, especially trauma history, and information about previous relationship problems and treatment experiences. After separate interviews, a conjoint interview can include assessment of the couple's relationship history, positive strengths and weaknesses, and how one partner understands the other's previous trauma and its effects on their relationship.

Getting details about problematic interactions can begin with direct observation (described above) and continue in a conjoint interview. One way to do this is to conduct a "chain analysis" of an argument or disagreement. This includes getting a step-by-step description of each partner's thoughts, emotional reactions, and actions (what he or she said and did in the moment), and how each person's behavior affected the other. It can be very useful to "map" it all out on a whiteboard or paper. This map illustrates their communication path and helps partners to understand each other better (Fruzzetti, 2006; Fruzzetti et al., 2007).

## Interventions

### Commitment to Therapy

In order to minimize the likelihood of dropout from treatment and maximize focused work in treatment, it is essential to orient partners to the treatment process and get a strong commitment early on. In DBT, commitment efforts try to identify, build, and accentuate the pros of treatment, including what clients can get out of treatment, while working to minimize the cons of the treatment, the things getting in the way, or what make the process difficult. Spending perhaps half a session on this to get a clear commitment at the beginning is important. This is followed up as needed throughout the course of treatment both to prevent dropout and to keep partners actively engaged in the treatment process.

## Treatment Target Hierarchy

Beginning during the assessment and commitment processes, the therapist and couple collaborate to make clear the general treatment goals and to establish a specific treatment target hierarchy. Based on assessment information, clear targets such as having effective communication skills, better understanding each other, providing more support and validation, reducing conflict, or increasing intimacy and closeness can be identified. Partners may have similar or quite different targets, but together they agree (along with the therapist) that achievement of these targets would go a long way toward satisfying their relationship goals. With each target, specific intervention strategies can then be identified and implemented as foci of each session.

# Structure and Strategies

## Structure

There is a minimal structure that the therapist employs in each session. This includes going over the client's diary card (to monitor and assess for the occurrence of primary and secondary targets, which helps organize the session agenda); completing a "chain analysis"; helping the clients to apply new skills as solutions; and ending with a commitment to practice relevant skills in order to manage similar situations in the future. The structure of each session is flexible but always built around these four activities, albeit with different targets.

The *diary card* or monitoring checklist helps the client and therapist keep track of targets and provides a way to track targets in order to set the session agenda. The diary card can include thoughts, actions, emotions, and skills as targets (cf. Fruzzetti et al., 2007, for an example of a partner diary card). This self-monitoring process helps to provide accurate weekly assessment and reporting. In addition, partners can be more motivated when able to view progress visually over time.

After going over the diary card, the therapist conducts a *chain analysis*, which identifies important moments in which partners need to change their behaviors (i.e., problematic emotional reactions, judgments, invalidating responses, inaccurate expression, and other things that led to poor outcomes in a particular interaction). Any behavioral chain that produced conflict or left the couple more distant can be assessed this way, and partners are encouraged to understand, accept, and validate their own and each other's behaviors as the chain unfolds.

As they begin to understand their own and the other's responses, and how they were reacting to each other, each partner (with help from the therapist) identifies skills that he or she could have used, in principle, that would have altered the problematic interaction (or chain) and likely would have led to a more satisfying outcome. These skills include anything from among the various skills available in DBT with families, which include the traditional DBT skills of mindfulness, distress tolerance, emotion regulation, and interpersonal effectiveness (Linehan, 1993b), as well as more relational DBT skills such as inhibiting invalidating responses, accurate expression (of emotion, wants, etc.), building or rebuilding positive relationship time, validation, mutual problem solving, and closeness (Fruzzetti, 2006). These skills will be discussed in more detail later in this chapter.

The couple then tries out these new skills in session. This strengthening and generalization of skills demonstrates how close each partner is to being able to engage in the interaction differently, and it gives the therapist opportunities to help them employ the skills, coach them, and help manage partner responses. If successful in the session, the resulting increased understanding and more regulated affect help increase motivation to build the skills further in daily life. Then, partners make a commitment to practice these alternative, more skillful behaviors to prevent a similar chain from happening in a similar situation in the future.

### Strategies and Skills

The long-term relationship goals of couple treatment with a trauma victim are to increase positive interactions and to reduce negative relationship patterns. To achieve this, the therapist needs to be dialectic, which includes the ability to be both understanding and accepting of the current interactions (including affective, cognitive, and behavioral components) and simultaneously focused on changing them (problem solving). Balancing acceptance and change is one of the cornerstone strategies of the therapist. Specifically, the therapist acknowledges the problematic behaviors and interactions, how partners come to behave that way, and how even destructive reactions make sense given their history (both individually and as a couple). Partners can then feel understood and accepted and become more committed to engaging the work. At the same time, of course, the therapist needs to block dysfunctional behaviors (the idea is that there is little value in practicing dysfunction in the session) and to push partners to create more skillful and effective alternatives.

Once specific treatment structures are established, specific interventions can be implemented. Although each couple with a trauma history reports different background and idiographic patterns of suffering, couple interventions can be divided into two categories based on their types of problems: (1) couples with a partner who has experienced childhood abuse and (2) couples with a partner who has a domestic violence history. Although overlapping, distinctive interventions for each population will be discussed, followed by more general treatment interventions in addition to those noted earlier (psychoeducation, providing functional support and active partner assistance in treatment).

## SPECIFIC TRAUMA-FOCUSED INTERVENTIONS WHEN A PARTNER EXPERIENCED CHILDHOOD ABUSE OR PREVIOUS DOMESTIC ABUSE

Victims who suffer from previous trauma often report a lot of psychological pain, including depression, anxiety, and relationship difficulties. Individual treatment and partner's support can effectively decrease these problems. At the same time, partners can work together to reduce aversive conflict that may be (at least in part) both a consequence and a cause of individual distress and psychopathology (e.g., Fruzzetti & Iverson, 2004). When a trauma victim is highly sensitive to any negative triggers in the current relationship, he or she may attribute that arousal and sensitivity to the current partner, and blaming the partner can happen often. The therapist can help the victim to recognize sensitivity and help the victim make more accurate attributions. For example, if the current partner has never threatened violence or engaged in any kind of related aggression, being mindful of this partner as safe is important. Fears of abuse are likely to be more related to the previous abuser. Knowing the current partner is a safe person can decrease the trauma aftereffects and begin to help correct emotional experiences with certain triggers (Johnson & Williams-Keeler, 1998).

Accurate expression and validation skills are helpful. For example, Jill witnessed her parents' violence when she was young. Her father would slam the door closed, which marked the beginning of the violent episode. Now Jill is with John who is a nonviolent and loving partner, with no history of violence in their relationship. However, when John slams the door (either accidentally, or in haste or frustration), Jill's arousal escalates and she re-experiences high levels of fear, anxiety, and mild panic attacks. Her panic may even have over-generalized such that she feels fear any time John is frustrated (whether in normative situations in their relationship or even in moments in life that have little or nothing to do with Jill). In this situation, the therapist can help Jill to be mindful about her relationship with John in the present, remembering that he is a safe person. In addition, Jill can validate her own arousal, saying it makes sense she has fear when John slams the door given her history. However, Jack is not her abusive father, and slamming the door does not mean that abuse is being initiated. John, of course, can gently and clearly restate his nonviolent commitment, both proactively and when he perceives Jill to be fearful. The therapist's position can be that although it may be valid to feel panic given Jill's history, it is not actually "valid" to withdraw or avoid John at these times. At the same time, John can validate Jill's responses because he can understand that she has higher sensitivity resulting from her trauma history. The next step for the therapist is to help Jill to express her experiences accurately about her feelings and thoughts when the trigger happens (fear is present because of prior experiences, not due to anything John is doing, but she may have other reactions to John in the present, which are important to discuss, just not in a way that confounds them with the fear). Jill's accurate expression will likely make it easier for John to respond with soothing, support, and validation, in part because he would be less defensive (not being incorrectly accused, explicitly nor implicitly, of being aggressive), and in part because he could understand better Jill's experience (he would not be left to imagine what her negative emotion is or what it is about). John's validating responses would decrease Jill's arousal, further helping her express herself accurately (Fruzzetti & Worrall, 2010), and prevent these small triggers from becoming retraumatization experiences.

Sometimes partners present ordinary relationship conflicts and distress without either partner describing any traumatic reactions, despite one of them having experienced prior family violence. Although it may seem like the victim does not have any trauma-related suffering (and, indeed, often he or she may not have any), there is a possibility that he or she has high sensitivity and reactivity that affect their relationship, in particular in conflict situations. In other words, a victim may be aroused quickly even with a small disagreement, and react more (either aggressively or by withdrawing at a low threshold of conflict). It may also take longer to calm down. It is important for the couple to notice the possibility of an impact coming from the previous trauma history on the current relationship and include this in their awareness and interventions. When there is lack of understanding about vulnerabilities like these, both the partner and the victim can be judgmental about victims' behaviors. The partner's improved understanding about the victim's lower threshold of arousal and reactivity can be helpful to validate the victim's experiences or behaviors and prevent a small conflict from getting worse. Additionally, supporting and encouraging the victim's efforts to self-manage can facilitate problem solving.

On the other hand, it is also important for partners not to attribute ordinary negative emotional reactions to one partner's trauma history or to his or her "overreacting." This can end up pathologizing one partner, whose reactions might be quite normative. Sorting out what parts of a partner's reactions are due to current, versus historical, stimuli is important and may require slowly reviewing the conflict situation via a detailed chain analysis, as described earlier.

Even though their current partners are not abusive and their conflicts seem ordinary, victims with domestic violence history may be more sensitive to triggers such as disagreements, arguments, or partner's anger expressions. When a victim is emotionally aroused, he or she is likely to pathologize his or her experiences with self-blame. This and other forms of self-invalidation are important behaviors to understand in this population. In a domestic violence setting, victims' normal thoughts, wants, and behaviors are invalidated by the perpetrators. After having abusive relationships with one or more partners, victims can become self-invalidating, which, in turn, results in lowered self-esteem, helplessness, hopelessness, and a variety of difficulties (Iverson et al., 2009). Therefore, victims especially need self-validation training to prevent from being judgmental and overwhelmed with self-blame. Additionally, being aware of one's emotional states and expressing them accurately needs to be included in skills training.

## WHEN VICTIMS HAD ABUSE HISTORY WITH A CURRENT PARTNER, BUT NOT CURRENT OR ONGOING VIOLENCE

In this case, a partner was abused with the current partner, but there has been no further violence in the relationship for some time, and the abuser has clearly (and effectively) committed to nonviolence. It is essential that the formerly abusive partner has both learned new self-management skills (evidenced by nonaggressive and nonthreatening responses across a variety of situations that previously included aggression) and been clear about his or her commitment to staying nonviolent. If the victim stays with this partner, he or she could be hypervigilant about the partner's moods all the time. On the one hand, this is completely sensible and protective. On the other hand, as time passes and the formerly abusive partner maintains his or her commitment to nonviolence, not adjusting to the new situation could become counterproductive (i.e., interfere with both partners' goals for a more loving relationship).

Understanding and accepting the prior victim's sensitivity and the other partner's combination of guilt and disappointment is the first step for this couple. It may take some time to develop trust and safety for the victim. Part of the "repair" from the prior abuser is to be able to tolerate the other partner's reactions, and his or her own ensuing guilt, all without escalation. On the other hand, this does not mean that both partners cannot do things that are disappointing or frustrating in the relationship; this is as normative as it is unavoidable. These disagreements still must be managed, just in a nonthreatening way. Then, specific activities to increase positive interaction and intimacy can follow, with both partners becoming increasingly mindful of the safety of the current situation, in the context of the more aggressive past history.

## Partner Relationship Skills

Although each couple has different history and assessment results, there are general targets that couples with trauma histories share: reducing relationship conflict and increasing intimacy, with awareness of the present, safe relationship. For a better understanding of the trauma survivor, psychoeducation needs to be made available to the spouse. In addition, specific skills to improve relationship functioning can be offered, including relationship mindfulness, inhibiting negative responding, being together actively and rebuilding their relationship, accurate expression, validation and acceptance, and closeness.

These skills are employed both to decrease conflict and emotion escalation and to build satisfaction, support, and intimacy.

## Relationship Mindfulness

Mindfulness is the core concept of DBT and the first skill couples learn. The general purpose of introducing mindfulness is to encourage an individual to be more clearly aware of the current moment, including their thoughts, emotions, sensations, desires, and other behaviors. For couples, relationship mindfulness (Fruzzetti, 2006; Fruzzetti & Fantozzi, 2008) includes first becoming aware of each other's presence and noticing and describing each other physically. In addition, partner's behaviors can be observed descriptively rather than in a judgmental way (not right or wrong). Sometimes, a partner can automatically jump to judgments without awareness. For example, one partner may notice the other partner's behavior ("She [or he] is just eating dinner"), describe how he or she feels ("I am lonely and sad that he [or she] is not looking at me, paying more attention to me"), and then attach a judgment immediately ("she's selfish" or "he's a jerk"). The consequences of being stuck with judgments can lead to inaccurate expression (e.g., either withdrawing from or attacking the partner). Mindfulness and relationship mindfulness skills help partners slow down their emotional reactivity, and then their verbal and nonverbal responses, to be more aware of their thoughts, feelings, and wants, and promote more accurate expressions. Even when a partner has a judgment, the target is to identify one's judgment and switch one's attention to noticing and describing the thing judged (the partner or partner's behaviors) and one's own experience (sensations, feelings, wants). These processes help keep emotional arousal from increasing to dysregulated levels.

## Being Together Actively

Couples with a traumatized partner often have low levels of intimacy. They can avoid emotional attachment, which is the main predictor of couple satisfaction (Gottman & Levenson, 1986). Many trauma victims are emotionally ambivalent about their partners. They want to share more time, but they are scared of being with them because of previous conflict or retraumatization memories. Of course, all couples have problems that need negotiating, and all encounter conflict situations regularly. Over time, partners can increasingly avoid each other and even neutral and positive interactions decrease.

The first step couples can do is to share time doing some activities. Even small and simple things such as being together in the same space (watching the same television show or eating breakfast in the same room), noticing each other, going out for recreational activities, sharing intellectual pursuits and spiritual experiences, spending time with friends and families can be satisfying for both partners. This is "being together when they are together," which is a key part of relationship mindfulness (Fruzzetti, 2006, p. 39). Positive time together can increase "we-ness" and help the couple to feel connected to each other with increased couple identity. Sharing time together does not necessarily mean spending more time together physically. Increasing awareness of one's partner while together, even when engaged in different activities (e.g., both of them are in the living room doing different things) can be sufficient to enhance their awareness of each other.

## Inhibit Negative Responding or Invalidating Responses

The next target for couples is to reduce negative or invalidating behaviors. Invalidation includes judgments (e.g., right versus wrong, good versus bad, should versus should not), criticism, or even contempt about valid or legitimate behaviors, thoughts, or feelings (Fruzzetti & Iverson, 2004). Partners need to identify their own hurtful responses, which result in further negative responses from the other and lead to destructive conflict. To decrease those invalidating responses, both partners are required to give up their old pattern of "what is right or wrong" (self-righteousness). The idea is that being "effective" in a conflict situation is more important than being right, at least in terms of meeting relationship goals. Even if their appraisals or criticisms are correct, there is no utility in saying them out loud and hurting their partner's feelings. By using mindfulness skills, each partner can notice increased arousal and the urge to invalidate the other partner. Then, switching attention to their long-term goals (like having a better relationship) rather than short-term goals (feeling "good" about being right) can allow a couple to reduce invalidating responses. Practicing relationship mindfulness can facilitate this.

## Accurate Expressions

To increase positive responses and decrease negative responses, partners have to express their thoughts, emotions, and wants accurately. If a partner expresses his or her judgments or secondary emotions (e.g., anger or fear when disappointment is more justified and normative) instead of more accurate, primary emotions, a partner may respond in the same negative way (e.g., judgments, anger, attack). Then, the conflict will escalate, and it is harder to decrease their arousal, solve their problems, and get back to more loving and supportive interactions. Of course, in order to express oneself accurately, a person first needs to identify wants, emotions, opinions, and so forth, descriptively. Mindfulness skills can be useful to become aware of genuine thoughts, emotions, and wants, and to express them more accurately. Another requirement for accurate expressions is a supportive and validating environment. Invaliding responses such as not paying enough attention or invalidating what the other partner is expressing are at best discouraging (and at worst punishing and escalating), and the partner will quickly stop trying to express accurately. Accurate expression, in part because it is descriptive and nonblaming, helps the other partner understand and makes it easier to validate (Fruzzetti & Worrall, 2010).

## Validating Responses

Validating is communicating one's understanding and acceptance of another's feelings, thoughts, behaviors, or experiences. Validating responses help the traumatized partner's arousal to decrease and helps promote accurate expression (and, consequently, decreases conflict escalation). To increase positive interactions, a therapist can give specific skills about what can be validated, how to validate the other person, and how to get validating responses. There are both verbal and nonverbal ways to validate individuals' feelings, thoughts, or behaviors.

Verbal validation has seven categories (Fruzzetti, 2006; Fruzzetti & Iverson, 2006): (1) simply paying attention and actively listening with appropriate eye contact, nodding, or leaning toward the other person in an open and nonthreatening way; (2) acknowledging the other's feelings or desires or point of view descriptively by summarizing, paraphrasing, and reflecting on what he or she is saying; (3) asking questions about the partner's perspective or experience to get detailed information, and to increase understanding (not to "challenge" the partner's experience); (4) understanding the partner's behaviors in the context of the partner's history (e.g., "it makes sense you are sensitive to the door slamming because you experienced it quite often when your parents were violent"); (5) normalizing the partner's experience and trying to understand his or her feelings (e.g., "of course you are disappointed in this situation; I would feel that way, too…anybody would"); (6) being genuine by treating the partner as an equal human being, not as fragile; and (7) self-disclosing one's own vulnerability to match the partner's vulnerability (e.g., if one individual says "I love you," the other partner can say "I love you, too").

It is also possible to validate nonverbally by providing behavioral support. It could be doing errands for the other partner when he or she is busy and treating the other the way you like to be treated in similar circumstances. When the trauma victim is experiencing some kind of flashback or other trauma effect, simply being with him or her, providing support (soothing, gentle touch, etc.), is another example of nonverbal validation. When validation is used appropriately, it decreases negative reactivity and arousal because the individual feels accepted and understood. Even though validation does not solve problems, per se, it facilitates problem-solving processes. It also builds trust, closeness, safety, and support in the relationship.

## Acceptance and Closeness

One of the common long-term goals for a couple with a traumatized partner is to improve the quality of their relationship by decreasing dysfunctional behaviors and increasing intimacy. However, there still could be things a partner wants to change about the other one, which are difficult or impossible to change (at least not immediately). Even though they are working hard to behave effectively using skills, there are things that cannot be changed. For example, a trauma victim's hypersensitivity or other vulnerabilities can be disappointing to the other partner. On the other hand, a nontraumatized partner's insensitivity or failure to pay "enough" attention can be something a trauma victim wants to change about the other partner. However, complaining, criticizing, or other efforts to change one's behaviors can make the partner feel more frustrated and unhappy and even interfere with desired changes. To get out of this spiral, the first step partners can do is to stop putting energy into changing their partner's behaviors. Instead, they can try to tolerate their partner's behaviors. Remember, their efforts to change have not been successful, and these efforts are in fact are making things worse. To decrease frustration and begin to let go of this negative situation, each partner needs to validate his or her own legitimate disappointment and soothe their own suffering. In addition, getting active together can be helpful by distracting the partner from his or her negative emotional states and increasing positive ones. Looking at a partner's problem behavior and understanding it in the context of the partner's history, experiences, and life is another beneficial way to accept those behaviors. Finally, being mindful of the more desirable aspects of the other person, of the relationship, is essential. The idea is not to minimize or invalidate the things that are bothersome, but rather to spend most of their relationship time engaging in the relationship as it is in its best sense, in its best moments, and not letting less desirable aspects of the other partner or the relationship permeate and detract from the more desirable ones.

## CONCLUSION

Research has demonstrated that trauma can have a harmful effect on the lives of trauma survivors, including their intimate relationships. Child abuse victims who experienced physical, psychological, or sexual abuse become sensitized to their trauma history and vulnerable to retraumatization later in their lives. In addition, their chronic negative emotions and emotion regulation difficulties can become barriers to trusting someone and having healthy interpersonal relationships, which, paradoxically, could help them overcome problems that resulted from the trauma. Domestic violence victims often have psychological difficulties similar to other trauma survivors. Frequent hypersensitivity and dysregulated emotion can get in the way of creating and enjoying a safe relationship in the future. Even when victims have partners who are not violent, the impact of their trauma history can still damage the quality of their relationships.

Many clinicians have found it useful to incorporate couple intervention into their work with trauma survivors. More knowledge about victims' sensitivity and reactivity and trauma's impact on their relationship will be helpful to understand victim partners' suffering and motivate partners to assist in treatment, both directly and indirectly. Both partners can help break the patterns of their conflict and prevent or reduce retraumatization experiences using interventions specifically targeting trauma-related interpersonal problems. In addition, having both partners in treatment can improve a couple's interactions that help reduce conflict and distress, whether it is or is not related to trauma. In this way, partners can create more peace and increase intimacy in their relationship.

## REFERENCES

Acitelli, L. K., & Antonucci, T. C. (1994). Gender differences in the link between marital support and satisfaction in order couples. *Journal of Personality and Social Psychology, 67*(4), 688–698.

Alexander, P. C. (2009). Childhood trauma, attachment, and abuse by multiple partners. *Psychological Trauma: Theory, Research, Practice, and Policy, 1*(1), 78–88.

Alexander, P. C., & Warner, S. (2003). Attachment theory and family systems theory as frameworks for understanding the intergenerational transmission of family violence. In P. Erdman & T. Caffery (Eds.), *Attachment and family systems: Conceptual, empirical, and therapeutic relatedness* (pp. 241–257). New York: Brunner-Routledge.

Allers, C. T., Benjack, K. J., & Allers, N. T. (1992). Unresolved childhood sexual abuse: Are older adults affected? *Journal of Counseling and Development, 71*(1), 14–17.

American Psychiatric Association. (1994). *Diagnostic and statistical manual of mental disorders* (4th ed.). Washington, DC: Author.

Babcock, J. C., Green, C. E., & Robbie, C. (2004). Does batterers' treatment work? A meta-analytic review of domestic violence treatment. *Clinical Psychology Review, 23*, 1023–1053.

Bandura, A. (1973). *Aggression: A social learning analysis*. Englewood Cliffs, NJ: Prentice Hall.

Beck, A. T., Rush, A. J., Shaw, B. F., & Emery, D. (1979). *Cognitive therapy of depression*. New York: Guilford Press.

Bernstein, D., & Fink, L. (1998). *Childhood trauma questionnaire: A retrospective self-report manual*. San Antonio, TX: Psychological Corporation.

Braun, B. G. (1988). The BASCK model of dissociation. *Progress in the Dissociative Disorders, 1*, 4–23.

Bremner, J. D., Southwick, S. M., & Charney, D. S. (1995). Etiological factors in the development of posttraumatic stress disorder. In C. M. Mazure (Ed.), *Does stress cause psychiatric illness?* (pp. 149–185). Washington, DC: American Psychiatric Association.

Briere, J., Elliott, D. M., & Harris, K. (2009). Trauma Symptom Inventory. *Journal of Interpersonal Violence, 10*(4), 387–401.

Browne, A., & Finkelhor, D. (1986). Impact of child sexual abuse: A review of the research. *Psychological Bulletin, 99*(1), 66–77.

Campbell, J. C., & Lewandowski, L. A. (1997). Mental and physical health effects of intimate partner on women and children. *Psychiatric Clinics of North America, 20*(2), 353–374.

Carroll, E. M., Rueger, D. B., Foy, D. W., & Donahoe, C. P. (1985). Vietnam combat Veterans with posttraumatic stress disorder: Analysis of marital and cohabitating adjustment. *Journal of Abnormal Psychology, 94*(3), 329–337.

Cattaneo, L., & Goodman, L. (2005). Risk factors for re-abuse in intimate partner violence: A cross-disciplinary critical review. *Trauma, Violence and Abuse, 6*, 141–175.

Classen, C., Field, N. P., Koopman, C., Nevill-Manning, K., & Spiegel, D. (2001). Interpersonal problems and their relationship to sexual retraumatization among women sexually abused in childhood. *Journal of Interpersonal Violence, 16*(6), 295–509.

Classen, C., Nevo, R., Koopman, C., Nevill-Manning, K., Gore-Felton, C., Rose, D. S., & Spiegel, D. (2002). Recent stressful life events, sexual revictimization, and their relationship with traumatic stress symptoms among women sexually abused in childhood. *Journal of Interpersonal Violence, 17*(12), 1274–1290.

Cloitre, M. (1998). Sexual retraumatization: Risk factors and prevention. In V. M. Follette, J. Ruzek, & F. R. Abueg (Eds.), *Cognitive-behavioral therapies for trauma* (pp. 278–304). New York: Guilford Press.

Cloitre, M., Cohen, L. R., & Scarvalone, P. (2002). Understanding retraumatization among childhood sexual abuse survivors: An interpersonal schema approach. *Journal of Cognitive Psychotherapy, 16*(1), 91–112.

Davidson, J. R., Hughes, D., Blazer, D. G., & George, L. K. (1991). Post-traumatic stress disorder in the community: An epidemiological study. *Psychological Medicine, 21*(3), 713–721.

Davies, J. M., & Frawley, M. G. (1994). *Treating the adult survivor of childhood sexual abuse: A psychoanalytic perspective.* New York: Basic Books.

DeBellis, M. D., Keshavan, M., Shifflett, H., Iyengar, S., Beers, S. R., & Hall, J. (2002). Brain structures in pediatric maltreatment-related PTSD: A sociodemographically matched study. *Biological Psychiatry, 52*, 1066–1078.

Dietrich, A. (2007). Childhood maltreatment and retraumatization: The role of affect dysregulation, interpersonal relatedness difficulties and posttraumatic stress disorder. *Journal of Trauma and Dissociation, 8*(4), 25–51.

DiLillo, D., & Long, P. (1999). Perceptions of couple functioning among female survivors of child sexual abuse. *Journal of Child Sexual Abuse, 7*(4), 59–76.

Dunford, F. W. (2000). The San Diego Navy Experiment: An assessment of interventions for men who assault their wives. *Journal of Consulting and Clinical Psychology, 68*(3), 468–476.

Ericksen, J. R., & Henderson, A. D. (1992). Diverging realities: Abused women and their children. In J. Campbell (Ed.), *Advocacy health care for battered women and their children* (pp. 138–155). Thousand Oaks, CA: Sage.

Fleming, J., Mullen, P. E., Sibthorpe, B., & Bammer, G. (1999). The long-term impact of childhood sexual abuse in Australian women. *Child Abuse and Neglect, 23*(2), 145–159.

Ford, D. A., & Regoli, M. J. (1992). The preventive impacts of policies for prosecuting wife batterers. In E. Buzawa & C. Buzawa (Eds.), *Domestic violence: The changing criminal justice response* (pp. 181–208). Westport, CT: Auburn House.

Fruzzetti, A. E. (2006). *The high conflict couples: A dialectic behavior therapy guide to finding peace, intimacy, and validation.* Oakland, CA: New Harbinger Press.

Fruzzetti, A. E., Crook, W., Erikson, K., Lee, J., & Worrall, J. M. (2009). Emotion regulation. In W. T. O'Donohue & J. E. Fisher (Eds.), *General principles and empirically
supported techniques of cognitive behavior therapy* (pp. 272–284). Hoboken, NJ:
Wiley.

Fruzzetti, A. E., & Fantozzi, B. (2008). Couple therapy and the treatment of borderline
personality and related disorders. In A. Gurman (Ed.), *Clinical handbook of couple
therapy* (4th ed., pp. 567–590). New York: Guilford Press.

Fruzzetti, A. E., & Jacobson, N. S. (1990). Toward a behavioral conceptualization of adult
intimacy: Implications for marital therapy. In E. Blechman (Ed.), *Emotions and the
family: For better or for worse* (pp. 117–135). Hillsdale, NJ: Lawrence Erlbaum
Associates.

Fruzzetti, A. E., & Jacobson, N. S. (1992). Couple assessment. In J. C. Rosen and
P. McReynolds (Eds.), *Advances in psychological assessment, Volume 8*
(pp. 201–224). New York: Plenum.

Fruzzetti, A. E., & Iverson, K. M. (2004). Couples dialectical behavior therapy: An
approach to both individual and relational distress. *Couples Research and Therapy,
10*, 8–13.

Fruzzetti, A. E., & Iverson, K. M. (2006). Intervening with couples and families to treat
emotion dysregulation and psychopathology. In D. K. Snyder, J. Simpson, & J. Hughes
(Eds.), *Emotion regulation in couples and families: Pathways to dysfunction and
health* (pp. 249–267). Washington, DC: American Psychological Association.

Fruzzetti, A. E., Santisteban, D. A., & Hoffman, P. D. (2007). Dialectical behavior therapy
with families. In L. A. Dimeff & K. Koerner (Eds.), *Dialectical behavior therapy
in clinical practice: Applications across disorders and settings* (pp. 222–244).
New York: Guilford Press.

Fruzzetti, A. E., & Worrall, J. M. (2010). Accurate expression and validating responses:
A transactional model for understanding individual and relationship distress.
In K. Sullivan & J. Davila (Eds.), *Support processes in intimate relationships*
(pp. 121–151). Oxford: Oxford University Press.

Gondolf, E. W. (1985). Anger and oppression in men who batter: Empiricist and feminist
perspectives and their implications for research. *Victimology: An International
Journal, 10*, 311–324.

Goodwin, J., Cheeves, K., & Connell, V. (1988). Defining a syndrome of severe symptoms
in survivors of severe incestuous abuse. *Dissociation: Progress in the Dissociative
Disorders, 1*(4), 11–16.

Gottman, J. M., & Levenson, R. W. (1986). Assessing the role of emotion in marriage.
*Behavioral Assessment, 8*(1), 31–48.

Gottman, J., & Rushe, R. (1995). Communication and social skills approaches to treating ailing marriages: A recommendation for a new marital therapy called "minimal
marital therapy." In W. O'Donohue & L. Krasner (Eds.), *Handbook of psychological
skills training: Clinical techniques and applications* (pp. 287–305). Needham
Heights, MA: Allyn & Bacon.

Grauerholz, L. (2000). An ecological approach to understanding sexual retraumatization: Linking personal, interpersonal, and sociocultural factors and processes. *Child
Maltreatment, 5*(1), 5–17.

Groer, M. W., Thomas, S. P., Evans, G. W., Helton, S., & Weldon, A. (2006). Inflammatory
effects and immune system correlates of rape. *Violence and Victims, 21*(6), 796–808.

Guterman, N. B., & Lee, Y. (2005). The role of fathers in risk for physical child abuse
and neglect: Possible pathways and unanswered questions. *Child Maltreatment,
10*, 136–149.

Harper, F., & Arias, I. (2009). The moderating role of parental warmth on the effects of exposure to family violence. *Violence and Victims, 18*(3), 353–367.

Henning, K., Leitenberg, H., Coffey, P., Turner, T., & Bennett, R. (1996). Long-term psychological and social impact of witnessing physical conflict between parents. *Journal of Interpersonal Violence, 11*(1), 35–91.

Herman, S. M. (1994). Marital satisfaction in the elderly. *Gerontology & Geriatrics Education, 14*(4), 69–79.

Heyman, R. E., & Schlee, K. (2003). Stopping wife abuse via physical aggression couples treatment. *Journal of Aggression, Maltreatment & Trauma, 7*(1–2), 135–157.

Heyman, R. E., & Smith, A. M. (2002). Do child abuse and interparental violence lead to adulthood family violence? *Journal of Marriage and Family, 64*(4), 864–870.

Irwin, H. J. (1999). Violent and nonviolent retraumatization of women abused in childhood. *Journal of Interpersonal Violence, 14*(10), 1095–1110.

Iverson, K. M., Shenk, C., & Fruzzetti, A. E. (2009). Dialectical behavior therapy for women victims of domestic violence: A pilot study. *Professional Psychology: Research and Practice, 40*(3), 242–248.

Jacobson, N. S., Gottman, J. M., Gortner, E., Berns, S., & Shortt, J. W. (1996). Psychological factors in the longitudinal course of battering: When do the couples split up? When does the abuse decrease? *Violence and Victims, 11*(4), 371–392.

Jaffe, P. G., Wolfe, D. A., & Wilson, S. K. (1990). *Children of battered women.* Thousand Oaks, CA: Sage.

Johnson, D., & Zlotnick, C. (2006). A cognitive-behavioral treatment for battered women with PTSD in shelters: Findings from a pilot study. *Journal of Traumatic Stress, 19*(4), 559–564.

Johnson, S. M., & Williams-Keeler, L. (1998). Creating healing relationships for couples dealing with trauma: The use of emotionally focused marital therapy. *Journal of Marital & Family Therapy, 24*(1), 25–40.

Julien, D., & Markman, H. J. (1991). Social support and social networks as determinants of individual and marital outcomes. *Journal of Social and Personal Relationships, 8*(4), 549–568.

Kalmuss, D. (1984). The intergenerational transmission of marital aggression. *Journal of Marriage & the Family, 46*(1), 11–19.

Kimerling, R., & Calhoun, K. S. (1994). Somatic symptoms, social support, and treatment seeking among sexual assault victims. *Journal of Consulting and Clinical Psychology, 62*(2), 333–340.

Koopman, C., Palesh, O., Marten, B., Thomson, B., Ismailji, T., Homes, D., & Butler, L. D. (2005). Child abuse and adult interpersonal trauma as predictors of posttraumatic stress disorder symptoms among women seeking treatment for intimate partner violence. In T. A. Corales (Eds.), *Focus on posttraumatic stress disorder research* (pp. 1–16). Hauppauge, NY: Nova Science.

LaTaillade, J. J., Epstein, N. B., & Werlinich, C. A. (2006). Conjoint treatment of intimate partner violence: A cognitive behavioral approach. *Journal of Cognitive Psychotherapy, 20*(4), 393–410.

Lieberman, A. F., & Pawl, J. H. (1988). Clinical applications of attachment theory. J. Belsky & T. Nezworski (Eds.), *Clinical implications of attachment* (pp. 327–351). Hillsdale, NJ: Lawrence Erlbaum Associates.

Linehan, M. M. (1993a). *Cognitive-behavioral treatment of borderline personality disorder.* New York: Guilford Press.

Linehan, M. M. (1993b). *Skills training manual for treating borderline personality disorder.* New York: Guilford Press.

Litz, B. T., Keane, T. M., Fisher, L., Marx, B., & Monaco, V. (1992). Physical health complaints in combat-related post-traumatic stress disorder: A preliminary report. *Journal of Traumatic Stress, 5*(1), 131–141.

Maker, A. H., Kemmelmeier, M., & Peterson, C. (1998). Long-term psychological consequences in women of witnessing parental physical conflict and experiencing abuse in childhood. *Journal of Interpersonal Violence, 13*(5), 574–589.

Markward, M. J. (1997). The impact of domestic violence on children. *Families in Society, 78*(1), 66–70.

McFarlane, A. C., & Yehuda, R. A. (1996). Resilience, vulnerability, and the course of posttraumatic reactions. In A. Bessel, A. C. McFarlane, & L. Weisaeth (Eds.), *The effects of overwhelming experience on mind, body, and society* (pp. 155–181). New York: Guilford Press.

Mullen, P. E., Martin, J. L., Anderson, J., & Romans, S. E. (1994). The effects of child sexual abuse on social, interpersonal and sexual function in adult life. *British Journal of Psychiatry, 165*(1), 35–47.

Nelson, B. S., & Wampler, K. S. (2000). Systemic effects of trauma in clinic couples: An exploratory study of secondary trauma resulting from childhood abuse. *Journal of Marital & Family Therapy, 26*(2), 171–184.

Noll, J. G., Horowitz, L. A., Bonanno, G. A., Trickett, P. K., & Putnam, F. W. (2003). Retraumatization and self-harm in females who experienced childhood sexual abuse: Results from a prospective study. *Journal of Interpersonal Violence, 18*(12), 1452–1471.

Peled, E. (1993). Secondary victims no more: Refocusing intervention with children. In J. L. Edleson & Z. C. Eisikovits (Eds.), *Future interventions with battered women and their families* (pp. 125–153). Thousand Oaks, CA: Sage.

Post, R. M., Weiss, S. R. B., & Smith, M. A. (1995). Sensitization and kindling: Implications for the evolving neural substrates of post-traumatic stress disorder. In M. J. Friedman, D. S. Charney, & A. Y. Deutch (Eds.), *Neurobiological and clinical consequences of stress: From normal adaptation to post-traumatic stress disorder* (pp. 203–224). Philadelphia, PA: Lippincott Williams & Wilkins.

Riggs, D. S. (2000). Marital and family therapy. In E. B. Foa, T. M., Keane, & M. J. Friedman (Eds.), *Effective treatments for PTSD: Practice guidelines from the International Society for Traumatic Stress Studies* (pp. 280–301). New York: Guilford Press.

Riggs, D. S., Byrne, C. A., Weathers, F. W., & Litz, B. T. (1998). The quality of the intimate relationships of male Vietnam Veterans: Problems associated with posttraumatic stress disorders. *Journal of Traumatic Stress, 11*(1), 87–101.

Roberts, W. R., Penk, W. E., Gearing, M. L., Robinowitz, R., Dolan, M. P., & Patterson, E. T. (1982). Interpersonal problems of Vietnam combat Veterans with symptoms of posttraumatic stress disorder. *Journal of Abnormal Psychology, 91*(6), 444–450.

Rogge, R., & Funk, J. (2007). Testing the ruler with item response theory: Increasing precision of measurement for relationship satisfaction with the couples satisfaction index. *Journal of Family Psychology, 21*(4), 572–583.

Salisbury, E. J., Henning, K., & Holdford, R. (2009). Fathering by partner-abusive men: Attitudes on children's exposure to interparental conflict and risk factors for child abuse. *Child Maltreatment, 14*, 232–242.

Schaefer, M. T., & Olson, D. H. (2007). Assessing intimacy: The Pair Inventory. *Journal of Marital and Family Therapy, 7*(1), 47–60.

Sonkin, D. J., Martin, D., & Walker, L. E. A. (1985). *The male batterer: A treatment approach.* New York: Springer.

Spanier, G. B. (1976). Measuring dyadic adjustment: New scales for assessing the quality of marriage and similar dyads. *Journal of Marriage and the Family, 38*(1), 15–28.

Stith, S. M., McCollum, E. E., Rosen, K., Locke, L. D., & Goldberg, P. D. (2005). Domestic violence-focused couples treatment. In J. L. Lebow (Eds.), *Handbook of clinical family therapy* (pp. 406–430). Hoboken, NJ: John Wiley & Sons.

Straus, M. A. (1991). Family violence in American families: Incidence rates, causes, and trends. In D. D. Knudsen & J. L. Miller (Eds.), *Abused and battered: Social and legal responses of family violence* (pp. 17–34). Hawthorne, NY: Aldine de Gruyter.

Straus, M. A., Hamby, S. L., Boney-McCoy, S., & Sugarman, D. B. (1996). The revised conflict tactics scales (CTS-2): Development and preliminary psychometric data. *Journal of Family Issues, 17*, 283–316.

Taylor, B. G., Davis, R. C., & Maxwell, C. D. (2001). The effects of a group batterer treatment program: A randomized experiment in Brooklyn. *Justice Quarterly, 18*(1), 171–201.

Tjaden, P., & Thoennes, N. (2000). Prevalence and consequences of male-to-female and female-to-male intimate partner violence as measured by the National Violence Against Women Survey. *Violence Against Women, 6*(2), 142–161.

U.S. Department of Justice. (2000). *Intimate partner violence*. Washington, DC.

Waysman, M., Mikulincer, M., Solomon, Z., & Weisenberg, M. (1993). Secondary traumatization among wives of posttraumatic combat Veterans: A family typology. *Journal of Family Psychology, 7*(1), 104–118.

Weiss, D. S., & Marmar, C. R. (1996). The Impact of Event Scale, revised. In J. Wilson & T. M. Keane (Eds.), Assessing psychological trauma and PTSD (pp. 399–411). New York: Guilford Press.

Woods, A. B., Page, G. G., O'Campo, P., Pugh, L. C., Ford, D., & Campbell, J. C. (2005). The mediation effect of posttraumatic stress disorder symptoms on the relationship of intimate partner violence and IFN-y levels. *American Journal of Community Psychology, 36*(1–2), 159–175.

Wurmser, L. (1987). Shame: The veiled companion of narcissism. In D. Nathanson (Ed.), *The many faces of shame* (pp. 64–92). New York: Guilford Press.

# Chapter 14

# Retraumatization Associated With Disabling Physical Injuries

*Melanie P. Duckworth, Tony Iezzi, and Erika M. Shearer*

Traumatic events can lead to serious physical injuries, and serious physical injuries can lead to significant traumatic stress reactions. Serious physical injuries usually require transportation via ambulance to an emergency department (ED), initial ED assessment of life-threatening and non-life-threatening injuries, treatment disposition, hospital admission, surgical and nonsurgical treatment, rehabilitation, postdischarge hospital follow-up, and outpatient follow-up in primary- and specialty-care settings. Events that involve physical injury can contribute to significant psychological distress by virtue of the parameters of the injury-causing event, the seriousness of the physical injuries sustained in the event, or the degree of functional and lifestyle compromise that result from physical injuries.

This chapter is designed to provide a general understanding of the nature and impact of physical injuries occurring in the context of potentially traumatizing events. Consistent with this overall aim, the chapter will focus on the following: (1) epidemiological data related to physical injuries; (2) theoretical models of physical injuries; (3) functional limitations and changes in quality of life that are associated with physical injury; (4) psychological conditions associated with physical injuries; (5) retraumatization in the context of physical injuries; (6) prevention and treatment of physical injuries; and (7) special issues related to the assessment and treatment of physical injuries. While an exhaustive review of injury contexts (e.g., community or domestic violence), injury mechanisms (e.g., blunt or piercing trauma), and injury types (e.g., fractures or contusions) is beyond the scope of this chapter, particular injury contexts, mechanisms, and types will be highlighted due to the richness of the empirical literature related to particular injuries or due to the likelihood of reinjury and retraumatization occurring in a particular injury context. Coverage of particular injury-causing and potentially traumatizing events in this chapter is selective and reflects content coverage within other chapters in this book.

## EPIDEMIOLOGICAL DATA RELATED TO PHYSICAL INJURIES

Physical injuries are commonly classified into one of two major categories based on the intent ascribed to the injury-causing event or behavior. Unintentional injuries are considered to be the result of events that are outside of human control or events that occur in the absence of any true intent to cause harm. Physical injuries that occur in the context of motor vehicle collisions (MVCs), falls, drownings, fires, and sporting and leisure activities are classified as unintentional injuries. Physical injuries that occur in the context of violence, whether self-inflicted or other-inflicted, are classified as intentional injuries. Across all injury contexts, physical injuries are prevalent and can increase the likelihood that more extreme and disabling psychological reactions will occur.

### Prevalence

Physical injuries are prevalent and are associated with significant mortality and morbidity. Physical injuries contribute most to the global burden of disease (Peden et al., 2004), with 16% of the world's burden of disease attributed to such injuries (Krug, Sharma, & Lozano, 2000). Statistics compiled by the World Health Organization (WHO) indicate that five million deaths occur annually as a result of injuries, with injury-related deaths accounting for 9% of all deaths throughout the world (Peden, McGee, & Sharma, 2002). MVCs are projected to be the second leading cause of worldwide death by the year 2020, with homicide and suicide identified as the 11th and 13th leading causes of death worldwide, respectively (Murray & Lopez, 1996). For the year 2003, physical injuries were designated as the leading cause of death for persons aged 1 to 44 years and the fifth leading cause of death across all age groups in the United States (CDC, 2006). It is estimated that 1 out of every 17 deaths in the United States is due to physical injury, with 67% of those deaths classified as unintentional deaths (Baker, O'Neill, Ginsberg, & Li, 1992). Findings related to the prevalence of injury deaths and the ranking of injury-causing events are consistent across population-based surveys and empirical studies of medically attended injured persons. In a large-scale retrospective study of 55,664 patients attending five trauma centers in San Diego, Potenza and colleagues (2004) determined that MVCs were the leading cause of physical injuries, while homicide and suicide were the leading causes of mortality.

Although fatal injuries are shockingly frequent, it must be acknowledged that the vast majority of persons who sustain physical injuries survive those injuries. Nonfatal injuries occur at rates that are exponentially higher than the rates of fatal injuries. The U.S. National Health Care Survey (NHCS) documented the occurrence of 76 million nonfatal, medically attended injuries for the year 2002 alone (Betz & Li, 2005). Using the Nationwide Inpatient Sample, the largest publically available database of acute-care hospital discharge records, Greenspan and colleagues (2006) examined discharge rates and frequencies for all injury-related hospitalizations in the United States for the year 2000 (Greenspan et al., 2006). They determined that 85% of all admissions were due to unintentional injuries, with falls identified as the leading cause of injury-related hospitalizations and ED visits. Fractures (56%) were the most common primary, nonfatal injury diagnosis, followed by internal organ injuries, open wounds, and sprains and strains. Although MVCs were the leading cause of injury mortality for the reporting year, MVCs accounted for a relatively smaller proportion (16%) of those medically attended, unintentional injuries.

Intentional injuries account for a considerably smaller proportion of hospitalizations and ED visits recorded by the Nationwide Inpatient Sample; however, the absolute number of intentional injuries is staggering. Greenspan and colleagues determined that self-inflicted injuries, most of which involved poisoning, accounted for approximately 136,000 injury-related hospital admissions, with assaults accounting for an additional 83,000 injury-related hospitalizations for the year 2000. Although unintentional injuries account for the larger proportion of injury-related hospitalizations and ED visits, data suggest that intentional injuries are more likely to require medical attendance. According to data from the NCHS, 90% of all treatment for intentional injuries occurs in EDs (Betz & Li, 2005).

Because of the significant mortality associated with intimate partner violence (IPV), and because of the significant individual, familial, and societal impacts of the nonfatal physical and psychological injuries that occur in the context of IPV, concerted efforts are being made to document, adjudicate, and prevent IPV. Investigations occurring in the United States suggest that 1,300 deaths and two million injuries are sustained each year as a function of IPV (CDC, 2006), with approximately one third of IPV incidents resulting in physical injuries that require medical attention (Tjaden & Thoennes, 2000). Women are particularly vulnerable in the context of IPV, with IPV serving as the single greatest cause of physical injury to women (Abbott, Johnson, Koziol-McLain, & Lowenstein, 1995). Among women murdered by an intimate partner, 44% had visited an ED for management of IPV-related injuries in the 2 years prior to their deaths (Crandall, Nathens, Kernic, Holt, & Rivara, 2004).

Research suggests that victims of traumatic injury are at increased risk for reinjury. Worrell and colleagues (2006) conducted a 9-year, retrospective, population-based study of initial injuries and reinjuries experienced by residents of the state of Washington. More than 113,000 persons identified as having had their first injury hospitalization were monitored for 5 years following initial injury and hospitalization to determine the number of hospitalizations and deaths that occurred during the 5-year follow-up period. After correcting for age, gender, and year of first injury, it was determined that for the 6-month to 5-year follow-up period, persons who suffered an injury experienced an injury risk ratio that was 2.6 times greater than that for the general population. Male gender, increasing age, and alcohol use were all associated with increased risk for reinjury. Previous injury conferred significant risk for an assault-related hospitalization in the year following initial injury, with injured persons experiencing a risk ratio for assault that was three times greater than that for the general population. Interestingly, injured persons tended to experience reinjury involving the same mechanism: 56% of first-time fallers fell again, and 55% of self-injurers had another self-inflicted injury. These researchers concluded that trauma victims were at increased risk of reinjury either because initial injuries predispose them to reinjury or because factors considered causative at the time of initial injury persist and contribute to reinjury.

## Cost

Physical injuries are expensive in terms of the direct (e.g., medical treatments) and indirect (e.g., income replacements benefits) costs associated with such injuries. Based on data compiled for the year 2000, the CDC (2006) has estimated that physical injuries account for 10% of the total medical expenditures for the United States, with annual injury-related expenditures totaling $224 billion when costs associated with rehabilitation and lost wages and productivity are included. Using data from 2000 National Vital Statistics System, Corso, Finkelstein, Miller, Fiebelkorn, and Zaloshnja (2006) examined the direct and indirect costs associated with medically treated injuries sustained by 50 million Americans (Corso et al., 2006). These medically treated injuries resulted in a lifetime cost of $406 billion, with nearly $80 billion of the overall cost associated with medical expenses and more than $320 billion of the cost associated with lost productivity. In a similar study, Corso, Mercy, Simon, Finkelstein, and Miller (2007) examined medical costs and productivity losses due to interpersonal and self-directed violence occurring in the United States. The total costs associated with nonfatal injuries and deaths due to violence in 2000 were estimated to be more than $70 billion, with

92% of this cost due to lost productivity. Each death due to assault resulted in $1.3 million in productivity losses, and each suicide resulted in $1 million in productivity losses. An estimated $5.6 billion were spent on medical care for more than 2.5 million injuries. The cost of health care related to IPV is estimated to be $5.8 billion (CDC, 2003). Moreover, $4.1 billion of this cost is for direct medical and mental health services.

The relative economic burden of physical injury is similar across Western countries. Over three million Canadians visited EDs in 2004 due to physical injuries (SMARTRISK, 2009). An examination of the economic burden of injuries sustained by Canadians for that year revealed the total cost of injuries to approach $20 billion, with direct costs accounting for 54% and indirect costs accounting for 46% of the total cost. Unintentional injuries accounted for 81% and intentional injuries accounted for 17% of all injury costs.


## Disability

Because physical injuries are often the result of potentially traumatizing events and because physical injuries may result in limitations in physical functioning that impact multiple lifestyle domains, injured persons are more likely to experience a combination of physical and psychological impairments that may lead to disability. Based on data from the Disability Supplement for the National Health Interview Survey (NHIS), Guerrero, Sniezak, and Sehgal (1999) estimated that 5.6 million Americans suffer from a disability due to injury, with 50% of these disabled persons experiencing disability due to falls and MVCs. Based on a subsequent analysis of NHIS data, Shults, Jones, Kresnow, Langlois, and Guerrero (2004) determined that 41% of working-aged individuals who experienced MVC-related disability were not able to return to work due to *ongoing* disability. Extrapolating from these data, the researchers estimated that 1.2 million adults who are living at home suffer from an MVC-related disability, with most MVC-related disability due to orthopedic impairment or intervertebral disc disorders (73%). Disability findings and the extrapolated population estimates from the Guerrero et al. and Shults et al. studies were confirmed by Airey, Chell, Rigby, Tennant, and Connelly's (2001) 5-year follow-up study of 367 persons who survived major traumatic injuries. The investigators found that, at the time of interview, 81% of this sample of injured persons had some form of disability in locomotion, behavior, continence, or intellectual functioning. At 5-year follow-up, 30% of the sample experienced complete recovery from their injuries and 50% remained moderately or severely disabled.

Although disability rates observed across the above described studies were relatively consistent, rates of disability are known to vary based on study setting, duration of follow-up, and definition of disability. Ameratunga, Norton, Bennett, and Jackson (2004) conducted a review of approximately

750 MVC studies, 19 of which were considered acceptable for the examination of disability following MVCs. Rates of disability across studies ranged from 2% to 87%, with disability rates observed to be somewhat lower among injured persons assessed in outpatient settings, EDs, and community settings (5% to 39%) than among injured persons who were admitted to hospitals (21% to 57%).

There is relatively less data related to intentional injuries and disability, due at least in part to issues of culpability and stigma that are sometimes associated with injuries that are the result of intentional events. Based on injury statistics for Canada, it is estimated that 83% of persons who sustain injuries consequent to acts of self-harm experience permanent total disability (SMARTRISK, 2009). Fifty percent of persons who sustain injuries in the context of violent assault experience permanent total disability. Based on a survey of 1,152 women, 54% of whom reported some type of interpersonal violence, Coker, Smith, and Fadden (2005) determined that women who had experienced interpersonal violence were twice as likely to report a disability, with the reported disability usually due to chronic pain or mental illness occurring consequent to interpersonal violence.

The findings described in this section highlight both the sheer prevalence of physical injuries as well as the sizable societal and physical costs associated with these injuries. At both the global and national levels, the costs associated with physical injuries are measured by a metric that combines both the years of life lost prematurely due to mortality as well as the years of life lost due to living in a compromised state as a consequence of physical injury. At the individual level, physically injured persons are required to deal with the residual effects of their injuries, which may include long-term functional limitations and disability. Because injured persons are at higher risk of reinjury, the negative health effects associated with each injury experience are likely to interact and make management of any one injury more challenging. Findings related to the prevalence and impact of physical injuries reviewed above highlight the importance of integrated, globally supported programs that reduce and prevent physical injuries through policy making, consistent implementation of safety regulations, and identification of environmental and personal factors associated with increased risk of injury.

## THEORETICAL MODELS EXPLAINING THE RELATION OF PHYSICAL INJURIES TO DISABILITY

A number of models have been forwarded that purport to explain the progression from physical injury to disability. Given the physical and psychological repercussions of physical injuries, etiological models of physical injury require an emphasis on the interaction between biological and environmental factors and the interaction between state and trait person factors. Although there is no one model of physical injury that would be considered the gold standard, there are a number of models that have heuristic utility in guiding research and clinical activities. In the current section, we review Haddon's Matrix, one of the earliest and most commonly used models of injury prevention; the International Classification of Functioning, Disability and Health, the WHO-approved model for classifying functional status and establishing treatment goals and outcomes; the Enabling-Disabling Process Model, a model forwarded by the Institute of Medicine and unique in its emphasis of societal-level influences on function and functional limitations; the Model of Trauma, Posttraumatic Stress Disorder, and Physical Health, a model that chronicles the progression from psychological injury to physical illness and disease; and the Model of Physical Injury, Trauma, and Disability, a model that emphasizes the interacting effects of pre-, peri-, and postinjury factors on both physical and psychological postinjury outcomes. Together, these models emphasize the integration of multiple indices of postinjury function, impairment, and disability and serve as exemplars for injury prevention and intervention efforts.

## Haddon Matrix

Haddon (1968) developed one of the first models that identified factors considered to be most relevant to the experience of disability following injury. Haddon's model has been used extensively in injury epidemiology and injury prevention research and has contributed significantly to the development of subsequently proffered models of injury and disability. The model, first used in the MVC context, is composed of two dimensions into which aspects of the injury-causing event and the injured person are categorized. The first dimension consists of three injury factors: host (e.g., person-related variables such as fatigue or alcohol use); agent/vector (e.g., vehicle-related variables such as age or weight of vehicle); and environment (e.g., physical and social-related variables, such as road conditions or public attitudes about drinking and driving). The second dimension consists of three injury phases: preinjury event phase (i.e., activities that will prevent the injury-causing event from occurring); injury event phase (i.e., activities that will prevent injury or reduce the seriousness of injury); and postinjury event phase (i.e., activities aimed at treating injuries and limiting injury-related disability). This model has considerable intuitive appeal and is relatively simple in its conceptualization. The second dimension of the matrix has been used effectively to organize the empirical literature related to the prediction of posttraumatic stress disorder (PTSD) (Brewin, Andrews, & Valentine, 2000; Ozer, Best, Lipsey, & Weiss, 2003) and whiplash/neck pain (Miro, Nieto, & Huguet, 2008).

## International Classification of Functioning, Disability, and Health

The International Classification of Functioning, Disability and Health (ICF) (World Health Organization, 1980, 2001) model, designed to accompany the International Classification of Diseases and Related Health Problems, 10th edition (ICD-10) (World Health Organization, 1992), provides a framework for conceptualizing both functioning and disability in association with specific health conditions. The ICF model relies on language that is universal, culturally sensitive, and interactive, and represents an integration of medical and social models of disability. The components (body functions and structures, activity, and participation) and contextual factors (environmental and personal factors) contained in this model of functioning and disability are dynamic and reciprocal. The ICF manual describes each of the key components and factors in extensive detail. The ICF model has received considerable research attention, with entire issues of professional journals (e.g., issues 11 and 12 of volume 25 of Disability and Rehabilitation, published in 2003, and issue 2 of volume 50 of Rehabilitation Psychology, published in 2005) devoted to explicating and promoting the model. However, researchers should be aware that the complexity of the model is better captured by the model description provided in the ICF manual than the figural representation of the model that is familiar to so many researchers and clinicians. The description of the ICF model that is forwarded in the manual would serve as a very useful template for constructing a testable model of health and disability (Johnston & Pollard, 2001).

## Enabling-Disabling Process Model

The Enabling-Disabling Process Model (Brandt & Pope, 1997) borrows heavily from Nagi's Disablement Model (1965). Nagi's model posits that disabling physical injury can be explained through four distinct but related concepts: pathology (molecular or tissue changes caused by disease or trauma); impairment (loss of mental, physiological, or biochemical function); functional limitation (an inability to perform a specific task); and disability (limitations in a person's ability to fulfill certain roles and tasks). The Enabling-Disabling Process Model elaborates on Nagi's model by emphasizing biological, psychological, and social factors that contribute to the disablement process and influence quality of life outcomes. This model expands upon Nagi's model by acknowledging the bidirectional relations among biological, psychological, and social factors and by providing for the possibility of full recovery from a previous disabled state. Although this model has been well recognized, it has not undergone extensive empirical evaluation.

## Model of Trauma, Posttraumatic Stress Disorder, and Physical Health

The previously described models were designed to provide more general conceptualizations of physical injury and disability. Schnurr and colleagues have developed a model that specifically charts the progression from psychological injury and traumatic stress to poor physical health (Schnurr & Green, 2004; Schnurr & Jankowski, 1999). Unlike other models of disability, this model does not require that an actual physical injury or medical condition serve as the circumstance that initiates physical or psychological symptoms and compromise. Instead, this model outlines the mediational influence of PTSD on the relation of trauma exposure to poor health. The model forwards two assumptions. The first assumption suggests that psychological distress, PTSD in particular, is necessary for adverse health outcomes to occur following exposure to a traumatic event. The second assumption is that psychological distress leads to adverse health outcomes via interacting biological, attentional, and behavioral pathways. While acknowledging the impact of depression on health, Schnurr and Green (2004) noted that PTSD has a distinct effect on physical health by virtue of the chronic and cumulative impacts (i.e., the allostatic load) of this stress response on physiological systems. The model has undergone empirical evaluation and has garnered some support (Ramchand, Marshall, Schell, & Jaycox, 2008; Sledjeski, Speisman, & Dierker, 2008; Weisberg et al., 2002).

## Model of Physical Injury, Trauma, and Disability

The Model of Physical Injury, Trauma, and Disability describes the interplay of physical and psychological factors that exert their influences from preinjury to peri-injury and from peri- to postinjury (Iezzi, 2008). It is important to recognize that preinjury physical risk factors (e.g., previous physical injuries, previous medical conditions, or physiological overreactivity) and preinjury psychological risk factors (e.g., childhood abuse, loss of significant others, or personal and familial history of depression occurring prior to the index injury) will influence baseline competencies and resources. At the time of the injury, most serious injury-causing events will involve physical concomitants (e.g., fractures or soft-tissue injuries) and psychological concomitants (e.g., depression or anxiety) that will alter the status of postinjury competencies and resources (e.g., the ability to work or activities of daily living) and influence postinjury recovery and function. Over time, the injured person's experience of postinjury pain, distress, and functional impairment will precipitate involvement in litigation related to pain and suffering and disruptions in function across multiple quality of life domains. Although conceived to explain MVC-related functional impairments and disability, the Model of

Physical Injury, Trauma, and Disability can be easily applied to the broader physical injury context. As is true for other more established models of injury-related disability, the Model of Physical Injury, Trauma, and Disability awaits empirical support.

Many of the traditional theoretical models that trace the progression from injury to impairment and disability place greater emphasis on peri- and postinjury factors that are considered to predict function and disability. These models would be enhanced by the recognition and integration of preinjury person and environment factors that are likely to influence exposure to as well as recovery from injury-causing events. Other models can be criticized for separating physical injuries and the functional consequences of physical injuries from the often co-occurring psychological impacts and impairments. Physical and psychological symptoms interact and have a significant effect on the injured person's overall clinical presentation. Serious physical injuries often result in psychological repercussions (e.g., depression and anxiety), and physiological repercussions (e.g., increased physiological arousal) that exacerbate physical symptoms (e.g., pain). The interplay between physical and psychological symptoms affects the injured person's quality of life. The poorer the quality of life a person experiences as a result of physical and psychological symptoms, the more likely it is that the injured person will become disabled. The cascade of effects that are seen consequent to physical injuries requires researchers and treating clinicians to embrace an etiological model that recognizes and addresses the many interacting aspects of physical, psychological, occupational, recreational, interpersonal, social, and familial functioning that determine quality of life and emotional well-being.

## FUNCTIONAL LIMITATIONS AND CHANGES IN QUALITY OF LIFE ASSOCIATED WITH PHYSICAL INJURIES

For some persons, the lingering and ongoing consequences of physical injury can be worse than the actual injuries. Physical injuries often result in chronic pain and discomfort, functional impairments, changes in the quality of life, long-term disability, and the need to pursue litigation to compensate for losses. Management of physical injuries may require that the injured person engage with multiple systems (e.g., legal, insurance, social services, policing, and government institutions), with some of these engagements being accurately characterized as adversarial in nature. The current section focuses on common sequelae associated with physical injuries, including chronic pain, functional impairments, changes in overall quality of life, and disability. Psychological distress often occurs as a consequence of serious physical injury. Traumatic events that involve serious physical injury can contribute to significant psychological distress by virtue of the parameters of the traumatic event, the seriousness of the physical injuries sustained in the event, or the degree of functional and lifestyle compromise that results from the physical injuries. Psychological distress and trauma associated with physical injury will be addressed in the following section.

## Chronic Pain

Regardless of injury context, mechanism, or type, physical injuries often result in the experience of pain. In fact, pain is the number one symptom reported in EDs (Cordell et al., 2002). Research suggests that pain, experienced pre-, peri-, or postinjury, is relevant to physical and psychological health outcomes experienced by injury survivors. In a follow-up evaluation of 480 persons who attended EDs for management of collision-related injuries, Atherton and colleagues (2006) determined that although a history of neck pain was not predictive of persistent postcollision neck pain, precollision widespread pain did contribute to increased risk of persistent neck pain following collision. This finding is supported by a number of studies of the relation of preinjury pain to postinjury pain (Carstensen et al., 2008; Walton, Pretty, MacDermid, & Teasell). In a study examining the contribution of peri-injury pain to the postinjury psychological health of 115 Level-I trauma center attendees, Norman, Stein, Dimsdale, and Hoyt (2008) determined that peri-injury pain was associated with an increased risk of PTSD in the months following injury. Knowledge of the amount of pain experienced at the time of hospitalization allowed for accurate classification of 65% of those injured persons who experienced PTSD at 4 and 8 months postinjury.

Persistent pain, either in isolation or in conjunction with other factors, can act to maintain postinjury physical and psychological impairments. Several studies have been performed to determine the contribution of persistent postinjury pain to the physical and psychological outcomes experienced by injury survivors. In one such study, Palyo and Beck (2005) evaluated the contribution of pain and PTSD to physical and psychosocial health outcomes experienced by 183 MVC survivors. Study findings revealed pain severity to be associated with both greater physical impairment and greater psychosocial impairment. In another study of the combined effects of persistent pain and posttraumatic stress on postinjury outcomes, Duckworth and Iezzi (2005) evaluated 152 patients who sustained physical injuries in the context of an MVC. Findings revealed that when compared to MVC survivors who endorsed chronic pain and a low number of posttraumatic stress symptoms, MVC survivors who endorsed chronic pain and a high number of posttraumatic stress symptoms evidenced more physical impairment, greater psychological distress, and poorer coping strategies; were more likely to be treated with antidepressants, pain, and other classes of medications; and were more likely to be recommended for psychological management of pain and psychological distress.

In the intentional injury context, physical injuries have been examined with respect to the frequency of occurrence of specific types of injuries, other medical problems occurring in association with violence-related physical injuries, injury-related pain, and injury-related psychological distress. The face, neck, upper back, breast, and abdomen have been identified as the most common locations for injuries sustained by women in the context of interpersonal violence (Mulleman, Lenaghan, & Pakieser, 1996). In a large-scale study that compared women who experienced IPV to women who denied any experience of IPV, IPV was determined to be related to chronic pain reports, with chronic pain being reported by more than twice as many women who reported the experience of IPV as women who denied any experience of IPV (Coker et al., 2005). Women who had experienced IPV were also more likely to report a disability due to chronic pain, with experiences of past and current IPV contributing equally to pain-related disability. Based on study findings, Coker et al. concluded that IPV is associated with all types of disability, and is particularly correlated with disability due to chronic pain and disability due to mental illness.

Wuest et al. (2009) evaluated the mediational effects of abuse-related injury and PTSD symptom severity on the relation of child abuse severity and assaultive (i.e., physical) and psychological (i.e., nonphysical) IPV severity to the severity of chronic pain reported by 309 women survivors of IPV. These researchers determined that the full model of predictors (child abuse severity and assaultive and psychological IPV severity) and mediators (abuse-related injury and PTSD symptom severity) contributed significantly to the prediction of chronic pain severity, with this combination of variables accounting for 38% of the variance in reports of chronic pain severity. Child abuse severity was determined to impact chronic pain severity directly and indirectly through abuse-related injury and PTSD symptom severity. Assaultive IPV severity was determined to impact chronic pain severity indirectly through abuse-related injury and PTSD symptom severity. Psychological IPV was determined to have a significant direct effect on chronic pain severity.

## Impairment, Changes in Quality of Life, and Disability

In the clinical context, injured persons often report that while they can cope with the actual physical injuries and the associated pain, they cannot cope with the limitations in function that are often a consequence of physical injury and pain. Injury- and pain-related limitations in function often include being unable to work, being unable to engage in activities of daily living, and being unable to engage fully in interpersonal relationships or other social pursuits. When present over time, these limitations in function often result in changes in quality of life, significant psychological distress, and disability, and may be more important to long-term postinjury adjustment than the actual injuries.

A considerable number of studies have been performed to evaluate the inter-acting effects of physical injuries, functional limitations, and injury-related psychological distress on the quality of life experienced by injury survivors. A select number of these studies are summarized below.

In an examination of both physical and psychiatric consequences of MVC involvement, Mayou, Bryant, and Duthie (1993) examined the medical, psychiatric, social/recreational, and occupational/financial outcomes experienced by 188 ED attendees at 3 months and at 1 year following MVC involvement. Medical outcome was established based on participants' reports of current medical symptoms, use of medical services, and disability. Nearly 25% of study participants reported psychiatric problems at 1-year follow-up. Among study participants with multiple injuries ($n = 114$), psychiatric consequences were significantly associated with the persistence of problems across all measured functional domains. Of those study participants who experienced multiple injuries and reported psychiatric consequences at 1-year follow-up, 71% experienced medical disability, 69% experienced moderate to major effects on work, 68% experienced financial problems, 75% experienced impairment in social functioning, and 77% experienced moderate to major effects on leisure pursuits.

These relations of injury and psychiatric compromise to functional compromise were borne out by findings from Mayou and Bryant's (2001) examination of the long-term medical, psychiatric, social/recreational, occupational/financial, and legal outcomes experienced by 1,148 consecutive ED attendees. Most ED attendees (81%) incurred MVC-related injuries, and most injuries (61%) were relatively minor. A smaller but significant number of ED attendees (21%) sustained injuries that required hospitalization. Of those persons reporting major physical problems at 3-month follow-up ($n = 57$), 81% reported a persistence of these major physical problems at 1-year follow-up. A significant number of participants (32%) evidenced symptoms of at least one psychological condition, with more severely injured participants being twice as likely to experience PTSD, travel anxiety, financial strain, and work problems at 1-year follow-up. This relation of injury severity to poor functional outcomes was also observed in a 3-year follow-up study of a sample of 546 MVC survivors (Mayou, Ehlers, & Bryant 2002).

In another large-scale study of the consequences of physical injury, Holbrook, Anderson, Sieber, Browner, and Hoyt (1999) used data from the Trauma Recovery project, an epidemiological study of traumatic injury patients recruited through four San Diego hospitals, to examine the functional, psychological, and quality of life outcomes experienced by 1,048 trauma patients. The majority of these patients sustained traumatic injuries consequent to MVCs, assaults, and falls. Patient outcomes were assessed at hospital discharge and at 6, 12, and 18 months postdischarge. At 18 months postdischarge, the vast majority of these trauma patients reported their health and well-being to be below the norm for healthy persons. It was determined that those trauma patients who experienced longer intensive care unit (ICU) stays, more depressive and PTSD symptoms postinjury, and declining social support, also experienced increased levels of disability.

Michaels et al. (2000) conducted baseline and 6- and 12-month follow-up evaluations of 247 patients admitted to a trauma center with intentional and unintentional injuries. The investigators were particularly interested in patients' general health, mental health, work status, and overall satisfaction with recovery at 12-month follow-up. After controlling for baseline mental health, injury severity, and physical functioning at 12-month follow-up, mental health at 12-month follow-up was predictive of general health, work status, and satisfaction with recovery. The authors interpreted these results as supporting the importance of mental health to posttrauma recovery of function across multiple functional and lifestyle domains. They went so far as to state that trauma centers that fail to assess and treat injury-related mental health outcomes are not fully attending to patients' needs.

Using a sample of 105 patients who sustained multiple severe injuries and who were admitted to a Level-I trauma center for treatment of intentional and unintentional injuries, Soberg and colleagues performed one study that evaluated the long-term functional outcomes experienced by these patients (Soberg, Bautz-Holter, Roise, & Finset, 2007) and a second study that examined factors predicting return to work among these patients (Soberg, Finset, Bautz-Holter, Sandvik, & Roise, 2007). Level-I trauma centers provide the highest level of surgical care to injured patients, and attendance at such a center suggests the relative severity of patients' physical injuries. Patients were assessed at 6 weeks after discharge, and at 1 and 2 years postinjury. Study findings indicated that disability scores at 2 years postinjury are best predicted by occupation, injury severity, pain, and physical, cognitive, and social function at 1 year postinjury, these variables accounting for 69% of the variance in disability scores. Study findings related to return to work revealed that 28% of injured patients had returned to work at 1-year follow-up, and 43% of injured patients had returned to work at 2-year follow-up. Several factors appeared to lessen the likelihood of return to work, including lower educational attainment, lengthier in-hospital rehabilitation (20 weeks or more), poorer general health, and lower physical, cognitive, and social functioning after returning home.

Campbell et al. (2002) and Coker, Smith, and Fadden (2005) examined the relation of injury to functional outcomes in the specific context of IPV. Campbell et al. (2002) compared the health status of 201 women who reported physical or sexual abuse to that of 240 women who had been involved in intimate relationships but had not experienced IPV. It was determined that abused women experienced a 50% to 70% increase in health problems, including central nervous system problems, gynecological problems, and stress-related problems. Those women who reported both physical and sexual abuse reported the greatest number of health problems.

Using data from a sample of 1,152 abused and nonabused women, Coker and colleagues (2005) examined the relation of IPV history and IPV frequency to past and current health and to the frequency and type of work-preventing disabilities reported by these women. Fifty-four percent of the total sample of women reported experiencing IPV at some time in their past, with 24% of those women indicating current involvement in a violent relationship. A little more than 19% of the full sample of women reported a work-preventing disability. Having a disability was associated with both past and current IPV, with the relation of disability to abuse being stronger for those women who reported current IPV. IPV was also associated with a host of psychological (e.g., depression or other mental illness) and medical conditions (e.g., nervous system injuries or disorders) considered to contribute to disability, with women reporting current IPV being more likely to experience these disability-causing conditions.

The studies summarized above lend support to the primacy of functional limitations in predicting quality of life following injury. The research literature also contains studies that confirm the limited influence of the actual injury on long-term functional outcomes. DePalma, Fedorka, and Simko (2003) examined the relation of severity of injury to quality of life in a sample of 64 severely injured individuals who were treated and discharged from a trauma center. Study participants were selected for participation based on having obtained extreme injury severity scores. The resulting sample experienced an average of 12 days in the ICU and an average hospital stay of 25 days. Using categories from the Sickness Impact Profile (SIP), these researchers determined that study participants experienced severe disruptions across most categories, with work, recreation, home management, sleep, and rest being the most affected domains of function. Although severe disruptions were observed across all SIP categories, study findings did not support a relation between severity of injury and quality of life. One explanation for the lack of support for this relation is the restriction in range of injury severity.

The findings from the DePalma et al. (2003) study were supported by the findings of Sluys, Haggmark, and Iselius (2005). In their examination of the relation of injury severity to long-term functional outcomes, Sluys and colleagues performed a 5-year follow-up survey of 205 patients, 93% of whom were hospitalized for treatment of blunt injuries sustained across a variety of injury contexts (e.g., MVCs) and 7% of whom were hospitalized for treatment of penetrating injuries sustained in context of stabbings and shootings. Poor long-term outcome (e.g., impaired physical functioning, bodily pain, and impaired mental health) was associated with a host of demographic, peri-injury, and postinjury factors, including older age, a greater number of in-hospital days, intensive care days, surgical procedures, in-hospital complications, and recurrent injury. Although considerable physical (68%) and psychological (41%) disabilities were evidenced by study participants at 5-year follow-up, injury severity did not predict quality of life 5 years postinjury.

Findings from studies that evaluate postinjury functional outcomes suggest that the relief experienced at surviving life-threatening physical injuries may not be sufficient to sustain persons who are faced with injury-related pain, functional impairment, and disability. These findings highlight the importance of being able to return to a productive life following physical injury. This would include returning to work, participating in activities of daily living, and maintaining healthy relationships and healthy psychological functioning. It may be concluded that satisfaction with overall outcome postinjury is as much a function of social, psychological, occupational, interpersonal, and financial well-being as it is a function of physical health.

## COMMON PSYCHOLOGICAL CONDITIONS ASSOCIATED WITH PHYSICAL INJURIES

An event is usually considered traumatic if it results in significant physical or psychological harm. Serious physical injuries usually require ED attendance or hospitalization and tend to result in significant pain, significant changes in role functioning (e.g., provider, partner, or parent), and significant changes in overall quality of life. For most seriously injured persons, the postinjury process is characterized by a sometimes variable but generally forward march toward recovery of function. For these injured persons, a return to normal activities of daily living and normal psychological functioning is much more likely. However, a substantial proportion of injured persons will experience permanent residual physical consequences of injury as well as event- and injury-related psychological distress. When present at the time of injury, psychological distress can magnify the immediate physical consequences of injury and interfere with primary intervention efforts. Long-term postinjury psychological distress can serve to maintain high levels of impairment and disability.

The type and intensity of psychological distress reactions that occur following physical injury are determined by parameters of the injury-causing event; the number and severity of physical injuries and associated impairments; the level of pain that accompanies injuries; and the level of compromise to various lifestyle domains and overall quality of life. A myriad of psychological distress reactions may occur consequent to physical injury; however, the relation between injury and psychological distress seems to be most reliable when distress occurs in the form of PTSD symptoms or depressive symptoms, the two types of psychological distress reactions found to occur most frequently following traumatic injury. For the purposes of this chapter, a brief review of the literature related to disorders of extreme stress and major depressive disorder (MDD) occurring in the context of physical injury is provided. Because of the influence of substance use on risk of both intentional and unintentional injury and because of the potential for abuse of medications used to manage injuries and injury-related pain and psychological distress, a brief review of the literature related to substance use disorders occurring in the context of physical injury is provided. For a more detailed presentation of psychological conditions associated with physical injuries, readers are referred to Duckworth (2008).

## Disorders of Extreme Stress

Physical injuries often serve as the initiating event for a variety of extreme stress responses, including acute stress disorder (ASD), PTSD, and Disorders of Extreme Stress Not Otherwise Specified (DESNOS). By definition, disorders of extreme stress require that the onset of symptoms be linked to the occurrence of a Criterion A traumatic event and that the response to the event be one of extreme horror, helplessness, and fear (*Diagnostic and Statistical Manual of Mental Disorders,* Fourth Edition, Text Revision, *DSM-IV-TR*) (American Psychiatric Association, 2000). An event is considered to be a Criterion A traumatic event if the event results in actual or possible death, serious injury, or threat of serious injury to self or others. A diagnosis of ASD, PTSD, or DESNOS also requires that the individual experience one or more symptoms of re-experiencing, behavioral and cognitive avoidance, affective numbing, and hyperarousal/hypervigilance, and that these symptoms cause significant distress or impairment across a number of functional domains (i.e., occupational, recreational, social, or interpersonal). The diagnostic criteria distinct to ASD, PTSD, and DESNOS are outlined below, and prevalence data related to the prevalence of each of these disorders in the physical injury context are briefly summarized.

### Acute Stress Disorder

ASD focuses on traumatic stress reactions that occur within 1 month of exposure to an event. The diagnosis of ASD also requires that the individual experience at least three of the following five dissociative symptoms: emotional numbing (e.g., a lack of interest in significant activities or pastimes) or affective restriction (e.g., reduced feelings of love for a family member or partner); reduced awareness of surroundings (e.g., being in a daze); derealization (e.g., feeling like the immediate sequence of events after an injury is not real); depersonalization (e.g., feeling that one's sense of self is altered while sitting trapped in a vehicle); and dissociative amnesia (e.g., remembering the ambulance ride to the hospital but not remembering the emergency room doctor requesting permission to amputate a peripheral extremity). Dissociative symptoms play a greater role in the conceptualization of ASD than PTSD.

Prevalence estimates for ASD tend to depend on a range of factors, including injury context, injury severity, and assessment method employed in establishing ASD cases. Estimates of ASD vary widely both within and across populations of injured persons, with ASD rates ranging from 1% to 16% among mixed-cause, severely injured, trauma center attendees (Creamer, O'Donnell, & Pattison, 2004; Mellman, David, Bustamante, Fins, & Esposito, 2001); from 12% to 14% among persons who sustained injury in various unintentional injury contexts (i.e., burnings, industrial accidents, and MVCs) (Bryant & Harvey, 1998a, 1998b, 1999a, 1999b); from 19% to 24% among persons injured during physical assault (Brewin, Andrews, Rose, & Kirk, 1999; Elklit & Brink, 2004); and at a rate of 30% among persons injured and hospitalized as a consequence of a terrorist attack (Balasinorwala, 2009).

## Posttraumatic Stress Disorder

The diagnostic formulation of PTSD has undergone several modifications since the inclusion of the disorder in the *DSM-III*. Changes over the years have focused on establishing certain events as sufficient to serve as a Criterion A traumatizing event, establishing responses as reflecting extreme stress, and better operationalizing the responses captured by the re-experiencing, avoidance, and hyperarousal symptom categories. In addition to requirements related to the endorsement of re-experiencing, avoidance/affective numbing, and hyperarousal/hypervigilance symptoms, the *DSM-IV-TR* provides diagnostic specifiers related to the onset and duration of PTSD symptoms. A diagnosis of acute PTSD is appropriate when PTSD symptoms are experienced for more than 1 month and less than 3 months. A diagnosis of chronic PTSD is appropriate if the duration of PTSD symptoms is greater than 3 months. A diagnosis of delayed onset PTSD is indicated if the onset of PTSD symptoms first occurs 6 months or more after the traumatic event.

PTSD prevalence estimates tend to vary depending on the type of traumatic event being studied and the method of recruitment, assessment, and data analysis used. In the unintentional injury context, considerable empirical attention has been paid to PTSD occurring consequent to MVCs. Norris (1992) determined that 23% of 1,000 adult survey participants had been involved in a serious MVC at some point in their lifetime, with nearly 12% of those MVC survivors reporting the experience of PTSD. Kessler, Sonnega, Bromet, Hughes, and Nelson (1995) noted that nearly 20% of 5,877 survey respondents in the National Comorbidity Study reported involvement in a serious MVC, with 6.5% of MVC survivors diagnosed with MVC-related PTSD (Kessler et al., 1995). In studies involving smaller samples, estimates for MVC-related PTSD have ranged from 1% (Malt, 1988) to 100% (Kuch, Cox, Evans, & Shulan, 1994), with estimates typically falling between 30% and 40% (Blanchard, Hickling, Taylor, & Loos, 1995; Koren, Arnon, & Klein, 1999; Zatzick et al., 2002). While acknowledging that MVCs occur less frequently than some potentially traumatizing events (e.g., IPV) and may be associated with less psychological distress than other potentially traumatizing events (e.g., criminal victimization), Norris (1992) described MVCs as the most significant type of traumatic event when frequency and impact are considered together. Nonetheless, rates of PTSD in the intentional injury context are also high. For example, it is estimated that between 30% and 80% of individuals who are sexually assaulted will develop PTSD (Kessler et al., 1995), and 20% to 39% of individuals who are physically assaulted will develop PTSD (Birmes et al., 2001; Brewin et al., 1999; Johansen, Wahl, Eilertsen, & Weisaeth, 2007; Kilpatrick & Acierno, 2003). The relation of intentional injury to PTSD appears to be particularly strong among women who have experienced criminal victimization, with women being twice as likely as men to experience PTSD following such events (Kilpatrick & Acierno, 2003).

Whether disasters are categorized as intentional (e.g., terrorist bombings) or unintentional (e.g., hurricane or nuclear accident), exposure to disasters is more common than expected, and PTSD is the most frequently studied psychological disorder in these disaster contexts (Norris et al., 2002). In a review of 284 studies of disasters and PTSD, Neria, Nandi, and Galea (2008) reported PTSD prevalence estimates to range from 30% to 40% in persons directly witnessing disasters, 10% to 20% in rescue workers, and 5% to 10% in the general population. Higher rates of PTSD tended to be associated with degree of physical injury, severity of property damage, and frequency of fatalities.

Prevalence estimates for PTSD vary across assessment time points; however, the general trend suggests that PTSD decreases over time. For studies evaluating PTSD at 12 months postevent, prevalence estimates range from 2% to 46% (Bryant & Harvey, 1995; Ehlers, Mayou, & Bryant, 1998; Koren, Arnon, & Klein, 1999; Mayou, Bryant, & Ehlers, 2001; Schnyder, Moergeli, Trentz, Klaghofer, & Buddeberg, 2001; Ursano et al., 1999). Remission rates have been used as estimates of changing PTSD prevalence over time. Using reported remission rates from studies evaluating the persistence of PTSD following MVCs, Blanchard and Hickling (2004) determined that, on average, 46% of MVC survivors are free of PTSD within 6 to 12 months following the MVC.

### Disorders of Extreme Stress Not Otherwise Specified/Complex Posttraumatic Stress Disorder (PTSD)

While the presenting problem for a number of physically injured persons might be injury-related physical limitations and psychological distress, a significant number of these persons present with very complicated preinjury background histories. These individuals report histories of childhood mental, physical, or sexual abuse, neglect, loss, serious physical injury or health conditions, interpersonal violence, personal or familial substance abuse, and personal or familial involvement with mental health professionals. Individuals with such complicated precollision histories may be conceptualized as having sustained repeated and extensive exposure to trauma. The diagnostic labels of DESNOS (Pelcovitz et al., 1997) and Complex PTSD (Courtois, 2004; Herman, 1992) have been developed to capture these more extreme and complicated experiences of PTSD. In essence, the study of retraumatization can probably best be encapsulated by these diagnostic labels.

DESNOS are characterized by alterations in the ability to modulate emotions, identity and sense of self, ongoing consciousness and memory, relations with perpetrators, relations with others, physical and medical status, and systems of meaning (van der Kolk, Roth, Pelcovitz, Sunday, & Spinazzola, 2005). Support for DESNOS is increasing (Courtois, 2004). Consistent with this impression, an entire issue of the *Journal of Traumatic Stress* was devoted to coverage of DESNOS/Complex PTSD (Schnurr, 2005). The *DSM-IV* (American Psychiatric Association, 1994) field trial for DESNOS did not lead to inclusion of these presentations as a separate diagnostic category, but it is hoped that this disorder will be included in the next edition of the *DSM* under anxiety disorders. Although there is a field trial study (Roth, Newman, Pelcovitz, van der Kolk, & Mandel, 1997), there are no studies that formally examine the occurrence of DESNOS/Complex PTSD in the physical injury context; however, there is little doubt that precollision traumas predict the occurrence of PTSD consequent to physical injury involvement. For illustration purposes, a study by Ramstad, Russo, and Zatzick (2004) is particularly relevant to this discussion. Using the National Comorbidity Study (NCS) trauma history screening instrument, these investigators evaluated the lifetime trauma histories of 251 hospitalized trauma surgery patients, 66 of whom sustained intentional injuries and 185 of whom sustained unintentional injuries. The researchers then compared the rates of lifetime exposure reported by these intentionally and unintentionally injured patients to the lifetime trauma rate reported by NCS participants (5873). Only 11% of NCS respondents reported four or more lifetime traumas, and 61% of intentionally injured patients and 40% of unintentionally injured patients reported four or more lifetime traumas. The researchers concluded that injured patients often bear both the burden of the current injury and an additional burden of significant traumas experienced prior to the current injury.

The importance of assessing and recognizing DESNOS/Complex PTSD has to do with its relevance for treatment outcome and prognosis. Psychological treatment of these more complicated cases requires more sessions than normal. There is no evidence to suggest that manualized treatment approaches will be effective with these presentations. In general, preinjury traumas can make an individual more vulnerable to the effects of a physical injury, but preinjury traumas should not be given more etiological importance than peri-injury or postinjury changes in physical and psychological functioning. In addition, the prognosis for someone identified as having DESNOS/Complex PTSD will likely be less than favorable. Clearly, more data related to prevalence and clinical characteristics of DESNOS/Complex PTSD are needed.

## Major Depressive Disorder

Injury-related depressive disorders occur with considerable frequency, but they have not received as much empirical attention, especially in comparison to PTSD. From a clinical standpoint, depression is a common consequence of physical injury that can serve to magnify residual physical consequences of injury and contribute to postinjury functional limitations and lifestyle impairment. Preinjury depression can make an individual more vulnerable to physical injury and more vulnerable to postinjury physical and psychological morbidity, including posttraumatic stress reactions.

A *DSM-IV-TR* diagnosis of MDD requires that at least five of the following nine symptoms be experienced on an almost daily basis for a period of at least 2 weeks (American Psychiatric Association, 2000): (1) feeling depressed or sad; (2) decreased interest or pleasure in almost all activities; (3) significant weight loss, weight gain, or changes in appetite; (4) insomnia or hypersomnia; (5) psychomotor agitation or retardation; (6) decreased energy or endurance; (7) feelings of worthlessness, helplessness, or hopelessness; (8) concentration and memory impairment; and (9) recurrent thoughts of death, and suicidal ideation or intent. A diagnosis of MDD requires that these symptoms significantly interfere with occupational, social, and other areas of functioning, and that symptoms not be better accounted for by another psychological condition (e.g., bereavement), by a general medical condition (e.g., diabetes), or by the physiological effects of a mood-altering substance (e.g., medication). Although the symptom criteria for MDD appear straightforward, in the context of physical injury, it can be particularly difficult to ascribe these symptoms to MDD rather than to some other aspect of the physical injury. For example, traumatic brain injury (TBI) can result in decreased energy, concentration, and memory impairment, sleep and appetite disturbances, and prominent feelings of worthlessness and helplessness. These TBI-related symptoms would be indistinguishable from those that define MDD.

Prevalence estimates for MDD largely depend upon the postinjury assessment interval. Michaels et al. (2000) determined that at the time of hospital admission, 19% of their sample of trauma patients experienced depression. Holbrook, Anderson, Sieber, Browner, and Hoyt (1998) determined that 60% of their sample of 1,048 trauma center attendees was depressed at hospital discharge. For studies of MDD occurring within the first 1 to 4 months following physical injury, MDD estimates range from 10% to 23% (Blanchard et al., 1995b; O'Donnell, Creamer, Pattison, & Atkin, 2004b; Shalev et al., 1998). For studies of MDD occurring 6 to 12 months following physical injury, MDD estimates range from 10% to 40% (Blanchard et al., 2004; Maes, Mylle, Delmeire, & Altamura, 2000; Michaels et al., 2000; O'Donnell et al., 2004b; Shalev et al., 1998). These established rates of postinjury MDD are consistent with clinical impressions regarding the significance of depression as a frequently occurring psychological consequence of traumatic injury.

MDD has frequently been identified as co-occurring with PTSD, with comorbidity estimates ranging from 26% to 59% across community, MVC, and mixed trauma samples (Blanchard et al., 1998; Frommberger et al., 1998; Kessler et al., 1995; Maes et al., 2000; O'Donnell et al., 2004b; Shalev et al., 1998). In their study of traumatic events and PTSD among urban-dwelling, young adults, Breslau, Davis, Andreski, and Peterson (1991) found that 39% of those young adults who evidenced PTSD also evidenced MDD. In a subsequent analysis of psychiatric disorders evidenced by urban-dwelling, young adults, Breslau, Davis, Peterson, and Schultz (1997) determined that MDD increases the risk for exposure to traumatic events, that preexisting depression increases a person's susceptibility to the PTSD-inducing effects of traumatic events, and that PTSD increases the risk for first onset of MDD. In a study evaluating the relation between MDD and PTSD in MVC survivors, Blanchard, Buckley, Hickling, and Taylor (1998) determined that nearly half of those MVC survivors who evidenced PTSD also evidenced MDD. This high rate of comorbidity between PTSD and MDD has been suggested by some to be evidence of a shared vulnerability (Breslau, Davis, Peterson, & Schultz, 2000; O'Donnell, Creamer, & Pattison (2004). Other researchers argue for the independence of the two disorders, noting that the two disorders are more distinguishable in the acute phases (O'Donnell et al., 2004a), and that the two disorders are associated with a number of nonoverlapping consequences (Blanchard et al., 1998)

## Substance-Related Disorders

Across all levels of engagement (i.e., use, intoxication, dependence, and abuse), ingestion of mood-altering substances increases risk of physical injury. When an individual's pattern of engagement with substances can be labeled as substance dependence or substance abuse, the pattern of engagement is considered to be disordered. According to the *DSM-IV-TR* (American Psychiatric Association, 2000), a diagnosis of substance dependence is applied when the pattern of substance use leads to significant distress and impairment as indicated by any three of the following: the experience of tolerance; the experience of withdrawal; an increase in the amount of substance that is consumed; the desire to cut down or stop substance use; an increase in the time dedicated to seeking, using, and recovering from substance use; reduced involvement in role functioning as a result of substance use; and continued substance use despite the knowledge that substance use is causing recurrent physical or psychological damage. The essential feature of substance abuse is the maladaptive pattern of substance use that results in multiple and recurrent adverse consequences. The diagnosis of substance abuse requires that an individual engage in recurrent substance use that (1) interferes with role functioning at work, school, or home; (2) occurs in hazardous situations (e.g., while operating a motor vehicle); (3) leads to legal ramifications (e.g., being charged or arrested for driving under the influence or for substance-related disorderly conduct); and (4) leads to persistent social or interpersonal problems (e.g., an increase in physical altercations or increase in marital discord). Research suggests that these substance-related disorders place individuals at a particularly high risk of physical injury, increase the likelihood of psychological distress and impairment consequent to physical injury, and impede physical and psychological recovery postinjury. The relation of substance use to risk of physical injury can be characterized as a dose-response relation (Baker & Chen, 2001). Research findings that document injury risk across substance engagement levels are presented immediately below.

Watt, Purdie, Roche, and McClure (2006) conducted a study that can be conceived as addressing some of the misconceptions held about the impact of beverage type, drinking setting, and drinking quantity on risk of physical injury (Watt et al., 2006). Using a sample of 593 patients who attended an ED for management of physical injuries, these researchers examined the relation of beverage type, drinking setting, and drinking quantity to injury risk across six different mechanisms of injury: being cut or pierced; being hit by or against something; being involved in an MVC; falling; overdosing; and other miscellaneous mechanisms. After controlling for a number of sociodemographic, situational, and substance use variables, it was observed that drinking in a licensed premise was associated with an increased risk of intentional injury. Low-risk drinking that occurred either at home or in locations other than a licensed premise was associated with an increased risk of MVC-related injury, while beverage type and drinking quantity were not differentially associated with injury risk across any of the six injury mechanisms studied. The researchers interpreted the study findings as indicating that acute alcohol consumption leads to a general increase in risk of physical injury to the drinker.

Being a current drinker is associated with an increased risk of mortality for every major cause of injury (Chen, Baker, & Li, 2005). National Highway Traffic Safety Administration (NHTSA) data suggest that alcohol is a factor in 41% of fatality-involved MVCs (NHTSA, 2003). Current drinking, whether characterized as light, moderate, or heavy, is associated with fatal injury across intentional and unintentional injury contexts (Chen et al., 2005). Acute alcohol intoxication has been linked to recurrent traumatic injury (Gentilello et al., 1999; Stockwell et al., 2002). Substance abuse and substance dependence have definite implications for physical injury. It has been estimated that 20% to 55% of persons hospitalized for trauma surgery have difficulties with substance abuse or dependence (Gentilello, Donovan, Dunn, & Rivara, 1995; Soderstrom et al., 1997).

In a comparison of data compiled on 5,549 persons who had sustained fatal injuries to data compiled on 42,698 controls who were representative of the general population, Chen, Baker, and Li (2005) determined current drinking (i.e., light, moderate, and heavy drinking) to be associated with fatal injury across intentional and unintentional injury contexts. These researchers observed that 37% of persons who suffered fatal falls, 59% percent of persons who died in MVCs, 70% of persons who committed suicide by hanging, and 74% of persons who committed suicide by drowning were current drinkers.

Borges and colleagues (2008) used data derived from the WHO Collaborative Study on Alcohol and Injuries to establish the contribution of alcohol use to traumatic injuries occurring in violent and nonviolent contexts. Results indicated that alcohol was a factor in 46% of violent injuries and 11.5% of nonviolent injuries. The authors indicated the risk of violence-related injury increased with drinking; higher levels of drinking were associated with a 15-fold increase in risk for violence-related injuries and a fourfold increase in risk for nonviolence-related injuries (Borges et al., 2008).

Substance dependence and abuse have been found to increase the likelihood that an individual will commit significant physical harm against the self and against another. Using data from a sample of 1,409 patients with intentionally caused TBI, Kim and Colantonio (2008) identified those factors that contributed most to TBIs occurring in the context of intentional self-harm or violent assault. Approximately 28% of intentional TBIs occurred in the context of self-harm (e.g., jumping from high places and using firearms), and 72% of intentional TBIs occurred in the context of violent assault (e.g., involvement in fights and brawls and being struck with an object). The researchers determined that self-inflicted TBIs were best predicted by alcohol or drug abuse history, younger age, and female gender, and that other-inflicted TBIs were best predicted by alcohol or drug abuse history, younger age, and male gender.

Using survey data from 350 patients who attended a family medicine practice that specialized in addiction, Reece (2008) examined the relation of lifetime traumas to medical conditions. The researchers identified 220 opioid-dependent patients among the 350 patients surveyed and compared those opioid-dependent patients to the remaining 130 patients, none of whom had a substance-related disorder. Reece observed that opioid-dependent patients committed more driving-related infractions and experienced more fractures, surgical operations, dental trauma, and assaults than did patients with no substance-related disorders.

With an urban, Level-I trauma center serving as the screening site, Prekker, Miner, Rockswold, and Biros (2009) screened 4,246 consecutive ED visits, with 1,036 of these visits due to physical injury. The majority of physical injury cases (75%) involved minor injuries, with only 11% of injury cases requiring hospital admission. Based on interview data obtained from 434 consenting injury patients, Prekker and colleagues determined that the likelihood of incurring a violence-related physical injury increased for persons of male gender, an annual income less than $5,000, a positive history of domestic violence, and heavy alcohol use.

Findings described in this section of the chapter highlight the importance of conceptualizing the physical injury context as one that requires routine assessment of those psychological conditions that increase the likelihood of injury as well as those psychological conditions that are common consequences of physical injury, that complicate recovery from physical injury, and that contribute to and maintain injury-related functional impairments. Assessment of psychological reactions to physical injury should involve repeat assessments, these assessments emphasizing what is practical given the assessment setting (e.g., use of brief screening inventories rather than diagnostic interviews in the hospital or primary-care settings) and scheduled to coincide with established time intervals for assessing recovery from physical injuries (e.g., at hospital admission, at hospital discharge, at first follow-up contact with the primary-care provider). In the initial hours and weeks following a physical injury, injured persons may experience transient symptoms of psychological distress that may be regarded as both predictable and within the normal range of responding given the nature of the injury-causing event or the extent of physical injuries sustained. For the majority of injured persons, these initial psychological reactions resolve along with recovery from physical injuries. When the injury-causing event is a psychologically traumatizing event, when sustained physical injuries are severe, and when injury-related functional impairments are extreme and far reaching, clinically significant psychological distress reactions are more likely. The course of intervention that would follow a postinjury diagnosis of MDD, PTSD, or substance abuse is relatively standard and would include consultation with and patient referral to a mental health professional who is experienced in comprehensively assessing and managing the interacting influences of physical and psychological injuries and impairments.

## RETRAUMATIZATION IN THE CONTEXT OF PHYSICAL INJURIES

For some, physical injuries represent one more trauma among a lifetime of traumatic events. Given this, the primary goals of psychological assessment in the physical injury context are the identification of prior traumatic events, evaluation of the physical and psychological injuries and impairments associated with those prior events, and recognition of the influence of prior traumatic events and traumatic reactions on physical and psychological recovery following the index injury-causing event. Prediction of psychological symptoms and impairments following physical injury requires an understanding of a complex web of interacting pre-, peri-, and postinjury factors that include but are not limited to the following: the biology of the individual; the experiential history of the individual; the social context of the individual; the individual's subjective appraisal of the injury-causing event; the enduring and fluctuating pattern of injury-related symptoms and functional impairments; and the system-level and societal reactions to both the injury-causing event and to the impact of the event on the individual (Duckworth, 2008).

The above described approach to assessing and integrating all the pre-, peri-, and postinjury factors that are relevant to psychological functioning postinjury is supported by findings described in two of the more comprehensive meta-analytic studies of PTSD predictors and symptoms (Brewin et al., 2000; Ozer et al., 2003). Brewin and colleagues selected 77 PTSD studies for inclusion in their meta-analysis. The selected studies involved evaluation of PTSD symptoms across a variety of trauma contexts, including combat, crime, natural disasters, MVCs, and other trauma contexts. Across the 77 studies, 14 variables were identified as potentially relevant to the prediction of PTSD symptoms among trauma victims: gender; age; socioeconomic status (SES); education; intelligence; race; psychiatric history; childhood abuse; previous trauma; other adverse childhood events; family psychiatric history; trauma history; social support; and life stress. The authors determined that education, previous trauma, general childhood adversity, trauma severity, lack of social support, and additional life stress were significant predictors of PTSD. When considered together, peri- and posttrauma factors such as trauma severity, lack of social support, and additional life stress were determined to have stronger predictive strength than pretrauma factors.

Ozer and colleagues (2003) performed a meta-analysis of PTSD studies that was similar to that undertaken by Brewin and colleagues (2000). These researchers selected 68 studies for evaluation; this set of studies included 21 studies that were not included in the Brewin et al. meta-analysis. The investigators identified seven potential predictors of PTSD: prior trauma; prior psychological adjustment; family history of psychopathology; perceived life threat during trauma; posttrauma social support; peritraumatic emotional responses; and peritraumatic dissociation. All predictors produced significant effects, with peritraumatic dissociation having the largest effect size. Consistent with the findings obtained by Brewin et al., Ozer and colleagues determined pretrauma variables such as family history, prior trauma, and prior adjustment to have the smallest effect sizes.

The two meta-analytic studies of PTSD symptoms and predictors summarized above should be considered particularly relevant to the assessment of individuals who survive traumatic injuries. Findings from these two studies may be useful to the process of conceptualizing the unique and interactive effects of those pre-, peri-, and postinjury factors that are thought to influence an individual's psychological reaction to physical injury and associated sequelae. One shortcoming that characterizes both of these meta-analytical studies is the lack of clarity related to the measurement of past traumas and past experiences of clinically significant traumatic stress reactions. The examination of retraumatization requires the examination of an individual's prior exposure to potentially traumatizing events and prior experience of clinically significant traumatic stress reactions in response to those events. Provided below are summaries of studies that have attempted to assess the impact of prior trauma exposures on psychological distress evidenced subsequent to an index injury.

Using the trauma history screen developed for the NCS, Zatzick and colleagues (2004) compared rates of prior trauma exposure reported by the NCS sample to the rates of prior trauma exposure reported by 251 injured, acute-care inpatients (Ramstad et al., 2004). Findings indicated that while 11% of the NCS sample reported four or more lifetime traumas, 45% of the injured, acute-care inpatients reported four or more lifetime traumas. When findings were considered with respect to injury intent, it was determined that unintentionally injured patients were five times more likely to have experienced prior physical attacks or assaults than NCS participants. Intentionally injured patients were 10 times more likely to have experienced a prior physical attack or assault and six times more likely to have experienced a prior life-threatening accident than NCS participants. This study represents one of the first examinations of prior trauma experienced by persons who have sustained an index injury and have been hospitalized for management of the index injury. In the same year, Zatzick and colleagues published findings from a study that evaluated physical injuries and psychological dysfunction occurring in the context of repeat trauma exposure (Zatzick et al., 2004). These researchers examined rates of prior trauma exposure and rates of current psychiatric diagnoses among 269 randomly selected injury survivors who attended Level-I trauma centers across two western cities. Nearly 68% of these injury survivors sustained unintentional injuries, with the remainder of injury survivors having sustained their injuries in the context of self-harm and violent assault. Approximately 48% of these injury survivors reported four or more traumas prior to the index injury and trauma center admission and more than 50% experienced immediate posttraumatic distress or alcohol abuse or dependence during the time of surgical admission. Regression analyses identified greater prior trauma, female gender, and nonwhite ethnicity as significant predictors of immediate posttraumatic distress.

Although the studies by Zatzick and colleagues (2004) are noteworthy for their inclusion of information related to both the number and type of prior traumas experienced by injury survivors, Irish and colleagues (2008) performed an evaluation of MVC patients that included many of the pretrauma variables identified by Ozer and colleagues (2003) and by Brewin and colleagues (2000) as important to the prediction of posttrauma PTSD. In an analysis of 180 MVC patients, these researchers tested the contribution of sociodemographic, distress, and trauma history variables to PTSD symptoms reported at 6 weeks and at 1 year postcollision. Findings revealed that at 6 weeks postcollision, sociodemographic (i.e., age, gender, and income), distress (i.e., depression), and trauma history (i.e., number of prior traumas, age at first trauma, interpersonal trauma history, and physical injury, life threat, and distress caused by prior trauma) variables accounted for approximately 39% of the variance in acute PTSD symptoms, with 7% of the explained variance accounted for by trauma history variables. The authors noted that the explanatory strength of this set of predictors was attributable to age, depression, and distress during a prior trauma. At 1 year postcollision, sociodemographic (i.e., age, gender, and income), distress (i.e., depression), and trauma history (i.e., number of types of traumas, life threat, and distress caused by prior trauma) variables accounted for approximately 36% of the variance in acute PTSD symptoms, with 6% of the explained variance accounted for by trauma history variables. The authors noted that the explanatory strength of this set of predictors was attributable largely to gender and depression, with income, number of types of traumas, and distress during a prior trauma contributing marginally to the prediction of chronic PTSD symptoms.

Findings from large-scale studies of European and South African populations confirm the strength of the relation between prior trauma exposure and psychological distress, especially distress occurring in the form of PTSD. In a large-scale study of more than 21,000 adults across six European countries, 8,797 adults were interviewed to establish rates of trauma exposure and PTSD prevalence (Darves-Bornoz et al., 2008). Findings revealed that, on average, respondents reported exposure to three traumatic events. The researchers performed a multivariate logistic regression to test the contribution of 28 potentially traumatic events (PTEs) to PTSD diagnosis at 12 months postevent. After controlling for gender, PTSD diagnosis was best predicted by six PTEs: being raped, being beaten by a partner, having experienced an undisclosed private event, having a child with serious illness, being beaten by a caregiver, and being stalked.

Using data from the South African Stress and Health Study (Williams et al., 2004), a large-scale survey of more than 4,000 South Africans, Williams and colleagues (2007) examined the relation of multiple traumas to nonspecific psychological distress. Reports of exposure to traumatic events indicated that 19% of participants experienced one traumatic event, 18% experienced two traumas, 13% experienced three traumas, and 16% experienced four or five traumas. Most noteworthy is that nearly 10% of survey respondents reported experiencing six or more traumas over a lifetime. The most common types of trauma included trauma to a close other, experienced by 43% of respondents; IPV, experienced by 30% of respondents; being a victim of crime, experienced by 25% of respondents; and threat to life, experienced by 25%. Those participants reporting six or more traumas were five times more likely to be highly distressed than participants experiencing fewer exposures to trauma. Although not reported, it can be assumed that many of the events of trauma experienced involved physical injury. It is also likely that physical injuries contributed to the psychological distress reported by survey participants. Surveys of trauma exposure that document physical injuries and that assess both nonclinical and clinical manifestations of trauma-related distress will serve best in elucidating the relations among these variables and the relation of these variables to short- and long-term functional outcomes.

In a study of the intersection of lifetime trauma exposure, PTSD, and physical health outcomes, Sledjeski, Speisman, and Dierker (2008) used a study from the National Comorbidity Survey-Replication (Kessler & Merikangas, 2004) to test the relation of trauma exposure (no exposure, exposure) and PTSD diagnosis (present, absent) to physical health status as indicated by the presence or absence of 15 different medical conditions. Of the 9,282 participants selected for inclusion in the study, 738 participants reported no exposure to trauma, 4,054 participants reported exposure to at least one Criterion A trauma in the absence of any experience of PTSD, and 574 participants reported exposure to at least one Criterion A trauma and met criteria for a diagnosis of PTSD. Findings revealed a graded relation between trauma exposure, PTSD, and medical conditions, with participants who experienced a qualifying trauma and PTSD having the highest likelihood of suffering chronic medical conditions, and those participants with no trauma exposure having the lowest likelihood of suffering chronic medical conditions. In addition, the participants who experienced a qualifying trauma and PTSD were more likely to be female, younger, have a lower annual income, lack health insurance, smoke, and have a history of MDD, other anxiety disorders, and substance abuse or substance dependence. Findings also suggested the importance of exposure to multiple traumas. With the exception of headaches, the relation of PTSD to the various medical conditions was explained by the number of lifetime traumas experienced. Overall, these researchers concluded that multiple traumas have a cumulative effect on physical health, and that the effect may be independent of PTSD.

In a similar study examining the relation of prior trauma exposure and lifetime psychiatric history to risk of physical injury, O'Donnell and colleagues (2009) recruited 1,167 patients with intentional (e.g., assaults) and unintentional injuries (e.g., transport crashes and falls) who received medical attention through five Australian trauma services over a 2-year period (O'Donnell et al., 2009). Data from Australian National Survey of Mental Health and Wellbeing indicate that 9% of Australians have experienced at least one traumatic event. O'Donnell and colleagues determined that 87% of their sample experienced at least one traumatic event prior to the index injury-related hospitalization. As many as 17% of those persons who were hospitalized with unintentional injuries and 28% of those hospitalized with intentional injuries reported experiencing more than four prior traumas. A psychiatric history was identified in 63% of the unintentional injury group and 78% of the intentional injury group. Rates of PTSD, MDD, alcohol dependence, and alcohol abuse were greater among persons who had sustained intentional injuries: 22% of intentionally injured patients and 13% of unintentionally injured persons were diagnosed with PTSD, 47% of intentionally injured patients and 30% of unintentionally injured persons were diagnosed with MDD, 37% of intentionally injured patients and 19% of unintentionally injured persons were diagnosed with alcohol dependence, and 53% of intentionally injured patients and 36% of unintentionally injured persons were diagnosed with alcohol abuse. The authors concluded that compared to population norms, intentional and unintentional injury survivors were at increased risk for reporting all types of trauma and all measured psychiatric diagnoses.

Dennis and colleagues (2009) examined the rates and types of trauma exposure, severity of psychological distress, presence of health conditions, and rates of health-care utilization among a sample of 148 Veteran and nonveteran community women, 72 of whom were diagnosed with PTSD, 24 of whom were diagnosed with MDD, and 52 of whom did not meet criteria for PTSD or MDD. Findings revealed rates of trauma exposure to be high across all groups, with 96% of women with PTSD, 79% of women with MDD, and 46% of women with neither diagnosis reporting three or more traumatic events. Findings revealed women with PTSD to have experienced significantly more traumatic life events and a significantly greater number of Criterion A events than did women with MDD or women with neither diagnosis. Across all three groups, death of a loved one was the most commonly reported traumatic event and the event cited by these women as the worst event. Women with PTSD were significantly more likely to endorse unexpected death or illness, adult physical assault, childhood physical violence, adult sexual assault, and accidents than women with neither PTSD nor MDD. Both the PTSD and MDD groups reported more physical health conditions than the control group, and the PTSD group was more likely to see a mental health provider than MDD and control groups. Finally, after controlling for diagnostic status, regression analysis for PTSD symptom severity revealed that trauma exposure with adult physical assault was associated with more severe PTSD and depressive symptoms.

For some persons, physical injuries represent another trauma in a lifetime of traumas. Because serious physical injuries are closely associated with increased psychological distress and negative health consequences, it is imperative that all pre-, peri-, and posttrauma factors that have been identified as influencing recovery from traumatic injury be considered when evaluating injured persons. Included among those trauma factors that predict recovery are sociodemographic factors (e.g., age); biological or medical factors (e.g., prior history of injury); psychological factors (e.g., prior trauma exposure and prior psychiatric history); and sociocultural factors (e.g., availability of social support). Altogether, the findings from these studies highlight the extent to which pre-, peri-, and posttraumatic injury factors can interact and contribute to increased psychological distress and long-term physical health problems.

## PREVENTION AND TREATMENT OF PHYSICAL INJURIES

One of the more interesting messages to be taken from the information provided in this chapter is that across intentional and unintentional contexts, injured persons do not appear to experience reinjury in a manner that is completely random. An individual who sustains injuries as a consequence of a fall is at disproportionately greater risk of suffering injuries due to another fall. An individual who self-injures is at disproportionately greater risk of suffering injuries due to another act of self-harm. Although unfortunate, this disproportionate risk of reinjury within the same injury context and as a function of the same injury mechanism establishes an injury pattern that may allow healthcare professionals to more accurately predict and prevent physical injuries. Primary injury prevention efforts can be considered the most effective means of reducing personal and societal costs related to physical injuries. Usually, injury prevention occurs in the form of educational efforts aimed at informing the public of the prevalence of injury-causing events and risk-avoidance behaviors. These educational efforts translate to prevention of injury as well as prevention of the physical and psychological morbidity, impairment, and disability that are the likely consequences of injury. Within the United States, the CDC is probably the best resource for information (e.g., fact sheets and research publications) related to injury prevention. Particularly beneficial are the CDC's efforts to provide information relevant to populations considered to be at greater risk of injury across injury contexts (e.g., Community-Based Interventions to Reduce Motor-Vehicle-Related Injuries, Effectiveness of Designated Driver Promotion, Preventing Violence Against Women: Program Activities Guide, and U.S. Fall Prevention Program). There are also a number of studies that have evaluated the effectiveness of injury prevention programs (Dicker et al., 2009; Nilsen, 2004; Rivara, Thompson, Beahler, & MacKenzie, 1999; Shults et al., 2009).

Once an injury has occurred, efforts to minimize the severity of the injury (secondary prevention) and to minimize the functional impairments associated with the injury (tertiary prevention) are necessarily complex. The success of such efforts depends on person-level variables, including prior history of physical injury, prior history of coping with physical injuries as well as insults of other types, availability and ability to access support within their own social network, availability and ability to access health care, and ability to negotiate compensation systems (e.g., the workers' compensation system, insurance companies, and the legal system), as well as system-level variables, including health-care initiatives and mass media campaigns designed to increase awareness of resources both to prevent injury-causing events and to limit the negative consequences of injury and the risk of reinjury.

Physical injuries, when sufficiently severe or when sufficiently overwhelming in their impacts, often involve physical and psychological dysfunction and often require medical and psychological management. Effective intervention around physical injuries, particularly those sustained in the context of trauma, requires an integration of biological, psychological, and social approaches to maximizing postinjury functioning. The field of physical injury intervention still can be characterized by the use of unidimensional approaches to managing singular aspects of physical injury, and a number of these unidimensional treatment approaches should be touted for both the effectiveness of the treatment approach and the extent to which the treatment approach attempts to capture additional aspects of physical injury. Examples of effective and more inclusive medical approaches to managing physical injuries are those forwarded by Richmond and colleagues (Richmond & Jacoby, 2008; Richmond, Thompson, Deatrick, & Kauder, 2000), Zatzick and colleagues (Wagner, Zatzick, Ghesquiere, & Jurkovich, 2007; Zatzick et al., 2004), and Hoyt, Holbrook, and colleagues (Dolich & Hoyt, 2008; Steim, Kerridge, Dimsdale, & Hoyt, 2007; Potenza et al., 2004). Examples of effective and more inclusive psychological approaches to managing physical injuries are those forwarded by O'Donnell and colleagues (O'Donnell, Bryant, Creamer, and Carty, 2008; O'Donnell et al., 2009) and Duckworth, Iezzi, and colleagues (Duckworth & Iezzi, 2010; Duckworth, Iezzi, & O'Donohue, 2008).

Although the literature pertaining to the treatment of psychological trauma occurring consequent to physical injury is relatively young, O'Donnell et al. (2008) provided a three-step, health services model that aims to improve the effectiveness of early psychological intervention following physical injuries. The first step of the model emphasizes the importance of screening injured persons for vulnerability to developing trauma-related distress. Such screening can occur in EDs, hospitals, specialists' offices, and primary-care offices and can be done with short self-report instruments. Psychological screening also provides an opportunity to educate and normalize the peritrauma psychological reactions experienced by injured persons. The second step in this model is to follow injured persons who have been identified as at risk. Patients undergo another screen via phone contact with a qualified mental health provider to determine ongoing psychological distress and potential psychological treatment needs. The third step in this model recommends that injured persons identified as experiencing psychological distress be invited to return for face-to-face assessment and to offer treatment as needed and as available. Although O'Donnell et al. (2008) proposed a model of early psychological intervention that derives from the empirical literature related to physical injuries, further research is required to establish the utility of this health services intervention model.

The psychological literature pertaining to the treatment of retraumatization is also relatively young; however, population data related to reinjury and repeat trauma exposure suggest that the treatment of psychological trauma related to any single event is likely occurring on a backdrop of previous injuries and previous traumatic exposures. There is a substantial literature related to the treatment of PTSD following single traumatic events and a growing recognition of the need to manage Complex PTSD following a series of exposures to traumatizing events and life circumstances. As a starting point for reviewing details related to the treatment of PTSD occurring across different trauma contexts, the reader is encouraged to examine the work of the following clinical researchers: Bryant and Harvey (2000); Courtois and

Ford (2009); Foa, Keane, & Friedman (2000); Follette and Ruzek (2006); Friedman, Keane, and Resick (2007); and Zayfert and Becker (2007).

## SPECIAL ISSUES RELATED TO PHYSICAL INJURIES

There are a number of factors that must be considered and accounted for when attempting to determine the degree to which any index physical injury will be associated with an experience of repeat traumatization. This section addresses those person and contextual factors that contribute to risk of physical injury and reinjury and those methodological issues that contribute to accurate estimation of the frequency of physical injuries and accurate appraisal of the physical, psychological, and social consequences of injury.

### The Injured Person

A number of person-specific factors are considered to influence risk of physical injury. Age and gender are demographic factors that are considered particularly relevant to injury risk. Epidemiological data suggest that age conveys differential risk for physical injury within and between injury contexts. For example, sexual violence is more prevalent during childhood than during any other developmental period. One third of lifetime rapes occur before age 12, and one half of lifetime rapes occur before age 18 (Betz & Li, 2007). Elderly persons experience unique injury risks. For the elderly, falls are the leading cause of injury deaths, nonfatal injuries, and trauma-related hospital admissions (CDC, 2006). Gender also appears to influence physical injury risk and the impact of physical injuries when they are sustained. Across all age groups, men experience higher rates of injury-related morbidity and mortality than do women (Betz & Li, 2007). Research suggests that women are more likely than men to develop PTSD and to experience poorer quality of life consequent to physical injuries (Holbrook & Hoyt, 2004; Holbrook, Hoyt, Stein, & Sieber, 2001).

Certain personality types or behavioral response styles appear to be associated with increased risk of physical injury. Risk-taking is one person factor that has been evaluated with respect to its influence on physical injury risk. In studies of the relation of risk-taking to injury, risk-taking has included unsafe or illegal volitional behaviors that are considered to increase injury risk (e.g., use of excessive speed while driving) as well as socially sanctioned activities that involve risk of injury (e.g., participation in competitive sports) (Turner, McClure, & Pirozzo, 2004). With the exception of sports that entail both risk and a high degree of skill, risk-taking has been documented to be consistently associated with increased risk of physical injury. Accident proneness (i.e., the tendency of an individual to experience more accidents than other demographically similar individuals) is another person factor considered important to estimating an individual's risk of physical injury and reinjury. Using reports from studies of physical injuries sustained in different injury contexts and across different populations, Visser, Pijl, Stolk, Neelman, and Rosmalen (2007) concluded that although the many operational definitions of accident proneness serve to limit the degree of consensus to be had around this construct, certain individuals experience accidents and accident-related health consequences at rates in excess of what would be expected by chance. It must be acknowledged that research related to person factors that influence reinjury is less than complete, and that findings related to risk-taking and accident proneness are inconclusive and require substantiation.

## The Injury Context

Physical injuries can result from intentional and unintentional actions or events, and even though psychological distress may be experienced in relation to any type of injury-causing action or event, some injury contexts seem to be associated with increased risk of psychological trauma. Across intentional and unintentional injury contexts, events associated with extreme injuries or extreme changes in life circumstances are likely to result in clinically significant traumatic stress reactions among exposed individuals (Neria et al., 2008). Events of interpersonal violence are associated with more significant and enduring traumatic stress reactions than accidental man-made disasters or natural disasters (Norris et al., 2002; Yehuda, 2002). When injuries that appear minor are associated with significant psychological distress and functional compromise, the injured person's history of previous physical and psychological injuries is likely to be relevant to the person's adjustment to the current injury.

## Evaluating Physical Injuries

### Definition of Injury

Physical injuries are generally classified according to injury intent, mechanism of injury, injury site, severity of injury, and context for injury management. Although these strategies for classifying injuries are frequently employed in research addressing injury prevalence and injury outcomes, it has been suggested that these classification strategies do not allow for the most accurate accounting of physical injuries or the causes and consequences of such injuries (Brasel, de Roon-Cassini, & Bradley, 2010; Cryer & Langley, 2008). Even when physical injuries are classified in a manner that suggests specificity (e.g., intentional TBI due to blunt force trauma), injury categories can capture very diverse injury experiences (e.g., a mild TBI resulting from being struck in the head by a fist versus a severe TBI resulting from a bomb blast), diverse injury management contexts (e.g., a decision to not undergo any medical evaluation or treatment of injury versus protracted hospitalization and repeat surgeries), and diverse outcomes (e.g., no apparent change in function versus permanent functional compromise and permanent disability).

Cryer and Langley (2008) recommend that when attempting to evaluate physical injuries, researchers explicate the case or theoretical definition of injury that is being used. According to Langley and Brenner (2004), physical injuries are most commonly defined based on the external causes of injury enumerated within the International Classification of Diseases (ICD) Supplementary Classification of External Causes of Injury and Poisoning (World Health Organization, 1977). This approach to defining physical injuries is akin to a case definition of injury. A case definition requires only that the researcher describe the injury in terms of the resulting anatomical or physiological damage and in terms of frequency of occurrence across different populations and across different time periods. A case definition of injury does not require that the researcher address any of the associated injury outcomes. A theoretical definition of injury requires that the researcher address both the cause and outcome of the injury. The energy definition of injury used by the WHO is an example of a theoretical definition of injury. A definition of injury that addresses cause and outcome is considered essential in ensuring that injuries are accurately classified and counted, in allowing for the identification of injury trends, in allowing international injury rate comparisons, and in guiding policy related to injury prevention and injury management. When the objective of a study is to provide an unbiased estimate of injury prevalence, incidence, association, or effect, the study should employ a theoretical definition of injury, should employ a case definition of injury (including the nature and quality of the date from which the case was obtained), and should provide a discussion of potential mismatches between theoretical and case definitions (Cryer & Langley, 2008). Also needed are clear and uniform definitions of the physical and psychological impairments and disabilities that may occur consequent to physical injuries. In the context of retraumatization, it is particularly important to document each injury-causing event, to determine the degree of physical and psychological trauma engendered by each injury-causing event, and to document the degree of physical and psychological impairment experienced consequent to each injury-causing event.

## Timing of Injury Assessment

The timing of injury assessment is important in determining the severity of physical injuries, in identifying associated limitations in function, in prioritizing treatment targets, and in predicting long-term outcomes. Injured persons are often faced with a challenging and variable course of physical and psychological recovery, with some injured persons taking significantly longer than others to reach maximal physical and psychological improvement. Although follow-up assessments usually evaluate injury-related outcomes over the 12-month period immediately following injury, study findings suggest that assessment of the full impact of physical injuries on all relevant domains of function (i.e., occupational/financial, interpersonal, social/recreational, and intrapersonal) and on overall quality of life requires lengthier follow-up periods (Holbrook et al., 1999; Holtslag, van Beeck, Lindeman, & Leenen, 2007; Mayou, Ehlers, & Bryant, 2002; Mayou, Tyndel, & Bryant, 1997).


## CONCLUSION

Physical injuries, by virtue of the frequency of occurrence, and by virtue of the associated functional limitations and lifestyle impairments, are considered a public health concern and warrant all the attention paid by health-care providers and policy makers. Several factors make the management and prevention of physical injuries an even greater global imperative. First, data related to the occurrence of physical injuries suggest that the experience of injury is not a random circumstance. A person who experiences an index injury is likely to experience a subsequent injury of that same type and is likely to report a prior history of physical injury. Similarly, individuals who experience an index PTE are likely to report a history of multiple exposures to PTEs. Some persons sustain physical injuries in the context of Criterion A traumatic events and on a backdrop of previous physical injuries and previous exposure to PTEs. In such instances, traumatic stress reactions that are evidenced in response to an index injury may be viewed as a direct result of exposure to the Criterion A traumatic event, as a direct result of the physical injuries and functional impairments, or as an event that exacerbates traumatic stress reactions evidenced in relation to some previous injury or trauma. When physical injuries serve as a context of retraumatization, it is essential that those pre-, peri-, and post-injury factors that best predict long-term physical and psychological recovery of function and quality of life be considered. It is imperative that medical professionals who are charged with evaluating and treating physical injuries recognize the need to evaluate potentially co-occurring psychological injuries that influence physical recovery, and mental health professionals who are charged with evaluating and managing traumatic stress reactions recognize the need to evaluate the impact of potentially co-occurring physical injuries that influence psychological recovery. This integrative and interdisciplinary approach to evaluating the impacts of trauma-related physical and psychological injuries is the most effective approach to reducing the personal and societal costs of injuries.

# REFERENCES

Abbot, J., Johnson, R., Koziol-McLain, J., & Lowenstein, S. R. (1995). Domestic violence against women: Incidence and prevalence in an emergency department population. *Journal of the American Medical Association, 273*, 1763–1767.

Airey, C. M., Chell, S. M., Rigby, A. S., Tennant, A., & Connelly, J. B. (2001). The epidemiology of disability and occupation handicap resulting from major traumatic injury. *Disability and Rehabilitation, 23*, 509–515.

Ameratunga, S. N., Norton, R. N., Bennett, D. A., & Jackson, R. T. (2004). Risk disability due to car crashes: A review of the literature and methodological issues. *Injury, International Journal of the Care of the Injured, 35*, 1116–1127.

American Psychiatric Association. (1994). *Diagnostic and statistical manual of mental disorders* (4th ed.). Washington, DC: Author.

American Psychiatric Association. (2000). *Diagnostic and statistical manual of mental disorders* (4th ed., text revision). Washington, DC: Author.

Atherton, K., Wiles, N. J., Lecky, F. E., Hawes, S. J., Silman, A. J., Macfarlane, G. J., & Jones, G. T. (2006). Predictors of persistent neck pain after whiplash injury. *Emergency Medicine Journal, 23*, 195–201.

Baker, S. P., & Chen, L. H. (2001). *Determination of characteristics of fatally injured drivers*. Washington, DC: National Highways Traffic Safety Administration.

Baker, S. P., O'Neill, B., Ginsberg, M. J., & Li, G. (1992). *The injury fact book* (2nd ed.). New York: Oxford University Press.

Balasinorwala, V. P. (2009). Acute stress disorder in victims after terror attacks in Mumbai, India. *British Journal of Psychiatry, 195*, 462.

Betz, M. E., & Li, G. (2005). Epidemiologic patterns of injuries treated in ambulatory care settings. *Annals of Emergency Medicine, 46*, 544–551.

Betz, M. E., & Li, G. (2007). Injury prevention and control. *Emergency Medicine Clinics of North America, 3*, 901–914.

Birmes, P., Carreras, D., Charlet, J. P., Warner, B. A., Lauque, D., & Schmitt, L. (2001). Peritraumatic dissociation and posttraumatic stress disorder in victims of violent assault. *Journal of Nervous and Mental Disease, 189*, 796–798.

Blanchard, E. B., Buckley, T. C., Hickling, E. J., & Taylor, A. E. (1998). Posttraumatic stress disorder and comorbid major depression: Is the correlation an illusion? *Journal of Anxiety Disorders, 12*, 21–37.

Blanchard, E. B., & Hickling, E. J. (2004). *After the crash: Psychological assessment and treatment of survivors of motor vehicle accidents* (2nd ed.). Washington, DC: American Psychological Association.

Blanchard, E. B., Hickling, E. J., Freidenberg, B. M., Malta, L. S., Kuhn, E., & Sykes, M. A. (2004). Two studies of psychiatric morbidity after motor vehicle accidents: Survivors 1 year after the crash. *Behaviour Research and Therapy, 42*, 569–583.

Blanchard, E. B., Hickling, E. J., Mitnick, N., Taylor, A. E., Loos, W. R., & Buckley, T. C. (1995a). The impact of severity of physical injury and the perception of life threat in the development of post-traumatic stress disorder in motor vehicle accident victims. *Behaviour Research and Therapy, 33*, 529–534.

Blanchard, E. B., Hickling, E. J., Taylor, A. E., Buckley, T. C., Loos, W. R., & Walsh, J. (1998). Effects of litigation settlements on posttraumatic stress symptoms in motor vehicle accident victims. *Journal of Traumatic Stress, 11*, 337–354.

Blanchard, E. B., Hickling, E. J., Taylor, A. E., & Loos, W. R. (1995b). Psychiatric morbidity associated with motor vehicle accidents. *Journal of Nervous and Mental Disease, 183*, 495–504.

Borges, G., Orozco, R., Cremonte, M., Buzi-Figlie, N., Cherpitel, C., & Poznyak, V. (2008). Alcohol and violence in the emergency department: A regional report from the WHO collaborative study on alcohol and injuries. *Salud Publica de Mexico, 50*, S6–S11.

Brandt, E. N., & Pope, A. M. (1997). *Enabling America: Assessing the role of rehabilitation science and engineering.* Washington, DC: National Academy of Science.

Brasel, K. J., deRoon-Cassini, T., & Bradley, C. T. (2010). Injury severity and quality of life: Whose perspective is important? *Journal of Trauma, 68*, 263–268.

Breslau, N., Davis, G. C., Peterson, E. L., & Schultz, L. R. (1997). Psychiatric sequelae of posttraumatic stress disorder in women. *Archives of General Psychiatry, 54*, 81–87.

Breslau, N., Davis, G. C., Peterson, E. L., & Schultz, L. R. (2000). A second look at comorbidity in victims of trauma: The posttraumatic stress disorder-major depression connection. *Biological Psychiatry, 48*, 902–909.

Breslau, N., Davis, T. C., Andreski, P., & Peterson, E. (1991). Traumatic events and posttraumatic stress disorder in an urban population of young adults. *Archives of General Psychiatrist, 48*, 216–222.

Brewin, C. R., Andrews, B., Rose, S., & Kirk, M. (1999). Acute stress disorder and posttraumatic disorder in victims of violent crime. *American Journal of Psychiatry, 156*, 360–366.

Brewin, C. R., Andrews, B., & Valentine, J. D. (2000). Meta-analysis of risk factors for posttraumatic stress disorder in trauma-exposed adults. *Journal of Consulting in Clinical Psychology, 68*, 748–766.

Bryant, R. A., & Harvey, A. G. (1995). Avoidant coping style and post-traumatic stress following motor vehicle accidents. *Behaviour Research and Therapy, 33*, 631–635.

Bryant, R. A., & Harvey, A. G. (2000). *Acute stress disorder: A handbook of theory, assessment, and treatment.* Washington, DC: American Psychological Association.

Bryant, R. A., & Harvey, A. G. (2003). The influence of litigation on maintenance of posttraumatic stress disorder. *Journal of Nervous and Mental Disease, 191*, 191–193.

Campbell, J., Jones, A. S., Dienemann, J., Kub, J., Schollenberger, J., O'Campo, P., ... Wynne, C. (2002). Intimate partner violence and physical health consequences. *Archives of Internal Medicine, 162*, 1157–1163.

Carstensen, T. B., Frostholm, L., Ørnbøl, E., Kongsted, A., Kasch, H., Jensen, T. S., & Fink, P. K. (2008). Post-trauma ratings of pre-collision pain and psychological distress predict poor outcome following acute whiplash trauma: A 12-month follow-up. *Pain, 139*, 248–259.

Cassidy, J. D., Carroll, L. J., Cote, P., Lemstra, M., Berglund, A., & Nygren, A. (2000). The effect of eliminating compensation for pain and suffering on the outcome of insurance. *New England Journal of Medicine, 342*, 1179–1186.

Centers for Disease Control and Prevention. (2003). *Costs of intimate partner violence against women in the United States.* Atlanta, GA: Author.

Centers for Disease Control and Prevention. (2004). Surveillance of fatal and nonfatal injuries in the United States, 2001. *Morbidity and Mortality Weekly Report, 53*, 1–57.

Centers for Disease Control and Prevention. (2006). *CDC injury fact book.* Atlanta, GA: Author.

Chen, L., Baker, S. P., & Li, G. (2005). Drinking history and risk of fatal injury: Comparison among specific injury causes. *Accident Analysis and Prevention, 37*, 245–251.

Coker, A. L., Smith, P. H., & Fadden, M. K. (2005). Intimate partner violence and disabilities among women attending family practice clinics. *Journal of Women's Health, 19*, 829–839.

Cordell, W. H., Keene, K. K., Giles, B. K., Jones, J. B., Jones, J. H., & Brizendine, E. J. (2002). The high prevalence of pain in emergency medical care. *American Journal of Emergency Medicine, 20,* 165–169.

Corso, P., Finkelstein, E., Miller, T., Fiebelkorn, I., & Zaloshnja, E. (2006). Incidence and lifetime costs of injuries in the United States. *Injury Prevention, 12,* 212–218.

Corso, P. S., Mercy, J. A., Simon, T. R., Finkelstein, E. A., & Miller, T. R. (2007). Medical costs and productivity losses due to interpersonal and self-directed violence in the United States. *American Journal of Preventative Medicine, 32,* 474–482.

Courtois, C. A. (2004). Complex trauma, complex reactions: Assessment and treatment. *Psychotherapy: Theory, Research, Practice, and Training, 41,* 412–425.

Courtois, C. C., & Ford, J. D. (Eds.). (2009). *Treating complex traumatic stress disorders.* New York: Guilford Press.

Crandall, M. L., Nathens, A. B., Kernic, M. A., Holt, V. L., & Rivara, F. P. (2004). Predicting future injury among women in abusive relationships. *Journal of Trauma, 56,* 906–912.

Creamer, M., O'Donnell, M. L., & Pattison, P. (2004). Acute stress disorder is of limited benefit in predicting post-traumatic stress disorder in people surviving traumatic injury. *Behaviour Research and Therapy, 42,* 315–328.

Cryer, C., & Langley, J. D. (2008). Studies need to make explicit the theoretical and case definitions of injury. *Injury Prevention, 14,* 74–77.

Darves-Bornoz, J., Alonso, J., de Girolamo, G., de Graaf, R., Haro, J. M., Kovess-Masfety, V., … Gasquet, I. (2008). Main traumatic events in Europe: PTSD in the European study of the epidemiology of mental disorders survey. *Journal of Traumatic Stress, 21,* 455–462.

Dennis, M. F., Flood, A. M., Reynolds, V., Araujo, G., Clancy, C. P., Barefoot, J. C., & Beckham, J. C. (2009). Evaluation of lifetime trauma exposure and physical health in women with posttraumatic stress disorder or major depressive disorder. *Violence Against Women, 15,* 618–627.

DePalma, J. A., Fedorka, P., & Simko, L. C. (2003). Quality of life experienced by severely injured trauma survivors. *AACN Clinical Issues: Advanced Practice in Acute & Critical Care Psychosocial Issues, 14,* 54–63.

Dicker, R. A., Jaeger, S., Knudson, M. M., Mackersie, R. C., Morabito, D. J., Antezana, J., & Texada, M. (2009). Where do we go from here? Interim analysis to forge ahead in violence prevention. *Journal of Trauma, 6,* 1169–1175.

Dolich, M. O., & Hoyt, D. B. (2008). Treatment of physical injury, acute pain and disability consequent to motor vehicle collisions. In M. P. Duckworth, T. Iezzi, & W. T. O'Donohue (Eds.), *Motor vehicle collisions: Medical, psychosocial, and legal consequences* (pp. 61–81). Oxford, UK: Elsevier.

Duckworth, M. P. (2008). Medicolegal issues associated with motor vehicle collisions: Psychological perspective. In M. P. Duckworth, T. Iezzi, & W. T. O'Donohue (Eds.), *Motor vehicle collisions: Medical, psychosocial, and legal consequences* (pp. 311–344). Oxford, UK: Elsevier.

Duckworth, M. P., & Iezzi, T. (2005). Chronic pain and posttraumatic stress symptoms in litigating motor vehicle accident victims. *Clinical Journal of Pain, 21,* 251–261.

Duckworth, M. P., & Iezzi, T. (2010). Physical injuries, pain, and psychological trauma: Pathways to disability. *Psychological Injury and Law, 3,* 241–253.

Duckworth, M. P., Iezzi, T., & O'Donohue. W. T. (Eds.). (2008). *Motor vehicle collisions: Medical, psychosocial, and legal consequences.* Oxford, UK: Elsevier.

Ehlers, A., Mayou, R. A., & Bryant, B. (1998). Psychological predictors of chronic posttraumatic stress disorder after motor vehicle accidents. *Journal of Abnormal Psychology, 107,* 508–519.

Elklit, A., & Brink, O. (2004). Acute stress disorder as a predictor of post-traumatic stress disorder in physical assault victims. *Journal of Interpersonal Violence, 19,* 709–726.

Foa, E. B., Keane, T. M., & Friedman, M. J. (2000). *Effective treatments for PTSD.* New York: Guilford Press.

Foa, E. B., & Rothbaum, B. O. (1998). *Treating the trauma of rape: Cognitive behavior therapy for PTSD.* New York: Guilford Press.

Follette, V. M., & Ruzek, J. I. (2006). *Cognitive-behavioral therapies for trauma.* New York: Guilford Press.

Friedman, M. J., Keane, T. M., & Resick, P. A. (Eds.). (2007). *Handbook of PTSD: Science and practice.* New York: Guilford Press.

Frommberger, U. H., Stieglitz, R., Nyberg, E., Schlickewei, W., Kuner, E., & Burger, M. (1998). Prediction of posttraumatic stress disorder by immediate reactions to trauma: A prospective study in road traffic accident victims. *European Archives of Psychiatry and Clinical Neuroscience, 248,* 316–321.

Gentilello, L. M., Donovan, D. M., Dunn, C. W., & Rivara, F. P. (1995). Alcohol interventions in trauma centers: Current practice and future directions. *Journal of the American Medical Association, 274,* 1043–1048.

Gentilello, L. M., Rivara, F. P., Donovan, D. M., Jurkovich, G. J., Daranciang, E., Dunn, C. W., … Ries, R. R. (1999). Alcohol interventions in a trauma center as a means of reducing the risk of injury recurrence. *Annals of Surgery, 230,* 473–480.

Greenspan, A. I., Coronado, V. G., MacKenzie, E. J., Shulman, J., Pierce, B., & Provenzano, G. (2006). Injury hospitalization: Using the nationwide inpatient sample. *Journal of Trauma, 61,* 1234–1243.

Guerrero, J. L., Sniezek, J. E., & Sehgal, M. (1999). The prevalence of disability from chronic conditions due to injury among adults ages 18–69 years: United States, 1994. *Disability and Rehabilitation, 21,* 187–192.

Haddon, W. (1968). The changing approach to the epidemiology, prevention, and amelioration of trauma: The transition to approaches etiologically rather than descriptively based. *American Journal of Public Health and the Nation's Health, 58,* 1431–1438.

Harris, I. A., Young, J. M., Rae, H., Jalaludin, B. B., & Solomon, M. J. (2008). Predictors of general health after major trauma. *Journal of Trauma, 64,* 969–974.

Harvey, A. G., & Bryant, R. A. (1998a). The relationship between acute stress disorder and posttraumatic stress disorder: A prospective evaluation of motor vehicle accident survivors. *Journal of Consulting and Clinical Psychology, 66,* 507–512.

Harvey, A. G., & Bryant, R. A. (1998b). Acute stress disorder after mild traumatic brain injury. *Journal of Nervous and Mental Disease, 186,* 333–337.

Harvey, A. G., & Bryant, R. A. (1999a). Acute stress disorder across trauma populations. *Journal of Nervous and Mental Disease, 187,* 443–446.

Harvey, A. G., & Bryant, R. A. (1999b). The relationship between acute stress disorder and posttraumatic stress disorder: A 2-year prospective evaluation. *Journal of Consulting and Clinical Psychology, 67,* 985–988.

Herman, J. L. (1992). Complex PTSD: A syndrome in survivors of prolonged and repeated trauma. *Journal of Traumatic Stress, 5,* 377–391.

Holbrook, T. L., Anderson, J. P., Sieber, W. J., Browner, D., & Hoyt, D. B. (1998). Outcome after major trauma: Discharge and 6-month follow-up results from the Trauma Recovery Project. *Journal of Trauma, 45,* 315–324.

Holbrook, T. L., Anderson, J. P., Sieber, W. J., Browner, D., & Hoyt, D. B. (1999). Outcome after major trauma: 12-month and 18-month follow-up results from the trauma recovery project. *Journal of Trauma, 46,* 765–771.

Holbrook, T. L., & Hoyt, D. B. (2004). The impact of major trauma: Quality-of-life outcomes are worse in women than in men, independent of mechanism and injury severity. *Journal of Trauma, 56,* 284–290.

Holbrook, T. L., Hoyt, D. B., Stein, M. B., & Sieber, W. J. (2001). Perceived threat to life predicts posttraumatic stress disorder after major trauma: Risk factors and functional outcome. *Journal of Trauma, 51,* 287–293.

Holtslag, H. R., van Beeck, E. F., Lindeman, E., & Leenen, L. P. H. (2007). Determinants of long-term functional consequences after major trauma. *Journal of Trauma, 62,* 919–927.

Iezzi, T. (2008). Medicolegal issues associated with motor vehicle collisions: Psychological perspective. In M. P. Duckworth, T. Iezzi, & W. T. O'Donohue (Eds.), *Motor vehicle collisions: Medical, psychosocial, and legal consequences* (pp. 503–539). Oxford, UK: Elsevier.

Irish, L., Ostrowski, S. A., Spoonster, E., van Dulmen, M., Sledjeski, E. M., & Delahanty, D. L. (2008). Trauma history characteristics and subsequent PTSD symptoms in motor vehicle accident victims. *Journal of Traumatic Stress, 21,* 377–384.

Jenewein, J., Wittman, L., Moergeli, H., Creutzig, J., & Schnyder, U. (2009). Mutual influence of posttraumatic stress disorder symptoms and chronic pain among injured accident survivors: A longitudinal study. *Journal of Traumatic Stress, 22,* 540–548.

Johnston, M., & Pollard, B. (2001). Consequences of disease: Testing the WHO international classification of impairments, disabilities and handicaps (ICIDH) model. *Social Science and Medicine, 53,* 1261–1273.

Kessler, R. C., & Merikangas, K. R. (2004). The National Comorbidity Survey Replication (NCS-R): Background and aims. *The International Journal of Methods in Psychiatric Research, 13,* 60–68.

Kessler, R. C., Sonnega, A., Bromet, E., Hughes, M., & Nelson, C. B. (1995). Posttraumatic stress disorder in the national comorbidity survey. *Archives of General Psychiatry, 52,* 1048–1060.

Kilpatrick, D. G., & Acierno, R. (2003). Mental health needs of crime victims: Epidemiology and outcomes. *Journal of Traumatic Stress, 16,* 119–132.

Kim, H., & Colantonio, A. (2008). Intentional traumatic brain injury in Ontario, Canada. *Journal of Trauma, 65,* 1287–1292.

Koren, D., Arnon, I., & Klein, E. (1999). Acute stress response and posttraumatic stress disorder traffic accident victims: A one-year prospective, follow-up study. *American Journal of Psychiatry, 156,* 367–373.

Krug, E. G., Sharma, G. K., & Lozano, R. (2000). The global burden of injuries. *American Journal of Public Health, 90,* 523–526.

Kuch, K., Cox, B. J., Evans, R. J., & Shulan, I. (1994). Phobias, panic and pain in 55 survivors of road accidents. *Journal of Anxiety Disorders, 8,* 181–187.

Langley, J., & Brenner, R. (2004). What is an injury? *Injury Prevention, 10,* 69–71.

Maes, M., Mylle, J., Delmeire, L., & Altamura, C. (2000). Psychiatric morbidity and comorbidity following accidental man-made traumatic events: Incidents and risk factors. *European Archives of Psychiatry and Clinical Sciences, 250,* 156–160.

Malt, U. (1988). The long-term psychiatric consequences of accidental injury: A longitudinal study of 107 adults. *British Journal of Psychiatry, 153,* 810–818.

Mayou, R., & Bryant, B. (2001). Outcome in consecutive emergency department attenders following a road traffic accident. *British Journal of Psychiatry, 179,* 528–534.

Mayou, R., Bryant, B., & Duthie, R. (1993). Psychiatric consequences of road traffic accidents. *British Medical Journal, 307,* 647–651.

Mayou, R., Bryant, B., & Ehlers, A. (2001). Prediction of psychological outcomes one year after a motor vehicle accident. *American Journal of Psychiatry, 158,* 1231–1238.

Mayou, R. A., Ehlers, A., & Bryant, B. (2002). Posttraumatic stress disorder after motor vehicle accidents: 3-year follow-up of a prospect of longitudinal study. *Behaviour Research and Therapy, 40,* 665–675.

Mayou, R., Tyndel, S., & Bryant, B. (1997). Long-term outcome of motor vehicle accident injury. *Psychosomatic Medicine, 59,* 578–584.

Mellman, T. A., David, D., Bustamante, V., Fins, A. I., & Esposito, K. (2001). Predictors of post-traumatic stress disorder following severe injury. *Depression and Anxiety, 14,* 226–231.

Michaels, A. J., Michaels, C. E., Smith, J. S., Moon, C. H., Peterson, C., & Long, B. B. (2000). Outcome from injury: General health, work status, and satisfaction 12 months after trauma. *Journal of Trauma: Injury, Infection, and Critical Care, 48,* 841–850.

Miro, J., Nieto, R., & Huguet, A. (2008). Predictive factors of chronic pain and disability in whiplash: A Delphi poll. *European Journal of Pain, 12,* 30–47.

Mulleman, R., Lenaghan, P. A., & Pakieser, R. A. (1996). Battered women: Injury locations and types. *Annals of Emergency Medicine, 28,* 486–492.

Murray, C. J. L., & Lopez, A. D. (1996). *Global burden of disease.* Cambridge, MA: Harvard University Press.

Nagi, S. Z. (1965). Some conceptual issues in disability and rehabilitation. In M. B. Sussman (Ed.), *Sociology and rehabilitation* (pp. 100–113). Washington, DC: American Sociological Association.

National Highway Traffic Safety Administration. (2003). *Traffic safety facts 2001—state alcohol estimates.* Washington, DC: Author

Neria, Y., Nandi, A., & Galea, S. (2008). Posttraumatic stress disorder following disasters: A systematic review. *Psychological Medicine, 38,* 467–480.

Nilsen, P. (2004). What makes community based injury prevention work? In search of evidence of effectiveness. *Injury Prevention, 10,* 268–274.

Norman, S. B., Stein, M. B., Dimsdale, J. E., & Hoyt, D. B. (2008). Pain in the aftermath of trauma is a risk factor for post-traumatic stress disorder. *Psychological Medicine, 38,* 533–542.

Norris, F. (1992). Epidemiology of trauma: Frequency and impact of different potentially traumatic events on different demographic groups. *Journal of Consulting and Clinical Psychology, 60,* 409–418.

Norris, F. H., Friedman, M. J., Watson, P. J., Byrne, C. M., Diaz, E., & Kaniasty, K. (2002). 60,000 disaster victims speak: Part I. An empirical review of the empirical literature, 1981–2001. *Psychiatry, 65,* 207–239.

O'Donnell, M. L., Bryant, R. A., Creamer, M., & Carty, J. (2008). Mental health following traumatic injury: Toward a health system model of early psychological intervention. *Clinical Psychology Review, 28,* 387–406.

O'Donnell, M. L., Creamer, M., Bryant, R. A., Schnyder, U., & Shalev, A. (2003). Posttraumatic disorders following injury: An empirical and methodological review. *Clinical Psychology Review, 23,* 587–603.

O'Donnell, M. L., Creamer, M., Elliot, P., Bryant, R., McFarlane, A., & Silove, D. (2009). Prior trauma and psychiatric history as risk factors for intentional and unintentional injury in Australia. *Journal of Trauma, 66,* 470–476.

O'Donnell, M. L., Creamer, M., & Pattison, P. (2004a). Posttraumatic stress disorder and depression following trauma: Understanding comorbidity. *American Journal of Psychiatry, 161,* 1390–1396.

O'Donnell, M. L., Creamer, M., Pattison, P., & Atkin, C. (2004b). Psychiatric morbidity following injury. *American Journal of Psychiatry, 161,* 507–514.

Ozer, E. J., Best, S. R., Lipsey, T. L., & Weiss, D. S. (2003). Predictors of posttraumatic stress disorder symptoms in adults: A meta-analysis. *Psychological Bulletin, 129,* 52–73.

Palyo, S. A., & Beck, J. G. (2005). Post-traumatic stress disorder symptoms, pain, and perceived life control: Associations with psychosocial and physical functioning. *Pain, 117,* 121–127.

Peden, M., McGee, K., & G. Sharma. (Eds.). (2002). *The injury chart book: A graphical overview of the global burden of injuries.* Geneva: World Health Organization.

Peden, M., Scurfield, R., Sleet, D., Mohan, D., Hyder, A. A., Jarawan, E., & Mathers, C. (Eds.). (2004). *World report on road traffic injury prevention.* Geneva: World Health Organization.

Pelcovitz, D., Van der Kolk, B. A., Roth, S., Mendel, F. S., Kaplan, S., & Resick, P. A. (1997). Development of a criteria set in a structured interview for disorders of extreme stress (SIDES). *Journal of Traumatic Stress, 10,* 3–17.

Potenza, B. M., Hoyt, D. B., Coimbra, R., Fortlage, D., Holbrook, T., & Hollingsworth-Fridlund, P. (2004). The epidemiology of serious and fatal injury in San Diego County over an 11-year period. *Journal of Trauma, 56,* 68–75.

Prekker, M. E., Miner, J. R., Rockswold, E. G., & Biros, M. H. (2009). The prevalence of injury of any type in an urban emergency department population. *Journal of Trauma, 66,* 1688–1695.

Ramchand, R., Marshall, G. N., Schell, T. L., & Jaycox, L. H. (2008). Posttraumatic distress and physical functioning: A longitudinal study of injured survivors of community violence. *Journal of Consulting and Clinical Psychology, 76,* 668–676.

Ramstad, S. M., Russo, J., & Zatzick, D. F. (2004). Is it an accident? Recurrent traumatic life events in Level I trauma center patients compared to the general population. *Journal of Traumatic Stress, 17,* 529–534.

Reece, A. S. (2008). Experience of road and other trauma by the opiate dependent patient: A survey report. *Substance Abuse Treatment, Prevention, and Policy, 3,* 1–12.

Richmond, T. S., & Jacoby, S. (2008). Emergency department trauma: The immediate aftermath of motor vehicle collisions. In M. P. Duckworth, T. Iezzi, & W. T. O'Donohue (Eds.), *Motor vehicle collisions: Medical, psychosocial, and legal consequences* (pp. 83–106). Oxford, UK: Elsevier.

Richmond, T. S., Thompson, H., Deatrick, J., & Kauder, D. (2000). Journey towards recovery following physical trauma. *Journal of Advanced Nursing, 32,* 1341–1347.

Rivara, F. P., Thompson, D. C., Beahler, C., & MacKenzie, E. J. (1999). Systematic reviews of strategies to prevent motor vehicle injuries. *American Journal of Preventative Medicine, 16,* 1–5.

Roth, S., Newman, E., Pelcovitz, D., van der Kolk, B., & Mandel, F. S. (1997). Complex PTSD in victims exposed to sexual and physical abuse: Results from the DSM-IV field trial for posttraumatic stress disorder. *Journal of Traumatic Stress, 10,* 539–555.

Schnurr, P. (Eds). (2005). Special section on complex trauma [Special issue]. *Journal of Traumatic Stress, 18*(5).

Schnurr, P. P., & Green, B. L. (2004). *Trauma and health: Physical health consequences of exposure to extreme stress.* Washington, DC: American Psychological Association.

Schnurr, P. P., & Jankowski, M. K. (1999). Physical health and post-traumatic stress disorder: Review and synthesis. *Seminars in Clinical Neuropsychiatry, 4*, 295–304.

Schnyder, U., Moergeli, H., Trentz, O., Klaghofer, R., & Buddeberg, C. (2001). Prediction of psychiatric morbidity in severely injured accident victims at one-year follow-up. *American Journal of Respiratory and Critical Care Medicine, 164*, 653–656.

Shalev, A. Y., Freedman, S., Peri, T., Brandes, D., Shar, T., Orr, S. P., & Pitman, R. K. (1998). Prospective study of posttraumatic stress disorder and depression following trauma. *American Journal of Psychiatry, 155*, 630–637.

Shults, R. A., Elder, R. W., Nichols, J. L., Sleet, D. A., Compton, R., & Chattopadhyay, S. K. (2009). Effectiveness of multicomponent programs with community mobilization for reducing alcohol-impaired driving. *American Journal of Preventative Medicine, 4*, 360–371.

Shults, R. A., Jones, B. H., Kresnow, M., Langlois, J. A., & Guerrero, J. L. (2004). Disability among adults injured in motor-vehicle crashes in the United States. *Journal of Safety Research, 35*, 447–452.

Sledjeski, E., Speisman, B., & Dierker, L. C. (2008). Does number of lifetime traumas explain the relationship between PTSD and chronic medical conditions? Answers from the National Comorbidity Survey-Replication (NCS-R). *Journal of Behavioral Medicine, 31*, 341–349.

Sluys, K., Haggmark, T., & Iselius, L. (2005). Outcome and quality of life 5 years after major trauma. *Journal of Trauma, 59*, 223–232.

SMARTRISK. (2009). *The economic burden of injury in Canada*. Toronto, ON: Author.

Soberg, H. L., Bautz-Holter, E., Roise, O., & Finset, A. (2007). Long-term multidimensional functional consequences of severe multiple injuries two years after trauma: A prospective longitudinal cohort study. *Journal of Trauma, 62*, 461–470.

Soberg, H. L., Finset, A., Bautz-Holter, E., Sandvik, L., & Roise, O. (2007). Return to work after severe multiple injuries: A multidimensional approach on status 1 and 2 year post-injury. *Journal of Trauma, 62*, 471–481.

Soderstrom, C. A., Dischinger, P. C., Smith, G. S., Hebel, J. R., McDuff, D. R., Gorelick, D. A., … Read, K. M. (1997). Alcoholism at the time of injury among trauma center patients: Vehicular crash victims compared with other patients. *Accident Analysis and Prevention, 29*, 715–721.

Stein, M. B., Kerridge, C., Dimsdale, J. E., & Hoyt, D. B. (2007). Pharmacotherapy to prevent PTSD: Results from a randomized controlled proof-of-concept trial in physically injured patients. *Journal of Traumatic Stress, 20*, 923–932.

Stockwell, T., McLeod, R., Stevens, M., Philips, M., Webb, M., & Jelinek, G. (2002). Alcohol consumption, setting, gender, and activity as predictors of injury: A population-based case-control study. *Journal of Studies of Alcohol, 63*, 372–379.

Tjaden, P., & Thoennes, N. (2000). *Full report of the Prevalence, Incidence, and Consequences of Intimate Partner Violence Against Women Survey*. Washington, DC: Department of Justice.

Turner, C., McClure, R., & Pirozzo, S. (2004). Injury and risk-taking behavior: A systematic review. *Accident Analysis and Prevention, 36*, 93–101.

Ursano, R. J., Fullerton, C. S., Epstein, R. S., Crowley, B., Kao, T., Vance, K., … Baum, A. (1999). Acute and chronic posttraumatic stress disorder in motor vehicle accident victims. *American Journal of Psychiatry, 156*, 589–595.

van der Kolk, B. A., Roth, S., Pelcovitz, D., Sunday, S., & Spinazzola, J. (2005). Disorders of extreme stress: The empirical foundation of a complex adaptation to trauma. *Journal of Traumatic Stress, 18*, 389–399.

Visser, E., Pijl, Y. J., Stolk, R. P., Neelman, J., & Rosmalen, J. G. M. (2007). Accident proneness, does it exist? A review and meta-analysis. *Accident Analysis and Prevention, 39*, 556–564.

Wagner, A. W., Zatzick, D. F., Ghesquiere, A., & Jurkovich, G. J. (2007). Behavioral activation as an early intervention for posttraumatic stress disorder and depression among physically injured trauma survivors. *Cognitive and Behavioral Practice, 14*, 341–349.

Walton, D. M., Pretty, J., MacDermid, J. C., & Teasell, R. W. (2009). Risk factors for persistent problems following whiplash injury: Results of a systematic review and meta-analysis. *Journal of Orthopedic Sports Physical Therapy, 39*, 334–350.

Watt, K., Purdie, D. M., Roche, A. M., & McClure, R. (2006). Acute alcohol consumption and mechanism of injury. *Journal of Studies in Alcohol, 67*, 14–21.

Weisberg, R. B., Bruce, S. E., Machan, J. T., Kessler, R. C., Culpepper, L., & Keller, M. B. (2002). Nonpsychiatric illness among primary care patients with trauma histories and posttraumatic stress disorder. *Psychiatric Services, 53*, 848–854.

Williams, D. R., Herman, A., Kessler, R. C., Sonnega, J., Seedat, S., Stein, D. J., … Wilson, C. M. (2004). The South Africa Stress and Health Study: Rationale and design. *Metabolic Brain Disease, 19*, 135–147.

Williams, S. L., Williams, D. R., Stein, D. J., Seedat, S., Jackson, P. B., & Moomal, H. (2007). Multiple traumatic events and psychological distress: The South Africa Stress and Health Study. *Journal of Traumatic Stress, 20*, 845–855.

World Health Organization, (1977). *International classification of diseases, injuries, and causes of death, 1975 revision*. Geneva: Author.

World Health Organization. (1980). *International classification of impairments, disabilities, and handicaps*. Geneva: Author.

World Health Organization. (1992). *International classification of diseases, injuries, and causes of death,* 10th edition (ICD-10). Geneva: Author.

World Health Organization. (2001). *International classification of functioning, disability, and health*. Geneva: Author.

Worrell, S. S., Koepsell, T. D., Sabath, D. R., Gentilello, L. M., Mock, C. N., & Nathens, A. B. (2006). The risk of reinjury in relation to time since first injury: A retrospective population-based study. *Journal of Trauma, 60*, 379–384.

Wuest, J., Ford-Gilboe, M., Merritt-Gray, M., Varcoe, C., Lent, B., Wilk, P., & Campbell, J. (2009). Abuse-related injury and symptoms of posttraumatic stress disorder as mechanisms of chronic pain in survivors of intimate partner violence. *American Academy of Pain Medicine, 10*, 739–747.

Yehuda, R. (2002) Post-traumatic stress disorder. *New England Journal of Medicine, 346*, 108–114.

Zatzick, D., Jurkovich, G., Russo, J., Roy-Bryne, P., Katon, W., Wagner, A., … Rivara, F. (2004). Posttraumatic distress, alcohol disorders, and recurrent trauma across Level I trauma centers. *Journal of Trauma, 57*, 360–366.

Zatzick, D. F., Kang, S., Muller, H., Russo, J. E., Rivara, F. P., Katon, W., … Roy-Byrne, P. (2002). Predicting posttraumatic distress in hospitalized trauma survivors with acute injuries. *American Journal of Psychiatry, 159*, 941–946.

Zatzick, D. F., Roy-Byrne, P., Russo, J., Rivara, F. P., Droesch, R., Wagner, A., … Katon, W. (2004). A randomized effectiveness trial of stepped collaborative care for acutely injured trauma survivors. *Archives of General Psychiatry, 61*, 498–506.

Zayfert, C., & Becker, C. B. (2007). *Cognitive behavioral therapy for PTSD: A case formulation approach*. New York: Guilford Press.

# Chapter 15

# Controversies Related to the Study and Treatment of Multiple Experiences of Trauma

*Sonja V. Batten and James A. Naifeh*

The past two decades have brought considerable advances in our understanding, assessment, and treatment of retraumatization. However, if this field is to continue meaningful advancement, it must evolve in theoretical sophistication and precise specifications of relevant constructs. As a first step in spurring scientific progress, we believe that those who work in this area should come to some level of consensus about what is meant by terms such as *revictimization, retraumatization,* and *multiple experiences of trauma.* Are these terms synonymous with one another, or do they point to subtly different constructs? Are we referring to all potentially traumatic events (PTEs) when we talk about retraumatization, or are only those PTEs that lead to symptoms relevant to this field? Without a greater level of conceptual clarity on these issues, we believe that the field of retraumatization will lack the appropriate framework to continue advancing in ways that will lead to improved clinical care and prevention. This chapter will highlight a series of questions and controversies related to the conceptual understanding of retraumatization, which we believe merit further attention due to their clinical, research, and policy implications.

As demonstrated throughout this volume, the issues related to multiple experiences of trauma are complex and multifaceted. At the most basic level, there is significant intricacy within the measurement and analysis of multiple traumatic events (see Roodman & Clum, 2001). Further complicating this work is the broad range of experiences that can be considered PTEs. For example, the word *retraumatization* can theoretically be used to refer to multiple incidences of the same type of PTE, as well as distinct experiences from different categories of events (e.g., sexual assault, combat, motor vehicle accidents) (Follette & Duckworth, this volume Chapter 16). Some researchers use the terms *retraumatization* or *revictimization* specifically to refer to PTEs that occur at different points in the developmental life span, although this characterization of the concept is not universal. The background data related to incidence, prevalence, and correlates of multiple traumatic experiences have been highlighted in the previous chapters of this text. Thus, this chapter will not summarize the epidemiological data on this topic. Instead, we will focus on cross cutting controversies that have clinical, research, and policy implications for the field of traumatic stress.

However, for a discussion of these controversies to be maximally productive, one must first attend to some basic issues regarding what constitutes retraumatization. Historical reviews of the literature demonstrate that researchers who began studying this area traditionally focused on multiple experiences of sexual trauma or interpersonal violence (for example, Koenig, Doll, O'Leary, & Pequegnat, 2004; Wyatt, Guthrie, & Notgrass, 1992). Hence, early literature often used the term *revictimization* due to the focus on those individuals who were victims of interpersonal trauma. However, research on multiply traumatized individuals has since expanded to include the impact of cumulative PTEs across more diverse categories (e.g., see Monson, this volume Chapter 10), and thus some writers have proposed a distinction between the more narrow term *revictimization* and the broader construct of *retraumatization* (Follette & Vijay, 2008). We believe that an expanded focus on diverse PTEs will likely prove important, as it may be problematic to generalize findings based on multiple interpersonal victimizations to the experience of multiple PTEs of all kinds.

## CONCEPTUALIZATION AND MEASUREMENT

As noted above, the definition of retraumatization continues to vary across studies. Definitional variation breeds disagreement and controversy, and it complicates efforts to synthesize research findings (for example, Roodman & Clum, 2001). To begin with, establishing psychometric support for instruments designed to assess retraumatization and its associated problems in functioning is critical in conducting meaningful research (Nunnally & Bernstein, 1994). However, lack of consensus regarding what constitutes retraumatization leads to wide variability in the language and focus of assessment instruments. Beyond the consequent problems stemming from an inability to draw conclusions across studies, these inconsistencies pose threats to instrument reliability and validity (Tourangeau, Rips, & Rasinski, 2000). If researchers in the field of retraumatization could come to at least a general consensus about the variables to be measured, it would greatly improve the construct validity of relevant assessment instruments. Subtle variations in the constructs that are studied by different researchers will otherwise impede the progressive development of scientific knowledge in this area. Similarly, without agreement on the constructs to be measured, researchers will be unable to reliably assess these variables across time and contexts. Consideration of several foundational issues may assist with reaching consensus on what is meant by the term *retraumatization*.

## Types of Potentially Traumatic Events (PTEs)

Much of the retraumatization literature has focused on the impact of interpersonal trauma (e.g., child abuse, sexual assault, domestic violence). However, interpersonal violence events constitute only a subset of a much broader range of human experiences that may be considered potentially traumatic (e.g., Kessler, Sonnega, Bromet, Hughes, & Nelson, 1995). For example, a motor vehicle accident (MVA) and the unexpected death of someone close both meet the *Diagnostic and Statistical Manual of Mental Disorders* (Fourth Edition) (*DSM-IV*) (American Psychiatric Association, 2000) definition of a stressor that can lead to posttraumatic stress disorder (PTSD, Criterion A1). Should multiple occurrences of these events, absent any other history of PTEs, fall under the umbrella of retraumatization, or do only certain types of events qualify? We would argue that the conceptualization and study of multiple PTE exposure must take all such events into account until there is evidence to justify their exclusion.

## PTE Exposure Within and Across Developmental Stages

Many studies on retraumatization have focused on the impact of adult trauma among those with a history of childhood trauma. Should conceptualizations of retraumatization be specific to PTEs that occur within or across certain developmental periods? Some studies have found that the rates and psychological correlates of retraumatization are much more significant when the initial traumatic event happens during early childhood rather than during adolescence or adulthood (Breslau, Chilcoat, Kessler, & Davis, 1999; Roodman & Clum, 2001). In light of such findings, should a history of multiple PTEs in adulthood be conceptualized in the same way as an extended trauma history that began in childhood? Adding (or removing) developmental constraints in determining whether someone meets criteria for retraumatization may have profound conceptual and applied implications (Alexander, this volume Chapter 8). Among researchers, varying emphasis on the importance of developmental factors can lead to a lack of methodological clarity (e.g., sampling procedures) and inconsistency in research findings.

## Context and Chronicity of PTEs

Some types of PTEs are more likely to occur repeatedly than others. For example, childhood sexual abuse (CSA) that is perpetrated by a family member may occur numerous times over several years. In that broad context of an invalidating environment, should each occurrence of CSA be counted as a separate event, or should those repeated instances of CSA be counted as a single PTE? An examination of the trauma literature suggests that the latter is far more common; however, the relevance of counting discrete instances of CSA is an empirical question that deserves greater attention. A similar issue arises for service members in a combat environment, where they may experience numerous combat-related PTEs during a single deployment or across multiple deployments (Kuhn, Hoffman, & Ruzek, this volume Chapter 9). How one defines the boundaries of PTEs within varying contexts will likely have a significant impact on research findings and conclusions that may be drawn from them. Without such clarity, this could lead to automatically characterizing all survivors of chronic childhood abuse, domestic violence, or combat as retraumatized. Conversely, aggregating 10 years of childhood sexual abuse or five combat deployments of 12 months each into a single "event" solely based on category of PTE is also likely to obscure important research findings. For example, among military service members deployed to Iraq, Hoge et al. (2004) found a linear relationship between number of firefights and PTSD symptom severity. This valuable information would have been lost if a combat deployment had been treated as a single PTE. Depending on the goals of a given analysis, either operationalization might be appropriate. However, a lack of consistency limits the generalizability of findings across populations and individual studies. We recommend that, whenever possible, researchers collect data in sufficient detail to allow for a fine-grained analysis of multiple PTEs, including the frequency, intensity, and duration of events that compose broad categories, such as childhood abuse or combat exposure.

## Psychological Outcomes of Prior PTEs

Researchers in the field of traumatic stress have drawn increasing recognition to the difference between a traumatic event and a *potentially* traumatic event (Bonanno & Mancini, 2008). The latter denotes only exposure to a stressor (e.g., one that meets PTSD Criterion A), and the former indicates that the stressor was actually associated with clinically significant levels of distress. This distinction is important, as numerous studies have shown that most individuals exposed to a PTE do not go on to develop significant psychological problems (Bonanno & Mancini, 2008; Breslau et al., 1998; Kessler et al., 1995; Norris, 1992; Resnick, Kilpatrick, Dansky, & Best, 1993). We believe that it is necessary to grapple with the issue of whether an individual's response to each PTE should be taken into account when determining whether that individual meets criteria for retraumatization. Should a history of multiple PTEs constitute retraumatization, or should the concept be limited to events associated with significant psychological sequelae? If the latter conceptualization is embraced, one must then define *significant psychological sequelae*. For example, is it necessary to establish that prior PTEs initially resulted in a diagnosable disorder or functional impairment for a person to be considered retraumatized following a subsequent PTE? There is considerable complexity in answering such questions. It may be, for instance, that subclinical distress associated with previous events can become exacerbated or elevated to clinical levels following exposure to a new stressor.

This issue has implications on both the population and individual levels. For researchers to be able to draw valid conclusions about the broad population of those who have been retraumatized, it may be important not simply to have individuals endorse PTEs on a checklist, but to further have them indicate if they experienced relevant symptoms following each PTE. Similarly, in a clinical context, a clinician may find it equally important to learn whether the individual client experienced symptoms of PTSD following prior PTEs (note that this depends to some extent upon one's theoretical orientation; for a functional analytic perspective, see Bonow & Follette, this volume Chapter 6). However, individuals may not always be able to retrospectively determine whether a given symptom was associated with any particular PTE, especially for distant childhood traumas and as the number of PTEs experienced across the lifespan increases.

With the impending publication of *DSM-5*, revisions to the PTSD construct are currently under consideration (American Psychiatric Association, 2010), and it is not yet known how these changes might impact the disorder's assessment and diagnosis. The current *DSM-IV* conceptualization of PTSD requires symptoms to be linked to a specified traumatic event (American Psychiatric Association, 2000), rather than to one's global history of PTEs. This process may be relatively straightforward for symptoms involving re-experiencing and active avoidance of identifiable internal and external trauma-related stimuli. However, endorsement of these symptoms alone is not sufficient for a diagnosis of PTSD. An individual must also endorse additional symptoms within the avoidance and hyperarousal clusters, none of which are clearly tied to a traumatic event (American Psychiatric Association, 2000). For example, generalized emotional numbing and irritability are not specific to any particular traumatic event. For individuals with a history of multiple PTEs, this potentially complicates the assessment process in two ways. First, the extent to which individuals can reliably attribute these latter symptoms to a particular PTE is unknown. A common method is to assess their temporal relation to the event (i.e., inquiring whether onset occurred after a given PTE) (Wilson & Keane, 2004). However, for individuals with multiple PTEs dating back to early childhood, the temporal relation of symptom onset to any particular PTE (e.g., "I don't know when that started. It seems like I've always been this way") may be uncertain (Wilson & Keane, 2004).

Second, it is possible that an individual may appear to meet full PTSD criteria through a combination of multiple PTEs, but not related to any single PTE. To illustrate, consider an individual who has been experiencing symptoms of emotional numbing (e.g., restricted range of affect, interpersonal detachment) and hyperarousal (e.g., hypervigilance, exaggerated startle response) since being sexually abused as a child but does not report significant re-experiencing symptoms related to the sexual abuse. What if this individual then experienced a severe MVA as an adult, resulting in persistent re-experiencing and avoidance, but no increase in emotional numbing or hyperarousal symptoms? A diagnosis of PTSD would technically be inappropriate, given that diagnostic criteria are not met for any one PTE, strictly speaking. However, not making the diagnosis of PTSD potentially disregards the individual's significant distress and functional impairment, all of which are trauma related. In a research context, this has implications for accurately identifying caseness, as well as factors related to risk and resilience. In a clinical context, this has implications for treatment planning and insurance reimbursement or other financial compensation.

## Importance of Conceptual Clarity

The issues described above all point to complex issues to be addressed, and several variations and combinations among them are possible. Improving the theories behind the conceptualization and measurement of retraumatization will undoubtedly help to move the science in this area (and consequently, related evidence-based treatments) forward (Follette & Houts, 1996). Failure to do so will perpetuate methodological inconsistencies within the retraumatization literature, hamper the development of more sophisticated assessment instruments, and complicate the process of determining for whom certain interventions are appropriate. Thoughtful researchers have the opportunity to advance the conceptualization and understanding of retraumatization through careful and explicit operationalization of variables and methodological consistency. Without engaging in this difficult work, the field of retraumatization may be doomed to an unfocused series of inconsistent research findings that have limited practical applications for prevention and treatment.

## CLINICAL CONSIDERATIONS

In many ways, the field of retraumatization highlights the tension between approaches to clinical assessment and treatment that are idiographic (i.e., highly particular and individualized) versus those that are traditionally nomothetic (i.e., universal and based on patterns seen in groups or populations) (Cone, 1986). It is certainly appropriate for therapists to use evidence-based knowledge of retraumatization to generate clinical hypotheses, but these hypotheses must be loosely held. PTEs, regardless of their number, type, or severity, are not deterministic experiences. As noted above, most individuals exposed to such events do not go on to develop significant psychopathology (Bonanno & Mancini, 2008; Breslau et al., 1998; Kessler et al., 1995; Norris, 1992; Resnick et al., 1993), and for those who do, a range of problematic responses is possible. In addition to peritraumatic factors, outcomes are also multiply determined by individual differences in genetic and biological vulnerabilities, personality characteristics, learning history, and culture (Friedman, Keane, & Resick, 2007). As a simplified example, responses to terrorism may vary considerably depending on whether terrorism is a novel or common occurrence in one's community (e.g., a small town in the middle of the United States versus a large city in Israel).

Thorough assessment is critical for ensuring appropriate diagnosis, case conceptualization, and treatment planning. Although this process is enhanced by self-report measures and structured interviews, existing assessment instruments may not adequately capture the complexity of multiple traumatic experiences and associated psychopathology. For example, extant measures of PTE exposure may emphasize certain types of events (e.g., interpersonal trauma) over others (e.g., accidents). Similarly, measures of trauma-related psychopathology may map well onto official diagnostic constructs (e.g., PTSD) while neglecting relevant psychological processes and functional dimensions that can be equally useful in treatment planning (e.g., emotion dysregulation, experiential avoidance) (Hayes, Wilson, Gifford, Follette, & Strosahl, 1996). This lack of theoretical specificity has implications not just for individualized treatment planning but also for the broader advancement of a scientific understanding of retraumatization (Follette & Houts, 1996). We previously noted that the research literature reveals a number of permutations in the definition of retraumatization. It would be unsurprising if there were even greater diversity in how clinicians conceptualize and define retraumatization, or even the extent to which they find it a necessary or useful construct for their clinical practice.

Taken together, these issues present potential challenges to the provision of appropriate clinical care. When the limitations of available assessment instruments are coupled with therapist assumptions about individuals who have experienced multiple PTEs, this may lead to inconsistencies in what questions are asked, how those questions are asked, and, ultimately, in diagnosis and treatment provision. Several practices can help to minimize these problems, including (1) awareness of the limits of clinical judgment and heuristics

(Garb & Boyle, 2004); (2) conscientious use of standardized assessment instruments, with awareness of their limitations (Garb, Lilienfeld, & Fowler, 2008); 3) use of behaviorally specific questions when inquiring about exposure to PTEs, rather than culturally loaded terms or descriptors with strong connotations (Fricker, Smith, Davis, & Hanson, 2003); and (4) treatment planning based on an ongoing functional analysis of behavior (Bonow & Follette, this volume Chapter 6), rather than simply a focus on past experiences.

## Complex PTSD and the Adequacy of Current Diagnostic Constructs

For many years, a number of theorists and researchers have suggested that the PTSD construct does not adequately capture the scope or severity of intra- and interpersonal difficulties resulting from exposure to repeated, prolonged psychological trauma. Many PTEs, such as MVAs, natural disasters, and rape, tend to be discrete, relatively brief events, and it is argued that the traditional conceptualization of PTSD most accurately represents the psychological sequelae associated with these types of experiences. However, other PTEs, such as repeated CSA or being held as a prisoner of war, are more chronic in nature, lasting months or years. It has been argued that chronic PTEs involving a prolonged period of total control by another are associated with a distinct constellation of psychological sequelae. This proposed syndrome, termed Complex PTSD or Disorders of Extreme Stress Not Otherwise Specified (DESNOS) (Herman, 1992), involves posttraumatic alterations in self-regulation, consciousness, self-perception, interpersonal functioning, somatization, and one's system of beliefs (Roth, Newman, Pelcovitz, Van der Kolk, & Mandel, 1997).

A primary argument against the reification of Complex PTSD/DESNOS as a new diagnostic construct involves concerns over whether it adds value above and beyond existing constructs. Many of its elements bear a marked resemblance to those of longstanding Axis II constructs, such as Borderline Personality Disorder (BPD) (American Psychiatric Association, 2000). Further, the *DSM-IV* Field Trials found that the vast majority of those meeting criteria for Complex PTSD/DESNOS also met criteria for PTSD (Roth et al., 1997). Thus, it may be argued that a new Complex PTSD/DESNOS diagnosis is unnecessary because the psychological phenomena it encompasses can be sufficiently communicated through the thoughtful application of existing diagnostic labels (e.g., a diagnosis of PTSD with comorbid features of BPD). One benefit of adopting this more conservative stance is that it helps to prevent redundancy across disorders, which may be a laudable goal given the ever-expanding *DSM* nosology. As the number of diagnoses multiplies with each iteration of the *DSM*, the incremental value of new constructs should ideally face greater scrutiny (Follette & Houts, 1996).

An additional complication is that, like PTSD, Complex PTSD/DESNOS specifies an etiological factor in the disorder's development (i.e., exposure to a prolonged, repeated PTE). This has proven to be a source of ongoing controversy within the PTSD literature, where numerous studies have found that individuals exposed to Criterion A and non-Criterion A stressors may endorse PTSD symptoms at comparable levels (for a review, see Weathers & Keane, 2007). Central to this controversy is disagreement over how broad the stressor criterion can become before the PTSD construct begins to lose meaning. It is likely that Complex PTSD/DESNOS would face a similar challenge, with clinicians and researchers alike debating whether "Event X" of "Duration Y" qualifies as a stressor.

These concerns aside, formalizing the Complex PTSD/DESNOS diagnosis could have some important potential benefits (Courtois, Ford, van der Kolk, & Herman, 2009). First, it may assist clinicians in recognizing and diagnosing trauma-related difficulties that are not captured by a standard PTSD assessment. These intra- and interpersonal difficulties may require special consideration during case conceptualization and treatment planning in order to maximize the benefits of a trauma-focused intervention. Second, it may reduce the stigma associated with symptoms that resemble BPD (Aviram, Brodsky, & Stanley, 2006). Reducing the stigma associated with diagnostic labels is a critical step toward ensuring that all clients are treated with compassion and respect. This may be particularly important for clients experiencing significant shame and distrust of others due to a history of interpersonal trauma.

This latter point also underscores an important caveat to this discussion: criticism of the Complex PTSD/DESNOS construct should not be viewed as an attempt to invalidate or diminish the very real struggles of individuals exposed to repeated, prolonged psychological trauma. It is not a question of whether those symptoms exist, but whether their existence warrants a unique diagnostic label, given the costs and benefits of such a decision. A functional contextual view of diagnostic categories would suggest that the clinical utility of a new category must be established on the basis of either homogeneous function or the source of behavioral control, rather than topographical features, before a new label is reified. Unless the new category truly contributes to treatment planning for uniform populations, communication between providers, the organization of research, or other ways of predicting and influencing behavior, its addition to the diagnostic nomenclature should be carefully considered (Follette, 1996).

## Applicability and Limitations of Existing PTSD Treatments

There is a strong and growing literature supporting the efficacy of cognitive-behavioral trauma-focused interventions, such as prolonged exposure (PE) (Foa, Hembree, & Rothbaum, 2007) and cognitive processing therapy (CPT)

(Resick & Schnicke, 1996). These empirically supported treatments (ESTs) have been found to significantly reduce the severity of PTSD and many of its associated features (e.g., depression, guilt) (Foa et al., 2005; Monson et al., 2006; Resick et al., 2008; Resick, Nishith, Weaver, Astin, & Feurer, 2002; Schnurr et al., 2007). However, current ESTs generally focus on one traumatic event at a time. Thus, although ESTs may be the first-line treatment for many multiply traumatized individuals, it should not be assumed that these interventions will be sufficient for all retraumatized clients.

There are few, if any, empirically derived guidelines for working with individuals traumatized by multiple events, whether those events are clearly distinct (e.g., natural disaster and rape) or part of a single, prolonged experience (e.g., years of domestic violence perpetrated by the same partner). It can be suggested that PE should first target the event with the most intrusive or distressing traumatic memories, as treatment gains will likely generalize to less upsetting traumatic events (Foa et al., 2007). However, these guidelines appear to be based largely on theory and clinical experience, rather than empirical data indicating which trauma should be addressed first. Further research is needed to optimize the selection of target traumatic events, and to determine whether targeting multiple events simultaneously is feasible or efficacious. If it is necessary to target more than one traumatic event in order to treat complex presentations, empirical data are also needed to validate which event should be addressed first and how many truly need to be targeted within exposure-based treatments.

In the meantime, treatment must be guided by ongoing assessment to determine the clinical relevance of all traumatic events and problems in functioning that could serve as treatment targets (Bonow & Follette, this volume Chapter 6). In doing so, clinicians must avoid making automatic assumptions based on the characteristics of the client or the traumatic event. For instance, imagine treating a male Veteran and a female Veteran, both of whom experienced combat and sexual assault while in the military (e.g., Murdoch, Polusny, Hodges, & O'Brien, 2004). Based on heuristics or one's prior clinical experience, there may be a tendency to devote greater attention to combat exposure when treating the man and to sexual assault when treating the woman Veteran. Such tendencies, while understandable, may invalidate a client's experience and ultimately jeopardize the success of his or her treatment. Until clear, empirically derived guidance is available, the clinician must work with the client to identify those traumatic events that have the most relevance to his or her symptoms (e.g., re-experiencing, sleep problems) and functioning (e.g., interpersonal relationships, occupational performance).


## POLICY ISSUES RELATED TO RETRAUMATIZATION

Research focused on understanding multiple experiences of traumatic events could be used to inform policy in many areas, including health care and personnel decisions. Thus, it is important that leaders across the public and private sectors understand the factors that may contribute to both rates of and responses to exposure to multiple PTEs. Many of these leaders will not have significant background in the field of traumatic stress, so it can be useful to begin with reminders about the basic underpinnings of this area of study. First, the experience of being exposed to a PTE is common; even being exposed to multiple PTEs over the course of a lifetime is not an uncommon experience (Breslau, Peterson, Poisson, Schultz, & Lucia, 2004; Kessler et al., 1995; Resnick et al., 1993). However, the most common response to a PTE is resilience—humans are amazingly able to rebound from these challenging experiences much of the time (Bonanno & Mancini, 2008). Thus, although policies may rightly be informed by ongoing research findings in the area of retraumatization, decisions must also be balanced by an understanding that these experiences are never deterministic for any given individual. Thoughtful policy makers might be able to sensitively craft policies that support and encourage those who have experienced or are likely to experience multiple traumatic events. At the same time, policies that promote sweeping generalizations about the health, fitness, or capabilities of those who have been exposed to multiple PTEs are likely to be discriminatory at best and harmful to individual and group functioning at worst.

For these reasons, it is important for health and personnel policy makers and leaders to be educated about the potential correlates of retraumatization and to be provided with a more nuanced understanding of what is and is not implied by such findings. We believe that it is the responsibility of experts in traumatic stress to explain research findings in a manner that conveys the complexity of these issues without overwhelming the audience with uncertainty. Balancing these competing demands is no simple task. Policy makers are required to make definitive, broad-reaching decisions based on population-level analyses, while researchers are generally aware of the limitations of any given research study and are thus much less comfortable making statements with 100% certitude. It is true that an understanding of the extant research will never provide a definitive answer that applies to all individuals. However, researchers and leaders in the field of traumatic stress cannot hide behind the intricacies of research design and analysis and avoid weighing in on important policy issues. Although the research literature will never be perfect or complete, it is important to be able to summarize what is known, so that new policies can be guided by the best information available.

Policy decisions will inevitably be made that affect those who have been exposed to traumatic stress and multiple PTEs. It is the responsibility of policy makers and leaders to recognize that these are complex issues and that experts in the field of traumatic stress can be invaluable in attempting to create policy and guidance that is fair, compassionate, and as justified as possible by the existing data. Policy makers have the unenviable challenge of having to balance parity and understanding on the individual level with the best interests of the unit, organization, or system. Just as it is important for researchers and clinicians to attend to the conceptualization and measurement issues highlighted earlier in this chapter, it is equally important for policy makers and leaders to be precise with their language to avoid unintended consequences from new policies designed to be responsive to issues of multiple traumatization. Similarly, those who draft policies that touch on these complex areas must also attend to the relevant assessment and definitional issues, so that data are not misused and do not result in drawing inappropriate conclusions.

## Examples of Potential Policy Dilemmas

### Pre-Employment Screening

One area in which potential controversies could arise involves pre-employment screening for a variety of occupations. If retraumatization research is conducted with sufficient specificity and demonstrates that a history of prior trauma (whether broadly defined or a specific type of trauma during a specific developmental period) is, in fact, a risk factor for development of PTSD or other mental health problems following exposure to a subsequent PTE during adulthood, this could have significant implications for many high-risk professions (including military service or combat deployments). As a purely hypothetical example, if it were to be found that experiencing physical abuse before the age of 12 significantly increases the likelihood of developing PTSD when a firefighter is exposed to a potentially traumatic event in adulthood, how should this information be handled? In this case, those who write personnel policy related to prescreening of potential firefighters might then choose to carefully assess the increased cost related to training, treatment, and attrition of firefighters with such a history. A purely economic analysis might lead decision makers to consider whether to allow individuals onto the force who had a history of childhood physical abuse (CPA). Although this type of analysis might be perfectly reasonable on one level, such a simplistic view of the impact of a childhood traumatic event on adult functioning does not take into account that no one event is deterministic on later functioning. As discussed earlier, knowing that someone has been exposed to one or even several PTEs may provide important information; however, these data still only account for a small amount of variance in predicting adult behavior and functioning, which are multiply determined. An overly simplistic view such as this also does not recognize that screening individuals out based on one risk factor likely deprives an organization of capable, talented applicants who could thrive and perform well even in stressful circumstances.

This is not to say that all individuals who have been exposed to a prior PTE are resilient and able to bounce back with no long-term effects. Some individuals will certainly have developed PTSD, depression, or other problems in functioning related to a prior trauma. In some circumstances, it may well be appropriate to screen for such problems depending on the demands and responsibilities of the position, as well as the likelihood that the individual will be exposed to further PTEs in the course of performing the job duties. For example, it may appear simpler to keep some individuals out of military occupational specialties that would expose them to combat. However, is such a decision truly fair to the individual who did not choose to experience a childhood trauma? Rather than making policies based on broad generalizations in any direction, leaders could instead focus efforts on building resilience to the benefit of the full workforce, including both those with and without a trauma history. Similar types of issues can come up in any setting in which individuals are likely to be exposed to PTEs, such as law enforcement and emergency response. Although policy makers may choose to attend to a variety of variables when directing personnel policy, a prior history of PTE exposure should not be the key determining factor.

### Compensation for Trauma-Related Problems

Another complex situation can arise with respect to disability compensation and benefits. Individuals may choose to file claims related to PTEs that they have experienced, whether through workers' compensation, federal disability compensation programs (including those for military service members and Veterans), or private lawsuits. If an individual is determined to have a prior history of PTE exposure, to what extent should the compensating authority be allowed to take the individual's previous history into account? Does it matter if the person had a diagnosis of PTSD earlier in life? Should the sequelae of a later trauma be considered less valid simply because the individual was previously exposed to a PTE? Or does ignoring these aspects of an individual's history place an undue burden on the agency that would be expected to compensate for the later traumatic event? These are not simple questions with singular answers. For example, the relevance of a childhood sexual trauma history to the development of PTSD following a motor vehicle accident or deployment stressor in adulthood depends on one's individual perspective, and policy makers and assessors should understand that their decisions in either direction have real consequences in individuals' lives.

## OVERARCHING ISSUES

Throughout this chapter, we have focused on the definitional and labeling issues related to the concept of retraumatization and the sequelae of multiple experiences of trauma. This is because, across clinical, research, and policy contexts, if one is not clear about what is being described, then the conclusions that are drawn will be imprecise and, at times, meaningless or even harmful.

If the term *retraumatization* were used simply as an objective description of multiple PTEs, defining it would be far less important. However, its meaning has moved well beyond an objective description of one's history. Rather, it has become synonymous in some contexts with a range of intra- and interpersonal problems that are more frequently associated with multiple experiences of trauma. Writers, researchers, and clinicians who deal frequently with these issues must ensure that the labels and terms they use are nonpejorative and do not assume or emphasize dysfunction or pathology. For example, as described above, early descriptions of this phenomenon were prone to use the term *revictimization*. Although, in some cases, this term may rightfully describe individuals who have been victims of violent crime and thus may be technically correct, the term *revictimization* has the potential to contribute to an overly negative assessment of the person's condition. By automatically describing a trauma survivor as a victim, one posits that the individual is expected to be affected negatively by these experiences. Use of this sort of language may implicitly lead clinicians, researchers, and the general public to focus on negative outcomes or pathology, rather than resilience. Although *retraumatized* is somewhat less pejorative and negative than *revictimized,* even this term does not take into account that every PTE is not necessarily an actual traumatic event, whether one is talking about the initial PTE or subsequent PTE(s). While recognizing that it can be awkward to use long, behaviorally specific, nonevaluative terms, we implore writers of the next wave of research findings and clinical guidance to pay careful attention to the potential, unintended consequences of the labels and terms that they choose to employ. Even subtle language choices can have implications.

A potential impediment to crystallizing some of the conceptual issues outlined in this chapter is the tendency of many trauma researchers to operate within conscribed niches or specialty areas (e.g., CSA, domestic violence, combat). This is certainly understandable, given individual interests, access to specific populations, and the practical limitations of keeping up with an ever-growing literature. However, future research efforts in this area must begin capturing the complexity of actual human experience, sufficiently expansive in its treatment of diverse PTEs across the lifespan. This would include broadening our scope to avoid overreliance on convenience samples of college students, or overrepresenting women due to the tendency of researchers to become interested in this niche as an outgrowth of a specialization in interpersonal trauma. Not only does such an unbalanced focus on retraumatized women neglect findings indicating that exposure to PTEs is more common among men (Kessler et al., 1995), it also maintains focus on PTEs that are more commonly reported among women (e.g., sexual assault), and may ultimately lead to the development of instruments or treatments that are not optimal for male respondents.

A final issue that may impede advancement of the retraumatization literature is related to oversensitivity on the part of some Institutional Review

Boards (IRBs) and funding agencies when evaluating trauma-focused research proposals (Newman, Risch, & Kassam-Adams, 2006). Anecdotal reports suggest that individuals on these committees who are not familiar with trauma research may worry that simply asking about PTEs will negatively impact the participants. A growing body of literature provides robust evidence that these concerns are unfounded (Ferrier-Auerbach, Erbes, & Polusny, 2009; Resick, Iverson, & Artz, 2009; Willebrand, 2008). In fact, many participants in trauma-focused studies report benefiting from their participation (Griffin, Resick, Waldrop, & Mechanic, 2003; for a review, see Newman & Kaloupek, 2004). Although any trauma-focused study may encounter these IRB and funding agency obstacles, there may be even more resistance to studies targeting individuals with multiple PTEs, because of a perception that these individuals are more "fragile" or have more psychological health problems. Thus, researchers can facilitate advancement of the retraumatization literature by educating colleagues and administrators that these studies can be conducted in a sensitive and responsible manner (Newman et al., 2006). For example, one might cite evidence from studies indicating that trauma-focused research is not harmful (see above). Additionally, one might point out that frequent re-experiencing symptoms are a core feature of PTSD; therefore, individuals who are truly traumatized are regularly confronted with trauma-related thoughts and images regardless of study participation. Based on a researcher's past experiences with particular IRBs or funding agencies, this information can be preemptively incorporated into research proposals, or submitted in response to specific concerns raised during the review process. Of course, as with any study proposal, researchers should clearly specify the precautions that will be taken to minimize participant harm, and how participants will be informed about available mental health resources, should the need arise.

## THE WAY AHEAD

In summary, exposures to potentially traumatic events, and even potential retraumatization, are common human experiences that should be attended to carefully at multiple levels. Because of the significant physical and psychological correlates of retraumatization, it is truly a public health concern to ensure proper assessment and treatment of the sequelae of these experiences for all individuals who are in need of such resources. However, even for those who are committed to working with and advocating for retraumatized populations, the issues are complex and do not lend themselves to simple clinical, research, or policy solutions. Exactly because these challenges are so important, retraumatization experts must ensure that their work is solidly grounded in both testable theory and valid research findings. In order to withstand potential criticisms or dismissals of the importance of these topics, those interested in retraumatization must be able to back up their passion and advocacy with empirical evidence whenever possible. We believe that attending thoughtfully and carefully to the controversial issues described in this chapter will provide the best opportunity to improve the lives of those who have been exposed to multiple traumas. Through iterative advances in assessment, treatment, and research, those committed to this field can continue to evolve the state of the knowledge to truly measure up to the complexity of the experiences of those who have survived multiple traumatic events.

## REFERENCES

American Psychiatric Association. (2000). *Diagnostic and statistical manual of mental disorders* (text revision). Washington, DC: Author.

American Psychiatric Association. (2010). DSM-5 development: 309.81 posttraumatic stress disorder. Retrieved May 18, 2010, from http://www.dsm5.org/ProposedRevisions/Pages/proposedrevision.aspx?rid=165.

Aviram, R. B., Brodsky, B. S., & Stanley, B. (2006). Borderline personality disorder, stigma, and treatment implications. *Harvard Review of Psychiatry, 14*, 249–256.

Bonanno, G. A., & Mancini, A. D. (2008). The human capacity to thrive in the face of potential trauma. *Pediatrics, 121*, 369–375.

Breslau, N., Chilcoat, H. D., Kessler, R. C., & Davis, G. C. (1999). Previous exposure to trauma and PTSD effects of subsequent trauma: Results from the Detroit Area Survey of Trauma. *American Journal of Psychiatry, 156*, 902–907.

Breslau, N., Kessler, R. C., Chilcoat, H. D., Schultz, L. R., Davis, G. C., & Andreski, P. (1998). Trauma and posttraumatic stress disorder in the community: The 1996 Detroit Area Survey of Trauma. *Archives of General Psychiatry, 55*, 626–632.

Breslau, N., Peterson, E. L., Poisson, L. M., Schultz, L. R., & Lucia, V. C. (2004). Estimating post-traumatic stress disorder in the community: Lifetime perspectives and the impact of typical traumatic events. *Psychological Medicine, 34*, 889–898.

Cone, J. D. (1986). Idiographic, nomothetic, and related perspectives in behavioral assessment. In R. O. Nelson & S. C. Hayes (Eds.), *Conceptual foundations of behavioral assessment* (pp. 111–128). New York: Guilford Press.

Courtois, C. A., Ford, J. D., van der Kolk, B. A., & Herman, J. L. (2009). *Treating complex traumatic stress disorders: An evidence-based guide*. New York: Guilford Press.

Ferrier-Auerbach, A. G., Erbes, C. R., & Polusny, M. A. (2009). Does trauma survey research cause more distress than other types of survey research? *Journal of Traumatic Stress, 22*, 320–323.

Foa, E. B., Hembree, E. A., Cahill, S. P., Rauch, S. A. M., Riggs, D. S., Feeny, N. C., & Yadin, E. (2005). Randomized trial of prolonged exposure for posttraumatic stress disorder with and without cognitive restructuring: Outcome at academic and community clinics. *Journal of Consulting and Clinical Psychology, 73*, 953–964.

Foa, E. B., Hembree, E. A., & Rothbaum, B. O. (2007). *Prolonged exposure therapy for PTSD: Emotional processing of traumatic experiences: Therapist guide*. New York: Oxford University Press.

Follette, V. M., & Vijay, A. (2008). Retraumatization. In G. Reyes, J. D. Elhai, & J. D. Ford (Eds.), *Encyclopedia of psychological trauma* (pp. 586–589). Hoboken, NJ: Wiley.

Follette, W. C. (1996). Introduction to the special section on the development of theoretically coherent alternatives to the DSM system. *Journal of Consulting and Clinical Psychology, 64*, 1117–1119.

Follette, W. C., & Houts, A. C. (1996). Models of scientific progress and the role of theory in taxonomy development: A case study of the DSM. *Journal of Consulting and Clinical Psychology, 64*, 1120–1132.

Fricker, A. E., Smith, D. W., Davis, J. L., & Hanson, R. F. (2003). Effects of context and question type on endorsement of childhood sexual abuse. *Journal of Traumatic Stress, 16*(3), 265–268.

Friedman, M. J., Keane, T. M., & Resick, P. A. (2007). *Handbook of PTSD: Science and practice.* New York: Guilford Press.

Garb, H. N., & Boyle, P. A. (2004). Understanding why some clinicians use pseudoscientific methods: Findings from research on clinical judgment. In S. O. Lilienfeld, S. J. Lynn, & J. M. Lohr (Eds.), *Science and pseudoscience in clinical psychology* (pp. 17–38). New York: Guilford Press.

Garb, H. N., Lilienfeld, S. O., & Fowler, K. A. (2008). Psychological assessment and clinical judgment. In J. E. Maddux & B. A. Winstead (Eds.), *Psychopathology: Foundations for a contemporary understanding* (2nd ed., pp. 103–124). New York: Taylor & Francis.

Griffin, M. G., Resick, P. A., Waldrop, A. E., & Mechanic, M. B. (2003). Participation in trauma research: Is there evidence of harm? *Journal of Traumatic Stress, 16*, 221–227.

Hayes, S. C., Wilson, K. G., Gifford, E. V., Follette, V. M., & Strosahl, K. (1996). Experiential avoidance and behavioral disorders: A functional dimensional approach to diagnosis and treatment. *Journal of Consulting and Clinical Psychology, 64*, 1152–1168.

Herman, J. L. (1992). Complex PTSD: A syndrome in survivors of prolonged and repeated trauma. *Journal of Traumatic Stress, 5*, 377–391.

Hoge, C. W., Castro, C. A., Messer, S. C., McGurk, D., Cotting, D. I., & Koffman, R. L. (2004). Combat duty in Iraq and Afghanistan: Mental health problems and barriers to care. *New England Journal of Medicine, 351*, 13–22.

Kessler, R. C., Sonnega, A., Bromet, E., Hughes, M., & Nelson, C. B. (1995). Posttraumatic stress disorder in the National Comorbidity Survey. *Archives of General Psychiatry, 52*(12), 1048–1060.

Koenig, L. J., Doll, L. S., O'Leary, A., & Pequegnat, W. (Eds.). (2004). *From child sexual abuse to adult sexual risk: Trauma, revictimization, and intervention.* Washington, DC: American Psychological Association.

Monson, C. M., Schnurr, P. P., Resick, P. A., Friedman, M. J., Young-Xu, Y., & Stevens, S. P. (2006). Cognitive processing therapy for Veterans with military-related posttraumatic stress disorder. *Journal of Consulting and Clinical Psychology, 74*, 898–907.

Murdoch, M., Polusny, M. A., Hodges, J., & O'Brien, N. (2004). Prevalence of in-service and post-service sexual assault among combat and noncombat veterans applying for Department of Veterans Affairs posttraumatic stress disorder disability benefits. *Military Medicine, 169*, 392–395.

Newman, E., & Kaloupek, D. G. (2004). The risks and benefits of participating in trauma-focused research studies. *Journal of Traumatic Stress, 17*(5), 383–394.

Newman, E., Risch, E., & Kassam-Adams, N. (2006). Ethical issues in trauma-related research: A review. *Journal of Empirical Research on Human Research Ethics, 1*, 29–46.

Norris, F. H. (1992). Epidemiology of trauma: Frequency and impact of different potentially traumatic events on different demographic groups. *Journal of Consulting and Clinical Psychology, 60*(3), 409–418.

Nunnally, J. C., & Bernstein, I. (1994). *Psychometric theory* (3rd ed.). New York: McGraw-Hill.

Resick, P. A., Galovski, T. E., Uhlmansiek, M. O., Scher, C. D., Clum, G. A., & Young-Xu, Y. (2008). A randomized clinical trial to dismantle components of cognitive processing therapy for posttraumatic stress disorder in female victims of interpersonal violence. *Journal of Consulting and Clinical Psychology, 75*, 243–258.

Resick, P. A., Iverson, K. M., & Artz, C. E. (2009). Paricipant reactions to a pretreatment research assessment during a treatment outcome study for PTSD. *Journal of Traumatic Stress, 22*, 316–319.

Resick, P. A., Nishith, P., Weaver, T. L., Astin, M. C., & Feurer, C. A. (2002). A comparison of cognitive-processing therapy with prolonged exposure and a waiting condition for the treatment of chronic posttraumatic stress disorder in female rape victims. *Journal of Consulting and Clinical Psychology, 70*, 867–879.

Resick, P. A., & Schnicke, M. K. (1996). *Cognitive processing therapy for rape victims: A treatment manual.* Newbury Park, CA: Sage.

Resnick, H. S., Kilpatrick, D. G., Dansky, B. S., & Best, C. L. (1993). Prevalence of civilian trauma and posttraumatic stress disorder in a representative national sample of women. *Journal of Consulting and Clinical Psychology 61*(6), 984–991.

Roodman, A. A., & Clum, G. A. (2001). Revictimization rates and method variance: A meta-analysis. *Clinical Psychology Review, 21*, 183–204.

Roth, S., Newman, E., Pelcovitz, D., Van der Kolk, B. A., & Mandel, F. S. (1997). Complex PTSD in victims exposed to sexual and physical abuse: Results from the DSM-IV Field Trial for posttraumatic stress disorder. *Journal of Traumatic Stress, 10*, 539–555.

Schnurr, P. P., Friedman, M. J., Engel, C. C., Foa, E. B., Shea, M. T., Chow, B. K., … Bernardy, N. (2007). Cognitive behavioral therapy for posttraumatic stress disorder in women: A randomized controlled trial. *Journal of the American Medical Association, 297*, 820–830.

Tourangeau, R., Rips, L. J., & Rasinski, K. (2000). *The psychology of survey response.* Cambridge, UK: Cambridge University Press.

Weathers, F. W., & Keane, T. M. (2007). The criterion A problem revisited: Controversies and challenges in defining and measuring psychological trauma. *Journal of Traumatic Stress, 20*, 107–121.

Willebrand, M. (2008). Presence of psychiatric morbidity and regrets about participation in trauma-related research—A pilot study. *General Hospital Psychiatry, 30*, 476–478.

Wilson, J. P., & Keane, T. M. (2004). *Assessing psychological trauma and PTSD* (2nd ed.). New York: Guilford Press.

Wyatt, G. E., Guthrie, D., & Notgrass, C. M. (1992). Differential effects of women's child sexual abuse and subsequent sexual revictimization. *Journal of Consulting and Clinical Psychology, 60*, 167–173.

# Chapter 16

# Conclusions and Future Directions in the Assessment, Treatment, and Prevention of Retraumatization

*Melanie P. Duckworth and Victoria M. Follette*

In editing the current retraumatization book, we considered it essential to clearly articulate our conceptualization of retraumatization and to place that conceptualization in the context of other ideas about repeat traumatization that are present in the empirical literature and in the arena of clinical practice. In defining *retraumatization* and in guiding contributors' use of the term, we defined a traumatic event as an event that results in actual or possible death, serious injury, or threat of serious injury to self or others and that elicits a response characterized by extreme horror, helplessness, and fear. We defined retraumatization as traumatic responding that occurs as a consequence of multiple exposures to physically or psychologically traumatizing events. Retraumatization can occur as a function of multiple exposures to one category of traumatic events (e.g., experiences of child and adult sexual assault) or as a function of multiple exposures across different categories of traumatic events (e.g., child physical abuse and involvement in a serious, injury-causing motor vehicle collision as an adult). While we recognize that the term *retraumatization* has been used in a more circumscribed way to capture distress that occurs with the retelling of a trauma narrative, we employed a more literal definition of retraumatization that emphasized traumatic stress reactions occurring consequent to multiple traumatic events. Our definition of retraumatization was forwarded to highlight the number and range of potentially traumatizing events to which an individual might be exposed over the developmental lifespan, to refine our thinking related to the distress reactions and functional compromise that are possible consequent to trauma exposure, and to increase the effectiveness of assessment and intervention efforts that are employed in response to an individual's exposure to multiple traumatizing events. This concluding chapter summarizes some of the major points contained within the book, highlights some of the ongoing controversies related to repeat trauma exposure and diagnostic accuracy in characterizing responses to trauma exposure, and provides some ideas related to the direction to be taken in identifying and evaluating those factors that most influence trauma exposure and retraumatization. Given the extensive literature reviews provided in the various content chapters that comprise the book, we structured this concluding chapter not as a further reference-based review of the literature but as a context for proposing directions for future research and practice efforts.

## USING THEORY TO CLARIFY THE CONCEPT OF RETRAUMATIZATION

In creating the structure for this book, we chose to include theoretical models that, on first blush, appear to be nonoverlapping explanations of retraumatization occurring consequent to an index traumatic event and some prior traumatizing event or events. This was done to provide the most inclusive review of theory related to the occurrence of traumatization and retraumatization following exposure to two or more traumatizing events. Cognitive behavioral conceptualizations of trauma exposure and traumatic stress responding emphasize those parameters and impacts of the traumatic event and those responses to traumatic event exposure that are most predictive of clinically significant distress reactions. Clinically significant distress reactions to a criterion relevant traumatic event are most likely to occur when the exposure elicits affective or physiological responses that include extreme fear and horror; cognitive responses that include perceptions of extreme threat, perceptions of helplessness, and peritraumatic dissociation; and behavioral responses that reflect behavioral inhibition. Cognitive behavioral conceptualizations of persistent, long-lasting traumatic stress reactions highlight the importance of the individual's pretrauma experiences (e.g., prior exposure to potentially traumatizing events) and pretrauma functioning across a variety of functional domains (e.g., academic or occupational attainment, prior psychiatric problems), these pretrauma variables serving as indications of prior life challenge and the breadth and flexibility of coping strategies acquired in the pretrauma life context. Cognitive behavioral conceptualizations of persistent, long-lasting traumatic stress reactions also emphasize those posttrauma factors (e.g., trauma-related physical impairments, use of avoidant and maladaptive coping strategies) that maintain psychological dysfunction and interfere with a return to baseline function.

The psychodynamic conceptualization of retraumatization that is presented offers a review of the historical conceptualizations of trauma, with emphasis placed on the refinement of trauma theories and the differing viewpoints within the psychodynamic tradition that continue to shape the views of psychodynamic psychotherapists and the broader field of trauma research and practice. Most appreciated within the psychodynamic conceptualization of retraumatization that is forwarded is description of trauma as occurring in the presence of an already established, person-specific pattern of perceiving and relating to the self, others, and the world and as manifested not only through traumatic stress reactions, but through problems in interpersonal relating that are best identified and addressed in the context of the therapeutic relationship. Early psychoanalytic approaches point to the developmental consequences of trauma exposure, with stage-specific successes, failures, and adaptations being influenced by the experience of trauma and influencing developmental achievements of subsequent stages.

Attachment theory is particularly relevant to traumatic stress occurring consequent to interpersonal violence. Caregiver attachment behaviors are considered important to the development of brain areas that are implicated in the processing of emotion and the regulation of emotional displays. The caregiver serves to establish certain behaviors as more or less effective and securing and maintaining access to the caregiver. When a caregiver's attachment behavior reflects secure attachment, and when a caregiver's reinforcement of the child's behavioral strategies for securing and maintaining interpersonal engagement engenders secure attachment, it increases the likelihood that emotion processing, emotion regulation, and attachment maintaining behaviors will positively affect future relationships. In the context of a secure attachment strategy, individuals who experience traumatic events are less likely to have negative impacts on their future relationships and are also less likely to attribute the effects of the traumatic events to themselves. Negative attachment styles, in particular an attachment style where an individual overengages with peers, may function to exacerbate negative effects of trauma as well as lead to further trauma in the context of domestic violence.

Attachment theory emphasizes the impact of interpersonal styles of relating on both trauma risk and trauma coping, but the theory of conservation of resources highlights the interacting individual- and system-level impacts of trauma and suggests that the long-term effects of trauma exposure and traumatic stress reactions are best assessed in terms of current and future resource loss. These researchers describe the process as one in which initial traumatization and initial coping resource loss lead to a cycle of repeat trauma exposure, retraumatization, and further resource loss that serves to compromise both mental and physical health over the lifespan. This model views system-level intervention as critical to stopping and preventing resource loss and allowing for individual-, family-, and community-level recovery following exposure to traumatizing events.

## THE CHALLENGE OF ASSESSING TRAUMATIC STRESS REACTIONS IN THE PRESENCE OF PRIOR TRAUMATIZATION

To account for the individual, contextual, and system-level variables that are relevant to the experience of retraumatization, assessment must be comprehensive, flexible, and ongoing. Prior to undertaking an assessment, individual variables relevant to the assessment process (e.g., age at time of assessment) and to the generation of an accurate trauma narrative (e.g., level of consciousness maintained during the event, memory for the event, postevent cognitive compromise, and time since the event) would need to be evaluated. Assessment would begin with an accounting of the potentially traumatizing event and all of the parameters of the event (e.g., event type, intensity and duration of exposure, presence and severity of physical injuries to the self or significant others, perceived responsibility or fault) that would contribute to the individual's experience of clinically significant traumatic stress reactions. Other forms of psychological distress may be experienced comorbid with traumatic stress reactions or in isolation. In assessing potential responses to trauma, those affective, cognitive, and behavioral responses most associated with trauma exposure (e.g., depression) and poorer posttrauma recovery (e.g., shame, peritraumatic dissociation, catastrophizing, and substance abuse) should be evaluated in terms of their function.

Other consequences of trauma exposure (e.g., disabling physical injury) that contribute to posttrauma functional compromise and resource loss should be assessed. Serious physical injuries are experienced in many trauma contexts, including child physical and sexual abuse, intimate partner violence, adult physical and sexual assault, combat, political violence, man-made and natural disasters, and motor vehicle collisions (MVCs). In all trauma contexts that involve serious physical injury, the assessor must obtain information sufficient to establish the magnitude of physical injuries, the nature (routine, urgent, or life-sustaining) of the medical procedures employed, the predicted course of recovery from physical injuries, the extent of injury- and pain-related physical limitations and functional impairments, and the level of psychological distress that is experienced consequent to injury-related changes in function and overall quality of life.

Based on the definition of retraumatization we have forwarded, assessment of traumatic stress reactions occurring consequent to any single event of trauma must include the assessment of all prior traumatic events, the physical and psychological consequences of those events (with particular emphasis on traumatic stress reactions), and the individual- and system-level changes in function and resources availability that resulted from prior traumatizing events. Prior trauma is considered to influence the likelihood of subsequent traumas and the intensity of psychological responses to subsequent traumas. A number of factors have been proposed to account for the relation of prior trauma to subsequent trauma and traumatic stress reactions, including threat perception and threat recognition; affective, behavioral, and cognitive avoidance; interpersonal overengagement; and psychiatric morbidity. The impacts of prior traumatic events may be specific to the event type. Assessment procedures should be sufficiently broad to capture these potential mediators and moderators of the relation of trauma to traumatization.

With comprehensive assessment and case formulation serving as the prerequisite for effective intervention, it is important that assessment of pre- and posttrauma functioning emphasize those domains of function that were undisturbed or recovered in the aftermath of trauma. Also important to effective treatment is the assessment of those adaptive coping strategies (e.g., problem solving and engaging social support resources) that were employed to successfully manage prior traumas and prior experiences of clinically significant trauma-related psychological distress.

## THE CHALLENGE OF TREATING TRAUMATIC STRESS REACTIONS IN THE PRESENCE OF PRIOR TRAUMATIZATION

It has been suggested that the treatment of traumatic stress reactions related to an index event of trauma frequently occurs in the presence of prior trauma exposure and prior traumatization. Treatment for retraumatization will incorporate many, if not all, of the empirically supported components of effective posttraumatic stress disorder (PTSD) treatment; however, the identification and prioritization of treatment targets, the selection of intervention strategies, the pacing of the change process, and the ultimate goals for therapy process and outcome will be guided by the documentation of prior trauma exposures and prior trauma-related intrapersonal, interpersonal, and environmental impacts. In the context of treating retraumatization, the treating professional will be required to assess for and document prior exposure to potentially traumatizing events; prior traumatization; prior trauma-related distress occurring in forms other than PTSD or occurring comorbid with PTSD; prior coping attempts (both adaptive and maladaptive); and prior impacts of trauma on function and resource availability at individual and system levels. Treatment for retraumatization requires that the treating professional's formulation of problems related to the current or index trauma be achieved with respect to prior traumatizing events and reactions.

Treatment of retraumatization requires explicit address of the impact of repeat trauma exposure on the traumatized individual's view of the self. The impact of traumatizing events on the individual's view of the self is implicit in statements that convey the individual's fear that he or she will be disproportionately impacted by or responsible for future traumas. Well-intentioned statements such as "bad things happen to everyone" are often used by laypersons and professionals to convey the universality and the randomness of trauma. Such statements would be more effective if they were reformulated to acknowledge that, while bad things do happen to everyone, individuals are not equal in their ability to access and utilize resources that allow for speedy and effective management of those bad things. Because coping resources are not always equally available, a necessary part of intervention will be informing and empowering traumatized individuals to identify and access such resources. The trauma and traumatic injury literatures attest to the fact that all types of trauma do not occur randomly. Less comfortable but potentially more empowering is the direct address of pretrauma, peritrauma, and posttrauma factors present in the traumatized individual's environment and in the traumatized individual's behavioral repertoire that may increase the risk of repeat trauma exposure and that may increase the likelihood of clinically significant psychological distress in response to such exposures.

Some professionals working in the area of trauma have used the term *retraumatization* to describe the distress that clients experience in the context of trauma-focused therapy. Trauma-focused therapy, through active and detailed recollections of traumatic events, can serve to occasion intense physiological arousal and emotional distress. However, this occasioning of intense arousal and distress should not be equated with the traumatic stress reactions that occur consequent to a Criterion A traumatic event. The context of psychotherapy is important to the processing of aspects and reminders of the trauma, and while psychotherapy can serve as a context for witnessing the impacts of trauma on interpersonal engagement, trauma-focused psychotherapy, when delivered appropriately, should not be considered a context for retraumatization.

## THE IMPORTANCE OF THE TRAUMA CONTEXT TO THE PREDICTION OF REPEAT TRAUMA EXPOSURE AND RETRAUMATIZATION

Certain trauma contexts, by their very nature, are associated with a particularly high risk of repeat trauma exposure. War is one such context. Individuals who experience combat are routinely exposed to situations in which physical injury and death of the self and others are far more than mere possibilities. Despite daily risk of exposure to potentially traumatic events (PTEs), the majority of combat personnel do not evidence clinically significant traumatic stress reactions. This absence of ill-effect is suggested to be a function of evaluations of mental fitness that occur at the point of initial selection into the military and at the point of deployment. For a sizable minority of combat personnel, exposure to PTEs is sufficient to trigger clinically significant traumatic stress reactions, compromise military performance, and impair overall function. In the context of war, the relation of trauma exposure to traumatic stress reactions is heightened by the frequency, duration, and intensity of combat exposure. Certain combat experiences heighten the risk of retraumatization. The experience of capture and imprisonment by the enemy is predictive of retraumatization. Also predictive of retraumatization is the dual experience of combat trauma and sexual assault. It can be hypothesized that both of these circumstances involve isolation (either actual or perceived) and a loss of peer support that serve to maintain stress reactions and heighten vulnerability to subsequent PTEs. It is important to recognize that any single experience of traumatization related to combat service may constitute retraumatization when that experience occurs on a backdrop of precombat traumas. In the absence of combat-related traumatic stress responses, the daily risk of exposure to PTEs and the survival coping that is required during combat may translate to an increased vulnerability to traumatic responding upon subsequent, post-combat exposure to trauma. To reduce the risk of traumatic reactions during and following combat service, adequate precombat preparation for the repeat occurrence of potentially traumatizing events, adequate postcombat assessment of civilian experiences of trauma, and comprehensive assessment of all behaviors that may be construed as reactions to traumatic events and that are likely to increase the risk of retraumatization are recommended.

Other trauma contexts are associated with repeat trauma exposure and retraumatization because the context (e.g., child physical or sexual abuse and intimate partner violence) involves some ongoing engagement between the individual who perpetrates the trauma and the individual who suffers the trauma. Traumatic events that involve interpersonal violence, when experienced in any developmental window, are associated with a myriad of distress reactions including traumatic stress reactions. When events of interpersonal violence are experienced in early development, these events have the potential to negatively impact physical and psychological health, cognitive abilities and intellectual attainment, coping skills acquisition and execution, and interpersonal relating. Children who experience child physical and sexual abuse are more likely to experience adult victimization. This increased risk of adult victimization may be a function of difficulties that arise from the initial childhood trauma. It is possible that the association between child physical and sexual abuse and adult intimate partner violence reflects alterations in threat perception and impaired patterns of interpersonal relating that result from victims living intimately with perpetrators of abuse and violence. The experience of child and adult victimization conveys an increased risk of clinically significant traumatic stress reactions as well as other distress reactions and problems in adjustment that persist and contribute to long-term resource loss.

A considerable amount of research is underway to identify the intrapersonal and interpersonal factors that contribute to victimization and revictimization. Although the number of factors proposed to contribute to risk of victimization and revictimization is large, these factors can be regarded as potential avenues for intervening to reduce victimization and to mitigate the negative effects of such victimization.

Across trauma contexts, the experience of serious physical injury is predictive of traumatic stress reactions and future risk for reinjury and retraumatization. When serious physical injuries occur consequent to a traumatizing event, the pain and discomfort associated with physical injuries, the procedures undergone to manage physical injuries, and the physical limitations and lifestyle changes imposed by those injuries may serve as reminders of the traumatizing event and may serve to maintain the intensity of traumatic stress reactions and functional compromise. Whether intentional or unintentional, whether interpersonal and due to the forces of nature, traumatizing events often involve both physical and psychological injury. Despite this overlap in the physical and psychological consequences of trauma, a nonoverlapping and discipline-specific approach is taken in evaluating and managing the consequences of traumas. The most achievable advance in treating individuals who have experienced multiple traumatizing events may occur as a consequence of increased integration of research efforts across fields of inquiry and intervention efforts across disciplines of care.

## ADDRESSING DEFINITIONAL AND DIAGNOSTIC CONTROVERSIES

Key to any effort to accurately identify, measure, and manage instances of retraumatization is the establishment of an operationally precise and universally employed definition of retraumatization. Currently, the study of both traumatization and retraumatization is tangled in controversies related to the following:

- What events are sufficient to cause clinically significant traumatic stress reactions?
- Whether retraumatization is best captured by repeat exposure to separate, diagnostically sufficient traumatic events, chronic exposure to one diagnostically sufficient traumatic event, or chronic exposure to some combination of potentially traumatizing and less than traumatizing, adverse life events.
- Whether retraumatization requires exposure to traumatizing events across multiple developmental stages or can occur as a consequence of multiple, within-stage exposures to traumatizing events.
- Whether trauma exposure is counted based on the larger trauma context or the separate PTEs that occur within that larger context.

Also debated is the validity and clinical utility of the different diagnostic labels and onset specifiers used to characterize traumatic stress reactions. Currently, the most debated issue relates to the concept of Complex PTSD and the inclusion of Complex PTSD as a disorder that is diagnostically distinct from PTSD. Supporters of Complex PTSD as a distinct disorder emphasize the individual's exposure to trauma and overwhelming life circumstances during early developmental stages, with the complexity of traumatic reactions being a function of both the nature (e.g., long-term sexual assault) and timing (e.g., sexual assault suffered from age 7 to age 13) of the traumatic event. Others view this conceptualization of trauma and traumatic stress reactions as loosening requirements related to PTSD-initiating events and as unnecessarily adding to the number and the level of redundancy across psychiatric diagnoses. These definitional and diagnostic controversies make clear the need to construct a definition of retraumatization that is sufficiently specific and sufficiently flexible. The definition of retraumatization that we have forwarded requires both evidence of prior exposure to one or more diagnostically sufficient PTEs and evidence of prior traumatization as a function of one or more of those prior exposures. This definition is specific in that it requires exposure to diagnostically sufficient traumatic events as well as the experience of clinically significant traumatic stress reactions. The definition is flexible with respect to the developmental stage or stages in which the traumatizing events are experienced, there being no requirement for psychological compromise during early development. Implicit in this is our view of repeat trauma exposure and repeat traumatization as having the ability to negatively and pervasively impact functioning, even when all traumas occur during adult stages of development.

## FUTURE DIRECTIONS IN RESEARCH AND PRACTICE: REFINING OUR UNDERSTANDING OF TRAUMA AND RETRAUMATIZATION

The larger goals of clinicians, researchers, and policy makers working in the area of trauma include the prevention of those PTEs that are preventable and the minimization of the physical and psychological impacts of those PTEs that cannot be avoided. Research suggests certain sociodemographic factors to predict exposure to certain types of PTEs. These findings can be used to develop prevention efforts that are both targeted and culturally sensitive. In targeting at-risk populations and in undertaking prevention efforts, it would be important to address those variables that account most directly for the increased risk (e.g., socioeconomic disadvantage) rather than variables that are more easily measured (e.g., race) but less appropriate targets for effecting the desired risk reduction (e.g., reducing crime-related violence). Prevention efforts should be designed not to simply maximize reach, but to ensure that the most at-risk populations are captured within these prevention efforts. The decision to engage around the prevention of certain types of PTEs presupposes some cost-benefit analysis, the outcome of the cost-benefit analysis being a function of how comprehensively costs and benefits are identified and the weight assigned to a given cost or benefit.

For many types of trauma, risk can be reduced but not totally ameliorated. Secondary prevention efforts related to trauma exposure would be aimed at minimizing the initial impacts of trauma exposure and reducing the likelihood of long-term negative consequences of exposure. In addition to effective prescreening of individuals who will be in positions that involve repeat exposure to PTEs (e.g., emergency first responders), secondary prevention should emphasize continuing education aimed at normalizing acute distress reactions; screening for and identifying acute reactions (e.g., increased use of substances to reduce stress) that are predictive of clinically significant distress reactions; creating a context for reviewing both the details of a given trauma and the feelings engendered by the trauma; calling attention to and celebrating the care efforts made, whether in an attempt to rescue or to recover trauma victims; and requiring periods of rest and recovery rather than awaiting requests for such periods. Tertiary prevention strategies would be employed when in the presence of clinically significant traumatic stress reactions, with the overall aim being management of traumatic stress reactions, restoration of psychological health, and restoration of function across lifestyle domains (interpersonal, occupational, recreational, and social). The likelihood of overall function and a satisfactory quality of life being restored is increased by adequate evaluation of all the separate and interacting pretrauma (e.g., history of prior traumatizing events, history of depression), peritrauma (e.g., life-threatening physical injuries, death of a loved one), and posttrauma (e.g., persisting pain, clinically significant psychological distress) factors that are considered to influence posttrauma adjustment. This would involve repeat evaluation of biological, psychological, and sociocultural health and accessible coping resources.

Although repeat trauma exposure has been researched within certain trauma contexts (e.g., sexual victimization), research related to retraumatization is in its infancy. Trauma researchers are beginning to address and debate the relative importance of the frequency of exposures to PTEs versus the experience of psychological injury consequent to such exposures. Attempts are being made to identify trauma contexts that convey higher risk of repeat trauma exposure, traumatic stress reactions, and associated functional compromise. Representatives of different medical and mental health disciplines are beginning to actively assess the contribution of physical injury to posttrauma psychological recovery and the contribution of psychological injury to posttrauma physical recovery. Currently, efforts are being made to refine diagnostic requirements related to the different disorders of extreme stress. Chief among the efforts being made to refine diagnostic criteria for PTSD are efforts to ensure clear and precise specification of events that would be sufficient to warrant clinically significant and diagnosable traumatic stress reactions. Many events, even those that cause extreme distress (e.g., divorce), that have ongoing and pervasive impacts (e.g., diagnosis of Alzheimer's), and that are considered by most individuals to be reprehensible (e.g., sexual harassment), may not be appropriate for designation as Criterion A events. With sufficiently clear specification of PTEs and sufficiently clear specification of age-specific expressions of traumatic stress reactions, trauma researchers can collaboratively move toward longitudinal evaluation of those individual, developmental, environmental, and societal factors that interactively serve to decrease resource availability and access, increase risk of repeat exposure to PTEs, and increase the likelihood of repeat experiences of traumatization.

# Index